Rules for Categorical Syllogisms

Rule 1:   *The middle term must be distributed at least once.*
Fallacy: Undistributed middle

Rule 2:   *If a term is distributed in the conclusion, then it must be distributed in the premise.*
Fallacy: Illicit major; illicit minor

Rule 3:   *Two negative premises are not allowed.*
Fallacy: Exclusive premises

Rule 4:   *A negative premise requires a negative conclusion, and a negative conclusion requires a negative premise.*
Fallacy: Drawing an affirmative conclusion from a negative premise; drawing a negative conclusion from affirmative premises

Rule 5:   *If both premises are universal, the conclusion cannot be particular.*
Fallacy: Existential fallacy

NOTE: If only Rule 5 is broken, the syllogism is valid from the Aristotelian standpoint if the critical term denotes actually existing things.

Truth Tables for the Propositional Operators

p	q	$\sim p$	$p \cdot q$	$p \lor q$	$p \supset q$	$p \equiv q$
T	T	F	T	T	T	T
T	F	F	F	T	F	F
F	T	T	F	T	T	F
F	F	T	F	F	T	T

Rules for the Probability Calculus

1. $P(A \text{ or not } A) = 1$
2. $P(A \text{ and not } A) = 0$
3. $P(A \text{ and } B) = P(A) \times P(B)$ (when A and B are independent)
4. $P(A \text{ and } B) = P(A) \times P(B \text{ given } A)$
5. $P(A \text{ or } B) = P(A) + P(B)$ (when A and B are mutually exclusive)
6. $P(A \text{ or } B) = P(A) + P(B) - P(A \text{ and } B)$
7. $P(A) = 1 - P(\text{not } A)$

www.wadsworth.com

www.wadsworth.com is the World Wide Web site for Wadsworth and is your direct source to dozens of online resources.

At *www.wadsworth.com* you can find out about supplements, demonstration software, and student resources. You can also send email to many of our authors and preview new publications and exciting new technologies.

www.wadsworth.com
Changing the way the world learns®

A Concise Introduction to Logic

NINTH EDITION

Patrick J. Hurley
University of San Diego

THOMSON
™
WADSWORTH

Australia • Canada • Mexico • Singapore • Spain
United Kingdom • United States

THOMSON

™

WADSWORTH

Publisher: *Holly J. Allen*
Philosophy Editor: *Steve Wainwright*
Assistant Editors: *Lee McCracken, Barbara Hillaker*
Editorial Assistant: *John Gahbauer*
Technology Project Manager: *Julie Aguilar*
Marketing Manager: *Worth Hawes*
Marketing Assistant: *Andrew Keay*
Advertising Project Manager: *Laurel Anderson*
Executive Art Director: *Maria Epes*
Print/Media Buyer: *Karen Hunt*

Permissions Editor: *Kiely Sisk*
Production Service: *Greg Hubit Bookworks*
Text Designer: *Susan Schmidler*
Copy Editor: *Richard Wingell*
Cover Designer: *Yvo Riezebos*
Cover Image: *Charly Franklin/Getty Images*
Cover Printer: *Phoenix Color Corporation*
Compositor: *Thompson Type*
Text Printer: *QuebecorWorld-Taunton*

For more information about our products,
contact us at:
Thomson Learning Academic Resource Center
1-800-423-0563

For permission to use material from this text
or product, submit a request online at
http://www.thomsonrights.com
Any additional questions about permissions
can be submitted by email to
http://www.thomsonrights.com

Library of Congress Control Number: 2004114135
Student Edition: ISBN: 0-534-58505-1
Instructor's Edition: ISBN: 0-495-00024-8
International Student Edition: ISBN: 0-495-00697-1
(Not for sale in the United States)

Wadsworth/Thomson Learning
10 Davis Drive
Belmont, CA 94002-3098
USA

Asia (including India)
Thomson Learning
5 Shenton Way
#01-01UIC Building
Singapore 068808

Australia/New Zealand
Thomson Learning Australia
102 Dodds Street
Southbank, Victoria 3006
Australia

Canada
Thomson Nelson
1120 Birchmount Road
Toronto, Ontario M1K 5G4
Canada

UK/Europe/Middle East/Africa
Thomson Learning
High Holborn House
50–51 Bedford Row
London WC1R 4LR
United Kingdom

Latin America
Thomson Learning
Seneca, 53
Colonia Polanco
11560 Mexico
D.F. Mexico

Spain (including Portugal)
Paraninfo
Calle/Magallanes, 25
28015 Madrid, Spain

It is wrong always, everywhere, and for anyone,
to believe anything upon insufficient evidence.

W. K. CLIFFORD

Preface

The most immediate benefit derived from the study of logic is the skill needed to construct sound arguments of one's own and to evaluate the arguments of others. In accomplishing this goal, logic instills a sensitivity for the formal component in language, a thorough command of which is indispensable to clear, effective, and meaningful communication. On a broader scale, by focusing attention on the requirement for reasons or evidence to support our views, logic provides a fundamental defense against the prejudiced and uncivilized attitudes that threaten the foundations of our democratic society. Finally, through its attention to inconsistency as a fatal flaw in any theory or point of view, logic proves a useful device in disclosing ill-conceived policies in the political sphere and, ultimately, in distinguishing the rational from the irrational, the sane from the insane.

To realize the benefits offered by the study of logic, one must thoroughly understand the central concepts of the subject and be able to apply them in actual situations. To promote the achievement of these goals, this text presents the central concepts of logic clearly and simply. Examples are used extensively, key terms are introduced in boldface type and defined in the glossary/index, and major points are illustrated in graphic boxes. Furthermore, to ensure sufficient practice in applying the basic principles, the book includes over 2,000 exercises selected to illustrate the main points and guard against the most typical mistakes. In most cases, every third exercise is answered in the back of the book.

Note to the Instructor

Learning Logic, the interactive tutorial program on the CD in the back of this book, has been pedagogically improved throughout and modified to conform to changes in the textbook. This program teaches the essential content of the book, leaving classroom time for troubleshooting and special interests. Even if you happen to be a confirmed skeptic when it comes to the alleged benefits of computerized instruction, I would urge you to take a close look at this program, because it really can simplify the task of teaching logic.

New technology offerings available with this edition include *iLrn*, *vMentor*, and *JoinIn*. *iLrn* is a powerful online course management system that provides assistance to students in working exercises in the textbook, and it offers instructors automated grading of tests and homework. *vMentor* is an online service that allows students to contact live tutors through their computer microphone for help with logic. Finally, *JoinIn* provides interactive classroom quizzing with immediate and anonymous results posted through PowerPoint. You can view demonstrations and find information on how to receive these programs at the Wadsworth philosophy website. Although all three services are free, *iLrn* and *vMentor* must be ordered at the time the book order is placed. The *JoinIn* software is available anytime through your Wadsworth campus representative.

Two of the more significant changes in the textbook can be found in Sections 4.7 and 6.6. In Section 4.7, a common mistake made by students in translating ordinary language statements into standard form categorical propositions is to mix up the subject and predicate terms of universal affirmative (**A** type) propositions. To help prevent this mistake, a rule is introduced that covers statements containing "if," "only if," "only," "unless," "what," "when," and several other words. This rule not only serves to simplify the explanation of how such statements should be treated, but it also points up the importance of preserving the syntactic or structural meaning of such statements in the translation.

In Section 6.6, a problem that occurs in identifying the form of ordinary language arguments arises from the fact that such arguments can be translated into the symbolism of propositional logic in different ways. As a result, one and the same argument can be identified as having different forms. To avoid this problem, certain liberties were taken in earlier editions of this book with disjunctive syllogism, modus tollens, and constructive dilemma that created the appearance of a conflict with the way these forms were treated in Chapter 7. For example, an argument was considered an instance of disjunctive syllogism regardless of whether the left or right disjunct was eliminated. To avoid this problem, double negation and commutativity are now explicitly introduced to allow translated arguments that are not exact instances of these forms to be rewritten so that they become exact instances.

In the prior edition of this book, a number of changes were introduced in connection with the Boolean–Aristotelian distinction. From the Aristotelian standpoint, universal statements about existing things imply the existence of the things talked about, but universal statements about nonexistent things do not imply the existence of those things. On the other hand, from the Boolean standpoint, universal statements never imply the existence of anything. In the current edition, this distinction is further refined and clarified. Basically, the two standpoints are considered to be pre-logical issues that must be faced before one proceeds to evaluate an argument in categorical logic. The Boolean standpoint is normally taken first, and then if an argument turns out invalid from that standpoint the Aristotelian standpoint can be taken.

Numerous smaller changes have been introduced in all nine chapters of this new edition. For example, the transition to a full-color format provides for a more effective presentation of Venn diagrams in Chapter 5. And in Chapter 7, five new natural deduction exercises have been added to each of the first four sections of that chapter. These exercises tend to be ones that have simpler solutions, so they ease the problem of the exercises increasing in difficulty too quickly. Finally, an appendix has been added that shows the applicability of logic to graduate-school entrance exams.

Note to the Student

Why study logic? This question is on a par with certain others: Why learn to read? Why develop one's writing skills? Why learn to add, subtract, multiply, divide? The answer is that these skills are needed to do anything well. Unlike the study of physics, chemistry, and microbiology, which are not essential to many other disciplines, logic is essential to every endeavor that involves any form of communication. The lawyer needs it to formulate arguments to a judge or jury, the physician needs it to give a credible rationale for the use of a medication, the businessperson needs it to write a coherent report, the anthropologist needs it to write a well-reasoned article, and literally everyone needs it in day-to-day dealings with friends, relatives, and associates. For these reasons, logic has played a foundational role in education for over two thousand years.

From a more pragmatic angle, logic is important to earning a good score on any of the several tests required for admission to graduate professional schools—the LSAT, GMAT, MCAT, and so on. Obviously the designers of these tests recognize that the ability to reason logically is a prerequisite to success in these fields. (See the appendix in the back of this book for sample questions.) Also, logic is a useful tool in relieving what has come to be called math anxiety. For whatever reason, there are countless students today who are terrified of any form of reasoning that involves abstract symbols. If you happen to be one of these students, you should find it relatively easy to master the use of logical symbols, and your newly found comfort with these symbols will carry over into the other, more difficult fields.

The CD included in the back of this book will help ensure your success in logic. It contains *Learning Logic*, which is an interactive multimedia program that will teach you the essential content of this textbook. To use it effectively your computer must be equipped with loudspeakers or headphones. *Learning Logic* follows the book chapter by chapter, and it contains thousands of practice problems that will solidify your grasp of the central concepts. I recommend to my own students that they begin by working through the material in *Learning Logic* for a certain chapter or section, and then turn to the exercises in the textbook. Finally, I suggest that they read through the presentation in the textbook.

As you begin working the exercises in the textbook, you will notice that most of them are tagged with the symbol **iLrn**. This symbol means that the exercise is included in an online program called *iLrn Logic*, which allows you to work exercises and submit them to your instructor via the Internet. If your instructor has ordered *iLrn,* you should have received a card packaged with your book that includes a PINcode. You will need this PINcode, along with an access code from your instructor, to gain entry to *iLrn.* Another service your instructor may have ordered is *vMentor*, an online tutoring service. Through *vMentor* you can contact live tutors for answers to questions you may have about logic. If you have this service available, your book will come with a card containing the needed information. Both *iLrn* and *vMentor* are available free of charge with your purchase of a new textbook.

Because proficiency in logic involves developing a skill, it helps to work through the practice problems in *Learning Logic* and the exercises in the textbook more than once. This will help you see that good reasoning (and bad reasoning, too) follows certain patterns whose identification is crucial to success in logic. As you progress, I think you will find that learning logic can be lots of fun, and working with the CD and the online resources should enhance your overall learning experience.

Alternative Course Approaches to the Textbook

Depending on the instructor's preferences, this textbook can be approached in several ways. The following chart presents possible approaches for three different kinds of course.

In general, the material in each chapter is arranged so that certain later sections can be skipped without affecting subsequent chapters. For example, those wishing a brief treatment of natural deduction in both propositional and predicate logic may want to skip the last three sections of Chapter 7 and the last four (or even five) sections of Chapter 8. Chapter 2 can be skipped altogether, although some may want to cover the first section of that chapter as an introduction to Chapter 3. Finally, the six sections of Chapter 9 depend only slightly on earlier chapters, so these sections can be treated in any order one chooses. However, Section 9.6 does depend in part on Section 9.5.

Type of course

	Traditional logic course	Informal logic course, critical reasoning course	Course emphasizing modern formal logic
Recommended material	Chapter 1 Chapter 3 Chapter 4 Chapter 5 Chapter 6 Sections 7.1–7.4	Chapter 1 Chapter 2 Chapter 3 Chapter 4 Sections 5.1–5.3 Sections 5.5–5.6 Sections 6.1–6.4 Section 6.6 Section 9.1 Sections 9.4–9.6 Writing Supplement	Chapter 1 Sections 4.1–4.3 Section 4.7 Sections 6.1–6.5 Chapter 7 Chapter 8 Truth Tree Supplement
Optional material	Chapter 2 Sections 7.5–7.7 Chapter 9	Section 5.4 Section 5.7 Section 6.5 Sections 9.2–9.3	Chapter 3 Sections 4.4–4.6 Sections 5.1–5.2 Section 5.7 Section 6.6

Acknowledgments

For their reviews and suggestions leading to this ninth edition I want to thank:

Thora Bayer, Xavier University of Louisiana; Andrew Botterell, University of Toronto; Drew Christie, University of New Hampshire; David Clowney, Rowan University; Michael J. Colson, Merced College; Pieranna Garavaso, University of Minnesota at Morris; Debby Hutchins, Boston College; Leemon McHenry, California State University, Northridge; Noel Merino, Humboldt State University; Fred Mills, Bowie State University; Jeff Mitchell,

Arkansas Tech University; Tony Roark, Boise State University; Ramon Tello, Shasta College; and Jan Thomas, University of Arkansas at Little Rock.

Of course, any errors or omissions that may remain are the result of my own oversight. Those who have contributed reviews and suggestions leading to the eight previous editions, and to whom I express my continued thanks, are:

James T. Anderson, University of San Diego; Carol Anthony, Villanova University; Harriet E. Baber, University of San Diego; Kent Baldner, Western Michigan University; James Baley, Mary Washington College; Jerome Balmuth, Colgate University; Victor Balowitz, State University of New York, College at Buffalo; Gary Baran, Los Angeles City College; Gregory Bassham, Kings College; David Behan, Agnes Scott College; John Bender, Ohio University, Athens; James O. Bennett, University of Tennessee, Knoxville; Robert Berman, Xavier University of Louisana; Joseph Bessie, Normandale Community College; John R. Bosworth, Oklahoma State University; Harold Brown, Northern Illinois University; Ken Buckman, University of Texas, Pan American; Robert Burch, Texas A&M University; Keith Burgess-Jackson, University of Texas, Arlington; James Campbell, University of Toledo; Joseph Keim Campbell, Washington State University; William Carroll, Coppin State University; Greg Cavin, Cypress College; Ping-Tung Chang, University of Alaska; Ralph W. Clarke, West Virginia University; William F. Cooper, Baylor University; Mike Coste, Front Range Community College; Ronald R. Cox, San Antonio College; Houston A. Craighead, Winthrop University; Donald Cress, Northern Illinois University, Dekalb; Drew Christie, University of new Hampshire; Jack Crumley, University of San Diego; Linda Damico, Kennesaw State University; William J. DeAngelis, Northeastern University; Paul DeVries, Wheaton College; Jill Dieterle, Eastern Michigan University; Beverly R. Doss and Richard W. Doss, Orange Coast College; William A. Drumin, King's College, Pennsylvania; Clinton Dunagan, Saint Philips College; Lenore Erickson, Cuesta College; Evan Fales, University of Iowa; Lewis S. Ford, Old Dominion University; Gary Foulk, Indiana State University, Terre Haute; LeAnn Fowler, Slippery Rock University; Thomas H. Franks, Eastern Michigan University; Bernard D. Freydberg, Slippery Rock University; Dick Gaffney, Siena College; George Gale, University of Missouri, Kansas City; Joseph Georges, El Camino College; Kevin Gibson, University of Colorado; Victor Grassian, Los Angeles Harbor College; J. Randall Groves, Ferris State University, Ken Hanly, Brandon University; Ronald Hill, University of San Diego; Lawrence Hinman, University of San Diego; Lynn Holt, Mississippi State University; R. I. G. Hughes, University of South Carolina, Columbia; Peter Hutcheson, Texas State University; Debby D. Hutchins, Boston College; William H. Hyde, Golden West College; Gary Jones, University of San Diego; Glenn C. Joy, Southwest Texas State University; Olin Joynton, North Harris County College; Glen Kessler, University of Virginia; Charles F. Kielkopf, Ohio State University; Moya Kinchla, Bakersfield College; Bernard W. Kobes, Arizona State University; Keith W. Krasemann, College of DuPage; Richard La Croix, State University College at Buffalo; Sandra LaFave, West Valley College, Saratoga, California; Richard Lee, University of Arkansas; Lory Lemke, University of Minnesota, Morris; Robert Levis, Pasadena City College; Chenyang Li, Monmouth College, Monmouth, Illinois; Ardon Lyon, City University of London; Scott MacDonald, University of Iowa; Robert McKay, Norwich University; Rick McKita, Colorado State University; Krishna Mallick, Salem State College; Thomas Manig, University of Missouri, Columbia; James Manns, University of Kentucky; Dalman Mayer, Bellevue Community College; Larry D. Mayhew, Western Kentucky University; Kenneth R. Merrill, University of Oklahoma; Thomas Michaud, Wheeling Jesuit College; Dolores Miller, University of Missouri, Kansas City; George D. Miller, DePaul University; Frederick Mills, Bowie State University; John Mize, Long Beach City College; Dwayne Mulder, California State University, Fresno; John D. Mullen, Dowling College; Henry Nardone, Kings College; Theresa Norman, South Texas Community College; David O'Connor, Seton Hall University;

Elane O'Rourke, Moorpark College; Rodney Peffer, University of San Diego; Linda Peterson, University of San Diego; Robert G. Pielke, El Camino College; Nelson Pole, Cleveland State University; Norman Prigge, Bakersfield State University; Gray Prince, West Los Angeles College; R. Puligandla, University of Toledo; T. R. Quigley, Oakland University; Nani Rankin, Indiana University at Kokomo; Robert Redmon, Virginia Commonwealth University; David Ring, Southern Methodist University; Phyllis Rooney, Oakland University; Beth Rosdatter, University of Kentucky; Paul A. Roth, University of Missouri, Saint Louis; Daniel Rothbart, George Mason University; Paul Santelli, Siena College; Stephen Satris, Clemson University; Philip Schneider, George Mason University; James D. Schumaker, University of North Carolina at Charlotte; Joseph G. Shay, Boston College; Arnold Smith, Youngstown State University; John-Christian Smith, Youngstown State University; Eric W. Snider, University of Toledo; Bob Snyder, Humboldt University; Joseph Snyder, Anne Arundel Community College; Lynne Spellman, University of Arkansas; Gordon Steinhoff, Utah State University; James Stuart, Bowling Green State University; John Sweigart, James Madison University; Clarendon Swift, Moorpark College; Wayne Swindall, California Baptist College; Bangs Tapscott, University of Utah; Richard Tieszen, San Jose State University; Larry Udell, West Chester University; William Uzgalis, Oregon State University; Thomas H. Warren, Solano College; Roy Weatherford, University of South Florida; David Weinburger, Stockton State College; Paul Weirich, University of Missouri, Columbia; Frank Wilson, Bucknell University; and W. Kent Wilson, University of Illinois, Chicago.

For their e-mail comments leading to the eighth edition I also want to thank:

Leonard Alvey, Jerry Balmuth, Marina Banchetti, Judith Barad, Bob Barrett, Lisa Bernasconi, Gary Bierly, Andrew Botterell, Denny Bradshaw, David S. Brown, Rick Burnor, Michael Byron, Alberto Carrillo, Zhen Chen, Mark J. Cherry, Kit R. Christensen, Alan Clark, Jonathan Cohen, Donna Curran, Linda Damico, Anthony Dangelantonio, Bill Davidson, Robert Deltete, Jill Dieterle, Jokhi Dinshaw, Paul R. Draper, Jim Druley, Lois Eveleth, Alan Fletcher, Mark W. Foreman, Peter S. Fosl, Mitchell Gabhart, Dick Gaffney, Jeanne Gallagher, Pieranna Garavaso, Marc Graney, Brenda S. Hines, Peter Hutcheson, Ewa Hyzy, Leo Ikamas, Dinshaw Jokhi, Jeffrey Koperski, Troy Kozma, Dean A. Kowalski, Russell Lascola, William F. Lawhead, Robert Lehe, Shellie Levine, Tim Lord, Marie A. Martin, Leemon McHenry, Rick McKita, Richard Miller, Frederick Mills, Louisa Moon, Luis F. Moreno, John D. Mullen, Griffin Nelson, Maurice Ngo, Te Norman, Nick Oweyssi, James Pearce, Rex Peterson, Shari M. Prior, Peter Pruim, Philip C. Ricards, Rodney C. Roberts, Linda Rollin, William A. Rottschaefer, John Sallstrom, Phil Schneider, Walter Schultz, Elizabeth Shadish, Katherine Shamey, David Sherry, Tim Snead, Bob Snyder, Lee Speer, Joe Spoerl, Allen Stairs, Nancy A. Stanlick, Mark Storey, S. Ruth Stuckel, James B. Stump, James E. Taylor, Rebecca Thall, Richard H. Toenjes, Patricia Turrisi, Nnachi Umennachi, Alec D. Walen, Margaret Walker, Donald M. Walter, June D. Watkins, Hugh Wilder, Steve White, Edward P. Whitman, Holly L. Wilson

Finally, it has been a pleasure working with production supervisor Greg Hubit and copy editor Richard Wingell. Also, I am grateful to Steven Wainwright, philosophy editor at Wadsworth Thomson, to assistant editor Lee McCracken, former assistant editor Anna Lustig, and to editorial assistant John Gahbauer for their help and support.

Contents

9 Induction 451

Basic Concepts

1.1 Arguments, Premises, and Conclusions

Logic may be defined as the organized body of knowledge, or science, that evaluates arguments. All of us encounter arguments in our day-to-day experience. We read them in books and newspapers, hear them on television, and formulate them when communicating with friends and associates. The aim of logic is to develop a system of methods and principles that we may use as criteria for evaluating the arguments of others and as guides in constructing arguments of our own. Among the benefits to be expected from the study of logic is an increase in confidence that we are making sense when we criticize the arguments of others and when we advance arguments of our own.

An **argument,** in its most basic form, is a group of statements, one or more of which (the premises) are claimed to provide support for, or reasons to believe, one of the others (the conclusion). All arguments may be placed in one of two basic groups: those in which the premises really do support the conclusion and those in which they do not, even though they are claimed to. The former are said to be good arguments (at least to that extent), the latter bad arguments. The purpose of logic, as the science that evaluates arguments, is thus to develop methods and techniques that allow us to distinguish good arguments from bad.

As is apparent from the above definition, the term "argument" has a very specific meaning in logic. It does not mean, for example, a mere verbal fight, as one might have with one's parent, spouse, or friend. Let us examine the features of this definition in greater detail. First of all, an argument is a group of statements. A **statement** is a sentence that is either true or false—in other words, typically a declarative sentence or a sentence component that could stand as a declarative sentence. The following sentences are statements:

> Chocolate truffles are loaded with calories.
> Melatonin helps relieve jet lag.
> Political candidates always tell the complete truth.
> No wives ever cheat on their husbands.
> Tiger Woods plays golf and Lindsay Davenport plays tennis.

The first two statements are true, the second two false. The last one expresses two statements, both of which are true. Truth and falsity are called the two possible **truth values** of a statement. Thus, the truth value of the first two statements is true, the truth value of the second two is false, and the truth value of the last statement, as well as that of its components, is true.

Unlike statements, many sentences cannot be said to be either true or false. Questions, proposals, suggestions, commands, and exclamations usually cannot, and so are not usually classified as statements. The following sentences are not statements:

Where is Khartoum?	(question)
Let's go to a movie tonight.	(proposal)
I suggest you get contact lenses.	(suggestion)
Turn off the TV right now.	(command)
Fantastic!	(exclamation)

The statements that make up an argument are divided into one or more premises and one and only one conclusion. The **premises** are the statements that set forth the reasons or evidence, and the **conclusion** is the statement that the evidence is claimed to support or imply. In other words, the conclusion is the statement that is claimed to follow from the premises. Here is an example of an argument:

All film stars are celebrities.
Halle Berry is a film star.
Therefore, Halle Berry is a celebrity.

The first two statements are the premises; the third is the conclusion. (The claim that the premises support or imply the conclusion is indicated by the word "therefore.") In this argument the premises really do support the conclusion, and so the argument is a good one. But consider this argument:

Some film stars are men.
Cameron Diaz is a film star.
Therefore, Cameron Diaz is a man.

In this argument the premises do not support the conclusion, even though they are claimed to, and so the argument is not a good one.

One of the most important tasks in the analysis of arguments is being able to distinguish premises from conclusions. If what is thought to be a conclusion is really a premise, and vice versa, the subsequent analysis cannot possibly be correct. Frequently, arguments contain certain indicator words that provide clues in identifying premises and conclusion. Some typical **conclusion indicators** are

therefore	accordingly	entails that
wherefore	we may conclude	hence
thus	it must be that	it follows that
consequently	for this reason	implies that
we may infer	so	as a result

Whenever a statement follows one of these indicators, it can usually be identified as the conclusion. By process of elimination the other statements in the argument are the premises. Example:

Tortured prisoners will say anything just to relieve the pain. Consequently, torture is not a reliable method of interrogation.

The conclusion of this argument is "Torture is not a reliable method of interrogation," and the premise is "Tortured prisoners will say anything just to relieve the pain."

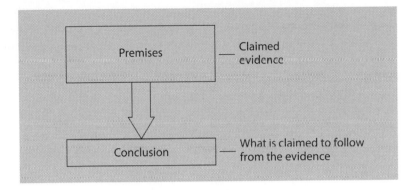

If an argument does not contain a conclusion indicator, it may contain a premise indicator. Some typical **premise indicators** are

since	in that	seeing that
as indicated by	may be inferred from	for the reason that
because	as	inasmuch as
for	given that	owing to

Any statement following one of these indicators can usually be identified as a premise. Example:

Expectant mothers should never use recreational drugs, since the use of these drugs can jeopardize the development of the fetus.

The premise of this argument is "The use of these drugs can jeopardize the development of the fetus," and the conclusion is "Expectant mothers should never use recreational drugs."

In reviewing the list of indicators, note that "for this reason" is a conclusion indicator, whereas "for the reason that" is a premise indicator. "For this reason" (except when followed by a colon) means for the reason (premise) that was just given, so what follows is the conclusion. On the other hand, "for the reason that" announces that a premise is about to be stated.

Sometimes a single indicator can be used to identify more than one premise. Consider the following argument:

It is vitally important that wilderness areas be preserved, for wilderness provides essential habitat for wildlife, including endangered species, and it is a natural retreat from the stress of daily life.

The premise indicator "for" goes with both "Wilderness provides essential habitat for wildlife, including endangered species," and "It is a natural retreat from the stress of daily life." These are the premises. By method of elimination, "It is vitally important that wilderness areas be preserved" is the conclusion.

Sometimes an argument contains no indicators. When this occurs, the reader/listener must ask himself or herself such questions as: What single statement is claimed (implicitly) to follow from the others? What is the arguer trying to prove? What is the main point in the passage? The answers to these questions should point to the conclusion. Example:

> The space program deserves increased expenditures in the years ahead. Not only does the national defense depend upon it, but the program will more than pay for itself in terms of technological spinoffs. Furthermore, at current funding levels the program cannot fulfill its anticipated potential.

The conclusion of this argument is the first statement, and all of the other statements are premises. The argument illustrates the pattern found in most arguments that lack indicator words: the intended conclusion is stated first, and the remaining statements are then offered in support of this first statement. When the argument is restructured according to logical principles, however, the conclusion is always listed *after* the premises:

P_1: The national defense is dependent upon the space program.
P_2: The space program will more than pay for itself in terms of technological spinoffs.
P_3: At current funding levels the space program cannot fulfill its anticipated potential.
C: The space program deserves increased expenditures in the years ahead.

When restructuring arguments such as this, one should remain as close as possible to the original version, while at the same time attending to the requirement that premises and conclusion be complete sentences that are meaningful in the order in which they are listed.

Note that the first two premises are included within the scope of a single sentence in the original argument. For the purposes of this chapter, compound arrangements of statements in which the various components are all claimed to be true will be considered as separate statements.

Passages that contain arguments sometimes contain statements that are neither premises nor conclusions. Only statements that are actually intended to support the conclusion should be included in the list of premises. If, for example, a statement serves merely to introduce the general topic, or merely makes a passing comment, it should not be taken as part of the argument. Examples:

> The claim is often made that malpractice lawsuits drive up the cost of healthcare. But if such suits were outlawed or severely restricted, then patients would have no means of recovery for injuries caused by negligent doctors. Hence the availability of malpractice litigation should be maintained intact.

> Currently 40 million Americans are without health insurance. When these people go to a hospital, they are routinely charged two to three times the normal cost for treatment. This practice, which covers the cost of treating indigent patients, is clearly unfair. For these reasons, a national health insurance program should be adopted. Politicians who oppose this change should be ashamed of themselves.

In the first argument, the opening statement serves merely to introduce the topic, so it is not part of the argument. The premise is the second statement, and the conclusion is the last statement. In the second argument, the final statement merely makes a passing comment, so it is not part of the argument. The premises are the first three statements, and the statement following "for these reasons" is the conclusion.

Closely related to the concepts of argument and statement are those of inference and proposition. An **inference,** in the technical sense of the term, is the reasoning process expressed by an argument. As we will see in the next section, inferences may be expressed not only through arguments but through conditional statements as well. In the loose sense of the term, "inference" is used interchangeably with "argument."

Analogously, a **proposition,** in the technical sense, is the meaning or information content of a statement. For the purposes of this book, however, "proposition" and "statement" are used interchangeably.

Note on the History of Logic

The person who is generally credited as the father of logic is the ancient Greek philosopher Aristotle (384–322 B.C.). Aristotle's predecessors had been interested in the art of constructing persuasive arguments and in techniques for refuting the arguments of others, but it was Aristotle who first devised systematic criteria for analyzing and evaluating arguments.

Aristotle's chief accomplishment is called **syllogistic logic,** a kind of logic in which the fundamental elements are *terms,* and arguments are evaluated as good or bad depending on how the terms are arranged in the argument. Chapters 4 and 5 of this textbook are devoted mainly to syllogistic logic. But Aristotle also deserves credit for originating **modal logic,** a kind of logic that involves such concepts as possibility, necessity, belief, and doubt. In addition, Aristotle catalogued a number of informal fallacies, a topic treated in Chapter 3 of this book.

After Aristotle's death, another Greek philosopher, Chrysippus (279–206 B.C.), one of the founders of the Stoic school, developed a logic in which the fundamental elements were *whole propositions.* Chrysippus treated every proposition as either true or false and developed rules for determining the truth or falsity of compound propositions from the truth or falsity of their components. In the course of doing so, he laid the foundation for the truth functional interpretation of the logical connectives presented in Chapter 6 of this book and introduced the notion of natural deduction, treated in Chapter 7.

For thirteen hundred years after the death of Chrysippus, relatively little creative work was done in logic. The physician Galen (A.D. 129–ca. 199) developed the theory of the compound categorical syllogism, but for the most part philosophers confined themselves to writing commentaries on the works of Aristotle and Chrysippus. Boethius (ca. 480–524) is a noteworthy example.

The first major logician of the Middle Ages was Peter Abelard (1079–1142). Abelard reconstructed and refined the logic of Aristotle and Chrysippus as communicated by Boethius, and he originated a theory of universals that traced the universal character of general terms to concepts in the mind rather than to "natures" existing outside the mind, as Aristotle had held. In addition, Abelard distinguished arguments that are valid because of their form from those that are valid because of their content, but he held that only formal validity is the "perfect" or conclusive variety. The present text follows Abelard on this point.

After Abelard, the study of logic during the Middle Ages blossomed and flourished through the work of numerous philosophers. A logical treatise by William of Sherwood (ca. 1200–1271) contains the first expression of the "Barbara, Celarent . . ." poem quoted in Section 5.1 of this book, and the *Summulae Logicales* of Peter of Spain (ca. 1210–1277) became the standard textbook in logic for three hundred years. However, the most original contributions from this period were made by William of Ockham (ca. 1285–1349). Ockham extended the theory of modal logic, conducted an exhaustive study of the forms of valid and invalid syllogisms, and further developed the idea of a metalanguage, a higher-level language used to discuss linguistic entities such as words, terms, and propositions.

Toward the middle of the fifteenth century, a reaction set in against the logic of the Middle Ages. Rhetoric largely displaced logic as the primary focus of attention; the logic of Chrysippus, which had already begun to lose its unique identity in the Middle Ages, was ignored altogether, and the logic of Aristotle was studied only in highly simplistic presentations. A reawakening did not occur until two hundred years later through the work of Gottfried Wilhelm Leibniz (1646–1716).

Leibniz, a genius in numerous fields, attempted to develop a symbolic language or "calculus" that could be used to settle all forms of disputes, whether in theology, philosophy, or international relations. As a result of this work, Leibniz is sometimes credited with being the father of symbolic logic. Leibniz's efforts to symbolize logic were carried into the nineteenth century by Bernard Bolzano (1781–1848).

With the arrival of the middle of the nineteenth century, logic commenced an extremely rapid period of development that has continued to this day. Work in symbolic logic was done by a number of philosophers and mathematicians, including Augustus DeMorgan (1806–1871), George Boole (1815–1864), William Stanley Jevons (1835–1882), and John Venn (1834–1923). The rule bearing DeMorgan's name is used in Chapter 7 of this book. Boole's interpretation of categorical propositions and Venn's method for diagramming them are covered in Chapters 4 and 5. At the same time a revival in inductive logic was initiated by the British philosopher John Stuart Mill (1806–1873), whose methods of induction are presented in Chapter 9.

Across the Atlantic, the American philosopher Charles Sanders Peirce (1839–1914) developed a logic of relations, invented symbolic quantifiers, and suggested the truth-table method for formulas in propositional logic. These topics are covered in Chapters 6 and 8 of this book. The truth-table method was completed independently by Emile Post (1897–1954) and Ludwig Wittgenstein (1889–1951).

Toward the end of the nineteenth century, the foundations of modern mathematical logic were laid by Gottlob Frege (1848–1925). His *Begriffsschrift* sets forth the theory of quantification presented in Chapter 8 of this text. Frege's work was continued into the twentieth century by Alfred North Whitehead (1861–1947) and Bertrand Russell (1872–1970), whose monumental *Principia Mathematica* attempted to reduce the whole of pure mathematics to logic. The *Principia* is the source of much of the symbolism that appears in Chapters 6, 7, and 8 of this text.

During the twentieth century, much of the work in logic has focused on the formalization of logical systems and on questions dealing with the completeness and consistency of such systems. A now-famous theorem proved by Kurt Goedel (1906–1978) states that in any formal system adequate for number theory there exists an undecidable formula—that is, a formula such that neither it nor its negation is derivable from the axioms of the system. Other developments include multivalued logics and the formalization of modal logic. Most recently, logic has made a major contribution to technology by providing the conceptual foundation for the electronic circuitry of digital computers.

EXERCISE 1.1

I. Each of the following passages contains a single argument. Using the letters "P" and "C," identify the premises and conclusion of each argument, writing premises first and conclusion last. List the premises in the order in which they make the most sense (usually the order in which they occur), and write both premises and conclusion in the form of separate declarative sentences. Indicator words may be eliminated once premises and conclusion have been appropriately labeled. The exercises marked with a star are answered in the back of the book.

★1. Titanium combines readily with oxygen, nitrogen, and hydrogen, all of which have an adverse effect on its mechanical properties. As a result, titanium must be processed in their absence.

(*Illustrated World of Science Encyclopedia*)

2. Since the good, according to Plato, is that which furthers a person's real interests, it follows that in any given case when the good is known, men will seek it.

(Avrum Stroll and Richard Popkin, *Philosophy and the Human Spirit*)

3. As the denial or perversion of justice by the sentences of courts, as well as in any other manner, is with reason classed among the just causes of war, it will follow that the federal judiciary ought to have cognizance of all causes in which the citizens of other countries are concerned.

(Alexander Hamilton, *Federalist Papers*, No. 80)

★4. When individuals voluntarily abandon property, they forfeit any expectation of privacy in it that they might have had. Therefore, a warrantless search or seizure of abandoned property is not unreasonable under the Fourth Amendment.

(Judge Stephanie Kulp Seymour, *United States v. Jones*)

5. Artists and poets look at the world and seek relationships and order. But they translate their ideas to canvas, or to marble, or into poetic images. Scientists try to find relationships between different objects and events. To express the order they find, they create hypotheses and theories. Thus the great scientific theories are easily compared to great art and great literature.

(Douglas C. Giancoli, *The Ideas of Physics*, 3rd edition)

6. The fact that there was never a land bridge between Australia and mainland Asia is evidenced by the fact that the animal species in the two areas are very different. Asian placental mammals and Australian marsupial mammals have not been in contact in the last several million years.

(T. Douglas Price and Gary M. Feinman, *Images of the Past*)

★7. Cuba's record on disaster prevention is impressive. After October 1963, when Hurricane Flora devastated the island and killed more than a thousand people, the Cuban government overhauled its civil defense system. It was so successful that when six powerful hurricanes thumped Cuba between1996 and 2002 only 16 people died. And when Hurricane Ivan struck Cuba in 2004 there was not a single casualty, but the same storm killed at least 70 people in other Caribbean countries.

(Newspaper clipping)

8. The classroom teacher is crucial to the development and academic success of the average student, and administrators simply are ancillary to this effort. For this reason, classroom teachers ought to be paid at least the equivalent of administrators at all levels, including the superintendent.

(Peter F. Falstrup, Letter to the Editor)

9. An agreement cannot bind unless both parties to the agreement know what they are doing and freely choose to do it. This implies that the seller who intends to enter a contract with a customer has a duty to disclose exactly what the customer is buying and what the terms of the sale are.

(Manuel G. Velasquez, "The Ethics of Consumer Production")

★10. Punishment, when speedy and specific, may suppress undesirable behavior, but it cannot teach or encourage desirable alternatives. Therefore, it is crucial to use positive techniques to model and reinforce appropriate behavior that the person can use in place of the unacceptable response that has to be suppressed.

(Walter Mischel and Harriet Mischel, *Essentials of Psychology*)

11. Profit serves a very crucial function in a free enterprise economy, such as our own. High profits are the signal that consumers want more of the output of the industry. High profits provide the incentive for firms to expand output and for more firms to enter the industry in the long run. For a firm of above-average efficiency, profits represent the reward for greater efficiency.

(Dominic Salvatore, *Managerial Economics,* 3rd edition)

12. Cats can think circles around dogs! My cat regularly used to close and lock the door to my neighbor's doghouse, trapping their sleeping Doberman inside. Try telling a cat what to do, or putting a leash on him—he'll glare at you and say, "I don't think so. You should have gotten a dog."

(Kevin Purkiser, Letter to the Editor)

★13. Since private property helps people define themselves, since it frees people from mundane cares of daily subsistence, and since it is finite, no individual should accumulate so much property that others are prevented from accumulating the necessities of life.

(Leon P. Baradat, *Political Ideologies, Their Origins and Impact*)

14. To every existing thing God wills some good. Hence, since to love any thing is nothing else than to will good to that thing, it is manifest that God loves everything that exists.

(Thomas Aquinas, *Summa Theologica*)

15. Women of the working class, especially wage workers, should not have more than two children at most. The average working man can support no more and the average working woman can take care of no more in decent fashion.

(Margaret Sanger, *Family Limitations*)

★16. Radioactive fallout isn't the only concern in the aftermath of nuclear explosions. The nations of planet Earth have acquired nuclear weapons with an explosive power equal to more than a million Hiroshima bombs. Studies suggest that explosion of only half these weapons would produce enough soot, smoke, and dust to blanket the Earth, block out the sun, and bring on a nuclear winter that would threaten the survival of the human race.

(John W. Hill and Doris K. Kolb, *Chemistry for Changing Times*, 7th edition)

17. An ant releases a chemical when it dies, and its fellows then carry it away to the compost heap. Apparently the communication is highly effective; a healthy ant painted with the death chemical will be dragged to the funeral heap again and again.

(Carol R. Ember and Melvin Ember, *Cultural Anthropology*, 7th edition)

18. Every art and every inquiry, and similarly every action and pursuit, is thought to aim at some good; and for this reason the good has rightly been declared to be that at which all things aim.

(Aristotle, *Nicomachean Ethics*)

★19. Poverty offers numerous benefits to the nonpoor. Antipoverty programs provide jobs for middle-class professionals in social work, penology, and public health. Such workers' future advancement is tied to the continued growth of bureaucracies dependent on the existence of poverty.

(J. John Palen, *Social Problems*)

20. Corn is an annual crop. Butcher's meat, a crop which requires four or five years to grow. As an acre of land, therefore, will produce a much smaller quantity of the one species of food than the other, the inferiority of the quantity must be compensated by the superiority of the price.

(Adam Smith, *The Wealth of Nations*)

21. Neither a borrower nor lender be
For loan oft loses both itself and friend,
And borrowing dulls the edge of husbandry.

(William Shakespeare, *Hamlet* I, 3)

★22. The stakes in whistleblowing are high. Take the nurse who alleges that physicians enrich themselves in her hospital through unnecessary surgery; the engineer who discloses safety defects in the braking systems of a fleet of new rapid-transit vehicles; the Defense Department official who alerts Congress to military graft and overspending: all know that they pose a threat to those whom they denounce and that their own careers may be at risk.

(Sissela Bok, "Whistleblowing and Professional Responsibility")

23. If a piece of information is not "job relevant," then the employer is not entitled qua employer to know it. Consequently, since sexual practices, political beliefs, associational activities, etc., are not part of the description of most jobs, that is, since they do not directly affect one's job performance, they are not legitimate information for an employer to know in the determination of the hiring of a job applicant.

(George G. Brenkert, "Privacy, Polygraphs, and Work")

24. Many people believe that a dark tan is attractive and a sign of good health, but mounting evidence indicates that too much sun can lead to health problems. One of the most noticeable effects is premature aging of the skin. The sun also contributes to certain types of cataracts, and, what is most worrisome, it plays a role in skin cancer.

(Joseph M. Moran and Michael D. Morgan, *Meteorology*, 4th edition)

★25. Contrary to the tales of some scuba divers, the toothy, gaping grin on the mouth of an approaching shark is not necessarily anticipatory. It is generally accepted that by constantly swimming with its mouth open, the shark is simply avoiding suffocation. This assures a continuous flow of oxygen-laden water into their mouths, over their gills, and out through the gill slits.

(Robert A. Wallace et al., *Biology: The Science of Life*)

26. Not only is the sky blue [as a result of scattering], but light coming from it is also partially polarized. You can readily observe this by placing a piece of Polaroid (for example, one lens of a pair of Polaroid sunglasses) in front of your eye and rotating it as you look at the sky on a clear day. You will notice a change in light intensity with the orientation of the Polaroid.

(Frank J. Blatt, *Principles of Physics*, 2nd edition)

27. Since the secondary light [from the moon] does not inherently belong to the moon and is not received from any star or from the sun, and since in the whole universe there is no other body left but the earth, what must we conclude? What is to be proposed? Surely we must assert that the lunar body (or any other dark and sunless orb) is illuminated by the earth.

(Galileo Galilei, *The Starry Messenger*)

★28. Anyone familiar with our prison system knows that there are some inmates who behave little better than brute beasts. But the very fact that these prisoners exist is a telling argument against the efficacy of capital punishment as a deterrent. If the death penalty had been truly effective as a deterrent, such prisoners would long ago have vanished.

("The Injustice of the Death Penalty," *America*)

29. Though it is possible that REM sleep and dreaming are not necessary in the adult, REM deprivation studies seem to suggest otherwise. Why would REM pressure increase with deprivation if the system is unimportant in the adult?

(Herbert L. Petri, *Motivation: Theory and Research,* 2nd edition)

30. World government and the balance of power are in many ways opposites. World government means one central authority, a permanent standing world police force, and clearly defined conditions under which this force will go into action. A balance of power system has many sovereign authorities, each controlling its own army, combining only when they feel like it to control aggression. To most people world government now seems unattainable.

(David W. Ziegler, *War, Peace, and International Politics,* 4th edition)

II. The following arguments were taken from magazine and newspaper editorials and letters to the editor. In most instances the main conclusion must be rephrased to capture the full intent of the author. Write out what you interpret the main conclusion to be.

★1. University administrators know well the benefits that follow notable success in college sports: increased applications for admissions, increased income from licensed logo merchandise, more lucrative television deals, post-season game revenue and more successful alumni fund drives. The idea that there is something ideal and pure about the amateur athlete is self-serving bunk.

(Michael McDonnell, Letter to the Editor)

2. In a nation of immigrants, people of diverse ethnic backgrounds must have a common bond through which to exchange ideas. How can this bond be accomplished if there is no common language? It is those who shelter the immigrant from learning English by encouraging the development of a multilingual society who are creating a xenophobic atmosphere. They allow the immigrant to surround himself with a cocoon of language from which he cannot escape and which others cannot penetrate.

(Rita Toften, Letter to the Editor)

3. The health and fitness of our children has become a problem partly because of our attitude toward athletics. The purpose of sports, especially for children, should be to make healthy people healthier. The concept of team sports

has failed to do this. Rather than learning to interact and cooperate with others, youngsters are taught to compete. Team sports have only reinforced the notion that the team on top is the winner, and all others are losers. This approach does not make sports appealing to many children, and some, especially among the less fit, burn out by the time they are twelve.

(Mark I. Pitman, "Young Jocks")

★4. College is the time in which a young mind is supposed to mature and acquire wisdom, and one can only do this by experiencing as much diverse intellectual stimuli as possible. A business student may be a whiz at accounting, but has he or she ever experienced the beauty of a Shakespearean sonnet or the boundless events composing Hebrew history? Most likely not. While many of these neoconservatives will probably go on to be financially successful, they are robbing themselves of the true purpose of collegiate academics, a sacrifice that outweighs the future salary checks.

(Robert S. Griffith, "Conservative College Press")

5. History has shown repeatedly that you cannot legislate morality, nor does anyone have a right to. The real problem is the people who have a vested interest in sustaining the multibillion-dollar drug industry created by the laws against drugs. The legalization of drugs would remove the thrill of breaking the law; it would end the suffering caused by unmetered doses, impurities, and substandard paraphernalia. A huge segment of the underground and extralegal economy would move into a legitimate economy, taking money away from criminals, eliminating crime and violence, and restoring many talented people to useful endeavor.

(Thomas L. Wayburn, Letter to the Editor)

6. Infectious disease is no longer the leading cause of death in this country, thanks to antibiotics, but there are new strains of bacteria that are resistant to—and others that grow only in the presence of—antibiotics. Yet Congress wants to cut the National Institutes of Health budget. Further cuts would leave us woefully unprepared to cope with the new microbes Mother Nature has cooking in her kitchen.

(Valina L. Dawson, Letter to the Editor)

★7. At a time when our religious impulses might help heal the pains and strains in our society, today's television pulpiteers preach intolerance, censure, and discrimination. They package a "believer life-style," and rail against everyone who doesn't fit it—homosexuals, communists, Jews and other non-Christians, sex educators, and so on. Such intolerance threatens to undermine the pluralism that marks our heritage. The packaging of that intolerance in slick Hollywood programming or under the guise of patriotic fervor is skillfully accomplished on many fronts. That, however, does not make it right.

(Peter G. Kreitler, "TV Preachers' Religious Intolerance")

8. Ideally, decisions about health care should be based on the doctor's clinical judgment, patient preference, and scientific evidence. Patients should always be presented with options in their care. Elective cesarean section, however, is not used to treat a problem but to avoid a natural process. An elective surgery like this puts the patient at unnecessary risk, increases the risk for complications in future deliveries, and increases health care costs.

(Anne Foster-Rosales, M.D., Letter to the Editor)

9. Parents who feel guilty for the little time they can (or choose to) spend with their children "pick up" after them—so the children don't learn to face the consequences of their own choices and actions. Parents who allow their children to fail are showing them greater love and respect.

(Susan J. Peters, Letter to the Editor)

★10. Most of the environmental problems facing us stem, at least in part, from the sheer number of Americans. The average American produces three quarters of a ton of garbage every year, consumes hundreds of gallons of gasoline, and uses large amounts of electricity (often from a nuclear power plant, coal burning, or a dam). The least painful way to protect the environment is to limit population growth.

(Craig M. Bradley, Letter to the Editor)

III. Define the following terms:

logic	conclusion	inference
argument	conclusion indicator	proposition
statement	premise indicator	truth value
premise		

IV. Answer "true" or "false" to the following statements:

1. The purpose of the premise or premises is to set forth the reasons or evidence given in support of the conclusion.
2. Some arguments have more than one conclusion.
3. All arguments must have more than one premise.
4. The words "therefore," "hence," "so," "since," and "thus" are all conclusion indicators.
5. The words "for," "because," "as," and "for the reason that" are all premise indicators.
6. In the strict sense of the terms, "inference" and "argument" have exactly the same meaning.
7. In most (but not all) arguments that lack indicator words, the conclusion is the first statement.
8. Any sentence that is either true or false is a statement.
9. Every statement has a truth value.
10. The person usually credited with being the father of logic is Aristotle.

1.2 Recognizing Arguments

Not all passages contain arguments. Because logic deals with arguments, it is important to be able to distinguish passages that contain arguments from those that do not. In general, a passage contains an argument if it purports to prove something; if it does not do so, it does not contain an argument. Two conditions must be fulfilled for a passage to purport to prove something:

1. At least one of the statements must claim to present evidence or reasons.
2. There must be a claim that the alleged evidence or reasons supports or implies something—that is, a claim that something follows from the alleged evidence.

As we have seen, the statements that claim to present the evidence or reasons are the premises, and the statement that the evidence is claimed to support or imply is the conclusion. It is not necessary that the premises present actual evidence or true reasons nor that the premises actually support the conclusion. But at least the premises must *claim* to present evidence or reasons, and there must be a *claim* that the evidence or reasons support or imply something.

The first condition expresses a **factual claim,** and deciding whether it is fulfilled often falls outside the domain of logic. Thus, most of our attention will be concentrated on whether the second condition is fulfilled. This second condition expresses what is called an **inferential claim.** The inferential claim is simply the claim that the passage expresses a certain kind of reasoning process—that something supports or implies something or that something follows from something. Such a claim can be either explicit or implicit.

An *explicit* inferential claim is usually asserted by premise or conclusion indicator words ("thus," "since," "because," "hence," "therefore," and so on). Example:

> Mad cow disease is spread by feeding parts of infected animals to cows, and this practice has yet to be completely eradicated. Thus, mad cow disease continues to pose a threat to people who eat beef.

The word "thus" expresses the claim that something is being inferred, so the passage is an argument.

An *implicit* inferential claim exists if there is an inferential relationship between the statements in a passage, but the passage contains no indicator words. Example:

> The genetic modification of food is risky business. Genetic engineering can introduce unintended changes into the DNA of the food-producing organism, and these changes can be toxic to the consumer.

The inferential relationship between the first statement and the other two constitutes an implicit claim that evidence supports something, so we are justified in calling the passage an argument. The first statement is the conclusion, and the other two are the premises.

In deciding whether there is a claim that evidence supports or implies something, keep an eye out for (1) indicator words and (2) the presence of an inferential relationship between the statements. In connection with these points, however, a word of caution is in order. First, the mere occurrence of an indicator word by no means guarantees the presence of an argument. For example, consider the following passages:

Since Edison invented the phonograph, there have been many technological developments.

Since Edison invented the phonograph, he deserves credit for a major technological development.

In the first passage the word "since" is used in a *temporal* sense. It means "from the time that." Thus, the first passage is not an argument. In the second passage "since" is used in a *logical* sense, and so the passage *is* an argument.

The second cautionary point is that it is not always easy to detect the occurrence of an inferential relationship between the statements in a passage, and the reader may have to review a passage several times before making a decision. In reaching such a decision, it sometimes helps to mentally insert the word "therefore" before the various statements to see whether it makes sense to interpret one of them as following from the others. Even with this mental aid, however, the decision whether a passage contains an inferential relationship (as well as the decision about indicator words) often involves a heavy dose of interpretation. As a result, not everyone will agree about every passage. Sometimes the only answer possible is a conditional one: "*If* this passage contains an argument, then these are the premises and that is the conclusion."

To assist in distinguishing passages that contain arguments from those that do not, let us now investigate some typical kinds of nonarguments. These include simple noninferential passages, expository passages, illustrations, explanations, and conditional statements.

Simple Noninferential Passages

Simple noninferential passages are unproblematic passages that lack a claim that anything is being proved. Such passages contain statements that could be premises or conclusions (or both), but what is missing is a claim that any potential premise supports a conclusion or that any potential conclusion is supported by premises. Passages of this sort include warnings, pieces of advice, statements of belief or opinion, loosely associated statements, and reports.

A **warning** is a form of expression that is intended to put someone on guard against a dangerous or detrimental situation. Examples:

Watch out that you don't slip on the ice.
Whatever you do, never confide personal secrets to Blabbermouth Bob.

If no evidence is given to prove that such statements are true, then there is no argument.

A **piece of advice** is a form of expression that makes a recommendation about some future decision or course of conduct. Examples:

You should keep a few things in mind before buying a used car. Test drive the car at varying speeds and conditions, examine the oil in the crankcase, ask to see service records, and, if possible, have the engine and power train checked by a mechanic.

Before accepting a job after class hours, I would suggest that you give careful consideration to your course load. Will you have sufficient time to prepare for classes and tests, and will the job produce an excessive drain on your energies?

As with warnings, if there is no evidence that is intended to prove anything, then there is no argument.

A **statement of belief** or **opinion** is an expression about what someone happens to believe or think about something. Examples:

> We believe that our company must develop and produce outstanding products that will perform a great service or fulfill a need for our customers. We believe that our business must be run at an adequate profit and that the services and products we offer must be better than those offered by competitors.
>
> (Robert D. Hay and Edmund R. Gray, "Introduction to Social Responsibility")

> When I can read the latte menu through the hole in my server's earlobe, something is seriously out of whack. What happened to an earring, maybe two, in each lobe. Now any surface is game. Brow, lip, tongue, cheek, nose. I've adjusted to untied shoelaces and pants that make mooning irrelevant. But when it comes to piercings, I just can't budge.
>
> (Debra Darvick, "Service with a Smile, and Plenty of Metal")

Because neither of these authors makes any claim that his or her belief or opinion is supported by evidence, or that it supports some conclusion, there is no argument.

Loosely associated statements may be about the same general subject, but they lack a claim that one of them is proved by the others. Example:

> Not to honor men of worth will keep the people from contention; not to value goods that are hard to come by will keep them from theft; not to display what is desirable will keep them from being unsettled of mind.
>
> (Lao-Tzu, *Thoughts from the Tao Te Ching*)

Because there is no claim that any of these statements provides evidence or reasons for believing another, there is no argument.

A **report** consists of a group of statements that convey information about some topic or event. Example:

> Even though more of the world is immunized than ever before, many old diseases have proven quite resilient in the face of changing population and environmental conditions, especially in the developing world. New diseases, such as AIDS, have taken their toll in both the North and the South.
>
> (Steven L. Spiegel, *World Politics in a New Era*)

These statements could serve as the premises of an argument; but because the author makes no claim that they support or imply anything, there is no argument. Another type of report is the news report:

> Witnesses said they heard a loud crack before a balcony gave way at a popular nightspot, dropping dozens of screaming people fourteen feet. At least eighty people were injured at the Diamond Horseshoe casino when they fell onto broken glass and splintered wood. Investigators are waiting for an engineer's report on the deck's occupancy load.
>
> (Newspaper clipping)

Again, because the reporter makes no claim that these statements imply anything, there is no argument.

One must be careful, though, with reports *about* arguments:

> "The Air Force faces a serious shortage of experienced pilots in the years ahead, because repeated overseas tours and the allure of high paying jobs with commercial airlines

are winning out over lucrative bonuses to stay in the service," says a prominent Air Force official.

(Newspaper clipping)

Properly speaking, this passage is not an argument, because the author of the passage does not claim that anything is supported by evidence. Rather, the author reports the claim by the Air Force official that something is supported by evidence. If such passages are interpreted as "containing" arguments, it must be made clear that the argument is not the author's but one made by someone about whom the author is reporting.

Expository Passages

An **expository passage** is a kind of discourse that begins with a topic sentence followed by one or more sentences that develop the topic sentence. If the objective is not to prove the topic sentence but only to expand it or elaborate it, then there is no argument. Examples:

> There are three familiar states of matter: solid, liquid, and gas. Solid objects ordinarily maintain their shape and volume regardless of their location. A liquid occupies a definite volume, but assumes the shape of the occupied portion of its container. A gas maintains neither shape nor volume. It expands to fill completely whatever container it is in.
>
> (John W. Hill and Doris K. Kolb, Chemistry for Changing Times, 7th ed.)

> There is a stylized relation of artist to mass audience in the sports, especially in baseball. Each player develops a style of his own—the swagger as he steps to the plate, the unique windup a pitcher has, the clean swinging and hard-driving hits, the precision quickness and grace of infield and outfield, the sense of surplus power behind whatever is done.
>
> (Max Lerner, America as a Civilization)

In each passage the topic sentence is stated first, and the remaining sentences merely develop and flesh out this topic sentence. These passages are not arguments because they lack an inferential claim. However, expository passages differ from simple noninferential passages (such as warnings and pieces of advice) in that many of them can also be taken as arguments. If the purpose of the subsequent sentences in the passage is not only to flesh out the topic sentence but also to prove it, then the passage is an argument. Example:

> Skin and the mucous membrane lining the respiratory and digestive tracts serve as mechanical barriers to entry by microbes. Oil gland secretions contain chemicals that weaken or kill bacteria on skin. The respiratory tract is lined by cells that sweep mucus and trapped particles up into the throat, where they can be swallowed. The stomach has an acidic pH, which inhibits the growth of many types of bacteria.
>
> (Sylvia S. Mader, Human Biology, 4th ed.)

In this passage the topic sentence is stated first, and the purpose of the remaining sentences is not only to *show how* the skin and mucous membranes serve as barriers to microbes but to *prove* that they do this. Thus, the passage can be taken as both an expository passage and an argument.

In deciding whether an expository passage should be interpreted as an argument, try to determine whether the purpose of the subsequent sentences in the passage is merely to develop the topic sentence or also to prove it. In borderline cases, ask yourself whether the topic sentence makes a claim that everyone accepts or agrees with. If it does, the passage is probably not an argument. In real-life situations authors rarely try to prove something that everyone already accepts. However, if the topic sentence makes a claim that many people do not accept or have never thought about, then the purpose of the remaining sentences may be both to prove the topic sentence as well as to develop it. If this be so, the passage is an argument.

Finally, if even this procedure yields no definite answer, the only alternative may be to say that *if* the passage is taken as an argument, then the first statement is the conclusion and the others are the premises.

Illustrations

An **illustration** consists of a statement about a certain subject combined with a reference to one or more specific instances intended to show what something means or how it is done. Illustrations are often confused with arguments because many of them contain indicator words such as "thus." Examples:

> Chemical elements, as well as compounds, can be represented by molecular formulas. Thus, oxygen is represented by "O_2," water by "H_2O," and sodium chloride by "$NaCl$."

> A deciduous tree is any tree that loses its leaves during the winter. For example, maples are deciduous. And so are elms, poplars, hawthorns, and alders.

These selections are not arguments because they make no claim that anything is being proved. In the first selection, the word "thus" indicates how something is done—namely, how chemical elements and compounds can be represented by formulas. In the second selection, the examples cited are intended to illustrate the meaning of the word "deciduous." It pins down the meaning by providing concrete instances.

However, as with expository passages, many illustrations can be taken as arguments. Such arguments are often called **arguments from example.** Here is an instance of one:

> Although most forms of cancer, if untreated, can cause death, not all cancers are life-threatening. For example, basal cell carcinoma, the most common of all skin cancers, can produce disfigurement, but it almost never results in death.

In this passage the example given is intended to prove the truth of "Not all cancers are life-threatening." Thus, the passage is best interpreted as an argument.

In deciding whether an illustration should be interpreted as an argument, one must determine whether the passage merely shows how something is done or what something means, or whether it also purports to prove something. In borderline cases it helps to note whether the claim being illustrated is one that practically everyone accepts or agrees with. If it is, the passage is probably not an argument. As we have already noted, in real-life situations authors rarely attempt to prove what everyone already accepts. But if the claim being illustrated is one that many people do not accept or have never thought about, then the passage may be interpreted as an argument.

Thus, in reference to the first two examples we considered, most people are aware that elements and compounds can be expressed by formulas—practically everyone knows that water is H_2O—and most people have at least a vague idea of what a deciduous tree is. But they may not have ever considered whether some forms of cancer are not life-threatening. This is one of the reasons for evaluating the first two examples as mere illustrations and the last one as an argument.

Explanations

One of the most important kinds of nonargument is the explanation. An **explanation** is a group of statements that purports to shed light on some event or phenomenon. The event or phenomenon in question is usually accepted as a matter of fact. Examples:

> The *Columbia* spacecraft disintegrated on reentry because its wing was damaged by flying foam debris during liftoff.
>
> The sky appears blue from the earth's surface because light rays from the sun are scattered by particles in the atmosphere.
>
> The AIDS virus causes sickness and death because it infects certain white blood cells called T cells, and these cells are essential to the body's immune system.

Every explanation is composed of two distinct components: the explanandum and explanans. The **explanandum** is the statement that describes the event or phenomenon to be explained, and the **explanans** is the statement or group of statements that purports to do the explaining. In the first example above, the explanandum is the statement "The *Columbia* spacecraft disintegrated on reentry," and the explanans is "Its wing was damaged by flying foam debris during liftoff."

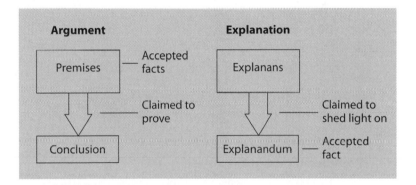

Explanations are sometimes mistaken for arguments because they often contain the indicator word "because." Yet explanations are not arguments because in an explanation the purpose of the explanans is to shed light on, or to make sense of, the explanandum event—not to prove that it occurred. In other words, the purpose of the explanans is to show *why* something is the case, while in an argument, the purpose of the premises is to prove *that* something is the case.

In the first example above, the fact that the *Columbia* disintegrated is known to nearly everyone. The statement that its wing was struck by flying foam debris during liftoff is not intended to prove *that* the spacecraft disintegrated but rather to show *why* it disintegrated. In the second example, the fact that the sky is blue is readily apparent. The intention of the passage is to explain *why* it appears blue—not to prove *that* it appears blue. Similarly, in the third example, virtually everyone knows that the AIDS virus causes sickness and death. The intention of the passage is to explain why this is so.

Thus, to distinguish explanations from arguments, identify the statement that is either the explanandum or the conclusion (usually this is the statement that precedes the word "because"). If this statement describes an accepted matter of fact, and if the remaining statements purport to shed light on this statement, then the passage is an explanation.

This method works for practically all passages that are either explanations or arguments (but not both). However, as with expository passages and illustrations, there are some passages that can be interpreted as both explanations and arguments. Example:

> Women become intoxicated by drinking a smaller amount of alcohol than men because men metabolize part of the alcohol before it reaches the bloodstream, whereas women do not.

The purpose of this passage could be to prove the first statement to those people who do not accept it as fact, and to shed light on that fact to those people who do accept it. Alternately, the passage could be intended to prove the first statement to a single person who accepts its truth on blind faith or incomplete experience, and simultaneously to shed light on this truth. Thus, the passage can be correctly interpreted as both an explanation and an argument.

Perhaps the greatest problem confronting the effort to distinguish explanations from arguments lies in determining whether something is an accepted matter of fact. Obviously what is accepted by one person may not be accepted by another. Thus, the effort often involves determining which person or group of people the passage is directed to—the intended audience. Sometimes the source of the passage (textbook, newspaper, technical journal, etc.) will decide the issue. But when the passage is taken totally out of context, ascertaining the source may prove impossible. In those circumstances the only possible answer may be to say that *if* the passage is an argument, then such-and-such is the conclusion and such-and-such are the premises.

Conditional Statements

A **conditional statement** is an "if . . . then . . ." statement; for example:

> If professional football games incite violence in the home, then the widespread approval given to this sport should be reconsidered.

> If Lance Armstrong has won the Tour de France six consecutive times, then he ranks as king of the hill in the world's most famous bicycle race.

Every conditional statement is made up of two component statements. The component statement immediately following the "if" is called the **antecedent,** and the one following the "then" is called the **consequent.** (Occasionally, the word "then" is left out, and occasionally the order of antecedent and consequent is reversed.) In the first example above, the antecedent is "professional football games incite violence in the home," and the consequent is "the widespread approval given to this sport should be reconsidered." In both of these examples, there is a meaningful relationship between antecedent and consequent. However, such a relationship need not exist for a statement to count as conditional. The statement "If Janet Jackson is a singer, then Denver is in Colorado" is just as much a conditional statement as those about professional football and Lance Armstrong.

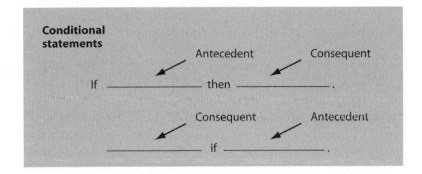

Conditional statements are not arguments, because they fail to meet the criteria given earlier. In an argument, at least one statement must claim to present evidence, and there must be a claim that this evidence implies something. In a conditional statement, there is no claim that either the antecedent or the consequent presents evidence. In other words, there is no assertion that either the antecedent or the consequent is true. Rather, there is only the assertion that *if* the antecedent is true, then so is the consequent. Of course, a conditional statement as a whole may present evidence because it asserts a relationship between statements. Yet when conditional statements are taken in this sense, there is still no argument, because there is then no separate claim that this evidence implies anything.

Some conditional statements are similar to arguments, however, in that they express the outcome of a reasoning process. As such, they may be said to have a certain inferential content. Consider the following:

> If Arnold Schwarzenegger was born a citizen of Austria, then he cannot be elected president of the United States.

> If Jennifer Lopez is Marc Anthony's wife, then Marc Anthony is Jennifer Lopez's husband.

The link between the antecedent and consequent of these conditional statements resembles the inferential link between the premises and conclusion of an argument. Yet there is a difference because the premises of an argument are claimed to be true, whereas no such claim is made for the antecedent of a conditional statement. Accordingly, these conditional statements are not arguments.* Yet their inferential content may be reexpressed to form arguments:

---

*In saying this we are temporarily ignoring the possibility of these statements being *enthymemes*. As we will see in Chapter 5, an enthymeme is an argument in which a premise or conclusion (or both) is implied but not stated. If, to the second example, we add the premise "Jennifer Lopez is Marc Anthony's wife" and the conclusion "Therefore, Marc Anthony is Jennifer Lopez's husband," we have a complete argument. To decide whether a conditional statement is an enthymeme, we must be familiar with the context in which it occurs.

Arnold Schwarzenegger was born a citizen of Austria.
Therefore, he cannot be elected president of the United States.

Jennifer Lopez is Marc Anthony's wife.
Therefore, Marc Anthony is Jennifer Lopez's husband.

Finally, while no single conditional statement is an argument, a conditional statement may serve as either the premise or the conclusion (or both) of an argument, as the following examples illustrate:

If Iran is developing nuclear weapons, then Iran is a threat to world peace.
Iran is developing nuclear weapons.
Therefore, Iran is a threat to world peace.

If borders are secure, then terrorists cannot enter the country.
If terrorists cannot enter the country, then acts of terrorism will be reduced.
Therefore, if borders are secure, then acts of terrorism will be reduced.

The relation between conditional statements and arguments may now be summarized as follows:

1. A single conditional statement is not an argument.
2. A conditional statement may serve as either the premise or the conclusion (or both) of an argument.
3. The inferential content of a conditional statement may be reexpressed to form an argument.

The first two rules are especially pertinent to the recognition of arguments. According to the first rule, if a passage consists of a single conditional statement, it is not an argument. But if it consists of a conditional statement together with some other statement, then, by the second rule, it *may* be an argument, depending on such factors as the presence of indicator words and an inferential relationship between the statements.

Conditional statements are especially important in logic because they express the relationship between necessary and sufficient conditions. *A* is said to be a sufficient condition for *B* whenever the occurrence of *A* is all that is needed for the occurrence of *B*. For example, being a dog is a sufficient condition for being an animal. On the other hand, *B* is said to be a necessary condition for *A* whenever *A* cannot occur without the occurrence of *B*. Thus, being an animal is a necessary condition for being a dog. These relationships are expressed in the following conditional statements:

If *X* is a dog, then *X* is an animal.
If *X* is not an animal, then *X* is not a dog.

The first statement says that being a dog is a sufficient condition for being an animal and the second that being an animal is a necessary condition for being a dog. However, a little reflection reveals that these two statements say exactly the same thing. Thus each expresses in one way a necessary condition and in another way a sufficient condition. The terminology of sufficient and necessary conditions will be used in later chapters to express definitions and causal connections.

Summary

In deciding whether a passage contains an argument, one should look for three things: (1) indicator words such as "therefore," "since," "because," and so on; (2) an inferential relationship between the statements; and (3) typical kinds of nonarguments. But remember that the mere occurrence of an indicator word does not guarantee the presence of an argument. One must check to see that the statement identified as the conclusion is intended to be supported by one or more of the other statements. Also keep in mind that in many arguments that lack indicator words, the conclusion is the first statement. Furthermore it helps to mentally insert the word "therefore" before the various statements before deciding that a statement should be interpreted as a conclusion. The typical kinds of nonarguments that we have surveyed are as follows:

warnings	reports
pieces of advice	expository passages
statements of belief	illustrations
statements of opinion	explanations
loosely associated statements	conditional statements

Keep in mind that these kinds of nonargument are not mutually exclusive, and that, for example, one and the same passage can sometimes be interpreted as both a report and a statement of opinion, or as both an expository passage and an illustration. The precise kind of nonargument a passage might be is nowhere near as important as correctly deciding whether or not it is an argument.

After working the exercises in this section, you may, if you wish, proceed directly to Section 1.6 ("Extended Arguments").

EXERCISE 1.2

I. Determine which of the following passages are arguments. For those that are, identify the conclusion. For those that are not, attempt to determine the kind of nonargument.

★1. The turkey vulture is called by that name because its red featherless head resembles the head of a wild turkey.

2. If public education fails to improve the quality of instruction in both primary and secondary schools, then it is likely that it will lose additional students to the private sector in the years ahead.

3. Freedom of the press is the most important of our constitutionally guaranteed freedoms. Without it, our other freedoms would be immediately threatened. Furthermore, it provides the fulcrum for the advancement of new freedoms.

★4. A mammal is a vertebrate animal that nurses its offspring. Thus, cats and dogs are mammals, as are sheep, monkeys, rabbits, and bears.

5. It is strongly recommended that you have your house inspected for termite damage at the earliest possible opportunity.

6. Mosquito bites are not always the harmless little irritations most of us take them to be. For example, some mosquitoes carry West Nile virus, and people who are infected can become very sick or even die.

★7. If stem-cell research is restricted, then future cures will not materialize. If future cures do not materialize, then people will die prematurely. Therefore, if stem-cell research is restricted, then people will die prematurely.

8. Fictional characters behave according to the same psychological probabilities as real people. But the characters of fiction are found in exotic dilemmas that real people hardly encounter. Consequently, fiction provides us with the opportunity to ponder how people react in uncommon situations, and to deduce moral lessons, psychological principles, and philosophical insights from their behavior.

(J. R. McCuen and A. C. Winkler, *Readings for Writers,* 4th edition)

9. I believe that it must be the policy of the United States to support free peoples who are resisting attempted subjugation by armed minorities or by outside pressures. I believe that we must assist free peoples to work out their own destinies in their own way. I believe that our help should be primarily through economic and financial aid, which is essential to economic stability and orderly political processes.

(President Truman, Address to Congress, 1947)

★10. Five college students who were accused of sneaking into the Cincinnati Zoo and trying to ride the camels pleaded no contest to criminal trespass yesterday. The students scaled a fence to get into the zoo and then climbed another fence to get into the camel pit before security officials caught them, zoo officials said.

(Newspaper clipping)

11. Mortality rates for women undergoing early abortions, where the procedure is legal, appear to be as low as or lower than the rates for normal childbirth. Consequently, any interest of the state in protecting the woman from an inherently hazardous procedure, except when it would be equally dangerous for her to forgo it, has largely disappeared.

(Justice Blackmun, *Roe v. Wade*)

12. The pace of reading, clearly, depends entirely upon the reader. He may read as slowly or as rapidly as he can or wishes to read. If he does not understand something, he may stop and reread it, or go in search of elucidation before continuing. The reader can accelerate his pace when the material is easy or less than interesting, and can slow down when it is difficult or enthralling. If what he reads is moving he can put down the book for a few moments and cope with his emotions without fear of losing anything.

(Marie Winn, *The Plug-In Drug*)

★13. I'm sick and tired of living in fear. I'm tired of plastic bags and duct tape. I'm tired of alerts telling me whether or not I can walk outside. America should be a bastion of hope. Jobs, affordable health care and respect from the world. These will bring hope, and hope is what prevents terrorism.

(Steve Mavros, Letter to the Editor)

14. Lions at Kruger National Park in South Africa are dying of tuberculosis. "All of the lions in the park may be dead within ten years because the disease is incurable, and the lions have no natural resistance," said the deputy director of the Department of Agriculture.

(Newspaper clipping)

15. Economics is of practical value in business. An understanding of the overall operation of the economic system puts the business executive in a better position to formulate policies. The executive who understands the causes and consequences of inflation is better equipped during inflationary periods to make more intelligent decisions than otherwise.

(Campbell R. McConnell, *Economics*, 8th edition)

★16. Bear one thing in mind before you begin to write your paper: Famous literary works, especially works regarded as classics, have been thoroughly studied to the point where prevailing opinion on them has assumed the character of orthodoxy.

(J. R. McCuen and A. C. Winkler, *Readings for Writers*, 4th edition)

17. Young people at universities study to achieve knowledge and not to learn a trade. We must all learn how to support ourselves, but we must also learn how to live. We need a lot of engineers in the modern world, but we do not want a world of modern engineers.

(Winston Churchill, *A Churchill Reader*, ed. Colin R. Coote)

18. No business concern wants to sell on credit to a customer who will prove unable or unwilling to pay his or her account. Consequently, most business organizations include a credit department which must reach a decision on the credit worthiness of each prospective customer.

(Walter B. Meigs and Robert F. Meigs, *Accounting*)

★19. For organisms at the sea surface, sinking into deep water usually means death. Plant cells cannot photosynthesize in the dark depths. Fishes and other animals that descend lose contact with the main surface food supply and themselves become food for strange deep-living predators.

(David H. Milne, *Marine Life and the Sea*)

20. Since the 1950s a malady called whirling disease has invaded U.S. fishing streams, frequently attacking rainbow trout. A parasite deforms young fish, which often chase their tails before dying, hence the name.

("Trout Disease—A Turn for the Worse," *National Geographic*)

21. Dachshunds are ideal dogs for small children, as they are already stretched and pulled to such a length that the child cannot do much harm one way or the other.

(Robert Benchley, quoted in *Cold Noses and Warm Hearts*)

★22. Atoms are the basic building blocks of all matter. They can combine to form molecules, whose properties are generally very different from those of the constituent atoms. Table salt, for example, a simple chemical compound formed from chlorine and sodium, resembles neither the poisonous gas nor the highly reactive metal.

(Frank J. Blatt, *Principles of Physics*, 2nd edition)

23. The coarsest type of humor is the *practical joke:* pulling away the chair from the dignitary's lowered bottom. The victim is perceived first as a person of consequence, then suddenly as an inert body subject to the laws of physics: authority is debunked by gravity, mind by matter; man is degraded to a mechanism.

(Arthur Koestler, *Janus: A Summing Up*)

24. If a man holding a belief which he was taught in childhood or persuaded of afterwards keeps down and pushes away any doubts which arise about it in his mind, purposely avoids the reading of books and the company of men that call in question or discuss it, and regards as impious those questions which cannot easily be asked without disturbing it—the life of that man is one long sin against mankind.

(W. K. Clifford, "The Ethics of Belief")

★25. It is usually easy to decide whether or not something is alive. This is because living things share many common attributes, such as the capacity to extract energy from nutrients to drive their various functions, the power to actively respond to changes in their environment, and the ability to grow, to differentiate, and to reproduce.

(Donald Voet and Judith G. Voet, *Biochemistry*, 2nd edition)

26. Words are slippery customers. The full meaning of a word does not appear until it is placed in its context. . . . And even then the meaning will depend upon the listener, upon the speaker, upon their entire experience of the language, upon their knowledge of one another, and upon the whole situation.

(C. Cherry, *On Human Communication*)

27. Haydn developed the string quartet from the eighteenth century *divertimento,* giving more substance to the light, popular form and scoring it for two violins, a viola, and a cello. His eighty-three quartets, written over the course of his creative lifetime, evolved slowly into a sophisticated form. Together they constitute one of the most important bodies of chamber music literature.

(Robert Hickok, *Exploring Music*)

★28. A person never becomes truly self-reliant. Even though he deals effectively with things, he is necessarily dependent upon those who have taught him to do so. They have selected the things he is dependent upon and determined the kinds and degrees of dependencies.

(B. F. Skinner, Beyond Freedom and Dignity)

29. There is no doubt that some businessmen conspire to shorten the useful life of their products in order to guarantee replacement sales. There is, similarly, no doubt that many of the annual model changes with which American (and other) consumers are increasingly familiar are not technologically substantive.

(Alvin Toffler, Future Shock)

30. Water is a good solvent for many different substances, and it picks them up as it moves through the environment. For example, rain water flowing over and under the ground dissolves minerals such as limestone.

(Gilbert Castellan et al., The World of Chemistry)

★31. In areas where rats are a problem, it is very difficult to exterminate them with bait poison. That's because some rats eat enough poison to die but others eat only enough to become sick and then learn to avoid that particular poison taste in the future.

(Rod Plotnik, Introduction to Psychology, 4th edition)

32. Men are less likely to develop osteoporosis until later in life than women and seldom suffer as severely because they have 30 percent more bone mass on the average and don't undergo the sudden drop in estrogen that occurs with menopause.

(Matt Clark, "The Calcium Craze," Newsweek)

33. Newspapers, radio, and television are essential for a democracy. They are the critical link between the people and their government. They provide information and analysis about policy issues, and they also sensitize policymakers to public opinion—which enables them to respond to the needs and desires of the population. Finally, the media play a critical role in reporting and evaluating the decisions of government.

(Stephen J. Wayne et al., The Politics of American Government)

★34. Nations are made in two ways, by the slow working of history or the galvanic force of ideas. Most nations are made the former way, emerging slowly from the mist of the past, gradually coalescing within concentric circles of shared sympathies, with an accretion of consensual institutions. But a few nations are formed and defined by the citizens' assent to a shared philosophy.

(George Will, "Lithuania and South Carolina")

35. Although the plane mirror is perhaps the oldest optical instrument known to man, it remains an important element in the modern arsenal of sophisticated optical devices. For example, the earth-moon laser-ranging experiments, initiated in 1969, rely on high-quality reflectors.

(Frank J. Blatt, Principles of Physics, 2nd edition)

II. The following selections were originally submitted as letters to the editor of newspapers and magazines. Determine which of them can, with good reason, be considered arguments. In those that can, identify the conclusion.

★1. What this country needs is a return to the concept of swift and certain justice. If we need more courts, judges and prisons, then so be it. And as for capital punishment, I say let the punishment fit the crime. When criminals behave more like humans, then we can start to treat them more humanely. In the meantime, I would like to see the Night Stalkers of our society swiftly executed rather than coddled by our courts and prisons.

(John Pearson)

2. The big problem with computers in elementary schools isn't their minimal educational value but the fact that they often replace science in the budget and curriculum. Our local Parent Teachers Association is throwing away science equipment as fervently as it raises money for more computers. I use computers extensively in the college physics classes I teach, so I appreciate their value in communications and advanced computation. But in elementary schools, too much is being sacrificed so that children can have all those pricey beige boxes.

(Roger G. Tobin)

3. Is there any country in the world that worries more about its kids having fun in school, making lessons exciting and relevant, and then is more disappointed with the result than the United States? We think learning is like buying a car or smoking a cigarette. Just get into the thing or draw a breath and you will be effortlessly transported to lands of pleasure and excitement.

(Charles M. Breinin)

★4. After reading your cover story, I find that cable TV has simply flooded our airwaves with more sex, violence, and teen-age punk junk. Now our children can spend even less time studying and we can spend more time in blank-space stares at the idiot box. Cable would be fine with more educational channels—and fewer cheap thrills aimed at narrow-minded bubble brains.

(Jacqueline Murray)

5. In opposing obligatory prayer in the public schools, I am not deserting my god (and I would like to think of myself as a Christian). On the contrary, it is perfectly possible that I am thus serving my god, who I believe wants his children to pray to him of their own free will and not because some legislator, who may or may not be motivated by truly religious considerations, forces them to.

(Philip D. Walker)

6. My own son returned from his public elementary school with a book on dinosaurs loaned to him by his first-grade "science" teacher. It depicted the beasts as fire-breathing dragons and said the Bible informs us they were this

way. God help us to achieve an educated and scientifically literate society, because these narrow-minded cretins won't.

(Bruce Strathdee)

★7. The poor quality of parenting and the lack in continuity of adult care provided to many U.S. children contribute to a passivity and a sense of helplessness that hobbles individuals for the remainder of their lives. Their subsequent unemployment, lack of education, and inability to make necessary life-style changes such as quitting an addiction can be attributed, in large part, to the helplessness they learned from childhood.

(William J. McCarthy)

8. Forty-one million Americans cannot afford health insurance in this time of global capitalism. At the same time, nine insurance executives earned more than $10 million last year, according to a recent study. If this is the celebrated triumph of capitalism over other forms of economic organization, what exactly did we win? Have we gained the world at the cost of our souls?

(Jason Reynolds)

9. The suggestion by sociobiologists that stepparent child abuse has evolutionary advantages is superficial. If there were evolutionary advantages to harming one's mate's offspring of a different parent, then by now there probably wouldn't be loving and generous stepparents around—and there are plenty. I know. I have a loving stepparent and am one.

(Ronald Cohen)

★10. The voting public is as full of bull as the politicians. As a result, we get the kind of officeholders we ask for. Show me a politician who will stand up and tell Americans the truth, and I'll show you a person who will never be elected.

(Huie Dixon)

III. The following statements represent conclusions for arguments. Each is expressed in the form of two alternatives. Select one of the alternatives for each conclusion, and then jot down several reasons that support it. Finally, incorporate your reasons into a written argument of at least 100 words that supports the conclusion. Include premise and conclusion indicators in some of your arguments, but not in all of them.

1. A constitutional amendment that outlaws flag burning should/should not be adopted.
2. Street drugs should/should not be legalized.
3. The death penalty should/should not be abolished.
4. Sanctions should/should not be imposed on students for using speech that is offensive to minorities.
5. Free health care should/should not be guaranteed to all citizens.
6. Same-sex marriages should/should not be recognized by the state.

7. The possession, ownership, and sale of handguns should/should not be outlawed.

8. Cigarettes should/should not be regulated as an addictive drug.

9. Affirmative action programs should/should not be abolished.

10. Doctors should/should not be allowed to assist terminally ill patients in committing suicide.

IV. Define the following terms:

argument from example	explanation
conditional statement	explanandum
antecedent	explanans
consequent	illustration
sufficient condition	expository passage
necessary condition	

V. Answer "true" or "false" to the following statements:

1. Any passage that contains an argument must contain a claim that something is supported by evidence or reasons.

2. In an argument, the claim that something is supported by evidence or reasons is always explicit.

3. Passages that contain indicator words such as "thus," "since," and "because" are always arguments.

4. In deciding whether a passage contains an argument, we should always keep an eye out for indicator words and the presence of an inferential relationship between the statements.

5. Some expository passages can be correctly interpreted as arguments.

6. Some passages containing "for example" can be correctly interpreted as arguments.

7. In deciding whether an expository passage or an illustration should be interpreted as an argument, it helps to note whether the claim being developed or illustrated is one that is accepted by everyone.

8. Some conditional statements can be reexpressed to form arguments.

9. In an explanation, the explanandum usually describes an accepted matter of fact.

10. In an explanation, the explanans is the statement or group of statements that does the explaining.

VI. Fill in the blanks with "necessary" or "sufficient" to make the following statements true. After the blanks have been filled in, express the result in terms of conditional statements.

★1. Being a tiger is a _____ condition for being an animal.

2. Being an animal is a _____ condition for being a tiger.

3. Drinking water is a _____ condition for quenching one's thirst.

★4. Having a racket is a _____ condition for playing tennis.

5. Pulling the cork is a _____ condition for drinking an expensive bottle of wine.

6. Stepping on a cat's tail is a _____ condition for making the cat yowl.

★7. Burning leaves is a _____ condition for producing smoke.

8. Paying attention is a _____ condition for understanding a lecture.

9. Taking a swim in the North Sea is a _____ condition for cooling off.

★10. Opening a door is a _____ condition for crossing the threshold.

VII. Page through a book, magazine, or newspaper and find two arguments, one with indicator words, the other without. Copy the arguments as written, giving the appropriate reference. Then identify the premises and conclusion of each.

1.3   Deduction and Induction

Arguments can be divided into two groups: deductive and inductive. A **deductive argument** is an argument in which the arguer claims that it is *impossible* for the conclusion to be false given that the premises are true. In such arguments the conclusion is claimed to follow *necessarily* from the premises. On the other hand, an **inductive argument** is an argument in which the arguer claims that it is *improbable* that the conclusion be false given that the premises are true. In these arguments the conclusion is claimed to follow only *probably* from the premises. Thus, deductive arguments are those that involve *necessary* reasoning, and inductive arguments are those that involve *probabilistic* reasoning. Examples:

> The meerkat is closely related to the suricat.
> The suricat thrives on beetle larvae.
> Therefore, probably the meerkat thrives on beetle larvae.

> The meerkat is a member of the mongoose family.
> All members of the mongoose family are carnivores.
> Therefore, it necessarily follows that the meerkat is a carnivore.

The first of these arguments is inductive, the second deductive.

The distinction between inductive and deductive arguments lies in the strength of an argument's inferential claim. In other words, the distinction lies in how strongly the conclusion is claimed to follow from the premises. Unfortunately, however, in most arguments the strength of this claim is not explicitly stated, so we must use our interpretive abilities to evaluate it. Three criteria that influence our decision about this claim are (1) the occurrence of special indicator words, (2) the *actual* strength of the inferential link between premises and conclusion, and (3) the form or style of argumentation the arguer uses.

The occurrence of special indicator words is illustrated in the examples we just considered. The word "probably" in the conclusion of the first argument suggests that the argument should be taken as inductive, and the word "necessarily" in the conclusion of the second suggests that the second argument be taken as deductive. Additional inductive indicators are "improbable," "plausible," "implausible," "likely," "unlikely," and "reasonable to conclude." Additional deductive indicators are "certainly," "absolutely," and "definitely." (Note that the phrase "it must be the case that" is ambiguous; "must" can indicate either probability or necessity).

Inductive and deductive indicator words often suggest the correct interpretation. However, if they conflict with one of the other criteria (discussed shortly), we should probably ignore them. Arguers often use phrases such as "it certainly follows that" for rhetorical purposes to add impact to their conclusion and not to suggest that the argument be taken as deductive. Similarly, some arguers, not knowing the distinction between inductive and deductive, will claim to "deduce" a conclusion when their argument is more correctly interpreted as inductive.

The second factor that bears upon our interpretation of an argument as inductive or deductive is the *actual* strength of the inferential link between premises and conclusion. If the conclusion actually does follow with strict necessity from the premises, the argument is clearly deductive. In such an argument it is impossible for the premises to be true and the conclusion false. On the other hand, if the conclusion does not follow with strict necessity but does follow probably, it is often best to consider the argument inductive. Examples:

> All entertainers are extroverts.
> David Letterman is an entertainer.
> Therefore, David Letterman is an extrovert.

> The vast majority of entertainers are extroverts.
> David Letterman is an entertainer.
> Therefore, David Letterman is an extrovert.

In the first example, the conclusion follows with strict necessity from the premises. If we assume that all entertainers are extroverts and that David Letterman is an entertainer, then it is impossible that David Letterman not be an extrovert. Thus, we should interpret this argument as deductive. In the second example, the conclusion does not follow from the premises with strict necessity, but it does follow with some degree of probability. If we assume that the premises are true, then based on that assumption it is probable that the conclusion is true. Thus, it is best to interpret the second argument as inductive.

Occasionally, an argument contains no indicator words, and the conclusion does not follow either necessarily or probably from the premises; in other words, it does not follow at all. This situation points up the need for the third factor to be taken into account, which is the character or form of argumentation the arguer uses.

Deductive Argument Forms

Many arguments have a distinctive character or form that indicates that the premises are supposed to provide absolute support for the conclusion. Five examples of such forms or kinds of argumentation are arguments based on mathematics, arguments from definition, and categorical, hypothetical, and disjunctive syllogisms.

An **argument based on mathematics** is an argument in which the conclusion depends on some purely arithmetic or geometric computation or measurement. For example, a shopper might place two apples and three oranges into a paper bag and then conclude that the bag contains five pieces of fruit. Or a surveyor might measure a square piece of land and, after determining that it is 100 feet on each side, conclude that it contains 10,000 square feet. Since all arguments in pure mathematics are deductive, we can usually consider arguments that depend on mathematics to be deductive as well. A noteworthy exception, however, is arguments that depend on statistics. As we will see shortly, such arguments are usually best interpreted as inductive.

An **argument from definition** is an argument in which the conclusion is claimed to depend merely upon the definition of some word or phrase used in the premise or conclusion. For example, someone might argue that because Claudia is mendacious, it follows that she tells lies, or that because a certain paragraph is prolix, it follows that it is excessively wordy. These arguments are deductive because their conclusions follow with necessity from the definitions of "mendacious" and "prolix."

A syllogism, in general, is an argument consisting of exactly two premises and one conclusion. Categorical syllogisms will be treated in greater depth in Chapter 5, but for now we will say that a **categorical syllogism** is a syllogism in which each statement begins with one of the words "all," "no," or "some." Example:

> All ancient forests are sources of wonder.
> Some ancient forests are targets of the timber industry.
> Therefore, some sources of wonder are targets of the timber industry.

Arguments such as these are nearly always best treated as deductive.

A **hypothetical syllogism** is a syllogism having a conditional statement for one or both of its premises. Examples:

> If Wal-Mart continues to grow, then suppliers will be squeezed even further.
> If suppliers are squeezed even further, then jobs will be forced overseas.
> Therefore, if Wal-Mart continues to grow, then jobs will be forced overseas.

> If Fox News is a propaganda machine, then it misleads its viewers.
> Fox news is a propaganda machine.
> Therefore, Fox news misleads its viewers.

Although certain forms of such arguments can sometimes be interpreted inductively, the deductive interpretation is usually the most appropriate.

A **disjunctive syllogism** is a syllogism having a disjunctive statement (i.e., an "either . . . or . . ." statement) for one of its premises. Example:

> Either global warming will be arrested, or hurricanes will become more intense.
> Global warming will not be arrested.
> Therefore, hurricanes will become more intense.

As with hypothetical syllogisms, such arguments are usually best taken as deductive. Hypothetical and disjunctive syllogisms will be treated in greater depth in Chapter 6.

Inductive Argument Forms

In general, inductive arguments are such that the content of the conclusion is in some way intended to "go beyond" the content of the premises. The premises of such an argument typically deal with some subject that is relatively familiar, and the conclusion then moves beyond this to a subject that is less familiar or that little is known about.

Such an argument may take any of several forms: predictions about the future, arguments from analogy, inductive generalizations, arguments from authority, arguments based on signs, and causal inferences, to name just a few.

A **prediction** is an argument that proceeds from our knowledge of the past to a claim about the future. For example, someone might argue that because certain meteorological phenomena have been observed to develop over a certain region of central Missouri, a storm will occur there in six hours. Or again, one might argue that because certain fluctuations occurred in the prime interest rate on Friday, the value of the dollar will decrease against foreign currencies on Monday. Nearly everyone realizes that the future cannot be known with certainty; thus, whenever an argument makes a prediction about the future, one is usually justified in considering the argument inductive.

An **argument from analogy** is an argument that depends on the existence of an analogy, or similarity, between two things or states of affairs. Because of the existence of this analogy, a certain condition that affects the better-known thing or situation is concluded to affect the similar, lesser-known thing or situation. For example, someone might argue that because Christina's Porsche is a great handling car, it follows that Angela's Porsche must also be a great handling car. The argument depends on the existence of a similarity, or analogy, between the two cars. The certitude attending such an inference is obviously probabilistic at best.

A **generalization** is an argument that proceeds from the knowledge of a selected sample to some claim about the whole group. Because the members of the sample have a certain characteristic, it is argued that all the members of the group have that same characteristic. For example, one might argue that because three oranges selected from a certain crate were especially tasty and juicy, all the oranges from that crate are especially tasty and juicy. Or again, one might argue that because six out of a total of nine members sampled from a certain labor union intend to vote for Johnson for union president, two-thirds of the entire membership intend to vote for Johnson. These examples illustrate the use of statistics in inductive argumentation.

An **argument from authority** is an argument that concludes something is true because a presumed expert or witness has said that it is. For example, a person might argue that earnings for Hewlett-Packard Corporation will be up in the coming quarter because of a statement to that effect by an investment counselor. Or a lawyer might argue that Mack the Knife committed the murder because an eyewitness testified to that effect under oath. Because the investment counselor and the eyewitness could be either mistaken or lying, such arguments are essentially probabilistic.

An **argument based on signs** is an argument that proceeds from the knowledge of a sign to a claim about the thing or situation that the sign symbolizes. The word "sign," as it is used here, means any kind of message (usually visual) produced by an intelligent being. For example, when driving on an unfamiliar highway one might see a sign indicating that the road makes several sharp turns one mile ahead. Based on this information, one might argue that the road does indeed make several sharp turns one mile ahead. Because the sign might be misplaced or in error about the turns, the conclusion is only probable.

A **causal inference** is an argument that proceeds from knowledge of a cause to a claim about an effect, or, conversely, from knowledge of an effect to a claim about a cause. For example, from the knowledge that a bottle of wine had been accidentally left in the freezer overnight, someone might conclude that it had frozen (cause to effect). Conversely, after tasting a piece of chicken and finding it dry and crunchy, one might conclude that it had been overcooked (effect to cause). Because specific instances of cause and effect can never be known with absolute certainty, one may usually interpret such arguments as inductive.

It should be noted that the various subspecies of inductive arguments listed here are not intended to be mutually exclusive. Overlaps can and do occur. For example, many causal inferences that proceed from cause to effect also qualify as predictions. The purpose of this survey is not to demarcate in precise terms the various forms of induction but rather to provide guidelines for distinguishing induction from deduction.

Keeping this in mind, we should take care not to confuse arguments in geometry, which are always deductive, with arguments from analogy or inductive generalizations. For example, an argument concluding that a triangle has a certain attribute (such as a right angle) because another triangle, with which it is congruent, also has that attribute might be mistaken for an argument from analogy. Similarly, an argument that concludes that all triangles have a certain attribute (such as angles totaling two right angles) because any particular triangle has that attribute might be mistaken for an inductive generalization. Arguments such as these, however, are always deductive, because the conclusion follows necessarily and with complete certainty from the premises.

One broad classification of arguments not listed in this survey is scientific arguments. Arguments that occur in science can be either inductive or deductive, depending on the circumstances. In general, arguments aimed at the *discovery* of a law of nature are usually considered inductive. Suppose, for example, that we want to discover a law that governs the time required for a falling body to strike the earth. We drop bodies of various weights from various heights and measure the time it takes them to fall. Comparing our measurements, we notice that the time is approximately proportional to the square root of the distance. From this we conclude that the time required for any body to fall is proportional to the square root of the distance through which it falls. Such an argument is best interpreted as an inductive generalization.

Another type of argument that occurs in science has to do with the *application* of known laws to specific circumstances. Arguments of this sort are often considered to be deductive—but only with certain reservations. Suppose, for example, that we want to apply Boyle's law for ideal gases to a container of gas in our laboratory. Boyle's law states that the pressure exerted by a gas on the walls of its container is inversely proportional to the volume. Applying this law, we conclude that when we reduce the volume of our laboratory sample by half, we will double the pressure. Considered purely as a mathematical computation, this argument is deductive. But if we acknowledge the fact that the conclusion pertains to the future and the possibility that Boyle's law may not work in the future, then the argument is best considered inductive.

A final point needs to be made about the distinction between inductive and deductive arguments. There is a tradition extending back to the time of Aristotle which holds that inductive arguments are those that proceed from the particular to the general, while deductive arguments are those that proceed from the general to the particular. (A **particular statement** is one that makes a claim about one or more particular members of a class, while a **general statement** makes a claim about *all* the members of a class.) It is true, of course, that many inductive and deductive arguments do work in this way; but this fact should not be used as a criterion for distinguishing induction from deduction. As a matter of fact, there are deductive arguments that proceed from the general to the general, from the particular to the particular, and from the particular to the general, as well as from the general to the particular; and there are inductive arguments that do the same. For example, here is a deductive argument that proceeds from the particular to the general:

> Three is a prime number.
> Five is a prime number.
> Seven is a prime number.
> Therefore, all odd numbers between two and eight are prime numbers.

And here is one that proceeds from the particular to the particular:

> Gabriel is a wolf.
> Gabriel has a tail.
> Therefore, Gabriel's tail is the tail of a wolf.

Here is an inductive argument that proceeds from the general to the particular:

> All emeralds previously found have been green.
> Therefore, the next emerald to be found will be green.

The other varieties are easy to construct. Thus, the progression from particular to general, and vice versa, cannot be used as a criterion for distinguishing induction from deduction.

Summary

To distinguish deductive arguments from inductive arguments, we attempt to evaluate the strength of the argument's inferential claim—how strongly the conclusion is claimed to follow from the premises. This claim is an objective feature of an argument, and it may or may not be related to the subjective intentions of the arguer.

To interpret an argument's inferential claim we look at three factors: special indicator words, the actual strength of the inferential link between premises and conclusion, and the character or form of argumentation. Given that we have more than one factor to look at, it is possible in a single argument for the occurrence of two of these factors to conflict with each other, leading to opposite interpretations. For example, in drawing a conclusion to a categorical syllogism (which is clearly deductive), an arguer might say "It probably follows that . . ." (which suggests induction). To help alleviate this conflict we can list the factors in order of importance:

1. Arguments in which the premises provide absolute support for the conclusion. Such arguments are always deductive.

2. Arguments having a specific deductive character or form (e.g., categorical syllogism). This factor is often of equal importance to the first, and, when present, it provides a clear-cut indication that the argument is deductive.

3. Arguments having a specific inductive character or form (e.g., a prediction). Arguments of this sort are nearly always best interpreted as inductive.

4. Arguments containing inductive indicator language (e.g., "It probably follows that . . ."). Since arguers rarely try to make their argument appear weaker than it really is, such language can usually be trusted. But if this language conflicts with one of the first two factors, it should be ignored.

5. Arguments containing deductive indicator language (e.g., "It necessarily follows that . . ."). Arguers occasionally use such language for rhetorical purposes, to make their argument appear stronger than it really is, so such language should be evaluated carefully.

6. Arguments in which the premises provide only probable support for the conclusion. This is the least important factor, and if it conflicts with any of the earlier ones, it should probably be ignored.

Unfortunately, many arguments in ordinary language are incomplete, so it often happens that none of these factors are clearly present. In such arguments it may be impossible to reach any definitive answer as to their inductive or deductive character.

EXERCISE 1.3

I. Determine whether the following arguments are best interpreted as being inductive or deductive. Also state the criteria you use in reaching your decision (i.e., the presence of indicator words, the nature of the inferential link between premises and conclusion, or the character or form of argumentation).

★1. Because triangle A is congruent with triangle B, and triangle A is isosceles, it follows that triangle B is isosceles.

2. The plaque on the leaning tower of Pisa says that Galileo performed experiments there with falling objects. It must be the case that Galileo did indeed perform those experiments there.

3. The rainfall in Seattle has been more than 15 inches every year for the past thirty years. Therefore, the rainfall next year will probably be more than 15 inches.

★4. No e-mail messages are eloquent creations. Some love letters are eloquent creations. Therefore, some love letters are not e-mail messages.

5. Amoco, Exxon, and Texaco are all listed on the New York Stock Exchange. It must be the case that all major American oil companies are listed on the New York Stock Exchange.

6. The longer a pendulum is, the longer it takes to swing. Therefore, when the pendulum of a clock is lengthened, the clock slows down.

★7. Paying off terrorists in exchange for hostages is not a wise policy, since such action will only lead them to take more hostages in the future.

8. The Matterhorn is higher than Mount Whitney, and Mount Whitney is higher than Mount Rainier. The obvious conclusion is that the Matterhorn is higher than Mount Rainier.

9. Although both front and rear doors were found open after the burglary, there were pry marks around the lock on the rear door and deposits of mud near the threshold. It must be the case that the thief entered through the rear door and left through the front.

★10. The *Encylopaedia Britannica* has an article on symbiosis. The *Encyclopedia Americana,* like the *Britannica,* is an excellent reference work. Therefore, the *Americana* probably also has an article on symbiosis.

11. Cholesterol is endogenous with humans. Therefore, it is manufactured inside the human body.

12. Either classical culture originated in Greece, or it originated in Egypt. Classical culture did not originate in Egypt. Therefore, classical culture originated in Greece.

★13. World-renowned physicist Stephen Hawking says that the condition of the universe at the instant of the Big Bang was more highly ordered than it is today. In view of Hawking's stature in the scientific community, we should conclude that this description of the universe is correct.

14. If Alexander the Great died from typhoid fever, then he became infected in India. Alexander the Great did die from typhoid fever. Therefore, he became infected in India.

15. Crater Lake, the deepest lake in the United States, was caused by a huge volcanic eruption 7700 years ago. Since human beings have lived around the mountain for more than 10,000 years, it is likely that people witnessed that eruption.

(National Park Service, "Crater Lake—Its History")

★16. Each element, such as hydrogen and iron, has a set of gaps—wavelengths that it absorbs rather than radiates. So if those wavelengths are missing from the spectrum, you know that that element is present in the star you are observing.

(Rick Gore, "Eyes of Science")

17. Because the apparent daily movement which is common to both the planets and the fixed stars is seen to travel from the east to the west, but the far slower single movements of the single planets travel in the opposite direction from west to east, it is therefore certain that these movements cannot depend on the common movement of the world but should be assigned to the planets themselves.

(Johannes Kepler, *Epitomy of Copernican Astronomy*)

18. Reserves of coal in the United States have an energy equivalent 33 times that of oil and natural gas. On a worldwide basis the multiple is about 10. By shifting to a coal-based economy, we could satisfy our energy requirements for at least a century, probably longer.

(William L. Masterson and Emil J. Slowinski, *Principles of Chemistry*)

★19. When the Romans occupied England, coal was burned. Since coal produces quite a bit of soot and sulfur dioxide, there must have been days almost 2000 years ago when the air in the larger towns was badly polluted.

(Stanley Gedzelman, *The Science and Wonders of the Atmosphere*)

20. The graphical method for solving a system of equations is an approximation, since reading the point of intersection depends on the accuracy with which the lines are drawn and on the ability to interpret the coordinates of the point.

(Karl J. Smith and Patrick J. Boyle, *Intermediate Algebra for College Students*)

21. That [the moons of Jupiter] revolve in unequal circles is manifestly deduced from the fact that at the longest elongation from Jupiter it is never possible to see two of these moons in conjunction, whereas in the vicinity of Jupiter they are found united two, three, and sometimes all four together.

(Galileo Galilei, *The Starry Messenger*)

★22. Lenses function by refracting light at their surfaces. Consequently, their action depends not only on the shape of the lens surfaces, but also on the indices of refraction of the lens material and the surrounding medium.

(Frank J. Blatt, *Principles of Physics,* 2nd edition)

23. Given present growth rates in underdeveloped countries, the limited practice of birth control, and the difficulty of slowing the current growth momentum, it can be said with virtual certainty that none of the people now reading this book will ever live in a world where the population is not growing.

(J. John Palen, *Social Problems*)

24. The interpretation of the laws is the proper and peculiar province of the courts. A constitution is, in fact, and must be regarded by the judges, as a fundamental law. It therefore belongs to them to ascertain its meaning, as well as the meaning of any particular act proceeding from the legislative body.

(Alexander Hamilton, *Federalist Papers,* No. 78)

★25. The Simpson incident had shown me that a dog was kept in the stables, and yet, though someone had been in and had fetched out a horse, he had not barked enough to arouse the two lads in the loft. Obviously the midnight visitor was someone whom the dog knew well.

(A. Conan Doyle, *Memoirs of Sherlock Holmes*)

26. Eternity is simultaneously whole. But time has a before and an after. Therefore time and eternity are not the same thing.

(Thomas Aquinas, *Summa Theologica*)

27. Ordinary things that we encounter every day are electrically neutral. Therefore, since negatively charged electrons are a part of everything, positively charged particles must also exist in all matter.

(James E. Brady and Gerard E. Humiston, *General Chemistry*)

★28. Animals that live on plant foods must eat large quantities of vegetation, and this consumes much of their time. Meat eaters, by contrast, have no need to eat so much or so often. Consequently, meat-eating hominines [early humans] may have had more leisure time available to explore and manipulate their environment; like lions and leopards, they would have time to spend lying around and playing.

(William A. Haviland, *Cultural Anthropology*, 8th edition)

29. [Psychologists] Wirtshafter and Davis noted that the glycerol content of the blood is related to the size of the fat cells [in the body]. Since the size of the fat cells would indicate something about the amount of stored fats, increases in blood glycerol should indicate increases in body weight.

(Herbert L. Petri, *Motivation: Theory and Research*, 2nd edition)

30. Because the moon moves relative to the earth so that it returns to the same position overhead after about 25 hours, there are two high and two low tides at any point every 25 hours.

(Douglas C. Giancoli, *The Ideas of Physics*, 3rd edition)

II. Define the following terms:

deductive argument	argument from analogy
inductive argument	generalization
argument based on mathematics	prediction
argument from definition	argument from authority
categorical syllogism	argument based on signs
hypothetical syllogism	causal inference
disjunctive syllogism	particular statement
	general statement

III. Answer "true" or "false" to the following statements:

1. In an inductive argument, it is intended that the conclusion contain more information than the premises.

2. In a deductive argument, the conclusion is not supposed to contain more information than the premises.

3. The form of argumentation the arguer uses may allow one to determine whether an argument is inductive or deductive.

4. The actual strength of the link between premises and conclusion may allow one to determine whether an argument is inductive or deductive.

5. A geometrical proof is an example of an inductive argument.

6. Most arguments based on statistical reasoning are deductive.

7. If the conclusion of an argument follows merely from the definition of a word used in a premise, the argument is deductive.

8. An argument that draws a conclusion about a thing based on that thing's similarity to something else is a deductive argument.

9. An argument that draws a conclusion that something is true because someone has said that it is, is a deductive argument.

10. An argument that presents two alternatives and eliminates one, leaving the other as the conclusion, is an inductive argument.

11. An argument that proceeds from knowledge of a cause to knowledge of an effect is an inductive argument.

12. If an argument contains the phrase "it definitely follows that," then we know for certain that the argument is deductive.

13. An argument that predicts what will happen in the future, based upon what has happened in the past, is an inductive argument.

14. Inductive arguments always proceed from the particular to the general.

15. Deductive arguments always proceed from the general to the particular.

IV. Page through a book, magazine, or newspaper and find two arguments, one inductive and the other deductive. Copy the arguments as written, giving the appropriate reference. Then identify the premises and conclusion of each.

1.4 Validity, Truth, Soundness, Strength, Cogency

This section introduces the central ideas and terminology required to evaluate arguments. We have seen that every argument makes two basic claims: a claim that evidence or reasons exist and a claim that the alleged evidence or reasons support something (or that something follows from the alleged evidence or reasons). The first is a factual claim, the second an inferential claim. The evaluation of every argument centers on the evaluation of these two claims. The more important of the two is the inferential claim, because if the premises fail to support the conclusion (that is, if the reasoning is bad), an argument is worthless. Thus we will always test the inferential claim first, and only if the premises do support the conclusion will we test the factual claim (that is, the claim that the premises present genuine evidence, or are true). The material that follows considers first deductive arguments and then inductive.

Deductive Arguments

The previous section defined a deductive argument as one in which the arguer claims that it is impossible for the conclusion to be false given that the premises are true. If this claim is true, the argument is said to be valid. Thus, a **valid deductive argument** is an argument in which it is impossible for the conclusion to be false given that the premises are true. In these arguments the conclusion follows with strict necessity from the premises. Conversely, an **invalid deductive argument** is a deductive argument in which it *is* possible for the conclusion to be false given that the premises are true. In these arguments the conclusion does not follow with strict necessity from the premises, even though it is claimed to.

An immediate consequence of these definitions is that there is no middle ground between valid and invalid. There are no arguments that are "almost" valid and "almost" invalid. If the conclusion follows with strict necessity from the premises, the argument is valid; if not, it is invalid.

To test an argument for validity we begin by assuming that all the premises are true, and then we determine if it is possible, in light of that assumption, for the conclusion to be false. Here is an example:

> All television networks are media companies.
> NBC is a television network.
> Therefore, NBC is a media company.

In this argument both premises are actually true, so it is easy to *assume* that they are true. Next we determine, in light of this assumption, if it is possible for the conclusion to be false. Clearly this is not possible. If NBC is included in the group of television networks (second premise) and if the group of television networks is included in the group of media companies (first premise), it necessarily follows that NBC is included in the group of media companies (conclusion). In other words, assuming the premises true and the conclusion false entails a strict *contradiction*. Thus the argument is valid.

Here is another example:

> All automakers are computer manufacturers.
> United Airlines is an automaker.
> Therefore, United Airlines is a computer manufacturer.

In this argument, both premises are actually false, but it is easy to assume that they are true. Every automaker could have a corporate division that manufactures computers. Also, in addition to flying airplanes, United Airlines could make cars. Next, in light of these assumptions, we determine if it is possible for the conclusion to be false. Again, we see that this is not possible, by the same reasoning as the previous example. Assuming the premises true and the conclusion false entails a contradiction. Thus, the argument is valid.

Another example:

> All banks are financial institutions.
> Wells Fargo is a financial institution.
> Therefore, Wells Fargo is a bank.

As in the first example, both premises of this argument are true, so it is easy to assume they are true. Next we determine, in light of this assumption, if it is possible for the conclusion to be false. In this case it *is* possible. If banks were included in one part of the group of financial institutions and Wells Fargo were included in another part, then Wells Fargo would *not* be a bank. In other words, assuming the premises true and the conclusion false does not involve any contradiction, and so the argument is invalid.

In addition to illustrating the basic idea of validity, these examples suggest an important point about validity and truth. In general, validity is not something that is uniformly determined by the actual truth or falsity of the premises and conclusion. Both the NBC example and the Wells Fargo example have actually true premises and an actually true conclusion, yet one is valid and the other invalid. The United Airlines example has actually false premises and an actually false conclusion, yet the argument is

Table 1.1 Deductive Arguments

	Valid	Invalid
True premises **True** conclusion	All wines are beverages. Chardonnay is a wine. Therefore, chardonnay is a beverage. [sound]	All wines are beverages. Chardonnay is a beverage. Therefore, chardonnay is a wine. [unsound]
True premises **False** conclusion	None exist	All wines are beverages. Ginger ale is a beverage. Therefore, ginger ale is a wine. [unsound]
False premises **True** conclusion	All wines are soft drinks. Ginger ale is a wine. Therefore, ginger ale is a soft drink. [unsound]	All wines are whiskeys. Chardonnay is a whiskey. Therefore, chardonnay is a wine. [unsound]
False premises **False** conclusion	All wines are whiskeys. Ginger ale is a wine. Therefore, ginger ale is a whiskey. [unsound]	All wines are whiskeys. Ginger ale is a whiskey. Therefore, ginger ale is a wine. [unsound]

valid. Rather, validity is something that is determined by the *relationship* between premises and conclusion. The question is not whether premises and conclusion are true or false, but whether the premises *support* the conclusion. In the examples of valid arguments the premises do support the conclusion, and in the invalid case they do not.

Nevertheless, there is *one* arrangement of truth and falsity in the premises and conclusion that does determine the issue of validity. Any deductive argument having actually true premises and an actually false conclusion is invalid. The reasoning behind this fact is fairly obvious. If the premises are actually true and the conclusion is actually false, then it certainly is *possible* for the premises to be true and the conclusion false. Thus, by the definition of invalidity, the argument is invalid.

The idea that any deductive argument having actually true premises and a false conclusion is invalid may be the most important point in all of deductive logic. The entire system of deductive logic would be quite useless if it accepted as valid any inferential process by which a person could start with truth in the premises and arrive at falsity in the conclusion.

Table 1.1 presents examples of deductive arguments that illustrate the various combinations of truth and falsity in the premises and conclusion. In the examples having false premises, both premises are false, but it is easy to construct other examples having only one false premise. When examining this table, note that the only combination of truth and falsity that does not allow for *both* valid and invalid arguments is true premises and false conclusion. As we have just seen, any argument having this combination is necessarily invalid.

The relationship between the validity of a deductive argument and the truth or falsity of its premises and conclusion, as illustrated in Table 1.1, is summarized as follows:

Premises	Conclusion	Validity
T	T	?
T	F	Invalid
F	T	?
F	F	?

A **sound argument** is a deductive argument that is *valid* and has *all true premises*. Both conditions must be met for an argument to be sound, and if either is missing the argument is unsound. Thus, an unsound argument is a deductive argument that is invalid, has one or more false premises, or both. Because a valid argument is one such that it is impossible for the premises to be true and the conclusion false, and because a sound argument does in fact have true premises, it follows that every sound argument, by definition, will have a true conclusion as well. A sound argument, therefore, is what is meant by a "good" deductive argument in the fullest sense of the term.

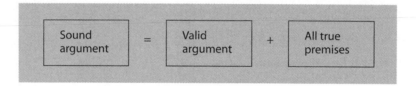

In connection with this definition of soundness, a single proviso is required: For an argument to be unsound, the false premise or premises must actually be needed to support the conclusion. An argument with a conclusion that is validly supported by true premises but with a superfluous false premise would still be sound. By similar reasoning, no addition of a false premise to an originally sound argument can make the argument unsound. Such a premise would be superfluous, and should not be considered part of the argument. Analogous remarks, incidentally, extend to induction.

Inductive Arguments

Section 1.3 defined an inductive argument as one in which the arguer claims that it is improbable that the conclusion be false given that the premises are true. If this claim is true, the argument is said to be strong. Thus, a **strong inductive argument** is an inductive argument in which it is improbable that the conclusion be false given that the premises are true. In such arguments, the conclusion does in fact follow probably from the premises. Conversely, a **weak inductive argument** is an argument in which the conclusion does not follow probably from the premises, even though it is claimed to.

The procedure for testing the strength of inductive arguments runs parallel to the procedure for deduction. First we assume the premises are true, and then we determine whether, based on that assumption, the conclusion is probably true. Example:

> All dinosaur bones discovered to this day have been at least 50 million years old. There-
> fore, probably the next dinosaur bone to be found will be at least 50 million years old.

In this argument the premise is actually true, so it is easy to assume that it is true. Based on that assumption, the conclusion is probably true, so the argument is strong. Here is another example:

> All meteorites found to this day have contained sugar. Therefore, probably the next mete-
> orite to be found will contain sugar.

The premise of this argument is obviously false. But if we assume the premise is true, then based on that assumption, the conclusion would probably be true. Thus, the argument is strong.

The next example is an argument from analogy:

> When a lighted match is slowly dunked into water, the flame is snuffed out. But gasoline
> is a liquid, just like water. Therefore, when a lighted match is slowly dunked into gaso-
> line, the flame will be snuffed out.

In this argument the premises are actually true and the conclusion is probably false. Thus, if we assume the premises are true, then, based on that assumption, it is not probable that the conclusion is true. Thus, the argument is weak.

Another example:

> During the past fifty years, inflation has consistently reduced the value of the American
> dollar. Therefore, industrial productivity will probably increase in the years ahead.

In this argument, the premise is actually true and the conclusion is probably true in the actual world, but the probability of the conclusion is in no way based on the assumption that the premise is true. Because there is no direct connection between inflation and increased industrial productivity, the premise is irrelevant to the conclusion and it provides no probabilistic support for it. The conclusion is probably true independently of the premise. As a result, the argument is weak.

This last example illustrates an important distinction between strong inductive arguments and valid deductive arguments. As we will see in later chapters, if the conclusion of a deductive argument is necessarily true independently of the premises, the argument is still considered valid. But if the conclusion of an inductive argument is probably true independently of the premises, the argument is weak.

These four examples show that in general the strength or weakness of an inductive argument results not from the actual truth or falsity of the premises and conclusion, but from the probabilistic support the premises give to the conclusion. The dinosaur argument has a true premise and probably true conclusion, and the meteorite argument has a false premise and a probably false conclusion; yet, both are strong because the premise of each provides probabilistic support for the conclusion. The industrial productivity argument has a true premise and a probably true conclusion, but the argument is weak because the premise provides no probabilistic support for the conclusion. Analogously to the evaluation of deductive arguments, the only arrangement of truth and falsity that establishes anything is true premises and probably false conclusion (as in the lighted match argument). Any inductive argument having true premises and a probably false conclusion is weak.

Table 1.2 Inductive Arguments

	Strong	Weak
True premise **Probably true conclusion**	All previous American presidents were men. Therefore, probably the next American president will be a man. [cogent]	A few American presidents were Federalists. Therefore, probably the next American president will be a man. [uncogent]
True premise **Probably false conclusion**	None exist	A few American presidents were Federalists. Therefore, probably the next American president will be a Federalist. [uncogent]
False premise **Probably true conclusion**	All previous American presidents were television debaters. Therefore, probably the next American president will be a television debater. [uncogent]	A few American presidents were Libertarians. Therefore, probably the next American president will be a television debater. [uncogent]
False premise **Probably false conclusion**	All previous American presidents were women. Therefore, probably the next American president will be a woman. [uncogent]	A few American presidents were Libertarians. Therefore, probably the next American president will be a Libertarian. [uncogent]

Table 1.2 presents the various possibilities of truth and falsity in the premises and conclusion of inductive arguments. Note that the only arrangement of truth and falsity that is missing for strong arguments is true premises and probably false conclusion.

The relationship between the strength of an inductive argument and the truth or falsity of its premises and conclusion, as illustrated in Table 1.2, is summarized as follows:

Premises	Conclusion	Strength
T	prob. T	?
T	prob. F	Weak
F	prob. T	?
F	prob. F	?

Unlike the validity and invalidity of deductive arguments, the strength and weakness of inductive arguments admit of degrees. To be considered strong, an inductive argument must have a conclusion that is more probable than improbable. In other words, the likelihood that the conclusion is true must be more than 50 percent, and as the probability increases, the argument becomes stronger. For this purpose, consider the following pair of arguments:

> This barrel contains 100 apples.
> Three apples selected at random were found to be ripe.
> Therefore, probably all 100 apples are ripe.

> This barrel contains 100 apples.
> Eighty apples selected at random were found to be ripe.
> Therefore, probably all 100 apples are ripe.

The first argument is weak and the second is strong. However, the first is not absolutely weak nor the second absolutely strong. Both arguments would be strengthened or weakened by the random selection of a larger or smaller sample. For example, if the size of the sample in the second argument were reduced to seventy apples, the argument would be weakened. The incorporation of additional premises into an inductive argument will also generally tend to strengthen or weaken it. For example, if the premise "One unripe apple that had been found earlier was removed" were added to either argument, the argument would be weakened.

A **cogent argument** is an inductive argument that is *strong* and has *all true premises;* if either condition is missing, the argument is uncogent. Thus, an uncogent argument is an inductive argument that is weak, has one or more false premises, or both. A cogent argument is the inductive analogue of a sound deductive argument and is what is

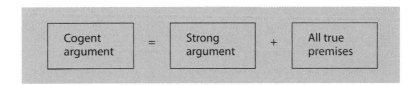

meant by a "good" inductive argument without qualification. Because the conclusion of a cogent argument is genuinely supported by true premises, it follows that the conclusion of every cogent argument is probably true.

There is a difference, however, between sound and cogent arguments in regard to the true premise requirement. In a sound argument it is necessary only that the premises be true and nothing more. Given such premises and good reasoning, a true conclusion is guaranteed. In a cogent argument, on the other hand, the premises must not only be true, but they must also not ignore some important piece of evidence that entails a quite different conclusion. This is called the *total evidence requirement.* As an illustration of the need for it, consider the following argument:

> Swimming in the Caribbean is usually lots of fun. Today the water is warm, the surf is gentle, and on this beach there are no dangerous currents. Therefore, it would be fun to go swimming here now.

If the premises reflect all the important factors, then the argument is cogent. But if they ignore the fact that several large dorsal fins are cutting through the water, then obviously the argument is not cogent. Thus, for cogency the premises must not only be true but also not overlook some important fact that requires a different conclusion.

Summary

For both deductive and inductive arguments, two separate questions need to be answered: (1) Do the premises support the conclusion? (2) Are all the premises true?

To answer the first question we begin by *assuming* the premises to be true. Then, for deductive arguments we determine whether, in light of this assumption, it *necessarily* follows that the conclusion is true. If it does, the argument is valid; if not, it is invalid. For inductive arguments we determine whether it *probably* follows that the conclusion is true. If it does, the argument is strong; if not, it is weak. For inductive arguments we keep in mind the requirements that the premises actually support the conclusion and that they not ignore important evidence. Finally, if the argument is either valid or strong, we turn to the second question and determine whether the premises are actually true. If all the premises are true, the argument is sound (in the case of deduction) or cogent (in the case of induction). All invalid deductive arguments are unsound, and all weak inductive arguments are uncogent.

The various alternatives open to statements and arguments may be diagrammed as follows. Note that in logic one never speaks of an argument as being "true" or "false," and one never speaks of a statement as being "valid," "invalid," "strong," or "weak."

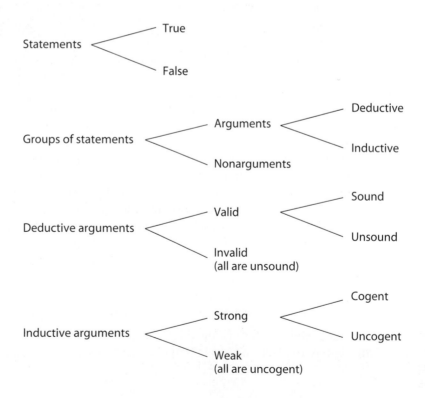

I. The following arguments are deductive. Determine whether each is valid or invalid, and note the relationship between your answer and the truth or falsity of the premises and conclusion. Finally, determine whether the argument is sound or unsound.

★1. Since *Moby Dick* was written by Shakespeare, and *Moby Dick* is a science fiction novel, it follows that Shakespeare wrote a science fiction novel.

2. Since London is north of Paris and south of Edinburgh, it follows that Paris is south of Edinburgh.

3. If George Washington was beheaded, then George Washington died. George Washington died. Therefore, George Washington was beheaded.

★4. The longest river in South America is the Amazon, and the Amazon flows through Brazil. Therefore, the longest river in South America flows through Brazil.

5. Since the Spanish-American War occurred before the American Civil War, and the American Civil War occurred after the Korean War, it follows that the Spanish-American War occurred before the Korean War.

6. The Empire State Building is taller than the Statue of Liberty, and the Statue of Liberty is taller than the Eiffel Tower. Therefore, the Empire State Building is taller than the Eiffel Tower.

★7. All leopards with lungs are carnivores. Therefore, all leopards are carnivores.

8. Chicago is a city in Michigan and Michigan is part of the United States. Therefore, Chicago is a city in the United States.

9. If Senator Hillary Clinton represents California, then she represents a western state. Hillary Clinton does not represent a western state. Therefore, she does not represent California.

★10. Every province in Canada has exactly one city as its capital. Therefore, since there are thirty provinces in Canada, there are thirty provincial capitals.

11. Since the Department of Defense Building in Washington, D.C., has the shape of a hexagon, it follows that it has seven sides.

12. Since Winston Churchill was English, and Winston Churchill was a famous statesman, we may conclude that at least one Englishman was a famous statesman.

★13. Since some fruits are green, and some fruits are apples, it follows that some fruits are green apples.

14. All physicians are individuals who have earned degrees in political science, and some lawyers are physicians. Therefore, some lawyers are persons who have earned degrees in political science.

15. The United States Congress has more members than there are days in the year. Therefore, at least two members of Congress have the same birthday.

II. The following arguments are inductive. Determine whether each is strong or weak, and note the relationship between your answer and the truth or falsity of the premise(s) and conclusion. Then determine whether each argument is cogent or uncogent.

★1. The grave marker at Arlington National Cemetery says that John F. Kennedy is buried there. It must be the case that Kennedy really is buried in that cemetery.

2. The ebb and flow of the tides has been occurring every day for millions of years. But nothing lasts forever. Therefore, probably the motion of the tides will die out within a few years.

3. The vast majority of Rose Bowl games (in Pasadena, CA) have been played in freezing cold weather. Therefore, probably the next Rose Bowl game will be played in freezing cold weather.

★4. Franklin Delano Roosevelt said that we have nothing to fear but fear itself. Therefore, women have no reason to fear serial rapists.

5. Most famous movie stars are millionaires. Leonardo Di Caprio is a famous movie star. Therefore, probably Di Caprio is a millionaire.

6. Constructing the great pyramid at Giza required lifting massive stone blocks to great heights. Probably the ancient Egyptians had some antigravity device to accomplish this feat.

★7. People have been listening to rock and roll music for over a hundred years. Probably people will still be listening to it a year from now.

8. Paleontologists have unearthed the fossilized bones of huge reptiles, which we have named dinosaurs. Tests indicate that these bones are more than 50 million years old. Therefore, probably dinosaurs really did roam the earth 50 million years ago.

9. The Declaration of Independence says that all men are endowed by their creator with certain unalienable rights. Therefore it probably follows that a creator exists.

★10. Coca-Cola is an extremely popular soft drink. Therefore, probably someone, somewhere, is drinking a Coke right this minute.

11. Every map of the United States shows that Alabama is situated on the Pacific coast. Therefore, Alabama must be a western state.

12. When Neil Armstrong landed on the moon, he left behind a gold plated Schwinn bicycle, which he used to ride around on the moon's surface. Probably that bicycle is still up there on the moon.

★13. African American athlete Jerome Bettis is able to withstand tremendous impacts on the football field. However, Venus Williams, like Jerome Bettis, is a great African American athlete. Therefore, Venus Williams should be able to withstand tremendous impacts on the football field.

14. Unlike monkeys, today's humans have feet that are not suited for grasping objects. Therefore, a thousand years from now, probably humans will still have feet that are not suited for grasping objects.

15. A random sample of twenty-five famous country and western singers, including Garth Brooks and Dolly Parton, revealed that every single one of them

studied music in Afghanistan. Therefore, probably the majority of famous country and western singers studied in Afghanistan.

III. Determine whether the following arguments are inductive or deductive. If an argument is inductive, determine whether it is strong or weak. If it is deductive, determine whether it is valid or invalid.

★1. Since Agatha is the mother of Raquel and the sister of Tom, it follows that Tom is the uncle of Raquel.

2. When a cook can't recall the ingredients in a recipe, it is appropriate that she refresh her memory by consulting the recipe book. Similarly, when a student can't recall the answers during a final exam, it is appropriate that she refresh her memory by consulting the textbook.

3. The sign on the highway leading into Denver, Colorado says that the city's elevation is 5280 feet. It must be the case that Denver is 1 mile high.

★4. Since Christmas is always on a Thursday, it follows that the day after Christmas is always a Friday.

5. This figure is a Euclidean triangle. Therefore, the sum of its angles is equal to two right angles.

6. By accident Karen baked her brownies two hours longer than she should have. Therefore, they have probably been ruined.

★7. After taking LSD, Alice said she saw a flying saucer land in the shopping center parking lot. Since Alice has a reputation for always telling the truth, we must conclude that a flying saucer really did land there.

8. Since Phyllis is the cousin of Denise, and Denise is the cousin of Harriet, it follows necessarily that Harriet is the cousin of Phyllis.

9. The picnic scheduled in the park for tomorrow will most likely be cancelled. It's been snowing for six days straight.

★10. Circle A has exactly twice the diameter of circle B. From this we may conclude that circle A has exactly twice the area of circle B.

11. Robert has lost consistently at blackjack every day for the past several days. Therefore, it is very likely that he will win today.

12. Since John loves Nancy and Nancy loves Peter, it follows necessarily that John loves Peter.

★13. This cash register drawer contains over 100 coins. Three coins selected at random were found to have dates earlier than 1945. Therefore, probably all of the coins in the drawer have dates earlier than 1945.

14. The Japanese attack on Pearl Harbor happened in either 1941 or 1951. But it didn't happen in 1941. Therefore, it happened in 1951.

15. Harry will never be able to solve that difficult problem in advanced calculus in the limited time allowed. He has never studied anything beyond algebra, and in that he earned only a C-.

★16. Since $x + y = 10$, and $x = 7$, it follows that $y = 4$.

17. If acupuncture is hocus pocus, then acupuncture cannot relieve chronic pain. But acupuncture can relieve chronic pain. Therefore, acupuncture is not hocus pocus.

18. If inflation heats up, then interest rates will rise. If interest rates rise, then bond prices will decline. Therefore, if inflation heats up, then bond prices will decline.

★19. Statistics reveal that 86 percent of those who receive flu shots do not get the flu. Jack received a flu shot one month ago. Therefore, he should be immune, even though the flu is going around now.

20. Since Michael is a Pisces, it necessarily follows that he was born in March.

IV. Define the following terms:

valid argument	strong argument
invalid argument	weak argument
sound argument	cogent argument
unsound argument	uncogent argument

V. Answer "true" or "false" to the following statements:

1. Some arguments, while not completely valid, are almost valid.
2. Inductive arguments admit of varying degrees of strength and weakness.
3. Invalid deductive arguments are basically the same as inductive arguments.
4. If a deductive argument has true premises and a false conclusion, it is necessarily invalid.
5. A valid argument may have a false premise and a false conclusion.
6. A valid argument may have a false premise and a true conclusion.
7. A sound argument may be invalid.
8. A sound argument may have a false conclusion.
9. A strong argument may have false premises and a probably false conclusion.
10. A strong argument may have true premises and a probably false conclusion.
11. A cogent argument may have a probably false conclusion.
12. A cogent argument must be inductively strong.
13. If an argument has true premises and a true conclusion, we know that it is a perfectly good argument.
14. A statement may legitimately be spoken of as "valid" or "invalid."
15. An argument may legitimately be spoken of as "true" or "false."

1.5   Argument Forms: Proving Invalidity

This section explores the idea that the validity of a deductive argument is determined by the argument's form. This idea was suggested in the arguments about wines and beverages presented in Table 1.1 in the previous section. All the arguments in the valid column have the same form, and all the arguments in the invalid column have the same form.

Yet, in the exercises at the end of that section we saw many cases of valid deductive arguments that did not have any recognizable form. How can we reconcile this fact with the claim that validity is determined by form? The answer is that these arguments are incomplete, so the form is not explicit. But once such arguments are completed and correctly phrased (which we address later in this book), the form becomes apparent. For example, consider the following valid argument:

Geese are migratory waterfowl, so they fly south for the winter.

This argument is missing a premise:

Migratory waterfowl fly south for the winter.

The argument can now be rephrased to make its form apparent:

All geese are migratory waterfowl.
All migratory waterfowl are birds that fly south for the winter.
Therefore, all geese are birds that fly south for the winter.

The form of the argument is:

All *A* are *B*.
All *B* are *C*.
All *A* are *C*.

This form is valid, and it captures the reasoning process of the argument. If we assume that the *A*s (whatever they might be) are included in the *B*s, and that the *B*s (whatever they might be) are included in the *C*s, then the *A*s must necessarily be included in the *C*s. This necessary relationship between the *A*s, *B*s, and *C*s is what makes the argument valid. This is what we mean when we say that the validity of a deductive argument is determined by its form.

Since validity is determined by form, it follows that any argument that has this valid form is a valid argument. Thus, we might substitute "daisies" for *A*, "flowers" for *B*, and "plants" for *C* and obtain the following valid argument:

All daisies are flowers.
All flowers are plants.
Therefore, all daisies are plants.

Any argument such as this that is produced by uniformly substituting terms or statements in place of the letters in an argument form is called a **substitution instance** of that form.

Let us now consider an invalid argument form:

All *A* are *B*.
All *C* are *B*.
All *A* are *C*.

In this argument form, if we assume that the *A*s are in the *B*s and that the *C*s are in the *B*s, it does not *necessarily* follow that the *A*s are in the *C*s. It would not follow if the *A*s were in one part of the *B*s and the *C*s were in another part, as the following diagram illustrates:

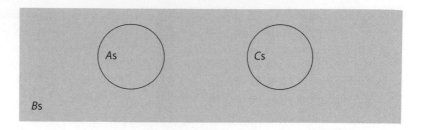

This diagram suggests that we can prove the form invalid if we can find a substitution instance having actually true premises and an actually false conclusion. In such a substitution instance the *A*s and the *C*s would be separated from each other, but they would both be included in the *B*s. If we substitute "cats" for *A*, "animals" for *B*, and "dogs" for *C*, we have such a substitution instance:

All *A* are *B*.	All cats are animals.	True
All *C* are *B*.	All dogs are animals.	True
All *A* are *C*.	Therefore, All cats are dogs.	False

This substitution instance proves the form invalid because it provides a concrete example of a case where the *A*s are in the *B*s, the *C*s are in the *B*s, but the *A*s are *not* in the *C*s.

Now, since the form is invalid, can we say that any argument that has this form is invalid? Unfortunately, the situation with invalid forms is not quite so simple as it is with valid forms. Every substitution instance of a valid form is a valid argument, but it is not the case that every substitution instance of an invalid form is an invalid argument. The reason is that some substitution instances of invalid forms are also substitution instances of valid forms.* However, we can say that any substitution instance of an invalid form is an invalid argument *provided* that it is not a substitution instance of any valid form. Thus we will say that an argument actually *has* an invalid form if it is a substitution instance of that form and it is not a substitution instance of any valid form.

The fact that some substitution instances of invalid forms are also substitution instances of valid forms means simply that we must exercise caution in identifying the form of an argument. However, cases of ordinary language arguments that can be interpreted as substitution instances of both valid and invalid forms are so rare that this book chooses to ignore them. With this in mind, consider the following argument:

---

*For example, the following valid argument is a substitution instance of the invalid form we have been discussing:

All bachelors are persons.
All unmarried men are persons.
Therefore, all bachelors are unmarried men.

However, because "bachelors" is equivalent in meaning to "unmarried men," the argument is also a substitution instance of this valid form:

All *A* are *B*.
All *A* are *B*.
All *A* are *A*.

All romantic novels are literary pieces.
All works of fiction are literary pieces.
Therefore, all romantic novels are works of fiction.

This argument clearly has the invalid form just discussed. This invalid form captures the reasoning process of the argument, which is obviously defective. Therefore, the argument is invalid, and it is invalid precisely because it has an invalid form.

Counterexample Method

A substitution instance having true premises and a false conclusion (like the cats-and-dogs example just constructed) is called a counterexample, and the method we have just used to prove the romantic-novels argument invalid is called the **counterexample method.** It consists of isolating the form of an argument and then constructing a substitution instance having true premises and a false conclusion. This proves the form invalid, which in turn proves the argument invalid. The counterexample method can be used to prove the invalidity of any invalid argument, but it cannot prove the validity of any valid argument. Thus, before the method is applied to an argument, the argument must be known or suspected to be invalid in the first place. Let us apply the counterexample method to the following invalid categorical syllogism:

Since some employees are not social climbers and all vice-presidents are employees, we may conclude that some vice-presidents are not social climbers.

This argument is invalid because the employees who are not social climbers might not be vice-presidents. Accordingly, we can *prove* the argument invalid by constructing a substitution instance having true premises and a false conclusion. We begin by isolating the form of the argument:

Some *E* are not *S*.
All *V* are *E*.
Some *V* are not *S*.

Next, we select three terms to substitute in place of the letters that will make the premises true and the conclusion false. The following selection will work:

E = animals
S = mammals
V = dogs

The resulting substitution instance is:

Some animals are not mammals.
All dogs are animals.
Therefore, some dogs are not mammals.

The substitution instance has true premises and a false conclusion and is therefore, by definition, invalid. Because the substitution instance is invalid, the form is invalid, and therefore the original argument is invalid.

In applying the counterexample method to categorical syllogisms, it is useful to keep in mind the following set of terms: "cats," "dogs," "mammals," "fish," and "animals." Most invalid syllogisms can be proven invalid by strategically selecting three of these terms and using them to construct a counterexample. Because everyone agrees about these terms, everyone will agree about the truth or falsity of the premises and conclusion of the counterexample. Also, in constructing the counterexample, it often helps to begin with the conclusion. First, select two terms that yield a false conclusion, and then select a third term that yields true premises. Another point to keep in mind is that the word "some" in logic always means "at least one." For example, the statement "Some dogs are animals" means "At least one dog is an animal"—which is true. Also note that this statement does not imply that some dogs are not animals.

Not all deductive arguments, of course, are categorical syllogisms. Consider, for example, the following hypothetical syllogism:

> If the government imposes import restrictions, the price of automobiles will rise. Therefore, since the government will not impose import restrictions, it follows that the price of automobiles will not rise.

This argument is invalid because the price of automobiles might rise even though import restrictions are not imposed. It has the following form:

> If G, then P.
> Not G.
> Not P.

This form differs from the previous one in that its letters stand for complete statements. G, for example, stands for "The government imposes import restrictions." If we make the substitution

> G = Abraham Lincoln committed suicide.
> P = Abraham Lincoln is dead.

we obtain the following substitution instance:

> If Abraham Lincoln committed suicide, then Abraham Lincoln is dead.
> Abraham Lincoln did not commit suicide.
> Therefore, Abraham Lincoln is not dead.

Since the premises are true and the conclusion false, the substitution instance is clearly invalid. Therefore, the form is invalid, and this proves the original argument invalid.

When applying the counterexample method to an argument having a conditional statement as a premise (such as the one above), it is recommended that the statement

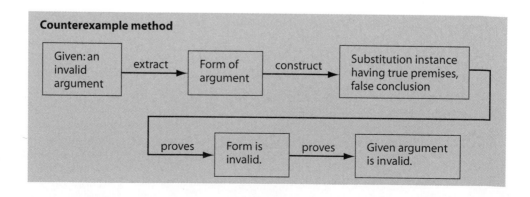

Counterexample method

Given: an invalid argument →extract→ Form of argument →construct→ Substitution instance having true premises, false conclusion

→proves→ Form is invalid. →proves→ Given argument is invalid.

substituted in place of the conditional statement express some kind of necessary connection. In the Lincoln example, the first premise asserts the necessary connection between suicide and death. There can be no doubt about the truth of such a statement. Furthermore, if it should turn out that the conclusion is a conditional statement, note that one sure way of producing a false conditional statement is by joining a true antecedent with a false consequent. For example, the conditional statement "If Lassie is a dog, then Lassie is a cat" is clearly false.

Being able to identify the form of an argument with ease requires a familiarity with the basic deductive argument forms. The first task consists in distinguishing the premises from the conclusion. Always write the premises first and the conclusion last. The second task involves distinguishing what we may call "form words" from "content words." To reduce an argument to its form, leave the form words as they are, and replace the content words with letters. For categorical syllogisms, the words "all," "no," "some," "are," and "not" are form words, and for hypothetical syllogisms the words "if," "then," and "not" are form words. Additional form words for other types of arguments are "either," "or," "both," and "and." For various kinds of hybrid arguments, a more intuitive approach may be needed. Here is an example:

> All movie stars are actors who are famous, because all movie stars who are famous are actors.

If we replace "movie stars," "actors," and "famous" with the letters M, A, and F, this argument has the following form:

> All M who are F are A.
> ———————————
> All M are A who are F.

Here is one possible substitution instance for this form:

> All humans who are fathers are men.
> Therefore, all humans are men who are fathers.

Because the premise is true and the conclusion false, the form is invalid and so is the original argument.

Using the counterexample method to prove arguments invalid requires a little ingenuity because there is no rule that will automatically produce the required term or statement to be substituted into the form. Any term or statement will work, of course, provided that it yields a substitution instance that has premises that are indisputably true and a conclusion that is indisputably false. Ideally, the truth value of these statements should be known to the average individual; otherwise, the substitution instance cannot be depended upon to prove anything. If, for example, P in the earlier hypothetical syllogism had been replaced by the statement "George Wilson is dead," the substitution instance would be useless, because nobody knows whether this statement is true or false.

The counterexample method is useful only for proving invalidity, because the only arrangement of truth and falsity that proves anything is true premises and false conclusion. If a substitution instance is produced having true premises and a true conclusion, it does *not* prove that the argument is valid. Furthermore, the method is useful only for deductive arguments because the strength and weakness of inductive arguments is only partially dependent on the form of the argument. Accordingly, no method that relates exclusively to the form of an inductive argument can be used to prove the argument weak.

I. Use the counterexample method to prove the following categorical syllogisms invalid. In doing so, follow the suggestions given in the text.

★1. All galaxies are structures that contain black holes in the center, so all galaxies are quasars, since all quasars are structures that contain black holes in the center.

2. Some evolutionists are not persons who believe in the Bible, for no creationists are evolutionists, and some persons who believe in the Bible are not creationists.

3. No patents are measures that discourage research and development, and all patents are regulations that protect intellectual property. Thus, no measures that discourage research and development are regulations that protect intellectual property.

★4. Some farm workers are not persons who are paid decent wages, because no illegal aliens are persons who are paid decent wages, and some illegal aliens are not farm workers.

5. Some politicians are persons who will stop at nothing to win an election, and no persons who will stop at nothing to win an election are true statesmen. Hence, no politicians are true statesmen.

6. All meticulously constructed timepieces are true works of art, for all Swiss watches are true works of art and all Swiss watches are meticulously constructed timepieces.

★7. No patrons of fast-food restaurants are health food addicts. Consequently, no patrons of fast-food restaurants are connoisseurs of fine desserts, since no connoisseurs of fine desserts are health food addicts.

8. Some toxic dumps are sites that emit hazardous wastes, and some sites that emit hazardous wastes are undesirable places to live near. Thus, some toxic dumps are undesirable places to live near.

9. All persons who assist others in suicide are persons guilty of murder. Accordingly, some individuals motivated by compassion are not persons guilty of murder, inasmuch as some persons who assist others in suicide are individuals motivated by compassion.

★10. Some school boards are not groups that oppose values clarification because some school boards are not organizations with vision, and some groups that oppose values clarification are not organizations with vision.

II. Use the counterexample method to prove each of the following arguments invalid.

★1. If animal species are fixed and immutable, then evolution is a myth. Therefore, evolution is not a myth, since animal species are not fixed and immutable.

2. If carbon dioxide is present in the atmosphere, then plants have a source of carbon. Hence, since plants have a source of carbon, carbon dioxide is present in the atmosphere.

3. If human rights are recognized, then civilization flourishes. If equality prevails, then civilization flourishes. Thus, if human rights are recognized, then equality prevails.

★4. If energy taxes are increased, then either the deficit will be reduced or conservation will be taken seriously. If the deficit is reduced, then inflation will be checked. Therefore, if energy taxes are increased, then inflation will be checked.

5. All homeless people who are panhandlers are destitute individuals. Therefore, all homeless people are destitute individuals.

6. Some wrestlers are colorful hulks, since some wrestlers are colorful and some wrestlers are hulks.

★7. All community colleges with low tuition are either schools with large enrollments or institutions supported by taxes. Therefore, all community colleges are institutions supported by taxes.

8. All merchandisers that are retailers are businesses that are inventory rotators. Therefore, all merchandisers are inventory rotators.

9. All diabetes victims are either insulin takers or glucose eliminators. Accordingly, some diabetes victims are glucose eliminators, since some diabetes victims are insulin takers.

★10. All FHA loans are living standard enhancers for the following reasons. All reverse mortgages that are FHA loans are either living standard enhancers or home equity depleters, and all reverse mortgages are home equity depleters.

1.6   Extended Arguments

The logical analysis of extended arguments, such as those found in editorials, essays, and lengthy letters to newspaper editors, involves numerous difficulties. Such arguments are often mixed together with fragments of reports, pieces of expository writing, illustrations, explanations, and statements of opinion. Proper analysis involves weeding out the extraneous material and isolating premises and conclusions. Another problem stems from the fact that lengthy arguments often involve complex arrangements of subarguments that feed into the main argument in various ways. Distinguishing one subargument from another is often a complicated task. And then there are some argumentative passages that involve completely separate strands of argumentation leading to separate conclusions. Again, distinguishing the strands and assigning premises to the right conclusion not only is problematic but often involves an element of creativity on the part of the analyst.

To facilitate the analysis of extended arguments, we will assign numerals to the various statements in the passage and use arrows to represent the inferential links. Example:

① The contamination of underground aquifers represents a pollution problem of catastrophic proportions. ② Half the nation's drinking water, which comes from these aquifers, is being poisoned by chemical wastes dumped into the soil for generations.

This argument is diagrammed as follows:

The diagram says that statement ②, the premise, supports statement ①, the conclusion.

In extended arguments we can identify two distinct patterns of argumentation, which we will name the vertical pattern and the horizontal pattern. The *vertical pattern* consists of a series of arguments in which a conclusion of a logically prior argument becomes a premise of a subsequent argument. Example:

> ① The selling of human organs, such as hearts, kidneys, and corneas, should be outlawed. ② Allowing human organs to be sold will inevitably lead to a situation in which only the rich will be able to afford transplants. This is so because ③ whenever something scarce is bought and sold as a commodity, the price always goes up. ④ The law of supply and demand requires it.

This argument is diagrammed as follows:

Vertical pattern

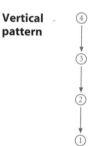

The diagram says that statement ①, which is the main conclusion, is supported by ②, which in turn is supported by ③, which in turn is supported by ④.

The *horizontal pattern* consists of a single argument in which two or more premises provide independent support for a single conclusion. If one of the premises were omitted, the other(s) would continue to support the conclusion in the same way. Example:

> ① The selling of human organs, such as hearts, kidneys, and corneas, should be outlawed. ② If this practice is allowed to get a foothold, people in desperate financial straits will start selling their own organs to pay their bills. Alternately, ③ those with a criminal bent will take to killing healthy young people and selling their organs on the black market. ④ In the final analysis, the buying and selling of human organs comes just too close to the buying and selling of life itself.

The diagram for this argument is as follows:

Horizontal pattern

This diagram says that statements ②, ③, and ④ support ① independently.

Two variations on the horizontal and vertical patterns occur when two or more premises support a conclusion *conjointly,* and when one or more premises supports *multiple* conclusions. The first variation occurs when the premises depend on one another in such a way that if one were omitted, the support that the others provide would be diminished or destroyed. The following argument illustrates the occurrence of conjoint premises:

> ① Getting poor people off the welfare rolls requires that we modify their behavior patterns. ② The vast majority of people on welfare are high school dropouts, single parents, or people who abuse alcohol and drugs. ③ These behavior patterns frustrate any desire poor people may have to get a job and improve their condition in life.

Statement ① is the conclusion. Taken separately, statements ② and ③ provide little or no support for ①, but taken together they do provide support. That is, ② and ③ support ① *conjointly.* This relationship between the premises is illustrated by the use of the brace in the following diagram:

Conjoint premises

The next example illustrates the occurrence of a multiple conclusion:

> ① Dropping out of school and bearing children outside of marriage are two of the primary causes of poverty in this country. Therefore, ② to eliminate poverty we must offer incentives for people to get high school diplomas. Also, ③ we must find some way to encourage people to get married before they start having children.

In this passage statement ① supports both ② and ③. Since no single argument can have more than one conclusion, the passage is correctly evaluated as consisting of two arguments. For our purposes, however, we will treat it as if it were a single argument by joining the two conclusions with a brace:

Multiple conclusion

Our symbolism is now sufficiently developed to analyze most arguments found in editorials and letters to the editor of newspapers and magazines. Consider the following argument, taken from a newspaper editorial:

> ① Government mandates for zero-emission vehicles won't work because ② only electric cars qualify as zero-emission vehicles, and ③ electric cars won't sell. ④ They are too expensive, ⑤ their range of operation Is too limited, and ⑥ recharging facilities are not generally available.
>
> (William Campbell, "Technology Is Not Good Enough")

We immediately see that ① is the main conclusion, and ② and ③ support ① conjointly. Also, ④, ⑤, and ⑥ support ③ independently. The argument pattern is as follows:

The next argument is taken from a letter to the editor:

> ① Rhinos in Kenya are threatened with extinction because ② poachers are killing them for their horn. Since ③ the rhino has no natural predators, ④ it does not need its horn to survive. Thus ⑤ there should be an organized program to capture rhinos in the wild and remove their horn. ⑥ Such a program would eliminate the incentive of the poachers.
>
> (Pamela C. Wagner, "Rhino Poaching")

First we search for the final conclusion. We select ⑤, because it is the ultimate point that the passage attempts to establish. Next we survey the premise and conclusion indicators. From this, we see that ② supports ① and ③ supports ④. Finally, we see that ①, ④, and ⑥ support ⑤. Yet these supporting statements depend on one another for their effect. Thus they support the final conclusion conjointly. The argument pattern is as follows:

The next argument is taken from a magazine article:

> ① Skating is a wonderful form of exercise and relaxation, but ② today's rollerbladers are a growing menace and ③ something should be done to control them. ④ Rollerbladers are oblivious to traffic regulations as ⑤ they breeze through red lights and ⑥ skim down the wrong way on one-way streets. ⑦ They pose a threat to pedestrians because ⑧ a collision can cause serious injury. ⑨ Rollerbladers are even a hazard to shopkeepers as ⑩ they zoom through stores and ⑪ damage merchandise.
>
> (Joan Schmidt, "Hell—On Wheels")

After reading the argument, we see that ① is merely an introductory sentence, and ② and ③ together compose the main conclusion. Also, ④, ⑦, and ⑨ support the main conclusion independently, while ⑤ and ⑥ support ④ independently, ⑧ supports ⑦, and ⑩ and ⑪ support ⑨ independently. The diagram is as follows:

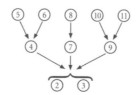

The next argument is taken from the science column of a newspaper:

① We can expect small changes to occur in the length of our calendar year for an indefinite time to come. ② This is true for two reasons. ③ First, the rotation of the earth exhibits certain irregularities. ④ And why is this so? ⑤ The rotation of any body is affected by its distribution of mass, and ⑥ the earth's mass distribution is continually subject to change. For example, ⑦ earthquakes alter the location of the tectonic plates. Also, ⑧ the liquid core of the earth sloshes as the earth turns, and ⑨ rainfall redistributes water from the oceans. The second reason is that ⑩ the motion of the tides causes a continual slowing down of earth's rotation. ⑪ Tidal motion produces heat, and ⑫ the loss of this heat removes energy from the system.

(Isaac Asimov, "As the World Turns")

Preliminary analysis reveals that the final conclusion is ①. Also, ② tells us that the supporting statements are divided into two basic groups, but since ② does not add any support, we can leave it out of the diagram. In the first group, ⑤ and ⑥ support ③ conjointly, while ⑦, ⑧, and ⑨ support ⑥ independently. ④ will not appear in the diagram, because it serves merely as a premise indicator. In the second group, ⑪ and ⑫ support ⑩ conjointly. Thus the argument pattern is as follows:

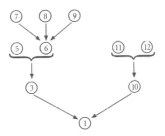

Our last example is taken from a letter to the editor of a newspaper:

① Community college districts save a great deal of money by hiring untenured part-time instructors, but ② the extensive use of these instructors is a disadvantage to the students. ③ Most part-time instructors are paid only 60 percent of what a full-time teacher earns, and as a result, ④ they are forced to teach five or six courses just to survive. ⑤ This detracts from the opportunity to consult with students outside the classroom. To make matters worse, ⑥ many part-timers are not even given office space. Furthermore, ⑦ the lower pay demoralizes the part-timer, and ⑧ the lack of tenure makes for constant financial insecurity. ⑨ Obviously these conditions render the instructor less receptive to student needs. Lastly, because ⑩ these part-timers are burning the candle from both ends, ⑪ they have no spare energy to improve their courses, and ⑫ many lack the enthusiasm to motivate their students. As a result, ⑬ the educational process is impaired.

(Gordon Dossett et al., "Part-Time College Instructors")

Preliminary analysis reveals that the main conclusion is not ① but ②. Also, we see three main reasons why part-timers are a disadvantage to students: They have little opportunity to consult with students, they are less receptive to student needs, and the educational process is impaired by ⑪ and ⑫. In the first main branch, the indicator "as a result" shows that ③ supports ④, and ④ and ⑥ independently support ⑤. In the second branch, ⑦ and ⑧ independently support ⑨. In the third, ⑩ supports both ⑪ and ⑫, which in turn support ⑬ independently. Here is the argument pattern:

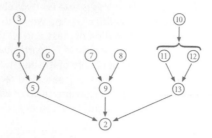

EXERCISE 1.6

I. The following arguments were abstracted from newspaper articles, editorials, and letters to the editor. Use the method presented in this section to construct argument patterns. If a statement is redundant or plays no role in the argument, do not include it in the pattern.

★1. ① The conditions under which many food animals are raised are unhealthy for humans. ② To keep these animals alive, large quantities of drugs must be administered. ③ These drugs remain in the animals' flesh and are passed on to the humans who eat it.

(Philip D. Oliver, "We Can Eat Ribs and Still Be Humane")

2. ① The development of carbon-embedded plastics, otherwise called "composits," is an important new technology because ② it holds the key for new aircraft and spacecraft designs. This is so because ③ these composits are not only stronger than steel but lighter than aluminum.

(Thomas H. Maugh II, "Composits—The Lightweight Champs of Aircraft Industry")

3. ① Homework stifles the thrill of learning in the mind of the student. ② It instills an oppressive learn-or-else discipline. ③ It quenches the desire for knowledge and the love of truth. For these reasons ④ homework should never be assigned.

(Colman McCarthy, "Homework's Tyranny Hobbles Promising Minds")

★4. ① When parents become old and destitute, the obligation of caring for them should be imposed on their children. ② Clearly, children owe a debt to their parents. ③ Their parents brought them into the world and cared for them when they were unable to care for themselves. ④ This debt could be appropriately discharged by having grown children care for their parents.

(Gary Jones, "The Responsibility of Parents")

5. ① Defending the war on drugs may not be fashionable, but the fact remains that ② hardcore drugs should remain illegal. ③ As long as hardcore drugs are

illegal, they are harder to get, and ④ the social stigma of being arrested deters many users.

(Charles Van DeVenter, "I'm Proof: The War on Drugs Is Working")

6. ① The rain forest of Brazil produces oxygen for the whole world, yet ② it yields no monetary return to that country. Given that ③ the industrialized nations consume the most oxygen, ④ those nations ought to pay Brazil an annual fee for the use of its rain forest.

(Diane B. Robinson, letter to the editor)

★7. ① It appears that animals may be able to predict earthquakes. ② Prior to a major quake in China, hundreds of snakes suddenly appeared from hibernation and froze to death in the snow, ③ fish were seen leaping from rivers and lakes, and ④ cows and horses refused to enter barns. Also, ⑤ prior to a quake in Fremont, California, a flood of callers reported strange behavior from their pets and domestic animals.

(Michael Bowker, "Can Animals Really Predict Earthquakes?")

8. ① Contributions to relief organizations are often wasted. ② Food sent to war torn countries rarely reaches its destination, because ③ food distribution is controlled by the warring groups, and ④ these groups sell the food to buy weapons and ammunition.

(Michael Maren, "The Faces of Famine")

9. ① Research leading to the development of a scramjet engine is worthwhile. ② Commercial aircraft incorporating such an engine could cross the Pacific in as little as two hours. ③ This would relieve the fatigue of flights from New York to Tokyo. Also, ④ such an engine could power future orbiting spacecraft.

(T. A. Heppenheimer, "A Plane for Space")

★10. ① There is a lot of pressure on untenured college teachers to dumb down their courses. ② Administrators tend to rehire teachers who bring in more money, and ③ teachers who dumb down their classes do precisely this. Why? Because ④ easier classes attract more students, and ⑤ more students means more money for the school.

(Lynne Drury Lerych, "Meeting the Bottom Line in the College Biz")

II. The following arguments were abstracted from the same sources as those in Part I of this exercise, but they are of gradually increasing difficulty. Use the method presented in this section to construct argument patterns. If a statement is redundant or plays no role in the argument, do not include it in the pattern.

★1. ① Many people believe that the crime of bribery cannot extend to campaign contributions. ② From a legal standpoint, however, countless campaign contributions are in fact bribes. ③ A bribe is anything of value or advantage given with the intent to unlawfully influence the person to whom it is given in his official capacity. ④ A campaign contribution is certainly something of value or advantage. Furthermore, ⑤ every contribution from a lobbyist or special interest group is given with the intent to influence voting, and ⑥ thousands of such contributions are made in every important election.

(Daniel Hays Lowenstein, "Can Candidates Run for Political Office Without Taking Bribes?")

2. ① America's farm policy desperately needs revamping. ② Seventy-three cents of every farm program dollar ends up in the pockets of the nation's super-farmers. As a result, ③ the mid-sized family farms are being squeezed out of existence. Also, ④ our farm policy courts environmental disaster. ⑤ Federal subsidies encourage farmers to use enormous amounts of fertilizer and pesticides. ⑥ These chemicals percolate down through the soil and pollute limited groundwater.

(Osha Gray Davidson, "Rise of America's Rural Ghetto")

3. ① Society values white lives more than black lives. This is clear from the fact that ② killers of whites are much more likely to be sentenced to death than killers of blacks. ③ Of the 1788 people currently on death row, 1713 were convicted of killing a white person. Yet ④ blacks are six times more likely to be murder victims than whites are. ⑤ In Florida, no one has ever been executed for murdering a black person, but ⑥ dozens have been executed for murdering white people.

(*Los Angeles Times* editorial, "Death and Race")

★4. ① Powerful new particle accelerators are important in high-energy physics, and ② they are worth their cost because ③ they will allow scientists to produce and capture significant quantities of Z particles. ④ Z particles result from the collision of positrons and electrons, and ⑤ particle accelerators are needed to achieve significant numbers of these collisions. ⑥ Z particles are thought to be the bearers of the weak nuclear force, and ⑦ learning the nature of this force may lead to the development of entirely new sources of energy.

(Lee Dye, "Linear Collider: Bold Gamble in Atomic Physics")

5. ① For years our country has been providing Japan unlimited access to our technology while getting little in return. ② Currently 7000 Japanese graduate students study science and engineering in the U.S., ③ while only 1000 Americans are engaged in similar studies in Japan. Also, ④ our government laboratories are open to the Japanese, but ⑤ Japanese laboratories are not open to Americans. ⑥ To remedy this imbalance, Japan should subsidize our universities, and also ⑦ it should help defray the costs of our laboratories.

(William C. Norris, "Technology Must Travel 2-Way Street")

6. ① All men crave material success because ② it serves as an insurance policy against sexual rejection. This is true because ③ women love men who are suc-

cessful. ④ Both men and women want power, and ⑤ success is the form of power women feel most deprived of. Thus, ⑥ women try to achieve it vicariously through men. ⑦ As the 5-foot 6-inch Dustin Hoffman once put it, "When I was in high school, women wouldn't touch me with a 10-foot pole. Now I can't keep them away with a 10-foot pole."

(Warren Farrell, "Success Story: From Frog to Prince")

★7. ① Cigarette consumption could be easily reduced by simply outlawing tailor-made cigarettes. ② The manufacture of tailor-made cigarettes to American standards is a high-tech industry. ③ It cannot be done in small illicit labs like the processing of PCP, cocaine or heroin. ④ The availability of quality tobacco for hand-rolling would discourage the development of an illegal tailor-made market. ⑤ Most people would not pay the premium prices demanded by an illicit market for a product of unknown quality. ⑥ They could roll a high-quality product for themselves. ⑦ Truly addicted persons would continue to smoke no matter how inconvenient. But ⑧ most would give it up as too much bother before it became a deeply ingrained habit.

(Richard Sand, "An Easy Way to Reduce Cigarette Consumption")

8. ① Flesh food is not a necessity in the human diet, as ② nutritionally adequate alternatives are readily available. ③ Many people in the world thrive on a nonmeat diet. ④ Indeed, vegetarian Seventh-Day Adventists in this country live an average of six years longer than their meat-eating counterparts. ⑤ The National Academy of Science warns that our fat-laden diet is directly responsible for much of the heart disease and cancer that afflict so many. ⑥ At a time when people are starving in certain parts of the world, it should be noted that a steer must consume sixteen pounds of grain and soy to produce one pound of meat. ⑦ The grain and soybeans we feed our meat-producing animals would feed every hungry mouth in the world many times over. ⑧ Cattle are competing with humans for food. ⑨ Clearly, a reassessment of the whole concept of killing and eating animals is in order.

(Suzanne Sutton, "Killing Animals for Food—Time for a Second Look")

9. ① The argument has been made that to cut down on teenage drunk driving we should increase the federal excise tax on beer. ② Such a measure, however, would almost certainly fail to achieve its intended result. ③ Teenagers are notoriously insensitive to cost. ④ They gladly accept premium prices for the latest style in clothes or the most popular record albums. And then, ⑤ those who drink and drive already risk arrest and loss of driving privileges. ⑥ They would not think twice about paying a little more for a six-pack. Finally, ⑦ the situation is not as bleak as it has been made to appear. ⑧ The fatality rate for teenage drivers is lower today than it has been in years.

(James C. Sanders, "Increased U.S. Tax on Beer")

★10. ① It has been widely acknowledged that the quality of undergraduate education in this country is diminishing. ② An often unrecognized cause of this malady is the exploitative way that universities as employers treat their part-time and temporary faculty members. ③ In many universities there are no formal guidelines for evaluating the work of these instructors. As a result, ④ poor instructors who solicit the favor of the department chairman are often retained over better ones who do not. ⑤ Another factor is the low pay given to these instructors. ⑥ In order to survive, many of them must accept heavy teaching loads spread out over three or four institutions. ⑦ The quality of instruction can only suffer when faculty members stretch themselves so thin. Lastly, because ⑧ part-time and temporary faculty are rarely members of the faculty senate, ⑨ they have no voice in university governance. But ⑩ without a voice, the shoddy conditions under which they work are never brought to light.

(Michael Schwalbe, "Part-Time Faculty Members Deserve a Break")

11. ① Doctors who attend elderly people in nursing homes often prescribe tranquilizers to keep these people immobile. ② This practice is often unwarranted, and ③ it often impairs the health of the patients. ④ These tranquilizers often have damaging side effects in that ⑤ they accentuate the symptoms of senility, and ⑥ they increase the likelihood of a dangerous fall because ⑦ they produce unsteadiness in walking. Furthermore, since ⑧ these medications produce immobility, ⑨ they increase the risk of bedsores. ⑩ Doctors at the Center for Aging and Health say that physicians who care for the elderly are simply prescribing too much medication.

(Hal Willard, "At 90, the Zombie Shuffle")

12. ① All of us have encountered motorists who will go to any length to get a parking spot within 20 feet of the door they expect to enter. ② This obsession with good parking spots transcends all logic. ③ It might take 5 minutes to secure the ideal spot in a store parking lot, ④ while a more distant spot that is immediately available is only a 40-second walk from the door. ⑤ Waiting for that ideal spot also results in frenzied nerves and skyrocketing blood pressure. ⑥ Inevitably the occupant of the desired space will preen her hair before departing, and ⑦ all the while the cars backed up behind the waiting driver are blaring their horns. ⑧ Parking a little farther away is usually easier and safer because ⑨ you can pull out more quickly, and ⑩ it avoids damage to car doors by adjacent parkers.

(Gwinn Owens, "A Ridiculous Addiction")

★13. ① The state has a right to intervene on behalf of unborn children, and ② this right should be implemented immediately. ③ While it may be true that a mere fetus has no rights, ④ surely a born child does have rights, and ⑤ these rights project backward to the time it was in the womb. This is true because ⑥ what happens to the child in the womb can have an impact throughout the child's life. ⑦ It is well known that alcohol and drug abuse by expectant mothers cause birth defects, and ⑧ these defects are not correctable after birth. ⑨ Granted, an expectant mother has the right to treat her own body as she chooses, but ⑩ this right does not extend to her unborn child. ⑪ Once a pregnant woman decides to give birth, she effectively transfers part of her rights over to her unborn child. ⑫ Unfortunately, however, the unborn child is incapable of securing these rights for itself. Thus, ⑬ the intervention of a higher power is justified.

(Alan Dershowitz, "Drawing the Line on Prenatal Rights")

14. ① A manned trip to Mars is a justified scientific goal because ② it affords a unique opportunity to explore the origins of the solar system and the emergence of life. However, ③ from a scientific standpoint, an initial landing on the tiny Martian moons, Phobos and Deimos, would be more rewarding than a landing on the planet itself. Because ④ the Martian terrain is rugged, ⑤ humans would not be able to venture far, ⑥ nor could they operate a robot vehicle without the use of a satellite, since ⑦ Mars's mountains would block their view. ⑧ Explorers on Phobos and Deimos could easily send robot vehicles to the planet's surface. ⑨ Using Mars's moons as a base would also be better than unmanned exploration directed from the Houston space center. Because ⑩ the distance is so great, ⑪ radio signals to and from Mars can take as long as an hour. Thus, ⑫ driving an unmanned rover from Earth, step by step, would be a time-consuming operation. ⑬ Sample returns to Earth would take months instead of hours, and ⑭ follow-on missions would be years apart instead of days, further slowing the process of exploration.

(S. Fred Singer, "The Case for Going to Mars")

15. ① There are lots of problems with the U.S. airline system, but ② deregulation isn't one of them. ③ Airline deregulation has delivered most of what it promised when enacted in 1978. ④ It has held down fares, ⑤ increased competition, ⑥ and raised the industry's efficiency. ⑦ Despite claims to the contrary, airline safety has not suffered. And, ⑧ with some exceptions, service to some cities and towns has improved. ⑨ On average, fares are lower today than in 1980. ⑩ Morrison and Winston estimate that fares are 20% to 30% below what they would be under regulation. ⑪ Competition has increased because ⑫ prior to deregulation airlines had protected routes. ⑬ After deregulation this changed. ⑭ Efficiency has also improved. ⑮ After deregulation the percentage of occupied seats jumped by 10% and miles traveled by 32%. ⑯ Despite fears that airlines would cut unprofitable service to small communities, most smaller cities and towns experienced a 20% to 30% increase in flight frequency. Lastly, ⑰ travel on U.S. airlines remains among the safest forms of transportation. ⑱ Between 1975 and 1985, deaths resulting from crashes totaled fewer than 3000.

(Robert J. Samuelson, "Let's Not Regulate the Deregulated Airlines")

III. Turn to the editorial pages of a newspaper and select an editorial that contains an argument. Keep in mind that some editorials are really reports and contain no arguments at all. Also, few editorials are as neat and straightforward as the selections presented in parts I and II of this exercise. Guest editorials on the opinion-editorial page (usually opposite the editorial page) are often better written than those on the editorial page. Analyze the argument (or arguments) according to the method presented in this section. Begin by placing a numeral at the beginning of each statement. Compound statements having components that are claimed to be true may be broken up into parts and the parts enumerated accordingly. Numerals should usually be placed after genuine premise and conclusion indicators even when they occur in the middle of a statement. Do *not*, however, break up conditional statements into antecedent and consequent. Proceed to identify the main conclusion (or conclusions) and determine how the other statements provide support. Any statement that does not play a direct role in the argument should be left out of the final argument pattern.

Summary

Logic is the study of the evaluation of arguments, which are lists of statements consisting of one or more premises and one conclusion. Premises can be distinguished from conclusion by the occurrence of indicator words ("hence," "therefore," "since," and so on) or an inferential relation among the statements. Because not all groups of statements are arguments, it is important to be able to distinguish arguments from nonarguments. This is done by attending to indicator words, the presence of an inferential relation among the statements, and typical kinds of nonarguments. Typical nonarguments include warnings, loosely associated statements, reports, expository passages, illustrations, conditional statements, and explanations.

Arguments are customarily divided into deductive and inductive. Deductive arguments are those in which the conclusion is claimed to follow necessarily from the premises, while inductive arguments are those in which the conclusion is claimed to follow only probably from the premises. The two can be distinguished by attending to special indicator words ("it necessarily follows that," "it probably follows that," and so on), the actual strength of the inferential relation, and typical forms or styles of deductive and inductive argumentation. Typical deductive arguments include arguments based on mathematics, arguments from definition, and categorical, hypothetical, and disjunctive syllogisms. Typical inductive arguments include predictions, arguments from analogy, generalizations, arguments from authority, arguments based on signs, and causal inferences.

The evaluation of arguments involves two steps: evaluating the link between premises and conclusion, and evaluating the truth of the premises. Deductive arguments in which the conclusion actually follows from the premises are said to be valid, and those that also have true premises are said to be sound. Inductive arguments in which the conclusion actually follows from the premises are said to be strong, and those that also have true premises are said to be cogent. The terms "true" and "false" apply not to arguments, but to statements. The truth and falsity of premises and conclusion is only indirectly related to validity, but any deductive argument having true premises and a false conclusion is invalid.

The validity of a deductive argument is determined by the form of the argument. An argument form that allows for a substitution instance having true premises and a false conclusion is an invalid form, and any argument having that form is an invalid argument. This fact leads to the counterexample method for proving invalidity. The method consists in identifying the form of a given invalid argument and then constructing a counterexample having premises that are indisputably true and a conclusion that is indisputably false.

The structure of longer arguments may be disclosed by the application of a method consisting of arrows and braces that show how the various premises support intermediate conclusions, and how the latter in turn support the main conclusion. Four basic argument patterns are the vertical pattern, horizontal pattern, conjoint premises, and multiple conclusion.

Language: Meaning and Definition

2.1 Varieties of Meaning

Ordinary language, as most of us are at least vaguely aware, serves various functions in our day-to-day lives. The twentieth-century philosopher Ludwig Wittgenstein thought the number of these functions to be virtually unlimited. Thus, among other things, language is used to

ask questions	tell jokes
tell stories	flirt with someone
tell lies	give directions
guess at answers	sing songs
form hypotheses	issue commands
launch verbal assaults	greet someone

and so on.

For our purpose, two linguistic functions are particularly important: (1) to convey information and (2) to express or evoke feelings. Consider, for example, the following statements:

> The death penalty, which is legal in thirty-six states, has been carried out most often in Georgia; however, since 1977 Texas holds the record for the greatest number of executions.
>
> The death penalty is a cruel and inhuman form of punishment in which hapless prisoners are dragged from their cells and summarily slaughtered only to satiate the bloodlust of a vengeful public.

The first statement is intended primarily to convey information about the death penalty, while the second is intended to persuade us that the death penalty is bad. The second accomplishes this function by engaging our feelings, and not, as in an argument, by establishing the truth of a claim.

These statements accomplish their respective functions through the distinct kinds of terminology in which they are phrased. Terminology that conveys information is said to have **cognitive meaning,** and terminology that expresses or evokes feelings is said to have **emotive meaning.** Thus, in the first statement the words "legal," "thirty-six," "most often," "Georgia," "record," and so on have primarily a cognitive meaning, while in the second statement the words "cruel," "inhuman," "hapless," "dragged," "slaughtered," "bloodlust," and "vengeful" have a strong emotive meaning. Of course, these latter words have cognitive meaning as well. "Cruel" means tending to hurt others, "inhuman" means inappropriate for humans, "hapless" means unfortunate, and so on.

The emotively charged statement about the death penalty illustrates two important points. The first is that statements of this sort usually have *both* cognitive meaning and emotive meaning. Therefore, since logic is concerned chiefly with cognitive meaning, it is important that we be able to distinguish and disengage the cognitive meaning of such statements from the emotive meaning. The second point is that part of the cognitive meaning of such statements is a value claim. A **value claim** is a claim that something is good, bad, right, wrong, or better, worse, more important or less important than some other thing. For example, the statement about the death penalty asserts the value claim that the death penalty is wrong or immoral. Such value claims are often the most important part of the cognitive meaning of emotive statements. Thus, for the purposes of logic, it is important that we be able to disengage the value claims of emotively charged statements from the emotive meaning and treat these claims as separate statements.

These observations suggest the reason that people use emotive terminology as often as they do: Value claims as such normally require evidence to support them. For example, the claim that the death penalty is immoral cannot simply stand by itself. It cries out for reasons to support it. But when value claims are couched in emotive terminology, the emotive "clothing" tends to obscure the fact that a value claim is being made, and it simultaneously gives psychological momentum to that claim. As a result, readers and listeners are inclined to swallow the value claim whole without any evidence. Furthermore, the intellectual laziness of many speakers and writers, combined with their inability to supply supporting reasons for their value claims, reinforces the desirability of couching such claims in emotive terminology.

Many people, for example, will refer to someone as "crazy," "stupid," or "weird" when they want to express the claim that what that person is doing is bad or wrong and when they are unable or unwilling to give reasons for this claim. Also, many people will refer to things or situations as "awesome" or "gross" for the same reasons. Those who happen to be listening, especially if they are friendly with the speaker, will often accept these claims without hesitation.

For a subtler example of emotive terminology, consider the word "harvest." This word evokes feelings associated with honest, hardworking farmers being rewarded for their labor in planting and tending their crops. To capitalize on this positive feeling, wood products companies speak of harvesting the trees in 200-year-old forests, even though they had nothing to do with planting them, and surgeons speak of harvesting the organs from the bodies of donors and the tissue from aborted fetuses. In all of these cases, the use of the word "harvest" is specifically calculated to elicit a favorable or agreeable response from the listener.

Let us now consider emotive terminology as it occurs in arguments. In arguments, emotive terminology accomplishes basically the same function as emotive terminology in statements. It allows the arguer to make value claims about the subject matter of the argument without providing evidence, and it gives the argument a kind of steamroller quality by which it tends to crush potential counterarguments before the reader or listener has a chance to think of them. This steamroller quality also tends to paralyze the logical thought processes of readers or listeners so that they are not able to see illogical arguments in their true light. These effects of emotive terminology can be avoided if the reader or listener will disengage the value claims and other cognitive meanings from the emotive meaning of the language and reexpress them as distinct premises.

Consider, for example, the following emotively charged argument taken from the letters to the editor section of a newspaper:

> Now that we know that the rocks on the moon are similar to those in our backyard and that tadpoles can exist in a weightless environment, and now that we have put the rest of the world in order, can we concentrate on the problems here at home? Like what makes people hungry and why is unemployment so elusive?
>
> (Robert J. Boland)

The conclusion of this argument is that our government should take money that has been spent on the space program and on international police actions and redirect it to solving domestic problems. The author minimizes the importance of the space program by covertly suggesting that it amounts to nothing more than work on ordinary rocks and tadpoles (which by themselves are relatively insignificant), and he exaggerates the scope of the international effort by covertly suggesting that it has solved every problem on earth but our own. Also, the phrase "put . . . in order" suggests that the international effort has been no more important than restoring order to a room in one's house. We might rephrase the argument in emotively neutral language, making the implicit suggestions and value claims explicit, as follows:

> The space program has been confined to work on ordinary rocks and tadpoles.
> Ordinary rocks and tadpoles are less important than domestic hunger and unemployment.
> Our international efforts have restored order to every nation on earth but our own.
> These efforts have been directed to problems that are less important than our own domestic problems.
> Therefore, our government should redirect funds that have been spent on these projects to solving our own domestic problems.

By restructuring the argument in this way, we can more easily evaluate the degree to which the premises support the conclusion. Inspection of the premises reveals that the first, third, and possibly fourth premises are false. Thus, the actual support provided by the premises is less than what we might have first expected. If the argument were to be rephrased a second time so that the premises turned out true (for example, the first premise might read "*Part* of the space program has been devoted to research on ordinary rocks and tadpoles"), the support given to the conclusion would still be weaker than the author intended.

Now that we have distinguished emotive meaning from cognitive meaning, let us explore some of the ways that cognitive meanings can be defective. Two of them are vagueness and ambiguity. A linguistic expression is said to be **vague** if there are borderline cases in which it is impossible to tell if the expression applies or does not apply. Vague expressions often allow for a continuous range of interpretations. The meaning is hazy, obscure, and imprecise. For example, words such as "love," "happiness," "peace," "excessive," "fresh," "rich," "poor," "normal," "conservative," and "polluted" are vague. We can rarely tell with any precision whether they apply to a given situation or not. How fresh does something have to be in order to be called fresh?

Vagueness can also affect entire statements. Such vagueness may arise not so much from the individual words as from the way in which the words are combined. For example, suppose someone were to say, "Today our job situation is more transparent." First, what is the meaning of "job situation"? Does it refer to finding a job, keeping a job, filling a job, completing a job, or bidding on a job? And what exactly does it mean for a job situation to be "transparent"? Does it mean that the job is more easily perceived or comprehended? That the job is more easily completed? That we can anticipate our future job needs more clearly? Or what else?

Not all cases of vagueness, however, are problematic. To describe an acquaintance as "tall" or "thin" often causes no trouble in ordinary conversation. Indeed, it may be overly burdensome to describe this person in more precise language. Trouble arises only when the language is not sufficiently precise for what the situation demands.

The other way in which cognitive meanings can be defective is ambiguity. An expression is said to be **ambiguous** when it can be interpreted as having more than one clearly distinct meaning in a given context. For example, words such as "light," "proper," "critical," "stress," "mad," "inflate," "chest," "bank," "sound," and "race" can be used ambiguously. Thus, if one were to describe a beer as a light pilsner, does this mean that the beer is light in color, light in calories, or light in taste? If one were to describe an action as proper, does this mean proper in a moral sense or proper in the sense of being socially acceptable? Or if one were to describe a person as critical, does this mean that the person is essential for a certain task or that the person tends to criticize others?

As is the case with vagueness, ambiguity can also affect entire statements. Such ambiguity often results from the way in which certain words are combined. For example, there was a newspaper headline that read, "Tuna are biting off the Washington coast." Does this mean that the tuna are nibbling away at the coastline or that fishermen are catching them off the coast? Presumably it means the latter. And another headline read, "College students are turning to vegetables." Does this mean that the students are metamorphosing into vegetables or that they are incorporating more vegetables into their diet? Again, the intended meaning is probably the latter.

The difference between ambiguity and vagueness is that vague terminology allows for a relatively continuous range of interpretations, whereas ambiguous terminology allows for multiple discrete interpretations. In a vague expression there is a blur of meaning, whereas in an ambiguous expression there is a mix-up of otherwise clear meanings. However, there are many forms of expression that are ambiguous in one context and vague in another. For example, the word "slow" in one context could mean either mentally retarded or physically slow, but when the word refers to physical slowness, it could be vague. How slow is slow? Similar remarks apply to "light," "fast," and "rich."

Ambiguity and vagueness are important in logic because there are countless occasions in which the evaluation of an argument leads to the observation, "Well, that depends on what you mean by . . ." Certain phraseology in the argument is vague or ambiguous, and its meaning must be clarified before any evaluation can proceed. For example, Scientologists argue that their organization should be exempt from paying taxes because, they claim, Scientology is a religion. Evaluating their argument requires that we clarify the meaning of "religion." Pro-life advocates argue that abortion is wrong because it results in the killing of human beings. But what is the meaning of "human being"? And some feminists argue that leering glances constitute sexual harassment. To evaluate their arguments we must clarify the meaning of "leering glances" and "sexual harassment."

The role of vagueness and ambiguity in arguments may be conveniently explored in the context of conflicting arguments between individuals. Such conflicts are called disputes:

> CLAUDIA: Mrs. Wilson abuses her children. And how do I know that? I saw her spank one of her kids the other day after the kid misbehaved.
>
> JANE: Don't be silly. Kids need discipline, and by disciplining her children, Mrs. Wilson is showing that she loves them.

Here the problem surrounds the vagueness of the words "abuse" and "discipline." When does discipline become abuse? The line separating the two is hazy at best, but unless it is clarified, disputes of this sort will never be resolved.

Another example:

> BRENDA: I'm afraid that Smiley is guilty of arson. Last night he confided to me that he was the one who set fire to the old schoolhouse.
>
> WARREN: No, you couldn't be more mistaken. In this country no one is guilty until proven so in a court of law, and Smiley has not yet even been accused of anything.

In this case the dispute arises over the ambiguity of the word "guilty." Brenda is using the word in the moral sense. Given that Smiley has admitted to setting fire to the old schoolhouse, it is very likely that he did indeed set fire to it and therefore is guilty of arson in the moral sense of the term. Warren, on the other hand, is using the word in the legal sense. Because Smiley has not been convicted in a court of law, he is not legally guilty of anything.

Disputes that arise over the meaning of language are called *verbal disputes*. But not all disputes are of this sort. Some disputes arise over a disagreement about facts, and these are called *factual disputes*. Example:

> KEITH: I know that Freddie stole a computer from the old schoolhouse. Barbara told me that she saw Freddie do it.
>
> PHYLLIS: That's ridiculous! Freddie has never stolen anything in his life. Barbara hates Freddie, and she is trying to pin the theft on him only to shield her criminal boyfriend.

Here the dispute centers on the factual issues of whether Barbara told the truth and whether Freddie stole the computer.

In dealing with disputes, the first question is whether the dispute is factual, verbal, or some combination of the two. If the dispute is verbal, then the second question to be answered is whether the dispute concerns ambiguity or vagueness.

EXERCISE 2.1

I. The following selection is taken from a speech delivered by George C. Wallace, former Governor of Alabama, on July 4, 1964. In this speech Wallace attacked

Lyndon Johnson's signing of the Civil Rights Act. The speech is liberally sprinkled with emotive terminology. Make a list of what you consider to be the twenty-five most highly charged words or phrases, and then indicate whether they are intended to evoke a favorable or an unfavorable attitude from the listener.

We come here today in deference to the memory of those stalwart patriots who on July 4, 1776, pledged their lives, their fortunes, and their sacred honor to establish and defend the proposition that governments are created by the people, empowered by the people, derive their just powers from the consent of the people, and must forever remain subservient to the will of the people.

Today, 188 years later, we celebrate that occasion and find inspiration and determination and courage to preserve and protect the great principles of freedom enunciated in the Declaration of Independence.

It is therefore a cruel irony that the President of the United States has only yesterday signed into law the most monstrous piece of legislation ever enacted by the United States Congress.

It is a fraud, a sham, and a hoax.

This bill will live in infamy. To sign it into law at any time is tragic. To do so upon the eve of the celebration of our independence insults the intelligence of the American people.

It dishonors the memory of countless thousands of our dead who offered up their very lives in defense of principles which this bill destroys.

Never before in the history of this nation have so many human and property rights been destroyed by a single enactment of the Congress. It is an act of tyranny. It is the assassin's knife stuck in the back of liberty.

With this assassin's knife and a blackjack in the hand of the federal force-cult, the left-wing liberals will try to force us back into bondage. Bondage to a tyranny more brutal than that imposed by the British Monarchy which claimed power to rule over the lives of our forefathers under sanction of the omnipotent black-robed despots who sit on the bench of the United States Supreme Court.

This bill is fraudulent in intent, in design and in execution.

It is misnamed. Each and every provision is mistitled. It was rammed through the Congress on the wave of ballyhoo, promotions, and publicity stunts reminiscent of P. T. Barnum.

It was enacted in an atmosphere of pressure, intimidation, and even cowardice, as demonstrated by the refusal of the United States Senate to adopt an amendment to submit the bill to a vote of the people.

To illustrate the fraud—it is not a civil rights bill. It is a federal penal code. It creates federal crimes which would take volumes to list and years to tabulate because it affects the lives of 192 million American citizens. Every person in every walk and station of life and every aspect of our daily lives become subject to the criminal provisions of this bill.

It threatens our freedom of speech, of assembly, of association, and makes the exercise of these freedoms a federal crime under certain conditions.

It affects our political rights, our right to trial by jury, our right to the full use and enjoyment of our private property, the freedom from search and seizure of our private property and possessions, the freedom from harassment by federal police and, in short, all the rights of individuals inherent in a society of free men.

Ministers, lawyers, teachers, newspapers, and every private citizen must guard his speech and watch his actions to avoid the deliberately imposed booby traps put into this bill. It is designed to make federal crimes of our customs, beliefs, and traditions.

Therefore, under the fantastic powers of the federal judiciary to punish for contempt of court and under their fantastic powers to regulate our most intimate aspects of our lives by injunction, every American citizen is in jeopardy and must stand guard against these despots.

II. The following selections were taken from the letters to the editor section of a newspaper. Each can be interpreted as expressing one or more arguments. Begin by identifying the conclusion of each. Then disengage the covert assumptions, value claims, and other cognitive assertions from the emotive language and translate them into emotively neutral premises. Use the two examples in the text as models. Finally, evaluate the restructured arguments. Some may turn out to be good ones.

★1. Why don't animal lovers do something about these dog sled races? Have you ever witnessed a race on television? Talk about torture. It's sickening to watch the dogs, panting and their tongues hanging out, pull a heavily laden sled with a driver through snow and ice in bitter cold.

(Joe Shapiro)

2. How anyone who has seen even one photo of the fly-covered, starving children in Somalia can still believe in a loving, everpresent, omnipotent God is beyond intelligent reasoning.

(William Blanchard)

3. The creationists have no right to impose their mistaken, ignorant, superstitious beliefs on others. They claim the constitutional right to the free exercise of religion. How about the rights of the majority of people who want their children taught the scientific truth about evolution—not fallacious myths and superstitions from primitive societies.

(Andrew M. Underhill, Jr.)

★4. God, guts, and guns made this great country of ours free, and you can bet your buns it will take more of the same to keep it that way. One of the very last things in this world we need is handgun control.

(R. Kinzie)

5. The insanity plea should be done away with; criminals should lose this easy way out. Killers can theoretically spend as little as six months in a mental hospital, then be released. It's time to take a stand for safety and put psychotic killers in prison.

(Keith Aikens)

6. Until now, the protest against the holocaust in our own nation has been vocal but far too small. The massacre of an unwanted generation through abortion and infanticide has sounded an alarm that should wake up every Christian. Helpless and guiltless little infants are mercilessly butchered daily in hospitals and clinics across our land. For the love of God, let us all urge the passage of the Human Life Bill, now before Congress.

(Jim Key)

★7. It's time to challenge all this nonsense about the "celebration of diversity" in our society. The more the schizophrenics preach the glories of diversity, the more we pull apart. This is not to deny appreciation of the ethnic roots, rituals, and foods, which add color to life. But to lay undue emphasis upon diversification results in destruction of the "social glue" that binds us together. Our forefathers framed one nation, indivisible. In the misguided effort to "celebrate" the uniqueness of every disparate culture and subculture, we betray our heritage and dilute our identities as Americans.

(Ruth M. Armstrong)

8. A kind and loving God surely favors the pro-choice attitude. He wants his world inhabited by happy, well-fed children with parents who love and care for them.

Our burgeoning population in Third World nations with constant famine and disease, and many other human miseries, could be relieved if the Catholic Church were to adjust more of its ancient policies to our current civilization.

(Art Bates)

9. Thousands of years of organized religion have done nothing to solve any problems and have almost always exacerbated them by promoting fear, superstition, and irrational mythologies. Kneeling in prayer to some supernatural entity seeking "divine guidance" or, even more implausibly, "divine intervention," is not only a waste of time, it is counterproductive because it lulls the supplicant into inactivity.

We must stand up, open our eyes and face life's challenges head-on in a problem-solving approach that is reality-based, empirical, and above all, rational.

(James W. Baugh)

★10. Liberalism has turned our welfare system from a social safety net into a hammock. We hand out money with few questions asked. When welfare recipients are asked for some contribution to our society in return, liberals scream that it's unconstitutional.

Liberalism has transformed our criminal justice system into one that cares more about the criminal's past childhood problems than for the victim. Liberalism in its never-ending quest for "social justice" has sacrificed the rights of the majority while continuing to push the rights of a few to new limits.

Liberalism has turned our school system from one of excellence to one where condoms and metal detectors are more important than prayer.

(Marc Sexton)

III. Determine whether the following disputes are verbal, factual, or some combination of the two. If verbal, discuss whether the dispute arises from vagueness or ambiguity.

★1. FRANK: Look at that huge tree that fell last night. It must have made a tremendous crash when it came down.

SHIRLEY: No, I'm afraid you're quite wrong. Sound is a perception, and perceptions depend on a perceiver. Therefore, since nobody was around here last night, there was no crash.

2. VICKIE: Yesterday I visited the exhibition of the work of Jean Michel Basquiat at the Central Gallery. What an interesting artist he is!

BARBARA: Don't be ridiculous! That's not art, it's just graffiti.

3. PHIL: That was a great basketball game last night. Shaquille O'Neal scored 37 points.

ARTHUR: Your statistics are all wet. O'Neal scored only 34 points.

★4. ROGER: I think modern society is becoming more and more violent every day. Just look at the increase in murder, rape, and robbery. Violence is clearly an evil that must be eradicated.

MARK: You might be right about the increase in crime, but the idea that violence is an evil is nonsense. Violence is quite natural. The universe was created in a tremendously violent Big Bang, the nuclear reactions that bring us sunlight are extremely violent, and insects and animals kill and devour one another all the time.

5. KATHY: I was saddened to hear about the death of your uncle. He was such a wonderful man. You must be consoled knowing that he's enjoying his heavenly reward.

ANNE: Thanks, but I'm afraid I don't know what you mean. If death is the end of life, how could my uncle be alive right now in heaven?

6. HEIDI: This morning I heard a lecture on the life of Jane Austen. She was such a wonderfully educated woman.

DAVID: That's not true at all. Jane Austen dropped out of school when she was only eleven, and she never even attended high school, much less college or graduate school.

★7. LESLIE: Your friend Paul told us that he would be visiting his parents in Knoxville this weekend. Therefore, he must not be at home.

DIANA: I agree that Paul is probably not at home, but you didn't hear him right. He said that his parents live in Nashville.

8. KARL: There's a euthanasia measure on the ballot today, and I think I'll vote for it. It seems reasonable that terminally ill patients should be allowed to be disconnected from life-support systems so that they can die peacefully and naturally.

SERGIO: You must be crazy! Euthanasia means giving people lethal injections, and that's clearly murder.

9. CHERYL: Tomorrow I'm going to the Metallica concert. Their music is fabulous.

OLIVER: You call that music? Really it's just noise, and incredibly loud noise at that.

★10. CAROL: Nelson could not have fought in the battle of Trafalgar, because that battle occurred in 1806, and Nelson died in 1804.

JUSTIN: Your knowledge of history is atrocious! Nelson did fight in Trafalgar, and the date was October 21, 1805.

11. ERIC: I've just signed up for Philosophy 502—Dr. Peterson's class in metaphysics. I know I'm going to enjoy it because I've always been fascinated by magic and ghosts.

LEAH: I'm afraid you're in for a surprise.

12. HAROLD: Professor Steinbeck is the most intelligent man I know. His lecture series on matter and consciousness was simply brilliant.

JOYCE: Steinbeck is actually an idiot. Yesterday I watched while he tried to get his car started. When it wouldn't start, he opened the hood, and he didn't even notice that someone had stolen the battery.

★13. THOMAS: George Foreman committed those crimes of child abuse through his own free choice. Nobody put a gun to his head. Therefore he should be punished for them.

EMILIE: That's not true. It's been established that Foreman was severely abused himself when he was a child, and such children have an irresistible obsession to abuse others when they grow up.

14. ANTHONY: The sun is much smaller than the earth. You see, it's just a small thing up there in the sky. Therefore, since the sun's gravitational attraction is proportional to its mass, the sun's gravity is less than the earth's.

CINDY: You are as stupid as they come. I agree the mass of the sun is less than that of the earth, but its volume is greater. Therefore, since gravitational attraction is proportional to volume, the sun's gravity is greater than the earth's.

15. MINDY: President Clinton should have been removed from office because he lied about having sexual relations with Monica Lewinsky.

KAREN: Don't be silly. President Clinton had only oral sex with Lewinsky, and oral sex does not constitute sexual relations.

★16. FRED: Today's professional athletes are overpaid. Many of them make millions of dollars a year.

SHAWN: I don't think they are overpaid at all. Just look at the owners of some of these teams. They make ten times as much as the athletes do.

17. BRIAN: That new morning-after pill, RU-486, causes abortion. Therefore, since abortion is wrong, you should never take that pill.

ELAINE: How ignorant you are! RU-486 merely prevents implantation of the fertilized ovum. Therefore, since the woman never gets pregnant, there is no abortion.

18. PENNY: In my mind, the use of marijuana should be legalized. After all, caffeine and alcohol are no less of a drug than marijuana, and it's not illegal to enjoy a glass of beer or drink a cup of coffee.

SAM: Your conclusion is way off. Beer and coffee are not drugs, they're foods.

★19. JERRY: In spite of the great strides technology has made in this country, poverty remains a terrible problem. Why, some people earn less than $10,000 per year. The government should do something about it.

FRANKIE: I hardly think that $10,000 per year constitutes poverty. Why, in many third world countries the majority of inhabitants earn less than $1,000 per year.

20. JOSEPH: Adult human beings have the right to marry whomever they please, as long as that person is not a close relative. From this it follows that homosexuals have the right to marry someone of their own sex.

STEPHEN: Your argument makes no sense. Rights are created by laws, and since there is no federal or state law that gives homosexuals the right to marry, they have no such right.

2.2   The Intension and Extension of Terms

The main task of logic is the evaluation of arguments. However, as we saw in the previous section, there are countless arguments in which this task leads to the observation, "Well, that depends on what you mean by . . ." Such an observation usually indicates that the meaning of certain words in the argument is vague or ambiguous. Clearing up the problem often involves supplying a definition. Thus, the study of meaning and definition is closely related to the main task of logic. In this section we continue our inquiry into aspects of linguistic meaning, and the results of this inquiry provide the basis for the theory of definition in the next section.

The basic units of any ordinary language are *words*. Our main concern in this chapter, however, is not with words in general but with terms. A **term** is any word or arrangement of words that may serve as the subject of a statement. Terms consist of proper names, common names, and descriptive phrases. Here are some examples:

Proper names	Common names	Descriptive phrases
Napoleon	animal	first president of the United States
North Dakota	restitution	
The United States	house	author of *Hamlet*
Senate	activity	books in my library
Gore Vidal	person	officers in the Swiss Navy
Robinson Crusoe		blue things
		those who study hard

Words that are not terms include verbs, nonsubstantive adjectives, adverbs, prepositions, conjunctions, and all nonsyntactic arrangements of words. The following words or phrases are not terms; none can serve as the subject of a statement:

dictatorial	moreover
runs quickly	craves
above and beyond	cabbages into again the forest

The last example is a nonsyntactic arrangement.

At this point it is important to distinguish the *use* of a word from the *mention* of a word. Without this distinction any word can be imagined to serve as the subject of a statement and, therefore, to count as a term. The word "wherever," for example, is not a term, but "wherever" (in quotes) can serve as the subject of a statement, such as "'Wherever' is an eight-letter word." But in this statement, it is not the word itself that is the subject but rather the *quoted* word. The word is said to be *mentioned*—not *used.* On the other hand, "wherever" is *used* in this statement: "I will follow you wherever you go." In distinguishing terms from nonterms one must be sure that the word or group of words can be *used* as the subject of a statement.

The previous section of this chapter explored the cognitive meaning of language in general. The cognitive meaning of terms comprises two kinds: intensional and extensional. The **intensional meaning** consists of the qualities or attributes that the term *connotes,* and the **extensional meaning** consists of the members of the class that the term *denotes.* For example, the intensional meaning of the term "cat" consists of the attributes of being furry, of having four legs, of moving in a certain way, of emitting certain sounds, and so on, while the extensional meaning consists of cats themselves— all the cats in the universe. The term connotes the attributes and denotes the cats.

The intensional meaning of a term is otherwise known as the **intension,** or **connotation,** and the extensional meaning is known as the **extension,** or **denotation.** "Intension" and "extension" are roughly equivalent to the more modern terms "sense" and "reference," respectively. Also, it should be noted that logic uses the terms "connotation" and "denotation" differently from the way they are used in grammar. In grammar, "connotation" refers to the subtle nuances of a word, whereas "denotation" refers to the word's direct and specific meaning.

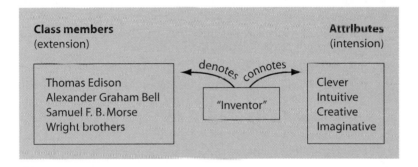

Exactly how a term connotes a set of attributes allows for at least two different interpretations. Some philosophers take an objective approach and hold that a term connotes whatever attributes something must have in order to be denoted by the term. Others take what might be called a subjective approach and hold that a term connotes the attributes that occur in the minds of the people who use that term. This book takes the latter approach.

In connection with this approach, however, we encounter the problem of terms connoting different things to different people. Thus, to a cat lover the term "cat" might connote the attributes of being cuddly and adorable, while to someone who hates cats it might connote the attributes of being obnoxious and disgusting. To avoid this problem, we restrict the meaning of connotation to what is usually called the conventional connotation. The **conventional connotation** of a term includes the attributes that the term *commonly* calls forth in the minds of competent speakers of the language. Under this interpretation, the connotation of a term remains more or less the same from person to person and from time to time.

The denotation of a term also typically remains the same from person to person, but it may change with the passage of time. The denotation of "currently living cat," for example, is constantly fluctuating as some cats die and others are born. The denotation of the term "cat," on the other hand, is presumably constant because it denotes all cats, past, present, and future.

Sometimes the denotation of a term can change radically with the passage of time. The terms "currently living dodo bird" and "current king of France," for example, at one time denoted actually existing entities, but today all such entities have perished. Accordingly, these terms now have what is called **empty extension.** They are said to denote the empty (or "null") class, the class that has no members. Other terms with empty extension include "unicorn," "leprechaun," "gnome," "elf," and "griffin." While these terms have empty extension, however, they do not have empty intension. "Currently living dodo bird" and "current king of France," as well as "unicorn," "elf," and "griffin," connote a variety of intelligible attributes.

The fact that some terms have empty extension leads us to an important connection between extension and intension—namely, that *intension determines extension.* The intensional meaning of a term serves as the criterion for deciding what the extension consists of. Because we know the attributes connoted by the term "unicorn," for example, we know that the term has empty extension. That is, we know that there are no four-legged mammals having a single straight horn projecting from their forehead. Similarly, the intension of the word "cat" serves as the criterion for determining what is and what is not a member of the class of cats.

One kind of term that raises problems for the intension-determines-extension rule is proper names. For example, the name "David" might not appear to have any intension, but it denotes the person who has this name. Although philosophers have disagreed about this, it would seem that proper names must have some kind of intension or we would not know what persons, if any, they denote. One possible solution to this problem is that names are shorthand symbols for descriptions or bundles of descriptions. For example, "David" could be shorthand for "the person who lives next door" or "the person who works at the corner store and who drives a green Chevy."

Another possible solution to the problem of proper names is that the intension of proper names consists of the causal chain of events leading from the point at which the name is first assigned to the point at which a certain person learns about the name. Thus, the first link in such a chain might be the baptismal event at which the name "David" is given to a certain infant, the second link would be the event in which a certain third party is informed of the first event, and so on. This entire chain of events extending through the linguistic community would then constitute the intension of "David." Thus, we conclude that for all terms, including proper names, intension determines extension.

The distinction between intension and extension may be further illustrated by comparing the way in which these concepts can be used to give order to random sequences of terms. Terms may be put in the order of increasing intension, increasing extension, decreasing intension, and decreasing extension. A series of terms is in the order of **in-**

creasing intension** when each term in the series (except the first) connotes more attributes than the one preceding it. In other words, each term in the series (except the first) is *more specific* than the one preceding it. (A term is specific to the degree that it connotes more attributes.) The order of **decreasing intension** is the reverse of that of increasing intension.

A series of terms is in the order of **increasing extension** when each term in the series (except the first) denotes a class having more members than the class denoted by the term preceding it. In other words, the class size gets larger with each successive term. **Decreasing extension** is, of course, the reverse of this order. Examples:

Increasing intension:	animal, mammal, feline, tiger
increasing extension:	tiger, feline, mammal, animal
decreasing intension:	tiger, feline, mammal, animal
decreasing extension:	animal, mammal, feline, tiger

These examples illustrate a fact pertaining to most such series: The order of increasing intension is usually the same as that of decreasing extension. Conversely, the order of decreasing intension is usually the same as that of increasing extension. There are some exceptions, however. Consider the following series:

> unicorn; unicorn with blue eyes; unicorn with blue eyes and green horn; unicorn with blue eyes, green horn, and a weight of over 400 pounds

Each term in this series has empty extension; so, while the series exhibits the order of increasing intension, it does not exhibit the order of decreasing extension. Here is another, slightly different, example:

> living human being; living human being with a genetic code; living human being with a genetic code and a brain; living human being with a genetic code, a brain, and a height of less than 100 feet

In this series none of the terms has empty extension, but each term has exactly the *same* extension as the others. Thus, while the intension increases with each successive term, once again the extension does not decrease.

EXERCISE 2.2

I. The following exercises deal with words and terms.

1. Determine which of the following words or groups of words are terms and which are nonterms.

extortion	Thomas Jefferson
laborious	Empire State Building
cunningly	annoy
practitioner	render satisfactory
seriousness	graceful dancer
forever	wake up
whoever studies	not only
interestingly impassive	tallest man on the squad
scarlet	mountaintop
reinvestment	between
therefore	since

2. Name some of the attributes connoted by the following terms. Express your answer with adjectives or adjectival phrases. Example: The term "elephant" connotes the attributes of being large, having tusks, having a trunk.

drum	wolf	fanatic	riot
politician	Mona Lisa	carrot	piano
devil	Statue of Liberty		

3. Name three items denoted by the terms in the left-hand column below and all items denoted by the terms in the right-hand column.

newspaper	tallest mountain on earth
scientist	prime number less than 10
manufacturer	governor of New York
river	language of Canada
opera	Scandinavian country

4. Put the following sequences of terms in the order of increasing intension:

★a. conifer, Sitka spruce, tree, spruce, plant

b. Italian sports car, car, vehicle, Maserati, sports car

c. doctor of medicine, person, brain surgeon, professional person, surgeon

d. wallaby, marsupial, mammal, animal, kangaroo

e. parallelogram, polygon, square, rectangle, quadrilateral

5. Construct a series of four terms that exhibits increasing intension but nondecreasing extension.

II. Answer "true" or "false" to the following statements:

1. All words have an intensional meaning and an extensional meaning.

2. The intensional meaning of a term consists of the attributes connoted by the term.

3. The extensional meaning of a term consists of the members of the class denoted by the term.

4. The extension of a term always remains the same with the passage of time.

5. Some terms have empty intension.

6. Some terms have empty extension.

7. The intension of a term determines the extension.

8. The intension of a term determines how specific the term is.

9. The order of increasing intension is always the same as that of decreasing extension.

10. "Leprechaun" and "unicorn" have the same extension.

2.3   Definitions and Their Purposes

Over the years philosophers have held various conflicting views about the purpose of definitions. For Plato, to mention just one, definitions were intended to explicate the meaning of certain eternal essences or forms, such as justice, piety, and virtue. For most logicians today, however, definitions are intended exclusively to explicate the meaning of *words*. In conformity with this latter position, we may define **definition** as a group of words that assigns a meaning to some word or group of words. Accordingly, every definition consists of two parts: the definiendum and the definiens. The **definiendum** is the word or group of words that is supposed to be defined, and the **definiens** is the word or group of words that does the defining. For example, in the definition " 'Tiger' means a large, striped, ferocious feline indigenous to the jungles of India and Asia," the word "tiger" is the definiendum, and everything after the word "means" is the definiens. The definiens is not itself the meaning of the definiendum; rather, it is the group of words that symbolizes (or that is supposed to symbolize) the *same* meaning as the definiendum. Because we presumably know in advance what the definiens symbolizes, we are led, via the definition, to understand what the definiendum symbolizes. It is in this way that the definition "assigns" a meaning to its definiendum.

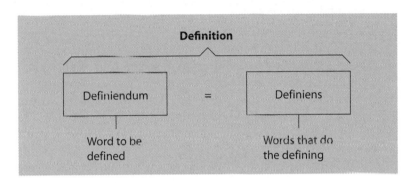

Once it has been decided that definitions explicate the meaning of words, other disagreements emerge among the philosophers. Some argue that since a definition is merely a rule that allows one set of words (the definiens) to be used in place of another set (the definiendum), definitions communicate no information at all about the subject matter of the definiendum. Others take the opposite tack and argue that since definitions result in a clarification of language, they provide a means for the discovery of deeper philosophical truths. It seems, however, that neither of these approaches is able to make good sense of all the various kinds of definitions that are actually employed in ordinary usage. As a result, instead of beginning their analysis of definitions with a set of a priori criteria, many logicians take a pragmatic approach and begin with a survey of the various kinds of definitions that are actually used and of the functions that they actually serve. This is the approach taken here.

Stipulative Definitions

A **stipulative definition** assigns a meaning to a word for the first time. This may involve either coining a new word or giving a new meaning to an old word. The purpose of a stipulative definition is usually to replace a more complex expression with a simpler one.

The need for a stipulative definition is often occasioned by some new phenomenon or development. For example, a few years ago the attempt was made at a certain zoo to crossbreed tigers and lions. Because of the genetic similarity of the two species, the attempt succeeded. Offspring were produced from a male tiger and a female lion and from a male lion and a female tiger. When the offspring were born, it became appropriate to give them names. Of course, the names "offspring of male tiger and female lion" and "offspring of male lion and female tiger" could have been used, but these names were hardly convenient. Instead, the names "tigon" and "liger" were selected. Any two new words would have sufficed equally well for naming the offspring— "topar" and "largine" for example—but "tigon" and "liger" were considered more appropriate, for obvious reasons. "Tigon" was taken to mean the offspring of a male tiger and a female lion, and "liger" the offspring of a male lion and a female tiger. These assignments of meanings were accomplished through stipulative definitions.

Another use for stipulative definitions is to set up secret codes. For example, during World War II, "Tora, Tora, Tora" was the code name Admiral Yamamoto transmitted to the war office in Tokyo signaling that the Japanese fleet had not been spotted in the hours preceding the bombing of Pearl Harbor; "Operation Barbarossa" was the name the Germans gave to the invasion of Russia; and "Operation Overlord" was the name the allied forces gave to the planned invasion of Normandy. More recently, "Operation Desert Storm" was the code name given to the military invasion of Iraq; and the campaign in Afghanistan, at least in its early phase, was called "Operation Enduring Freedom." Law enforcement organizations have adopted similar code names for sting operations against organized crime.

Because people are continually coming up with new creations, whether it be food concoctions, inventions, modes of behavior, or kinds of apparel, stipulative definitions are continually being introduced to name them. The invention of computers provides a prime example. Today we have dozens of new terms or new uses of old terms that did not exist a few years ago: "cyberspace," "e-mail," "browser," "hacker," "dot-com," "hardware," "software," "download," "web site," "webmaster," "server," "boot," "barcode," "mouse," "modem," "cookies," and "spam"—to name just a few. Earlier, in the area of biology, when a certain excretion of the pancreas was refined to its pure form, the word "insulin" was chosen to name it, and the word "penicillin" was chosen for an antibacterial substance produced by certain *Penicillium* molds. In mathematics, the symbol "10^5" was chosen as a simple substitute for "$10 \times 10 \times 10 \times 10 \times 10$."

Because a stipulative definition is a completely arbitrary assignment of a meaning to a word for the first time, there can be no such thing as a "true" or "false" stipulative definition. Furthermore, for the same reason, a stipulative definition cannot provide any new information about the subject matter of the definiendum. The fact that the word "tigon" was selected to replace "offspring of a male tiger and a female lion" tells us nothing new about the nature of the animal in question. One stipulative definition may, however, be more or less convenient or more or less appropriate than another.

Stipulative definitions are misused in verbal disputes when one person covertly uses a word in a peculiar way and then proceeds to assume that everyone else uses that word in the same way. Under these circumstances that person is said to be using the word "stipulatively." In such cases the assumption that other persons use the word in the same way is rarely justified.

Lexical Definitions

A **lexical definition** is used to report the meaning that a word already has in a language. Dictionary definitions are all instances of lexical definitions. Thus, in contrast with a stipulative definition, which assigns a meaning to a word for the first time, a lexical definition may be true or false depending on whether it does or does not report the way a word is actually used. Because words are frequently used in more than one way, lexical definitions have the further purpose of eliminating the ambiguity that would otherwise arise if one of these meanings were to be confused with another.

As we saw in the first section of this chapter, an expression is **ambiguous** when it can be interpreted as having two or more clearly distinct meanings in a given context. Words such as "light," "mad," and "bank" can be used ambiguously. Because a lexical definition lists the various meanings that a word can have, a person who consults such a definition is better prepared to avoid ambiguous constructions of his or her own and to detect those of others. Undetected ambiguity causes the most trouble. In many cases the problem lies not with the obvious differences in meaning that words such as "light" and "bank" may have but with the subtle shadings of meaning that are more likely to be confused with one another. For example, if a woman is described as "nice," any number of things could be intended. She could be fastidious, refined, modest, pleasant, attractive, or even lewd. A good lexical definition will distinguish these various shadings and thereby guard against the possibility that two such meanings will be unconsciously jumbled together into one.

Precising Definitions

The purpose of a **precising definition** is to reduce the vagueness of a word. As we saw in the first section of this chapter, an expression is **vague** if there are borderline cases in which it is impossible to tell if the word applies or does not apply. Words such as "fresh," "rich," and "poor" are vague. Once the vagueness of such words is reduced by a precising definition, one can reach a decision as to the applicability of the word to a specific situation. For example, if legislation were ever introduced to give direct financial assistance to the poor, a precising definition would have to be supplied specifying exactly who is poor and who is not. The definition "'Poor' means having an annual income of less than $4,000 and a net worth of less than $20,000" is an example of a precising definition.

Whenever words are taken from ordinary usage and used in a highly systematic context such as science, mathematics, medicine, or law, they must always be clarified by means of a precising definition. The terms "force," "energy," "acid," "element," "number," "equality," "contract," and "agent" have all been given precising definitions by specific disciplines.

Sometimes the substance of a court trial may revolve around the precise usage of a term. A trial in California addressed the question of whether a man who had ridden a bicycle while intoxicated violated the motor vehicle code. The question concerned whether, for these purposes, a bicycle could be considered a "vehicle." The court decided in the affirmative, and the decision amounted to an incremental extension of an already existent precising definition of the word "vehicle."

Another example involves the practice of surgical transplantation of vital organs. Before a heart transplant can be conducted, the donor must be dead; otherwise the surgeon will be accused of murder. If the donor is dead for too long, however, the success of the transplant will be imperiled. But exactly when is a person considered to be dead? Is it when the heart stops beating, when the person stops breathing, when rigor mortis sets in, or some other time? The question involves the meaning of the term "moment of death." The courts have decided that "moment of death" should be taken to mean the moment the brain stops functioning, as measured by an electroencephalograph. This decision amounts to the acceptance of a precising definition for "moment of death."

A precising definition differs from a stipulative definition in that the latter involves a purely arbitrary assignment of meaning, whereas the assignment of meaning in a precising definition is not at all arbitrary. A great deal of care must be taken to ensure that the assignment of meaning in a precising definition is appropriate and legitimate for the context within which the term is to be employed.

Theoretical Definitions

A **theoretical definition** assigns a meaning to a word by suggesting a theory that gives a certain characterization to the entities that the term denotes. Such a definition provides a way of viewing or conceiving these entities that suggests deductive consequences, further investigation (experimental or otherwise), and whatever else would be entailed by the acceptance of a theory governing these entities. The definition of the term "heat" found in texts dealing with the kinetic theory of heat provides a good example: "'Heat' means the energy associated with the random motion of the molecules of a substance." This definition does more than merely assign a meaning to a word; it provides a way of conceiving the physical phenomenon that is heat. In so doing, it suggests the deductive consequence that as the molecules of a substance speed up, the temperature of the substance increases. In addition, it suggests a number of experiments—experiments investigating the relationship between molecular velocity and the phenomena of radiation, gas pressure, molecular elasticity, and molecular configuration. In short, this definition of "heat" provides the impetus for an entire theory about heat.

Other examples of theoretical definitions are the definition of "light" as a form of electromagnetic radiation and the definition of "force," "mass," and "acceleration" in Newton's second law of motion as expressed in the equation "$F = MA$." The latter is a kind of contextual definition in which each term is defined in terms of the other two. Both definitions entail numerous deductive consequences about the phenomena involved and suggest numerous avenues of experimental investigation.

Not all theoretical definitions are associated with science. Many terms in philosophy, such as "substance," "form," "cause," "change," "idea," "good," "mind," and "God," have been given theoretical definitions. In fact, most of the major philosophers in history have given these terms their own peculiar theoretical definitions, and this fact accounts in part for the unique character of their respective philosophies. For example, Gottfried Wilhelm Leibniz's definition of "substance" in terms of what he called "monads" laid the foundation for his metaphysical theory, and John Stuart Mill's definition of "good" as the greatest happiness of the greatest number provided the underpinnings for his utilitarian theory of ethics.

Like stipulative definitions, theoretical definitions are neither true nor false, strictly speaking. The reason is that theoretical definitions function as proposals to see or interpret some phenomenon in a certain way. Since proposals have no truth value, neither do theoretical definitions. They may, however, be more or less interesting or more or less fruitful, depending on the deductive consequences they entail and on the outcome of the experiments they suggest.

Persuasive Definitions

The purpose of a **persuasive definition** is to engender a favorable or unfavorable attitude toward what is denoted by the definiendum. This purpose is accomplished by assigning an emotionally charged or value-laden meaning to a word while making it appear that the word really has (or ought to have) that meaning in the language in which it is used. Thus, persuasive definitions amount to a certain synthesis of stipulative, lexical, and, possibly, theoretical definitions backed by the rhetorical motive to engender a certain attitude. As a result of this synthesis, a persuasive definition masquerades as an honest assignment of meaning to a term while condemning or blessing with approval the subject matter of the definiendum. Here are some examples of opposing pairs of persuasive definitions:

"Abortion" means the ruthless murdering of innocent human beings.
"Abortion" means a safe and established surgical procedure whereby a woman is relieved of an unwanted burden.

"Liberal" means a drippy-eyed do-gooder obsessed with giving away other people's money.
"Liberal" means a genuine humanitarian committed to the goals of adequate housing and health care and of equal opportunity for all of our citizens.

"Capitalism" means the economic system in which individuals are afforded the God-given freedom to own property and conduct business as they choose.
"Capitalism" means the economic system in which humanity is sacrificed to the wanton quest for money, and mutual understanding and respect are replaced by alienation, greed, and selfishness.

"Taxation" means the procedure by means of which our commonwealth is preserved and sustained.
"Taxation" means the procedure used by bureaucrats to rip off the people who elected them.

The objective of a persuasive definition is to influence the attitudes of the reader or listener; thus, such definitions may be used with considerable effectiveness in political speeches and editorial columns. While persuasive definitions may, like lexical definitions, be evaluated as either true or false, the primary issue is neither truth nor falsity but the effectiveness of such definitions as instruments of persuasion.

I. Determine whether the following definitions are stipulative, lexical, precising, theoretical, or persuasive.

★1. "Blind" means, for federal income tax purposes, either the inability to see better than 20/200 in the better eye with glasses or having a field of vision of 20 degrees or less.

2. "Football" means a sport in which modern-day gladiators brutalize one another while trying to move a ridiculously shaped "ball" from one end of the playing field to the other.

3. "Wristovision" means a miniature television set that can be worn on the wrist.

★4. "Diffident" means lacking confidence in oneself; characterized by modest reserve.

5. "Magnetism" means a property of certain substances such as iron, cobalt, and nickel that arises from the spin of the electrons in the unfilled inner shell of the atoms that compose the substance.

6. "Fiduciary" means having to do with a confidence or trust; a person who holds something in trust.

★7. "Politician" means a person of unquestioned honesty and integrity whom the people, in their collective wisdom, have duly elected to guide the ship of state and protect it from the reefs and shoals that threaten it on every side.

8. "Intoxicated," for purposes of driving a car in many states, means having a blood-alcohol content of 0.1% (.001) or greater.

9. "Gweed" means a thoroughly immature person who feigns intellectual prowess; a total loser.

★10. "Sound" means a compression wave in air or some other elastic medium having a frequency ranging (for humans) from 20 to 20,000 vibrations per second.

11. "Radioactive area" means, for purposes of the U.S. Nuclear Regulatory Commission, any area accessible to individuals in which there exists radiation at such levels that a major portion of the body could receive in any one hour a dose in excess of 5 millirems or in any five consecutive days a dose in excess of 100 millirems.

12. "Neurosis" means a chronic emotional disturbance that arises from suppressed or forgotten emotional stress (such as resentment, hostility, aggression, or guilt) experienced in early childhood.

★13. "Scaling" means a sport in which people race four-wheel drive vehicles up the face of boulder-strewn hillsides.

14. "Smoker" means a rude and disgusting individual who callously emits noxious tobacco fumes into the air, threatening the health and comfort of everyone in the vicinity.

15. "Diadem" means an ornamental headband worn as a badge of royalty; a crown.

★16. "Psychiatry" means the fortuitous melding of modern medicine with psychology that promises relief to thousands of poor, desperate souls who suffer the pains of emotional disorder.

17. "Gene" means the hereditary unit that occupies a fixed chromosomal locus, which through transcription has a specific effect on phenotype and which can mutate to various allelic forms.

18. "Subgression" means moving oneself and one's family to a subterranean bomb shelter for the purpose of escaping nuclear attack.

★19. "Intractable" means not easily governed; obstinate; unruly; not disposed to be taught.

20. "Recession" means, for purposes of the National Bureau of Economic Research, two consecutive quarters of negative growth in real GNP or in aggregate output for the entire economy.

21. "Gravity" means a force that results from the universal attraction that every particle of matter has for every other particle, and which varies directly with the mass of the particles and inversely with the square of the distance between them.

★22. "Assault" means, for legal purposes, an intentional and unprivileged act resulting in the apprehension of an immediate harmful or offensive contact.

23. "Television" means the electronic medium that keeps an entire nation of viewers in a state of seminarcosis by feeding them a steady stream of inane drivel.

24. "Obelisk" means an upright, four-sided pillar that terminates in a pyramid; a dagger.

★25. "Aereomobile" means a vehicle that is normally driven on the ground but that has the capability of flying through the air to avoid traffic congestion.

II. The following exercises involve constructing definitions:

1. Invent stipulative definitions for two new words that you wish to introduce into the language for the first time.

2. Construct lexical definitions for "capital" and "depression," and indicate two different meanings for each.

3. Construct precising definitions for "middle-aged" and "alcoholic." Interpret both words as relating to people and specify the purpose for which the definitions are to be used.

4. Construct theoretical definitions for "energy" and "atom."

5. Construct opposing pairs of persuasive definitions for "conservative" and "socialism."

III. Answer "true" or "false" to the following statements:

1. From the standpoint of logic, many definitions are concerned not with words but with things.

2. The definiendum is the word or term that is supposed to be defined.

3. The definiens is the word or group of words that assigns a meaning to the word being defined.

4. A stipulative definition is either true or false.

5. A lexical definition reports the way a word is actually used in a language.

6. One of the purposes of a lexical definition is to guard against the ambiguous use of a word.

7. The meaning given to a word by a precising definition is completely arbitrary.

8. Theoretical definitions are either true or false, just as are lexical definitions.

9. Theoretical definitions provide a theoretical characterization of the entity or entities denoted by the word being defined.

10. The purpose of a persuasive definition is to influence attitudes.

2.4   Definitional Techniques

In the last section we presented a survey of some of the kinds of definitions actually in use and the functions they are intended to serve. In this section we will investigate some of the techniques used to produce these definitions. These techniques may be classified in terms of the two kinds of meaning, intensional and extensional, discussed in Section 2.2.

Extensional (Denotative) Definitions

An **extensional definition** is one that assigns a meaning to a term by indicating the members of the class that the definiendum denotes. There are at least three ways of indicating the members of a class: pointing to them, naming them individually, and naming them in groups. The three kinds of definitions that result are called, respectively, demonstrative or ostensive definitions, enumerative definitions, and definitions by subclass.

Demonstrative (ostensive) definitions are probably the most primitive form of definition. All one need know to understand such a definition is the meaning of pointing. As the following examples illustrate, such definitions may be either partial or complete, depending on whether all or only some of the members of the class denoted by the definiendum are pointed to:

"Chair" means this and this and this—as you point to a number of chairs, one after the other.

"Washington Monument" means that—as you point to it.

If you were attempting to teach a foreigner your own native language, and neither of you understood a word of each other's language, demonstrative definition would almost certainly be one of the methods you would use.

Because demonstrative definitions are the most primitive, they are also the most limited. In addition to the limitations affecting all extensional definitions (which will be discussed shortly), there is the obvious limitation that the required objects be available for being pointed at. For example, if one wishes to define the word "sun" and it happens to be nighttime, or the word "dog" and none happens to be in the vicinity, a demonstrative definition cannot be used.

Demonstrative definitions differ from the other kinds of definitions in that the definiens is constituted at least in part by a gesture—the gesture of pointing. Since the definiens in any definition is a group of words, however, a gesture, such as pointing, must count as a word. While this conclusion may appear strange at first, it is supported by the fact that the "words" in many sign languages consist exclusively of gestures.

Enumerative definitions assign a meaning to a term by naming the members of the class the term denotes. Like demonstrative definitions, they may also be either partial or complete. Examples:

"Actress" means a person such as Nicole Kidman, Emma Thompson, or Demi Moore.

"Baltic state" means Estonia, Latvia, or Lithuania.

Complete enumerative definitions are usually more satisfying than partial ones because they identify the definiendum with greater assurance. Relatively few classes, however, can be completely enumerated. Many classes, such as the class of real numbers greater than 1 but less than 2, have an infinite number of members. Others, such as the class of stars and the class of persons, while not infinite, have still too many members to enumerate. Therefore, anything approximating a complete enumerative definition of terms denoting these classes is clearly impossible. Then there are others—the class of insects and the class of trees, for example—the vast majority of whose members have no names. For terms that denote these classes, either a demonstrative definition or a definition by subclass is the more appropriate choice.

A **definition by subclass** assigns a meaning to a term by naming subclasses of the class denoted by the term. Such a definition, too, may be either partial or complete, depending on whether the subclasses named, when taken together, include all the members of the class or only some of them. Examples:

"Tree" means an oak, pine, elm, spruce, maple, and the like.

"Flower" means a rose, lily, daisy, geranium, zinnia, and the like.

"Cetacean" means either a whale, a dolphin, or a porpoise.

"Fictional work" means either a poem, a play, a novel, or a short story.

The first two are partial, the second two complete. As with definitions by enumeration, complete definitions by subclass are more satisfying than partial ones; but because relatively few terms denote classes that admit of a conveniently small number of subclasses, complete definitions by subclass are often difficult, if not impossible, to provide.

Extensional definitions are chiefly used as techniques for producing lexical and stipulative definitions. Lexical definitions are aimed at communicating how a word is actually used, and one of the ways of doing so is by identifying the members of the class that the word denotes. Dictionaries frequently include references to the individual members (or to the subclasses) of the class denoted by the word being defined. Sometimes they even include a kind of demonstrative definition when they provide a picture of the object that the word denotes. Not all lexical definitions have to occur in dictionaries, however. A lexical definition can just as well be spoken, as when one person attempts to explain orally to another how a word is used in a language. Such attempts, incidentally, often have recourse to all three kinds of extensional definition.

Stipulative definitions are used to assign a meaning to a word for the first time. This task may be accomplished by all three kinds of extensional definition. For example, a biologist engaged in naming and classifying types of fish might assign names to the specific varieties by pointing to their respective tanks (demonstrative definition), and then she might assign a class name to the whole group by referring to the names of the specific varieties (definition by subclass). An astronomer might point via his telescope to a newly discovered comet and announce, "That comet will henceforth be known as 'Henderson's Comet'" (demonstrative definition). The organizer of a children's game might make the stipulation: "John, Mary, and Billy will be called 'Buccaneers,' and Judy, George, and Nancy will be 'Pirates'" (enumerative definition).

Although it is conceivable that extensional definitions could also serve as techniques for theoretical and persuasive definitions (though this would be highly unusual), extensional definitions by themselves cannot properly serve as precising definitions for the following reason. The function of a precising definition is to clarify a vague word, and vagueness is a problem affecting intensional meaning. Because the intension is imprecise, the extension is indefinite. To attempt to render the intension precise by exactly specifying the extension (as with an extensional definition) would be tantamount to having extension determine intension—which cannot be done.

The principle that intension determines extension, whereas the converse is not true, underlies the fact that all extensional definitions suffer serious deficiencies. For example, in the case of the demonstrative definition of the word "chair," if all the chairs pointed to are made of wood, observers might get the idea that "chair" means "wood" instead of something to sit on. Similarly, they might get the idea that "Washington Monument" means "tall" or "pointed" or any of a number of other things. From the definition of "actress," readers or listeners might think that "actress" means "woman"—which would include countless individuals who have nothing to do with the stage or screen. From the definition of "tree" they might get the idea that "tree" means "firmly planted in the ground," which would also include the pilings of a building. And they might think that "cetacean" means "aquatic animal," which includes salmon, tuna, squid, manatees, and so on. In other words, it makes no difference how many individuals or subclasses are named in an extensional definition, there is no assurance that listeners or readers will get the *intensional* meaning. Extensions can *suggest* intensions, but they cannot *determine* them.

Intensional (Connotative) Definitions

An **intensional definition** is one that assigns a meaning to a word by indicating the qualities or attributes that the word connotes. Because at least four strategies may be used to indicate the attributes a word connotes, there are at least four kinds of intensional definitions: synonymous definition, etymological definition, operational definition, and definition by genus and difference.

A **synonymous definition** is one in which the definiens is a single word that connotes the same attributes as the definiendum. In other words, the definiens is a synonym of the word being defined. Examples:

"Physician" means doctor.

"Intentional" means willful.

"Voracious" means ravenous.

"Observe" means see.

When a single word can be found that has the same intensional meaning as the word being defined, a synonymous definition is a highly concise way of assigning a meaning. Many words, however, have subtle shades of meaning that are not connoted by any other single word. For example, the word "wisdom" is not exactly synonymous with either "knowledge," "understanding," or "sense"; and "envious" is not exactly synonymous with either "jealous" or "covetous."

An **etymological definition** assigns a meaning to a word by disclosing the word's ancestry in both its own language and other languages. Most ordinary English words have ancestors either in old or middle English or in some other language such as Greek, Latin, or French, and the current English meaning (as well as spelling and pronunciation) is often closely tied to the meaning (and spelling and pronunciation) of these ancestor words. For example, the English word "license" is derived from the Latin verb *licere,* which means to be permitted, and the English word "captain" derives from the Latin noun *caput,* which means head.

Etymological definitions have special importance for at least two reasons. The first is that the etymological definition of a word often conveys the word's root meaning or seminal meaning from which all other associated meanings are derived. Unless one is familiar with this root meaning, one often fails to place other meanings in their proper light or to grasp the meaning of the word when it is used in its most proper sense. For example, the word "principle" derives from the Latin word *principium,* which means beginning or source. Accordingly, the "principles of physics" are those fundamental laws that provide the "source" of the science of physics. The English word "efficient" derives from the Latin verb *efficere,* which means to bring about. Thus, the "efficient cause" of something (such as the motion of a car) is the agent that actually brings that thing about (the engine).

The second reason for the importance of etymological definitions is that if one is familiar with the etymology of one English word, one often has access to the meaning of an entire constellation of related words. For example, the word "orthodox" derives from the two Greek words *ortho,* meaning right or straight, and *doxa,* meaning belief or opinion. From this, one might grasp that "orthopedic" has to do with straight bones (originally in children—*pais* in Greek means child), and that "orthodontic" has to do with straight teeth (*odon* in Greek means tooth). Similarly, if one is familiar with the etymological definition of "polygon" (from the Greek words *poly,* meaning many, and *ganos* meaning angle), one might grasp the meanings of "polygamy" (from *gamos,* meaning marriage) and "polygraph" (from *graphein,* meaning to write). A polygraph is a lie detector that simultaneously records pulse rate, blood pressure, respiration, and so on.

An **operational definition** assigns a meaning to a word by specifying certain experimental procedures that determine whether or not the word applies to a certain thing. Examples:

One substance is "harder than" another if and only if one scratches the other when the two are rubbed together.

A subject has "brain activity" if and only if an electroencephalograph shows oscillations when attached to the subject's head.

A "potential difference" exists between two conductors if and only if a voltmeter shows a reading when connected to the two conductors.

A solution is an "acid" if and only if litmus paper turns red when dipped into it.

Each of these definitions prescribes an operation to be performed. The first prescribes that the two substances in question be rubbed together, the second that the electroencephalograph be connected to the patient's head and observed for oscillations, the third that the voltmeter be connected to the two conductors and observed for deflection, and the fourth that the litmus paper be placed in the solution and observed for color change. Unless it specifies such an operation, a definition cannot be an operational definition. For example, the definition "A solution is an 'acid' if and only if it has a pH of less than 7," while good in other respects, is not an operational definition because it prescribes no operation.

Operational definitions were invented for the purpose of tying down relatively abstract concepts to the solid ground of empirical reality. In this they succeed fairly well; yet, from the standpoint of ordinary language usage, they involve certain deficiencies. One of these deficiencies concerns the fact that operational definitions usually convey only *part* of the intensional meaning of a term. Certainly "brain activity" means more than oscillations on an electroencephalograph, just as "acid" means more than blue litmus paper turning red. This deficiency becomes more acute when one attempts to apply operational definitions to terms outside the framework of science. For example, no adequate operational definition could be given for such words as "love," "respect," "freedom," and "dignity." Within their proper sphere, however, operational definitions are quite useful and important. It is interesting to note that Einstein developed his special theory of relativity in partial response to the need for an operational definition of simultaneity.

A **definition by genus and difference** assigns a meaning to a term by identifying a genus term and one or more difference words that, when combined, convey the meaning of the term being defined. Definition by genus and difference is more generally applicable and achieves more adequate results than any of the other kinds of intensional definition. To explain how it works, we must first explain the meanings of the terms "genus," "species," and "specific difference."

In logic, "genus" and "species" have a somewhat different meaning than they have in biology. In logic, "genus" simply means a relatively larger class, and "species" means a relatively smaller subclass of the genus. For example, we may speak of the genus animal and the species mammal, or of the genus mammal and the species feline, or of the genus feline and the species tiger, or the genus tiger and the species Bengal tiger. In other words, genus and species are merely relative classifications.

The "specific difference," or "difference," is the attribute or attributes that distinguish the various species within a genus. For example, the specific difference that distinguishes tigers from other species in the genus feline would include the attributes of being large, striped, ferocious, and so on. Because the specific difference is what distinguishes the species, when a genus is qualified by a specific difference, a species is identified. Definition by genus and difference is based on this fact. It consists of combining a term denoting a genus with a word or group of words connoting a specific difference so that the combination identifies the meaning of the term denoting the species.

Let us construct a definition by genus and difference for the word "ice." The first step is to identify a genus of which ice is the species. The required genus is water. Next we must identify a specific difference (attribute) that makes ice a special form of water. The required difference is frozen. The completed definition may now be written out:

Species		Difference	Genus
"Ice"	means	frozen	water.

A definition by genus and difference is easy to construct. Simply select a term that is more general than the term to be defined, then narrow it down so that it means the same thing as the term being defined. Examples:

Species		Difference	Genus
"Daughter"	means	female	offspring.
"Husband"	means	married	man.
"Doe"	means	female	deer.
"Fawn"	means	very young	deer.
"Skyscraper"	means	very tall	building.

Other examples are more sophisticated:

"Tent" means a collapsible shelter made of canvas or other material that is stretched and sustained by poles.

"Tent" is the species, "shelter" is the genus, and "collapsible" and "made of canvas . . ." the difference.

Definition by genus and difference is the most effective of the intensional definitions for producing the five kinds of definition discussed in Section 2.3. Stipulative, lexical, precising, theoretical, and persuasive definitions can all be constructed according to the method of genus and difference. Lexical definitions are typically definitions by genus and difference, but they also often include etymological definitions. Operational definition can serve as the method for constructing stipulative, lexical, precising, and persuasive definitions, but because of the limitations we have noted, it typically could not be used to produce a *complete* lexical definition. Other techniques would have to be used in addition. Synonymous definition may be used to produce only lexical definitions. Since, in a synonymous definition, the definiendum must have a meaning before a synonym can be found, this technique cannot be used to produce stipulative definitions, and the fact that the definiens of such a definition contains no more information than the definiendum prohibits its use in constructing precising, theoretical, and persuasive definitions.

This account of definitions is inevitably incomplete. At the beginning of the chapter we mentioned that all words—not just terms—stand in need of definitions, but the account given here is based on the intension and extension of *terms*. Nevertheless, many of the techniques developed here can be applied to words in general, and even to symbols. For example, in Chapters 6 and 8 we will present definitions of various symbols that are used in modern logic to connect one statement with another and to translate ordinary language statements into symbolic form. When these symbols were introduced many years ago, it was accomplished through stipulative definitions. Also, as we will see in Chapter 6, some of these symbols are defined by certain tables, called "truth tables," which establish each symbol's meaning under all possible arrangements

2.1 Correlation of Definitional Techniques with Types of Definition

This technique	Can produce this type of definition				
	Stipulative	**Lexical**	**Precising**	**Theoretical**	**Persuasive**
Demonstrative	yes	yes	no	(unusual)	(unusual)
Enumerative	yes	yes	no	(unusual)	(unusual)
Subclass	yes	yes	no	(unusual)	(unusual)
Synonymous	no	yes	no	no	no
Etymological	yes	yes	no	no	no
Operational	(limited)	yes	yes	(unusual)	(unusual)
Genus & Difference	yes	yes	yes	yes	yes

of truth values. These definitions are probably best described as extensional, and they are similar in some ways to demonstrative definitions and enumerative definitions.

The applicability of the seven definitional techniques in producing the five kinds of definition is summarized in Table 2.1.

EXERCISE 2.4

I. Determine whether the following are demonstrative definitions, enumerative definitions, definitions by subclass, synonymous definitions, etymological definitions, operational definitions, or definitions by genus and difference.

★1. "Plant" means something such as a tree, a flower, a vine, or a cactus.

2. "Hammer" means a tool used for pounding.

3. A triangle is "equilateral" if and only if a compass, when placed sequentially on two vertices and properly adjusted, strikes through the other two vertices.

★4. "State" means something such as Ohio, Arkansas, Minnesota, and Tennessee.

5. "Angel" is a word that originates from the Greek word *angelos,* which means messenger.

6. "Neophyte" means beginner.

★7. "House" means this:

8. "Painting" means something like da Vinci's *Mona Lisa,* van Gogh's *Starry Night,* Botticelli's *Birth of Venus,* or Rembrandt's *Night Watch.*

9. "Dessert" means something such as pie, cake, cookies, or ice cream sundaes.

★10. "Hot" means, for an electric iron, that your wetted finger sizzles when placed momentarily in contact with it.

11. "Universe" originates from the Latin word *universus,* which means whole or entire.

12. "Mountain" means something such as Everest, Rainier, Whitney, or McKinley.

★13. "Hurricane" means a storm having winds of at least 73 miles per hour that originates at sea.

14. A substance is "translucent" if and only if when held up to a strong light some of the light comes through.

15. "Insect" means something such as a fly, an ant, a wasp, or a caterpillar.

★16. "Poignant" is a word derived from the Latin word *pungere,* which means to prick, pierce, or sting.

17. "Facade" means face.

18. "Prime number" means a number greater than one that is divisible only by itself and one.

★19. "Language" means something such as French, German, Spanish, English, and so on.

20. "Tree" means this, and this, and this (as you point to a number of trees).

21. "Oak" means a tree that bears acorns.

★22. "Rapier" means sword.

23. An "electric current" flows in a circuit if and only if an ammeter connected in series with the circuit shows a reading.

24. "Philosopher" means someone such as Plato, Aristotle, Descartes, or Kant.

★25. "Professional person" means a person such as a doctor, a lawyer, a professor, or an architect.

26. "Error" means mistake.

27. "Tale" is a word that derives from the Old English word *talu,* which means talk.

★28. "Truck" means a vehicle used for hauling.

29. "Done" means, in reference to a baking cake, that a wooden toothpick poked into the center comes out clean.

30. "Musical composition" means something such as a symphony, a concerto, a sonata, or a toccata.

II. The following exercises involve constructing definitions.

1. Construct a partial enumerative definition for the following terms by naming three members of the class the term denotes. Then find a nonsynonymous term that these members serve equally well to define. Example: "Poet" means a person such as Wordsworth, Coleridge, or Shelley. A nonsynonymous term is "Englishman."

   ★a. skyscraper
   b. corporation
   c. island
   d. composer
   e. novel

2. Construct a complete enumerative definition for the following terms:
   a. ocean
   b. continent

3. Construct a definition by subclass for the following terms by naming three subclasses of the class the term denotes. Then find a nonsynonymous term that these subclasses serve equally well to define.

★a. animal

b. fish

c. vehicle

d. gemstone

e. polygon

4. Construct a complete definition by subclass for the following terms:

a. quadrilateral

b. circulating American coin

5. Construct synonymous definitions for the following terms:

★a. intersection

b. fabric

c. nucleus

d. abode

e. wedlock

f. cellar

g. summit

h. apparel

6. Construct operational definitions for the following words:

★a. genius

b. ferromagnetic

c. fluorescent

d. alkaline

e. polarized (light)

7. Construct definitions by genus and difference for the following terms. In each definition identify the genus term.

★a. drake

b. biologist

c. felony

d. widow

e. library

8. Consult a dictionary to find the etymological roots of the following words, and then explain how they relate to the conventional meaning of these words.

★a. morphology

b. isomorphic

c. isotropic

d. phototropic

    e. photography

    f. lithography

    g. lithology

    h. psychology

III. Answer "true" or "false" to the following statements:

1. The technique of extensional definition may be used to produce precising definitions.

2. The technique of extensional definition may be used to produce stipulative and lexical definitions.

3. Most extensional definitions convey the precise intensional meaning of a term.

4. An intensional definition conveys the meaning of a term by indicating the members of the class the term denotes.

5. In a synonymous definition the definiens must be a single word.

6. The technique of synonymous definition may be used to construct precising definitions.

7. Operational definitions typically convey the entire intensional meaning of a word.

8. The species is a subclass of the genus.

9. The specific difference is an attribute or set of attributes that identifies a species.

10. Definition by genus and difference may be used to produce stipulative, lexical, precising, theoretical, and persuasive definitions.

2.5   Criteria for Lexical Definitions

Because the function of a lexical definition is to report the way a word is actually used in a language, lexical definitions are the ones we most frequently encounter and are what most people mean when they speak of the "definition" of a word. Accordingly, it is appropriate that we have a set of rules that we may use in constructing lexical definitions of our own and in evaluating the lexical definitions of others. While some of these rules apply to the other kinds of definitions as well, the unique functions that are served by stipulative, precising, theoretical, and persuasive definitions prescribe different sets of criteria.

Rule 1: A Lexical Definition Should Conform to the Standards of Proper Grammar

A definition, like any other form of expression, should be grammatically correct. Examples of definitions that are grammatically *incorrect* are as follows:

    Vacation is when you don't have to go to work or school.

    Furious means if you're angry at someone.

    Cardiac is like something to do with the heart.

The corrected versions are:

"Vacation" means a period during which activity is suspended from work or school.

"Furious" means a condition of being angry.

"Cardiac" means pertaining to, situated near, or acting on the heart.

Technically the definiendum should be put in quotation marks or italics, but this convention is not always followed.

Rule 2: A Lexical Definition Should Convey the Essential Meaning of the Word Being Defined

The word "human" is occasionally defined as featherless biped. Such a definition fails to convey the essential meaning of "human" as the word is used in ordinary English. It says nothing about the important attributes that distinguish humans from the other animals—namely, the capacity to reason and to use language on a sophisticated level. A more adequate definition would be "'Human' means the animal that has the capacity to reason and to speak."

If a lexical definition is to be given in terms of an operational definition or in terms of any of the forms of extensional definition, it should usually be supplemented by one of the other forms of intensional definition, preferably definition by genus and difference. As we have noted, from the standpoint of ordinary language usage an operational definition often conveys only part of the intensional meaning of a word, and this part frequently misses the essential meaning altogether. As for extensional definitions, at best they can only *suggest* the essential meaning of a word; they cannot *determine* it precisely. As a result, no adequate lexical definition can consist exclusively of extensional definitions.

Rule 3: A Lexical Definition Should Be Neither Too Broad nor Too Narrow

If a definition is too broad, the definiens includes too much; if it is too narrow, the definiens includes too little. If, for example, "bird" were defined as any warm-blooded animal having wings, the definition would be too broad because it would include bats, and bats are not birds. If, on the other hand, "bird" were defined as any warm-blooded, feathered animal that can fly, the definition would be too narrow because it would exclude ostriches, which cannot fly.

The only types of lexical definitions that tend to be susceptible to either of these deficiencies are synonymous definitions and definitions by genus and difference. With synonymous definitions, one must be careful that the definiens really is a synonym of the definiendum. For example, the definition "'king' means ruler" is too broad because many rulers are not kings. "Ruler" is not genuinely synonymous with "king." As for definitions by genus and difference, one must ensure that the specific difference narrows the genus in exactly the right way. Both of the above definitions of "bird" are definitions by genus and difference in which the specific difference fails to restrict the genus in exactly the right manner.

Rule 4: A Lexical Definition Should Avoid Circularity

Sometimes the problem of circularity appears in connection with *pairs* of definitions. The following pair is circular:

"Science" means the activity engaged in by scientists.

"Scientist" means anyone who engages in science.

At other times a definition may be intrinsically circular. Of the following, the first is a synonymous definition, the second a definition by genus and difference:

"Quiet" means quietude.

"Silence" means the state of being silent.

Certain operational definitions also run the risk of circularity:

"Time" means whatever is measured by a clock.

Surely a person would have to know what "time" means before he or she could understand the purpose of a clock.

Rule 5: A Lexical Definition Should Not Be Negative When It Can Be Affirmative

Of the following two definitions, the first is affirmative, the second negative:

"Concord" means harmony.

"Concord" means the absence of discord.

Some words, however, are intrinsically negative. For them, a negative definition is quite appropriate. Examples:

"Bald" means lacking hair.

"Darkness" means the absence of light.

Rule 6: A Lexical Definition Should Avoid Figurative, Obscure, Vague, or Ambiguous Language

A definition is *figurative* if it involves metaphors or tends to paint a picture instead of exposing the essential meaning of a term. Examples:

"Architecture" means frozen music.

"Camel" means a ship of the desert.

A definition is *obscure* if its meaning is hidden as a result of defective or inappropriate language. One source of obscurity is overly technical language. Compare these two definitions:

"Bunny" means a mammalian of the family Leporidae of the order Lagomorpha whose young are born furless and blind.

"Bunny" means a rabbit.

The problem lies not with technical language as such but with *needlessly* technical language. Because "bunny" is very much a nontechnical term, no technical definition is needed. On the other hand, some words are intrinsically technical, and for them only a technical definition will suffice. Example:

"Neutrino" means a quasi-massless lepton obeying Fermi-Dirac statistics and having one-half quantum unit of spin.

A definition is *vague* if it lacks precision or if its meaning is blurred—that is, if there is no way of telling exactly what class of things the definiens refers to. Example:

> "Democracy" means a kind of government where the people are in control.

This definition fails to identify the people who are in control, how they exercise their control, and what they are in control of.

A definition is *ambiguous* if it lends itself to more than one distinct interpretation. Example:

> "Triangle" means a figure composed of three straight lines in which all the angles are equal to 180°.

Does this mean that each angle separately is equal to 180° or that the angles taken together are equal to 180°? Either interpretation is possible given the ambiguous meaning of "all the angles are equal to 180°."

Rule 7: A Lexical Definition Should Avoid Affective Terminology

Affective terminology is any kind of word usage that plays upon the emotions of the reader or listener. It includes sarcastic and facetious language and any other kind of language that is liable to influence attitudes. Examples:

> "Communism" means that "brilliant" invention of Karl Marx and other foolish political visionaries in which the national wealth is supposed to be held in common by the people.

> "Theism" means belief in that great Santa Claus in the sky.

The second example also violates Rule 5 because it contains a metaphor.

Rule 8: A Lexical Definition Should Indicate the Context to Which the Definiens Pertains

This rule applies to any definition in which the context of the definiens is important to the meaning of the definiendum. For example, the definition " 'Deuce' means a tie in points toward a game or in games toward a set" is practically meaningless without any reference to tennis. Whenever the definiendum is a word that means different things in different contexts, a reference to the context is important. Examples:

> "Strike" means (in baseball) a pitch at which a batter swings and misses.
> "Strike" means (in bowling) the act of knocking down all the pins with the first ball of a frame.
> "Strike" means (in fishing) a pull on a line made by a fish in taking the bait.

It is not always necessary to make *explicit* reference to the context, but at least the phraseology of the definiens should indicate the context.

EXERCISE 2.5

Criticize the following definitions in light of the eight rules for lexical definitions:

★1. A sculpture is a three-dimensional image made of marble.

2. "Elusory" means elusive.

3. "Birdie" means sinking the ball in one stroke under par.

★4. A cynic is a person who knows the price of everything and the value of nothing.

(Oscar Wilde)

5. "Semantics" is when somebody studies words.

6. "iPod" means a handheld electronic device weighing about six ounces and featuring a single click-wheel on one side.

★7. A theist is anyone who is not an atheist or an agnostic.

8. "Intelligence" means whatever is measured by an IQ test.

9. A symphony is a musical piece written for full orchestra.

★10. Feminism is a militant movement originated by a group of deviant women for the purpose of undermining the natural distinction between the sexes.

11. "Wood" means fibrous, lignified cellulose.

12. Logic is the study of arguments including definitions.

★13. "Truculent" is if you're cruel or fierce.

14. A house is a structure made of wood or stone intended for human habitation.

15. Satire is a kind of glass, wherein beholders do generally discover everybody's face but their own.

(Jonathan Swift)

★16. A carpenter's square is a square used by a carpenter.

17. "Safety" means a play in which a player grounds the ball behind his own goal line when the ball was caused to cross the goal line by his own team.

18. Puberty: the time in life in which the two sexes begin first to be acquainted.

(Johnson's Dictionary)

★19. "Normal" means an attribute possessed by people who are able to get on in the world.

20. An organic substance is any substance that is not inorganic.

21. Faith is the bird that sings when the dawn is still dark.

(Rabindranath Tagore)

★22. "Schooner" means sort of like a sailboat.

23. "Faith" means reason succumbing to insecurity.

24. "Gammon" means, in backgammon, a victory in which one player defeats another before he can remove any of his men from the board.

★25. A cello is a stringed musical instrument played with a bow.

26. Tobacco is a plant grown in the southeastern United States that, when enjoyed in the form of cigars and cigarettes, produces a most delightful and satisfying taste and aroma.

27. History is the unfolding of miscalculations.

(Barbara Tuchman)

★28. "Clock" means a manufactured device featuring two pointers that rotate past a set of numerals ranging from 1 to 12.

29. "Soap" means saponified glyceride.

30. Mackerel: a sea-fish.

(Johnson's Dictionary)

★31. "Anchorperson" means an electronic media guru who has great looks but less than average intelligence and who brings canned news to people incapable of reading a newspaper.

32. "Diet" means like when you cut back on your calories.

33. Animal: a living creature corporeal, distinct, on the one side, from pure spirit, on the other, from pure matter.

(Johnson's Dictionary)

★34. "Pen" means an instrument used for writing on paper.

35. Wine is an alcoholic beverage made from grapes.

Summary

Terminology that conveys information is said to have cognitive meaning, and terminology that expresses or evokes feelings is said to have emotive meaning. Statements expressed in emotive terminology often make value claims; when these statements occur in arguments, it is appropriate to disengage the value claims from the emotive language and express them as separate premises. Two ways in which cognitive meanings can be defective are vagueness and ambiguity. Vagueness involves a blur of meaning, whereas ambiguity involves a mix-up of otherwise clear meanings.

A term is a word or group of words that can serve as the subject of a statement. All terms have intensional meaning (intension or connotation), and those terms that refer to actually existing things also have extensional meaning (extension or denotation). The intensional meaning of a term consists of the attributes that the term connotes, and the extensional meaning consists of the members of the class that the term denotes. Terms that refer to nonexistent things are said to have empty extension.

A definition is a group of words that assigns a meaning to a word or group of words. The definiendum is the word or group of words being defined, and the definiens is the word or group of words that does the defining. Because definitions can serve different purposes, there are different kinds of definitions. Stipulative definitions assign a meaning to a word when it first comes into use, lexical definitions report the meaning that a word already has within a given linguistic community, precising definitions reduce the vagueness of a word, theoretical definitions suggest a theory that gives a certain characterization to the entities that the term denotes, and persuasive definitions are used to influence the attitude of people in the community toward the things the word denotes.

The two kinds of meaning that words have, intensional and extensional, can be used as the basis for producing definitions. Extensional definitions assign a meaning to a word by identifying the things that the word denotes, and intensional definitions accomplish the same purpose by identifying the attributes that the word connotes.

Among the extensional definitions, demonstrative definitions "point" to the things in question, enumerative definitions name various individuals in the class, and definitions by subclass identify subclasses of those things. Among the intensional definitions, synonymous definitions equate the word being defined with another word that connotes the same attributes, etymological definitions disclose the word's ancestry, operational definitions specify experimental procedures for determining whether the word applies to a certain thing, and definitions by genus and difference identify a larger class of things and then narrow it down so that it matches the class that the word refers to.

There are rules that govern the construction of lexical definitions. Such definitions should conform to grammatical standards, convey the essential meaning of the word being defined, be neither too broad nor too narrow, avoid circularity, avoid negative, figurative, obscure, vague, ambiguous, and affective language, and indicate the context to which the defininiens pertains.

2

3 Informal Fallacies

3.1 Fallacies in General

A **fallacy** is a defect in an argument that consists in something other than merely false premises. As we will see, fallacies can be committed in many ways, but usually they involve either a mistake in reasoning or the creation of some illusion that makes a bad argument appear good (or both). A fallacy that involves a mistake in reasoning is sometimes called a *non sequitur* (which, in Latin, means "it does not follow"). Both deductive and inductive arguments may contain fallacies; if they do, they are either unsound or uncogent, depending on the kind of argument. Conversely, if an argument is unsound or uncogent, it has one or more false premises or it contains a fallacy (or both).

Fallacies are usually divided into two groups: formal and informal. A **formal fallacy** is one that may be identified by merely examining the form or structure of an argument. Fallacies of this kind are found only in deductive arguments that have identifiable forms. Chapter 1 presented some of these forms: categorical syllogisms, disjunctive syllogisms, and hypothetical syllogisms. The following categorical syllogism contains a formal fallacy:

> All bullfights are grotesque rituals.
> All executions are grotesque rituals.
> Therefore, all bullfights are executions.

This argument has the following form:

> All *A* are *B*.
> All *C* are *B*.
> ———————
> All *A* are *C*.

By merely examining this form, one can see that it is invalid. The fact that *A*, *B*, and *C* stand respectively for "bullfights," "grotesque rituals," and "executions" is irrelevant in detecting the fallacy. The problem may be traced to the second premise. If the letters *C* and *B* are interchanged, the form becomes valid, and the original argument, with the same change introduced, also becomes valid (but unsound).

Here is an example of a formal fallacy that occurs in a hypothetical syllogism:

If apes are intelligent, then apes can solve puzzles.
Apes can solve puzzles.
Therefore, apes are intelligent.

This argument has the following form:

If *A* then *B*.
B.
―――――――
A.

In this case, if *A* and *B* are interchanged in the first premise, the form becomes valid, and the original argument, with the same change, also becomes valid. This fallacy and the one that precedes it will be discussed in later chapters.

In distinguishing formal from informal fallacies, remember that formal fallacies occur only in deductive arguments. Thus, if a given argument is inductive, it cannot contain a formal fallacy. Also, keep an eye out for standard deductive argument forms such as categorical syllogisms and hypothetical syllogisms. If such an argument is invalid because of an improper arrangement of terms or statements, it commits a formal fallacy. Section 1.5 investigated some of these forms and gave instruction on distinguishing the form from the content of an argument. All of the exercises at the end of that section commit formal fallacies.

Informal fallacies are those that can be detected only by examining the content of the argument. Consider the following example:

The Brooklyn Bridge is made of atoms.
Atoms are invisible.
Therefore, the Brooklyn Bridge is invisible.

To detect this fallacy one must know something about bridges—namely, that they are large visible objects, and even though their atomic components are invisible, this does not mean that the bridges themselves are invisible.

Or consider this example:

A chess player is a person.
Therefore, a bad chess player is a bad person.

To detect this fallacy one must know that the meaning of the word "bad" depends on what it modifies, and that being a bad chess player is quite different from being a bad person.

The various informal fallacies accomplish their purpose in so many different ways that no single umbrella theory covers them all. Some fallacies work by getting the reader or listener to feel various emotions, such as fear, pity, or camaraderie, and then attaching a certain conclusion to those emotions. Others attempt to discredit an opposing argument by associating it with certain pejorative features of its author. And then there are those that appeal to various dispositions on the part of the reader or listener, such as superstition or mental laziness, to get him or her to accept a conclusion. By studying the typical ways in which arguers apply these techniques, one is less likely to be fooled by the fallacious arguments posed by others or to stumble blindly into fallacies when constructing arguments for one's own use.

Since the time of Aristotle, logicians have attempted to classify the various informal fallacies. Aristotle himself identified thirteen and separated them into two groups. The work of subsequent logicians has produced dozens more, rendering the task of classifying them even more difficult. The presentation that follows divides twenty-two informal fallacies into five groups: fallacies of relevance, fallacies of weak induction, fallacies of presumption, fallacies of ambiguity, and fallacies of grammatical analogy. The final section of the chapter considers the related topics of detecting and avoiding fallacies in the context of ordinary language.

EXERCISE 3.1

iLrn Determine whether the fallacies committed by the following arguments are formal fallacies or informal fallacies.

★1. If Rasputin was really mad, then he deceived Czar Nicholas II. Rasputin was not really mad. Therefore, he did not deceive Czar Nicholas II.

2. Everything that runs has feet. The Columbia River runs very swiftly. Therefore, the Columbia River has feet.

3. All persons who believe we create our own reality are persons who lack social responsibility. All persons governed by selfish motives are persons who lack social responsibility. Therefore, all persons who believe we create our own reality are persons governed by selfish motives.

★4. The ship of state is like a ship at sea. No sailor is ever allowed to protest orders from the captain. For the same reason, no citizen should ever be allowed to protest presidential policies.

5. Renowned violinist Pinchas Zukerman has said, "When it comes to vodka, Smirnoff plays second fiddle to none." We must therefore conclude that Smirnoff is the best vodka available.

6. If the Chinese government systematically kills its unwanted orphans, then the Chinese government is immoral. The Chinese government is indeed immoral. Therefore, the Chinese government systematically kills its unwanted orphans.

★7. Sarah Jessica Parker, Ben Affleck, and Julia Roberts are Democrats. Therefore, it must be the case that all Hollywood stars are Democrats.

8. House Majority Leader Tom DeLay argues that stem-cell research is immoral. But DeLay is an ultra-right-wing lunatic who is incapable of thinking objectively about anything. Obviously his argument is nonsense.

9. If plastic guns are sold to the public, then terrorists will carry them aboard airliners undetected. If plastic guns are sold to the public, then airline hijackings will increase. Therefore, if terrorists carry plastic guns aboard airliners undetected, then airline hijackings will increase.

★10. Some corporate mergers are arrangements that produce layoffs. Some arrangements that produce layoffs are occasions of economic unrest. Therefore, some corporate mergers are occasions of economic unrest.

3.2   Fallacies of Relevance

The **fallacies of relevance** share the common characteristic that the arguments in which they occur have premises that are *logically* irrelevant to the conclusion. Yet the premises may appear to be *psychologically* relevant, so the conclusion may *seem* to follow from the premises, even though it does not follow logically. In a good argument the premises provide genuine evidence in support of the conclusion. In an argument that commits a fallacy of relevance, on the other hand, the connection between premises and conclusion is emotional. To identify a fallacy of relevance, therefore, one must be able to distinguish genuine evidence from various forms of emotional appeal.

1. Appeal to Force (*Argumentum ad Baculum*: Appeal to the "Stick")

The fallacy of **appeal to force** occurs whenever an arguer poses a conclusion to another person and tells that person either implicitly or explicitly that some harm will come to him or her if he or she does not accept the conclusion. The fallacy always involves a threat by the arguer to the physical or psychological well-being of the listener or reader, who may be either a single person or a group of persons. Obviously, such a threat is logically irrelevant to the subject matter of the conclusion, so any argument based on such a procedure is fallacious. The *ad baculum* fallacy often occurs when children argue with one another:

> *Child to playmate:* "Teletubbies" is the best show on TV; and if you don't believe it, I'm going to call my big brother over here and he's going to beat you up.

But it occurs among adults as well:

> *Secretary to boss:* I deserve a raise in salary for the coming year. After all, you know how friendly I am with your wife, and I'm sure you wouldn't want her to find out what's been going on between you and that sexpot client of yours.

The first example involves a physical threat, the second a psychological threat. While neither threat provides any genuine evidence that the conclusion is true, both provide evidence that someone might be injured. If the two types of evidence are confused with each other, both arguer and listener may be deluded into thinking that the conclusion is supported by evidence, when in fact it is not.

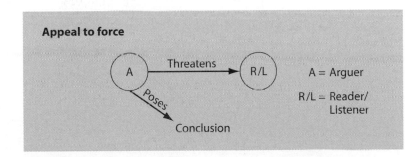

Appeal to force

Threatens

A → R/L

Poses

Conclusion

A = Arguer

R/L = Reader/Listener

The appeal to force fallacy usually accomplishes its purpose by psychologically impeding the reader or listener from acknowledging a missing premise that, if acknowledged, would be seen to be false or at least questionable. The two examples just given can be interpreted as concealing the following premises, both of which are most likely false:

> If my brother forces you to admit that "Teletubbies" is the best show on TV, then "Teletubbies" is in fact the best show.

> If I succeed in threatening you, then I deserve a raise in salary.

The conclusion of the first argument is that "Teletubbies" is the best show on TV. But just because someone is forced into saying that it is does not mean that such is the case. Similarly, the conclusion of the second argument is that the secretary deserves a raise in salary. But if the boss is threatened into raising the secretary's salary, this does not mean that the secretary deserves a raise. Many of the other informal fallacies can be interpreted as accomplishing their purpose in this way.

2. Appeal to Pity
(*Argumentum ad Misericordiam*)

The **appeal to pity** fallacy occurs when an arguer attempts to support a conclusion by merely evoking pity from the reader or listener. This pity may be directed toward the arguer or toward some third party. Example:

> *Taxpayer to judge:* Your Honor, I admit that I declared thirteen children as dependents on my tax return, even though I have only two. But if you find me guilty of tax evasion, my reputation will be ruined. I'll probably lose my job, my poor wife will not be able to have the operation that she desperately needs, and my kids will starve. Surely I am not guilty.

The conclusion of this argument is "Surely I am not guilty." Obviously, the conclusion is not *logically* relevant to the arguer's set of pathetic circumstances, although it is *psychologically* relevant. If the arguer succeeds in evoking pity from the listener or reader, the latter is likely to exercise his or her desire to help the arguer by accepting the argument. In this way the reader or listener may be fooled into accepting a conclusion that is not supported by any evidence. The appeal to pity is quite common and is often used by students on their instructors at exam time and by lawyers on behalf of their clients before judges and juries.

Of course, some arguments that attempt to evoke sympathetic feelings from the reader or listener are not fallacious. We might call them *arguments from compassion*.

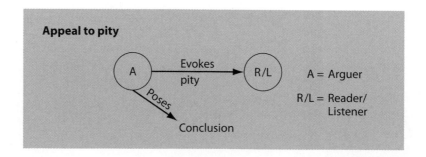

Appeal to pity

A → Evokes pity → R/L

A → Poses → Conclusion

A = Arguer

R/L = Reader/Listener

Such arguments differ from the fallacious appeal to pity in that, in addition to evoking compassion on behalf of some person, they supply information about why that person is genuinely deserving of help or special consideration. Whenever possible these nonfallacious arguments should show that the person in question is a victim of circumstances and not responsible for the dire straits he finds himself in, that the recommended help or special consideration is not illegal or inappropriate, and that it will genuinely help the person in question. In contrast to such arguments, the appeal to pity proceeds by ignoring all of these considerations and attempts to support a conclusion by merely evoking pity from the reader or listener.

3. Appeal to the People (*Argumentum ad Populum*)

Nearly everyone wants to be loved, esteemed, admired, valued, recognized, and accepted by others. The **appeal to the people** uses these desires to get the reader or listener to accept a conclusion. Two approaches are involved, one of them direct, the other indirect.

The *direct approach* occurs when an arguer, addressing a large group of people, excites the emotions and enthusiasm of the crowd to win acceptance for his or her conclusion. The objective is to arouse a kind of mob mentality. This is the strategy used by nearly every propagandist and demagogue. Adolf Hitler was a master of the technique, but it is also used with some measure of success by speechmakers at Democratic and Republican national conventions. Waving flags and blaring music add to the overall effect. Because the individuals in the audience want to share in the camaraderie, the euphoria, and the excitement, they find themselves accepting any number of conclusions with ever-increasing fervor.

An appeal to negative emotions, such as suspicion and fear, can also generate a mob mentality. These emotions have produced many a lynching, and they led to the internment of Japanese Americans during World War II. Also, the direct approach is not limited to oral discourse. The same effect can be accomplished in writing. By using such emotionally charged phraseology as "fighter of communism," "champion of the free enterprise system," and "defender of the working man," polemicists can awaken the same kind of mob mentality as they would if they were speaking.

In the *indirect approach* the arguer aims his or her appeal not at the crowd as a whole but at one or more individuals separately, focusing on some aspect of their

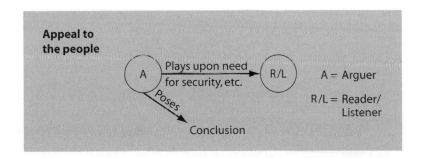

relationship to the crowd. The indirect approach includes such specific forms as the bandwagon argument, the appeal to vanity, and the appeal to snobbery. All are standard techniques of the advertising industry.

Here is an example of the **bandwagon argument:**

> Of course you want to buy Zing toothpaste. Why, 90 percent of America brushes with Zing.

The idea is that you will be left behind or left out of the group if you do not use the product.

The **appeal to vanity** often associates the product with someone who is admired, pursued, or imitated, the idea being that you, too, will be admired and pursued if you use it. The current television and billboard ads for the U.S. Marine Corps provide an example. The ads show a strong, handsome man in uniform holding a gleaming sword, and the caption reads:

> The Few, the Proud, the Marines.

The message is that if you join the Marines, then you, too, will be admired and respected, just like the handsome man in the uniform.

The **appeal to snobbery** depends on a similar kind of association.

> A Rolls-Royce is not for everyone. If you qualify as one of the select few, this distinguished classic may be seen and driven at British Motor Cars, Ltd.
> (By appointment only, please.)

Needless to say, the indirect approach is used by others besides advertisers:

> *Mother to child:* You want to grow up and be just like Wonder Woman, don't you? Then eat your liver and carrots.

These examples illustrate how the indirect version of the appeal to the people can overlap the false cause fallacy, which is presented in Section 3.3. Thus, the previous example might be interpreted to suggest that eating liver and carrots will *cause* one to become just like Wonder Woman. If so, the fallacy could be identified as false cause.

Both the direct and indirect approaches of the *ad populum* fallacy have the same basic structure:

> You want to be accepted/included-in-the-group/loved/esteemed....Therefore, you should accept XYZ as true.

In the direct approach the arousal of a mob mentality produces an immediate feeling of belonging for each person in the crowd. Each person feels united with the crowd, which evokes a sense of strength and security. When the crowd roars its approval of the conclusions that are then offered, anyone who does not accept them automatically cuts himself or herself off from the crowd and risks the loss of his or her security, strength, and acceptance. The same thing happens in the indirect approach, but the context and technique are somewhat subtler.

4. Argument Against the Person (*Argumentum ad Hominem*)

This fallacy always involves two arguers. One of them advances (either directly or implicitly) a certain argument, and the other then responds by directing his or her attention not to the first person's argument but to the first person *himself*. When this occurs, the second person is said to commit an **argument against the person.**

The argument against the person occurs in three forms: the *ad hominem* abusive, the *ad hominem* circumstantial, and the *tu quoque*. In the **ad hominem abusive,** the second person responds to the first person's argument by verbally abusing the first person. Example:

> Before he died, poet Allen Ginsberg argued in favor of legalizing pornography. But Ginsberg's arguments are nothing but trash. Ginsberg was a marijuana-smoking homosexual and a thoroughgoing advocate of the drug culture.

Because Ginsberg's being a marijuana-smoking homosexual and advocate of the drug culture is irrelevant to whether the premises of his argument support the conclusion, this argument is fallacious.

Not all cases of the *ad hominem* abusive are as blunt as this one, but they are just as fallacious. Example:

> William Buckley has argued in favor of legalizing drugs such as cocaine and heroin. But Buckley is just another one of those upper-crust intellectuals who is out of touch with real America. No sensible person should listen to his pseudo-solutions.

Again, whether Buckley is an upper-crust intellectual has nothing to do with whether his premises support his conclusion.

The **ad hominem circumstantial** begins the same way as the *ad hominem* abusive, but instead of heaping verbal abuse on his or her opponent, the respondent attempts to discredit the opponent's argument by alluding to certain circumstances that affect the opponent. By doing so the respondent hopes to show that the opponent is predisposed to argue the way he or she does and should therefore not be taken seriously. Here is an example:

> The Dalai Lama argues that China has no business in Tibet and that the West should do something about it. But the Dalai Lama just wants the Chinese to leave so he can return as leader. Naturally he argues this way. Therefore, we should reject his arguments.

The author of this argument ignores the substance of the Dalai Lama's argument and attempts to discredit it by calling attention to certain circumstances that affect the Dalai Lama—namely, that he wants to return to Tibet as its leader. But the fact that the Dalai Lama happens to be affected by these circumstances is irrelevant to whether

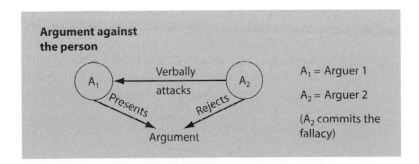

Argument against the person

A_1 — Verbally attacks → A_2

A_1 Presents → Argument ← Rejects A_2

A_1 = Arguer 1

A_2 = Arguer 2

(A_2 commits the fallacy)

his premises support a conclusion. The *ad hominem* circumstantial is easy to recognize because it always takes this form: "Of course Mr. X argues this way; just look at the circumstances that affect him."

The ***tu quoque*** ("you too") fallacy begins the same way as the other two varieties of the *ad hominem* argument, except that the second arguer attempts to make the first appear to be hypocritical or arguing in bad faith. The second arguer usually accomplishes this by citing features in the life or behavior of the first arguer that conflict with the latter's conclusion. In effect, the second arguer says, "How dare you argue that I should stop doing *X*; why, you do (or have done) *X* yourself." Example:

> *Child to parent:* Your argument that I should stop stealing candy from the corner store is no good. You told me yourself just a week ago that you, too, stole candy when you were a kid.

Obviously, whether the parent stole candy is irrelevant to whether the parent's premises support the conclusion that the child should not steal candy.

It is important to keep in mind that the purpose of an *ad hominem* argument is to discredit another person's argument by placing its author in a bad light. Thus, for the fallacy to be committed, there must always be two arguers (at least implicitly). If it should turn out that the person being attacked is not an arguer, then the personal comments made by the attacker may well be relevant to the conclusion that is drawn. In general, personal observations are relevant to conclusions about what kind of person someone is (good, bad, stingy, trustworthy, and so forth) and whether a person has done something. Example:

> International terrorist Osama bin Laden planned the destruction of the World Trade Center, killing thousands of innocent people, and he supports terrorist causes all over the world. Bin Laden is therefore a wicked and irresponsible person.

The conclusion is not that Bin Laden's argument is bad but that Bin Laden himself is bad. Because the premises give relevant support to this conclusion, the argument commits no fallacy. Another example:

> Shakespeare cannot possibly have written the thirty-six plays attributed to him, because the real Shakespeare was a two-bit country businessman who barely finished the fourth grade in school and who never left the confines of his native England.

The conclusion is not that some argument of Shakespeare's is bad but that Shakespeare did not write certain plays. Again, since the premises are relevant to this conclusion, the argument commits no *ad hominem* fallacy.

Determining what kind of person someone is includes determining whether that person is trustworthy. Thus personal comments are often relevant in evaluating whether a person's proclamations or statements, unsupported by evidence, warrant our belief. Examples of such statements include promises to do something, testimony given by a witness, and testimonials in support of a product or service. Here is an example of an argument that discredits a witness:

> Mickey has testified that he saw Freddy set fire to the building. But Mickey was recently convicted on ten counts of perjury, and he hates Freddy with a passion and would love to see him sent to jail. Therefore, you should not believe Mickey's testimony.

This argument commits no fallacy. The conclusion is not that you should reject Mickey's argument but rather that you should reject his testimony. Testimony is not argument, and the fact that the witness is a known liar and has a motive to lie now is relevant to whether we should believe him. Furthermore, note that the conclusion is not that Mickey's statement is literally false but rather that we should not *believe* the statement. It is quite possible that Mickey really did see Freddy set fire to the building and that Mickey's statement to that effect is true. But if our only reason for believing this statement is the mere fact that Mickey has made it, then given the circumstances, we are not justified in that belief. Personal factors are never relevant to truth and falsity as such, but they are relevant to believability.

Yet there is often a close connection between truth and believability, and this provides one of the reasons why *ad hominem* arguments are often effective. In evaluating any argument there are always two issues to be considered: the quality of the reasoning and the truth of the premises. As we have noted, both are irrelevant to the personal characteristics of the arguer. But whether we *accept* the premises as true may depend on the credibility of the arguer. Knowing that the arguer is biased or has a motive to lie may provide good grounds for distrusting the premises. Another reason why *ad hominem* arguments are effective is that they engage the emotions of readers and listeners and thereby motivate them to transfer their negative feelings about the arguer onto the argument.

5. Accident

The fallacy of **accident** is committed when a general rule is applied to a specific case it was not intended to cover. Typically, the general rule is cited (either directly or implicitly) in the premises and then wrongly applied to the specific case mentioned in the conclusion. Two examples:

> Freedom of speech is a constitutionally guaranteed right. Therefore, John Q. Radical should not be arrested for his speech that incited the riot last week.

> Property should be returned to its rightful owner. That drunken sailor who is starting a fight with his opponents at the pool table lent you his .45-caliber pistol, and now he wants it back. Therefore, you should return it to him now.

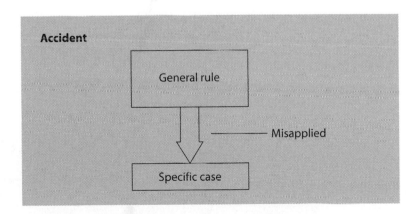

In the first example, the general rule is that freedom of speech is normally guaranteed, and the specific case is the speech made by John Q. Radical. Because the speech incited a riot, the rule does not apply. In the second example, the general rule is that property should be returned to its rightful owner, and the specific case is the sailor who wants his gun returned. The rule does not apply because the return of the property might result in serious injury or death.

The fallacy of accident gets its name from the fact that one or more accidental features of the specific case make it an exception to the rule. In the first example the accidental feature is that the speech incited a riot; in the second example, the accidental features are that the sailor is drunk, that he is starting a fight, and that the property in question is dangerous.

6. Straw Man

The **straw man** fallacy is committed when an arguer distorts an opponent's argument for the purpose of more easily attacking it, demolishes the distorted argument, and then concludes that the opponent's real argument has been demolished. By so doing, the arguer is said to have set up a straw man and knocked it down, only to conclude that the real man (opposing argument) has been knocked down as well. Example:

> Mr. Goldberg has argued against prayer in the public schools. Obviously Mr. Goldberg advocates atheism. But atheism is what they used to have in Russia. Atheism leads to the suppression of all religions and the replacement of God by an omnipotent state. Is that what we want for this country? I hardly think so. Clearly Mr. Goldberg's argument is nonsense.

Like the argument against the person fallacy, the straw man fallacy involves two arguers. Mr. Goldberg, who is the first arguer, has presented an argument against prayer in the public schools. The second arguer then attacks Goldberg's argument by equating it with an argument for atheism. He then attacks atheism and concludes that Goldberg's argument is nonsense. Since Goldberg's argument had nothing to do with atheism, the second argument commits the straw man fallacy.

As this example illustrates, the kind of distortion the second arguer resorts to is often an attempt to exaggerate the first person's argument or make it look more extreme than it really is. Here are two more examples:

> The garment workers have signed a petition arguing for better ventilation on the work premises. Unfortunately, air conditioning is expensive. Air ducts would have to be run throughout the factory, and a massive heat exchange unit installed on the roof. Also,

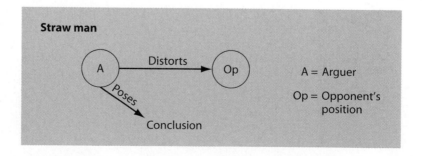

Straw man

A = Arguer

Op = Opponent's position

the cost of operating such a system during the summer would be astronomical. In view of these considerations the petition must be rejected.

The student status committee has presented us with an argument favoring alcohol privileges on campus. What do the students want? Is it their intention to stay boozed up from the day they enter as freshmen till the day they graduate? Do they expect us to open a bar for them? Or maybe a chain of bars all over campus? Such a proposal is ridiculous!

In the first argument, the petition is merely for better ventilation in the factory—maybe a fan in the window during the summer. The arguer exaggerates this request to mean an elaborate air conditioning system installed throughout the building. He then points out that this is too expensive and concludes by rejecting the petition. A similar strategy is used in the second argument. The arguer distorts the request for alcohol privileges to mean a chain of bars all over campus. Such an idea is so patently outlandish that no further argument is necessary.

7. Missing the Point (*Ignoratio Elenchi*)

All the fallacies we have discussed thus far have been instances of cases where the premises of an argument are irrelevant to the conclusion. **Missing the point** illustrates a special form of irrelevance. This fallacy occurs when the premises of an argument support one particular conclusion, but then a different conclusion, often vaguely related to the correct conclusion, is drawn. Whenever one suspects that such a fallacy is being committed, he or she should be able to identify the *correct* conclusion, the conclusion that the premises *logically* imply. This conclusion must be significantly different from the conclusion that is actually drawn. Examples:

Crimes of theft and robbery have been increasing at an alarming rate lately. The conclusion is obvious: we must reinstate the death penalty immediately.

Abuse of the welfare system is rampant nowadays. Our only alternative is to abolish the system altogether.

At least two correct conclusions are implied by the premise of the first argument: either "We should provide increased police protection in vulnerable neighborhoods" or "We should initiate programs to eliminate the causes of the crimes." Reinstating the death penalty is not a logical conclusion at all. Among other things, theft and robbery are not

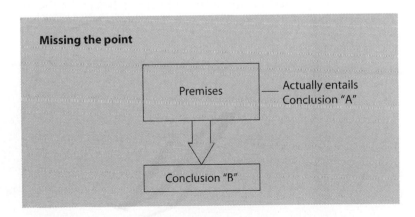

Missing the point

Premises — Actually entails Conclusion "A"

Conclusion "B"

capital crimes. In the second argument the premises logically suggest some systematic effort to eliminate the cheaters rather than eliminating the system altogether.

Ignoratio elenchi means "ignorance of the proof." The arguer is ignorant of the logical implications of his or her own premises and, as a result, draws a conclusion that misses the point entirely. The fallacy has a distinct structure all its own, but in some ways it serves as a catchall for arguments that are not clear instances of one or more of the other fallacies. An argument should not be identified as a case of missing the point, however, if one of the other fallacies fits.

8. Red Herring

This fallacy is closely associated with missing the point (*ignoratio elenchi*). The **red herring** fallacy is committed when the arguer diverts the attention of the reader or listener by changing the subject to a different but sometimes subtly related one. He or she then finishes by either drawing a conclusion about this different issue or by merely presuming that some conclusion has been established. By so doing, the arguer purports to have won the argument. The fallacy gets its name from a procedure used to train hunting dogs to follow a scent. A red herring (or bag of them) is dragged across the trail with the aim of leading the dogs astray. Since red herrings have an especially potent scent (caused in part by the smoking process used to preserve them), only the best dogs will follow the original scent.

To use the red herring fallacy effectively, the arguer must change the original subject of the argument without the reader or listener noticing it. One way of doing this is to change the subject to one that is subtly related to the original subject. Here are two examples of this technique:

> Environmentalists are continually harping about the dangers of nuclear power. Unfortunately, electricity is dangerous no matter where it comes from. Every year hundreds of people are electrocuted by accident. Since most of these accidents are caused by carelessness, they could be avoided if people would just exercise greater caution.

> There is a good deal of talk these days about the need to eliminate pesticides from our fruits and vegetables. But many of these foods are essential to our health. Carrots are an excellent source of vitamin A, broccoli is rich in iron, and oranges and grapefruits have lots of vitamin C.

Both arguments commit the red herring fallacy. In the first, the original issue is whether nuclear power is dangerous. The arguer changes this subject to the danger of

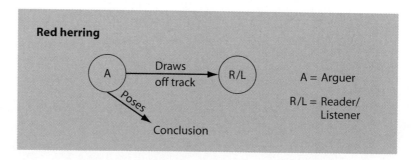

Red herring

A   Draws off track   R/L

Poses

Conclusion

A = Arguer

R/L = Reader/Listener

electrocution and proceeds to draw a conclusion about that. The new subject is clearly different from the possibility of nuclear explosion or meltdown, but the fact that both are related to electricity facilitates the arguer's goal of leading someone off the track. In the second argument, the original issue is pesticides, and the arguer changes it to the value of fruits and vegetables in one's diet. Again, the fact that the second topic is related to the first assists the arguer in committing the fallacy. In neither case does the arguer draw a conclusion about the original topic, but by merely diverting the attention of the reader or listener, the arguer creates the presumption of having won the argument.

A second way of using the red herring effectively is to change the subject to some flashy, eye-catching topic that is virtually guaranteed to distract the listener's attention. Topics of this sort include sex, crime, scandal, immorality, death, and any other topic that might serve as the subject of gossip. Here is an example of this technique:

> Professor Conway complains of inadequate parking on our campus. But did you know that last year Conway carried on a torrid love affair with a member of the English Department? The two used to meet every day for clandestine sex in the copier room. Apparently they didn't realize how much you can see through that fogged glass window. Even the students got an eyeful. Enough said about Conway.

The red herring fallacy can be confused with the straw man fallacy because both have the effect of drawing the reader/listener off the track. This confusion can usually be avoided by remembering the unique ways in which they accomplish this purpose. In the straw man, the arguer begins by distorting an opponent's argument and concludes by knocking down the distorted argument. In the red herring, on the other hand, the arguer ignores the opponent's argument (if there is one) and subtly changes the subject. Thus, to distinguish the two fallacies, one should attempt to determine whether the arguer has knocked down a distorted argument or simply changed the subject. Also keep in mind that straw man always involves two arguers, at least implicitly, whereas a red herring often does not.

Both the red herring and straw man fallacies are susceptible of being confused with missing the point, because all three involve a similar kind of irrelevancy. To avoid this confusion, one should note that both red herring and straw man proceed by generating a new set of premises, whereas missing the point does not. Straw man draws a conclusion from new premises that are obtained by distorting an earlier argument, and red herring, if it draws any conclusion at all, draws one from new premises obtained by changing the subject. Missing the point, however, draws a conclusion from the original premises. Also, in the red herring and straw man, the conclusion, if there is one, is *relevant* to the premises from which it is drawn; but in missing the point, the conclusion is *irrelevant* to the premises from which it is drawn. Finally, remember that missing the point serves in part as a kind of catchall fallacy, and a fallacious argument should not be identified as a case of missing the point if one of the other fallacies clearly fits.

EXERCISE 3.2

iLrn I. Identify the fallacies of relevance committed by the following arguments, giving a brief explanation for your answer. If no fallacy is committed, write "no fallacy."

★1. The position open in the accounting department should be given to Frank Thompson. Frank has six hungry children to feed, and his wife desperately needs an operation to save her eyesight.

2. President George W. Bush argues that we should open up the Arctic National Wildlife Refuge for oil drilling. But Bush just wants to reward his rich cronies in the oil industry who got him elected. Thus, we can hardly take Bush's argument seriously.

3. The school board argues that our schools are in desperate need of repair. But the real reason our students are falling behind is that they spend too much time with their computers. Becoming educated means a lot more than learning how to point and click. The school board should send a letter to the parents urging them to monitor their kids' computer time.

★4. Whoever thrusts a knife into another person should be arrested. But surgeons do precisely this when operating. Therefore, surgeons should be arrested.

5. You should read Irving Stone's latest novel right away. It's sold over a million copies, and practically everyone in the Manhattan cocktail circuit is talking about it.

6. Friedrich Nietzsche's philosophy is not worth the paper it's printed on. Nietzsche was an immoral reprobate who went completely insane from syphilis before he died.

★7. Surely you welcome the opportunity to join our protective organization. Think of all the money you will lose from broken windows, overturned trucks, and damaged merchandise in the event of your not joining.

8. Senator Barrow advocates increased Social Security benefits for the poor. It is regrettable that the senator finds it necessary to advocate socialism. Socialism defeats initiative, takes away promised rewards, and leads directly to inefficiency and big government. It was tried for years in Eastern Europe, and it failed miserably. Clearly, socialism is no good.

9. Something is seriously wrong with high school education these days. After ten years of decline, SAT scores are still extremely low, and high school graduates are practically incapable of reading and writing. The obvious conclusion is that we should close the schools.

★10. The editors of the *Daily Register* have accused our company of being one of the city's worst water polluters. But the *Daily Register* is responsible for much more pollution than we are. After all, they own the Western Paper Company, and that company discharges tons of chemical residue into the city's river every day.

11. If 20 percent of adult Americans are functionally illiterate, then it's no wonder that morons get elected to public office. In fact, 20 percent of adult Americans *are* functionally illiterate. Therefore, it's no wonder that morons get elected to public office.

12. Ladies and gentlemen, today the lines of battle have been drawn. When the din of clashing armor has finally died away, the Republican party will emerge victo-

rious! We are the true party of the American people! We embody the values that all real Americans hold sacred! We cherish and protect our founding fathers' vision that gave birth to the Constitution! We stand for decency and righteousness; for self-determination and the liberty to conduct our affairs as each of us freely chooses! In the coming election, victory will be ours, so help us God!

★13. We've all heard the argument that too much television is the reason our students can't read and write. Yet, many of today's TV shows are excellent. "The West Wing" says a lot about the inner workings of our government, "Law and Order" explores ethical issues in our criminal justice system, and "60 Minutes" exposes a great variety of scams and illegal practices. Today's TV is just great!

14. Surely architect Norris is not responsible for the collapse of the Central Bank Tower. Norris has had nothing but trouble lately. His daughter eloped with a child molester, his son committed suicide, and his alcoholic wife recently left for Las Vegas with his retirement savings.

15. The First Amendment to the Constitution prevents the government from interfering with the free exercise of religion. The liturgical practice of the Religion of Internal Enlightenment involves human sacrifice. Therefore, it would be wrong for the government to interfere with this religious practice.

★16. Former anti-terrorism czar Richard Clark argues in his book that the Iraq war was a terrible mistake and that it undermines the war on terrorism. But it's clear that Clark makes these outlandish claims merely to drum up sales for his book. Thus, we really shouldn't take his arguments seriously.

17. Professor Pearson's arguments in favor of the theory of evolution should be discounted. Pearson is a cocaine-snorting sex pervert and, according to some reports, a member of the Communist party.

18. Rudolf Höss, commandant of the Auschwitz concentration camp, confessed to having exterminated one million people, most of whom were Jews, in the Auschwitz gas chamber. We can only conclude that Höss was either insane or an extremely evil person

★19. Brewing magnate Joseph Coors has argued that government should get off the back of the American businessman. Obviously, Coors wants to abolish government altogether. Yet without government there would be no defense, no judicial system, no Social Security, and no health and safety regulations. None of us wants to forgo these benefits. Thus we can see that Coors's argument is absurd.

20. I know that some of you oppose the appointment of David Cole as the new sales manager. Upon further consideration, however, I am confident you will find him well qualified for the job. If Cole is not appointed, it may become necessary to make severe personnel cutbacks in your department.

21. Animal rights activists say that animals are abused in biomedical research labs. But consider this: Pets are abused by their owners every day. Probably 25 percent of pet owners should never get near animals. Some cases of abuse are enough to make you sick.

★22. Of course you want to buy a pair of Slinky fashion jeans. Slinky jeans really show off your figure, and all the Hollywood starlets down on the Strip can be seen wearing them these days.

23. Actress Andie MacDowell says that it's healthy to drink milk. But the dairy industry pays MacDowell thousands of dollars to make these ads. Therefore, we should not take her testimonials too seriously.

24. Dr. Morrison has argued that smoking is responsible for the majority of health problems in this country and that every smoker who has even the slightest concern for his or her health should quit. Unfortunately, however, we must consign Dr. Morrison's argument to the trash bin. Only yesterday I saw none other than Dr. Morrison himself smoking a cigar.

★25. Mr. Rhodes is suffering from amnesia and has no recollection whatever of the events of the past two weeks. We can only conclude that he did not commit the crime of murdering his wife a week ago, as he has been accused of doing.

II. Answer "true" or "false" to the following statements:

1. In the appeal to force, the arguer physically attacks the listener.

2. In the direct variety of the appeal to the people, the arguer attempts to create a kind of mob mentality.

3. If an arguer attempts to discredit a promise or court room testimony by pointing out that the witness or the person making the promise is a liar, then the arguer commits an *argumentum ad hominem* (argument against the person) fallacy.

4. The *argumentum ad hominem* always involves two arguers.

5. In the *argumentum ad hominem* circumstantial, the circumstances cited by the second arguer are intended precisely to malign the character of the first arguer.

6. In the *tu quoque* fallacy, the arguer threatens the reader or listener.

7. In the fallacy of accident, a general rule is applied to a specific case where it does not fit.

8. In the straw man fallacy, an arguer often distorts another person's argument by making it look more extreme than it really is.

9. Whenever one suspects that a missing the point fallacy is being committed, one should be able to state the conclusion that is logically implied by the premises.

10. In the red herring fallacy, the arguer attempts to lead the reader or listener off the track.

III. Identify the arguments in the following dialogue, then discuss each of them in terms of the fallacies presented in this section. You should be able to find at least one case of each fallacy.

"Thanks for saving us a seat," Jodie says to her friend Frank, as she and Liz sit down with coffee cups in hand in the crowded cafeteria.
"No problem," Frank says.

"We were late getting out of Professor Conklin's social problems class," Jodie says disgustedly. "He's such a jerk! He always keeps us late, and he's the most arrogant snob I've ever met."

"I've heard that," Frank says. "What's he covering in class now?"

"Sexual harassment in the workplace," Jodie replies. "But that *is* a real problem these days."

"How so?"

"Well, my friend Amelia is a dispatcher for a trucking company, and she's told me about dozens of times she's been a victim of sexual harassment. The truckers have *Playboy* centerfolds tacked up all over the place, they constantly leer at her, they're always asking her for dates. One of them even pats her rear when she leans over at the drinking fountain."

Frank laughs. "Well, there is such a thing as the First Amendment, which supposedly guarantees freedom of expression. You wouldn't want to deny these guys their freedom of expression, would you?"

"Freedom of expression, my eye!" explodes Jodie, looking incredulously at Frank. "Patting someone's rear isn't freedom of expression, it's abusive physical contact. So it's not protected by the First Amendment. Men! The trouble with you, Frank, is you're a typical man. If you were a woman, you'd see these things for what they are," she says, looking at Liz for support.

Liz nods her head in strong agreement.

"Well," says Frank, "I think your friend is lucky to have a job, what with all the people out of work these days. I've got a friend who's spent half his retirement savings just putting food on the table for his family, after losing his job. He was in the construction business, which is dead right now. And in other parts of the country it's even worse. You should tell Amelia to quit complaining."

"Stop giving me the runaround," demands Jodie, offended. "The trouble with you men is, you always look at women as sex objects. That makes sexual harassment inevitable."

"What do you mean?" protests Frank. "It's you women who treat us men like sex objects. What about all your makeup and perfume? And the tight pants and all the see-through stuff you wear? You think men are just a pack of animals—nothing but instinct—and you think that will make us fall for you. Isn't that how you see us?"

"I won't dignify that with a reply," fumes Jodie. "Anyone who isn't blind can see that Amelia's being victimized by those truckers. If you can't see it, maybe pouring this hot coffee over your thick head will wake you up!" she threatens.

"Calm down," says Frank with a startled look. "Everyone is beginning to stare at us. Okay, suppose I agree that Amelia is a victim. The question is, what do we do about it?"

"To begin with," says Jodie firmly, "the trucking company should transfer Amelia out of dispatch and give her a better job, like executive secretary in the regional office. Her husband ran out on her recently, leaving her with all five kids—and little Tommy needs braces. She could really use the extra money."

"You're joking!" Frank laughs sarcastically. "Didn't you tell me once that Amelia never finished high school and is functionally illiterate? She could never handle a job like that."

Thinking for a moment, Jodie then replies, "Well, maybe you're right. But at least the company should adopt a policy forbidding all forms of sexual harassment. Maybe that would make the truckers see how abusive they are, and then they might stop acting that way. Practically every company in the country has such a policy, but Amelia's bosses are dragging their feet."

"Okay. But then how do you define sexual harassment?" Frank asks. "'Cause if you can't define it, any policy is useless."

"Well, I don't exactly know," Jodie hesitates. "I'll have to think about that."

"Aha! I knew it!" exclaims Frank, triumphantly. "You can't define it, which means you don't even know if it exists! If you weren't such a radical feminist, you would see that all these claims of sexual harassment are hooey."

"Me, radical?" Jodie explodes. "The truth is you're a radical sexist. What you're saying is, women are only chattel, like they were 200 years ago, and men can use or abuse them any way they please. Liz, that's what he's saying, isn't it?"

"Absolutely," Liz affirms.

"What a crazy argument," says Frank scornfully. "What you're saying is, we should abolish all distinctions between men and women and create a unisex society in which everyone acts like a bunch of robots. Isn't that right, Liz?"

"No, not at all," insists Liz. "She's trying to—"

"You're completely insane, Frank," Jodie interrupts, rising determinedly from her chair, "and your arguments are wacko!" She then throws the remains of her coffee at Frank. The other students who have been listening to the heated argument rise up shouting, "Right on, Jodie!" Some begin chanting, "End sex harassment! End sex harassment!" As more students join the demonstration, they surround Frank, gesturing crudely.

Angry and humiliated, he breaks away and dashes out the door.

3.3 Fallacies of Weak Induction

The **fallacies of weak induction** occur not because the premises are logically irrelevant to the conclusion, as is the case with the eight fallacies of relevance, but because the connection between premises and conclusion is not strong enough to support the conclusion. In each of the following fallacies, the premises provide at least a shred of evidence in support of the conclusion, but the evidence is not nearly good enough to cause a reasonable person to believe the conclusion. Like the fallacies of relevance, however, the fallacies of weak induction often involve emotional grounds for believing the conclusion.

9. Appeal to Unqualified Authority (*Argumentum ad Verecundiam*)

We saw in Chapter 1 that an argument from authority is an inductive argument in which an arguer cites the authority or testimony of another person in support of some conclusion. The **appeal to unqualified authority** fallacy is a variety of the argument from authority and occurs when the cited authority or witness lacks credibility. There are several reasons why an authority or witness might lack credibility. The person might lack the requisite expertise, might be biased or prejudiced, might have a motive to lie or disseminate "misinformation," or might lack the requisite ability to perceive or recall. The following examples illustrate these reasons:

> Dr. Bradshaw, our family physician, has stated that the creation of muonic atoms of deuterium and tritium hold the key to producing a sustained nuclear fusion reaction at room temperature. In view of Dr. Bradshaw's expertise as a physician, we must conclude that this is indeed true.

This conclusion deals with nuclear physics, and the authority is a family physician. Because it is unlikely that a physician would be an expert in nuclear physics, the argument commits an appeal to unqualified authority.

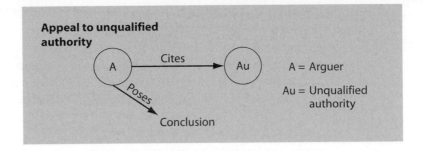

Appeal to unqualified authority

A —Cites→ Au

A —Poses→ Conclusion

A = Arguer

Au = Unqualified authority

> David Duke, former Grand Wizard of the Ku Klux Klan, has stated, "Jews are not good Americans. They have no understanding of what America is." On the basis of Duke's authority, we must therefore conclude that the Jews in this country are un-American.

As an authority, David Duke is clearly biased, so his statements cannot be trusted.

> James W. Johnston, Chairman of R. J. Reynolds Tobacco Company, testified before Congress that tobacco is not an addictive substance and that smoking cigarettes does not produce any addiction. Therefore, we should believe him and conclude that smoking does not in fact lead to any addiction.

If Mr. Johnston had admitted that tobacco is addictive, it would have opened the door to government regulation, which could put his company out of business. Thus, because Johnston had a clear motive to lie, we should not believe his statements.

> Old Mrs. Furguson (who is practically blind) has testified that she saw the defendant stab the victim with a bayonet while she was standing in the twilight shadows 100 yards from the incident. Therefore, members of the jury, you must find the defendant guilty.

Here the witness lacks the ability to perceive what she has testified to, so her testimony is untrustworthy.

Of course if an authority is credible, the resulting argument will contain no fallacy. Example:

> The county tax collector issued a press release stating that property tax revenues are higher this year than last. Therefore, we conclude that these revenues are indeed higher this year.

Normally a county tax collector would be considered a qualified expert in the area of tax revenues, so assuming the tax collector has no reason to lie, this argument is inductively strong.

In deciding whether a person is a qualified authority, one should keep two important points in mind. First, the person might be an authority in more than one field. For example, a chemist might also be an authority in biology, or an economist might also be an authority in law. The second point is that there are some areas in which practically no one can be considered an authority. Such areas include politics, morals, and religion. For example, if someone were to argue that abortion is immoral because a certain philosopher or religious leader has said so, the argument would be weak regardless of the authority's qualifications. Many questions in these areas are so hotly contested that there is no conventional wisdom an authority can depend on.

10. Appeal to Ignorance (*Argumentum ad Ignorantiam*)

When the premises of an argument state that nothing has been proved one way or the other about something, and the conclusion then makes a definite assertion about that thing, the argument commits an **appeal to ignorance.** The issue usually involves something that is incapable of being proved or something that has not yet been proved. Example:

> People have been trying for centuries to provide conclusive evidence for the claims of astrology, and no one has ever succeeded. Therefore, we must conclude that astrology is a lot of nonsense.

Conversely, the following argument commits the same fallacy.

> People have been trying for centuries to disprove the claims of astrology, and no one has ever succeeded. Therefore, we must conclude that the claims of astrology are true.

The premises of an argument are supposed to provide positive evidence for the conclusion. The premises of these arguments, however, tell us nothing about astrology; rather, they tell us about what certain unnamed and unidentified people have tried unsuccessfully to do. This evidence may provide some slight reason for believing the conclusion, but certainly not sufficient reason.

These examples do, however, lead us to the first of two important exceptions to the appeal to ignorance. The first stems from the fact that if qualified researchers investigate a certain phenomenon within their range of expertise and fail to turn up any evidence that the phenomenon exists, this fruitless search by itself constitutes positive evidence about the question. Consider, for example, the following argument:

> Teams of scientists attempted over a number of decades to detect the existence of the luminiferous aether, and all failed to do so. Therefore, the luminiferous aether does not exist.

The premises of this argument are true. Given the circumstances, it is likely that the scientists in question would have detected the aether if in fact it did exist. Since they

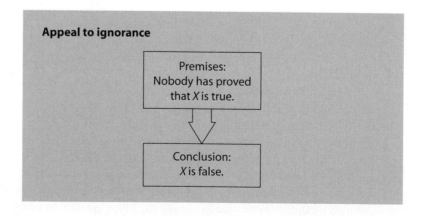

Appeal to ignorance

Premises:
Nobody has proved
that *X* is true.

Conclusion:
X is false.

did not detect it, it probably does not exist. Thus, we can say that the above argument is inductively strong (but not deductively valid).

As for the two arguments about astrology, if the attempts to prove or disprove the astrological claims had been done in a systematic way by qualified experts, it is more likely that the arguments would be good. Exactly what is required to qualify someone to investigate astrological claims is, of course, difficult to say. But as these arguments stand, the premises state nothing about the qualifications of the investigators, and so the arguments remain fallacious.

It is not *always* necessary, however, that the investigators have *special* qualifications. The kinds of qualifications needed depend on the situation. Sometimes the mere ability to see and report what one sees is sufficient. Example:

> No one has ever seen Mr. Andrews drink a glass of wine, beer, or any other alcoholic beverage. Probably Mr. Andrews is a nondrinker.

Because it is highly probable that if Mr. Andrews were a drinker, somebody would have seen him drinking, this argument is inductively strong. No special qualifications are needed to be able to see someone take a drink.

The second exception to the appeal to ignorance relates to courtroom procedure. In the United States and Canada, among other countries, a person is presumed innocent until proven guilty. If the prosecutor in a criminal trial fails to prove the guilt of the defendant beyond reasonable doubt, counsel for the defense may justifiably argue that his or her client is not guilty. Example:

> Members of the jury, you have heard the prosecution present its case against the defendant. Nothing, however, has been proved beyond a reasonable doubt. Therefore, under the law, the defendant is not guilty.

This argument commits no fallacy because "not guilty" means, in the legal sense, that guilt beyond a reasonable doubt has not been proved. The defendant may indeed have committed the crime of which he or she is accused, but if the prosecutor fails to prove guilt beyond a reasonable doubt, the defendant is considered "not guilty."

11. Hasty Generalization (Converse Accident)

Hasty generalization is a fallacy that affects inductive generalizations. In Chapter 1 we saw that an inductive generalization is an argument that draws a conclusion about all members of a group from evidence that pertains to a selected sample. The fallacy occurs when there is a reasonable likelihood that the sample is not representative of the group. Such a likelihood may arise if the sample is either too small or not randomly selected. Here are two examples:

> After only one year the alternator went out in Mr. O'Grady's new Chevrolet. Mrs. Dodson's Oldsmobile developed a transmission problem after six months. The obvious conclusion is that cars made by General Motors are just a pile of junk these days.

> Ten Arab fundamentalists hijacked planes and crashed them into the World Trade Center in New York City. The message is clear: Arabs are nothing but a pack of religious fanatics prone to violence.

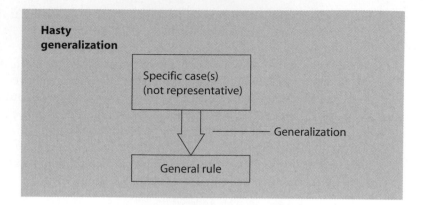

Hasty generalization

Specific case(s) (not representative)

Generalization

General rule

In these arguments a conclusion about a whole group is drawn from premises that mention only a few instances. Because such small, atypical samples are not sufficient to support a general conclusion, each argument commits a hasty generalization. The second example indicates how hasty generalization plays a role in racial (and religious) prejudice.

The mere fact that a sample may be small, however, does not necessarily mean that it is atypical. On the other hand, the mere fact that a sample may be large does not guarantee that it is typical. In the case of small samples, various factors may intervene that render such a sample typical of the larger group. Examples:

> Ten milligrams of substance Z was fed to four mice, and within two minutes all four went into shock and died. Probably substance Z, in this amount, is fatal to mice in general.

> On three separate occasions I drank a bottle of Figowitz beer and found it flat and bitter. Probably I would find every bottle of Figowitz beer flat and bitter.

Neither of these arguments commits the fallacy of hasty generalization because in neither case is there any likelihood that the sample is atypical of the group. In the first argument the fact that the mice died in only two minutes suggests the existence of a causal connection between eating substance Z and death. If there is such a connection, it would hold for other mice as well. In the second example the fact that the taste of beer typically remains constant from bottle to bottle causes the argument to be strong, even though only three bottles were sampled.

In the case of large samples, if the sample is not random, it may not be typical of the larger group. Example:

> One hundred thousand voters from Orange County, California, were surveyed on their choice for governor, and 68 percent said they intend to vote for the Republican candidate. Clearly the Republican candidate will be elected.

Even though the sample cited in this argument is large, the argument commits a hasty generalization. The problem is that Orange County is overwhelmingly Republican, so the mere fact that 68 percent intend to vote for the Republican candidate is no indication of how others in the state intend to vote. In other words, the survey was not conducted randomly, and for this reason the argument is fatally flawed. The need for randomness in samples is discussed further in Section 9.4 of this book.

Hasty generalization is otherwise called "converse accident" because it proceeds in a direction opposite to that of accident. Whereas accident proceeds from the general to the particular, converse accident moves from the particular to the general. The premises cite some characteristic affecting one or more atypical instances of a certain class, and the conclusion then applies that characteristic to all members of the class.

12. False Cause

The fallacy of **false cause** occurs whenever the link between premises and conclusion depends on some imagined causal connection that probably does not exist. Whenever an argument is suspected of committing the false cause fallacy, the reader or listener should be able to say that the conclusion depends on the supposition that X causes Y, whereas X probably does not cause Y at all. Examples:

> During the past two months, every time that the cheerleaders have worn blue ribbons in their hair, the basketball team has been defeated. Therefore, to prevent defeats in the future, the cheerleaders should get rid of those blue ribbons.

> Successful business executives are paid salaries in excess of $100,000. Therefore, the best way to ensure that Ferguson will become a successful executive is to raise his salary to at least $100,000.

> There are more laws on the books today than ever before, and more crimes are being committed than ever before. Therefore, to reduce crime we must eliminate the laws.

The first argument depends on the supposition that the blue ribbons caused the defeats, the second on the supposition that a high salary causes success, and the third on the supposition that laws cause crime. In no case is it likely that any causal connection exists.

The first argument illustrates a variety of the false cause fallacy called *post hoc ergo propter hoc* ("after this, therefore on account of this"). This variety of the fallacy presupposes that just because one event precedes another event the first event causes the second. Obviously, mere temporal succession is not sufficient to establish a causal connection. Nevertheless, this kind of reasoning is quite common and lies behind most forms of superstition. (Example: "A black cat crossed my path and later I tripped and sprained my ankle. It must be that black cats really are bad luck.")

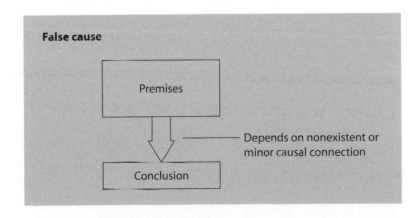

False cause

Premises

Conclusion

Depends on nonexistent or minor causal connection

The second and third arguments illustrate a variety of the false cause fallacy called *non causa pro causa* ("not the cause for the cause"). This variety is committed when what is taken to be the cause of something is not really the cause at all and the mistake is based on something other than mere temporal succession. In reference to the second argument, success as an executive causes increases in salary—not the other way around—so the argument mistakes the cause for the effect. In reference to the third argument, the increase in crime is, for the most part, only coincidental with the increase in the number of laws. Obviously, the mere fact that one event is coincidental with another is not sufficient reason to think that one caused the other.

A third variety of the false cause fallacy, and one that is probably committed more often than either of the others in their pure form, is *oversimplified cause*. This variety occurs when a multitude of causes is responsible for a certain effect but the arguer selects just one of these causes and represents it as if it were the sole cause. Here are some examples:

> The quality of education in our grade schools and high schools has been declining for years. Clearly, our teachers just aren't doing their job these days.

> Today, all of us can look forward to a longer life span than our parents and grandparents. Obviously, we owe our thanks to the millions of dedicated doctors who expend every effort to ensure our health.

In reference to the first argument, the decline in the quality of education is caused by many factors, including lack of discipline in the home, lack of parental involvement, too much television, and drug use by students. Poor teacher performance is only one of these factors and probably a minor one at that. In the second argument, the efforts of doctors are only one among many factors responsible for our longer life span. Other, more important factors include a better diet, more exercise, reduced smoking, safer highways, and more stringent occupational safety standards.

The oversimplified cause fallacy is usually motivated by self-serving interests. Sometimes the arguer wants to take undeserved credit for himself or give undeserved credit to some movement with which he or she is affiliated. At other times, the arguer wants to heap blame on an opponent or shift blame from himself or herself onto some convenient occurrence. Instances of the fallacy can resemble either the *post hoc* or the *non causa pro causa* varieties in that the alleged cause can occur either prior to or concurrently with the effect. It differs from the other varieties of false cause fallacy in that the single factor selected for credit or blame is often partly responsible for the effect, but responsible to only a minor degree.

The last variety of false cause we will consider is called the *gambler's fallacy*. This fallacy is committed whenever the conclusion of an argument depends on the supposition that independent events in a game of chance are causally related. Here is an example:

> A fair coin was flipped five times in a row, and each time it came up heads. Therefore, it is extremely likely that it will come up tails on the next flip.

In fact, it is no more likely that the coin will come up tails on the next flip than it was on the first flip. Each flip is an independent event, so earlier flips have no causal influence on later ones. Thus, the fact that the earlier flips came up heads does not increase the likelihood that the next flip will come up tails.

For the gambler's fallacy to be committed, it is essential that the events be independent or nearly independent. Such events include rolls of a pair of fair (unloaded) dice, spins of a fair roulette wheel, and selections of lottery winning numbers. Events are not completely independent whenever the skill of the gambler affects the outcome. Thus, poker, blackjack, and horse-race betting provide less-than-perfect candidates for the gambler's fallacy.

The false cause fallacy is often convincing because it is often difficult to determine whether two phenomena are causally related. A lengthy time lapse between the operation of the cause and the occurrence of the effect can exacerbate the problem. For example, the thirty-year interval between exposure to asbestos and the onset of asbestosis impeded the recognition of a causal connection. Also, when two events are causally related, it may be hard to determine the degree of relatedness. Thus, there may be some connection between the electromagnetic field produced by high voltage transmission lines and leukemia, but the connection may be extremely slight. Finally, when a causal connection is recognized, it may be difficult to determine which is the cause and which is the effect. For example, an allergic reaction may be connected with an episode of anxiety, but it may be hard to tell if the allergy causes the anxiety or if the anxiety causes the allergy.

The realm of human action constitutes another area in which causal connections are notoriously difficult to establish. For example, the attorneys for accused murderer Dan White argued that Twinkies, Coke, and potato chips caused him to kill San Francisco Mayor George Moscone. Other attorneys have blamed their clients' crimes on PMS, rap music, childhood abuse, mental retardation, and hallucinations. The complex nature of human motivation renders all such causal claims difficult to evaluate. The situation may become even worse when a whole nation of people are involved. Thus, the recent drop in crime rates has been attributed to "three strikes" laws, but it is difficult to say whether this or some other factor is really responsible.

One point that should be kept in mind when establishing causal connections is that statistical correlations by themselves often reveal little about what is actually going on. For example, if all that we knew about smoking and lung cancer was that the two frequently occur together, we might conclude any number of things. We might conclude that both have a common cause, such as a genetic predisposition, or we might conclude that lung cancer is a disease contracted early in life and that it manifests itself in its early stages by a strong desire for tobacco. Fortunately, in the case of smoking and lung cancer there is more evidence than a mere statistical correlation. This additional evidence inclines us to believe that the smoking is a cause of the cancer.

13. Slippery Slope

The fallacy of **slippery slope** is a variety of the false cause fallacy. It occurs when the conclusion of an argument rests upon an alleged chain reaction and there is not sufficient reason to think that the chain reaction will actually take place. Here is an example:

> Immediate steps should be taken to outlaw pornography once and for all. The continued manufacture and sale of pornographic material will almost certainly lead to an increase in sex-related crimes such as rape and incest. This in turn will gradually erode the moral fabric of society and result in an increase in crimes of all sorts. Eventually a

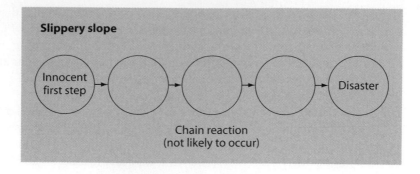

Slippery slope

Innocent first step → ○ → ○ → ○ → Disaster

Chain reaction
(not likely to occur)

complete disintegration of law and order will occur, leading in the end to the total collapse of civilization.

Because there is no good reason to think that the mere failure to outlaw pornography will result in all these dire consequences, this argument is fallacious. An equally fallacious counterargument is as follows:

> Attempts to outlaw pornography threaten basic civil rights and should be summarily abandoned. If pornography is outlawed, censorship of newspapers and news magazines is only a short step away. After that there will be censorship of textbooks, political speeches, and the content of lectures delivered by university professors. Complete mind control by the central government will be the inevitable result.

Both arguments attempt to persuade the reader or listener that the welfare of society rests on a "slippery slope" and that a single step in the wrong direction will result in an inevitable slide all the way to the bottom.

The slippery slope fallacy can involve various kinds of causality. For example, someone might argue that removing a single brick from a building would set off a chain reaction leading to the destruction of the building, or that chopping down a tall tree would set off a cascade of falling trees leading to the destruction of the forest. These arguments depend on pure physical causality. On the other hand, someone might argue that starting a rumor about the health of the economy would set off a chain reaction leading to the collapse of the stock market. Such an argument would depend on the kind of causality found in interpersonal communications. Or someone might argue that planting a seed of doubt in a person's mind about the faithfulness of his or her spouse would gnaw away at that person, leading to the breakup of the marriage. Such an argument would depend on the kind of causality that links mental states.

Deciding whether a slippery slope fallacy has been committed can be difficult when there is uncertainty whether the alleged chain reaction will or will not occur. This question is discussed in Section 3.5. But many slippery slopes rest on a mere emotional conviction on the part of the arguer that a certain action or policy is bad, and the arguer attempts to trump up support for his or her position by citing all sorts of dire consequences that will result if the action is taken or the policy followed. In such cases there is usually little problem in identifying the argument as a slippery slope.

14. Weak Analogy

This fallacy affects inductive arguments from analogy. As we saw in Chapter 1, an argument from analogy is an argument in which the conclusion depends on the existence of an analogy, or similarity, between two things or situations. The fallacy of **weak analogy** is committed when the analogy is not strong enough to support the conclusion that is drawn. Example:

> Harper's new car is bright blue, has leather upholstery, and gets excellent gas mileage. Crowley's new car is also bright blue and has leather upholstery. Therefore, it probably gets excellent gas mileage, too.

Because the color of a car and the choice of upholstery have nothing to do with gasoline consumption, this argument is fallacious.

The basic structure of an argument from analogy is as follows:

> Entity A has attributes $a, b, c,$ and z.
> Entity B has attributes a, b, c.
> Therefore, entity B probably has attribute z also.

Evaluating an argument having this form requires a two-step procedure: (1) Identify the attributes $a, b, c, \ldots$ that the two entities A and B share in common, and (2) determine how the attribute z, mentioned in the conclusion, relates to the attributes $a, b, c, \ldots$ If some causal or systematic relation exists between z and $a, b,$ or c, the argument is strong; otherwise it is weak. In the argument above, the two entities share the attributes of being cars; the attributes entailed by being a car, such as having four wheels; and the attributes of color and upholstery material. Because none of these attributes is systematically or causally related to good gas mileage, the argument is fallacious.

As an illustration of when the requisite systematic or causal relation does and does not exist, consider the following arguments:

> The flow of electricity through a wire is similar to the flow of water through a pipe. Obviously a large-diameter pipe will carry a greater flow of water than a pipe of small diameter. Therefore, a large-diameter wire should carry a greater flow of electricity than a small-diameter wire.

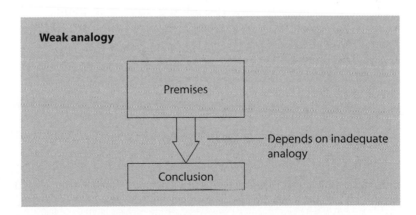

Weak analogy

Premises → Conclusion — Depends on inadequate analogy

The flow of electricity through a wire is similar to the flow of water through a pipe. When water runs downhill through a pipe, the pressure at the bottom of the hill is greater than it is at the top. Thus, when electricity flows downhill through a wire, the voltage should be greater at the bottom of the hill than at the top.

The first argument is good and the second is fallacious. Both arguments depend on the similarity between water molecules flowing through a pipe and electrons flowing through a wire. In both cases there is a systematic relation between the diameter of the pipe/wire and the amount of flow. In the first argument this systematic relation provides a strong link between premises and conclusion, and so the argument is a good one. But in the second argument a causal connection exists between difference in elevation and increase in pressure that holds for water but not for electricity. Water molecules flowing through a pipe are significantly affected by gravity, but electrons flowing through a wire are not. Thus, the second argument is fallacious.

The theory and evaluation of arguments from analogy is one of the most complex and elusive subjects in all of logic. Additional material on arguments from analogy appears in Sections 3.5 and 9.1 of this text.

EXERCISE 3.3

iLrn I. Identify the fallacies of weak induction committed by the following arguments, giving a brief explanation for your answer. If no fallacy is committed, write "no fallacy."

1. The *Daily News* carried an article this morning about three local teenagers who were arrested on charges of drug possession. Teenagers these days are nothing but a bunch of junkies.

2. If a car breaks down on the freeway, a passing mechanic is not obligated to render emergency road service. For similar reasons, if a person suffers a heart attack on the street, a passing physician is not obligated to render emergency medical assistance.

3. There must be something to psychical research. Three famous physicists—Oliver Lodge, James Jeans, and Arthur Stanley Eddington—took it seriously.

★4. The secretaries have asked us to provide lounge areas where they can spend their coffee breaks. This request will have to be refused. If we give them lounge areas, next they'll be asking for spas and swimming pools. Then it will be racquetball courts, tennis courts, and fitness centers. Expenditures for these facilities will drive us into bankruptcy.

5. The accumulation of pressure in a society is similar to the build-up of pressure in a boiler. If the pressure in a boiler increases beyond a critical point, the boiler will explode. Accordingly, if a government represses its people beyond a certain point, the people will rise up in revolt.

6. A few minutes after Governor Harrison finished his speech on television, a devastating earthquake struck southern Alaska. For the safety of the people up there, it is imperative that Governor Harrison make no more speeches.

★7. No one has ever been able to prove the existence of extrasensory perception. We must therefore conclude that extrasensory perception is a myth.

8. Lester Brown, universally respected author of the yearly *State of the World* report, has said that the destruction of tropical rain forests is one of the ten most serious worldwide problems. Thus, it must be the case that this is indeed a very serious problem.

9. America's business leaders are all a bunch of crooks. Just look at the facts. Dennis Kowslowski ripped off millions of dollars from Tyco Corporation, Jeffrey Skilling and Andy Fastow did the same with Enron, Bernie Ebbers defrauded the investors of WorldCom, and the Rigas family stole millions from Adelphia.

★10. U.S. Senator Tom Coburn says that lesbianism is rampant in the Oklahoma schools. This must indeed be true, because surely the senator couldn't be mistaken about the schools in his own home state.

11. Probably no life exists on Venus. Teams of scientists have conducted exhaustive studies of the planet's surface and atmosphere, and no living organisms have been found.

12. We don't dare let the animal rights activists get their foot in the door. If they sell us on the idea that dogs, cats, and dolphins have rights, next it will be chickens and cows. That means no more chicken Kiev or prime rib. Next it will be worms and insects. This will lead to the decimation of our agricultural industry. The starvation of the human race will follow close behind.

★13. No one would buy a pair of shoes without trying them on. Why should anyone be expected to get married without premarital sex?

14. No one has proved conclusively that America's nuclear power plants constitute a danger to people living in their immediate vicinity. Therefore, it is perfectly safe to continue to build nuclear power plants near large metropolitan centers.

15. There are more churches in New York City than in any other city in the nation, and more crimes are committed in New York City than anywhere else. So, if we are to eliminate crime, we must abolish the churches.

II. Answer "true" or "false" to the following statements:

1. If an arguer cites a statement by a recognized expert in support of a conclusion and the statement falls within the expert's range of expertise, then the arguer commits an appeal to unqualified authority.

2. If an arguer cites a statement in support of a conclusion and the statement reflects the strong bias of its author, then the arguer commits an appeal to unqualified authority.

3. In the appeal to ignorance, the arguer accuses the reader or listener of being ignorant.

4. If an attorney for the defense in an American or Canadian criminal trial argues that the prosecution has proved nothing beyond a reasonable doubt about the guilt of the defendant, then the attorney commits an appeal to ignorance.

5. Hasty generalization always proceeds from the particular to the general.

6. The *post hoc ergo propter hoc* variety of the false cause fallacy presumes that X causes Y merely because X happens before Y.

7. If an argument concludes that X causes Y simply because X and Y occur over the same time interval, then the argument commits the *non causa pro causa* variety of the false cause fallacy.

8. If the conclusion of an argument depends on the occurrence of a chain reaction of events, and there is good reason to believe that the chain reaction will actually occur, the argument commits a slippery slope fallacy.

9. The fallacy of weak analogy always depends on an alleged similarity between two things or situations.

10. If an argument from analogy depends on a causal or systematic relationship between certain attributes, and there is good reason to believe that this relationship exists, then the argument commits no fallacy.

iLrn III. Identify the fallacies of relevance and weak induction committed by the following arguments. If no fallacy is committed, write "no fallacy."

★1. On our first date, George had his hands all over me, and I found it nearly impossible to keep him in his place. A week ago Tom gave me that stupid line about how, in order to prove my love, I had to spend the night with him. Men are all alike. All any of them want is sex.

2. Tagging by graffiti artists has become a terrible problem in recent years. Obviously our schools are stifling the creative spirit of these young people.

3. North Korean dictator Kim Jong Il has promised not to let any of his nuclear weapons fall into the hands of terrorists. But Kim is erratic, dishonest, corrupt, and possibly even insane. Therefore, we should not trust his promises for a minute.

★4. Vice President Dick Cheney argues in favor of legalizing same-sex civil unions. And why does he argue for this? Because his daughter is a lesbian, and he wants to maintain peace on the home front. For this reason, we should ignore Cheney's argument.

5. What the farmer sows in the spring he reaps in the fall. In the spring he sows $8-per-bushel soybeans. Therefore, in the fall he will reap $8-per-bushel soybeans.

6. World-renowned physicist Stephen Hawking claims that black holes do not gobble up everything that falls into them without leaving a trace, but that something is always left behind. Given Hawking's stature as a scientist and the many years he has worked on this problem, we should conclude that this is indeed the case.

★7. Emily has bought over 100 tickets on the weekly state lottery, and she has never won anything. Therefore, the likelihood increases every week that she will win something if she continues to buy tickets.

8. Johnny, of course I deserve the use of your bicycle for the afternoon. After all, I'm sure you wouldn't want your mother to find out that you played hooky today.

9. Practically everyone downloads music free of charge from the Internet these days. Therefore, you should have no qualms about doing this yourself.

★10. Ellen Quinn has argued that logic is not the most important thing in life. Apparently Ellen advocates irrationality. It has taken two million years for the human race to achieve the position that it has, and Ellen would throw the whole thing into the garbage. What utter nonsense!

11. When water is poured on the top of a pile of rocks, it always trickles down to the rocks on the bottom. Similarly, when rich people make lots of money, we can expect this money to trickle down to the poor.

12. Extensive laboratory tests have failed to prove any deleterious side effects of the new pain killer lexaprine. We conclude that lexaprine is safe for human consumption.

★13. Environmentalists accuse us of blocking the plan to convert Antarctica into a world park. In fact, nothing could be further from the truth. Antarctica is a huge continent teeming with life. It is the home of millions of penguins, seals, sea birds, and sea lions. Also, great schools of finfish and whales inhabit its coastal waters.

14. Media host Howard Stern cites over a thousand reasons why George W. Bush is doing a rotten job as president. But Stern is nothing but a vulgar, smutmouthed freak who will say anything for shock value. Nobody should listen to his arguments.

15. The operation of a camera is similar in many ways to the operation of an eye. If you are to see anything in a darkened room, the pupils of your eyes must first dilate. Accordingly, if you are to take a photograph (without flash) in a darkened room, the aperture of the camera lens must first be increased.

★16. Certainly Miss Malone will be a capable and efficient manager. She has a great figure, a gorgeous face, and tremendous poise, and she dresses very fashionably.

17. At a news conference in Europe, President George W. Bush stated, "Africa is a nation that suffers from incredible disease." Apparently Africa is now a nation.

18. Dear Internal Revenue Service: I received a notice that my taxes are being audited for last year. But you have no right to do this. The deadline for filing a return was April 15, and I filed my tax return on April 12—a full three days before the deadline.

★19. To prevent dangerous weapons from being carried aboard airliners, those seeking to board must pass through a magnetometer and submit to a possible pat-down search. Therefore, to prevent alcohol and drugs from being carried into rock concerts, it is appropriate that those entering submit to similar search procedures.

20. Mr. Flemming's arguments against the rent control initiative on the September ballot should be taken with a grain of salt. As a landlord he would naturally be expected to oppose the initiative.

21. India is suffering a serious drought, thousands of children are dying of starvation in their mothers' arms, and homeless beggars line the streets of the

major cities. Surely we must give these poor downtrodden people the chance of bettering their condition in America, the land of wealth and opportunity.

★22. Members of the jury, you have heard Shirley Gaines testify that the defendant did not offer to perform acts of prostitution for the undercover police officer. But Gaines is a known prostitute herself and a close friend of the defendant. Also, only a year ago she was convicted of twelve counts of perjury. Therefore, you should certainly discount Gaines's testimony.

23. It is ridiculous to hear that man from Peru complaining about America's poverty. Peru has twice as much poverty as America has ever had.

24. Angela complains that the problems on the algebra test were too hard. But have you ever seen the way Angela flirts with that good-looking quarterback on the football team? She's constantly batting those long, black eyelashes at him, and her tight-fitting sweaters leave nothing to the imagination. Angela should pay more attention to her studies.

★25. Nobody has ever proved that immoral behavior by elected officials erodes public morality. Therefore, we must conclude that such behavior does not erode public morality.

26. Freedom of speech is guaranteed by the First Amendment. Therefore, your friend was acting within his rights when he shouted "Fire! Fire!" in that crowded theater, even though it was only a joke.

27. No one, upon encountering a watch lying on a forest trail, would expect that it had simply appeared there without having been made by someone. For the same reason, no one should expect that the universe simply appeared without having been made by some being.

★28. On Monday I drank ten rum and Cokes, and the next morning I woke up with a headache. On Wednesday I drank eight gin and Cokes, and the next morning I woke up with a headache. On Friday I drank nine bourbon and Cokes, and the next morning I woke up with a headache. Obviously, to prevent further headaches I must give up Coke.

29. Former Senate majority leader Trent Lott announced in a press conference that homosexuality is a sin. In view of Mr. Lott's expertise in religious matters, we must conclude that homosexuality is a sin, just as he claims.

30. Some of the parents in our school district have asked that we provide bilingual education in Spanish. This request will have to be denied. If we provide this service, then someone will ask for bilingual education in Greek. Then it will be German, French, and Hungarian. Polish, Russian, Chinese, Japanese, and Korean will follow close behind. We certainly can't accommodate all of them.

IV. Identify the arguments in the following dialogue, then discuss each of them in terms of the fallacies presented in this section and the previous section. You should be able to find at least one case of each fallacy.

"Hi! Glad you could make it," Ralph says to his friend Claudia at a Friday night party. "Hey, you just missed a great discussion that Tom, Ruben, and I were having about abduction by extraterrestrials. Ruben just left, but he said he's been reading this book by Whitley Strieber—I think it's called *Transformation*—in which Strieber describes being kidnapped by creatures from outer space."

"Good grief! You don't actually believe that nonsense, do you?" Claudia asks incredulously.

"Well, I don't think Strieber would lie. Also, Ruben told us an amazing personal story. He was out camping a year ago, and after he'd killed off a couple of six-packs of Moosehead, he says he saw a UFO. So, I think we have to conclude there really are UFOs."

"What a joke!" Claudia laughs scornfully. "Ruben was probably hallucinating. By the way, didn't he fail most of his classes last semester? His parents are spending a fortune for his education, and all he does is party, sleep, and ignore his studies. I think that's immoral. As for Strieber, does he give any evidence?"

"As a matter of fact, he does," Ralph replies smugly. "Apparently, a few years ago, he was driving with his wife on some country road, when both of them experienced an unusual blackout. When they woke up, they were thirty-five miles further down the road, and they had no recollection of how they got there. Later, both began having dreams about extraterrestrials performing experiments on them while they were on board their spacecraft. Extraterrestrials must have abducted them, then hypnotized them so they wouldn't remember what had happened."

"Oh yeah, now I remember who Strieber is," answers Claudia, caustically. "He's that weirdo who dreams up all kinds of fantastic stories just so he can write books about them and make lots of money. If you give that sickie one minute of your time, then you're crazier than he is."

"I think you're prejudiced," Ralph says. "Why, recent surveys show that 64 percent of the American public believe in UFOs, and the number is growing every day. That alone should convince you they're real."

"You've got to be kidding," Claudia mutters, shaking her head in disbelief.

"Well then, consider this," insists Ralph. "There are hundreds of people out there who've had similar dreams and the same unaccounted for time lapses. They can't all be fantasizing."

"I know that Strieber is a kook," Claudia persists, "so all the others must be, too."

"Now, now, aren't we jumping to conclusions?" her friend asks condescendingly.

"Not at all. First it was UFOs and little green men. Now those little creatures are abducting people and experimenting on them. Before long they'll be manipulating our genes and trying to infiltrate the human race. In the end, everyone will suspect everyone else of being an alien, mass terror will prevail, and civilization will collapse!" Claudia exclaims in mock horror.

"Don't be a fool!" Ralph barks, irritated. "The problem with you is, you're an agnostic. Obviously, you're saying we should refuse to believe in anything we can't clearly see or touch. So, logically, God doesn't exist, and there is no immortal soul. Tom, that's what she's saying, isn't it?"

"More or less," Tom agrees halfheartedly.

"Again, not at all," Claudia responds. "What I'm saying is, people have to be just a little bit critical about what they believe. Apparently you believe any cockamamie story that comes your way. You're just so gullible. If you keep it up, everyone and their dog will take you for a ride."

"Oh yeah? If I were you, I'd take a close look at my own beliefs," Ralph gibes. "Didn't I see you reading the astrology column just the other day? Nobody in their right mind believes in astrology. Maybe I should start screaming 'Claudia believes in astrology! Claudia believes in astrology!' Then everyone will gawk at you, and that sexy physics major you're dying to get a date with will think you're a nut."

"Oh, shut up!" says Claudia, blushing. "I may read the astrology column, but I certainly don't believe it. I just read it for fun. But, the fact is, during the past twenty-five years there have been thousands of alleged sightings of UFOs, and not a single one has led to any solid evidence of their existence. What do you make of that?"

"I think we should look at this situation the other way around," Ralph says. "Up until now, nobody has shown that UFOs *don't* exist, so I think we should give those people who claim they have seen them the benefit of the doubt. We should believe in UFOs and extraterrestrials until the sightings are proven false."

"Well, okay. Let's suppose, just for the sake of argument, that I admit the existence of UFOs and their little green drivers. How are we supposed to respond to them? What are we supposed to do?" Claudia asks.

"For starters, we should extend an open invitation to them," answers Ralph. "They may come from a dying planet where millions of their compatriots desperately struggle for survival. Their sun may be burning out, their water supply exhausted, and their soil poisoned with toxic chemicals. Surely they deserve a second chance on a new planet."

"Maybe so," Claudia says in a patronizing tone. "And now that you mention it, we probably have a legal obligation to let them in. Our current immigration laws say that we have to admit at least ten thousand applicants annually, from every major nation. If those aliens would just sign the right papers, we'd have to give them permanent residency. However, what worries me is, they may have the wrong intentions. After all, didn't they conduct experiments on those people they abducted?"

"Yes, but don't we experiment on animals? If the animals don't complain, why should we? Also, medical experimentation often leads to wonderful new cures. I'm certain we have nothing to worry about," says Ralph, proud of his logic.

"Humph! I hope you're right. Well, I've got to go now—and don't let any green men kidnap you," Claudia says with a barb.

"And you, either," Ralph answers.

3.4   Fallacies of Presumption, Ambiguity, and Grammatical Analogy

The **fallacies of presumption** include begging the question, complex question, false dichotomy, and suppressed evidence. These fallacies arise not because the premises are irrelevant to the conclusion or provide insufficient reason for believing the conclusion but because the premises presume what they purport to prove. *Begging the question* presumes that the premises provide adequate support for the conclusion when in fact they do not, and *complex question* presumes that a question can be answered by a simple "yes," "no," or other brief answer when a more sophisticated answer is needed. *False dichotomy* presumes that an "either . . . or . . ." statement presents jointly exhaustive alternatives when in fact it does not, and *suppressed evidence* presumes that no important evidence has been overlooked by the premises when in fact it has.

The **fallacies of ambiguity** include *equivocation* and *amphiboly*. These fallacies arise from the occurrence of some form of ambiguity in either the premises or the conclusion (or both). As we saw in Section 2.1, an expression is ambiguous if it is susceptible to different interpretations in a given context. The words "light" and "bank" are ambiguous, as is the statement "Tuna are biting off the Washington coast." When the conclusion of an argument depends on a shift in meaning of an ambiguous word or phrase or on the wrong interpretation of an ambiguous statement, the argument commits a fallacy of ambiguity.

The **fallacies of grammatical analogy** include *composition* and *division*. Arguments that commit these fallacies are grammatically analogous to other arguments that are good in every respect. Because of this similarity in linguistic structure, such fallacious arguments may appear good yet be bad.

15. Begging the Question (*Petitio Principii*)

The fallacy of **begging the question** is committed whenever the arguer creates the illusion that inadequate premises provide adequate support for the conclusion by leaving out a possibly false (shaky) key premise, by restating a possibly false premise as the conclusion, or by reasoning in a circle. The latin name for this fallacy, *petitio principii*, means "request for the source." The actual source of support for the conclusion is not apparent, and so the argument is said to beg the question. After reading or hearing the argument, the observer is inclined to ask, "But how do you know *X*?" where *X* is the needed support.

The first, and most common, way of committing this fallacy is by leaving a possibly false key premise out of the argument while creating the illusion that nothing more is needed to establish the conclusion. Examples:

> Murder is morally wrong. This being the case, it follows that abortion is morally wrong.

> Of course humans and apes evolved from common ancestors. Just look how similar they are.

> It's obvious that the poor in this country should be given handouts from the government. After all, these people earn less than the average citizen.

> Clearly, terminally ill patients have a right to doctor-assisted suicide. After all, many of these people are unable to commit suicide by themselves.

The first of these arguments begs the question "How do you know that abortion is a form of murder?" The second begs the question "Does the mere fact that humans and apes look similar imply that they evolved from common ancestors?" And the third

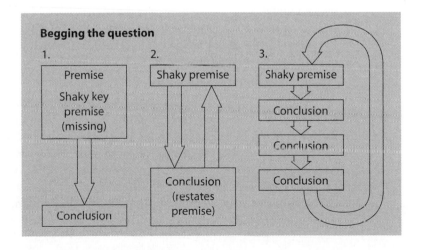

Begging the question

1. Premise / Shaky key premise (missing) → Conclusion

2. Shaky premise → Conclusion (restates premise)

3. Shaky premise → Conclusion → Conclusion → Conclusion

and fourth beg the questions "Just because the poor earn less than the average citizen, does this imply that the government should give them handouts?" and "Just because terminally ill patients cannot commit suicide by themselves, does it follow that they have a right to a doctor's assistance?"

These questions indicate that something has been left out of the original arguments. Thus, the first argument is missing the premise, "Abortion is a form of murder"; the second is missing the premise, "If humans and apes look similar, then they have common ancestors"; and so on. These premises are crucial for the soundness of the arguments. If the arguer is unable to establish the truth of these premises, then the arguments prove nothing. However, in most cases of begging the question, this is precisely the reason why such premises are left unstated. The arguer is *not* able to establish their truth, and by employing rhetorical phraseology such as "of course," "clearly," "this being the case," and "after all," the arguer hopes to create the illusion that the stated premise, by itself, provides adequate support for the conclusion when in fact it does not.

The same form of begging the question often appears in arguments concerning religious topics to justify conclusions about the existence of God, the immortality of the soul, and so on. Example:

> The world in which we live displays an amazing degree of organization. Obviously this world was created by an intelligent God.

This argument begs the question, "How do you know that the organization in the world could only have come from an intelligent creator?" Of course the claim that it did come from an intelligent creator may well be true, but the burden is on the arguer to prove it. Without supporting reasons or evidence, the argument proves nothing. Yet most people who are predisposed to believe the conclusion are likely to accept the argument as a good one. The same can be said of most arguments that beg the question, and this fact suggests another reason why arguers resort to this fallacy: Such arguments tend to reinforce preexisting inclinations and beliefs.

The second form of *petitio principii* occurs when the conclusion of an argument merely restates a possibly false premise in slightly different language. In such an argument, the premise supports the conclusion, and the conclusion tends to reinforce the premise. Examples:

> Capital punishment is justified for the crimes of murder and kidnapping because it is quite legitimate and appropriate that someone be put to death for having committed such hateful and inhuman acts.

> Anyone who preaches revolution has a vision of the future for the simple reason that if a person has no vision of the future he could not possibly preach revolution.

In the first argument, saying that capital punishment is "justified" means the same thing as saying that it is "legitimate and appropriate," and in the second argument the premise and the conclusion say exactly the same thing. However, by repeating the same thing in slightly different language, the arguer creates the illusion that independent evidence is being presented in support of the conclusion, when in fact it is not. Both arguments contain rhetorical phraseology ("hateful and inhuman," "*simple* reason," and "could not possibly") that help effect the illusion. The first argument begs the question, "How do you know that capital punishment really is legitimate and appropriate?" and the second begs the question, "How do you know that people who preach revolution really do have a vision of the future?"

The third form of *petitio principii* involves circular reasoning in a chain of inferences having a first premise that is possibly false. Here is an example:

> Ford Motor Company clearly produces the finest cars in the United States. We know they produce the finest cars because they have the best design engineers. This is true because they can afford to pay them more than other manufacturers. Obviously they can afford to pay them more because they produce the finest cars in the United States.

Upon encountering this argument, the attentive reader is inclined to ask, "Where does this reasoning begin? What is its source?" Since the argument goes in a circle, it has no beginning or source, and as a result it proves nothing. Of course, in this example the circularity is rather apparent, so the argument is not likely to convince anyone. Cases in which circular reasoning may convince involve long and complex arguments having premises that depend on one another in subtle ways and a possibly false key premise that depends on the conclusion.

In all cases of begging the question, the arguer uses some linguistic device to create the illusion that inadequate premises provide adequate support for a conclusion. Without such an illusion, the fallacy is not committed. Thus, the following arguments commit no fallacy:

> No dogs are cats.
> Therefore, no cats are dogs.

> London is in England and Paris is in France.
> Therefore, Paris is in France and London is in England.

In both of these examples, the premise amounts to little more than a restatement of the conclusion. Yet both arguments are sound because they are valid and have true premises. No fallacy is committed because no illusion is created to make inadequate premises appear as adequate. We will study arguments of this sort in Chapters 4 and 7.

Here is another example:

> Rome is in Germany or Rome is in Germany.
> Therefore, Rome is in Germany.

This argument is valid, but it is unsound because it has a false premise. However, it commits no fallacy because, again, no illusion is created to cover anything up. Arguments having this form also appear in Chapter 7.

As with these examples, arguments that beg the question are normally valid. This is easy to see. Any argument that includes the conclusion as one of the premises is clearly valid, and those forms of the fallacy that leave a key premise out of the argument become valid when that key premise is introduced. The problem with arguments that beg the question is that they are usually unsound, or at least not clearly sound, because the premise needed to provide adequate support for the conclusion is, at best, of uncertain truth value. Because such arguments presume the truth of this premise, begging the question is called a fallacy of presumption.

16. Complex Question

The fallacy of **complex question** is committed when two (or more) questions are asked in the guise of a single question and a single answer is then given to both of them. Every complex question presumes the existence of a certain condition. When the respondent's answer is added to the complex question, an argument emerges that establishes the presumed condition. Thus, although not an argument as such, a complex question involves an implicit argument. This argument is usually intended to trap the respondent into acknowledging something that he or she might otherwise not want to acknowledge. Examples:

> Have you stopped cheating on exams?
> Where did you hide the marijuana you were smoking?

Let us suppose the respondent answers "yes" to the first question and "under the bed" to the second. The following arguments emerge:

> You were asked whether you have stopped cheating on exams. You answered "yes." Therefore, it follows that you have cheated in the past.

> You were asked where you hid the marijuana you were smoking. You replied "under the bed." It follows that you were in fact smoking marijuana.

On the other hand, let us suppose that the respondent answers "no" to the first question and "nowhere" to the second. We then have the following arguments:

> You were asked whether you have stopped cheating on exams. You answered "no." Therefore, you continue to cheat.

> You were asked where you hid the marijuana you were smoking. You answered "nowhere." It follows that you must have smoked all of it.

Obviously, each of the questions is really two questions:

> Did you cheat on exams in the past? If you did cheat in the past, have you stopped now?

> Were you smoking marijuana? If you were smoking it, where did you hide it?

If respondents are not sophisticated enough to identify a complex question when one is put to them, they may answer quite innocently and be trapped by a conclusion that is supported by no evidence at all; or, they may be tricked into providing the evidence themselves. The correct response lies in resolving the complex question into its component questions and answering each separately.

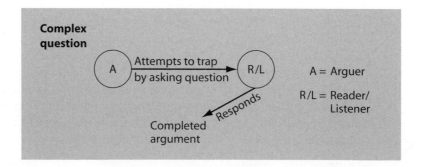

The fallacy of complex question should be distinguished from another kind of question known in law as a leading question. A *leading question* is one in which the answer is in some way suggested in the question. Whether or not a question is a leading one is important in the direct examination of a witness by counsel. Example:

Tell us, on April 9, did you see
    the defendant shoot the
    deceased?   (leading question)
Tell us, what did you see on
    April 9?   (straight question)

Leading questions differ from complex questions in that they involve no logical fallacies—that is, they do not attempt to trick the respondent into admitting something he or she does not want to admit. To distinguish the two, however, it is sometimes necessary to know whether prior questions have been asked. Here are some additional examples of complex questions:

Are you going to be a good little boy and eat your hamburger?
Is George Hendrix still telling lies?
How long must I put up with your snotty behavior?
When are you going to stop talking nonsense?

17. False Dichotomy

The fallacy of **false dichotomy** is committed when a disjunctive ("either . . . or . . .") premise presents two unlikely alternatives as if they were the only ones available, and the arguer then eliminates the undesirable alternative, leaving the desirable one as the conclusion. Such an argument is clearly valid, but since the disjunctive premise is false, or at least probably false, the argument is typically unsound. The fallacy is often committed by children when arguing with their parents, by advertisers, and by adults generally. Here are three examples:

Either you let me attend the Dixie Chicks concert or I'll be miserable for the rest of my life. I know you don't want me to be miserable for the rest of my life, so it follows that you'll let me attend the concert.

Either you use Ultra Guard deodorant or you risk the chance of perspiration odor. Surely you don't want to risk the chance of perspiration odor. Therefore, you will want to use Ultra Guard deodorant.

Either you buy only American-made products or you don't deserve to be called a loyal American. Yesterday you bought a new Toyota. It's therefore clear that you don't deserve to be called a loyal American.

In none of these arguments does the disjunctive premise present the only alternatives available, but in each case the arguer tries to convey that impression. For example, in the first argument, the arguer tries to convey the impression that he or she either goes to the concert or faces a lifetime of misery, and that no other alternatives are possible. Clearly, however, this is not the case.

The fallacious nature of false dichotomy lies in the illusion created by the arguer that the disjunctive premise presents jointly exhaustive alternatives. If it did, the premise would be true of necessity. For example, the statement "Either Reno is in

Nevada, or it is not in Nevada" presents jointly exhaustive alternatives and is true of necessity. But in the fallacy of false dichotomy, the two alternatives not only fail to be jointly exhaustive, but they are not even likely. As a result, the disjunctive premise is false, or at least probably false. Thus, the fallacy amounts to making a false or probably false premise appear true.

If one of the alternatives in the disjunctive premise is true, then the fallacy is not committed. For example, the following argument is valid and sound:

> Either Seattle is in Washington, or it is in Oregon.
> Seattle is not in Oregon.
> Therefore, Seattle is in Washington

False dichotomy is otherwise called "false bifurcation" and the "either-or fallacy." Also, in most cases the arguer expresses only the disjunctive premise and leaves it to the reader or listener to supply the missing statements:

> Either you buy me a new mink coat, or I'll freeze to death when winter comes.
> Either I continue smoking, or I'll get fat and you'll hate to be seen with me.

The missing premise and conclusion are easily introduced.

18. Suppressed Evidence

Chapter 1 explained that a cogent argument is an inductive argument with good reasoning and true premises. The requirement of true premises includes the proviso that the premises not ignore some important piece of evidence that outweighs the presented evidence and entails a very different conclusion. If an inductive argument does indeed ignore such evidence, then the argument commits the fallacy of **suppressed evidence.** Consider, for example, the following argument:

> Most dogs are friendly and pose no threat to people who pet them. Therefore, it would be safe to pet the little dog that is approaching us now.

If the arguer ignores the fact that the little dog is excited and foaming at the mouth (which suggests rabies), then the argument commits a suppressed evidence fallacy. This fallacy is classified as a fallacy of presumption because it works by creating the presumption that the premises are both true and complete when in fact they are not.

Perhaps the most common occurrence of the suppressed evidence fallacy appears in inferences based on advertisements. Nearly every ad neglects to mention certain negative features of the product advertised. As a result, an observer who sees or hears an advertisement and then draws a conclusion from it may commit the fallacy of suppressed evidence. Example:

> The ad for Kentucky Fried Chicken says, "Buy a bucket of chicken and have a barrel of fun!" Therefore, if we buy a bucket of that chicken, we will be guaranteed to have lots of fun.

The ad fails to state that the fun does not come packaged with the chicken but must be supplied by the buyer. Also, of course, the ad fails to state that the chicken is loaded with fat and that the buyer's resultant weight gain may not amount to a barrel of fun. By ignoring these facts, the argument based on the ad is fallacious.

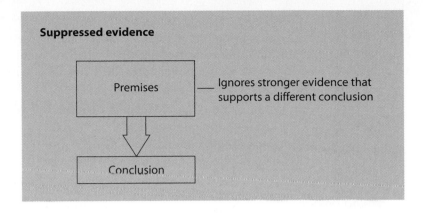

Suppressed evidence

Premises —— Ignores stronger evidence that supports a different conclusion

Conclusion

Another way that an arguer can commit the suppressed evidence fallacy is by ignoring important events that have occurred with the passage of time that render an inductive conclusion improbable. Here is an example:

> During the past fifty years, Poland has enjoyed a rather low standard of living. Therefore, Poland will probably have a low standard of living for the next fifty years.

This argument ignores the fact that Poland was part of the Soviet bloc during most of the past fifty years, and this fact accounts for its rather low standard of living. However, following the collapse of the Soviet Union, Poland became an independent nation, and its economy is expected to improve steadily during the next fifty years.

Yet another form of suppressed evidence is committed by arguers who quote passages out of context from sources such as the Bible, the Constitution, and the Bill of Rights to support a conclusion that the passage was not intended to support. Consider, for example, the following argument against gun control:

> The Second Amendment to the Constitution states that the right of the people to keep and bear arms shall not be infringed. But a law controlling handguns would infringe the right to keep and bear arms. Therefore, a law controlling handguns would be unconstitutional.

In fact, the Second Amendment reads, "A well regulated militia being necessary to the security of a free state, the right of the people to keep and bear arms shall not be infringed." In other words, the amendment states that the right to bear arms shall not be infringed when the arms are necessary for the preservation of a well-regulated militia. Because a law controlling handguns (pistols) would have little effect on the preservation of a well-regulated militia, it is unlikely that such a law would be unconstitutional.

The suppressed evidence fallacy is similar to the form of begging the question in which the arguer leaves a key premise out of the argument. The difference is that suppressed evidence leaves out a premise that requires a *different* conclusion, while that form of begging the question leaves out a premise that is needed to support the *stated* conclusion. However, because both fallacies proceed by leaving a premise out of the argument, there are cases where the two fallacies overlap.

19. Equivocation

The fallacy of **equivocation** occurs when the conclusion of an argument depends on the fact that a word or phrase is used, either explicitly or implicitly, in two different senses in the argument. Such arguments are either invalid or have a false premise, and in either case they are unsound. Examples:

> Some triangles are obtuse. Whatever is obtuse is ignorant. Therefore, some triangles are ignorant.

> Any law can be repealed by the legislative authority. But the law of gravity is a law. Therefore, the law of gravity can be repealed by the legislative authority.

> We have a duty to do what is right. We have a right to speak out in defense of the innocent. Therefore, we have a duty to speak out in defense of the innocent.

> A mouse is an animal. Therefore, a large mouse is a large animal.

In the first argument "obtuse" is used in two different senses. In the first premise it describes a certain kind of angle, while in the second it means dull or stupid. The second argument equivocates on the word "law." In the first premise it means statutory law, and in the second it means law of nature. The third argument uses "right" in two senses. In the first premise "right" means morally correct, but in the second it means a just claim or power. The fourth argument illustrates the ambiguous use of a relative word. The word "large" means different things depending on the context. Other relative words that are susceptible to this same kind of ambiguity include "small," "good," "bad," "light," "heavy," "difficult," "easy," "tall," "short," and so on.

To be convincing, an argument that commits an equivocation must use the equivocal word in ways that are subtly related. Of the three examples given above, only the third might fulfill this requirement. Since both uses of the word "right" are related to ethics, the unalert observer may not notice the shift in meaning. Another technique is to spread the shift in meaning out over the course of a lengthy argument. Political speechmakers often use phrases such as "equal opportunity," "gun control," "national security," and "environmental protection" in one way at the beginning of a speech and in quite another way at the end. A third technique consists in using such phrases one

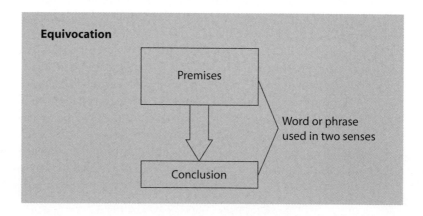

way in a speech to one group and in a different way in a speech to an opposing group. If the same people are not present at both speeches, the equivocation is not detected.

20. Amphiboly

The fallacy of **amphiboly** occurs when the arguer misinterprets an ambiguous statement and then draws a conclusion based on this faulty interpretation. The original statement is usually asserted by someone other than the arguer, and the ambiguity usually arises from a mistake in grammar or punctuation—a missing comma, a dangling modifier, an ambiguous antecedent of a pronoun, or some other careless arrangement of words. Because of this ambiguity, the statement may be understood in two clearly distinguishable ways. The arguer typically selects the unintended interpretation and proceeds to draw a conclusion based upon it. Here are some examples:

> The tour guide said that standing in Greenwich Village, the Empire State Building could easily be seen. It follows that the Empire State Building is in Greenwich Village.

> John told Henry that he had made a mistake. It follows that John has at least the courage to admit his own mistakes.

> Professor Johnson said that he will give a lecture about heart failure in the biology lecture hall. It must be the case that a number of heart failures have occurred there recently.

The premise of the first argument contains a dangling modifier. Is it the observer or the Empire State Building that is supposed to be standing in Greenwich Village? The factually correct interpretation is the former. In the second argument the pronoun "he" has an ambiguous antecedent; it can refer either to John or to Henry. Perhaps John told Henry that *Henry* had made a mistake. In the third argument the ambiguity concerns what takes place in the biology lecture hall; is it the lecture or the heart failures? The correct interpretation is probably the former. The ambiguity can be eliminated by inserting commas ("Professor Johnson said that he will give a lecture, about heart failure, in the biology lecture hall") or by moving the ambiguous modifier ("Professor Johnson said that he will give a lecture in the biology lecture hall about heart failure"). Ambiguities of this sort are called *syntactical ambiguities*.

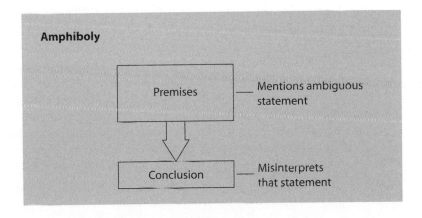

Amphiboly

Premises — Mentions ambiguous statement

Conclusion — Misinterprets that statement

Two areas where cases of amphiboly cause serious problems involve contracts and wills. The drafters of these documents often express their intentions in terms of ambiguous statements, and alternate interpretations of these statements then lead to different conclusions. Examples:

> Mrs. Hart stated in her will, "I leave my 500-carat diamond necklace and my pet chinchilla to Alice and Theresa." Therefore, we conclude that Alice gets the necklace and Theresa gets the chinchilla.

> Mr. James signed a contract that reads, "In exchange for painting my house, I promise to pay David $5000 and give him my new Cadillac only if he finishes the job by May 1." Therefore, since David did not finish until May 10, it follows that he gets neither the $5000 nor the Cadillac.

In the first example, the conclusion obviously favors Alice. Theresa is almost certain to argue that the gift of the necklace and chinchilla should be shared equally by her and Alice. Mrs. Hart could have avoided the dispute by adding either "respectively" or "collectively" to the end of the sentence. In the second example, the conclusion favors Mr. James. David will argue that the condition that he finish by May 1 affected only the Cadillac and that he therefore is entitled to the $5000. The dispute could have been avoided by properly inserting a comma in the language of the promise.

Amphiboly differs from equivocation in two important ways. First, equivocation is always traced to an ambiguity in the meaning of a *word* or *phrase*, whereas amphiboly involves a syntactical ambiguity in a *statement*. The second difference is that amphiboly usually involves a mistake made by the arguer in interpreting an ambiguous statement made by someone else, whereas the ambiguity in equivocation is typically the arguer's own creation. If these distinctions are kept in mind, it is usually easy to distinguish amphiboly from equivocation. Occasionally, however, the two fallacies occur together, as the following example illustrates:

> The *Great Western Cookbook* recommends that we serve the oysters when thoroughly stewed. Apparently the delicate flavor is enhanced by the intoxicated condition of the diners.

First, it is unclear whether "stewed" refers to the oysters or to the diners, and so the argument commits an amphiboly. But if "stewed" refers to the oysters it means "cooked," and if it refers to the diners it means "intoxicated." Thus, the argument also involves an equivocation.

21. Composition

The fallacy of **composition** is committed when the conclusion of an argument depends on the erroneous transference of an attribute from the parts of something onto the whole. In other words, the fallacy occurs when it is argued that because the parts have a certain attribute, it follows that the whole has that attribute too and the situation is such that the attribute in question cannot be legitimately transferred from parts to whole. Examples:

> Maria likes anchovies. She also likes chocolate ice cream. Therefore, it is certain that she would like a chocolate sundae topped with anchovies.

Each player on this basketball team is an excellent athlete. Therefore, the team as a whole is excellent.

Each atom in this piece of chalk is invisible. Therefore, the chalk is invisible.

Sodium and chlorine, the atomic components of salt, are both deadly poisons. Therefore, salt is a deadly poison.

In these arguments the attributes that are transferred from the parts onto the whole are designated by the words "Maria likes," "excellent," "invisible," and "deadly poison," respectively. In each case the transference is illegitimate, and so the argument is fallacious.

Not every such transference is illegitimate, however. Consider the following arguments:

Every atom in this piece of chalk has mass. Therefore, the piece of chalk has mass.

Every component in this picket fence is white. Therefore, the whole fence is white.

In each case an attribute (having mass, being white) is transferred from the parts onto the whole, but these transferences are quite legitimate. Indeed, the fact that the atoms have mass is the very reason *why* the chalk has mass. The same reasoning extends to the fence. Thus, the acceptability of these arguments is attributable, at least in part, to the *legitimate* transference of an attribute from parts onto the whole.

These examples illustrate the fact that the fallacy of composition is indeed an informal fallacy. It cannot be discovered by a mere inspection of the form of an argument—that is, by the mere observation that an attribute is being transferred from parts onto the whole. In addition, detecting this fallacy requires a general knowledge of the situation and of the nature of the attribute being transferred. The critic must be certain that, given the situation, the transference of this particular attribute is not allowed.

Further caution is required by the fact that composition is sometimes confused with hasty generalization. The only time this confusion is possible is when the "whole" is a

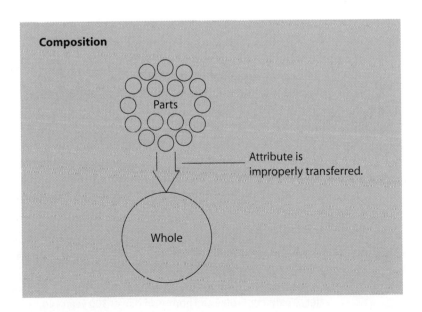

Composition

Parts

Attribute is improperly transferred.

Whole

class (such as the class of people in a city or the class of trees in a forest), and the "parts" are the members of the class. In such a case composition proceeds from the members of the class to the class itself. Hasty generalization, on the other hand, proceeds from the specific to the general. Because it is sometimes easy to mistake a statement about a class for a general statement, composition can be mistaken for hasty generalization. Such a mistake can be avoided if one is careful to keep in mind the distinction between these two kinds of statements. This distinction falls back on the difference between the **collective** and the **distributive** predication of an attribute. Consider the following statements:

> Fleas are small.
> Fleas are numerous.

The first statement is a general statement. The attribute of being small is predicated distributively; that is, it is assigned (or distributed) to each and every flea in the class. Each and every flea in the class is said to be small. The second statement, on the other hand, is a statement about a class as a whole, or what we will call a "class statement." The attribute of being numerous is predicated collectively; in other words, it is assigned not to the individual fleas but to the *class* of fleas. The meaning of the statement is not that each and every flea is numerous but that the class of fleas is large.

To distinguish composition from hasty generalization, therefore, the following procedure should be followed. Examine the conclusion of the argument. If the conclusion is a general statement—that is, a statement in which an attribute is predicated distributively to each and every member of a class—the fallacy committed is hasty generalization. But if the conclusion is a class statement—that is, a statement in which an attribute is predicated collectively to a class as a whole—the fallacy is composition. Example:

> Less gasoline is consumed by a car than by a truck. Therefore, less gasoline is consumed in the United States by cars than by trucks.

At first sight this argument might appear to proceed from the specific to the general and, consequently, to commit a hasty generalization. But in fact the conclusion is not a general statement at all but a class statement. The conclusion states that the whole class of cars uses less gas than does the whole class of trucks (which is false, because there are many more cars than trucks). Since the attribute of using less gasoline is predicated collectively, the fallacy committed is composition.

22. Division

The fallacy of **division** is the exact reverse of composition. As composition goes from parts to whole, division goes from whole to parts. The fallacy is committed when the conclusion of an argument depends on the erroneous transference of an attribute from a whole (or a class) onto its parts (or members). Examples:

> Salt is a nonpoisonous compound. Therefore, its component elements, sodium and chlorine, are nonpoisonous.

> This jigsaw puzzle, when assembled, is circular in shape. Therefore, each piece is circular in shape.

> The Royal Society is over 300 years old. Professor Thompson is a member of the Royal Society. Therefore, Professor Thompson is over 300 years old.

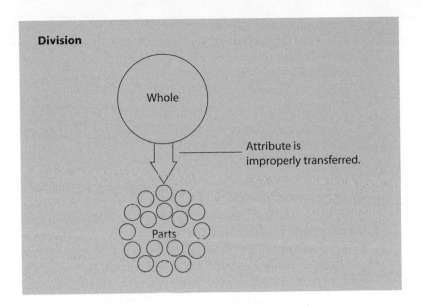

Division

Whole

Attribute is improperly transferred.

Parts

In each case the attribute, designated respectively by the terms "nonpoisonous," "circular in shape," and "over 300 years old," is illegitimately transferred from the whole or class onto the parts or members. As with the fallacy of composition, however, this kind of transference is not always illegitimate. The following arguments contain no fallacy:

> This piece of chalk has mass. Therefore, the atoms that compose this piece of chalk have mass.

> This field of poppies is uniformly orange in color. Therefore, the individual poppies are orange in color.

Obviously, one must be acquainted with the situation and the nature of the attribute being transferred to decide whether the fallacy of division is actually committed.

Just as composition can sometimes be confused with hasty generalization (converse accident), division can sometimes be confused with accident. As with composition, this confusion can occur only when the "whole" is a class. In such a case, division proceeds from the class to the members, while accident proceeds from the general to the specific. Thus, if a class statement is mistaken for a general statement, division may be mistaken for accident. To avoid such a mistake, one should analyze the premises of the argument. If the premises contain a general statement, the fallacy committed is accident; but if they contain a class statement, the fallacy is division. Example:

> Stanley Steamers have almost disappeared.
> This car is a Stanley Steamer.
> Therefore, this car has almost disappeared.

The first premise is not a general statement but a class statement. The attribute of having almost disappeared is predicated collectively. Accordingly, the fallacy committed is division, not accident.

This example also illustrates how cases of division that involve class statements can include a subtle form of equivocation. In the conclusion, the word "disappeared" means fading from vision, as when the lights are turned down; but in the first premise it means rarely seen. The equivocation is a kind of secondary fallacy that results from the primary fallacy, which is division.

The next example shows how division turns up in arguments dealing with averages.

> The average American family has 2.5 children.
> The Jones family is an average American family.
> Therefore, the Jones family has 2.5 children.

The statement "The average American family has 2.5 children" is not a general statement, but rather a class statement. The sense of the statement is not that each and every family has 2.5 children, but that the class of families is reducible to 55 percent children and 45 percent adults. Thus, once again, the fallacy is division, and not accident.

In our account of composition and division, we have presented examples of arguments that commit these fallacies in conjunction with other, structurally similar arguments that do not. Because of the structural similarity between arguments that do and do not commit these fallacies, composition and division are classified as fallacies of grammatical analogy.

SUMMARY OF INFORMAL FALLACIES

Fallacies of Relevance

Appeal to force: Arguer threatens reader/listener.

Appeal to pity: Arguer elicits pity from reader/listener.

Appeal to the people (direct): Arguer arouses mob mentality.

Appeal to the people (indirect): Arguer appeals to reader/listener's desire for security, love, respect, etc.

Argument against the person (abusive): Arguer verbally abuses other arguer.

Argument against the person (circumstantial): Arguer presents other arguer as predisposed to argue this way.

Argument against the person (*tu quoque*): Arguer presents other arguer as hypocrite.

Accident: General rule is applied to a specific case it was not intended to cover.

Straw man: Arguer distorts opponent's argument and then attacks the distorted argument.

Missing the point: Arguer draws conclusion different from that supported by premises.

Red herring: Arguer leads reader/listener off track.

Fallacies of Weak Induction

Appeal to unqualified authority: Arguer cites untrustworthy authority.

Appeal to ignorance: Premises report that nothing is known or proved, and then a conclusion is drawn.

Hasty generalization: Conclusion is drawn from atypical sample.

False cause: Conclusion depends on nonexistent or minor causal connection.

Slippery slope: Conclusion depends on unlikely chain reaction.

Weak analogy: Conclusion depends on defective analogy.

Fallacies of Presumption
Begging the question: Arguer creates the illusion that inadequate premises are adequate by leaving out a key premise, by restating the conclusion as a premise, or by reasoning in a circle.

Complex question: Multiple questions are concealed in a single question.

False dichotomy: "Either ... or ..." statement hides additional alternatives.

Suppressed evidence: Arguer ignores important evidence that requires a different conclusion.

Fallacies of Ambiguity
Equivocation: Conclusion depends on a shift in meaning of a word or phrase.

Amphiboly: Conclusion depends on the wrong interpretation of a syntactically ambiguous statement.

Fallacies of Grammatical Analogy
Composition: Attribute is wrongly transferred from parts to whole.

Division: Attribute is wrongly transferred from whole to parts.

EXERCISE 3.4

iLrn I. Identify the fallacies of presumption, ambiguity, and grammatical analogy committed by the following arguments, giving a brief explanation for your answer. If no fallacy is committed, write "no fallacy."

★1. Either we require forced sterilization of Third World peoples or world population will explode and all of us will die. We certainly don't want to die, so we must require forced sterilization.

2. Every sentence in this paragraph is well written. Therefore, the paragraph is well written.

3. An athlete is a human being. Therefore, a good athlete is a good human being.

★4. James said that he saw a picture of a beautiful girl stashed in Stephen's locker. We can only conclude that Stephen has broken the rules, because girls are not allowed in the locker room.

5. Why is it so difficult for you to reach a decision?

6. Water will quench one's thirst. Water is composed of hydrogen and oxygen. Therefore, hydrogen and oxygen will quench one's thirst.

★7. People who lack humility have no sense of beauty because everyone who has a sense of beauty also has humility.

8. Butane is combustible. Therefore, it burns.

9. Honey, this postcard just arrived, and it says we have won a free airline trip. All we have to do is call the toll-free number to claim it. If we call the number, we can go to Paris in June!

★10. If Thomas gives Marie a ring, then Thomas and Marie will be engaged. Thomas did give Marie a ring. In fact, he phoned her just the other night. Therefore, Thomas and Marie are engaged.

11. Alex, I heard your testimony in court earlier today. Tell me, why did you lie on the witness stand?

12. Johnson is employed by the General Services Administration, and everyone knows that the GSA is the most inefficient branch of the government. Therefore, Johnson must be an inefficient worker.

★13. All men are mortal. Therefore, some day man will disappear from the earth.

14. Each and every cell in this carrot is 90 percent water. Therefore, the entire carrot is 90 percent water.

15. George said that he was interviewing for a job drilling oil wells in the supervisor's office. We can only conclude that the supervisor must have an awfully dirty office.

★16. During the fifty years that Mr. Jones worked, he contributed $90,000 to Social Security. Now that he is retired, he stands to collect $200,000 from the system. Obviously he will collect a much greater monetary value than he contributed.

17. Either you marry me right now or I'll be forced to leave you and never speak to you again. I'm sure you wouldn't want me to do that. Therefore, you'll marry me right now.

18. Either Meg Ryan or Britney Spears is a popular singer. Meg Ryan is not a popular singer. Therefore, Britney Spears is a popular singer.

★19. Switzerland is 48 percent Protestant. Heidi Gilsing is a Swiss. Therefore, Heidi Gilsing is 48 percent Protestant.

20. Picasso is the greatest artist of the twentieth century. We know that this is so because art critics have described him in these terms. These art critics are correct in their assessment because they have a more keenly developed sense of appreciation than the average person. This is true because it takes a more keenly developed sense of appreciation to realize that Picasso is the greatest artist of the twentieth century.

21. An atomic bomb causes more damage than a conventional bomb. Therefore, during World War II more damage was caused by atomic bombs than by conventional bombs.

★22. Sylvia, I saw you shopping for wine the other day. Incidentally, are you still drinking excessively?

23. The author warns about numerous computational errors in his accounting text. Therefore, he must have written it very carelessly.

24. Emeralds are seldom found in this country, so you should be careful not to misplace your emerald ring.

★25. Of course abortion is permissible. After all, a woman has a right to do as she pleases with her own body.

II. Answer "true" or "false" to the following statements:

1. Arguments that commit the fallacy of begging the question are normally valid.

2. The effect of begging the question is to hide the fact that a premise may not be true.

3. The correct way of responding to a complex question is to divide the question into its component questions and answer each separately.

4. False dichotomy always involves an "either . . . or . . ." statement, at least implicitly.

5. The fallacy of equivocation arises from a syntactical defect in a statement.

6. The fallacy of amphiboly usually involves the ambiguous use of a single word.

7. Amphiboly usually arises from the arguer's misinterpreting a statement made by someone else.

8. The fallacy of composition always proceeds from whole to parts.

9. The fallacy of division always proceeds from parts to whole.

10. A general statement makes an assertion about each and every member of a class.

11. A class statement makes an assertion about a class as a whole.

12. In the statement "Divorces are increasing," an attribute is predicated distributively.

13. In the statement "Waistlines are increasing," an attribute is predicated distributively.

14. Composition and division involve the distributive predication of an attribute.

15. Equivocation and amphiboly are classified as fallacies of ambiguity.

iLrn III. Identify the fallacies of relevance, weak induction, presumption, ambiguity, and grammatical analogy committed by the following arguments, giving a brief explanation for your answer. If no fallacy is committed, write "no fallacy."

★1. In his *History of the American Civil War*, Jeffry Noland argues that the war had little to do with slavery. However, as a historian from Alabama, Noland could not possibly present an accurate account. Therefore, his arguments should be discounted.

2. Mr. Wilson said that on July 4 he went out on the veranda and watched the fireworks go up in his pajamas. We conclude that Mr. Wilson must have had an exciting evening.

3. Televangelist Jerry Falwell said that God's anger with feminism led to the destruction of the World Trade Center. Given Falwell's closeness to God, we have no alternative than to blame the feminists for this atrocity.

★4. A crust of bread is better than nothing. Nothing is better than true love. Therefore, a crust of bread is better than true love.

5. Every member of the Delta Club is over 70 years old. Therefore, the Delta Club must be over 70 years old.

6. Of course you should eat Wheaties. Wheaties is the breakfast of champions, you know.

★7. It's obvious that animals have rights. Just look at how powerless they are in comparison with modern humans.

8. The idea that black people in this country live in poverty is ridiculous. Look at Bill Cosby. He's a millionaire. And so are Denzel Washington and Oprah Winfrey.

9. No one has ever proved that the human fetus is not a person with rights. Therefore, abortion is morally wrong.

★10. California condors are rapidly disappearing. This bird is a California condor. Therefore, this bird should disappear any minute now.

11. When a car breaks down so often that repairs become pointless, the car is thrown on the junk heap. Similarly, when a person becomes old and diseased, he or she should be mercifully put to death.

12. The twenty-story Carson Building is constructed of concrete blocks. Each and every concrete block in the structure can withstand an earthquake of 9.5 on the Richter scale. Therefore, the building can withstand an earthquake of 9.5 on the Richter scale.

★13. Terrorists from the Middle East have crossed our borders and traveled through the country at will. Obviously the Immigration Service has not been doing its job.

14. This administration is not anti-German, as it has been alleged. Germany is a great country. It has contributed immensely to the world's artistic treasury. Goethe and Schiller made magnificent contributions to literature, and Bach, Beethoven, Wagner, and Brahms did the same in music.

15. Paul, it was great to see you at the party the other night. Everyone there was doing crack. Incidentally, how long have you been dealing that stuff?

16. Rod Paige, Secretary of Education for the Bush administration, said that the National Education Association is a terrorist organization. Given Paige's vast knowledge in these matters, we can only conclude that the NEA is indeed a terrorist organization.

17. Senator Kennedy's arguments in favor of health care for the poor and aged should be ignored. Kennedy is a do-gooder who supports this kind of legislation only to get his name in the newspapers.

18. Professor Andrews, surely I deserve a B in logic. I know that I have gotten F's on all the tests, but if you give me an F for my final grade, I will lose my scholarship. That will force me to drop out of school, and my poor, aged parents, who yearn to see me graduate, will be grief-stricken for the rest of their lives.

★19. Molecules are in constant random motion. The Statue of Liberty is composed of molecules. Therefore, the Statue of Liberty is in constant random motion.

20. Either we have prayer in our public schools or the moral fabric of society will disintegrate. The choice should be obvious.

21. White sheep eat more than black sheep (because there are more of them). Therefore, this white sheep eats more than that black sheep.

★22. If someone rents a piece of land and plants crops on it, the landlord is never permitted to come and take those crops for himself when harvest time arrives. Similarly, if couples enlist the services of a surrogate mother to provide them with a baby, the mother should never be allowed to welch on the deal and keep the baby for herself once it is born.

23. Motives and desires exert forces on people, causing them to choose one thing over another. But force is a physical quantity, governed by the laws of physics. Therefore, human choices are governed by the laws of physics.

24. Each and every brick in the completely brick-faced Wainright Building has a reddish brown color. Therefore, the Wainright Building has a reddish brown color.

★25. Humanitarian groups have argued in favor of housing for the poor. Apparently what they want is another high-density project. Unfortunately, these projects have been tried in the past and have failed. In no time they turn into ghettos with astronomical rates of crime and delinquency. Chicago's Cabrini-Green is a prime example. Clearly, these humanitarian arguments are not what they seem.

26. Pauline said that after she had removed her new mink coat from the shipping carton she threw it into the trash. We conclude that Pauline has no appreciation for fine furs.

27. We know that induction will provide dependable results in the future because it has always worked in the past. Whatever has consistently worked in the past will continue to work in the future, and we know that this is true because it has been established by induction.

★28. What goes up must come down. The price of housing has been going up for years. Therefore, it will surely come down soon.

29. Mr. Prime Minister, I am certain you will want to release the members of our National Liberation Group whom you currently hold in prison. After all, I'm sure you will want to avoid having car bombs go off in the centers of your most heavily populated cities.

30. San Diego has the same latitude as Yuma, Arizona, and San Diego enjoys moderate temperatures through the summer months. Therefore, probably Yuma enjoys moderate temperatures through the summer months.

★31. We're all familiar with the complaint that over 40 million Americans are without health insurance. But America's doctors, nurses, and hospitals are among the best in the world. Thousands of people come from abroad every year to be treated here. Clearly there is nothing wrong with our health care system.

32. Real estate mogul Donald Trump argues that good management is essential to any business. But who is he to talk? Trump's own mismanagement drove Trump Hotels and Casino Resorts into bankruptcy twice in twelve years.

33. The farmers of our state have asked that we introduce legislation to provide subsidies for soybeans. Unfortunately, we will have to turn down their request. If we give subsidies to the soybean farmers, then the corn and wheat growers will ask for the same thing. Then it will be the cotton growers, citrus growers, truck farmers, and cattle raisers. In the end, the cost will be astronomical.

★34. The travel brochure states that walking up O'Connell Street, the statue of Parnell comes into view. Apparently that statue has no trouble getting around.

35. Criminals are basically stupid, because anyone who isn't basically stupid wouldn't be a criminal.

36. Professor Glazebrooks's theory about the origin of the Martian craters is undoubtedly true. Rudolph Orkin, the great concert pianist, announced his support of the theory in this morning's newspaper.

★37. Mr. Franklin has lost at the craps table for the last ten throws of the dice. Therefore, it is extremely likely that he will win on the next throw.

38. Raising a child is like growing a tree. Sometimes violent things, such as cutting off branches, have to be done to force the tree to grow straight. Similarly, corporal punishment must sometimes be inflicted on children to force them to develop properly.

39. Good steaks are rare these days, so don't order yours well done.

★40. The Book of Mormon is true because it was written by Joseph Smith. Joseph Smith wrote the truth because he was divinely inspired. We know that Joseph Smith was divinely inspired because the Book of Mormon says that he was, and the Book of Mormon is true.

41. The students attending Bradford College come from every one of the fifty states. Michelle attends Bradford College. Therefore, Michelle comes from every one of the fifty states.

42. Rhubarb pie is a dessert. Therefore, whoever eats rhubarb pie eats a dessert.

★43. The vast majority of car accidents occur within twenty miles of one's home. Apparently it is much more dangerous to drive close to home than far away from home.

44. Either you're with us or you're with the terrorists. The choice should be easy.

45. Nobody has ever proved that weapons of mass destruction do not exist in Iraq. Therefore, those weapons must be in that country somewhere.

★46. On Friday I took Virginia out to dinner. She told me that if I wasn't interested in a serious relationship, I should forget about dating her. On Saturday I took Margie to a film. When we discussed it afterward over a drink, she couldn't understand why I wasn't interested in babies. Women are all alike. All they want is a secure marriage.

47. Dozens of species of plants and animals are being wiped out every year, even though we have laws to prevent it. Clearly, we should repeal the Endangered Species Act.

48. People are driving their cars like maniacs tonight. There must be a full moon.

★**49.** A line is composed of points. Points have no length. Therefore, a line has no length.

50. Are you in favor of the ruinous economic policy of the Democratic Platform Committee?

IV. Identify the arguments in the following dialogue, then discuss each of them in terms of the fallacies presented in this section and the previous section. You should be able to find at least one case of each fallacy.

"Thanks for giving me a lift home," Paul says to his friend Steve, as they head toward the freeway.

"No problem; it's on my way," says Steve.

"Uh oh," warns Paul suddenly, "watch out ahead. Looks like the police have pulled somebody over."

"Thanks," Steve says. "Hope they don't beat the guy up."

"Not a chance," says Paul. "Why would you say that?"

"You're an optimist," answers Steve. "Most cops are animals; they beat up on anybody they want to. You remember Rodney King, don't you? Those cops in L.A. put King in the hospital for no reason at all. That should prove I'm right."

"I think you're overreacting," Paul says. "Daryl Gates, the L.A. police chief at the time, said the King incident was an aberration. Since he was chief, I think we should take him at his word."

"But Gates was a lunatic who refused to acknowledge even our most basic rights," Steve persists. "Also, if you recall, he was forced to resign after the King incident. I know we don't live in L.A., but our police department is just as bad as theirs. So you can bet that our friend back there is just as abusive as any of them."

"Wait a minute," Paul argues. "As far as I know, nobody has ever proved that our police force is the slightest bit violent. You've no right to draw such a conclusion."

"Well, listen to this," Steve counters, as he changes lanes and turns onto the freeway. "About a week ago, I was with my friend Casey. When I left him, he was perfectly okay, but he was picked up for going through a stop sign on the way home. I saw him a couple of days later, and he had a big bruise under his right eye. The cop who stopped Casey must have hit him with his baton."

"Hold on. Did you ask Casey what happened?"

"No. I didn't have to," says Steve, a bit righteously. "I asked Casey's wife what happened between Casey and the cop, and she said he hit him. Those were her exact words, so that was good enough for me. I bet the cop's a maniac."

"Good grief," answers his friend. "How long will it take you to get over your warped view of things?"

"My way of looking at things isn't warped," Steve insists. "The problem is, you and I are both white. If you were black, you'd see things differently. Police brutality toward African Americans is way out of hand."

"Well," counters Paul, "a study done recently by an independent agency might interest you. According to that study, for every African American whom the police use force against, there's a white person they also use force against. That proves the police treat African Americans no worse than they do whites."

"I've never heard of that study, but it seems to me there must be something wrong with it," insists Steve.

"Well, the results of that study are borne out in my experience," says Paul. "I've been pulled over three or four times in the past couple of years, and the officers have always been extremely courteous. I can only conclude that the vast majority of these allegations of police brutality are the product of fertile imaginations."

"Again, your naiveté amazes me," Steve answers, dumbfounded. "First of all, you forget that you're white and you drive a new Mercedes. Don't you think that makes a difference? In fact, that's the trouble with all these arguments that downplay police brutality. They're all concocted by white people."

"Well, the fact remains that we have a major crime problem in this country," Paul argues. "Combating crime requires a few concessions, and you do want to combat crime, don't you?"

"Sure," Steve replies grudgingly, "but at what expense? Do innocent people have to get their heads bashed in?"

"Well, I think what it comes down to is this," says Paul. "Either you allow the police to use whatever force they find necessary, or the criminals will take over this country. Now you certainly don't want that to happen, do you?"

"No, but that's the crucial question," Steve says, exiting from the freeway. "When and how much force is necessary?"

"Well, you remember when the police apprehended that serial killer a few weeks ago? When the police made the arrest, the killer attacked them. So, the police can use force when attacked."

"I agree," responds Steve thoughtfully. "But what about the way the police treated those peaceful right-to-lifers who were demonstrating in front of the abortion clinic the other day? Many of them were elderly and posed no physical threat. But the cops used those contraptions—what do you call them, nimchucks, nomchucks, I don't know—to squeeze the old folks' wrists, causing great pain and injury, and they hit the old people on the head with their batons. Do you think that was necessary?"

"Of course it was," answers Paul, agitatedly. "Those people attacked the police—they hurled epithets at them."

"Honestly, I don't know how we've managed to stay friends all these years," Steve says with some frustration. "By the way, do you know what it says on the back of all police cars? It says 'To Protect and Serve.' Now if you hired a servant to take care of you, you'd get rid of him if he disobeyed you. Right?"

"Probably."

"Well, isn't it true," Steve asks, "that whenever a police officer disobeys one of us taxpayers, that officer should be fired?"

"That may be stretching it a bit," Paul laughs.

"But seriously," continues Steve, "I think what we need is some screening device to keep violent types from ever becoming cops."

"Well, you'll be happy to know that exactly such a device has been used for the past twenty-one years," Paul states. "Before entering the police academy, every applicant goes through a battery of psychological tests that positively eliminates all the macho types and the ones prone to violence. This ensures the individual officers are nonviolent, so we know the entire police force is nonviolent."

"Hmm. Maybe your so-called solution is really the problem," Steve suggests, as he pulls up in front of Paul's house. "We've had psychological testing for twenty-one years, and all that time, police violence has been on the rise. Perhaps we should get rid of the testing program."

"Well, I don't know about the logic of that," Paul muses, stepping out of the car. "But like you said, we've been friends for a long time, so I guess we can disagree. Thanks for the ride and the discussion. See you tomorrow!"

"Sure," Steve murmurs. "Tomorrow."

3.5 Fallacies in Ordinary Language

This section addresses two topics. The first concerns the challenge of detecting the fallacies of others in ordinary language, and the second relates to the goal of avoiding fallacies in one's own arguments.

Detecting Fallacies

Most of the informal fallacies that we have seen thus far have been clear-cut, easily recognizable instances of a specific mistake. When fallacies occur in ordinary usage, however, they are often neither clear-cut nor easily recognizable. The reason is that there are innumerable ways of making mistakes in arguing, and variations inevitably occur that may not be exact instances of any specifically named fallacy. In addition, one fallacious mode of arguing may be mixed together with one or more others, and the strands of reasoning may have to be disentangled before the fallacies can be named. Yet another problem arises from the fact that arguments in ordinary language are rarely presented in complete form. It often happens that a premise or conclusion is left unexpressed, which may obscure the nature of the evidence that is presented or the strength of the link between premises and conclusion.

Consider, for example, the following letter that appeared in a newspaper:

> God, I am sick of "women's rights"! Every time one turns on the news we hear about some form of discrimination against some poor female who wants to be a fireman—or some "remark" that suggests or implies women are inferior to men.
>
> I, for one, do not want to be rescued by a "woman fireman," especially if I am a 6-foot-2 male and she is a 5-foot-6 female.
>
> Why is it that women find their "role" so degrading? What is wrong with being a wife and mother, staying home while the male goes out and "hunts for food" and brings it home to his family?
>
> I don't think women have proven themselves to be as inventive, as capable (on the average) of world leadership, as physically capable, or as "courageous" as men. They have yet to fight a war (the average American woman) and let's face it ladies, who wants to?
>
> Whether a person is female, black, white, handicapped—whatever ability is what counts in the final analysis. Women cannot demand "equality"—no one can—unless it is earned.
>
> When push comes to shove and a damsel is in distress, she is hard-pressed to protect herself and usually has to be rescued by a man. Until I can move a piano, beat off a potential robber or rapist, or fight a war, I am quite content to be a woman, thank you.
>
> (Patricia Kelley)

This letter can be interpreted as committing a number of fallacies. The phrase "poor female who wants to be a fireman" suggests a mild *ad hominem* abusive, and equating women's rights in general with the right to be a firefighter suggests a straw man. The second paragraph commits another straw man fallacy by supposing that the job of firefighter inevitably entails such activities as climbing up ladders and rescuing people. Surely there are many male firefighters who cannot do this. The same paragraph also can be interpreted as begging the question: Do women who want to be firefighters want the specific job of rescuing tall men?

The third paragraph throws out a red herring. The issue is whether women have the right to be considered for a job of their choice and whether they must be paid as much as a man in the same situation. Whether there is something wrong with being a wife and mother is quite a different issue. Also, the reference to men hunting for food suggests a possible begging of the question: Are we still locked into a "hunter-gatherer" social structure?

The paragraph about whether women have proved themselves to be as inventive, capable, and courageous as men begs yet another question: Assuming, for the sake of argument, that this is true, have women been allowed to occupy roles in society where such inventiveness, capability, and courageousness can be demonstrated? Furthermore, this paragraph commits a red herring fallacy and/or misses the point: Even if women have not proved this, what does that have to do with the issue? Most jobs do not require any high degree of inventiveness or courage or a capacity for world leadership.

The paragraph about ability begs yet another question: Is it in fact the case that women have less ability? I am not aware that anything of the sort has ever been proved. Finally, the last paragraph throws out another red herring. What does moving pianos (bare-handed?) and beating off rapists have to do with most jobs or the question of equal pay for equal work?

Probably the single most important requirement for detecting fallacies in ordinary language is alertness. The reader or listener must pay close attention to what the arguer is saying. What is the conclusion? What are the reasons given in support of the conclusion? Are the reasons relevant to the conclusion? Do the reasons support the conclusion? If the reader or listener is half asleep, or lounging in that passive, drugged-out state that attends much television viewing, then none of these questions will receive answers. Under those circumstances the reader or listener will never be able to detect informal fallacies, and he or she will accept even the worst reasoning without the slightest hesitation.

Avoiding Fallacies

Why do people commit informal fallacies? Unfortunately, this question admits of no simple, straightforward answer. The reasons underlying the commission of fallacies are complex and interconnected. However, we can identify three factors that lead to most of the informal mistakes in reasoning. The first is intent. Many fallacies are committed intentionally. The arguer may know full well that his or her reasoning is defective but goes ahead with it anyway because of some benefit for himself or herself or some other person. All of the informal fallacies we have studied can be used for that purpose, but some of them are particularly well suited. These include the appeal to force, appeal to pity, appeal to the people, straw man, *ad hominem*, complex question, false dichotomy, and suppressed evidence. Here is such a case of appeal to force:

> I deserve a chocolate sundae for dessert, and if you don't buy me one right now, I'll start screaming and embarrass you in front of all of the people in this restaurant.

And here is a case of false dichotomy that conveys the appearance of being intentionally committed:

> Either you take me on a Caribbean cruise, or I'll have a nervous breakdown. It's up to you.

The key to avoiding fallacies that are intentionally committed probably lies in some form of moral education. The arguer must come to realize that using intellectually dishonest means to acquire something he or she does not deserve is just another form of cheating.

The situation becomes more complicated, however, when the sought-after goal is morally justified. Arguers sometimes use fallacious reasoning intentionally to trick a person into doing something that is really for that person's own good. Here is a false dichotomy of that sort:

> Either you control your eating and get regular exercise, or you'll have a heart attack and die. The choice is yours.

Given the beneficial consequences of controlled eating and regular exercise, some moral philosophers will find nothing wrong with this argument. Others will contend that manipulating someone into doing something violates human dignity. In either event, such arguments are logically unacceptable.

The second factor that leads to the commission of informal fallacies is a careless mental posture combined with an emotional disposition favoring or opposing some person or thing. The careless mental posture opens the door, so to speak, to fallacious reasoning, and the emotional disposition pushes the arguer through it. Even people who are thoroughly versed in the informal fallacies occasionally succumb to the deadly combination of mental carelessness and emotional impetus. For example, arguments such as the following *ad hominem* abusive can sometimes be heard in the halls of university philosophy departments:

> Professor Ballard's argument in favor of restructuring our course offering isn't worth a hoot. But what would you expect from someone who publishes in such mediocre journals. And did you hear Ballard's recent lecture on Aristotle? It was total nonsense.

When people who should know better are confronted with the fact that their argument commits a common fallacy, they often admit with embarrassment that they have not been thinking and then revise their argument according to logical principles. In contrast, people who are not familiar with the distinction between good and fallacious reasoning will likely deny that there is anything wrong with their argument. Thus, the key to avoiding fallacies that arise from mental carelessness lies in developing a thorough familiarity with the informal fallacies combined with a habitual realization of how emotions affect people's reasoning. Everyone should realize that unchecked emotions are an open invitation to illogical reasoning, and they can lead a person to commit quite blindly every one of the fallacies we have studied thus far.

The third factor that leads to the commission of informal fallacies is far more difficult to contend with than the first two. It consists in the influence of what we might call the "worldview" of the arguer. By worldview we mean a cognitive network of beliefs, attitudes, habits, memories, values, and other elements that conditions and renders meaningful the world in which we live. Beginning in infancy, our worldview emerges quietly and unconsciously from enveloping influences—culture, language, gender, religion, politics, and social and economic status. As we grow older, it continues to develop through the shaping forces of education and experience. Once it has taken root, our worldview determines how each of us sizes up the world in which we live. Given a set of circumstances, it indicates what is reasonable to believe and what is unreasonable.

In connection with the construction and evaluation of arguments, an arguer's worldview determines the answer to questions about importance, relevance, causal connections, the qualifications of authorities, whether a sample is typical or atypical of a group, what can and cannot be taken for granted, and other factors. However, because these determinations inevitably involve unexamined presuppositions, the arguer's worldview can lead to the commission of informal fallacies. All of the fallacies we have studied so far are likely candidates, but the ones especially susceptible are appeal to pity, straw man, missing the point, appeal to unqualified authority, hasty generalization, false cause, slippery slope, weak analogy, begging the question, false dichotomy, and suppressed evidence.

Thus, a person with a victim mentality may think that his pathetic circumstances really justify some favorable treatment; an uncritical conservative may cite with complete confidence the authority of Rush Limbaugh; a person with a racist worldview may conclude that the errant behavior of a handful of Asians, African Americans, or Hispanics really is typical of the larger class; a person with a liberal worldview may quite innocently distort an opponent's argument by equating it with fascism; a pro-life arguer may consider it obvious that the fetus is a person with rights, while a pro-choice arguer may take it for granted that the fetus is not a person with rights, and so on. Consider, for example, the following argument from analogy:

> A court trial is like a professional football game. In a professional football game, the most important thing is winning. Similarly, in a trial, the most important thing is winning.

This argument is consistent with the worldview of many, if not most, lawyers. Lawyers are trained as advocates, and when they enter a courtroom they see themselves going into battle for their clients. In any battle, winning is the most important objective. But this viewpoint presupposes that truth and justice are either unattainable in the courtroom or of secondary importance. Thus, while many lawyers would evaluate this argument as nonfallacious, many nonlawyers would reject it as a weak analogy.

For another example, consider the following causal inference:

> After enslaving most of Eastern Europe for nearly fifty years, the evil Soviet empire finally collapsed. Obviously God listened to our prayers.

This argument reflects the worldview of many theists. It presupposes that there is a God, that God listens to prayers, that God is affected by prayers, that God has the power to influence the course of history, and that God does influence the course of history. While the theist is likely to consider this argument a good one, the atheist will reject it as a blatant case of false cause.

To avoid fallacies that arise from the influence of worldviews, the arguer must acknowledge and critique his or her presuppositions. Doing so inclines the arguer to couch his or her arguments in language that takes those presuppositions into account. The result is nearly always an argument that is more intelligently crafted, and, it is hoped, more persuasive. However, the task of recognizing and critiquing one's presuppositions is not easy. Presuppositions are intrinsically linked to one's worldview, and many people are not even aware that they have a worldview. The reason is that worldviews are formed through a process that is largely unconscious. Thus, the arguer must first recognize that he or she has a worldview and must then exercise constant vigilance over the presuppositions it comprises.

Even after one's presuppositions have been exposed and thoroughly critiqued, however, there is no guarantee that one's arguments will agree with the arguments of others who have critiqued their worldviews. This is because a person's worldview reflects the unique perspective that person has on the world. No two people share exactly the same perspective. Nevertheless, disclosing and critiquing the presuppositions in one's worldview lays a foundation for meaningful communication with other reasonable arguers, and it provides a context of reasonableness for working out disagreements.

In summary, the three factors that are probably responsible for most informal fallacies are intention, mental carelessness combined with emotional dispositions, and unexamined worldviews. However, these factors rarely occur in isolation. In the vast majority of cases, two, or all three, conspire to produce fallacious reasoning. This fact exacerbates the difficulty in avoiding informal fallacies in one's own arguments and in detecting fallacies in the arguments of others.

Now let us consider some cases of real-life arguments in light of the factors we have just discussed. All are taken from letters to the editors of newspapers and magazines. The first relates to affirmative action programs:

> I'm a nonracist, nonsexist, white male born in 1969, who has never owned a slave, treated anyone as inferior because of his or her race, or sexually harassed a female co-worker. In other words, I don't owe women or minorities a thing. Since when are people required to pay for the sins of their predecessors simply because they belong to the same race or gender.
>
> (Ben Gibbons)

The author of this argument presupposes that racist and sexist patterns in society have not benefitted him in any way. Among other things, he presupposes that his white ancestors in no way benefitted from their being white and that none of these benefits passed down to him. On the other hand, given that he has received such benefits, he may presuppose that he is not obligated to pay any of them back. Of course none of these things may have occurred, but the author should at least address these issues. Because he does not address them, the argument begs the question.

The next argument relates to second-hand smoke from cigarettes:

> Now, besides lung cancer and other nasty business, second-hand smoke causes deafness and impotence. Was second-hand smoke a problem when people heated their homes solely by fireplaces? How about those romantic teepees with the smoke hole at the top? And what about fireplaces in new homes? Let's have some research about the problems caused by these as well as barbecues. A little cancer with your hot dog, anyone?
>
> (Pat Sharp)

This argument seems to commit the fallacy of equivocation. The arguer begins by using "second-hand smoke" to refer to the smoke from burning tobacco, and then uses the term to refer to the smoke from fireplaces, teepee fires, and barbecues. Smoke from burning tobacco is clearly not the same thing as smoke from burning wood or charcoal. Alternately, the argument might be seen to beg the question: "But do people burn tobacco in their fireplaces and barbecues?" These fallacies probably arise either from the intentions of the author or from carelessness in failing to distinguish the two kinds of second-hand smoke. In either event, the author is probably hostile to government efforts to control second-hand tobacco smoke in confined areas.

The next argument deals with gun control:

> Detroit, the seventh largest city and one with strict gun laws, had 596 homicides last year. In the same year Phoenix, the ninth largest city and one that at the time did not require gun owners to be licensed, had 136 homicides. Criminals don't fear the toothless criminal-justice system, but they do fear armed citizens.
>
> (Paul M. Berardi)

This argument commits a false cause fallacy. The author presupposes that the availability of guns caused Phoenix to have a lower homicide rate than Detroit. The arguer also presupposes that Detroit and Phoenix are comparable as to homicide rate merely because they are roughly the same size. As a result, the argument involves a weak analogy and also begs the question. The additional factors of emotion and intent may also be present. The arguer probably hates the prospect of gun control, and he may be fully aware of the fact that Phoenix and Detroit are not comparable for his purpose, but he went ahead with the comparison anyway.

The next argument deals with religious fundamentalism:

> If we compromise God's word, we compromise the truth. To say that the fundamentalist is a loud shrill voice drowning out religious moderation implies that diluted truth is better than absolute truth.
>
> (Gerald Gleason)

This argument begs the question. The arguer presupposes that there is a God, that God has spoken, that God has revealed his intentions to fundamentalist preachers, and that those preachers accurately report the word of God. The argument also seems to reflect an emotional disposition in favor of religious fundamentalism.

The last argument we will consider relates to English as the official U.S. language:

> This great country has been held together for more than 200 years because of one simple thing: the English language.
> There are two things we must do: Make English the official language of the United States and do away with bilingual education.
>
> (David Moisan)

This argument misses the point. The arguer presupposes that making English the official language would guarantee that all citizens speak it and that doing away with bilingual education would accelerate the learning process of immigrant children. The argument may also reflect the fear that many feel in connection with the changes our society is experiencing as a result of recent immigration.

EXERCISE 3.5

iLrn I. Most of the following selections were taken from letters to the editors of newspapers and magazines. Identify any fallacies that may be committed, giving a brief explanation for your answer. Then, if a fallacy is identified, discuss the possible factors that led the arguer to commit the fallacy.

★1. Exporting cigarettes [to Asia] is good business for America; there is no reason we should be prohibited from doing so. Asians have been smoking for decades; we are only offering variety in their habit. If the Asians made tobacco smoking illegal, that would be a different situation. But as long as it is legal, the decision is up to the smokers. The Asians are just afraid of American supremacy in the tobacco industries.

(Pat Monohan)

2. When will these upper-crust intellectuals realize that the masses of working people are not in cozy, cushy, interesting, challenging, well-paying jobs, professions and businesses? My husband is now 51; for most of the last 33 years he has worked in the same factory job, and only the thought of retiring at 62 has sustained him. When he reaches that age in 11 years, who will tell him that his aging and physically wracked body must keep going another two years? My heart cries out for all the poor souls who man the assembly lines, ride the trucks or work in the fields or mines, or in the poorly ventilated, hot-in-summer, cold-in-winter factories and garages. Many cannot afford to retire at 62, 65, or even later. Never, never let them extend the retirement age. It's a matter of survival to so many.

(Isabel Fierman)

3. Women in military combat is insane. No society in its right mind would have such a policy. The military needs only young people and that means the only women who go are those in their child-bearing years. Kill them off and society will not be able to perpetuate itself.

(Jack Carman)

★4. Dear Ann: I've read that one aspirin taken every other day will reduce the risk of heart attack. Why not take two and double the protection?

(Boston)

5. The American Civil Liberties Union did a study that found that in the last 80 years it believes twenty-five innocent people have been executed in the United States. This is unfortunate. But, there are innocent people who die each year in highway accidents. Out of 40,000 deaths, how many deaths are related to driving while intoxicated? How many more thousands are injured and incur financial ruin or are invalids and handicapped for the remainder of their lives?

(Mahlon R. Braden)

6. Mexico's president expresses legitimate concern when he questions supplying oil to Americans who are unwilling to apply "discipline" in oil consumption. In view of the fact that his country's population is expected to double in only twenty-two years, isn't it legitimate for us to ask when Mexicans will apply the discipline necessary to control population growth and quit dumping their excess millions over our borders?

(Wayne R. Bartz)

★7. A parent would never give a ten-year-old the car keys, fix him or her a martini, or let him or her wander at night through a dangerous part of town. The same holds true of the Internet. Watch what children access, but leave the Net alone. Regulation is no substitute for responsibility.

(Bobby Dunning)

8. How would you feel to see your children starving and have all doors slammed in your face? Isn't it time that all of us who believe in freedom and human rights stop thinking in terms of color and national boundaries? We should open our arms and hearts to those less fortunate and remember that a time could come when we might be in a similar situation.

(Lorna Doyle)

9. A capital gains tax [reduction] benefits everyone, not just the "rich," because everyone will have more money to invest or spend in the private economy, resulting in more jobs and increasing prosperity for all. This is certainly better than paying high taxes to a corrupt, self-serving and incompetent government that squanders our earnings on wasteful and useless programs.

(David Miller)

★10. After reading "Homosexuals in the Churches," I'd like to point out that I don't know any serious, capable exegetes who stumble over Saint Paul's denunciation of homosexuality. Only a fool (and there seem to be more and more these days) can fail to understand the plain words of Romans, Chapter one. God did not make anyone "gay." Paul tells us in Romans 1 that homosexuals become that way because of their own lusts.

(LeRoy J. Hopper)

11. When will they ever learn—that the Republican Party is not for the people who voted for it?

(Alton L. Stafford)

12. Before I came to the United States in July, 1922, I was in Berlin where I visited the famous zoo. In one of the large cages were a lion and a tiger. Both respected each other's strength. It occurred to me that it was a good illustration of "balance of power." Each beast followed the other and watched each other's moves. When one moved, the other did. When one stopped, the other stopped.

In today's world, big powers or groups of powers are trying to maintain the status quo, trying to be as strong as or stronger than the other. They realize a conflict may result in mutual destruction. As long as the countries believe there is a balance of power we may hope for peace.

(Emilie Lackow)

★13. Doctors say the birth of a baby is a high point of being a doctor. Yet a medical survey shows one out of every nine obstetricians in America has stopped delivering babies.

Expectant mothers have had to find new doctors. In some rural areas, women have had to travel elsewhere to give birth.

How did this happen? It's part of the price of the lawsuit crisis.

The number of lawsuits Americans file each year is on the rise. Obstetricians are among the hardest hit—almost three out of four have faced a malpractice claim. Many have decided it isn't worth the risk.

(Magazine ad by the Insurance Information Institute)

14. The conservative diatribe found in campus journalism comes from the mouths of a handful of affluent brats who were spoon-fed through the '80s. Put them on an ethnically more diverse campus, rather than a Princeton or a Dartmouth, and then let us see how long their newspapers survive.

(David Simons)

15. I see that our courts are being asked to rule on the propriety of outlawing video games as a "waste of time and money."

It seems that we may be onto something here. A favorable ruling would open the door to new laws eliminating show business, spectator sports, cocktail lounges, the state of Nevada, public education and, of course, the entire federal bureaucracy.

(A. G. Dobrin)

★16. The death penalty is the punishment for murder. Just as we have long jail terms for armed robbery, assault and battery, fraud, contempt of court, fines for speeding, reckless driving and other numerous traffic violations, so must we have a punishment for murder. Yes, the death penalty will not deter murders any more than a speeding ticket will deter violating speed laws again, but it is the punishment for such violation!

(Lawrence J. Barstow)

17. Would you rather invest in our nation's children or Pentagon waste? The choice is yours.

(Political ad)

18. My gun has protected me, and my son's gun taught him safety and responsibility long before he got hold of a far more lethal weapon—the family car. Cigarettes kill many times more people yearly than guns and, unlike guns, have absolutely no redeeming qualities. If John Lennon had died a long, painful and expensive death from lung cancer, would you have devoted a page to a harangue against the product of some of your biggest advertisers—the cigarette companies?

(Silvia A. DeFreitas)

★19. If the advocates of prayers in public schools win on this issue, just where will it end? Perhaps next they will ask for prayers on public transportation? Prayers by government workers before they start their job each day? Or maybe, mandatory prayers in public restaurants before starting each meal might be a good idea.

(Leonard Mendelson)

20. So you want to ban smoking in all eating establishments? Well, you go right ahead and do that little thing. And when the 40 percent of smokers stop eating

out, the restaurants can do one of two things: close, or raise the price of a $20 dinner 40 percent to $28.

(Karen Sawyer)

21. Pigeons are forced to leave our city to battle for life. Their struggle is an endless search for food. What manner of person would watch these hungry creatures suffer from want of food and deny them their survival? These helpless birds are too often ignored by the people of our city, with not the least bit of compassion shown to them. Pigeons are God's creatures just as the so-called human race is. They need help.

(Leslie Ann Price)

★22. You take half of the American population every night and set them down in front of a box watching people getting stabbed, shot and blown away. And then you expect them to go out into the streets hugging each other?

(Mark Hustad)

23. So you think that putting the worst type of criminal out of his misery is wrong. How about the Americans who were sent to Korea, to Vietnam, to Beirut, to Central America? Thousands of good men were sacrificed supposedly for the good of our country. At the same time we were saving and protecting Charles Manson, Sirhan Sirhan [Robert Kennedy's murderer], and a whole raft of others too numerous to mention.

(George M. Purvis)

24. The fact is that the hype over "acid rain" and "global warming" is just that: hype. Take, for example, Stephen Schneider, author of *Global Warming*. In his current "study" he discusses a "greenhouse effect of catastrophic proportions," yet twenty years ago Schneider was a vocal proponent of the theory of a "new ice age."

(Urs Furrer)

★25. Just as our parents did for us, my husband and I rely solely on Christian Science for all the health needs of our four sons and find it invaluable for the quick cure of whatever ailments and contagions they are subject to. One particular healing that comes to mind happened several years ago when our youngest was a toddler. He had a flu-type illness that suddenly became quite serious. We called a Christian Science practitioner for treatment and he was completely well the next morning.

(Ellen Austin)

26. As somebody who has experienced the tragedy of miscarriage—or spontaneous abortion—at eight weeks, I greatly resent the position that a fetus is not a baby. I went through the grief of losing a baby, and no one should tell me otherwise.

(Ann Fons)

27. How can we pledge allegiance to the flag of the United States of America and not establish laws to punish people who burn the flag to make a statement? We

are a people who punish an individual who libels another person but will not seek redress from an individual who insults every citizen of this great country by desecrating the flag.

(William D. Lankford)

★28. The notion of "buying American" is as misguided as the notion of buying Wisconsin, or Oshkosh, Wisconsin, or South Oshkosh, Wisconsin. For the same reasons that Wisconsin increases its standard of living by trading with the rest of the nation, America increases its standard of living by trading with the rest of the world.

(Phillip Smith)

29. We've often heard the saying, "Far better to let 100 guilty men go free than to condemn one innocent man." What happens then if we apply the logic of this argument to the question, "Is a fetus an unborn human being?" Then is it not better to let 100 fetuses be born rather than to mistakenly kill one unborn human being? This line of reasoning is a strictly humanist argument against abortion.

(James Sebastian)

30. In our society it is generally considered improper for a man to sleep, shower, and dress amid a group of women to whom he normally would be sexually attracted. It seems to me, then, to be equally unacceptable that a gay man sleep, shower, and dress in a company of men to whom, we assume, he would be no less sexually attracted.

(Mark O. Temple)

★31. I say "bravo" and "right on!" Now we have some real-life humane heroes to look up to! These brave people [a group of animal liberators] went up against the insensitive bureaucratic technology, and won, saving former pet animals from senseless torture.

If researchers want to experiment, let them use computers, or themselves—but not former pet animals! I know it's bad enough they use monkeys and rats, but if those animals are bred knowing nothing else but these Frankensteins abusing them it's different (but not better) than dogs or cats that have been loved and petted all their lives to suddenly be tortured and mutilated in the name of science. End all animal research! Free all research animals!

Right on, animal liberators!

(Linda Magee)

32. Dear Ann: Recently I was shopping downtown in 20-below-zero weather. A stranger walked up to me and said, "I wonder how many beautiful rabbits died so you could have that coat?" I noticed she was wearing a down coat, so I asked if the geese they got the down from to make her coat were still alive. She looked surprised. Obviously she had never given it a thought.

If people are so upset about cruelty to animals, why don't they go after the folks who refuse to spend the money to have their pets neutered and spayed? Thousands of dogs are put to death every year because the animal pounds can't feed and house them. Talk about cruelty to animals—that's the best example there is.

("Baby It's Cold Outside")

33. I prayed for the U.S. Senate to defeat the prayer amendment—and it did. There is a God.

(Richard Carr)

★34. People of the Philippines, I have returned! The hour of your redemption is here! Rally to me! Let the indomitable spirit of Bataan and Corregidor lead on! As the lines of battle roll forward to bring you within the zone of operations, rise and strike! For future generations of your sons and daughters, strike! Let no heart be faint! Let every arm be steeled! The guidance of divine God points the way! Follow in his name to the Holy Grail of righteous victory!

(General Douglas MacArthur)

35. As the oldest of eleven children (all married), I'd like to point out our combined family numbers more than 100 who vote only for pro-life candidates. Pro-lifers have children, pro-choicers do not.

(Mrs. Kitty Reickenback)

36. I am 12 years old. My class had a discussion on whether police used unnecessary force when arresting the people from Operation Rescue.

My teacher is an ex-cop, and he demonstrated police holds to us. They don't hurt at all unless the person is struggling or trying to pull away. If anybody was hurt when they were arrested, then they must have been struggling with the officers trying to arrest them.

(Ben Torre-Bueno)

★37. As corporate farms continue to gobble up smaller family farms, they control a larger percentage of the grain and produce raised in the United States. Some have already reached a point in size where, if they should decide to withhold their grain and produce from the marketplace, spot shortages could occur and higher prices would result. The choice is to pay us family farmers now or pay the corporations later.

(Delwin Yost)

38. If you buy our airline ticket now you can save 60 percent, and that means 60 percent more vacation for you.

(Radio ad)

39. Why all the flap about atomic bombs? The potential for death is always with us. Of course, if you just want something to worry about, go ahead. Franklin D. Roosevelt said it: "The only thing we have to fear is fear itself."

(Lee Flemming Reese)

★40. September 17 marked the anniversary of the signing of the U.S. Constitution. How well have we, the people, protected our rights? Consider what has happened to our private-property rights.

"Property has divine rights, and the moment the idea is admitted into society that property is not as sacred as the laws of God, anarchy and tyranny begin." John Quincy Adams, 1767–1848, Sixth President of the United States.

Taxes and regulations are the two-edged sword which gravely threatens the fabric of our capitalistic republic. The tyranny of which Adams speaks is with us today in the form of government regulators and regulations which have all but destroyed the right to own property. Can anarchy be far behind?

(Timothy R. Binder)

41. Evolution would have been dealt serious setbacks if environmentalists had been around over the eons trying to save endangered species.

Species are endangered because they just do not fit the bigger picture any more as the world changes. That's not bad. It's just life.

In most cases we have seen the "endangered species" argument is just a ruse; much deeper motives usually exist, and they are almost always selfish and personal.

(Tom Gable)

42. The problem that I have with the pro-choice supporters' argument is that they make "choice" the ultimate issue. Let's face facts. No one has absolute freedom of choice sanctioned by the law. One can choose to rob a bank, but it's not lawful. Others can choose to kill their one-year-old child, but it is not legal. Why then should a woman have the legal right to take the life of her unborn child?

(Loretta S. Horn)

★43. If a car or truck kills a person, do politicians call for car control or truck control? And call in all cars/trucks?

If a child burns down a house do we have match control or child control and call in all of each?

Gun control and confiscation is equally as pathetic a thought process in an age of supposed intelligence.

(Pete Hawes)

44. I was incensed to read in your article about the return of anti-Semitism that New York City Moral Majority Leader Rev. Dan C. Fore actually said that "Jews have a God-given ability to make money, almost a supernatural ability . . ." I find it incredibly ironic that he and other Moral Majority types conveniently overlook the fact that they, too, pack away a pretty tidy sum themselves through their fund-raising efforts. It is sad that anti-Semitism exists, but to have this prejudice voiced by leaders of religious organizations is deplorable. These people are in for quite a surprise come Judgment Day.

(John R. Murks)

45. Are Americans so stupid they don't realize that every time they pay thousands of dollars for one of those new "economical" Japanese cars, they are simultaneously making the U.S. bankrupt and giving the Japanese enough money to buy all of America?

(Sylvia Petersen Young)

★46. Why are people so shocked that Susan Smith apparently chose to kill her children because they had become an inconvenience? Doesn't this occur every day in abortion clinics across the country? We suspect Smith heard very clearly the message many feminists have been trying to deliver about the expendable nature of our children.

(Kevin and Diana Cogan)

47. What's wrong with kids today? Answer: nothing, for the majority of them. They are great.

Witness the action of two San Diego teenage boys recently, when the Normal Heights fire was at its worst. They took a garden hose to the roof of a threatened house—a house belonging to four elderly sisters, people they didn't even know. They saved the house, while neighboring houses burned to the ground.

In the Baldwin Hills fire, two teenage girls rescued a blind, retired Navy man from sure death when they braved the flames to find him, confused, outside his burning house. He would probably have perished if they hadn't run a distance to rescue him.

(Theodore H. Wickham)

48. Now that Big Brother has decided that I must wear a seatbelt when I ride in a car, how long will it take before I have to wear an inner tube when I swim in my pool, a safety harness when I climb a ladder, and shoes with steel-reinforced toecaps when I carry out the garbage?

(G. R. Turgeon)

★49. Dear Ann: I was disappointed in your response to the girl whose mother used the strap on her. The gym teacher noticed the bruises on her legs and backside and called it "child abuse." Why are you against strapping a child when the Bible tells us in plain language that this is what parents should do?

The Book of Proverbs mentions many times that the rod must be used. Proverbs 23:13 says: "Withhold not correction from the child for if thou beatest him with the rod he shall not die." Proverbs 23:14 says: "Thou shalt beat him with the rod and shalt deliver his soul from death."

There is no substitute for a good whipping. I have seen the results of trying to reason with kids. They are arrogant, disrespectful and mouthy. Parents may wish for a more "humane" way, but there is none. Beating children is God's way of getting parents to gain control over their children.

(Davisville, W. Va.)

50. The Fourth Amendment guarantees our right to freedom from unreasonable search and seizure. It does not prohibit *reasonable* search and seizure. The matter of sobriety roadblocks to stop drunk drivers boils down to this: Are such roadblocks reasonable or unreasonable? The majority of people answer: "Reasonable." Therefore, sobriety roadblocks should not be considered to be unconstitutional.

(Haskell Collier)

51. The Supreme Court recently ruled that a police department in Florida did not violate any rights of privacy when a police helicopter flew over the back yard of a suspected drug dealer and noticed marijuana growing on his property. Many people, including groups like the Anti-Common Logic Union, felt that the suspect's right to privacy outweighed the police department's need to protect the public at large.

 The simple idea of sacrificing a right to serve a greater good should be allowed in certain cases. In this particular case the danger to the public wasn't extremely large; marijuana is probably less dangerous than regular beer. But anything could have been in that back yard—a load of cocaine, an illegal stockpile of weapons, or other major threats to society.

(Matt Cookson)

★52. I am 79 and have been smoking for 60 years. My husband is 90 and has inhaled my smoke for some 50 years with no bad effects.

 I see no reason to take further steps to isolate smokers in our restaurants and public places, other than we now observe.

 Smokers have taken punishment enough from neurotic sniffers, some of whom belong in bubbles. There are plenty of injudicious fumes on our streets and freeways.

(Helen Gans)

53. The mainstream press finds itself left behind by talk radio, so they try to minimize its importance. Americans are finding the true spirit of democracy in community and national debate. Why should we be told what to believe by a news weekly or the nightly news when we can follow public debate as it unfolds on talk radio?

(Adam Abbott)

54. The issue is not whether we should subsidize the arts, but whether anyone should be able to force someone else to subsidize the arts. You and I are free to *give* any amount of our money to any artistic endeavor we wish to support. When the government gets involved, however, a group of bureaucrats is given the power to *take* our money and give it to the arts they wish to support. We are not consulted. That is not a way to promote a responsible culture. That is tyranny.

(Jerry Harben)

★55. Who are these Supreme Court justices who have the guts to OK the burning of our flag?

 If the wife or daughter of these so-called justices were raped, could the rapist be exonerated because he took the First Amendment? That he was just expressing himself? How about murder in the same situation?

(Robert A. Lewis)

56. I have one question for those bleeding hearts who say we should not have used the atomic bomb: If the nation responsible for the Rape of Nanking, the

Manchurian atrocities, Pearl Harbor and the Bataan Death March had invented the bomb first, don't you think they would have used it? So do I.

(Bill Blair)

57. Since when did military service become a right, for gays or anyone else? The military has always been allowed to discriminate against people who don't meet its requirements, including those who are overweight or too tall or too short. There is an adequate supply of personnel with the characteristics they need. And there is no national need for gays in the military.

(William R. Cnossen)

★58. There is something very wrong about the custom of tipping. When we go to a store, we don't decide what a product is worth and pay what we please; we pay the price or we leave. Prices in coffee bars and restaurants should be raised, waiters should be paid a decent wage, and the words "no tipping" should be clearly visible on menus and at counters.

(George Jochnowitz)

59. Most Americans do not favor gun control. They know that their well-being depends on their own ability to protect themselves. So-called "assault rifles" are used in few crimes. They are not the weapon of choice of criminals, but they are for people trying to protect themselves from government troops.

(Larry Herron)

60. Holding a gun, a thief robs John Q. Public of thousands of dollars. Holding a baby, an unmarried mother robs taxpayers of thousands of dollars. If one behavior is considered a crime, then so should the other.

(Louis R. Ward)

II. Turn to the editorial pages of a newspaper or the letters column of a magazine and find an instance of a fallacious argument in the editorials or letters to the editor. Identify the premises and conclusion of the argument and write an analysis at least one paragraph in length identifying the fallacy or fallacies committed and the factors that may have led the arguer to commit them.

Summary

A fallacy is a mistake in an argument that arises from something other than merely false premises. Usually fallacies involve defects in reasoning or the creation of an illusion that makes a bad argument appear good. Fallacies can be either formal or informal. A formal fallacy is one that can be detected by analyzing the form of an argument; such fallacies affect only deductive arguments. An informal fallacy is one that can be identified only by analyzing the content of an argument; such fallacies can affect both deductive and inductive arguments.

The fallacies of relevance occur when the premises of an argument are not relevant to the conclusion. Cases of such irrelevance occur in premises that threaten the observer, elicit pity from the observer, create a mob mentality in a group of observers, appeal to the observer's desire for security, verbally abuse an opposing arguer, present an opposing arguer as predisposed to argue as he does, present an opposing arguer as a hypocrite, misapply a general rule, distort an opponent's argument, or lead the observer off the track. A kind of catch-all fallacy, missing the point, occurs when an arguer draws a conclusion different from the one implied by the premises.

The fallacies of weak induction occur when the premises, although possibly relevant to the conclusion, provide insufficient support for the conclusion. Cases of such inadequate support occur when the arguer cites an authority who is not qualified, draws a conclusion from premises that give no positive evidence, draws a conclusion from an atypical sample, depends on a nonexistent or minor causal connection, depends on a chain reaction that is unlikely to occur, or draws a conclusion from an analogy that is not close enough to support it.

The fallacies of presumption occur when the premises presume what they purport to prove. Such presumptions occur when the arguer creates the illusion that inadequate premises are adequate, asks a question that comprises two or more questions, uses a disjunctive statement that falsely claims to exhaust the available alternatives, or ignores important evidence that requires a different conclusion.

The fallacies of ambiguity occur when the conclusion depends on some form of linguistic ambiguity. Either a word or phrase is used in more than one sense or the wrong interpretation is given to an ambiguous statement.

The fallacies of grammatical analogy occur when a defective argument appears good owing to a grammatical similarity to some argument that is not fallacious. Such grammatical similarities occur in arguments that wrongly transfer an attribute from parts to a whole or from a whole to its parts.

Fallacies that occur in real-life argumentation are harder to detect than those in manufactured examples because they may not exactly fit the structure of the named fallacies and because several fallacies can be woven together in a single passage. Three factors that underlie the commission of fallacies in real-life argumentation are the intent of the arguer, mental carelessness combined with unchecked emotions, and unexamined presuppositions in the arguer's worldview.

4 Categorical Propositions

4.1 The Components of Categorical Propositions

In Chapter 1 we saw that a proposition (or statement—here we are ignoring the distinction) is a sentence that is either true or false. A proposition that relates two classes, or categories, is called a **categorical proposition**. The classes in question are denoted respectively by the **subject term** and the **predicate term**, and the proposition asserts that either all or part of the class denoted by the subject term is included in or excluded from the class denoted by the predicate term. Here are some examples of categorical propositions:

Atkins dieters avoid carbohydrates.
Snowmobiles do not belong in Yellowstone National Park.
Many of today's cell phones contain cameras.
Not all romances have a happy ending.
Michael Moore shoots documentaries.

The first statement asserts that the entire class of Atkins dieters is included in the class of things that avoid carbohydrates, the second that the entire class of snowmobiles is excluded from the class of things that belong in Yellowstone National Park, and the third that part of the class of today's cell phones is included in the class of things that contain cameras. The fourth statement asserts that part of the class of romances is excluded from the class of things that have a happy ending, and the last statement asserts that the class that has Michael Moore as its single member is included in the class of persons who shoot documentaries.

Since any categorical proposition asserts that either all or part of the class denoted by the subject term is included in or excluded from the class denoted by the predicate term, it follows that there are exactly four types of categorical propositions: (1) those that assert that the whole subject class is included in the predicate class, (2) those that assert that part of the subject class is included in the predicate class, (3) those that assert that the whole subject class is excluded from the predicate class, and (4) those that assert that part of the subject class is excluded from the predicate class. A categorical proposition that expresses these relations with complete clarity is one that is in stan-

dard form. A categorical proposition is in standard form if and only if it is a substitution instance of one of the following four forms:

> All S are P.
> No S are P.
> Some S are P.
> Some S are not P.

Many categorical propositions, of course, are not in standard form because, among other things, they do not begin with the words "all," "no," or "some." In the final section of this chapter we will develop techniques for translating categorical propositions into standard form, but for now we may restrict our attention to those that are already in standard form.

The words "all," "no," and "some" are called **quantifiers** because they specify how much of the subject class is included in or excluded from the predicate class. The first form above asserts that the whole subject class is included in the predicate class, the second that the whole subject class is excluded from the predicate class, and so on. (Incidentally, in formal deductive logic the word "some" always means at least one.) The letters "S" and "P" stand respectively for the subject and predicate terms, and the words "are" and "are not" are called the **copula** because they link (or "couple") the subject term with the predicate term.

Consider the following example:

> All members of the American Medical Association are persons holding degrees from recognized academic institutions.

This standard-form categorical proposition is analyzed as follows:

quantifier:	all
subject term:	members of the American Medical Association
copula:	are
predicate term:	persons holding degrees from recognized academic institutions

In resolving standard-form categorical propositions into their four components, one must keep these components separate. They do not overlap each other. In this regard it should be noted that "subject term" and "predicate term" do not mean the same thing in logic that "subject" and "predicate" mean in grammar. The *subject* of the above statement includes the quantifier "all," but the *subject term* does not. Similarly, the *predicate* includes the copula "are," but the *predicate term* does not.

Two additional points should be noted about standard-form categorical propositions. The first is that the form "All S are not P" is *not* a standard form. This form is ambiguous and can be rendered as either "No S are P" or "Some S are not P," depending on the content. The second point is that there are exactly three forms of quantifiers and two forms of copulas. Other texts allow the various forms of the verb "to be" (such as "is," "is not," "will," and "will not") to serve as the copula. For the sake of uniformity, this book restricts the copula to "are" and "are not." The last section of this chapter describes techniques for translating these alternate forms into the two accepted ones.

The theory of categorical propositions was originated by Aristotle, and it has constituted one of the core topics in logic for over 2,000 years. It remains important even today because many of the statements we make in ordinary discourse are either categorical propositions as they stand or are readily translatable into them. Standard-form categorical propositions represent an ideal of clarity in language, and a familiarity with the relationships that prevail among them provides a backdrop of precision for all kinds of linguistic usage. In Chapter 5 we will see how categorical propositions may be combined to produce *categorical syllogisms*, a kind of argumentation that is closely related to the most basic forms of human reasoning.

EXERCISE 4.1

iLrn In the following categorical propositions identify the quantifier, subject term, copula, and predicate term.

★1. Some airport screeners are officials who harass frail grandmothers.

2. No persons who live near airports are persons who appreciate the noise of jets.

3. All oil-based paints are products that contribute significantly to photochemical smog.

★4. Some preachers who are intolerant of others' beliefs are not television evangelists.

5. All trials in which a coerced confession is read to the jury are trials in which a guilty verdict can be reversed.

6. Some artificial hearts are mechanisms that are prone to failure.

★7. No sex education courses that are taught competently are programs that are currently eroding public morals.

8. Some universities that emphasize research are not institutions that neglect undergraduate education.

4.2 Quality, Quantity, and Distribution

Quality and quantity are attributes of categorical propositions. In order to see how these attributes pertain, it is useful to rephrase the meaning of categorical propositions in class terminology:

Proposition	Meaning in class notation
All *S* are *P*.	Every member of the *S* class is a member of the *P* class; that is, the *S* class is included in the *P* class.
No *S* are *P*.	No member of the *S* class is a member of the *P* class; that is, the *S* class is excluded from the *P* class.
Some *S* are *P*.	At least one member of the *S* class is a member of the *P* class.
Some *S* are not *P*.	At least one member of the *S* class is not a member of the *P* class.

The **quality** of a categorical proposition is either affirmative or negative depending on whether it affirms or denies class membership. Accordingly, "All *S* are *P*" and "Some *S* are *P*" have **affirmative** quality, and "No *S* are *P*" and "Some *S* are not *P*" have **negative** quality.

The **quantity** of a categorical proposition is either universal or particular depending on whether the statement makes a claim about *every* member or just *some* member of the class denoted by the subject term. "All *S* are *P*" and "No *S* are *P*" each assert something about every member of the S class and thus are **universal.** "Some S are P" and "Some S are not P" assert something about one or more members of the S class and hence are **particular.**

Note that the quantity of a categorical proposition may be determined through mere inspection of the quantifier. "All" and "no" immediately imply universal quantity, while "some" implies particular. But categorical propositions have no "qualifier." In universal propositions the quality is determined by the quantifier, and in particular propositions it is determined by the copula.

It should also be noted that particular propositions mean no more and no less than the meaning assigned to them in class notation. The statement "Some S are P" does *not* imply that some S are not P, and the statement "Some S are not P" does *not* imply that some S are P. It often *happens*, of course, that substitution instances of these statement forms are both true. For example, "Some apples are red" is true, as is "Some apples are not red." But the fact that one is true does not *necessitate* that the other be true. "Some zebras are animals" is true (because at least one zebra is an animal), but "Some zebras are not animals" is false. Similarly, "Some turkeys are not fish" is true, but "Some turkeys are fish" is false. Thus, the fact that one of these statement forms is true does not *logically imply* that the other is true, as these substitution instances clearly prove.

Since the early Middle Ages the four kinds of categorical propositions have commonly been designated by letter names corresponding to the first four vowels of the Roman alphabet: **A, E, I, O.** The universal affirmative is called an **A** proposition, the universal negative an **E** proposition, the particular affirmative an **I** proposition, and the particular negative an **O** proposition. Tradition has it that these letters were derived from the first two vowels in the Latin words *affirmo* ("I affirm") and *nego* ("I deny"), thus:

		n
Universal	A	E
	f	
	f	g
Particular	I	O
	r	
	m	
	o	

The material presented thus far in this section may be summarized as follows:

Proposition	Letter name	Quantity	Quality
All S are P.	**A**	universal	affirmative
No S are P.	**E**	universal	negative
Some S are P.	**I**	particular	affirmative
Some S are not P.	**O**	particular	negative

Unlike quality and quantity, which are attributes of *propositions*, **distribution** is an attribute of the *terms* (subject and predicate) of propositions. A term is said to be distributed if the proposition makes an assertion about every member of the class denoted by the term; otherwise, it is undistributed. Stated another way, a term is distributed if and only if the statement assigns (or distributes) an attribute to every member of the class denoted by the term. Thus, if a statement asserts something about every member of the S class, then S is distributed; if it asserts something about every member of the P class, then P is distributed; otherwise S and P are undistributed.

Let us imagine that the members of the classes denoted by the subject and predicate terms of a categorical proposition are contained respectively in circles marked with the letters "S" and "P." The meaning of the statement form "All S are P" may then be represented by the following diagram:

The S circle is contained in the P circle, which represents the fact that every member of S is a member of P. (Of course, should S and P represent terms denoting identical classes, the two circles would overlap exactly.) Through reference to the diagram, it is clear that "All S are P" makes a claim about every member of the S class, since the statement says that every member of S is in the P class. But the statement does not make a claim about every member of the P class, since there may be some members of P that are outside of S. Thus, by the definition of "distributed term" given above, S is distributed and P is not. In other words, for any universal affirmative (**A**) proposition, the subject term, whatever it may be, is distributed, and the predicate term is undistributed.

Let us now consider the universal negative (**E**) proposition. "No S are P" states that the S and P classes are separate, which may be represented as follows:

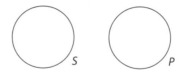

This statement makes a claim about every member of S and every member of P. It asserts that every member of S is separate from every member of P, and also that every member of P is separate from every member of S. Accordingly, by the definition above, both the subject and predicate terms of universal negative (**E**) propositions are distributed.

The particular affirmative (**I**) proposition states that at least one member of S is a member of P. If we represent this one member of S that we are certain about by an asterisk, the resulting diagram looks like this:

Since the asterisk is inside the *P* class, it represents something that is simultaneously an *S* and a *P*; in other words, it represents a member of the *S* class that is also a member of the *P* class. Thus, the statement "Some *S* are *P*" makes a claim about one member (at least) of *S* and also one member (at least) of *P*, but not about all members of either class. Hence, by the definition of distribution, neither *S* nor *P* is distributed.

The particular negative (**O**) proposition asserts that at least one member of *S* is not a member of *P*. If we once again represent this one member of *S* by an asterisk, the resulting diagram is as follows:

Since the other members of *S* may or may not be outside of *P*, it is clear that the statement "Some *S* are not *P*" does not make a claim about every member of *S*, so *S* is not distributed. But, as may be seen from the diagram, the statement does assert that every member of *P* is separate and distinct from this one member of *S* that is outside the *P* circle. Thus, in the particular negative (**O**) proposition, *P* is distributed and *S* is undistributed.

At this point the notion of distribution may be somewhat vague and elusive. Unfortunately, there is no simple and easy way to make the idea graphically clear. The best that can be done is to repeat some of the things that have already been said. First of all, distribution is an attribute or quality that the subject and predicate terms of a categorical proposition may or may not possess, depending on the kind of proposition. If the proposition in question is an **A** type, then the subject term, whatever it may be, is distributed. If it is an **E** type, then both terms are distributed; if an **I** type, then neither; and if an **O** type, then the predicate. If a certain term is *distributed* in a proposition, this simply means that the proposition says something about every member of the class that the term denotes. If a term is *undistributed*, the proposition does not say something about every member of the class.

An easy way to remember the rule for distribution is to keep in mind that universal (**A** and **E**) statements distribute their subject terms and negative (**E** and **O**) statements distribute their predicate terms. As an aid to remembering this arrangement, the following mnemonic may be useful: "Unprepared Students Never Pass." Attending to the first letter in these words may help one recall that Universals distribute Subjects, and Negatives distribute Predicates. Another mnemonic that accomplishes the same purpose is "Any Student Earning B's Is Not On Probation." In this mnemonic the first letters may help one recall that **A** statements distribute the Subject, **E** statements distribute Both terms, **I** statements distribute Neither term, and **O** statements distribute the Predicate.

Finally, we note that the attribute of distribution, while not particularly important to subsequent developments in this chapter, is essential to the evaluation of syllogisms in the next chapter.

The material of this section may now be summarized as follows:

Proposition	Letter name	Quantity	Quality	Terms distributed
All S are P.	A	universal	affirmative	S
No S are P.	E	universal	negative	S and P
Some S are P.	I	particular	affirmative	none
Some S are not P.	O	particular	negative	P

EXERCISE 4.2

iLrn I. For each of the following categorical propositions identify the letter name, quantity, and quality. Then state whether the subject and predicate terms are distributed or undistributed.

★1. No butterfly ballots are trustworthy election tools.

2. All governments that bargain with terrorists are governments that encourage terrorism.

3. Some symphony orchestras are organizations on the brink of bankruptcy.

★4. Some Chinese leaders are not thoroughgoing opponents of capitalist economics.

5. All human contacts with benzene are potential causes of cancer.

6. No labor strikes are events welcomed by management.

★7. Some hospitals are organizations that overcharge the Medicare program.

8. Some affirmative action plans are not programs that result in reverse discrimination.

iLrn II. Change the quality but not the quantity of the following statements:

★1. All drunk drivers are threats to others on the highway.

2. No wildlife refuges are locations suitable for condominium developments.

3. Some slumlords are persons who eventually wind up in jail.

★4. Some CIA operatives are not champions of human rights.

III. Change the quantity but not the quality of the following statements:

★1. All owners of pit bull terriers are persons who can expect expensive lawsuits.

2. No tax proposals that favor the rich are fair proposals.

3. Some grade school administrators are persons who choke the educational process.

★4. Some residents of Manhattan are not people who can afford to live there.

iLrn IV. Change both the quality and the quantity of the following statements:

★1. All oil spills are events catastrophic to the environment.

2. No alcoholics are persons with a healthy diet.

3. Some Mexican vacations are episodes that end with gastrointestinal distress.

★4. Some corporate lawyers are not persons with a social conscience.

4.3   Venn Diagrams and the Modern Square of Opposition

Aristotle and Boole

Before we can address the two main topics of this section, we must say a few words about the meaning of universal (**A** and **E**) propositions. Consider these two **A** propositions:

All Henry's students are achievers.

All unicorns are one-horned animals.

The first proposition suggests that Henry does indeed have some students. In other words, the statement appears to have existential import. It suggests that one or more things denoted by the subject term actually exist. On the other hand, no such suggestion is made by the statement about unicorns. The statement is true, because unicorns, by definition, have a single horn. But the statement does not seem to suggest that unicorns actually exist.

    Thus, the question arises, Should universal propositions be interpreted as implying that the things talked about actually exist? Or should they be interpreted as implying no such thing? In response to this question, logicians have taken two different approaches. Aristotle held that universal propositions about existing things have existential import. In other words, such statements imply the existence of the things talked about:

Aristotelian Standpoint

All pheasants are birds.   Implies the existence of pheasants.

No pine trees are maples.   Implies the existence of pine trees.

All satyrs are vile creatures.   Does not imply the existence of satyrs.

The first two statements have existential import because their subject terms denote actually existing things. The third statement has no existential import because satyrs do not exist.

    On the other hand, the nineteenth-century logician George Boole held that no universal propositions have existential import. Such statements never imply the existence of the things talked about:

Boolean Standpoint

All trucks are vehicles.	Does not imply the existence of trucks.
No roses are daisies.	Does not imply the existence of roses.
All werewolves are monsters.	Does not imply the existence of werewolves.

We might summarize these results by saying that the Aristotelian standpoint is "open" to existence. When things exist, the Aristotelian standpoint recognizes that existence, and universal statements about those things have existential import. In other words, existence counts for something from the Aristotelian standpoint. On the other hand, the Boolean standpoint is "closed" to existence. When things exist, the Boolean statement does not recognize that existence, and universal statements about those things have no existential import.

The Aristotelian standpoint differs from the Boolean standpoint only with regard to universal (**A** and **E**) propositions. The two standpoints are identical with regard to particular (**I** and **O**) propositions. Both the Aristotelian and the Boolean standpoints recognize that particular propositions make a positive assertion about existence. For example, from both standpoints, the statement "Some cats are animals" asserts that at least one cat exists, and that cat is an animal. Also, from both standpoints, "Some fish are not mammals" asserts that at least one fish exists, and that fish is not a mammal. Thus, from both standpoints, the word "some" implies existence.*

Adopting either the Aristotelian or the Boolean standpoint amounts to accepting a set of ground rules for interpreting the meaning of universal propositions. Either standpoint can be adopted for any categorical proposition or any argument composed of categorical propositions. Taking the Aristotelian standpoint amounts to recognizing that universal statements about existing things convey evidence about existence. Conversely, for a statement to convey such evidence, the Aristotelian standpoint must be taken and the subject of the statement must denote actually existing things. Taking the Boolean standpoint, on the other hand, amounts to ignoring any evidence about existence that universal statements might convey.

Because the Boolean standpoint is neutral about existence, it is simpler than the Aristotelian standpoint, which recognizes existential implications. For this reason, we will direct our attention first to arguments considered from the Boolean standpoint. Later, in Section 4.5, we will extend our treatment to the Aristotelian standpoint.

Venn Diagrams

From the Boolean standpoint, the four kinds of categorical propositions have the following meaning. Notice that the first two (universal) propositions imply nothing about the existence of the things denoted by *S*:

---

*In ordinary language, the word "some" occasionally implies something less than actual existence. For example, the statement "Some unicorns are tender-hearted" does not seem to suggest that unicorns actually exist, but merely that among the group of imaginary things called "unicorns," there is a subclass of tender-hearted ones. In the vast majority of cases, however, "some" in ordinary language implies existence. The logical "some" conforms to these latter uses.

All *S* are *P*. = No members of *S* are outside *P*.
No *S* are *P*. = No members of *S* are inside *P*.
Some *S* are *P*. = At least one *S* exists, and that *S* is a *P*.
Some *S* are not *P*. = At least one *S* exists, and that *S* is not a *P*.

Adopting this interpretation of categorical propositions, the nineteenth-century logician John Venn developed a system of diagrams to represent the information they express. These diagrams have come to be known as **Venn diagrams.**

A Venn diagram is an arrangement of overlapping circles in which each circle represents the class denoted by a term in a categorical proposition. Because every categorical proposition has exactly two terms, the Venn diagram for a single categorical proposition consists of two overlapping circles. Each circle is labeled so that it represents one of the terms in the proposition. Unless otherwise required, we adopt the convention that the left-hand circle represents the subject term, and the right-hand circle the predicate term. Such a diagram looks like this:

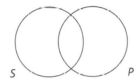

The members of the class denoted by each term should be thought of as situated inside the corresponding circle. Thus, the members of the *S* class (if any such members exist) are situated inside the *S* circle, and the members of the *P* class (if any such members exist) are situated inside the *P* circle. If any members are situated inside the area where the two circles overlap, then such members belong to both the *S* class and the *P* class. Finally, if any members are situated outside both circles, they are members of neither *S* nor *P*.

Suppose, for example, that the *S* class is the class of Americans and the *P* class is the class of farmers. Then, if we use numerals to identify the four possible areas, the diagram looks like this:

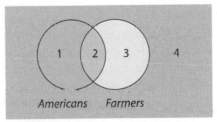

Anything in the area marked "1" is an American but not a farmer, anything in the area marked "2" is both an American and a farmer, and anything in the area marked "3" is a farmer but not an American. The area marked "4" is the area outside both circles; thus, anything in this area is neither a farmer nor an American.

We can now use Venn diagrams to represent the information expressed by the four kinds of categorical proposition. To do this we make a certain kind of mark in a diagram.

Two kinds of marks are used: shading an area and placing an X in an area. Shading an area means that the shaded area is empty,* and placing an X in an area means that at least one thing exists in that area. The X may be thought of as representing that one thing. If no mark appears in an area, this means that nothing is known about that area; it may contain members or it may be empty. Shading is always used to represent the content of universal (**A** and **E**) propositions, and placing an X in an area is always used to represent the content of particular (**I** and **O**) propositions. The content of the four kinds of categorical propositions is represented as follows:

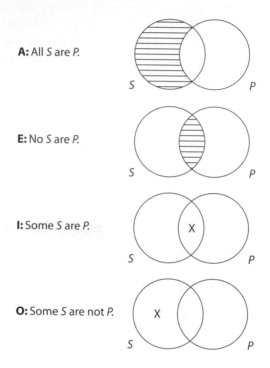

A: All *S* are *P*.

E: No *S* are *P*.

I: Some *S* are *P*.

O: Some *S* are not *P*.

Recall that the **A** proposition asserts that no members of *S* are outside *P*. This is represented by shading the part of the *S* circle that lies outside the *P* circle. The **E** proposition asserts that no members of *S* are inside *P*. This is represented by shading the part of the *S* circle that lies inside the *P* circle. The **I** proposition asserts that at least one *S* exists and that *S* is also a *P*. This is represented by placing an X in the area where the *S* and *P* circles overlap. This X represents an existing thing that is both an *S* and a *P*. Finally, the **O** proposition asserts that at least one *S* exists, and that *S* is not a *P*. This is represented by placing an X in the part of the *S* circle that lies outside the *P* circle. This X represents an existing thing that is an *S* but not a *P*.

Because there is no X in the diagrams that represent the universal propositions, these diagrams say nothing about existence. For example, the diagram for the **A** proposition merely asserts that nothing exists in the part of the *S* circle that lies outside the *P*

---

*In many mathematics texts, shading an area of a Venn diagram indicates that the area is *not* empty. The significance of shading in logic is exactly the opposite.

circle. The area where the two circles overlap and the part of the *P* circle that lies outside the *S* circle contain no marks at all. This means that something might exist in these areas, or they might be completely empty. Similarly, in the diagram for the **E** proposition, no marks appear in the left-hand part of the *S* circle and the right-hand part of the *P* circle. This means that these two areas might contain something or, on the other hand, they might not.

The Modern Square of Opposition

Let us compare the diagram for the **A** proposition with the diagram for the **O** proposition. The diagram for the **A** proposition asserts that the left-hand part of the *S* circle is empty, whereas the diagram for the **O** proposition asserts that this same area is not empty. These two diagrams make assertions that are the exact opposite of each other. As a result, their corresponding statements are said to contradict each other. Analogously, the diagram for the **E** proposition asserts that the area where the two circles overlap is empty, whereas the diagram for the **I** proposition asserts that the area where the two circles overlap is not empty. Accordingly, their corresponding propositions are also said to contradict each other. This relationship of mutually contradictory pairs of propositions is represented in a diagram called the **modern square of opposition.** This diagram, which arises from the modern (or Boolean) interpretation of categorical propositions, is represented as follows:

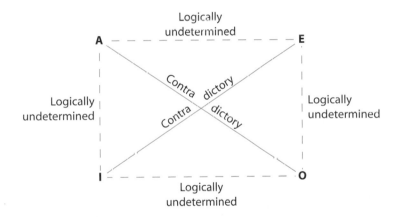

If two propositions are related by the **contradictory relation,** they necessarily have opposite truth value. Thus, if a certain **A** proposition is given as true, the corresponding **O** proposition must be false. Similarly, if a certain **I** proposition is given as false, the corresponding **E** proposition must be true. But no other inferences are possible. In particular, given the truth value of an **A** or **O** proposition, nothing can be determined about the truth value of the corresponding **E** or **I** propositions. These propositions are said to have **logically undetermined** truth value. Like all propositions, they do have a truth value, but logic alone cannot determine what it is. Similarly, given the truth value of an **E** or **I** proposition, nothing can be determined about the truth value of the corresponding **A** or **O** propositions. They, too, are said to have logically undetermined truth value.

Testing Immediate Inferences

Since the modern square of opposition provides logically necessary results, we can use it to test certain arguments for validity. We begin by assuming the premise is true, and we enter the pertinent truth value in the square. We then use the square to compute the truth value of the conclusion. If the square indicates that the conclusion is true, the argument is valid; if not, the argument is invalid. Here is an example:

> Some trade spies are not masters at bribery.
> Therefore, it is false that all trade spies are masters at bribery.

Arguments of this sort are called **immediate inferences** because they have only one premise. Instead of reasoning from one premise to the next, and then to the conclusion, we proceed immediately to the conclusion. To test this argument for validity, we begin by assuming that the premise, which is an **O** proposition, is true, and we enter this truth value in the square of opposition. We then use the square to compute the truth value of the corresponding **A** proposition. By the contradictory relation, the **A** proposition is false. Since the conclusion claims that the **A** proposition is false, the conclusion is true, and therefore the argument is valid. Arguments that are valid from the Boolean standpoint are said to be **unconditionally valid** because they are valid regardless of whether their terms refer to existing things.

Note that the conclusion of this argument has the form "It is false that all S are P." Technically, statements of this type are not standard-form propositions because, among other things, they do not begin with a quantifier. To remedy this difficulty we adopt the convention that statements having this form are equivalent to " 'All S are P' is false." Analogous remarks apply to the negations of the **E**, **I**, and **O** statements.

Here is another example:

> It is false that all meteor showers are common spectacles.
> Therefore, no meteor showers are common spectacles.

We begin by assuming that the premise is true. Since the premise claims that an **A** proposition is false, we enter "false" into the square of opposition. We then use the square to compute the truth value of the corresponding **E** proposition. Since there is no relation that links the **A** and **E** propositions, the **E** proposition has undetermined truth value. Thus, the conclusion of the argument has undetermined truth value, and the argument is invalid.

We can also use Venn diagrams to test immediate inferences for validity. To do so we begin by using letters to represent the terms, and we then draw Venn diagrams for the premise and conclusion. If the information expressed by the conclusion diagram is contained in the premise diagram, the argument is valid; if not, it is invalid. Here is the symbolized form of the trade spies argument that we tested earlier.

> Some T are not M.
> Therefore, it is false that all T are M.

The next step is to draw two Venn diagrams, one for the premise and the other for the conclusion. The premise diagram is easy; all we need do is place an X in the left-hand part of the T circle. But drawing the conclusion is a bit more complicated. First we consider how we would diagram "All T are M." We would shade the left-hand part of the *T* circle. But since the conclusion asserts that "All *T* are *M*" is *false,* we do just the opposite: we place an *X* in the left-hand part of the *T* circle. Here are the completed diagrams:

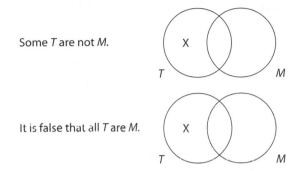

Some *T* are not *M.*

It is false that all *T* are *M.*

Now, to evaluate the argument, we look to see whether the information expressed by the conclusion diagram is also expressed by the premise diagram. The conclusion diagram asserts that something exists in the left-hand part of the *T* circle. Since this information is also expressed by the premise diagram, the argument is valid. In this case, the diagram for the conclusion is identical to the diagram for the premise, so it is clear that premise and conclusion assert exactly the same thing. However, as we will see in Section 4.5, for an argument to be valid, it is not necessary that premise and conclusion assert exactly the same thing. It is only necessary that the premise assert *at least as much* as the conclusion.

Here is the symbolized version of the second argument evaluated earlier:

It is false that all *M* are *C.*
Therefore, no *M* are *C.*

In diagramming the premise, we do just the opposite of what we would do to diagram "All *M* are *C.*" Instead of shading the left-hand part of the *M* circle, we place an X in that area. For the conclusion we shade the area where the two circles overlap:

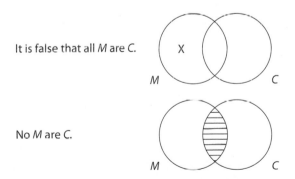

It is false that all *M* are *C.*

No *M* are *C.*

Here, the conclusion diagram asserts that the overlap area is empty. Since this information is not contained in the premise diagram, the argument is invalid.

We conclude with a special example:

All cell phones are wireless devices.
Therefore, some cell phones are wireless devices.

The completed Venn diagrams are as follows:

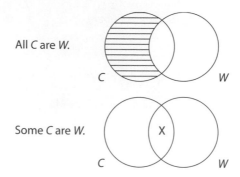

All C are W.

C   W

Some C are W.

C   W

The information of the conclusion diagram is not contained in the premise diagram, so the argument is invalid. However, if the premise were interpreted as having existential import, then the *C* circle in the premise diagram would not be empty. Specifically, there would be members in the overlap area. This would make the argument valid.

Arguments of this sort are said to commit the existential fallacy. From the Boolean standpoint, the **existential fallacy** is a formal fallacy that is committed whenever an argument is invalid merely because the premise is interpreted as lacking existential import. In Section 4.5, additional forms of this fallacy will be explored. For now, we can identify two forms of the fallacy that arise from the Boolean standpoint:

Existential fallacy

All *A* are *B*.
Therefore, some *A* are *B*.

No *A* are *B*.
Therefore, some *A* are not *B*.

EXERCISE 4.3

I. Draw Venn diagrams for the following propositions.

★1. No life decisions are happenings based solely on logic.

2. All electric motors are machines that depend on magnetism.

3. Some political campaigns are mere attempts to discredit opponents.

★4. Some rock music lovers are not fans of Madonna.

5. All redistricting plans are sources of controversy.

6. No tax audits are pleasant experiences for cheaters.

★7. Some housing developments are complexes that exclude children.

8. Some cruise ships are not steam-driven vessels.

iLrn II. Use the modern square of opposition to determine whether the following immediate inferences are valid or invalid from the Boolean standpoint.

★1. No sculptures by Rodin are boring creations.
Therefore, all sculptures by Rodin are boring creations.

2. It is false that some lunar craters are volcanic formations.
Therefore, no lunar craters are volcanic formations.

3. All trial lawyers are persons with stressful jobs.
Therefore, some trial lawyers are persons with stressful jobs.

★4. All dry martinis are dangerous concoctions.
Therefore, it is false that some dry martinis are not dangerous concoctions.

5. It is false that no jazz musicians are natives of New Orleans.
Therefore, some jazz musicians are not natives of New Orleans.

6. Some country doctors are altruistic healers.
Therefore, some country doctors are not altruistic healers.

★7. No fertility drugs are solutions to every problem.
Therefore, it is false that all fertility drugs are solutions to every problem.

8. It is false that no credit cards are things that contain holograms.
Therefore, some credit cards are things that contain holograms.

9. It is false that some stunt pilots are not colorful daredevils.
Therefore, it is false that some stunt pilots are colorful daredevils.

★10. No vampires are avid connoisseurs of garlic bread.
Therefore, it is false that some vampires are avid connoisseurs of garlic bread.

11. No talk radio shows are accurate sources of information.
Therefore, some talk radio shows are not accurate sources of information.

12. Some stellar constellations are spiral-shaped objects.
Therefore, no stellar constellations are spiral-shaped objects.

★13. It is false that some soap bubbles are not occasions of glee.
Therefore, some soap bubbles are occasions of glee.

14. It is false that all weddings are light-hearted celebrations.
Therefore, some weddings are not light-hearted celebrations.

15. It is false that some chocolate soufflés are desserts containing olives.
Therefore, it is false that all chocolate soufflés are desserts containing olives.

iLrn III. Use Venn diagrams to evaluate the immediate inferences in Part II of this exercise. Identify any that commit the existential fallacy.

4.4   Conversion, Obversion, and Contraposition

For a preliminary glimpse into the content of this section, consider the statement "No dogs are cats." This statement claims that the class of dogs is separated from the class of cats. But the statement "No cats are dogs" claims the same thing. Thus, the two statements have the same meaning and the same truth value. For another example, consider the statement "Some dogs are not retrievers." This statement claims there is at least one dog outside the class of retrievers. But the statement "Some dogs are non-retrievers" claims the same thing, so again, the two statements have the same meaning and the same truth value.

Conversion, obversion, and contraposition are operations that can be performed on a categorical proposition, resulting in a new statement that may or may not have the same meaning and truth value as the original statement. Venn diagrams are used to determine how the two statements relate to each other.

Conversion

The simplest of the three operations is **conversion,** and it consists in switching the subject term with the predicate term. For example, if the statement "No foxes are hedgehogs" is converted, the resulting statement is "No hedgehogs are foxes." This new statement is called the converse of the given statement. To see how the four types of categorical propositions relate to their converse, compare the following sets of Venn diagrams:

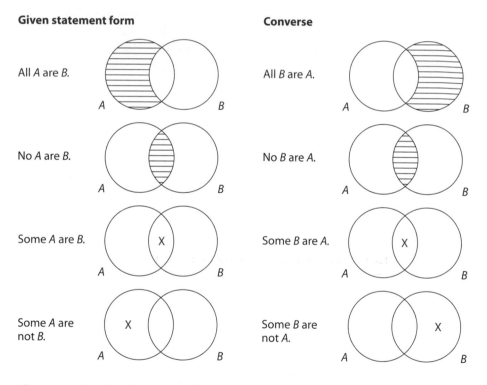

Given statement form

All *A* are *B*.

No *A* are *B*.

Some *A* are *B*.

Some *A* are not *B*.

Converse

All *B* are *A*.

No *B* are *A*.

Some *B* are *A*.

Some *B* are not *A*.

If we examine the diagram for the **E** statement, we see that it is identical to that of its converse. Also, the diagram for the **I** statement is identical to that of its converse. This means that the **E** statement and its converse are logically equivalent, and the **I** statement and its converse are logically equivalent. Two statements are said to be **logically equivalent** when they necessarily have the same truth value. Thus, converting an **E** or **I** statement gives a new statement that always has the same truth value (and the same meaning) as the given statement. These equivalences are strictly proved by the Venn diagrams for the **E** and **I** statements.

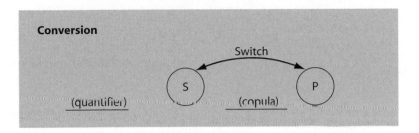

On the other hand, the diagram for the **A** statement is clearly not identical to the diagram for its converse, and the diagram for the **O** statement is not identical to the diagram for its converse. Also, these pairs of diagrams are not the exact opposite of each other, as is the case with contradictory statements. This means that an **A** statement and its converse are logically unrelated as to truth value, and an **O** statement and its converse are logically unrelated as to truth value. In other words, converting an **A** or **O** statement gives a new statement whose truth value is logically undetermined in relation to the given statement. The converse of an **A** or **O** statement does have a truth value, of course, but logic alone cannot tell us what it is.

Because conversion yields necessarily determined results for **E** and **I** statements, it can be used as the basis for immediate inferences having these types of statements as premises. The following argument forms are valid:

No *A* are *B*.
Therefore, no *B* are *A*.

Some *A* are *B*.
Therefore, some *B* are *A*.

Since the conclusion of each argument form necessarily has the same truth value as the premise, if the premise is assumed true, it follows necessarily that the conclusion is true. On the other hand, the next two argument forms are invalid. Each commits the fallacy of **illicit conversion:**

All *A* are *B*.
Therefore, all *B* are *A*.

Some *A* are not *B*.
Therefore, some *B* are not *A*.

Two examples of arguments that commit the fallacy of illicit conversion are:

All cats are animals.   (True)
Therefore, all animals are cats.   (False)

Some animals are not dogs.   (True)
Therefore, some dogs are not animals.   (False)

Obversion

Obversion is more complicated than conversion, and it requires two steps: (1) changing the quality (without changing the quantity), and (2) replacing the predicate with its term complement. The first part of this operation was treated in Exercise 4.2. It consists in changing "No *S* are *P*" to "All *S* are *P*" and vice versa, and changing "Some *S* are *P*" to "Some *S* are not *P*" and vice versa.

The second step requires understanding the concept of *class complement*. The complement of a class is the group consisting of everything outside the class. For example, the complement of the class of dogs is the group that includes everything that is not a dog (cats, fish, trees, and so on). Now the **term complement** is the word or group of words that denotes the class complement. For terms consisting of a single word, the term complement is usually formed by simply attaching the prefix "non" to the term. Thus, the complement of the term "dog" is "non-dog," the complement of the term "book" is "non-book," and so on.

The relationship between a term and its complement can be illustrated by a Venn diagram. For example, if a single circle is allowed to represent the class of dogs, then everything outside the circle represents the class of non-dogs:

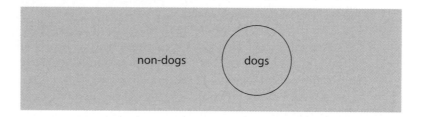

We now have everything we need to form the obverse of categorical propositions. First we change the quality (without changing the quantity), and then we replace the predicate term with its term complement. For example, if we are given the statement "All horses are animals," then the obverse is "No horses are non-animals"; and if we are given the statement "Some trees are maples," then the obverse is "Some trees are not non-maples." To see how the four types of categorical propositions relate to their obverse, compare the following sets of Venn diagrams:

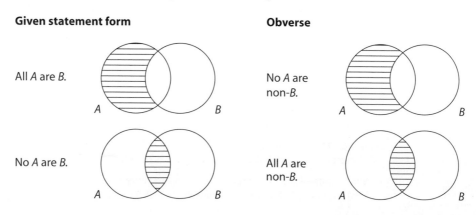

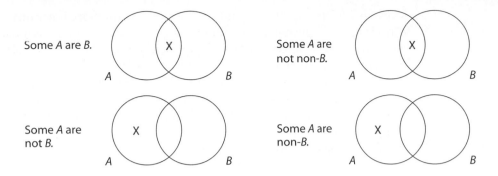

Some *A* are *B*.

Some *A* are not non-*B*.

Some *A* are not *B*.

Some *A* are non-*B*.

To see how the obverse diagrams are drawn, keep in mind that "non-*B*" designates the area outside the *B* circle. Thus, "No *A* are non-*B*" asserts that the area where *A* overlaps non-*B* is empty. This is represented by shading the left-hand part of the *A* circle. "All *A* are non-*B*" asserts that all members of *A* are outside *B*. This means that no members of *A* are inside *B*, so the area where *A* overlaps *B* is shaded. "Some *A* are not non-*B*" asserts that at least one member of *A* is not outside *B*. This means that at least one member of *A* is inside *B*, so an X is placed in the area where *A* and *B* overlap. Finally, "Some *A* are non-*B*" asserts that at least one member of *A* is outside *B*, so an X is placed in the left-hand part of the *A* circle.

Now if we examine these pairs of diagrams, we see that the diagram for each given statement form is identical to the diagram for its obverse. This means that each of the four types of categorical proposition is logically equivalent to (and has the same meaning as) its obverse. Thus, if we obvert an **A** statement that happens to be true, the resulting statement will be true; if we obvert an **O** statement that happens to be false, the resulting statement will be false, and so on.

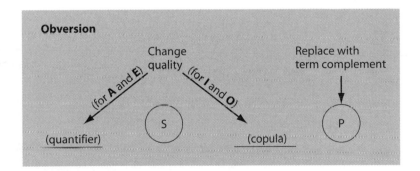

Obversion

Change quality

(for **A** and **E**)

(for **I** and **O**)

Replace with term complement

(quantifier)

S

(copula)

P

It is easy to see that if a statement is obverted and then obverted again, the resulting statement will be identical to the original statement. For example, the obverse of "All horses are animals" is "No horses are non-animals." To obvert the latter statement we again change the quality ("no" switches to "all") and replace "non-animals" with its term complement. The term complement is produced by simply deleting the prefix "non." Thus, the obverse of the obverse is "All horses are animals."

When a term consists of more than a single word, more ingenuity is required to form its term complement. For example, if we are given the term "animals that are not native to America," it would not be appropriate to form the term complement by writing "non-animals that are not native to America." Clearly it would be better to write "animals native to America." Even though this is technically not the complement of the given term, the procedure is justified if we allow a reduction in the scope of discourse. This can be seen as follows. Technically the term complement of "animals that are not native to America" denotes all kinds of things such as ripe tomatoes, battleships, gold rings, and so on. But if we suppose that we are talking *only* about animals (that is, we reduce the scope of discourse to animals), then the complement of this term is "animals native to America."

As is the case with conversion, obversion can be used to supply the link between the premise and the conclusion of immediate inferences. The following argument forms are valid:

All *A* are *B*.
Therefore, no *A* are non-*B*.

Some *A* are *B*.
Therefore, some *A* are not non-*B*.

No *A* are *B*.
Therefore, all *A* are non-*B*.

Some *A* are not *B*.
Therefore, some *A* are non-*B*.

Because the conclusion of each argument form necessarily has the same truth value as its premise, if the premise is assumed true, it follows necessarily that the conclusion is true.

Contraposition

Like obversion, **contraposition** requires two steps: (1) switching the subject and predicate terms and (2) replacing the subject and predicate terms with their term complements. For example, if the statement "All goats are animals" is contraposed, the resulting

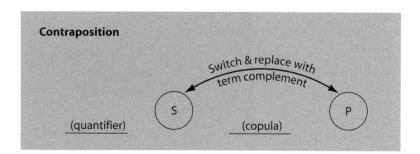

statement is "All non-animals are non-goats." This new statement is called the contrapositive of the given statement. To see how all four types of categorical propositions relate to their contrapositive, compare the following sets of diagrams:

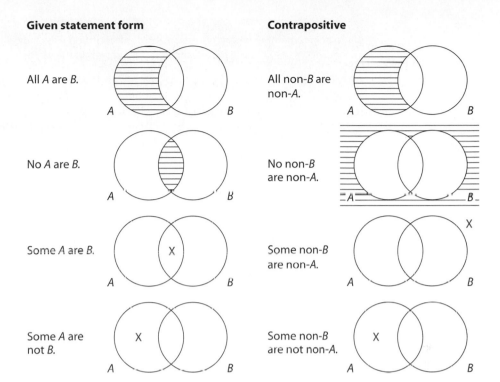

Given statement form		Contrapositive	
All *A* are *B*.		All non-*B* are non-*A*.	
No *A* are *B*.		No non-*B* are non-*A*.	
Some *A* are *B*.		Some non-*B* are non-*A*.	
Some *A* are not *B*.		Some non-*B* are not non-*A*.	

To see how the first diagram on the right is drawn, remember that "non-*A*" designates the area outside *A*. Thus, "All non-*B* are non-*A*" asserts that all members of non-*B* are outside *A*. This means that no members of non-*B* are inside *A*. Thus, we shade the area where non-*B* overlaps *A*. "No non-*B* are non-*A*" asserts that the area where non-*B* overlaps non-*A* is empty. Since non-*B* is the area outside the *B* circle and non-*A* is the area outside the *A* circle, the place where these two areas overlap is the area outside both circles. Thus, we shade this area. "Some non-*B* are non-*A*" asserts that something exists in the area where non-*B* overlaps non-*A*. Again, this is the area outside both circles, so we place an X in this area. Finally, "Some non-*B* are not non-*A*" asserts that at least one member of non-*B* is outside non-*A*. This means that at least one member of non-*B* is inside *A*, so we place an X in the area where non-*B* overlaps *A*.

Now, inspection of the diagrams for the **A** and **O** statements reveals that they are identical to the diagrams of their contrapositive. Thus, the **A** statement and its contrapositive are logically equivalent (and have the same meaning), and the **O** statement and its contrapositive are logically equivalent (and have the same meaning). On the other hand, the diagrams of the **E** and **I** statements are neither identical to nor the exact opposite of the diagrams of their contrapositives. This means that contraposing an **E** or **I** statement gives a new statement whose truth value is logically undetermined in relation to the given statement.

To help remember when conversion and contraposition yield logically equivalent results, note the second and third vowels in the words:

C O N V E R S I O N

C O N T R A P O S I T I O N

As with conversion and obversion, contraposition may provide the link between the premise and the conclusion of an argument. The following argument forms are valid:

All *A* are *B*.
Therefore, all non-*B* are non-*A*.

Some *A* are not *B*.
Therefore, some non-*B* are not non-*A*.

On the other hand, the following argument forms are invalid. Each commits the fallacy of **illicit contraposition:**

Some *A* are *B*.
Therefore, some non-*B* are non-*A*.

No *A* are *B*.
Therefore, no non-*B* are non-*A*.

Two examples of arguments that commit the fallacy of illicit contraposition are:

No dogs are cats.   (True)
Therefore, no non-cats are non-dogs.   (False)

Some animals are non-cats.   (True)
Therefore, some cats are non-animals.   (False)

In regard to the first argument, an example of something that is both a non-cat and a non-dog is a pig. Thus, the conclusion implies that no pigs are pigs, which is false. In regard to the second argument, if both premise and conclusion are obverted, the premise becomes "Some animals are not cats," which is true, and the conclusion becomes "Some cats are not animals," which is false.

Both illicit conversion and illicit contraposition are formal fallacies: they can be detected through mere examination of the form of an argument.

Finally, it should be noted that the Boolean interpretation of categorical propositions has prevailed throughout this section. This means that the results obtained are unconditional, and they hold true regardless of whether the terms in the propositions denote actually existing things. Thus, they hold for propositions about unicorns and leprechauns just as they do for propositions about dogs and animals. These results are summarized in the following table.

Conversion: Switch subject and predicate terms.

Given statement	Converse	Truth value
E: No *S* are *P.*	No *P* are *S.*	Same truth value as given statement
I: Some *S* are *P.*	Some *P* are *S.*	
A: All *S* are *P.*	All *P* are *S.*	Undetermined truth value
O: Some *S* are not *P.*	Some *P* are not *S.*	

Obversion: Change quality, replace predicate with term complement.

Given statement	Obverse	Truth value
A: All *S* are *P.*	No *S* are non-*P.*	Same truth value as given statement
E: No *S* are *P.*	All *S* are non-*P.*	
I: Some *S* are *P.*	Some *S* are not non-*P.*	
O: Some *S* are not *P.*	Some *S* are non-*P.*	

Contraposition: Switch subject and predicate terms, and replace each with its term complement.

Given statement	Contrapositive	Truth value
A: All *S* are *P.*	All non-*P* are non-*S.*	Same truth value as given statement
O: Some *S* are not *P.*	Some non-*P* are not non-*S.*	
E: No *S* are *P.*	No non-*P* are non-*S.*	Undetermined truth value
I: Some *S* are *P.*	Some non-*P* are non-*S.*	

EXERCISE 4.4

iLrn I. Exercises 1 through 6 provide a statement, its truth value in parentheses, and an operation to be performed on that statement. Supply the new statement and the truth value of the new statement. Exercises 7 through 12 provide a statement, its truth value in parentheses, and a new statement. Determine how the new statement was derived from the given statement and supply the truth value of the new statement.

Given statement	Operation	New statement	Truth value
★1. No *A* are non-*B.* (T)	conv.	_____	_____
2. Some *A* are *B.* (T)	contrap.	_____	_____
3. All *A* are non-*B.* (F)	obv.	_____	_____
★4. All non-*A* are *B.* (F)	contrap.	_____	_____
5. Some non-*A* are not *B.* (T)	conv.	_____	_____
6. Some non-*A* are non-*B.* (T)	obv.	_____	_____
★7. No non-*A* are non-*B.* (F)	_____	No *B* are *A.*	_____
8. Some *A* are not non-*B.* (T)	_____	Some *A* are *B.*	_____
9. All *A* are non-*B.* (F)	_____	All non-*B* are *A.*	_____
★10. No non-*A* are *B.* (F)	_____	All non-*A* are non-*B.*	_____
11. Some non-*A* are not *B.* (T)	_____	Some non-*B* are not *A.*	_____
12. Some *A* are non-*B.* (F)	_____	Some non-*B* are *A.*	_____

iLrn II. Perform the operations of conversion, obversion, and contraposition as indicated.

1. Convert the following propositions and state whether the converse is logically equivalent or not logically equivalent to the given proposition.

   ★a. All hurricanes are storms intensified by global warming.

   b. No sex-change operations are completely successful procedures.

   c. Some murals by Diego Rivera are works that celebrate the revolutionary spirit.

   d. Some forms of carbon are not substances with a crystalline structure.

2. Obvert the following propositions and state whether the obverse is logically equivalent or not logically equivalent to the given proposition.

   ★a. All radically egalitarian societies are societies that do not preserve individual liberties.

   b. No cult leaders are people who fail to brainwash their followers.

   c. Some college football coaches are persons who do not slip money to their players.

   d. Some budgetary cutbacks are not actions fair to the poor.

3. Contrapose the following propositions and state whether the contrapositive is logically equivalent or not logically equivalent to the given proposition.

   ★a. All physicians whose licenses have been revoked are physicians ineligible to practice.

   b. No unpersecuted migrants are migrants granted asylum.

   c. Some politicians who do not defend Social Security are politicans who do not want to increase taxes.

   d. Some opponents of gay marriage are not opponents of civil unions.

III. Use conversion, obversion, and contraposition to determine whether the following arguments are valid or invalid. For those that are invalid, name the fallacy committed.

★1. All commodity traders are gamblers who risk sudden disaster.
   Therefore, all gamblers who risk sudden disaster are commodity traders.

2. No child abusers are persons who belong in day-care centers.
   Therefore, all child abusers are persons who do not belong in day-care centers.

3. Some states having limited powers are not slave states.
   Therefore, some free states are not states having unlimited powers.

★4. Some insane people are illogical people.
   Therefore, some logical people are sane people.

5. Some organ transplants are not sensible operations.
   Therefore, some organ transplants are senseless operations.

6. No individuals who laugh all the time are persons with a true sense of humor.
   Therefore, no persons with a true sense of humor are individuals who laugh all the time.

★7. All periods when interest rates are high are times when businesses tend not to expand.

Therefore, all times when businesses tend to expand are periods when interest rates are low.

8. Some swimsuits are not garments intended for the water.

Therefore, some garments intended for the water are not swimsuits.

9. No promises made under duress are enforceable contracts.

Therefore, no unenforceable contracts are promises made in the absence of duress.

★10. All ladies of the night are individuals with low self-esteem.

Therefore, no ladies of the night are individuals with high self-esteem.

11. Some graffiti writers are artists relieving pent-up frustrations.

Therefore, some artists relieving pent-up frustrations are graffiti writers.

12. Some peaceful revolutions are episodes that erupt in violence.

Therefore, some episodes that do not erupt in violence are nonpeaceful revolutions.

★13. Some insurance companies are not humanitarian organizations.

Therefore, some humanitarian organizations are not insurance companies.

14. Some fire-breathing dragons are lizards that languish in soggy climates.

Therefore, some fire-breathing dragons are not lizards that flourish in soggy climates.

15. All hired killers are criminals who deserve the death penalty.

Therefore, all criminals who deserve the death penalty are hired killers.

★16. No nonprescription drugs are medicines without adverse effects.

Therefore, no medicines with adverse effects are prescription drugs.

17. All fossil fuels are unrenewable energy sources.

Therefore, no fossil fuels are renewable energy sources.

18. Some distant galaxies are not spiral-shaped arrangements.

Therefore, some spiral-shaped arrangements are not distant galaxies.

★19. All unpleasant experiences are things we do not like to remember.

Therefore, all things we like to remember are pleasant experiences.

20. Some pro-lifers are not people concerned with child welfare.

Therefore, some pro-lifers are people unconcerned with child welfare.

4.5

The Traditional Square of Opposition

In Section 4.3 we adopted the Boolean standpoint, and we saw how the modern square of opposition applies regardless of whether the propositions refer to actually existing things. In this section, we adopt the Aristotelian standpoint, which recognizes that universal propositions about existing things have existential import. For such propositions the traditional square of opposition becomes applicable. Like the modern square, the **traditional square of opposition** is an arrangement of lines that illustrates logically necessary relations among the four kinds of categorical propositions. However, because the Aristotelian standpoint recognizes the additional factor of existential import, the traditional square supports more inferences than does the modern square. It is represented as follows:

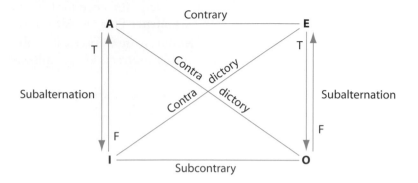

The four relations in the traditional square of opposition may be characterized as follows:

Contradictory = opposite truth value
Contrary = at least one is false (not both true)
Subcontrary = at least one is true (not both false)
Subalternation = truth flows downward, falsity flows upward

The **contradictory** relation is the same as that found in the modern square. Thus, if a certain **A** proposition is given as true, the corresponding **O** proposition is false, and vice versa, and if a certain **A** proposition is given as false, the corresponding **O** proposition is true, and vice versa. The same relation holds between the **E** and **I** propositions. The contradictory relation thus expresses complete opposition between propositions.

The **contrary** relation differs from the contradictory in that it expresses only partial opposition. Thus, if a certain **A** proposition is given as true, the corresponding **E** proposition is false (because at least one must be false), and if an **E** proposition is given as true, the corresponding **A** proposition is false. But if an **A** proposition is given as false, the corresponding **E** proposition could be *either* true or false without violating the "at least one is false" rule. In this case, the **E** proposition has logically undetermined truth value. Similarly, if an **E** proposition is given as false, the corresponding **A** proposition has logically undetermined truth value.

These results are borne out in ordinary language. Thus, if we are given the actually true **A** proposition "All cats are animals," the corresponding **E** proposition "No cats are animals" is false, and if we are given the actually true **E** proposition "No cats are dogs," the corresponding **A** proposition "All cats are dogs" is false. Thus, the **A** and **E** propositions cannot both be true. However, they can both be false. "All animals are cats" and "No animals are cats" are both false.

The **subcontrary** relation also expresses a kind of partial opposition. If a certain **I** proposition is given as false, the corresponding **O** proposition is true (because at least one must be true), and if an **O** proposition is given as false, the corresponding **I** proposition is true. But if either an **I** or an **O** proposition is given as true, then the corresponding proposition could be either true or false without violating the "at least one is true" rule. Thus, in this case the corresponding proposition would have logically undetermined truth value.

Again, these results are borne out in ordinary language. If we are given the actually false **I** proposition "Some cats are dogs," the corresponding **O** proposition "Some cats are not dogs" is true, and if we are given the actually false **O** proposition "Some cats are not animals," the corresponding **I** proposition "Some cats are animals" is true. Thus, the **I** and **O** propositions cannot both be false, but they can both be true. "Some animals are cats" and "Some animals are not cats" are both true.

The **subalternation** relation is represented by two arrows: a downward arrow marked with the letter "T" (true), and an upward arrow marked with an "F" (false). These arrows can be thought of as pipelines through which truth values "flow." The downward arrow "transmits" only truth, and the upward arrow only falsity. Thus, if an **A** proposition is given as true, the corresponding **I** proposition is true also, and if an **I** proposition is given as false, the corresponding **A** proposition is false. But if an **A** proposition is given as false, this truth value cannot be transmitted downward, so the corresponding **I** proposition will have logically undetermined truth value. Conversely, if an **I** proposition is given as true, this truth value cannot be transmitted upward, so the corresponding **A** proposition will have logically undetermined truth value. Analogous reasoning prevails for the subalternation relation between the **E** and **O** propositions. To remember the direction of the arrows for subalternation, imagine that truth descends from "above," and falsity rises up from "below."

Now that we have explained these four relations individually, let us see how they can be used together to determine the truth values of corresponding propositions. The first rule of thumb that we should keep in mind when using the square to compute more than one truth value is always to use contradiction first. Now, let us suppose that we are told that the nonsensical proposition "All adlers are bobkins" is true. Suppose further that adlers actually exist, so we are justified in using the traditional square of opposition. By the contradictory relation, "Some adlers are not bobkins" is false. Then, by either the contrary or the subalternation relation, "No adlers are bobkins" is false. Finally, by either contradictory, subalternation, or subcontrary, "Some adlers are bobkins" is true.

Next, let us see what happens if we assume that "All adlers are bobkins" is false. By the contradictory relation, "Some adlers are not bobkins" is true, but nothing more can be determined. In other words, given a false **A** proposition, both contrary and subalternation yield undetermined results, and given a true **O** proposition (the one whose truth value we just determined), subcontrary and subalternation yield undetermined results. Thus, the corresponding **E** and **I** propositions have logically undetermined truth value. This result illustrates two more rules of thumb. Assuming that we always use the contradictory relation first, if one of the remaining relations yields a logically undetermined truth value, the others will as well. The other rule is that whenever one statement turns out to have logically undetermined truth value, its contradictory will also. Thus, statements having logically undetermined truth value will always occur in pairs, at opposite ends of diagonals on the square.

Testing Immediate Inferences

Next, let us see how we can use the traditional square of opposition to test immediate inferences for validity. Here is an example:

> All Swiss watches are true works of art.
> Therefore, it is false that no Swiss watches are true works of art.

To evaluate this argument, we begin, as usual, by assuming the premise is true. Since the premise is an **A** proposition, by the contrary relation the corresponding **E** proposition is false. But this is exactly what the conclusion says, so the argument is valid.

Here is another example:

> Some viruses are structures that attack T-cells.
> Therefore, some viruses are not structures that attack T-cells.

Here the premise and conclusion are linked by the subcontrary relation. According to that relation, if the premise is assumed true, the conclusion has logically undetermined truth value, and so the argument is invalid. It commits the formal fallacy of **illicit subcontrary.** Analogously, arguments that depend on an incorrect application of the contrary relation commit the formal fallacy of **illicit contrary,** and arguments that depend on an illicit application of subalternation commit the formal fallacy of **illicit subalternation.** Some forms of these fallacies are as follows:

Illicit contrary

It is false that all *A* are *B*.
Therefore, no *A* are *B*.

It is false that no *A* are *B*.
Therefore, all *A* are *B*.

Illicit subcontrary

Some *A* are *B*.
Therefore, it is false that some *A* are not *B*.

Some *A* are not *B*.
Therefore, some *A* are *B*.

Illicit subalternation

Some *A* are not *B*.
Therefore, no *A* are *B*.

It is false that all *A* are *B*.
Therefore, it is false that some *A* are *B*.

Cases of the incorrect application of the contradictory relation are so infrequent that an "illicit contradictory" fallacy is not usually recognized.

As we saw at the beginning of this section, for the traditional square of opposition to apply, the Aristotelian standpoint must be adopted, and the propositions to which it is applied must assert something about actually existing things. The question may now be asked, What happens when the Aristotelian standpoint is adopted but the propositions are about things that do not exist? The answer is that another fallacy, the **existential fallacy,** is committed. From the Aristotelian standpoint the existential fallacy is committed whenever contrary, subcontrary, and subalternation are used (in an otherwise correct way) with propositions about things that do not exist. The existential fallacy occurs only in connection with these three relations. It does not occur in connection with the contradictory relation, which holds in the same way with nonexisting things as it does with existing things. The following inferences commit the existential fallacy:

> All witches who fly on broomsticks are fearless women.
> Therefore, some witches who fly on broomsticks are fearless women.
>
> No wizards with magical powers are malevolent beings.
> Therefore, it is false that all wizards with magical powers are malevolent beings.

The first depends on an otherwise correct use of the subalternation relation, and the second on an otherwise correct use of the contrary relation. If flying witches and magical wizards actually existed, both arguments would be valid. But since they do not exist, both arguments are invalid and commit the existential fallacy.

In summary, the existential fallacy can be committed in either of two ways. As we saw in Section 4.3, from the Boolean standpoint, the existential fallacy is committed whenever an argument is invalid merely because the premise is interpreted as lacking existential import. Thus, the argument "All cats are animals; therefore, some cats are animals" commits the existential fallacy from the Boolean standpoint. On the other hand, from the Aristotelian standpoint, the existential fallacy is committed whenever the validity of an argument depends on existential import and the requisite things do not exist. Thus, the argument "All unicorns are animals; therefore, some unicorns are animals" commits the existential fallacy from the Aristotelian standpoint. Any argument that commits the existential fallacy from the Aristotelian standpoint also commits it from the Boolean standpoint, but the converse obviously is not true.

Existential fallacy examples — Two standpoints

All cats are animals.
Some cats are animals. } Boolean: Invalid, existential fallacy
                           Aristotelian: Valid

All unicorns are animals.
Some unicorns are animals. } Boolean: Invalid, existential fallacy
                              Aristotelian: Invalid, existential fallacy

---

The phrase **conditionally valid** applies to an argument after the Aristotelian standpoint has been adopted and we are not certain if the subject term of the premise denotes actually existing things. For example, the following argument is conditionally valid:

> All students who failed the exam are students on probation.
> Therefore, some students who failed the exam are students on probation.

The validity of this argument rests on whether there were in fact any students who failed the exam. The argument is either valid or invalid, but we lack sufficient information about the meaning of the premise to tell which is the case. Once it becomes known that there are indeed some students who failed the exam, we can assert that the argument is valid from the Aristotelian standpoint. But if there are no students who failed the exam, the argument is invalid because it commits the existential fallacy.

Similarly, all argument *forms* that depend on valid applications of contrary, subcontrary, and subalternation are conditionally valid because we do not know if the letters in the propositions denote actually existing things. For example, the following argument form, which depends on the contrary relation, is conditionally valid:

All *A* are *B*.
Therefore, it is false that no *A* are *B*.

If "dogs" and "animals" are substituted in place of *A* and *B*, respectively, the resulting argument is valid. But if "unicorns" and "animals" are substituted, the resulting argument is invalid because it commits the existential fallacy. In Section 4.3, we noted that all arguments (and argument forms) that are valid from the Boolean standpoint are **unconditionally valid.** They are valid regardless of whether their terms denote actually existing things.

Now that we have seen how the traditional square of opposition, by itself, is used to test arguments for validity, let us see how it can be used together with the operations of conversion, obversion, and contraposition to prove the validity of arguments that are given as valid. Suppose we are given the following valid argument:

All inappropriate remarks are faux pas.
Therefore, some faux pas are not appropriate remarks.

To prove this argument valid, we select letters to represent the terms, and then we use some combination of conversion, obversion, and contraposition together with the traditional square to find the intermediate links between premise and conclusion:

All non-*A* are *F*.	(assumed true)
Some non-*A* are *F*.	(true by subalternation)
Some *F* are non-*A*.	(true by conversion)
Therefore, some *F* are not *A*.	(true by obversion)

The premise is the first line in this proof, and each succeeding step is validly derived from the one preceding it by the relation written in parentheses at the right. Since the conclusion (which is the last step) follows by a series of three necessary inferences, the argument is valid.

Various strategies can be used to construct proofs such as this, but one useful procedure is to concentrate first on obtaining the individual terms as they appear in the conclusion, then attend to the order of the terms, and finally use the square of opposition to adjust quality and quantity. As the above proof illustrates, however, variations on this procedure are sometimes necessary. The fact that the predicate of the conclusion is "*A*," while "non-*A*" appears in the premise, leads us to think of obversion. But using obversion to change "non-*A*" into "*A*" requires that the "non-*A*" in the premise be moved into the predicate position via conversion. The latter operation, however, is valid only on **E** and **I** statements, and the premise is an **A** statement. The fact that the conclusion is a particular statement suggests subalternation as an intermediate step, thus yielding an **I** statement that can be converted.

iLrn I. Use the traditional square of opposition to find the answers to these problems. When a statement is given as false, simply enter an "F" into the square of opposition and compute (if possible) the other truth values.

★1. If "All fashion fads are products of commercial brainwashing" is true, what is the truth value of the following statements?

    a. No fashion fads are products of commercial brainwashing.

    b. Some fashion fads are products of commercial brainwashing.

    c. Some fashion fads are not products of commercial brainwashing.

2. If "All fashion fads are products of commercial brainwashing" is false, what is the truth value of the following statements?

    a. No fashion fads are products of commercial brainwashing.

    b. Some fashion fads are products of commercial brainwashing.

    c. Some fashion fads are not products of commercial brainwashing.

3. If "No sting operations are cases of entrapment" is true, what is the truth value of the following statements?

    a. All sting operations are cases of entrapment.

    b. Some sting operations are cases of entrapment.

    c. Some sting operations are not cases of entrapment.

★4. If "No sting operations are cases of entrapment" is false, what is the truth value of the following statements?

    a. All sting operations are cases of entrapment.

    b. Some sting operations are cases of entrapment.

    c. Some sting operations are not cases of entrapment.

5. If "Some assassinations are morally justifiable actions" is true, what is the truth value of the following statements?

    a. All assassinations are morally justifiable actions.

    b. No assassinations are morally justifiable actions.

    c. Some assassinations are not morally justifiable actions.

6. If "Some assassinations are morally justifiable actions" is false, what is the truth value of the following statements?

    a. All assassinations are morally justifiable actions.

    b. No assassinations are morally justifiable actions.

    c. Some assassinations are not morally justifiable actions.

★7. If "Some obsessive-compulsive behaviors are not curable diseases" is true, what is the truth value of the following statements?

    a. All obsessive-compulsive behaviors are curable diseases.

    b. No obsessive-compulsive behaviors are curable diseases.

    c. Some obsessive-compulsive behaviors are curable diseases.

8. If "Some obsessive-compulsive behaviors are not curable diseases" is false, what is the truth value of the following statements?

  a. All obsessive-compulsive behaviors are curable diseases.

  b. No obsessive-compulsive behaviors are curable diseases.

  c. Some obsessive-compulsive behaviors are curable diseases.

iLrn II. Use the traditional square of opposition to determine whether the following arguments are valid or invalid. Name any fallacies that are committed.

★1. All advocates of school prayer are individuals who insist on imposing their views on others.
Therefore, some advocates of school prayer are individuals who insist on imposing their views on others.

2. It is false that no jailhouse informants are persons who can be trusted.
Therefore, some jailhouse informants are not persons who can be trusted.

3. All homemakers are persons with real jobs.
Therefore, it is false that no homemakers are persons with real jobs.

★4. It is false that some trolls are not creatures who live under bridges.
Therefore, it is false that no trolls are creatures who live under bridges.

5. Some campus romances are episodes plagued by violence.
Therefore, some campus romances are not episodes plagued by violence.

6. Some pornographic publications are materials protected by the First Amendment.
Therefore, it is false that no pornographic publications are materials protected by the First Amendment.

★7. It is false that all mainstream conservatives are persons who support free legal services for the poor.
Therefore, no mainstream conservatives are persons who support free legal services for the poor.

8. It is false that some forms of human creativity are activities amenable to mathematical analysis.
Therefore, it is false that all forms of human creativity are activities amenable to mathematical analysis.

9. It is false that some tooth fairies are daytime visitors.
Therefore, some tooth fairies are not daytime visitors.

★10. It is false that some orthodox psychoanalysts are not individuals driven by a religious fervor.
Therefore, it is false that some orthodox psychoanalysts are individuals driven by a religious fervor.

11. Some starship captains are not members of the Federation.
Therefore, it is false that all starship captains are members of the Federation.

12. It is false that some network news programs are exercises in mediocrity.
Therefore, it is false that no network news programs are exercises in mediocrity.

★13. No flying reindeer are animals who get lost in the fog.
Therefore, it is false that all flying reindeer are animals who get lost in the fog.

14. It is false that no leveraged buyouts are deals unfair to workers.
Therefore, all leveraged buyouts are deals unfair to workers.

15. It is false that some wood ticks are not carriers of Lyme disease.
Therefore, some wood ticks are carriers of Lyme disease.

iLrn III. Exercises 1 through 10 provide a statement, its truth value in parentheses, and an operation to be performed on that statement. Supply the new statement and the truth value of the new statement. Exercises 11 through 20 provide a statement, its truth value in parentheses, and a new statement. Determine how the new statement was derived from the given statement and supply the truth value of the new statement. Take the Aristotelian standpoint in working these exercises and assume that the terms refer to actually existing things.

Given statement	Operation/relation	New statement	Truth value
★1. All non-A are B. (T)	contrap.	_____	_____
2. Some A are non-B. (F)	subalt.	_____	_____
3. No A are non-B. (T)	obv.	_____	_____
★4. Some non-A are not B. (T)	subcon.	_____	_____
5. No A are non-B. (F)	contradic.	_____	_____
6. No A are B. (T)	contrap.	_____	_____
★7. All non-A are B. (T)	contrary	_____	_____
8. Some A are not non-B. (F)	obv.	_____	_____
9. No A are non-B. (F)	conv.	_____	_____
★10. Some non-A are non-B. (F)	subcon.	_____	_____
11. Some non-A are not B. (T)	_____	All non-A are B.	_____
12. Some A are non-B. (T)	_____	Some non-B are A.	_____
★13. All non-A are B. (F)	_____	No non-A are non-B.	_____
14. Some non-A are not B. (T)	_____	No non-A are B.	_____
15. All A are non-B. (F)	_____	All non-B are A.	_____
★16. Some non-A are non-B. (F)	_____	No non-A are non-B.	_____
17. Some A are not non-B. (T)	_____	Some B are not non-A.	_____
18. No non-A are B. (T)	_____	Some non-A are not B.	_____
★19. No A are non-B. (F)	_____	All A are non-B.	_____
20. Some non-A are B. (F)	_____	Some non-A are not B.	_____

iLrn IV. Use either the traditional square of opposition or conversion, obversion, or contraposition to determine whether the following arguments are valid or invalid. For those that are invalid, name the fallacy committed.

★1. It is false that some jogging events are not aerobic activities.
Therefore, it is false that no jogging events are aerobic activities.

2. No meat-eating vegetarians are individuals with a high protein diet.
   Therefore, no individuals with a high protein diet are meat-eating vegetarians.

3. Some jobs in health care are not glamorous occupations.
   Therefore, some jobs in health care are glamorous occupations.

★4. Some terminally ill patients are patients who do not want to live.
   Therefore, some patients who want to live are recovering patients.

5. All Barbie dolls are toys that engender a false sense of values.
   Therefore, no Barbie dolls are toys that engender a true sense of values.

6. All flying elephants are jolly pachyderms.
   Therefore, some flying elephants are jolly pachyderms.

★7. It is false that some international terrorists are political moderates.
   Therefore, some international terrorists are not political moderates.

8. No pet hamsters are animals that need much attention.
   Therefore, it is false that all pet hamsters are animals that need much attention.

9. Some hedge fund managers are not responsible investors.
   Therefore, some responsible investors are not hedge fund managers.

★10. It is false that all substances that control cell growth are hormones.
   Therefore, no substances that control cell growth are hormones.

11. Some cases of whistle-blowing are actions disloyal to employers.
   Therefore, some cases of whistle-blowing are not actions loyal to employers.

12. No stolen computer chips are easy items to trace.
   Therefore, no difficult items to trace are computer chips that are not stolen.

★13. Some economists are followers of Ayn Rand.
   Therefore, some economists are not followers of Ayn Rand.

14. All porcelain figurines are fragile artifacts.
   Therefore, it is false that some porcelain figurines are not fragile artifacts.

15. Some pleasant recollections are not missed opportunities.
   Therefore, some availed opportunities are not unpleasant recollections.

V. Use the traditional square of opposition together with conversion, obversion, and contraposition to prove that the following arguments are valid. Show each intermediate step in the deduction.

★1. All insurance policies are cryptically written documents.
   Therefore, some cryptically written documents are insurance policies.

2. No gemstones that do not contain chromium are emeralds.
   Therefore, some stones that are not emeralds are not gemstones that contain chromium.

3. It is false that some ficus benjaminas are untemperamental house plants.
   Therefore, all ficus benjaminas are temperamental house plants.

★4. All exogenous morphines are addictive substances.
   Therefore, it is false that all addictive substances are endogenous morphines.

5. No persons who do not advocate free-enterprise economics are fundamental-ist Christians.
Therefore, it is false that some fundamentalist Christians are not persons who advocate free enterprise economics.

6. It is false that some Gothic cathedrals are buildings that do not feature pointed arches.
Therefore, some buildings that feature pointed arches are Gothic cathedrals.

★7. Some persons who recognize paranormal events are not non-scientists.
Therefore, it is false that no scientists are persons who recognize paranormal events.

8. It is false that no unhealthy things to ingest are food additives.
Therefore, some food additives are not healthy things to ingest.

9. It is false that some illegal searches are not sobriety checkpoints.
Therefore, some sobriety checkpoints are not legal searches.

★10. It is false that some feminists are not advocates of equal pay for equal work.
Therefore, it is false that all advocates of equal pay for equal work are non-feminists.

4.6   Venn Diagrams and the Traditional Standpoint

Earlier in this chapter we saw how Venn diagrams can be used to represent the content of categorical propositions from the Boolean standpoint. With a slight modification they can also be used to represent the content of categorical propositions from the traditional, or Aristotelian, standpoint. These modified Venn diagrams can then be used to prove the relationships of the traditional square of opposition, and also to test the validity of immediate inferences from the traditional standpoint.

The difference between the Boolean standpoint and the Aristotelian standpoint concerns only universal (**A** and **E**) propositions. From the Boolean standpoint, universal propositions have no existential import, but from the Aristotelian standpoint they do have existential import when their subject terms refer to actually existing things. For example, from the Boolean standpoint the statement "All raccoons are pests" does not imply the existence of anything, but from the Aristotelian standpoint it implies the existence of raccoons. Thus, if we are to construct a Venn diagram to represent such a statement from the Aristotelian standpoint, we need to introduce some symbol that represents this implication of existence.

The symbol that we will introduce for this purpose is an X surrounded by a circle. Like the X's that we have used up until now, this circled X signifies that something exists in the area in which it is placed. However, the two symbols differ in that the uncircled X represents the positive claim of existence made by particular (**I** and **O**) propositions, whereas the circled X represents the implication of existence made by universal propositions about actually existing things. Such statements may be diagrammed from the Aristotelian standpoint as follows:

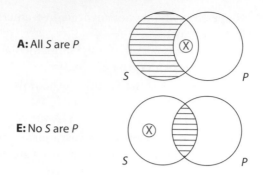

A: All *S* are *P*

E: No *S* are *P*

In the diagram for the **A** statement, the left-hand part of the *S* circle is shaded, so if there are any members of *S*, they must be in the area where the two circles overlap. Thus, a circled X is placed in the overlap area. In the diagram for the **E** statement, the overlap area is shaded, so if there are any members of *S* they must be in the left-hand part of the *S* circle. Thus, a circled X is placed in this area.

The diagrams for the **I** and **O** statements are the same from the Aristotelian standpoint as they are from the Boolean:

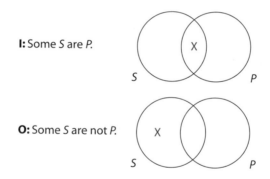

I: Some *S* are *P*.

O: Some *S* are not *P*.

Proving the Traditional Square of Opposition

We can now use this modified Venn diagram technique to prove the relations of the traditional square of opposition. Having such a proof is important because up until now these relations have only been illustrated with various examples; they have not been proved. The accompanying figure reproduces the traditional square of opposition together with Venn diagrams that represent the Aristotelian interpretation of the four standard-form propositions.

Let us begin with the contradictory relation. If the **A** statement is given as true, then the left-hand part of the *S* circle is empty. This makes the **O** statement false, be-

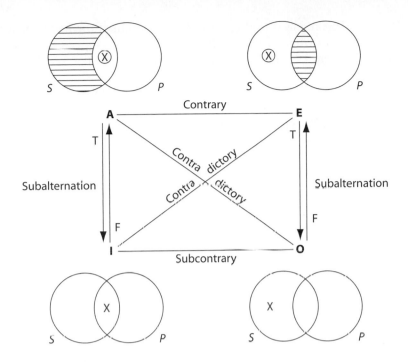

cause it claims that the left-hand part of the S circle is not empty. And if the **O** statement is given as true, then the left-hand part of the S circle is not empty, which makes the **A** statement false. On the other hand, if the **O** statement is given as false, then the left-hand part of the S circle is empty. However, given that some members of S exist, they must be in the overlap area. This double outcome makes the **A** statement true. Also, if the **A** statement is given as false, then either the left-hand part of the S circle is not empty, or the overlap area is empty (or both). If the left-hand part of the S circle is not empty, then the **O** statement is true. Alternately, if the overlap area is empty, then, given that some members of S exist, they must be in the left-hand part of the S circle, and, once again, the **O** statement is true. Analogous reasoning applies for the relation between the **E** and **I** statements.

Next, turning to the contrary relation. If the **A** statement is given as true, then the overlap area is not empty, which makes the **E** statement false. By analogous reasoning, if the **E** statement is given as true, the overlap area is empty, which makes the **A** statement false. However, if the **A** statement is given as false (making the **O** statement true), then the **E** statement could be either true or false depending on whether or not the overlap area is empty. Thus, in this case the **E** statement would have logically undetermined truth value. By analogous reasoning, if the **E** statement is given as false (making the **I** statement true), the **A** statement could be either true or false depending on whether or not the left-hand part of the S circle is empty. Thus, the **A** statement would have logically undetermined truth value.

Turning next to the subcontrary relation, if the **I** statement is given as false, then the area where the *S* and *P* circles overlap is empty. Given that at least one *S* exists, there must be something in the left-hand part of the *S* circle, which makes the **O** statement true. By analogous reasoning, if the **O** statement is given as false, there must be something in the overlap area, making the **I** statement true. But if the **I** statement is given as true, then the **O** statement could be either true or false depending on whether something exists in the left-hand part of the *S* circle. Thus the **O** statement would have undetermined truth value. Similarly, if the **O** statement is given as true, then the **I** statement could be either true or false depending on whether something exists in the overlap area. Thus, the **I** statement would have undetermined truth value.

Finally, we consider subalternation. If the **A** statement is given as true, then something exists in the area where the *S* and *P* circles overlap, which makes the **I** statement true as well. And if the **I** statement is given as false, then the overlap area is empty, making the **A** statement false. But if the **A** statement is given as false (making the **O** statement true), then the **I** statement could be either true or false depending on whether something exists in the overlap area. Thus, the **I** statement would have logically undetermined truth value. And if the **I** statement is given as true, then the **A** statement could be either true or false depending on whether or not the left-hand part of the *S* circle is empty. Thus, the **A** statement would have logically undetermined truth value. Analogous reasoning applies for the subalternation relation between the **E** and **O** statements.

Testing Immediate Inferences

The modified Venn diagram technique involving circled X's can be used to test immediate inferences from the Aristotelian standpoint. The only requirement is that the subject and predicate terms of the conclusion be the same as those of the premise. Such inferences depend on the square of opposition and do not involve the operations of conversion, obversion, and contraposition. Venn diagrams can also be used to test inferences involving these latter operations, but a further modification must be introduced.

Since any argument that is valid from the Boolean standpoint is also valid from the Aristotelian standpoint, it is often simpler first to test the argument from the Boolean standpoint. If the argument is valid, then it is valid from both standpoints. But if the argument is invalid from the Boolean standpoint, then it can be tested from the Aristotelian standpoint. Let us begin by testing an inference *form* for validity:

> All *A* are *B*.
> Therefore, some *A* are *B*.

First, we draw Venn diagrams from the Boolean standpoint for the premise and conclusion:

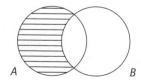

Some *A* are *B*.
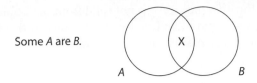

The information of the conclusion diagram is not represented in the premise diagram, so the inference form is not valid from the Boolean standpoint. Thus, we adopt the Aristotelian standpoint and assume for the moment that the subject of the premise (*A*) denotes at least one existing thing. This thing is represented by placing a circled X in the open area of that circle:

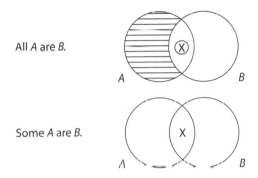

All *A* are *B*.

Some *A* are *B*.

Now the information of the conclusion diagram *is* represented in the premise diagram. Thus, the inference form is conditionally valid from the Aristotelian standpoint. It is valid on condition that the circled X represents at least one existing thing.

To test a complete inference we begin by testing its form. Here is an example:

No penguins are birds that can fly.
Therefore, it is false that all penguins are birds that can fly.

First, we reduce the immediate inference to its form and test it from the Boolean standpoint:

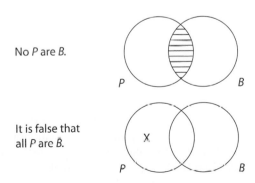

No *P* are *B*.

It is false that all *P* are *B*.

Since the inference form is not valid from the Boolean standpoint, we adopt the Aristotelian standpoint and assume for the sake of this test that the subject of the premise (*P*) denotes at least one existing thing:

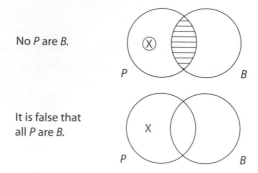

No *P* are *B*.

It is false that
all *P* are *B*.

The Venn diagrams show that the inference form is conditionally valid from the Aristotelian standpoint. It is valid on condition that the circled X represents at least one existing thing. Since the circled X is in the *P* circle, the final step is to see if the term in the inference corresponding to *P* denotes something that exists. The term in question is "penguins," and at least one penguin actually exists. Thus, the condition is fulfilled, and the inference is valid from the Aristotelian standpoint.

Another example:

> All sugarplum fairies are delicate creatures.
> Therefore, some sugarplum fairies are delicate creatures.

This immediate inference has the same form as the first one we tested. The form is not valid from the Boolean standpoint, but it is conditionally valid from the Aristotelian standpoint:

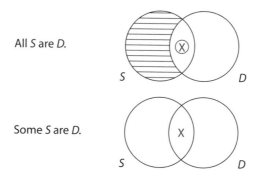

All *S* are *D*.

Some *S* are *D*.

The final step is to see if the circled X represents at least one existing thing. The circled X is in the *S* circle and *S* stands for "sugarplum fairies," which do not exist. Thus, the requisite condition is not fulfilled, and the inference is not valid from the Aristotelian standpoint. The inference commits the existential fallacy.

The steps involved in testing an immediate inference from the Aristotelian standpoint may now be summarized:

1. Reduce the inference to its form and test it from the Boolean standpoint. If the form is valid, proceed no further. The inference is valid from both standpoints.

2. If the inference form is invalid from the Boolean standpoint, then adopt the Aristotelian standpoint and look to see if the left-hand premise circle is partly shaded. If it is, enter a circled X in the unshaded part and retest the form.

3. If the inference form is conditionally valid, determine if the circled X represents something that exists. If it does, the condition is fulfilled, and the inference is valid from the Aristotelian standpoint. If it does not, the inference is invalid, and it commits the existential fallacy from the Aristotelian standpoint.

EXERCISE 4.6

I. Use the modified Venn diagram technique to determine if the following immediate inference forms are valid from the Boolean standpoint, conditionally valid from the Aristotelian standpoint, or invalid.

★1. Some *A* are not *B*.
   Therefore, no *A* are *B*.

2. It is false that some *A* are *B*.
   Therefore, it is false that all *A* are *B*.

3. It is false that no *A* are *B*.
   Therefore, some *A* are *B*.

★4. All *A* are *B*.
   Therefore, it is false that no *A* are *B*.

5. Some *A* are *B*.
   Therefore, it is false that some *A* are not *B*.

6. Some *A* are not *B*.
   Therefore, it is false that all *A* are *B*.

★7. It is false that some *A* are *B*.
   Therefore, no *A* are *B*.

8. It is false that some *A* are not *B*.
   Therefore, some *A* are *B*.

9. It is false that all *A* are *B*.
   Therefore, no *A* are *B*.

★10. No *A* are *B*.
   Therefore, some *A* are not *B*.

iLrn II. Use the modified Venn diagram technique to determine if the following immediate inferences are valid from the Boolean standpoint, valid from the Aristotelian standpoint, or invalid. Identify any inferences that commit the existential fallacy from either standpoint.

★1. No summer romances are banal pastimes.
   Therefore, it is false that some summer romances are banal pastimes.

2. It is false that some people who hunger for wealth are not victims of their obsession.
Therefore, some people who hunger for wealth are victims of their obsession.

3. No lamps containing genies are ordinary sources of light.
Therefore, some lamps containing genies are not ordinary sources of light.

★4. It is false that some duck hunters are animal rights activists.
Therefore, some duck hunters are not animal rights activists.

5. All repressive political regimes are insults to human dignity.
Therefore, no repressive political regimes are insults to human dignity.

6. It is false that all skating rinks are playgrounds for amateurs.
Therefore, some skating rinks are not playgrounds for amateurs.

★7. All pixies who slide down moonbeams are fun-loving daredevils.
Therefore, it is false that no pixies who slide down moonbeams are fun-loving daredevils.

8. It is false that some graduate teaching assistants are not underpaid laborers.
Therefore, it is false that no graduate teaching assistants are underpaid laborers.

9. Some housing projects are developments riddled with crime.
Therefore, it is false that no housing projects are developments riddled with crime.

★10. It is false that some thunderstorms are quiescent phenomena.
Therefore, all thunderstorms are quiescent phenomena.

11. No flower gardens are creations that feature skunk weed.
Therefore, it is false that all flower gardens are creations that feature skunk weed.

12. It is false that no incendiary devices are contraptions that misfire.
Therefore, some incendiary devices are not contraptions that misfire.

★13. It is false that some pet lovers are people who think that animals are mere machines.
Therefore, it is false that all pet lovers are people who think that animals are mere machines.

14. No werewolves are creatures who lurk about in the daytime.
Therefore, it is false that all werewolves are creatures who lurk about in the daytime.

15. Some soccer games are not thrilling events to watch.
Therefore, no soccer games are thrilling events to watch.

4.7   Translating Ordinary Language Statements into Categorical Form

Although few statements that occur in ordinary written and oral expression are categorical propositions in standard form, many of them can be translated into standard-form propositions. Such translation has two chief benefits. The first is that the operations and inferences pertinent to standard-form categorical propositions (contrary, subcontrary, etc.) become applicable to these statements. The second is that such statements, once translated, are completely clear and unambiguous as to their meaning. Many statements in ordinary language are susceptible to multiple interpretations, and each interpretation represents one possible mode of translation. The effort to translate such statements discloses the various interpretations and thus helps prevent misunderstanding and confusion.

Translating statements into categorical form is like any other kind of translation in that no set of specific rules can be given that will cover every possible form of phraseology. Yet one general rule always applies: Understand the *meaning* of the given statement, and then reexpress it in a new statement that has a quantifier, subject term, copula, and predicate term. Some of the forms of phraseology that are typically encountered are terms without nouns, nonstandard verbs, singular propositions, adverbs and pronouns, unexpressed and nonstandard quantifiers, conditional statements, exclusive propositions, "the only," and exceptive propositions.

1. Terms Without Nouns

The subject and predicate terms of a categorical proposition must contain either a plural noun or a pronoun that serves to denote the class indicated by the term. Nouns and pronouns denote classes, while adjectives (and participles) connote attributes. If a term consists of only an adjective, a plural noun or pronoun should be introduced to make the term genuinely denotative. Examples:

Some roses are red.	Some roses are red *flowers*.
All tigers are carnivorous.	All tigers are carnivorous *animals*.

2. Nonstandard Verbs

According to the position adopted earlier in this chapter, the only copulas that are allowed in standard-form categorical propositions are "are" and "are not." Statements in ordinary usage often incorporate other forms of the verb "to be." Such statements may be translated as the following examples illustrate:

Some college students will become educated.	Some college students *are persons who* will become educated.
Some dogs would rather bark than bite.	Some dogs *are animals that* would rather bark than bite.

In other statements no form of the verb "to be" occurs at all. These may be translated as the following examples indicate:

Some birds fly south during the winter.	Some birds *are animals that* fly south during the winter.
All ducks swim.	All ducks *are swimmers*. or All ducks *are animals that* swim.

3. Singular Propositions

A singular proposition is a proposition that makes an assertion about a specific person, place, thing, or time. Singular propositions are typically translated into universals by means of a parameter. A **parameter** is a phrase that, when introduced into a statement, affects the form but not the meaning. Some parameters that may be used to translate singular propositions are:

persons identical to
places identical to
things identical to
cases identical to
times identical to

For example, the statement "Socrates is mortal" may be translated as "All persons identical to Socrates are persons who are mortal." Because only one person is identical to Socrates, namely Socrates himself, the term "persons identical to Socrates" denotes the class that has Socrates as its only member. In other words, it simply denotes Socrates. Such a translation admittedly leaves some of the original information behind, because singular statements usually have existential import, whereas universal statements do not—at least from the Boolean standpoint. But if such translations are interpreted from the Aristotelian standpoint, the existential import is preserved. Here are some examples:

George went home.	All *persons identical to* George are *persons who* went home.
Sandra did not go shopping.	No *persons identical to* Sandra are *persons who* went shopping.
There is a radio in the bedroom.	All *places identical to* the bedroom are *places* there is a radio. or *Some* radios are *things* in the bedroom.
The moon is full tonight.	All *things identical to* the moon are *things that* are full tonight. or All *times identical to* tonight are *times* the moon is full.
I hate gin.	All *persons identical to* me are *persons who* hate gin. or All *things identical to* gin are *things that* I hate.

In translating singular statements, note that the parameter "persons identical to" is *not* the same as "persons similar to" or "persons like." There may be many persons *like* Socrates, but there is only one person *identical to* Socrates. Also note that parameters should *not* be used when the term in question already has a plural noun (or pronoun) that denotes the intended class. Such use is not wrong, technically, but it is redundant. Example:

Diamonds are carbon allotropes.

Correct: All diamonds are carbon allotropes.

Redundant: All things identical to diamonds are things identical to carbon allotropes.

4. Adverbs and Pronouns

When a statement contains a spatial adverb such as "where," "wherever," "anywhere," "everywhere," or "nowhere," or a temporal adverb such as "when," "whenever," "anytime," "always," or "never," it may be translated in terms of "places" or "times," respectively. Statements containing pronouns such as "who," "whoever," "anyone," "what," "whatever," or "anything" may be translated in terms of "persons" or "things," respectively. Examples:

He always wears a suit to work.

All *times* he goes to work are *times* he wears a suit.

He is always clean shaven.

All *times* are *times* he is clean shaven.

She never brings her lunch to school.

No *times* she goes to school are *times* she brings her lunch.

Nowhere on earth are there any unicorns.

No *places* on earth are *places* there are unicorns.

Whoever works hard will succeed.

All *persons* who work hard are *persons* who will succeed.

Whenever he wins he celebrates.

All *times* he wins are *times* he celebrates.

She goes where she chooses.

All *places* she chooses to go are *places* she goes.

She does what she wants.

All *things* she wants to do are *things* she does.

Notice the order of the subject and predicate terms in the last four examples. When translating statements such as these it is often easy to confuse the subject term with the predicate term. However, since these statements are all translated as **A** type categorical propositions, such as mix-up amounts to committing the fallacy of illicit conversion. To prevent it from happening, keep this rule in mind: For "W" words ("who," "what," "when," "where," "whoever," "whatever," "whenever," "wherever"), the language following the "W" word goes into the subject term of the categorical proposition.

5. Unexpressed Quantifiers

Many statements in ordinary usage have quantifiers that are implied but not expressed. In introducing the quantifiers one must be guided by the most probable meaning of the statement. Examples:

Emeralds are green gems.	*All* emeralds are green gems.
There are lions in the zoo.	*Some* lions are animals in the zoo.
A tiger is a mammal.	*All* tigers are mammals.
A fish is not a mammal.	*No* fish are mammals.
A tiger roared.	*Some* tigers are animals that roared.
Children are human beings.	*All* children are human beings.
Children live next door.	*Some* children are persons who live next door.

6. Nonstandard Quantifiers

In some ordinary language statements, the quantity is indicated by words other than the three standard form quantifiers. Such words include "few," "a few," "not every," "anyone," and various other forms. Another problem occurs when the quantifier "all" is combined with the copula "are not." As we have already seen, statements of the form "All *S* are not *P*" are *not* standard-form propositions. Depending on their meaning, they should be translated as either "No *S* are *P*" or "Some *S* are not *P*." When the intended meaning is "Some *S* are not *P*," the meaning may be indicated by placing oral emphasis on the word "All." For example, "*All* athletes are not superstars" means "Some athletes are not superstars." Here are some additional examples:

A few soldiers are heroes.	*Some* soldiers are heroes.
Anyone who votes is a citizen.	*All* voters are citizens.
Not everyone who votes is a Democrat.	*Some* voters are not Democrats.
Not a single dog is a cat.	*No* dogs are cats.
All newborns are not able to talk.	*No* newborns are people able to talk.
All prisoners are not violent.	*Some* prisoners are not violent persons.
Few sailors entered the regatta.	*Some* sailors are persons who entered the regatta *and some* sailors are not persons who entered the regatta.

Notice that this last statement beginning with "few" cannot be translated as a single categorical proposition. Such statements (and some beginning with "a few") must be translated as a compound arrangement of an **I** proposition and an **O** proposition. Statements beginning with "almost all" and "not quite all" must be handled in the same way. When these statements occur in arguments, the arguments must be treated in the same way as those containing exceptive propositions, which will be discussed shortly.

7. Conditional Statements

When the antecedent and consequent of a conditional statement talk about the same thing, the statement can usually be translated into categorical form. Such statements are always translated as universals. Language following the word "if" goes in the subject term of the categorical proposition, and language following "only if" goes in the predicate term. Examples:

If it's a mouse, then it's a mammal.	All mice are mammals.
If a bear is hungry, then it is dangerous.	All hungry bears are dangerous animals.
Jewelry is expensive if it is made of gold.	All pieces of jewelry made of gold are expensive things.
A car is a Camry only if it's a Toyota.	All Camrys are Toyotas.

Conditional statements having a negated consequent are usually best translated as **E** propositions. Examples:

If it's a turkey, then it's not a mammal.	No turkeys are mammals.
If an animal has four legs, then it is not a bird.	No four-legged animals are birds.
A knife will cut only if it isn't dull.	No knives that cut are dull knives.

The word "unless" means "if not." Since language following the word "if" goes in the subject, statements containing "unless" are translated as categorical propositions having negated subject terms. Examples:

Tomatoes are edible unless they are spoiled.	All unspoiled tomatoes are edible tomatoes.
Unless a boy misbehaves he will be treated decently.	All boys who do not misbehave are boys who will be treated decently.

8. Exclusive Propositions

Many propositions that involve the words "only," "none but," "none except," and "no . . . except" are exclusive propositions. Efforts to translate them into categorical propositions often lead to confusing the subject term with the predicate term. To avoid such confusion keep in mind that language following "only," "none but," "none except," and "no . . . except" goes in the predicate term of the categorical proposition. For example, the statement "Only executives can use the silver elevator" is translated "All persons who can use the silver elevator are executives." If it were translated "All executives are persons who can use the silver elevator," the translation would be incorrect. Examples:

Only elected officials will attend the convention.	All persons who will attend the convention are elected officials.
None but the brave deserve the fair.	All persons who deserve the fair are brave persons.
No birds except peacocks are proud of their tails.	All birds proud of their tails are peacocks.
He owns only blue-chip stocks.	All stocks he owns are blue-chip stocks.
She invited only wealthy socialites.	All persons she invited are wealthy socialites.

For a statement involving "only," "none but," "none except," and "no . . . except" to be a genuinely exclusive proposition, the word that follows these words must be a *plural* noun or pronoun. If the word that follows "only," "none but," or the like designates an *individual*, the statement really asserts two things. For example, the statement

"Only Megan painted a picture" asserts that Megan painted a picture *and* that no other person painted a picture. Thus it would be translated as two statements: "All persons identical to Megan are persons who painted a picture, *and* all persons who painted a picture are persons identical to Megan." This section of the book will ignore cases where the word following "only," "none but," or the like designates an individual.

Also note that many English statements containing "only" are ambiguous owing to the fact that "only" can be interpreted as modifying alternate words in the statement. Consider, for example, the statement "He only jogs after sunset." Does this mean "He is the only person who jogs after sunset" or "He jogs and does not walk after sunset" or "The only time he jogs is after sunset"? If the statement's context does not provide an answer, the translator is free to pick any of these senses for translation. This same ambiguity, incidentally, affects the last two examples above. Accordingly, they might also be translated "All things he owns are blue-chip stocks" and "All socialites she invited are wealthy persons."

9. "The Only"

Statements beginning with the words "the only" are translated differently from those beginning with "only." For example, the statement "The only cars that are available are Chevrolets" means "If a car is available, then it is a Chevrolet." This in turn is translated as "All cars that are available are Chevrolets." In other words, language following "the only" goes in the subject term of the categorical proposition. Examples:

The only animals that live in this canyon are skunks.	All animals that live in this canyon are skunks.
Accountants are the only ones who will be hired.	All those who will be hired are accountants.

Statements involving "the only" are similar to those involving "only" in this one respect: When the statement is about an *individual*, two statements are needed to translate it. For example, "The only person who painted a picture is Megan" means that Megan painted a picture, *and* no other person painted a picture. The statement is equivalent in meaning to "Only Megan painted a picture." Thus it is translated "All persons identical to Megan are persons who painted a picture, *and* all persons who painted a picture are persons identical to Megan." Statements involving "the only" that refer to individuals are ignored throughout the remainder of this chapter.

10. Exceptive Propositions

Propositions of the form "All except *S* are *P*" and "All but *S* are *P*" are exceptive propositions. They must be translated not as single categorical propositions but as pairs of conjoined categorical propositions. Statements that include the phrase "none except," on the other hand, are exclusive (not exceptive) propositions. "None except" is synonymous with "none but." Some examples of exceptive propositions are:

All except students are invited.	No students are invited persons, and all nonstudents are invited persons.

| All but managers must report to the president. | No managers are persons who must report to the president, and all nonmanagers are persons who must report to the president. |

Because exceptive propositions cannot be translated into single categorical propositions, many of the simple inferences and operations pertinent to categorical propositions cannot be applied to them. Arguments that contain exceptive propositions as premises or conclusion can be evaluated only through the application of extended techniques. This topic is taken up in the next chapter.

Key word (to be eliminated)	Translation hint
whoever, wherever, always, anyone, never, etc.	use "all" together with persons, places, times
a few	"some"
if ... then	use "all" or "no"
unless	"if not"
only, none, but, none except, no ... except	use "all"
the only	use "all"
all but, all except, few	two statements required
not every, not all	"some ... are not"
there is, there are	"some"

Rule for A propositions

Language following these words goes in the subject term: "if," "the only," and W words ("who," "what," "when," "where," "whoever," "whatever," "whenever," "wherever").

Language following these words goes in the predicate term: "only if," "only," "none

EXERCISE 4.7

iLrn I. Translate the following into standard-form categorical propositions:

★1. Any bank that makes too many risky loans will fail.

2. Women military officers are not eligible for combat duty.

3. Terrorist attacks succeed whenever security measures are lax.

★4. Bromine is extractable from seawater.

5. Not all guilt feelings are psychological aberrations.

6. Every jazz fan admires Duke Ellington.

★7. If it's a halogen, then it isn't chemically inert.

8. A television show that depicts violence incites violence.

9. Manipulators do not make good marriage partners.

★10. None but pirate ships fly the Jolly Roger.

11. She gains weight whenever she's depressed.

12. She's depressed whenever she gains weight.

★13. A man is a bachelor only if he is unmarried.

14. Warmth always relieves pain.

15. Joseph J. Thomson discovered the electron.

★16. A few organic silicones are used as lubricants.

17. Only nuclear-powered vehicles are suitable for deep space exploration.

18. Comets are the only heavenly bodies with tails.

★19. There is a giant star in the Tarantula Nebula.

20. If a pregnant woman drinks alcohol, she risks giving birth to a deformed child.

21. No shellfish except oysters make pearls.

★22. Only those given to flights of fancy believe Noah's ark lies beneath the snows of Ararat.

23. The electroscope is a device for detecting static electricity.

24. Occasionally there are concerts in Central Park.

★25. Berlin was the setting for the 1936 Olympic Games.

26. The Kentucky Derby is never run in January.

27. The only way to get rid of a temptation is to yield to it.

★28. Where there's smoke, there's fire.

29. Lunar eclipses do not occur unless the moon is full.

30. Radio transmissions are disrupted whenever sunspot activity increases.

★31. If an ore isn't radioactive, then it isn't pitchblende.

32. All but the rats left the sinking ship.

33. A pesticide is dangerous if it contains DDT.

★34. John Grisham writes only novels about lawyers.

35. He who hesitates is lost.

36. Modern corporations are all run in the interest of their managers.

★37. Unless the sun is shining, a rainbow cannot occur.

38. Whoever suffers allergic reactions has a weakened immune system.

39. All fruits except pineapples ripen after they are picked.

★40. Few corporate raiders are known for their integrity.

41. Monkeys are found in the jungles of Guatemala.

42. Monkeys are mammals.

★43. I like strawberries.

44. All passengers are not allowed to smoke on board the aircraft.

45. All flowers are not fragrant.

★46. Cynthia travels where she wants.

47. Bats are the only true flying mammals.

48. Not every river runs to the sea.

★49. Physicists do not understand the operation of superconductors.

50. A few apartment dwellers are victimized by incessant noise.

51. There are forced labor camps in China.

★52. Whatever increases efficiency improves profitability.

53. Dolphins are swimming between the breakers.

54. Feathers are not heavy.

★55. Few picnics are entirely free of ants.

56. A civil right is unalienable if it is a human right.

57. She says what she pleases.

★58. None but computer buffs are Net surfers.

59. An animal is a feline only if it is a cat.

60. Renee does whatever she is told to do.

II. The following exercises contain typical mistakes that students make in attempting to translate statements into standard form. Correct the errors and redundancies in these attempted translations.

★1. Some of the third-generation computers are things that are machines that take dictation.

2. All cars identical to BMWs are the only cars that young lawyers drive.

3. All vertebrates except cartilaginous fishes are animals with a bony skeleton.

★4. No downhill skiers are effective competitors if they suffer from altitude sickness.

5. All substances like cobalt are things that are substances identical to ferromagnetic metals.

6. No persons identical to nuclear pacifists are persons who believe a just war is possible.

★7. All persons identical to matadors are not performers who succumb easily to fear.

8. All companies identical to Google are looking forward to a bright future.

9. No toxic dumps are ecological catastrophes unless they leak.

★10. All crocodiles are things identical to dangerous animals when they are hungry.

Summary

A categorical proposition is a proposition that relates two classes (or categories). Standard-form categorical propositions occur in four forms and are composed of a quantifier ("all," "no," "some"), a subject term, a copula ("are," "are not"), and a predicate term. A standard-form categorical proposition has either affirmative or negative *quality*, depending on whether it joins or separates the subject and predicate classes, and universal or particular *quantity*, depending on whether it relates all or only a part of the subject class to the predicate class. The subject and predicate terms are said to be *distributed* or *undistributed* depending on whether the proposition makes an assertion about all or only a part of the class denoted by the term in question. Each standard-form proposition is given a letter name (**A, E, I, O**) that reflects its quantity and quality.

Categorical propositions having universal quantity allow for two different interpretations. According to the Aristotelian interpretation, **A** and **E** propositions about actually existing things imply the existence of those things, but according to the Boolean interpretation, **A** and **E** propositions never imply the existence of anything. The content of a standard-form proposition may be represented in a Venn diagram, which consists of two overlapping circles. Placing an X in an area indicates that the area is not empty, and shading an area indicates that the area is empty. The modern square of opposition is a diagram that applies to the Boolean interpretation; it indicates that the **A** and **O** propositions contradict each other and that the **E** and **I** propositions contradict each other.

Conversion, obversion, and contraposition are operations that can be performed on standard-form propositions; they result in a new proposition that is either logically equivalent or not logically equivalent to the original proposition. Two propositions that are logically equivalent necessarily have the same truth value. Conversion gives logically equivalent results for **E** and **I** propositions, obversion does so for all four, and contraposition, for **A** and **O**. The formal fallacies of illicit conversion and illicit contraposition result from the application of conversion and contraposition to propositions that do not yield logically equivalent results.

The traditional square of opposition applies to the Aristotelian interpretation of categorical propositions when the subject term refers to actually existing things; it shows how each kind of proposition relates to the other three. The contrary relation, holding between the **A** and **E** propositions, asserts that at least one is false. Subcontrary, holding between **I** and **O**, asserts that at least one is true. Subalternation, holding between **A** and **I** and between **E** and **O**, indicates that truth "flows" downward and falsity upward. Contradiction holds as in the modern square. The formal fallacies of illicit contrary, illicit subcontrary, and illicit subalternation result from incorrect applications of these relations. The existential fallacy results from applying the traditional square to propositions whose subject terms denote nonexistent things.

The Venn diagram technique, which typically applies to the Boolean interpretation of categorical propositions, can be modified to apply to the Aristotelian interpretation. The modification consists in introducing a circled X, which represents the temporary assumption of existence, into the unshaded part of the subject circle for **A** and **E** propositions. Once modified, the Venn diagram technique can be used to prove the relationships of the traditional square of opposition and to test immediate inferences from the Aristotelian standpoint.

Categorical propositions that are not in standard form can be translated into standard-form propositions. The chief requirements are that the new proposition have a proper quantifier, subject term, copula, and predicate term and that it have the same meaning as the original proposition.

5 Categorical Syllogisms

5.1 Standard Form, Mood, and Figure

In the general sense of the term, a **syllogism** is a deductive argument consisting of two premises and one conclusion. Provisionally we shall define a **categorical syllogism** as a syllogism consisting of three categorical propositions and containing a total of three different terms, each of which appears twice in distinct propositions. (We will give a more precise definition shortly.) The following argument is a categorical syllogism:

> All soldiers are patriots.
> No traitors are patriots.
> Therefore, no traitors are soldiers.

The three terms in a categorical syllogism are given names depending on their position in the argument. The **major term,** by definition, is the predicate of the conclusion, and the **minor term** is the subject of the conclusion. The **middle term,** which provides the middle ground between the two premises, is the one that occurs once in each premise and does not occur in the conclusion. Thus, for the argument above, the major term is "soldiers," the minor term is "traitors," and the middle term is "patriots."

The premises of a categorical syllogism are also given names. The **major premise,** by definition, is the one that contains the major term, and the **minor premise** is the one that contains the minor term. Thus, in the syllogism above, the major premise is "All soldiers are patriots," and the minor premise is "No traitors are patriots." Now that we are supplied with these definitions, we may proceed to the idea of standard form. A categorical syllogism is said to be in **standard form** when the following four conditions are met:

1. All three statements are standard-form categorical propositions.
2. The two occurrences of each term are identical.
3. Each term is used in the same sense throughout the argument.
4. The major premise is listed first, the minor premise second, and the conclusion last.

The first condition requires that each statement have a proper quantifier, subject term, copula, and predicate term. The second condition is clear. The third rules out the possibility of equivocation. For example, if a syllogism containing the word "men" used that term in the sense of human beings in one statement and in the sense of male human beings in another statement, the syllogism would really contain more than three terms and would therefore not be in standard form. Finally, the fourth condition merely requires that the three statements be listed in the right order.

The syllogism about soldiers is in standard form because all four conditions are fulfilled. However, the following syllogism is not in standard form because the fourth condition is violated:

All watercolors are paintings.
Some watercolors are masterpieces.
Therefore, some paintings are masterpieces.

To put this syllogism into standard form the order of the premises must be reversed. The major premise (the one containing "masterpieces," which is the predicate of the conclusion) must be listed first, and the minor premise (the one containing "paintings," which is the subject of the conclusion) must be listed second.

Now that we have a definition of "standard form," we can give a more precise definition of categorical syllogism. A **categorical syllogism** is a deductive argument consisting of three categorical propositions that is capable of being translated into standard form. For an argument to qualify as a categorical syllogism it is not necessary that all three statements be standard-form categorical propositions, but if they are, the analysis is greatly simplified. For this reason, all of the syllogisms presented in the first four sections of this chapter will consist of statements that are in standard form. In later sections, techniques will be developed for translating non-standard-form syllogisms into equivalent arguments that are in standard form.

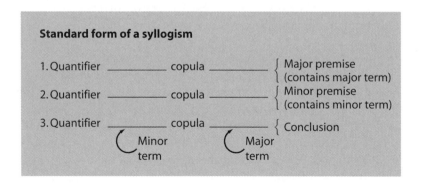

After a categorical syllogism has been put into standard form, its validity or invalidity may be determined through mere inspection of the form. The individual form of a syllogism consists of two factors: mood and figure. The **mood** of a categorical syllogism consists of the letter names of the propositions that make it up. For example, if the major premise is an **A** proposition, the minor premise an **O** proposition, and the conclusion an **E** proposition, the mood is **AOE.** To determine the mood of a categorical syllogism, one must first put the syllogism into standard form; the letter name of the statements may then be noted to the side of each. The mood of the syllogism is then designated by the order of these letters, reading the letter for the major premise first, the letter for the minor premise second, and the letter for the conclusion last.

The **figure** of a categorical syllogism is determined by the location of the two occurrences of the middle term in the premises. Four different arrangements are possible. If we let *S* represent the subject of the conclusion (minor term), *P* the predicate of the conclusion (major term), and *M* the middle term, and leave out the quantifiers and copulas, the four possible arrangements may be illustrated as follows:

Figure 1		Figure 2		Figure 3		Figure 4	
Ⓜ	P	P	Ⓜ	Ⓜ	P	P	Ⓜ
S	Ⓜ	S	Ⓜ	Ⓜ	S	Ⓜ	S
S	P	S	P	S	P	S	P

In the first figure the middle term is top left, bottom right; in the second, top right, bottom right, and so on. Example:

No painters are sculptors.
Some sculptors are artists.
Therefore, some artists are not painters.

This syllogism is in standard form. The mood is **EIO** and the figure is four. The form of the syllogism is therefore designated as **EIO**-4.

To assist in remembering how the four figures are defined, imagine the four possible arrangements of the middle term as depicting the outline of a shirt collar:

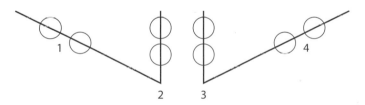

The only problem with this device is that it may lead you to confuse the second figure with the third. To avoid this confusion, keep in mind that for these two figures the *S* and *P* terms go on the same "collar flap" as the middle term. Thus, for the second figure, *S* and *P* are to the left of the middle term, and for the third figure they are to the right.

Since there are four kinds of categorical propositions and there are three categorical propositions in a categorical syllogism, there are 64 possible moods ($4 \times 4 \times 4 = 64$). And since there are four different figures, there are 256 different forms of categorical syllogisms ($4 \times 64 = 256$).

Once the mood and figure of a syllogism is known, the validity of the syllogism can be determined by checking the mood and figure against a list of valid syllogistic forms. To do this, first adopt the Boolean standpoint and look to see if the syllogism's form appears on the following list of unconditionally valid forms. If it does, the syllogism is valid from the Boolean standpoint. In other words, it is valid regardless of whether its terms denote actually existing things.

Unconditionally valid forms

Figure 1	Figure 2	Figure 3	Figure 4
AAA	EAE	IAI	AEE
EAE	AEE	AII	IAI
AII	EIO	OAO	EIO
EIO	AOO	EIO	

If the syllogism does not appear on the list of unconditionally valid forms, then adopt the Aristotelian standpoint and look to see if the syllogism's form appears on the following list of conditionally valid forms. If it does, the syllogism is valid from the Aristotelian standpoint on condition that a certain term (the "critical" term) denotes actually existing things. The required condition is stated in the last column.

Conditionally valid forms

Figure 1	Figure 2	Figure 3	Figure 4	Required condition
AAI	AEO		AEO	S exists
EAO	EAO			
		AAI	EAO	M exists
		EAO		
			AAI	P exists

For example, the **AAI**-1 is valid from the Aristotelian standpoint if the subject of the conclusion (the minor term) denotes actually existing things. The **EAO**-3 is valid if the middle term denotes actually existing things. Thus, if we are given an **AAI**-1 syllogism and the minor term is "cats," then the syllogism is valid from the Aristotelian standpoint. But if the minor term is "unicorns," then the syllogism is invalid. On the other hand, if the minor term is "students who failed the exam" and we are not certain if there are any such students, then the syllogism is conditionally valid.

The relationship between the Aristotelian standpoint and the Boolean standpoint is illustrated in the following bar graph:

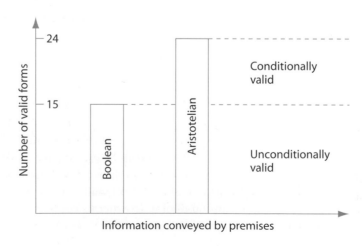

The graph shows that when the premises of a syllogistic form are recognized as conveying information about existence, an additional nine forms become valid.

It is interesting, from a historical perspective, to recall that logic students during the Middle Ages used to memorize a little poem that served as a rule of thumb for distinguishing valid from invalid syllogisms. The vowels in the words identified the mood, and the words "prioris," "secundae," and so on the figure.

> Barbara, Celarent, Darii, Ferioque prioris;
> Cesare, Camestres, Festino, Baroco secundae;
> Tertia, Darapti, Disamis, Datisi, Felapton,
> Bocardo, Ferison habet: quarta insuper addit
> Bramantip, Camenes, Dimaris, Fesapo, Fresison.

For example, the "Barbara" syllogism (this designation is still encountered today) is **AAA**-1, "Celarent" is **EAE**-1, and so on. This poem conforms substantially to the two lists above, except that five forms have been left out. The reason these forms were left out is that the logicians of that time considered them weak: They draw a particular conclusion from premises that would support a (stronger) universal conclusion. For example, the weaker **AAI**-1 is left out in favor of the stronger **AAA**-1. Needless to say, few students today depend on this poem to distinguish valid from invalid syllogisms.

We have seen how, given the syllogism, we can obtain the mood and figure. But sometimes we need to go in the reverse direction: from the mood and figure to the syllogistic form. Let us suppose we are given the form **EIO**-4. To reconstruct the syllogistic form is easy. First use the mood to determine the skeleton of the form:

E	No _____ are _____.
I	Some _____ are _____.
O	Some _____ are not _____.

Then use the figure to determine the arrangement of the middle terms:

E	No _____ are *M*.
I	Some *M* are _____.
O	Some _____ are not _____.

Finally, supply the major and minor terms, using the letters "*S*" and "*P*" to designate the subject and predicate of the conclusion. The predicate of the conclusion is always repeated in the first premise, and the subject of the conclusion is repeated in the second premise:

E	No *P* are *M*.
I	Some *M* are *S*.
O	Some *S* are not *P*.

EXERCISE 5.1

iLrn I. The following syllogisms are in standard form. Identify the major, minor, and middle terms, and the mood and figure of each. Then use the two lists of valid syllogistic forms to determine whether each is valid from the Boolean standpoint, valid from the Aristotelian standpoint, or invalid.

★1. All neutron stars are things that produce intense gravity.
All neutron stars are extremely dense objects.
Therefore, all extremely dense objects are things that produce intense gravity.

2. No insects that eat mosquitoes are insects that should be killed.
All dragonflies are insects that eat mosquitoes.
Therefore, no dragonflies are insects that should be killed.

3. No environmentally produced diseases are inherited afflictions.
Some psychological disorders are not inherited afflictions.
Therefore, some psychological disorders are environmentally produced diseases.

★4. No persons who mix fact with fantasy are good witnesses.
Some hypnotized persons are persons who mix fact with fantasy.
Therefore, some hypnotized persons are not good witnesses.

5. All ozone molecules are good absorbers of ultraviolet rays.
All ozone molecules are things destroyed by chlorine.
Therefore, some things destroyed by chlorine are good absorbers of ultraviolet rays.

iLrn II. Put the following syllogisms into standard form using letters to represent the terms, and name the mood and figure. Then use the two lists of valid syllogistic forms to determine whether each is valid from the Boolean standpoint, valid from the Aristotelian standpoint, or invalid.

★1. No Republicans are Democrats, so no Republicans are big spenders, since all big spenders are Democrats.

2. Some latchkey children are not kids who can stay out of trouble, for some youngsters prone to boredom are latchkey children, and no kids who can stay out of trouble are youngsters prone to boredom.

3. No rent control proposals are regulations welcomed by landlords, and all regulations welcomed by landlords are measures that allow a free hand in raising rents. Therefore, some rent control proposals are measures that allow a free hand in raising rents.

★4. Some insects that feed on milkweed are not foods suitable for birds, inasmuch as no monarch butterflies are foods suitable for birds and all monarch butterflies are insects that feed on milkweed.

5. No illegal aliens are persons who have a right to welfare payments, and some migrant workers are illegal aliens. Thus, some persons who have a right to welfare payments are migrant workers.

6. Some African nations are not countries deserving military aid, because some African nations are not upholders of human rights, and all countries deserving military aid are upholders of human rights.

★7. All pranksters are exasperating individuals, consequently some leprechauns are exasperating individuals, since all leprechauns are pranksters.

8. Some racists are not persons suited to be immigration officials, given that some humanitarians are not persons suited to be immigration officials, and no humanitarians are racists.

9. No persons who respect human life are terrorists, and all airline hijackers are terrorists. Hence, no airline hijackers are persons who respect human life.

★10. Some silicates are crystalline substances, because all silicates are oxygen compounds, and some oxygen compounds are not crystalline substances.

III. Reconstruct the syllogistic forms from the following combinations of mood and figure.

★1. **OAE**-3

2. **EIA**-4

3. **AII**-3

★4. **IAE**-1

5. **AOO**-2

6. **EAO**-4

★7. **AAA**-1

8. **EAO**-2

9. **OEI**-3

★10. **OEA**-4

IV. Construct the following syllogisms:

★1. An **EIO**-2 syllogism with these terms: *major:* dogmatists; *minor:* theologians; *middle:* scholars who encourage free thinking.

2. An unconditionally valid syllogism in the first figure with a particular affirmative conclusion and these terms: *major:* persons incapable of objectivity; *minor:* Supreme Court justices; *middle:* lockstep ideologues.

3. An unconditionally valid syllogism in the fourth figure having two universal premises and these terms: *major:* teenage suicides; *minor:* heroic episodes; *middle:* tragic occurrences.

★4. A valid syllogism having mood **OAO** and these terms: *major:* things capable of replicating by themselves; *minor:* structures that invade cells; *middle:* viruses.

5. A valid syllogism in the first figure having a universal negative conclusion and these terms: *major:* guarantees of marital happiness; *minor:* prenuptial agreements; *middle:* legally enforceable documents.

V. Answer "true" or "false" to the following statements:

1. Every syllogism is a categorical syllogism.

2. Some categorical syllogisms cannot be put into standard form.

3. The statements in a categorical syllogism need not be expressed in standard form.

4. The statements in a standard-form categorical syllogism need not be expressed in standard form.

5. In a standard-form categorical syllogism the two occurrences of each term must be identical.

6. The major premise of a standard-form categorical syllogism contains the subject of the conclusion.

7. To determine its mood and figure, a categorical syllogism must first be put into standard form.

8. In a standard-form syllogism having Figure 2, the two occurrences of the middle term are on the right.

9. The unconditionally valid syllogistic forms are valid from both the Boolean and Aristotelian standpoints.

10. The conditionally valid syllogistic forms are invalid if the requisite condition is not fulfilled.

5.2   Venn Diagrams

Venn diagrams provide the most intuitively evident and, in the long run, easiest to remember technique for testing the validity of categorical syllogisms. The technique is basically an extension of the one developed in Chapter 4 to represent the information content of categorical propositions. Because syllogisms contain three terms, whereas propositions contain only two, the application of Venn diagrams to syllogisms requires three overlapping circles.

These circles should be drawn so that seven areas are clearly distinguishable within the diagram. The second step is to label the circles, one for each term. The precise order of the labeling is not critical, but we will adopt the convention of always assigning the lower left circle to the subject of the conclusion, the lower right circle to the predicate of the conclusion, and the top circle to the middle term. This convention is easy to remember because it conforms to the arrangement of the terms in a standard-form syllogism: The subject of the conclusion is on the lower left, the predicate of the conclusion is on the lower right, and the middle term is in the premises, above the conclusion.

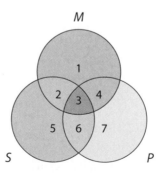

Anything in the area marked "1" is an *M* but neither an *S* nor a *P*, anything in the area marked "2" is both an *S* and an *M* but not a *P*, anything in the area marked "3" is a member of all three classes, and so on.

The test procedure consists of transferring the information content of the premises to the diagram and then inspecting the diagram to see whether it necessarily implies the truth of the conclusion. If the information in the diagram does do this, the argument is valid; otherwise it is invalid.

The use of Venn diagrams to evaluate syllogisms usually requires a little practice before it can be done with facility. Perhaps the best way of presenting the technique is through illustrative examples, but a few preliminary pointers are needed:

1. Marks (shading or placing an X) are entered only for the premises. No marks are made for the conclusion.

2. If the argument contains one universal premise, this premise should be entered first in the diagram. If there are two universal premises, either one can be done first.

3. When entering the information contained in a premise, one should concentrate on the circles corresponding to the two terms in the statement. While the third circle cannot be ignored altogether, it should be given only minimal attention.

4. When inspecting a completed diagram to see whether it supports a particular conclusion, one should remember that particular statements assert two things. "Some *S* are *P*" means "At least one *S* exists *and* that *S* is a *P*"; "Some *S* are not *P*" means "At least one *S* exists *and* that *S* is not a *P*."

5. When shading an area, one must be careful to shade *all* of the area in question. Examples:

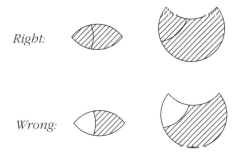

6. The area where an X goes is always initially divided into two parts. If one of these parts has already been shaded, the X goes in the unshaded part. Examples:

If one of the two parts is not shaded, the X goes on the line separating the two parts. Examples:

Right:

This means that the X may be in either (or both) of the two areas—but it is not known which one.

7. An X should never be placed in such a way that it dangles outside of the diagram, and it should never be placed on the intersection of two lines.

Wrong: *Wrong:*

Boolean Standpoint

Because the Boolean standpoint does not recognize universal premises as having existential import, its approach to testing syllogisms is simpler and more general than that of the Aristotelian standpoint. Hence, we will begin by testing syllogisms from that standpoint and proceed, later in this section, to the Aristotelian standpoint. Here is an example:

1. No *P* are *M*.   **EAE**-2
   All *S* are *M*.
   No *S* are *P*.

Since both premises are universal, it makes no difference which premise we enter first in the diagram. To enter the major premise, we concentrate our attention on the *M* and *P* circles, which are highlighted with color:

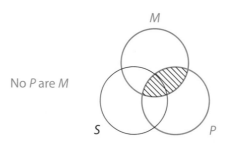

We now complete the diagram by entering the minor premise. In doing so, we concentrate our attention on the *S* and *M* circles, which are highlighted with color:

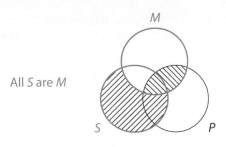

All S are M

The conclusion states that the area where the S and P circles overlap is shaded. Inspection of the diagram reveals that this area is indeed shaded, so the syllogistic form is valid. Because the form is valid from the Boolean standpoint, it is **unconditionally valid.** In other words, it is valid regardless of whether its premises are recognized as having existential import.

Here is another example:

2. All *M* are *P*.   **AEE**-1
   No *S* are *M*.
   No *S* are *P*.

Again, both premises are universal, so it makes no difference which premise we enter first in the diagram. To enter the major premise, we concentrate our attention on the *M* and *P* circles:

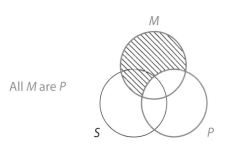

All *M* are *P*

To enter the minor premise, we concentrate our attention on the *M* and *S* circles:

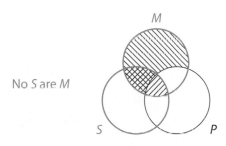

No *S* are *M*

Again, the conclusion states that the area where the *S* and *P* circles overlap is shaded. Inspection of the diagram reveals that only part of this area is shaded, so the syllogistic form is invalid.

Another example:

> 3. Some *P* are *M*. **IAI**-4
>   All *M* are *S*.
>   Some *S* are *P*.

We enter the universal premise first. To do so, we concentrate our attention on the *M* and *S* circles:

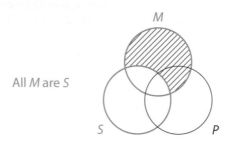

To enter the particular premise, we concentrate our attention on the *M* and *P* circles. This premise tells us to place an X in the area where the *M* and *P* circles overlap. Because part of this area is shaded, we place the X in the remaining area:

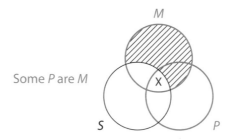

The conclusion states that there is an X in the area where the *S* and *P* circles overlap. Inspection of the diagram reveals that there is indeed an X in this area, so the syllogistic form is valid.

The examples that follow are done in a single step.

> 4. All *P* are *M*. **AOO**-2
>   Some *S* are not *M*.
>   Some *S* are not *P*.

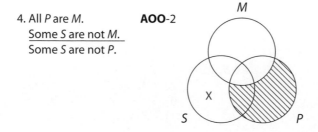

The universal premise is entered first. The particular premise tells us to place an X in the part of the S circle that lies outside the M circle. Because part of this area is shaded, we place the X in the remaining area. The conclusion states that there is an X that is inside the S circle but outside the P circle. Inspection of the diagram reveals that there is indeed an X in this area, so the syllogistic form is valid.

5. Some *M* are *P.*   **IAI-1**
   All *S* are *M.*
   Some *S* are *P.*

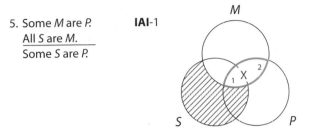

As usual, we enter the universal premise first. In entering the particular premise, we concentrate on the area where the *M* and *P* circles overlap. (For emphasis, this area is colored in the diagram.) Because this overlap area is divided into two parts (the areas marked "1" and "2"), we place the X on the line (arc of the *S* circle) that separates the two parts. The conclusion states that there is an X in the area where the *S* and *P* circles overlap. Inspection of the diagram reveals that the single X is dangling outside of this overlap area. We do not know if it is in or out. Thus the syllogistic form is invalid.

6. All *M* are *P.*   **AOO-1**
   Some *S* are not *M.*
   Some *S* are not *P.*

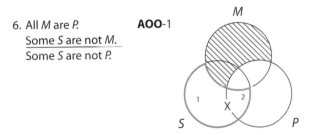

In entering the particular premise, we concentrate our attention on the part of the *S* circle that lies outside the *M* circle (colored area). Because this area is divided into two parts (the areas marked "1" and "2"), we place the X on the line (arc of the *P* circle) separating the two areas. The conclusion states that there is an X that is inside the *S* circle but outside the *P* circle. There *is* an X in the *S* circle, but we do not know whether it is inside or outside the *P* circle. Hence, the argument is invalid.

7. All *M* are *P.*   **AAA-1**
   All *S* are *M.*
   All *S* are *P.*

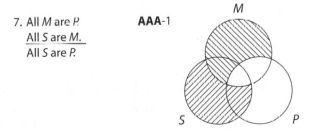

This is the "Barbara" syllogism. The conclusion states that the part of the *S* circle that is outside the *P* circle is empty. Inspection of the diagram reveals that this area is indeed empty. Thus, the syllogistic form is valid.

8. Some *M* are not *P*.   **OIO**-1
   Some *S* are M.
   Some *S* are not *P*.

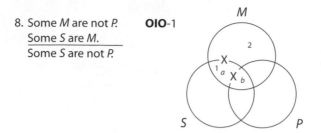

In this diagram no areas have been shaded, so there are two possible areas for each of the two X's. The X from the first premise goes on the line (arc of the *S* circle) separating areas 1 and 2, and the X from the second premise goes on the line (arc of the *P* circle) separating areas *a* and *b*. The conclusion states that there is an X that is inside the *S* circle but outside the *P* circle. We have no certainty that the X from the first premise is inside the *S* circle, and while the X from the second premise is inside the *S* circle, we have no certainty that it is outside the *P* circle. Hence, the syllogistic form is invalid.

We have yet to explain the rationale for placing the X on the boundary separating two areas when neither of the areas is shaded. Consider this argument:

No *P* are *M*.
Some *S* are not *M*.
Some *S* are *P*.

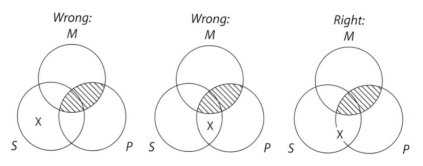

In each of the three diagrams the content of the first premise is represented correctly. The problem concerns placing the X from the second premise. In the first diagram the X is placed inside the *S* circle but outside both the *M* circle and the *P* circle. This diagram asserts: "At least one *S* is not an *M* and it is also not a *P*." Clearly the diagram says more than the premise does, and so it is incorrect. In the second diagram the X is placed inside the *S* circle, outside the *M* circle, and inside the *P* circle. This diagram asserts: "At least one *S* is not an *M*, but it is a *P*." Again, the diagram says more than the premise says, and so it is incorrect. In the third diagram, which is done correctly, the X is placed on the boundary between the two areas. This diagram asserts: "At least one *S* is not an *M*, and it may or may not be a *P*." In other words, nothing at all is said about *P*, and so the diagram represents exactly the content of the second premise.

Aristotelian Standpoint

The syllogistic forms we have tested thus far are valid or invalid from the Boolean standpoint, which does not recognize universal premises as having existential import. We now shift to the Aristotelian standpoint, where existential import can make a difference to validity. To test a syllogism from the Aristotelian standpoint, we follow basically the same procedure we followed in Section 4.6 to test immediate inferences:

1. Reduce the syllogism to its form and test it from the Boolean standpoint. If the form is valid, proceed no further. The syllogism is valid from both standpoints.

2. If the syllogistic form is invalid from the Boolean standpoint, then adopt the Aristotelian standpoint and look to see if there is a Venn circle that is completely shaded except for one area. If there is, enter a circled X in that area and retest the form.

3. If the syllogistic form is conditionally valid, determine if the circled X represents something that exists. If it does, the condition is fulfilled, and the syllogism is valid from the Aristotelian standpoint.

In regard to step 2, if the diagram contains no Venn circle completely shaded except for one area, then the syllogism is invalid from the Aristotelian standpoint. However, if it does contain such a Venn circle, then we place a circled X in the one unshaded area. This circled X represents the temporary assumption that the Venn circle in question is not empty.

In regard to step 3, if the circled X does not represent something that exists, then the syllogism is invalid. As we will see in Section 5.3, such syllogisms commit the existential fallacy from the Aristotelian standpoint.

The list of conditionally valid syllogistic forms presented in Section 5.1 names nine forms that are valid from the Aristotelian standpoint if a certain condition is fulfilled. The following syllogism has one of those forms:

9. No fighter pilots are tank commanders.
   All fighter pilots are courageous individuals.
   Therefore, some courageous individuals are not tank commanders.

First we reduce the syllogism to its form and test it from the Boolean standpoint:

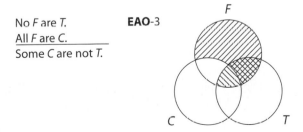

No *F* are *T*.
All *F* are *C*.
Some *C* are not *T*.

EAO-3

The conclusion asserts that there is an X that is inside the *C* circle but outside the *T* circle. Inspection of the diagram reveals no X's at all, so the syllogistic form is invalid from the Boolean standpoint. Proceeding to step 2, we adopt the Aristotelian standpoint and, noting that the *F* circle is all shaded except for one area, we enter a circled X in that area:

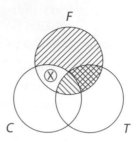

The diagram now indicates that the syllogistic form is conditionally valid, so we proceed to step 3 and determine whether the circled X represents something that actually exists. Since the circled X represents an *F*, and since *F* stands for fighter pilots, the circled X does represent something that exists. Thus, the condition is fulfilled, and the syllogism is valid from the Aristotelian standpoint.

Here is another example:

10. All reptiles are scaly animals.
All currently living tyrannosaurs are reptiles.
Therefore, some currently living tyrannosaurs are scaly animals.

First we test the syllogistic form from the Boolean standpoint:

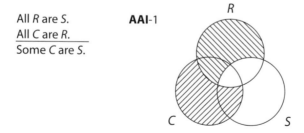

The conclusion asserts that there is an X in the area where the *C* and *S* circles overlap. Since the diagram contains no X's at all, the syllogistic form is invalid from the Boolean standpoint. Proceeding to step 2, we adopt the Aristotelian standpoint. Then, after noticing that the *C* circle is all shaded except for one area, we enter a circled X in that area:

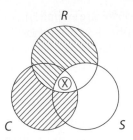

R

C   S

The diagram now indicates that the syllogistic form is conditionally valid, so we proceed to the third step and determine whether the circled X represents something that actually exists. Since the circled X represents a C, and C stands for currently living tyrannosaurs, the circled X does not represent something that actually exists. Thus, the condition is not fulfilled, and the syllogism is invalid. As we will see in the next section of this chapter, the syllogism commits the existential fallacy from the Aristotelian standpoint.

In determining whether the circled X stands for something that exists, we always look to the Venn circle that is all shaded except for one area. If the term corresponding to that circle denotes existing things, then the circled X represents one of those things. In some diagrams, however, there may be two Venn circles that are all shaded except for one area, and each may contain a circled X in the unshaded area. In these cases we direct our attention only to the circled X needed to draw the conclusion. If that circled X stands for something that exists, the argument is valid; if not, it is invalid.

EXERCISE 5.2

iLrn   I. Use Venn diagrams to determine whether the following standard-form categorical syllogisms are valid from the Boolean standpoint, valid from the Aristotelian standpoint, or invalid. Then, identify the mood and figure, and cross-check your answers with the lists of valid syllogisms found in Section 5.1.

★1. All corporations that overcharge their customers are unethical businesses.
Some unethical businesses are investor-owned utilities.
Therefore, some investor-owned utilities are corporations that overcharge their customers.

2. No AIDS victims are persons who pose an immediate threat to the lives of others.
Some kindergarten children are AIDS victims.
Therefore, some kindergarten children are not persons who pose an immediate threat to the lives of others.

3. No individuals truly concerned with the plight of suffering humanity are persons motivated primarily by self-interest.
All television evangelists are persons motivated primarily by self-interest.
Therefore, some television evangelists are not individuals truly concerned with the plight of suffering humanity.

★4. All high-fat diets are diets high in cholesterol.
Some diets high in cholesterol are not healthy food programs.
Therefore, some healthy food programs are not high-fat diets.

5. No concertos are symphonies.
   No symphonies are string quartets.
   Therefore, no string quartets are concertos.

6. All compounds that destroy the ozone layer are environmental hazards.
   All chlorofluorocarbons are compounds that destroy the ozone layer.
   Therefore, all chlorofluorocarbons are environmental hazards.

★7. No pediatricians are individuals who jeopardize the health of children.
   All faith healers are individuals who jeopardize the health of children.
   Therefore, no faith healers are pediatricians.

8. Some individuals prone to violence are not men who treat others humanely.
   Some police officers are individuals prone to violence.
   Therefore, some police officers are not men who treat others humanely.

9. Some automated teller machines are places criminals lurk.
   All places criminals lurk are places to be avoided at night.
   Therefore, some places to be avoided at night are automated teller machines.

★10. No corporations that defraud the government are organizations the government should deal with.
   Some defense contractors are not organizations the government should deal with.
   Therefore, some defense contractors are not corporations that defraud the government.

11. All circular triangles are plane figures.
   All circular triangles are three-sided figures.
   Therefore, some three-sided figures are plane figures.

12. All supernovas are objects that emit massive amounts of energy.
   All quasars are objects that emit massive amounts of energy.
   Therefore, all quasars are supernovas.

★13. No persons who profit from the illegality of their activities are persons who want their activities legalized.
   All drug dealers are persons who profit from the illegality of their activities.
   Therefore, no drug dealers are persons who want their activities legalized.

14. Some individuals who risk heart disease are persons who will die young.
   Some smokers are individuals who risk heart disease.
   Therefore, some smokers are persons who will die young.

15. Some communications satellites are rocket-launched failures.
   All communications satellites are devices with antennas.
   Therefore, some devices with antennas are rocket-launched failures.

★16. All currently living dinosaurs are giant reptiles.
   All giant reptiles are ectothermic animals.
   Therefore, some ectothermic animals are currently living dinosaurs.

17. All survivalists are persons who enjoy simulated war games.
   No persons who enjoy simulated war games are soldiers who have tasted the agony of real war.
   Therefore, all soldiers who have tasted the agony of real war are survivalists.

18. No persons majoring in greed are individuals concerned about the welfare of society.
Some college students are persons majoring in greed.
Therefore, some college students are not individuals concerned about the welfare of society.

★19. No aspirin-based pain relievers are ibuprofens.
All aspirin-based pain relievers are analgesics.
Therefore, some analgesics are not ibuprofens.

20. Some snowflakes are not uniform solids.
All snowflakes are six-pointed crystals.
Therefore, some six-pointed crystals are not uniform solids.

iLrn II. Use Venn diagrams to obtain the conclusion that is validly implied by each of the following sets of premises. If no conclusion can be validly drawn, write "no conclusion."

★1. No *P* are *M*.
All *S* are *M*.

6. No *M* are *P*.
Some *S* are not *M*.

2. Some *P* are not *M*.
Some *M* are *S*.

★7. All *M* are *P*.
All *S* are *M*.

3. Some *M* are *P*.
All *S* arc *M*.

8. All *P* are *M*.
All *S* are *M*.

★4. Some *M* are not *P*.
All *M* are *S*.

9. No *P* are *M*.
Some *M* are *S*.

5. Some *P* are *M*.
All *M* are *S*.

★10. No *P* arc *M*.
No *M* are *S*.

III. Answer "true" or "false" to the following statements:

1. In the use of Venn diagrams to test the validity of syllogisms, marks are sometimes entered in the diagram for the conclusion.

2. When an X is placed on the arc of a circle, it means that the X could be in either (or both) of the two areas that the arc separates.

3. If an X lies on the arc of a circle, the argument cannot be valid.

4. When representing a universal statement in a Venn diagram, one always shades two of the seven areas in the diagram (unless one of these areas is already shaded).

5. If a completed diagram contains two X's, the argument cannot be valid.

6. If the conclusion asserts that a certain area is shaded, and inspection of the diagram reveals that only half that area is shaded, the argument is valid.

7. If the conclusion asserts that a certain area contains an X and inspection of the diagram reveals that only half an X appears in that area, the argument is valid.

8. If the conclusion is in the form "All S are P," and inspection of the diagram reveals that the part of the S circle that is outside the P circle is shaded, then the argument is valid.

9. If, in a completed diagram, three areas of a single circle are shaded, and placing an X in the one remaining area would make the conclusion true, then the argument is valid from the Aristotelian standpoint but not from the Boolean standpoint.

10. If, in a completed diagram, three areas of a single circle are shaded, but the argument is not valid from the Boolean standpoint, then it must be valid from the Aristotelian standpoint.

5.3   Rules and Fallacies

The idea that valid syllogisms conform to certain rules was first expressed by Aristotle. Many such rules are discussed in Aristotle's own account, but logicians of today generally settle on five or six.* If any one of these rules is violated, a specific formal fallacy is committed and, accordingly, the syllogism is invalid. Conversely, if none of the rules is broken, the syllogism is valid. These rules may be used as a convenient cross-check against the method of Venn diagrams. We will first consider the rules as they apply from the Boolean standpoint, and later in the section shift to the Aristotelian standpoint.

Boolean Standpoint

Of the five rules presented in this section, the first two depend on the concept of distribution, the second two on the concept of quality, and the last on the concept of quantity. In applying the first two rules it may help to recall either of the two mnemonic devices presented in Chapter 4: "Unprepared Students Never Pass" and "Any Student Earning B's Is Not On Probation." These mnemonics help one remember that the four categorical propositions distribute their terms as follows:

Statement type	Terms distributed
A	subject
E	subject, predicate
I	none
O	predicate

Here is the first rule.

---

*Some texts include a rule stating that the three terms of a categorical syllogism must be used in the same sense throughout the argument. In this text this requirement is included as part of the definition of "standard form" and is subsequently incorporated into the definition of "categorical syllogism." See Section 5.1.

Rule 1: The middle term must be distributed at least once.

Fallacy: *Undistributed middle.*

Example: All sharks are fish.
<u>All salmon are fish.</u>
All salmon are sharks.

In this standard-form categorical syllogism the middle term is "fish." In both premises "fish" occurs as the predicate of an **A** proposition and therefore it is not distributed in either premise. Thus, the syllogism commits the fallacy of undistributed middle and is invalid. If the major premise were rewritten to read "All fish are sharks," then "fish" would be distributed in that premise and the syllogism would be valid. But, of course, it would still be unsound because the rewritten premise would be false.

The logic behind Rule 1 may be explained by recounting how the middle term accomplishes its intended purpose, which is to provide a common ground between the subject and predicate terms of the conclusion. Let us designate the minor, major, and middle terms by the letters S, P, and M, respectively, and let us suppose that M is distributed in the major premise. By definition, P is related to the *whole* of the M class. Then, when the M class is related either in whole or in part to S, S and P necessarily become related. Analogous reasoning prevails if we suppose that M is distributed in the minor premise. But if M is undistributed in both premises, S and P may be related to *different parts* of the M class, in which case there is no common ground for relating S and P. This is exactly what happens in our fish example. The terms "salmon" and "sharks" are related to different parts of the fish class, so no common ground exists for relating them together.

Rule 2: If a term is distributed in the conclusion, then it must be distributed in a premise.

Fallacies: *Illicit major; illicit minor.*

Examples: All horses are animals.
<u>Some dogs are not horses.</u>
Some dogs are not animals.

All tigers are mammals.
<u>All mammals are animals.</u>
All animals are tigers.

In the first example the major term, "animals," is distributed in the conclusion but not in the major premise, so the syllogism commits the fallacy of illicit major, or, more precisely, "illicit process of the major term." In the second example the minor term, "animals," is distributed in the conclusion but not in the minor premise. The second example therefore commits the fallacy of illicit minor, or "illicit process of the minor term."

In applying this rule, one must always examine the conclusion first. If no terms are distributed in the conclusion, Rule 2 cannot be violated. If one or both terms in the conclusion are distributed, then the appropriate premise must be examined. If the term distributed in the conclusion is also distributed in the premise, then the rule is not violated. But, if the term is not distributed in the premise, the rule is violated and the syllogism is invalid. In applying Rule 2 (and also Rule 1), you may find it helpful to begin by marking all the distributed terms in the syllogism—either by circling them or by labeling them with a small letter "d."

The logic behind Rule 2 is easy to understand. Let us once again designate the minor, major, and middle terms by the letters S, P, and M, respectively, and let us suppose that a certain syllogism commits the fallacy of illicit major. The conclusion of that syllogism then makes an assertion about every member of the P class, but the major premise makes an assertion about only some members of the P class. Because the minor premise, by itself, says nothing at all about the P class, the conclusion clearly contains information not contained in the premises, and the syllogism is therefore invalid. Analogous reasoning applies to the fallacy of illicit minor.

Rule 2 becomes intuitively plausible when it is recognized that distribution is a positive attribute. Granting this, an argument that has a term distributed in the conclusion but not in the premises has *more* in the conclusion than it does in the premises and is therefore invalid. Of course, it is always permissible to have more in a premise than appears in the conclusion, so it is perfectly all right for a term to be distributed in a premise but not in the conclusion.

Rule 3: Two negative premises are not allowed.

Fallacy: *Exclusive premises.*

Example: No fish are mammals.
Some dogs are not fish.
_____
Some dogs are not mammals.

This syllogism may be seen to be invalid because it has true premises and a false conclusion. The defect is attributable to the fact that it has two negative premises.

Upon reflection, Rule 3 should be fairly obvious. Let S, P, and M once again designate the minor, major, and middle terms. Now, if the P class and the M class are separate either wholly or partially, and the S class and the M class are separate either wholly or partially, nothing is said about the relation between the S class and the P class. These two classes may be either distinct or identical in whole or in part. Venn diagrams may be used effectively to illustrate the fact that no conclusion can be validly drawn from two negative premises.

Rule 4: A negative premise requires a negative conclusion, and a negative conclusion requires a negative premise.

Fallacy: *Drawing an affirmative conclusion from a negative premise.*
or
Drawing a negative conclusion from affirmative premises.

Examples: All crows are birds.
Some wolves are not crows.
_____
Some wolves are birds.

All triangles are three-angled polygons.
All three-angled polygons are three-sided polygons.
_____
Some three-sided polygons are not triangles.

These arguments may be seen to be invalid because each has true premises and a false conclusion. The first draws an affirmative conclusion from a negative premise, and the second draws a negative conclusion from affirmative premises.

An alternate formulation of Rule 4 is: Any syllogism having exactly one negative *statement* is invalid. Thus, if the conclusion alone is negative, or if one premise is negative while the other premise and the conclusion are affirmative, the syllogism is invalid.

The logic behind Rule 4 may be seen as follows. If S, P, and M once again designate the minor, major, and middle terms, an affirmative conclusion always states that the S class is contained either wholly or partially in the P class. The only way that such a conclusion can follow is if the S class is contained either wholly or partially in the M class, and the M class wholly in the P class. In other words, it follows only when both premises are affirmative. But if, for example, the S class is contained either wholly or partially in the M class, and the M class is separate either wholly or partially from the P class, such a conclusion will never follow. Thus, an affirmative conclusion cannot be drawn from negative premises.

Conversely, a negative conclusion asserts that the S class is separate either wholly or partially from the P class. But if both premises are affirmative, they assert class inclusion rather than separation. Thus, a negative conclusion cannot be drawn from affirmative premises.

As a result of the interaction of these first four rules, it turns out that no valid syllogism can have two particular premises. This result is convenient to keep in mind, because it allows us to identify as invalid any standard-form syllogism in which both premises start with "some." We will not give any separate rule to this effect, however, because it is logically derivable from the first four rules.

Rule 5: If both premises are universal, the conclusion cannot be particular.

Fallacy: *Existential fallacy.*

Example: All mammals are animals.
                 All tigers are mammals.
                 Some tigers are animals.

The example has two universal premises and a particular conclusion, so it violates Rule 5. It commits the existential fallacy from the Boolean standpoint. The reason the syllogism is invalid from the Boolean standpoint is that the conclusion asserts that tigers exist, whereas the premises are interpreted as making no such assertion. From the Boolean standpoint, universal premises are not recognized as having existential import.

Aristotelian Standpoint

Any categorical syllogism that breaks one of the first four rules is invalid from the Aristotelian standpoint. However, if a syllogism breaks only Rule 5, it is valid from the Aristotelian standpoint on condition that the critical term denotes at least one existing thing. (The critical term is the term listed in the right-hand column of the conditionally valid list of syllogistic forms.) In the example given in connection with Rule 5, the critical term is "tigers," and the syllogism breaks no other rules, so it is valid from the

Aristotelian standpoint. The conclusion asserts that tigers exist, and the Aristotelian standpoint recognizes that the premises convey evidence of their existence. On the other hand, consider the following example:

All mammals are animals.
All unicorns are mammals.
Some unicorns are animals.

In this example, the critical term is "unicorns." Since unicorns do not exist, the Aristotelian standpoint does not recognize that the premises convey evidence of their existence. Thus, the syllogism is invalid from the Aristotelian standpoint, and it commits the existential fallacy from that standpoint. Of course, it also commits the existential fallacy from the Boolean standpoint.

In addition to consulting the list, one way of identifying the critical term is to draw a Venn diagram. The critical term is the one that corresponds to the circle that is all shaded except for one area. In the case of two such circles, it is the one that corresponds to the Venn circle containing the circled X upon which the conclusion depends. Another way of identifying the critical term is through examination of the distributed terms in the syllogism. The critical term is the one that is *superfluously distributed*. In other words, it is the term that, in the premises, is distributed in more occurrences than is necessary for the syllogism to obey all the rules. Here are three examples:

All M^d are P.   No M^d are P^d.   All P^d are M.
All S^d are M.   All M^d are S.   All M^d are S.
Some S are P.   Some S are not P^d.   Some S are P.

The distributed terms are tagged with a small "d." In the first syllogism, M must be distributed to satisfy Rule 1, but S, in the second premise, need not be distributed to satisfy any rule. Thus, by the *superfluous distribution rule,* S is the term that must denote actually existing things for the syllogism to be valid from the Aristotelian standpoint. In the second syllogism, P must be distributed in the first premise to satisfy Rule 2, and M must be distributed once to satisfy Rule 1; but M is distributed twice. Thus, M is the term that must denote existing things for the syllogism to be valid from the Aristotelian standpoint. In the third syllogism, M must be distributed to satisfy Rule 1, but P need not be distributed to satisfy any rule. Thus, in this syllogism, P is the critical term.

You may recall that the existential fallacy from the Boolean standpoint first appeared in Section 4.3, where it arose in connection with the modern square of opposition. Also, the existential fallacy from the Aristotelian standpoint first appeared in Section 4.5, where it arose in connection with the traditional square of opposition. The two versions of the existential fallacy that appear in connection with Rule 5 stem from the same mistake as it relates to categorical syllogisms.

Proving the Rules

The foregoing discussion has shown that if a syllogism breaks any one of the five rules, it cannot be valid from the Boolean standpoint. Thus, we have shown that each of the rules is a *necessary* condition for validity. The question remains, however, whether a syllogism's breaking none of the rules is a *sufficient* condition for validity. In other words, does the fact that a syllogism breaks none of the rules guarantee its validity?

The answer to this question is "yes," but unfortunately there appears to be no easy, shortcut method for proving this fact. Therefore, if you are willing to take your instructor's word for it, you may stop reading this section now and proceed to the exercises. The proof that follows is somewhat tedious, and it proceeds by considering four classes of syllogisms having **A, E, I,** and **O** propositions for their conclusions.

Let us first suppose we are given a valid syllogism having an **A** proposition for its conclusion. Once again, suppose that *P, S,* and *M* designate the major, minor, and middle terms, respectively. Then, by Rules 1 and 2, both *M* and *S* are distributed in the premises. Further, by Rule 4, both premises are affirmative. Now, since **I** propositions distribute neither term, and **A** propositions distribute only one term, both premises must be **A** propositions, and *S* must be distributed in one and *M* in the other. Accordingly, the premises are "All *S* are *M*" and "All *M* are *P.*" If we now combine these premises with the conclusion, "All *S* are *P,*" we can determine by simple reasoning or a Venn diagram that the syllogism is valid. Note that only Rules 1, 2, and 4 were used in producing this first step in our proof, but the resulting syllogism obeys the unused rules as well. A similar process applies to the steps that follow.

Next, we consider a syllogism having an **E** proposition for its conclusion. By Rules 1 and 2, all three terms are distributed in the premises, and by Rules 3 and 4, one premise is negative and the other affirmative. Because three terms are distributed in the premises and there are only two premises, one of the premises must distribute two terms. Accordingly, this premise must be an **E** proposition. Furthermore, the other premise, which is affirmative, and which distributes the third term, must be an **A** proposition. From this we conclude that there are four possible sets of premises. "All *S* are *M*" and "No *M* are *P*" (or its converse), and "All *P* are *M*" and "No *M* are *S*" (or its converse). Since converting an **E** proposition has no effect on validity, we may ignore the converse of these propositions. If we now combine the two given sets of premises with the conclusion, "No *S* are *P,*" simple reasoning or a pair of Venn diagrams will establish the validity of the two resulting syllogisms.

Next, consider a syllogism having an **I** proposition for its conclusion. By Rule 1, *M* is distributed in at least one premise, and by Rule 4, both premises are affirmative. Further, by Rule 5, both premises cannot be universal. Thus, at least one premise is an **I** proposition. However, since the other premise distributes a term, that premise must be an **A** proposition. Accordingly, the four possible sets of premises are "All *M* are *S*" and "Some *M* are *P*" (or its converse), and "All *M* are *P*" and "Some *M* are *S*" (or its converse). Again, since converting an **I** proposition has no effect on validity, we may ignore the converse of these propositions. Then if we combine the two given pairs of premises with the conclusion, "Some *S* are *P,*" simple reasoning or a pair of Venn diagrams will establish the validity of the two resulting syllogisms.

Last, we consider a syllogism having an **O** proposition for its conclusion. By Rules 1 and 2, both *M* and *P* are distributed in the premises. Also, by Rules 3 and 4, one premise is negative and the other affirmative, and by Rule 5, both premises cannot be universal. However, both premises cannot be particular (**I** and **O**), because then only one term would be distributed. Therefore, the premises are either **A** and **O** or **E** and **I**. In regard to the first of these alternatives, either *M* is the subject of the **A** statement and *P* is the predicate of the **O,** or *P* is the subject of the **A** statement and *M* is the predicate of the

O. This gives the premises as "All *M* are *S*" and "Some *M* are not *P*," and "All *P* are *M*" and "Some *S* are not *M*." When these pairs of premises are combined with the conclusion, "Some *S* are not *P*," simple reasoning or a pair of Venn diagrams will establish the validity of the two resulting syllogisms. Finally, considering the other alternative (**E** and **I**), the resulting four sets of premises are "No *M* are *P*" (or its converse) and "Some *M* are *S*" (or its converse). Again ignoring the converted propositions, simple reasoning or a Venn diagram will establish the validity of the single resulting syllogism.

This procedure proves that the five rules collectively provide a sufficient condition for the validity of any syllogism from the Boolean standpoint. Since eight distinct inferences or Venn diagrams were needed to accomplish it, this shows that there are really only eight significantly distinct syllogisms that are valid from the Boolean standpoint. The other seven are variations of these that result from converting one of the premises. For syllogisms having particular conclusions and universal premises about existing things, an analogous procedure can be used to prove that the first four rules collectively provide a sufficient condition for the validity of any syllogism from the Aristotelian standpoint.

EXERCISE 5.3

iLrn I. Reconstruct the following syllogistic forms and use the five rules for syllogisms to determine if they are valid from the Boolean standpoint, valid from the Aristotelian standpoint, or invalid. For those that are conditionally valid, identify the condition that must be fulfilled. For those that are invalid from either the Boolean or Aristotelian standpoint, name the fallacy or fallacies committed. Check your answers by constructing a Venn diagram for each.

★1. **AAA**-3	11. **AII**-2
2. **IAI**-2	12. **AIO**-3
3. **EIO**-1	★13. **AEE**-4
★4. **AAI**-2	14. **EAE**-4
5. **IEO**-1	15. **EAO**-3
6. **EOO**-4	★16. **EEE**-1
★7. **EAA**-1	17. **EAE**-1
8. **AII**-3	18. **OAI**-3
9. **AAI**-4	★19. **AOO**-2
★10. **IAO**-3	20. **EAO**-1

iLrn II. Use the five rules to determine whether the following standard-form syllogisms are valid from the Boolean standpoint, valid from the Aristotelian standpoint, or invalid. For those that are invalid from either the Boolean or Aristotelian standpoint, name the fallacy or fallacies committed. Check your answer by constructing a Venn diagram for each.

★1. Some nebulas are clouds of gas.
Some clouds of gas are objects invisible to the naked eye.
Therefore, some objects invisible to the naked eye are nebulas.

2. No individuals sensitive to the difference between right and wrong are people who measure talent and success in terms of wealth.
All corporate takeover experts are people who measure talent and success in terms of wealth.
Therefore, no corporate takeover experts are individuals sensitive to the difference between right and wrong.

3. No endangered species are creatures loved by the timber industry.
All spotted owls are endangered species.
Therefore, some spotted owls are not creatures loved by the timber industry.

★4. Some cases of affirmative action are not measures justified by past discrimination.
No cases of affirmative action are illegal practices.
Therefore, some illegal practices are not measures justified by past discrimination.

5. All transparent metals are good conductors of heat.
All transparent metals are good conductors of electricity.
Therefore, some good conductors of electricity are good conductors of heat.

6. All members of the National Rifle Association are persons opposed to gun control.
All members of the National Rifle Association are law-abiding citizens.
Therefore, all law-abiding citizens are persons opposed to gun control.

★7. No searches based on probable cause are violations of Fourth Amendment rights.
Some warrantless searches are violations of Fourth Amendment rights.
Therefore, some warrantless searches are not searches based on probable cause.

8. All war zones are places where abuse of discretion is rampant.
Some places where abuse of discretion is rampant are international borders.
Therefore, some international borders are war zones.

9. All inside traders are persons subject to prosecution.
Some executives with privileged information are not persons subject to prosecution.
Therefore, some executives with privileged information are inside traders.

★10. All successful flirts are masters at eye contact.
All masters at eye contact are persons genuinely interested in others.
Therefore, some persons genuinely interested in others are successful flirts.

III. Answer "true" or "false" to the following statements:

1. If a categorical syllogism violates one of the first four rules, it may still be valid.

2. If a valid syllogism has an **E** statement as its conclusion, then both the major and minor terms must be distributed in the premises.

3. If a syllogism has two **I** statements as premises, then it is invalid.

4. If a syllogism has an **E** and an **O** statement as premises, then no conclusion follows validly.

5. If a syllogism has an **I** statement as its conclusion, then Rule 2 cannot be violated.

6. If a valid syllogism has an **O** statement as its conclusion, then its premises can be an **A** and an **I** statement.

7. If a valid syllogism has an **E** statement as a premise, then its conclusion can be an **A** statement.

8. If a syllogism breaks only Rule 5 and its three terms are "dogs," "cats," and "animals," then the syllogism is valid from the Boolean standpoint.

9. If a syllogism breaks only Rule 5 and its three terms are "dogs," "cats," and "animals," then the syllogism is valid from the Aristotelian standpoint.

10. If a syllogism breaks only Rule 5 and its three terms are "elves," "trolls," and "gnomes," then the syllogism is valid from the Aristotelian standpoint.

5.4 Reducing the Number of Terms

Categorical syllogisms, as they occur in ordinary spoken and written expression, are seldom phrased according to the precise norms of the standard-form syllogism. Sometimes quantifiers, premises, or conclusions are left unexpressed, chains of syllogisms are strung together into single arguments, and terms are mixed together with their negations in a single argument. The final four sections of this chapter are concerned with developing techniques for reworking such arguments in order to render them testable by Venn diagrams or by the rules for syllogisms.

In this section we consider arguments that contain more than three terms but that can be modified to reduce the number of terms to three. Consider the following:

All photographers are non-writers.
Some editors are writers.
Therefore, some non-photographers are not non-editors.

This syllogism is clearly not in standard form because it has six terms: "photographers," "editors," "writers," "non-photographers," "non-editors," and "non-writers." But because three of the terms are complements of the other three, the number of terms can be reduced to a total of three, each used twice in distinct propositions. To accomplish the reduction, we can use the three operations of conversion, obversion, and contraposition discussed in Chapter 4. But, of course, since the reworked syllogism must be equivalent in meaning to the original one, we must use these operations only on the kinds of statements for which they yield logically equivalent results. That is, we must use conversion only on **E** and **I** statements and contraposition only on **A** and **O** statements. Obversion yields logically equivalent results for all four kinds of categorical statements.

Let us rewrite our six-term argument using letters to represent the terms, and then obvert the first premise and contrapose the conclusion in order to eliminate the negated letters:

Symbolized argument	**Reduced argument**
All P are non-W.	No P are W.
Some E are W.	Some E are W.
Some non-P are not non-E.	Some E are not P.

Because the first premise of the original argument is an **A** statement and the conclusion an **O** statement, and because the operations performed on these statements yield logically equivalent results, the reduced argument is equivalent in meaning to the original argument. The reduced argument is in standard syllogistic form and may be evaluated either with a Venn diagram or by the five rules for syllogisms. The application of these methods indicates that the reduced argument is valid. We conclude, therefore, that the original argument is also valid.

It is not necessary to eliminate the negated terms in order to reduce the number of terms. It is equally effective to convert certain nonnegated terms into negated ones. Thus, instead of obverting the first premise of the above argument and contraposing the conclusion, we could have contraposed the first premise and converted and then obverted the second premise. The operation is performed as follows:

Symbolized argument	**Reduced argument**
All *P* are non-*W*.	All *W* are non-*P*.
Some *E* are *W*.	Some *W* are not non-*E*.
Some non-*P* are not non-*E*.	Some non-*P* are not non-*E*.

The reduced argument is once again equivalent to the original one, but now we must reverse the order of the premises to put the syllogism into standard form:

Some *W* are not non-*E*.
All *W* are non-*P*.
Some non-*P* are not non-*E*.

When tested with a Venn diagram or by means of the five rules, this argument will, of course, also be found valid, and so the original argument is valid. When using a Venn diagram, no unusual method is needed; the diagram is simply lettered with the three terms "*W*," "non-*E*," and "non-*P*."

The most important point to remember in reducing the number of terms is that conversion and contraposition must never be used on statements for which they yield undetermined results. That is, conversion must never be used on **A** and **O** statements, and contraposition must never be used on **E** and **I** statements. The operations that are allowed are summarized as follows:

Conversion:	No *S* are *P*.	No *P* are *S*.
	Some *S* are *P*.	Some *P* are *S*.
Obversion:	All *S* are *P*.	No *S* are non-*P*.
	No *S* are *P*.	All *S* are non-*P*.
	Some *S* are *P*.	Some *S* are not non-*P*.
	Some *S* are not *P*.	Some *S* are non-*P*.
Contraposition:	All *S* are *P*.	All non-*P* are non-*S*.
	Some *S* are not *P*.	Some non-*P* are not non-*S*.

EXERCISE 5.4

Rewrite the following arguments using letters to represent the terms, reduce the number of terms, and put the arguments into standard form. Then test the new forms with Venn diagrams or by means of the five rules for syllogisms to determine the validity or invalidity of the original arguments.

★1. Some intelligible statements are true statements, because all unintelligible statements are meaningless statements and some false statements are meaningful statements.

2. Some persons who do not regret their crimes are convicted murderers, so some convicted murderers are persons insusceptible of being reformed, since all persons susceptible of being reformed are persons who regret their crimes.

3. All Peace Corps volunteers are persons who have witnessed poverty and desolation, and all persons insensitive to human need are persons who have failed to witness poverty and desolation. Thus, all Peace Corps volunteers are persons sensitive to human need.

★4. Some unintentional killings are not punishable offenses, inasmuch as all cases of self-defense are unpunishable offenses, and some intentional killings are cases of self-defense.

5. All aircraft that disintegrate in flight are unsafe planes. Therefore, no poorly maintained aircraft are safe planes, because all well-maintained aircraft are aircraft that remain intact in flight.

6. No objects that sink in water are chunks of ice, and no objects that float in water are things at least as dense as water. Accordingly, all chunks of ice are things less dense than water.

★7. Some proposed flights to Mars are inexpensive ventures, because all unmanned space missions are inexpensive ventures, and some proposed flights to Mars are not manned space missions.

8. All schools driven by careerism are institutions that do not emphasize liberal arts. It follows that some universities are not institutions that emphasize liberal arts, for some schools that are not driven by careerism are universities.

9. No cases of AIDS are infections easily curable by drugs, since all diseases that infect the brain are infections not easily curable by drugs, and all diseases that do not infect the brain are cases other than AIDS.

★10. Some foreign emissaries are persons without diplomatic immunity, so some persons invulnerable to arrest and prosecution are foreign emissaries, because no persons with diplomatic immunity are persons vulnerable to arrest and prosecution.

5.5   Ordinary Language Arguments

Many arguments that are not standard-form categorical syllogisms as written can be translated into standard-form syllogisms. Such translation often utilizes techniques developed in the last section of Chapter 4—namely, inserting quantifiers, modifying subject and predicate terms, and introducing copulas. The goal, of course, is to produce an argument consisting of three standard-form categorical propositions that contain a total of three different terms, each of which occurs twice in distinct propositions. Once translated, the argument can be tested by means of a Venn diagram or the rules for syllogisms.

Since the task of translating arguments into standard-form syllogisms involves not only converting the component statements into standard form but adjusting these statements one to another so that their terms occur in matched pairs, a certain amount of practice may be required before it can be done with facility. In reducing the terms to three matched pairs it is often helpful to identify some factor common to two or all three propositions and to express this common factor through the strategic use of parameters. For example, if all three statements are about people, the term "people" or "people identical to" might be used; or if they are about times or places, the term "times" or "times identical to" or the term "places" or "places identical to" might be used. Here is an example:

> Whenever people put off marriage until they are older, the divorce rate decreases. Today, people are putting off marriage until they are older. Therefore, the divorce rate is decreasing today.

The temporal adverbs "whenever" and "today" suggest that "times" should be used as the common factor. Following this suggestion, we have:

> All times people put off marriage until they are older are times the divorce rate decreases. All present times are times people put off marriage until they are older. Therefore, all present times are times the divorce rate decreases.

This is a standard-form categorical syllogism. Notice that each of the three terms is matched with an exact duplicate in a different proposition. To obtain such a matchup, it is sometimes necessary to alter the wording of the original statement just slightly. Now if we adopt the convention

> M = times people put off marriage until they are older
> D = times the divorce rate decreases
> P = present times

the syllogism may be symbolized as follows:

> All M are D.
> All P are M.
> All P are D.

This is the so-called "Barbara" syllogism and is, of course, valid. Here is another example:

> Boeing must be a manufacturer because it hires riveters, and any company that hires riveters is a manufacturer.

For this argument the parameter "companies" suggests itself:

> All companies identical to Boeing are manufacturers, because all companies identical to Boeing are companies that hire riveters, and all companies that hire riveters are manufacturers.

The first statement, of course, is the conclusion. When the syllogism is written in standard form, it will be seen that it has, like the previous syllogism, the form **AAA**-1.
Another example:

> If a piece of evidence is trustworthy, then it should be admissible in court. Polygraph tests are not trustworthy. Therefore, they should not be admissible in court.

To translate this argument it is not necessary to use a single common factor:

> All trustworthy pieces of evidence are pieces of evidence that should be admissible in court. No polygraph tests are trustworthy pieces of evidence. Therefore, no polygraph tests are pieces of evidence that should be admissible in court.

This syllogism commits the fallacy of illicit major and is therefore invalid.

As was mentioned in Section 4.7, arguments containing an exceptive proposition must be handled in a special way. Let us consider one that contains an exceptive proposition as a premise:

> All of the jeans except the Levi's are on sale. Therefore, since the Calvin Klein jeans are not Levi's, they must be on sale.

The first premise is translated as two conjoined categorical propositions: "No Levi's are jeans on sale," and "All jeans that are not Levi's are jeans on sale." These give rise to two syllogisms:

> No Levi's are jeans on sale.
> No Calvin Klein jeans are Levi's.
> Therefore, all Calvin Klein jeans are jeans on sale.

> All jeans that are not Levi's are jeans on sale.
> No Calvin Klein jeans are Levi's.
> Therefore, all Calvin Klein jeans are jeans on sale.

The first syllogism, which is in standard form, is invalid because it has two negative premises. The second one, on the other hand, is not in standard form, because it has four terms. If the second premise is obverted, so that it reads "All Calvin Klein jeans are jeans that are not Levi's," the syllogism becomes an **AAA**-1 standard-form syllogism, which is valid.

Each of these two syllogisms may be viewed as a pathway in which the conclusion of the original argument might follow necessarily from the premises. Since it does follow via the second syllogism, the original argument is valid. If both of the resulting syllogisms turned out to be invalid, the original argument would be invalid.

EXERCISE 5.5

Translate the following arguments into standard-form categorical syllogisms, then use Venn diagrams or the rules for syllogisms to determine whether each is valid or invalid. See Section 4.7 for help with the translation.

★1. Physicists are the only scientists who theorize about the nature of time, and Stephen Hawking certainly does that. Therefore, Stephen Hawking must be a physicist.

2. Whenever suicide rates decline, we can infer that people's lives are better adjusted. Accordingly, since suicide rates have been declining in recent years, we can infer that people's lives have been better adjusted in recent years.

3. Environmentalists purchase only fuel-efficient cars. Hence Hummers must not be fuel-efficient, since environmentalists do not purchase them.

★4. Whoever wrote the Declaration of Independence had a big impact on civilization, and Thomas Jefferson certainly had that. Therefore, Thomas Jefferson wrote the Declaration of Independence.

5. There are public schools that teach secular humanism. Therefore, since secular humanism is a religion, there are public schools that teach religion.

6. Anyone who led America into the space age will live in history. Therefore, John Glenn will live in history, because he led America into the space age.

★7. Shania Twain sings what she wants. Hence, since Shania sings country songs, it follows that she must want to sing country songs.

8. Not all interest expenses are tax-deductible. Home mortgage payments are interest expenses. Thus, they are not tax-deductible.

9. If a marriage is based on a meshing of neuroses, it allows little room for growth. If a marriage allows little room for growth, it is bound to fail. Therefore, if a marriage is based on a meshing of neuroses, it is bound to fail.

★10. Television viewers cannot receive scrambled signals unless they have a decoder. Whoever receives digital satellite signals receives scrambled signals. Therefore, whoever receives digital satellite signals has a decoder.

11. Wherever icebergs are present, threats to shipping exist. Icebergs are not present in the South Pacific. Hence, there are no threats to shipping in the South Pacific.

12. According to surveys, there are college students who think that Africa is in North America. But anyone who thinks that has no knowledge of geography. It follows that there are college students who have no knowledge of geography.

★13. Diseases carried by recessive genes can be inherited by offspring of two carriers. Thus, since cystic fibrosis is a disease carried by recessive genes, it can be inherited by offspring of two carriers.

14. All of the movies except the chick flicks were exciting. Hence, the action films were exciting, because none of them are chick flicks.

15. Autistic children are occasionally helped by aversive therapy. But aversive therapy is sometimes inhumane. Thus, autistic children are sometimes helped by inhumane therapy.

5.6 Enthymemes

An **enthymeme** is an argument that is expressible as a categorical syllogism but that is missing a premise or a conclusion. Examples:

> The corporate income tax should be abolished; it encourages waste and high prices.

> Animals that are loved by someone should not be sold to a medical laboratory, and lost pets are certainly loved by someone.

The first enthymeme is missing the premise "Whatever encourages waste and high prices should be abolished," and the second is missing the conclusion "Lost pets should not be sold to a medical laboratory."

Enthymemes occur frequently in ordinary spoken and written English for a number of reasons. Sometimes it is simply boring to express every statement in an argument. The listener or reader's intelligence is called into play when he or she is required to supply a missing statement, and his or her interest is thereby sustained. On other occasions the arguer may want to slip an invalid or unsound argument past an unwary listener or reader, and this aim may be facilitated by leaving a premise or conclusion out of the picture.

Many enthymemes are easy to convert into syllogisms. The reader or listener must first determine what is missing, whether premise or conclusion, and then introduce the missing statement with the aim of converting the enthymeme into a good argument. Attention to indicator words will often provide the clue as to the nature of the missing statement, but a little practice can render this task virtually automatic. The missing statement need not be expressed in categorical form; expressing it in the general context of the other statements is sufficient and is often the easier alternative. Once this is done, the entire argument may be translated into categorical form and then tested with a Venn diagram or by the rules for syllogisms. Example:

Venus completes its orbit in less time than the Earth, because Venus is closer to the sun.

Missing premise: Any planet closer to the sun completes its orbit in less time than the Earth.

Translating this argument into categorical form, we have

All planets closer to the sun are planets that complete their orbit in less time than the Earth.
All planets identical to Venus are planets closer to the sun.
All planets identical to Venus are planets that complete their orbit in less time than the Earth.

This syllogism is valid (and sound).

Any enthymeme (such as the one about Venus) that contains an indicator word is missing a premise. This may be seen as follows. If an enthymeme contains a conclusion indicator, then the conclusion follows it, which means that the missing statement is a premise. On the other hand, if the enthymeme contains a premise indicator, then the conclusion precedes it, which means, again, that the missing statement is a premise.

If, however, an enthymeme contains no indicator words at all (such as the two enthymemes at the beginning of this section), then the missing statement could be either a premise or a conclusion. If the two given statements are joined by a word such as "and," "but," "moreover," or some similar conjunction, the missing statement is usually a conclusion. If not, the first statement is usually the conclusion, and the missing statement is a premise. To test this latter alternative, it may help to mentally insert the word "because" between the two statements. If this insertion makes sense, the missing statement is a premise.

After the nature of the missing statement has been determined, the next task is to write it out. To do so, one must first identify its terms. This can be done by taking account of the terms that are given. Two of the terms in the given statements will match up with each other. Once this pair of terms is found, attention should be focused on the other two terms. These are the ones that will be used to form the missing statement. In constructing the missing statement, attention to the rules for syllogisms may be helpful (if the resulting syllogism is to be valid). For example, if the missing statement is a conclusion and one of the given premises is negative, the missing conclusion must be negative. Or if the missing statement is a premise and the stated conclusion is universal, the missing premise must be universal.

The enthymemes that we have considered thus far have been fairly straightforward. The kinds of enthymemes that occur in letters to the editor of magazines and newspapers often require a bit more creativity to convert into syllogisms. Consider the following:

> The motorcycle has served as basic transportation for the poor for decades. It deserves to
> be celebrated.

> (William B. Fankboner)

The conclusion is the last statement, and the missing premise is that any vehicle that has served as basic transportation for the poor for decades deserves to be celebrated. The enthymeme may be written as a standard form syllogism as follows:

> All vehicles that have served as basic transportation for the poor for decades are vehicles
> that deserve to be celebrated.
> All vehicles identical to the motorcycle are vehicles that have served as basic transporta-
> tion for the poor for decades.
> Therefore, all vehicles identical to the motorcycle are vehicles that deserve to be
> celebrated.

The syllogism is valid and arguably sound. Here is another example:

> I know several doctors who smoke. In a step toward my own health, I will no longer be
> their patient. It has occurred to me that if they care so little about their own health,
> how can they possibly care about mine?

> (Joan Boyer)

In this argument the author draws three connections: the connection between doctors' smoking and doctors' caring about their own health, between doctors' caring about their own health and doctors' caring about the author's health, and between doctors' caring about the author's health and doctors who will have the author as a patient. Two arguments are needed to express these connections:

> All doctors who smoke are doctors who do not care about their own health.
> All doctors who do not care about their own health are doctors who do not care about my
> health.
> Therefore, all doctors who smoke are doctors who do not care about my health.

And,

> All doctors who smoke are doctors who do not care about my health.
> All doctors who do not care about my health are doctors who will not have me as a patient.
> Therefore, all doctors who smoke are doctors who will not have me as a patient.

Notice that the conclusion of the first argument becomes a premise in the second argument. To put these arguments into final standard form the order of the premises must be reversed. Both arguments are valid, but probably not sound.

I. In the following enthymemes determine whether the missing statement is a premise or a conclusion. Then supply the missing statement, attempting whenever possible to convert the enthymeme into a valid argument. The missing statement need not be expressed as a standard-form categorical proposition.

★1. Some police chiefs undermine the evenhanded enforcement of the law, because anyone who fixes parking tickets does that.

2. Any form of cheating deserves to be punished, and plagiarism is a form of cheating.

3. *Lord of the Rings* is a great film. After all, it won eleven Oscars.

★4. A few fraternities have dangerous initiation rites, and those that do have no legitimate role in campus life.

5. Only nonprofit organizations are exempt from paying taxes, so churches must be exempt.

6. All of the operas except Mozart's were well performed, and *Carmen* was not written by Mozart.

★7. Not all phone calls are welcome, but those from friends are.

8. Higher life forms could not have evolved through merely random processes, because no organized beings could have evolved that way.

9. None but great novels are timeless, and *The Brothers Karamazov* is a great novel.

★10. The humpback whale population has been decreasing in recent years because the humpback is being overhunted.

11. Wherever water exists, human life can be sustained, and water exists on the moon.

12. If a symphony orchestra has effective fund-raisers, it will survive; and the Cleveland symphony has survived for years.

★13. Mechanistic materialists do not believe in free will because they think that everything is governed by deterministic laws.

14. A contract to buy land is not enforceable unless it's in writing; but our client's contract to buy land *is* in writing.

15. The only telescopes that are unaffected by the atmosphere are orbiting telescopes, and the Hubble telescope is in orbit.

II. Translate the enthymemes in Part I of this exercise into standard-form categorical syllogisms and test them for validity.

III. The following enthymemes were originally submitted as letters to the editor of magazines and newspapers. Convert them into valid standard-form syllogisms. In some cases two syllogisms may be required.

★1. If the Defense Department is so intent on fighting alcohol abuse, why does it make alcohol so readily available and acceptable? Alcohol is tax free at post liquor stores, and enlisted men's and officers' clubs make drinking almost a mandatory facet of military life.

(Diane Lynch)

2. All aid to Israel should be stopped at once. Why should the American tax-payer be asked to send billions of dollars to Israel when every city in the United States is practically broke and millions of people are out of work?

(Bertha Grace)

3. Suicide is not immoral. If a person decides that life is impossible, it is his or her right to end it.

(Donald S. Farrar)

★4. The best way to get people to read a book is to ban it. The fundamentalist families in Church Hill, Tennessee, have just guaranteed sales of *Macbeth, The Diary of Anne Frank, The Wizard of Oz* and other stories.

(Paula Fleischer)

5. The budget deficit will not be brought under control because to do so would require our elected leaders in Washington to do the unthinkable—act coura-geously and responsibly.

(Bruce Crutcher)

6. The Constitution bans any law that is so vague that "men of common intelli-gence must necessarily guess at its meaning." Sexual harassment laws, how-ever, are so vague that no one knows what they mean.

(Hans Bader)

★7. College students of today are the higher-income taxpayers of tomorrow. Con-gress should consider financial aid as an investment in the financial future of our country.

(Carol A. Steimel)

8. Our genes and our environment control our destinies. The idea of conscious choice is ridiculous. Yes, prisons should be designed to protect society, but they should not punish the poor slobs who were headed for jail from birth.

(Paul R. Andrews)

9. Encouraging toy-gun play gives children a clear message that the best way to deal with frustration and conflict is with a gun. Is this the message that we want to be sending our kids?

(Patricia Owen)

★10. The U.S. surgeon general's latest report on cigarettes and cancer is an interest-ing example of natural selection in the late twentieth century. The intelligent members of our species will quit smoking, and survive. The dummies will continue to puff away.

(Kelly Kinnon)

IV. Page through a magazine or newspaper and identify five topics of current interest. Construct an enthymeme involving each topic.

5.7 Sorites

A **sorites** is a chain of categorical syllogisms in which the intermediate conclusions have been left out. The name is derived from the Greek word *soros*, meaning "heap," and is pronounced "sō rī tēz." The plural form is also "sorites." Here is an example:

> All bloodhounds are dogs.
> All dogs are mammals.
> No fish are mammals.
> Therefore, no fish are bloodhounds.

The first two premises validly imply the intermediate conclusion "All bloodhounds are mammals." If this intermediate conclusion is then treated as a premise and put together with the third premise, the final conclusion follows validly. The sorites is thus composed of two valid categorical syllogisms and is therefore valid. The rule in evaluating a sorites is based on the idea that a chain is only as strong as its weakest link. If any of the component syllogisms in a sorites is invalid, the entire sorites is invalid.

A sorites is in **standard form** when each of the component propositions is in standard form, when each term occurs twice, when the predicate of the conclusion is in the first premise, and when each successive premise has a term in common with the preceding one.* The sorites presented above, for example, is in standard form. Each of the propositions is in standard form, each term occurs twice, the predicate of the conclusion, "bloodhounds," is in the first premise, the other term in the first premise, "dogs," is in the second premise, and so on.

The procedure to be followed in evaluating a sorites is (1) put the sorites into standard form, (2) introduce the intermediate conclusions, and (3) test each component syllogism for validity. If each component is valid, the sorites is valid. Consider the following sorites form:

> No *B* are *C*.
> Some *E* are *A*.
> All *A* are *B*.
> All *D* are *C*.
> ——————
> Some *E* are not *D*.

To put the sorites form into standard form, the premises must be rearranged:

> All *D* are *C*.
> No *B* are *C*.
> All *A* are *B*.
> Some *E* are *A*.
> ——————
> Some *E* are not *D*.

Next, the intermediate conclusions are drawn. Venn diagrams are useful in performing this step, and they serve simultaneously to check the validity of each component syllogism:

---

*Actually, there are two definitions of standard form: the Goclenian and the Aristotelian. The one given here is the Goclenian. In the Aristotelian version, the premises are arranged so that the *subject* of the conclusion occurs in the first premise.

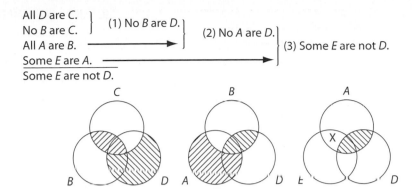

All *D* are *C*.
No *B* are *C*.
All *A* are *B*.
Some *E* are *A*.
Some *E* are not *D*.

(1) No *B* are *D*.

(2) No *A* are *D*.

(3) Some *E* are not *D*.

The first intermediate conclusion, "No *B* are *D*," is drawn from the first two premises. The second, "No *A* are *D*," is drawn from the first intermediate conclusion and the third premise. And the third conclusion, which is identical to the final conclusion, is drawn from the second intermediate conclusion and the fourth premise. Since all conclusions are drawn validly, the sorites is valid.

If, at any designated step in the procedure, no conclusion can be validly drawn—as, for example, if the first two premises are negative or contain undistributed middle terms—then the sorites is invalid. Sometimes immediate inspection will disclose that a certain sorites is invalid. For example, any sorites having two (or more) negative premises or two (or more) particular premises is invalid. Before any such inspection is attempted, however, one must be certain that the terms occur in pairs. Sometimes the operations of conversion, obversion, and contraposition must be used to reduce the number of terms in a sorites, and obversion, of course, affects the quality of the statements on which it is used.

EXERCISE 5.7

I. Rewrite the following sorites in standard form, reducing the number of terms when necessary. Then supply the intermediate conclusions and test with Venn diagrams.

★1. No *B* are *C*.
Some *D* are *C*.
All *A* are *B*.
Some *D* are not *A*.

2. No *C* are *D*.
All *A* are *B*.
Some *C* are not *B*.
Some *D* are not *A*.

3. No *S* are *M*.
All *F* are *S*.
Some *M* are *H*.
All *E* are *F*.
Some *H* are not *E*.

★4. Some *T* are *K*.
No *K* are *N*.
Some *C* are *Q*.
All *T* are *C*.
Some *Q* are not *N*.

5. No *A* are non-*B*.
No *C* are *B*.
All non-*A* are non-*D*.
No *D* are *C*.

6. All *M* are non-*P*.
Some *M* are *S*.
All *K* are *P*.
Some non-*K* are not non-*S*.

★7. All non-*U* are non-*V*.
No *U* are non-*W*.
All *V* are *Y*.
No *X* are *W*.
_____
All *Y* are non-*X*.

8. All *D* are non-*C*.
All non-*B* are non-*A*.
Some *E* are *D*.
All *B* are *C*.
_____
Some non-*A* are not non-*E*.

9. All non-*L* are non-*K*.
Some *K* are *M*.
All *P* are non-*L*.
No non-*N* are *M*.
No *Q* are non-*P*.
_____
Some *N* are not *Q*.

★10. All *R* are *S*.
No non-*V* are *T*.
No *Q* are non-*R*.
No non-*Q* are *P*.
All *T* are non-*S*.
_____
All *V* are non-*P*.

II. The following sorites are valid. Rewrite each sorites in standard form, using letters to represent the terms and reducing the number of terms whenever necessary. Then use Venn diagrams to prove each one valid.

★1. Whatever produces oxygen supports human life.
Rain forests produce oxygen.
Nothing that supports human life should be destroyed.
_____
Rain forests should not be destroyed.

2. No restrictive trade policies fail to invite retaliation.
Trade wars threaten our standard of living.
Some Japanese trade policies are restrictive.
Policies that invite retaliation lead to a trade war.
_____
Some Japanese trade policies threaten our standard of living.

3. Anything that poisons drinking water causes disease and death.
Chemicals percolating through the soil contaminate aquifers.
Dumped chemicals percolate through the soil.
Whatever contaminates aquifers poisons drinking water.
_____
Dumped chemicals cause disease and death.

★4. Nothing that is brittle is ductile.
Superconductors are all ceramics.
Only ductile things can be pulled into wires.
Ceramics are brittle.
_____
Superconductors cannot be pulled into wires.

5. Some college students purchase their term papers.
Any cheat is expelled from college.
No one will achieve his career goals who is expelled.
No one who purchases term papers is other than a cheat.
_____
Some college students will not achieve their career goals.

6. Creation science does not favor the teaching of evolution.
Nothing should be taught that frustrates the understanding of life.
Whatever opposes the teaching of evolution impedes the learning of biology.

Anything that enhances the understanding of life fosters the learning of biology.
Creation science should not be taught.

★7. Whoever gives birth to crack babies increases future crime rates.
Some pregnant women use crack.
None but criminals increase future crime rates.
Pregnant crack users never give birth to anything but crack babies.
Some pregnant women are criminals.

8. Whatever retards population growth increases food availability.
Anything that prevents starvation enhances life.
Birth control measures never accelerate population growth.
Anything that enhances life should be encouraged.
Whatever increases food availability prevents starvation.
Birth control measures should not be discouraged.

9. A few countries allow ivory trading.
Whatever country resists elephant killing discourages poachers.
Any country that allows ivory trading encourages poachers.
No country that promotes the extinction of elephants should escape the condemnation of the civilized world.
Any country that supports elephant killing promotes the extinction of elephants.
A few countries should be condemned by the civilized world.

★10. Anything that promotes skin cancer causes death.
Whatever preserves the ozone layer prevents the release of chlorofluorocarbons.
Nothing that resists skin cancer increases ultraviolet radiation.
Anything that destroys the ozone layer increases ultraviolet radiation.
There are packaging materials that release chlorofluorocarbons.
Nothing that causes death should be legal.
Some packaging materials should be illegal.

III. The following sorites are taken from Lewis Carroll's *Symbolic Logic*. All are valid. Rewrite each sorites in standard form, using letters to represent the terms and reducing the number of terms whenever necessary. Then use Venn diagrams to prove each one valid.

★1. No ducks waltz.
No officers ever decline to waltz.
All my poultry are ducks.
My poultry are not officers.

2. No experienced person is incompetent.
Jenkins is always blundering.
No competent person is always blundering.
Jenkins is inexperienced.

3. No terriers wander among the signs of the zodiac.
Nothing that does not wander among the signs
of the zodiac is a comet.

Nothing but a terrier has a curly tail.
<u>No comet has a curly tail.</u>

★4. All hummingbirds are richly colored.
No large birds live on honey.
<u>Birds that do not live on honey are dull in color.</u>
All hummingbirds are small.

5. All unripe fruit is unwholesome.
All these apples are wholesome.
<u>No fruit grown in the shade is ripe.</u>
These apples were grown in the sun.

6. All my sons are slim.
No child of mine is healthy who takes no exercise.
All gluttons who are children of mine are fat.
<u>No daughter of mine takes any exercise.</u>
All gluttons who are children of mine are unhealthy.

★7. The only books in this library that I do not recommend for reading
are unhealthy in tone.
The bound books are all well-written.
All the romances are healthy in tone.
<u>I do not recommend you to read any of the unbound books.</u>
All the romances in this library are well-written.

8. No interesting poems are unpopular among people of real taste.
No modern poetry is free from affectation.
All your poems are on the subject of soap bubbles.
No affected poetry is popular among people of real taste.
<u>No ancient poem is on the subject of soap bubbles.</u>
All your poems are uninteresting.

9. All writers who understand human nature are clever.
No one is a true poet unless he can stir the hearts of men.
Shakespeare wrote *Hamlet.*
No writer who does not understand human nature can
stir the hearts of men.
<u>None but a true poet could have written *Hamlet.*</u>
Shakespeare was clever.

★10. I trust every animal that belongs to me.
Dogs gnaw bones.
I admit no animals into my study unless they beg when told to do so.
All the animals in the yard are mine.
I admit every animal that I trust into my study.
<u>The only animals that are really willing to beg when told to do so are dogs.</u>
All the animals in the yard gnaw bones.

Summary

A categorical syllogism is a deductive argument consisting of three categorical propositions and containing a total of three different terms, each of which appears twice in distinct propositions. In a standard-form categorical syllogism, the propositions are all in standard form, the two occurrences of each term are identical, each term is used in the same sense throughout the argument, and the major premise is listed first, the minor premise second, and the conclusion last. The major premise is the one that contains the major term (which by definition is the predicate of the conclusion), and the minor premise is the one that contains the minor term (which by definition is the subject of the conclusion). The middle term is the one that appears twice in the premises.

The validity of a standard-form syllogism is determined by its form, and the form is identified in terms of mood and figure. The mood consists of the letter names of the propositions that compose the syllogism, and the figure is determined by the location of the two occurrences of the middle term in the premises. From the Boolean standpoint, a syllogism is either valid or invalid regardless of whether its terms denote actually existing things. From the Aristotelian standpoint, a syllogism is either valid, conditionally valid, or invalid. A conditionally valid syllogism is called valid once it is known that the critical term denotes actually existing things.

Venn diagrams for syllogisms consist of three overlapping circles, with each circle representing a term. To test a syllogism for validity, the content of the premises is represented in the diagram, and the diagram is then inspected to see if it supports the conclusion. In representing the content of the premises, X's and shading are entered into the diagram in basically the same way as they are for two-circle diagrams. The Venn diagram technique applies immediately to syllogisms interpreted from the Boolean standpoint, but it can be modified to test syllogisms from the Aristotelian standpoint.

The validity of categorical syllogisms can also be tested by the application of five rules. A syllogism is valid if and only if (1) its middle term is distributed in at least one premise, (2) a term distributed in the conclusion is also distributed in the premise, (3) at least one premise is affirmative, (4) a negative conclusion occurs with a negative premise and vice versa, and (5) a particular conclusion (should there be one) occurs with a particular premise. If only the last rule is violated, the syllogism is valid from the Aristotelian standpoint on condition that the critical term denotes actually existing things, but it is not valid from the Boolean standpoint.

An argument containing more than three terms, wherein one is a complement of another, may be reduced to a standard-form syllogism by applying the operations of conversion, obversion, and contraposition. These operations must be used only when they yield logically equivalent results, and the goal is to produce an argument containing three terms wherein each is matched with an identical term in a different proposition.

Syllogisms expressed in ordinary language can be translated into standard form by applying the techniques developed in Section 4.7. Enthymemes are quasi-syllogisms that are missing a premise or conclusion. They can be converted into syllogisms by supplying the missing statement. A sorites is a chain of syllogisms in which the intermediate conclusions have been deleted. Testing a sorites consists in putting it into standard form, supplying the intermediate conclusions, and testing each syllogism in the chain.

6 Propositional Logic

6.1 Symbols and Translation

Earlier chapters showed that the validity of a deductive argument is purely a function of its form. By knowing the form of an argument, we can often tell immediately whether it is valid or invalid. Unfortunately, however, ordinary linguistic usage often obscures the form of an argument. To dispel this obscurity, logic introduces various simplifying procedures. In Chapter 5, letters were used to represent the terms in a syllogism, and techniques were developed to reduce syllogisms to what is called standard form. In this chapter, form recognition is facilitated through the introduction of special symbols called **operators,** or **connectives.** When arguments are expressed in terms of these symbols, determining validity often becomes a matter of mere visual inspection.

In the two previous chapters, the fundamental elements were terms. In propositional logic, however, the fundamental elements are whole statements (or propositions). Statements are represented by letters, and these letters are then combined by means of the operators to form more complex symbolic representations.

To understand the symbolic representation used in propositional logic, it is necessary to distinguish what are called simple statements from compound statements. A **simple statement** is one that does not contain any other statement as a component. Here are some examples:

> Fast foods tend to be unhealthy.
> James Joyce wrote *Ulysses.*
> Parakeets are colorful birds.
> The monk seal is threatened with extinction.

Any convenient upper-case letter may be selected to represent each statement. Thus *F* might be selected to represent the first, *J* the second, *P* the third, and *M* the fourth. As will be explained shortly, lower-case letters are reserved for use as statement variables.

A **compound statement** is one that contains at least one simple statement as a component. Here are some examples:

> It is not the case that Al-Quaeda is a humanitarian organization.
> Dianne Reeves sings jazz, and Christina Aguilera sings pop.

Either people get serious about conservation or energy prices will skyrocket.
If the world's nations spurn international law, then future wars are guaranteed.
The Broncos will win if and only if they run the ball.

Using letters to stand for the simple statements, these compound statements may be represented as follows:

It is not the case that *A*.
D and *C*.
Either *P* or *E*.
If *W* then *F*.
B if and only if *R*.

In the first example, note that the statement is compound even though it contains only a single component (*A*). In general, negative statements are interpreted as compound units consisting of an affirmative statement and the phrase "it is not the case that."

The expressions "it is not the case that," "and," "or," "if . . . then . . . ," and "if and only if" are translated by logical operators. The five logical operators are as follows:

Operator	Name	Logical function	Used to translate
~	tilde	negation	not, it is not the case that
•	dot	conjunction	and, also, moreover
v	wedge	disjunction	or, unless
⊃	horseshoe	implication	if . . . then . . . , only if
≡	triple bar	equivalence	if and only if

Saying that logical operators are used to "translate" these English expressions does not mean that the expressions and the operators are identical. As in any translation (from English to French, for example), a certain distortion of meaning occurs. The meaning of such English expressions as "and," "or," and "if and only if" are often vague and may vary with context, whereas the meaning of the logical operators is clear, precise, and invariable. Thus, when we say that the logical operators may be used to translate expressions in ordinary language, we mean that the operators capture a certain aspect of their correlative English expressions. The precise character of this aspect is spelled out in the next section of this chapter. The purpose of this section is to develop a familiarity with the logical operators through practice in translation.

When we use the operators to translate the previous examples of compound statements, the results are as follows:

It is not the case that *A*   ~*A*
D and *C*.   *D* • *C*
Either *P* or *E*.   *P* v *E*
If *W* then *F*.   *W* ⊃ *F*
B if and only if *R*.   *B* ≡ *R*

The statement ~*A* is called a **negation.** The statement *D* • *C* is called a **conjunctive statement** (or a **conjunction**), and the statement *P* v *E* is called a **disjunctive statement** (or a **disjunction**); in the conjunctive statement, the components *D* and *C* are called **conjuncts,** and in the disjunctive statement the components *P* and *E* are called **disjuncts.** The statement *W* ⊃ *F* is called a **conditional statement,** and it expresses the relation of **material implication.** Its components are called **antecedent** (*W*) and **consequent** (*F*). Lastly, *B* ≡ *R* is called a **biconditional statement,** and it expresses the relation of **material equivalence.**

Let us now use the logical operators to translate additional English statements. The tilde symbol is used to translate any negated simple proposition:

Rolex does not make computers.	~ *R*
It is not the case that Rolex makes computers.	~ *R*
It is false that Rolex makes computers.	~ *R*

As these examples show, the tilde is always placed *in front* of the proposition it negates. All of the other operators are placed *between* two propositions. Also, unlike the other operators, the tilde cannot be used to connect two propositions. Thus, *G* ~ *H* is not a proper expression. But the tilde is the only operator that can immediately follow another operator. Thus, it would be proper to write *G* • ~*H*. In the Rolex examples, the tilde is used to negate a simple proposition, but it can also be used to negate a compound proposition—for example ~(*G* • *F*). In this case the tilde negates the entire expression inside the parentheses.

This last example allows us the opportunity to define what is called the main operator in a statement. The **main operator** is that operator in a compound statement that governs the largest component(s) in the statement. In the example just given, the main operator is the tilde, because it governs everything that follows it—namely, (*G* • *F*). The dot, on the other hand, is not the main operator because it governs only the two simple statements inside the parentheses. On the other hand, in the statement *H* • ~(*K* ∨ *M*), the dot is the main operator because it governs both *H* and ~(*K* ∨ *M*), whereas the tilde governs only the expression in parentheses.

> These statements are all **negations.** The main operator is a tilde.
>
> ~*B*
> ~(*G* ⊃ *H*)
> ~[(*A* ≡ *F*) • (*C* ≡ *G*)]

The dot symbol is used to translate such conjunctions as "and," "also," "but," "however," "yet," "still," "moreover," "although," and "nevertheless":

Tiffany sells jewelry, and Gucci sells cologne.	*T* • *G*
Tiffany sells jewelry, but Gucci sells cologne.	*T* • *G*
Tiffany sells jewelry; however, Gucci sells cologne.	*T* • *G*
Tiffany and Ben Bridge sell jewelry.	*T* • *B*

Note that the last example is equivalent in meaning to "Tiffany sells jewelry, and Ben Bridge sells jewelry." To translate such a statement as a conjunction of two simple statements, the original statement must be equivalent to a compound statement in English. For example, the statement "Mary and Louise are friends" is *not* equivalent in meaning to "Mary is a friend, and Louise is a friend," so this statement cannot be translated as $M \cdot L$.

These statements are all **conjunctions.** The main operator is a dot.

$K \cdot \sim L$

$(E \lor F) \cdot (G \lor H)$

$[(R \supset T) \lor (S \supset U)] \cdot [(W \equiv X) \lor (Y \equiv Z)]$

The wedge symbol is used to translate "or" and "unless." A previous chapter explained that "unless" is equivalent in meaning to "if not." This equivalence holds in propositional logic as well, but in propositional logic it is usually simpler to equate "unless" with "or." For example, the statement "You won't graduate unless you pass freshman English" is equivalent to "Either you pass freshman English or you won't graduate" and also to "If you don't pass freshman English, then you won't graduate." As the next section demonstrates, the wedge symbol has the meaning of "and/or"— that is, "or" in the inclusive sense. Although "or" and "unless" are sometimes used in an exclusive sense, the wedge is usually used to translate them.

The word "either," which is often used to introduce disjunctive statements, has primarily a punctuational meaning. The placement of this word often tells us where parentheses and brackets must be introduced in the symbolic expression. If parentheses or brackets are not needed, "either" does not affect the translation. A similar point applies to the word "both," which is often used to introduce conjunctive statements. Here are some disjunctive statements:

Aspen allows snowboards or Telluride does.	$A \lor T$
Either Aspen allows snowboards or Telluride does.	$A \lor T$
Aspen allows snowboards unless Telluride does.	$A \lor T$
Unless Aspen allows snowboards, Telluride does.	$A \lor T$

From the English sense of these statements, it should be clear that $A \lor T$ is logically equivalent to $T \lor A$. Also $T \cdot G$ is logically equivalent to $G \cdot T$. Logically equivalent propositions necessarily have the same truth value.

These statements are all **disjunctions.** The main operator is a wedge.

$\sim C \lor \sim D$

$(F \cdot H) \lor (\sim K \cdot \sim L)$

$[S \cdot (I \supset U)] \lor [X \cdot (Y \equiv Z)]$

The horseshoe symbol is used to translate "if . . . then . . . ," "only if," and similar expressions that indicate a conditional statement. The expressions "in case," "provided that," "given that," and "on condition that" are usually translated in the same way as "if." By customary usage, the horseshoe symbol is also used to translate "implies." Although "implies" is used most properly to describe the relationship between the premises and conclusion of an argument, we may accept this translation as an alternate meaning for "implies."

The function of "only if" is, in a sense, just the reverse of "if." For example, the statement "You will catch a fish only if your hook is baited" does not mean "If your hook is baited, then you will catch a fish." If it meant this, then everyone with a baited hook would catch a fish. Rather, the statement means "If your hook is not baited, then you will not catch a fish," which is logically equivalent to "If you catch a fish, then your hook was baited." To avoid mistakes in translating "if" and "only if" remember this rule: The statement that follows "if" is always the antecedent, and the statement that follows "only if" is always the consequent. Thus "C only if H" is translated $C \supset H$, whereas "C if H" is translated $H \supset C$. Additional examples:

If Purdue raises tuition, then so does Notre Dame.	$P \supset N$
Notre Dame raises tuition if Purdue does.	$P \supset N$
Purdue raises tuition only if Notre Dame does.	$P \supset N$
Cornell cuts enrollment provided that Brown does.	$B \supset C$
Cornell cuts enrollment on condition that Brown does.	$B \supset C$
Brown's cutting enrollment implies that Cornell does.	$B \supset C$

In translating conditional statements, it is essential not to confuse antecedent with consequent. The statement $A \supset B$ is not logically equivalent to $B \supset A$.

These statements are all **conditionals** (material implications). The main operator is a horseshoe.

$H \supset {\sim}J$
$(A \lor C) \supset (D \cdot E)$
$[K \lor (S \cdot {\sim}T)] \supset [{\sim}F \lor (M \cdot O)]$

The horseshoe symbol is also used to translate statements phrased in terms of sufficient conditions and necessary conditions. Event A is said to be a **sufficient condition** for event B whenever the occurrence of A is all that is required for the occurrence of B. On the other hand, event A is said to be a **necessary condition** for event B whenever B cannot occur without the occurrence of A. For example, having the flu is a sufficient condition for feeling miserable, whereas having air to breathe is a necessary condition for survival. Other things besides having the flu might cause a person to feel miserable, but that by itself is sufficient; other things besides having air to breathe are required for survival, but without air survival is impossible. In other words, air is necessary.

To translate statements involving sufficient and necessary conditions into symbolic form, place the statement that names the sufficient condition in the antecedent of the conditional and the statement that names the necessary condition in the consequent. The mnemonic device "SUN" may be conveniently used to keep this rule in mind. Turn-

6

ing the U sideways creates $S \supset N$, wherein S and N designate sufficient and necessary conditions, respectively. Whatever is given as a sufficient condition goes in the place of the S, and whatever is given as a necessary condition goes in the place of the N:

Hilton's opening a new hotel is a sufficient condition for Marriott's doing so.	$H \supset M$
Hilton's opening a new hotel is a necessary condition for Marriott's doing so.	$M \supset H$

The triple bar symbol is used to translate the expressions "if and only if" and "is a necessary and sufficient condition for":

JFK tightens security if and only if O'Hare does.	$J \equiv O$
JFK's tightening security is a sufficient and necessary condition for O'Hare's doing so.	$J \equiv O$

Analysis of the first statement reveals that $J \equiv O$ is logically equivalent to $(J \supset O) \cdot (O \supset J)$. The statement "JFK tightens security only if O'Hare does" is translated $J \supset O$, and "JFK tightens security if O'Hare does" is translated $O \supset J$. Combining the two English statements, we have $(J \supset O) \cdot (O \supset J)$, which is just a longer way of writing $J \equiv O$. A similar analysis applies to the second statement. Because the order of the two conjuncts can be reversed, $J \equiv O$ is logically equivalent to $O \equiv J$. However, when translating such statements, we adopt the convention that the letter representing the first English statement is written to the left of the triple bar, and the letter representing the second English statement is written to the right of the triple bar. Thus, the examples above are translated $J \equiv O$, and not $O \equiv J$.

These statements are all **biconditionals** (material equivalences). The main operator is a triple bar.

$M \equiv {\sim}T$
$(B \lor D) \equiv (A \cdot C)$
$[K \lor (F \supset I)] \equiv [{\sim}L \cdot (G \lor H)]$

Whenever more than two letters appear in a translated statement, parentheses, brackets, or braces must be used to indicate the proper range of the operators. The statement $A \cdot B \lor C$, for example, is ambiguous. When parentheses are introduced, this statement becomes either $(A \cdot B) \lor C$ or $A \cdot (B \lor C)$. These two statements are not logically equivalent. Thus, with statements such as these, some clue must be found in the English statement that indicates the correct placement of the parentheses in the symbolic statement. Such clues are usually given by commas and semicolons, by such words as "either" and "both," and by the use of a single predicate in conjunction with two or more subjects. The following examples illustrate the correct placement of parentheses and brackets:

Prozac relieves depression and Allegra combats allergies, or Zocor lowers cholesterol.	$(P \cdot A) \lor Z$

Prozac relieves depression, and Allegra combats allergies or Zocor lowers cholesterol.	$P \cdot (A \lor Z)$
Either Prozac relieves depression and Allegra combats allergies or Zocor lowers cholesterol.	$(P \cdot A) \lor Z$
Prozac relieves depression and either Allegra combats allergies or Zocor lowers cholesterol.	$P \cdot (A \lor Z)$
Prozac relieves depression or both Allegra combats allergies and Zocor lowers cholesterol.	$P \lor (A \cdot Z)$
Prozac relieves depression and Allegra or Zocor lowers cholesterol.	$P \cdot (A \lor Z)$
If Merck changes its logo, then if Pfizer increases sales, then Lilly will reorganize.	$M \supset (P \supset L)$
If Merck's changing its logo implies that Pfizer increases sales, then Lilly will reorganize.	$(M \supset P) \supset L$
If Schering and Pfizer lower prices or Novartis downsizes, then Warner will expand production.	$[(S \cdot P) \lor N] \supset W$

> **Do not confuse these three statement forms:**
>
> | | |
> |---|---|
> | A if B | $B \supset A$ |
> | A only if B | $A \supset B$ |
> | A if and only if B | $A \equiv B$ |

When a tilde appears in a symbolic expression, by convention it is considered to affect only the unit that immediately follows it. For example, in the expression $\sim K \lor M$ the tilde affects only the K; in the expression $\sim(K \lor M)$ it affects the entire expression inside the parentheses. In English, the expression "It is not the case that K or M" is ambiguous, because the range of the negating words is indefinite. To eliminate this ambiguity, we now adopt the convention that the negating words are considered to affect only the unit that follows them. Thus "It is not the case that K or M" is translated $\sim K \lor M$.

The statement "Not both S and T" is translated $\sim(S \cdot T)$. By an important rule called *DeMorgan's rule*, this statement is logically equivalent to $\sim S \lor \sim T$. For example, the statement "Not both Steven and Thomas were fired" is equivalent in meaning to "Either Stephen was not fired or Thomas was not fired." Because the former statement is *not* equivalent in meaning to "Stephen was not fired and Thomas was not fired," $\sim(S \cdot T)$ is *not* logically equivalent to $\sim S \cdot \sim T$. Analogously, the statement "Not either S or T" is translated $\sim(S \lor T)$, which by DeMorgan's rule is logically equivalent to $\sim S \cdot \sim T$. For example, "Not either Steven or Thomas was fired" is equivalent in meaning to "Steven was not fired and Thomas was not fired." Thus $\sim(S \lor T)$ is *not* logically equivalent to $\sim S \lor \sim T$. The following examples illustrate these points:

Megan is not a winner, but Kathy is.	$\sim M \cdot K$
Not both Megan and Kathy are winners.	$\sim(M \cdot K)$

Both Megan and Kathy are not winners.	$\sim M \cdot \sim K$
Not either Megan or Kathy is a winner.	$\sim (M \lor K)$
Neither Megan nor Kathy is a winner.	$\sim (M \lor K)$
Either Megan or Kathy is not a winner.	$\sim M \lor \sim K$

Notice the function of "either" and "both":

Not either A or B.	$\sim (A \lor B)$
Either not A or not B.	$\sim A \lor \sim B$
Not both A and B.	$\sim (A \cdot B)$
Both not A and not B.	$\sim A \cdot \sim B$

The symbolic expressions that we have used throughout this section to translate meaningful, unambiguous English statements are called **well-formed formulas** (**WFFs**). "WFFs" is usually pronounced "woofs." A well-formed formula is a *syntactically* correct arrangement of symbols. In English, for example, the expression "there is a cat on the porch" is syntactically correct, but "Porch on the is cat a there" is not syntactically correct. Some examples of symbolic arrangements that are *not* well-formed formulas are "$A \supset \lor B$," "$A \cdot B (\lor C)$," and "$\sim \lor B \equiv \supset C$."

Summary	Operator
not, it is not the case that, it is false that	$\sim$
and, yet, but, however, moreover, nevertheless, still, also, although, both, additionally, furthermore	$\cdot$
or, unless	$\lor$
if ... then, only if, implies, given that, in case, provided that, on condition that, sufficient condition for, necessary condition for (Note: Do not confuse antecedent with consequent!)	$\supset$
if and only if, is equivalent to, sufficient and necessary condition for	$\equiv$

EXERCISE 6.1

iLrn   I. Translate the following statements into symbolic form using capital letters to represent affirmative English statements:

  ★1. California does not allow smoking in restaurants.

  2. Florida has a major theme park but Maine does not.

  3. Either AMC or Loews gives student discounts.

★4. Both FedEx and UPS deliver overnight.

5. If Nintendo produces an alien game, then so does Sega.

6. Nintendo produces an alien game if Sega does.

★7. Michael J. Fox will be cured if and only if stem-cell research succeeds.

8. Matt Damon comes to the party only if Ben Affleck comes.

9. ImClone's earnings will improve given that Erbitux cures cancer.

★10. The Colts' winning the Superbowl implies that Peyton Manning is a great quarterback.

11. Mary-Kate Olsen does not appear in a movie unless Ashley does.

12. Alabama restricts abortion rights only if Georgia and Mississippi do.

★13. The President supports campaign reform and either the House adopts universal health care or the Senate approves missile defense.

14. Either the President supports campaign reform and the House adopts universal health care or the Senate approves missile defense.

15. Not both Hertz and Avis rent limousines.

★16. Both Hertz and Avis do not rent limousines.

17. Either Motrin or Contac cures headaches.

18. Not either Mylanta or Pepcid cures headaches.

★19. Neither Mylanta nor Pepcid cures headaches.

20. Either Mylanta or Pepcid does not cure headaches.

21. If Canada subsidizes exports, then if Mexico opens new factories, then the United States raises tariffs.

★22. If Canada's subsidizing exports implies that Mexico opens new factories, then the United States raises tariffs.

23. DMX abandons explicit lyrics if and only if neither Columbia nor BMG stops advertising.

24. If Iraq launches bioterrorist attacks, then either Peter Jennings or Brian Williams will report them.

★25. Either Oregon does not allow same-sex marriages or if Nevada legalizes prostitution then so does Arizona.

26. If either Eminem or Dr. Dre attend the charity concert, then neither Britney Spears nor Christina Aguilera will attend.

27. If the *New York Times* and the *Washington Post* suppress free speech, then either CNN or MSNBC will get higher ratings.

★28. Panasonic or Samsung introduces a new widescreen TV given that both Hitachi and Toshiba do not do so.

29. Jennifer Capriatti wins tournaments, and Barry Bonds hits homers or Marshall Faulk runs touchdowns.

30. Jennifer Capriati wins tournaments and Barry Bonds hits homers, or Marshall Faulk runs touchdowns.

★31. Yosemite and Kings Canyon restrict vehicle traffic unless Bryce and Zion do not.

32. Jennifer Lopez goes to the premiere provided that Marc Anthony does, but Ben Affleck does not.

33. Either Ashanti or Beyonce wear a red dress to the Grammys but it is not the case that both do.

★34. Microsoft does not acknowledge a monopoly; however, if Intel lays off workers, then either Dell or Apple will have job applicants.

35. It is not the case that both Budweiser changes its formula and Miller or Heineken closes a brewery.

36. It is not the case that either Delta Zeta serves alcohol or the Glee Club and Honor Society serve soft drinks.

★37. If Spike Lee writes a movie, then if Denzel Washington stars in it, then Paramount and MGM will compete for it.

38. If HBO films a special, then if Showtime expands viewership, then Bravo's launching an ad campaign implies that Encore features oldies.

39. It is not the case that either Bart and Lisa do their chores or Lenny and Karl blow up the power plant.

★40. It is not the case that both McDonald's or Burger King closes early and Taco Bell or KFC closes late.

41. Michael Douglas's having an affair is a sufficient condition for Catherine Zeta-Jones's divorcing him.

42. Michael Douglas's having an affair is a necessary condition for Catherine Zeta-Jones's divorcing him.

★43. Michael Douglas's having an affair is a necessary and sufficient condition for Catherine Zeta-Jones's divorcing him.

44. Outkast's winning a Grammy is a sufficient condition for the White Stripes to be jealous, only if Janet Jackson's Superbowl prank is a necessary condition for Jessica Simpson's being asked to sing the anthem.

45. Nike and Adidas give out free shoes if and only if Reebok or Converse lowers prices.

★46. It is not the case that both *Cosmo*'s changing its cover implies that *Glamour* does and *Time*'s increasing circulation implies that *Newsweek* does.

47. Domino's delivers for free if Pizza Hut adds new toppings, provided that Round Table airs more commercials.

48. Verizon's offering free long distance implies that AT&T does, given that Qualcomm's inventing new circuits implies that neither Nokia nor Ericsson sells inferior phones.

★49. If the Gap's advertising a sale and Abercrombie's selling more clothes are sufficient and necessary conditions for Old Navy's cutting costs, then neither Nordstrom nor Saks attracts new customers.

50. *Friends* going off the air is a necessary condition for Joey's getting a spin-off; moreover, Will and Grace's having more guest stars and Donald Trump's firing more candidates is a sufficient condition for NBC's getting better ratings.

6

II. Translate the following statements into symbolic form using capital letters to represent affirmative English statements.

★1. Unless we reduce the incidence of child abuse, future crime rates will increase.

2. If pharmaceutical makers conceal test results, they are subject to substantial fines.

3. High-definition television is a technological marvel, but it is expensive.

★4. Cigarette manufacturers are neither honest nor socially responsible.

5. Psychologists and psychiatrists do not both prescribe antidepressant drugs.

6. If health maintenance organizations cut costs, then either preventive medicine is emphasized or the quality of care deteriorates.

★7. A necessary condition for a successful business venture is good planning.

8. If cocaine is legalized, then its use may increase but criminal activity will decline.

9. Ozone depletion in the atmosphere is a sufficient condition for increased cancer rates.

★10. If affirmative action programs are dropped, then if new programs are not created, then minority applicants will suffer.

11. If Internet use continues to grow, then more people will become cyberaddicts and normal human relations will deteriorate.

12. Human life will not perish unless either we poison ourselves with pollution or a large asteroid collides with the earth.

★13. Cooling a group of atoms to absolute zero and keeping them bunched together is a necessary and sufficient condition for producing a Bose-Einstein condensate.

14. If motion pictures contain subliminal sex messages or if they challenge the traditional family, then conservative politicians call for censorship.

15. Either clear-cutting in national forests is halted and old growth trees are allowed to stand, or salmon runs will be destroyed and bird habitats obliterated.

★16. Three-strikes laws will be enforced and longer sentences imposed only if hundreds of new prisons are built, and that will happen only if taxes are increased.

17. The Ebola virus is deadly, but it will become a major threat to humanity if and only if it becomes airborne and a vaccine is not developed.

18. If evolutionary biology is correct, then higher life-forms arose by chance, and if that is so, then it is not the case that there is any design in nature and divine providence is a myth.

★19. If banks charge fees for teller-assisted transactions, then more people will use ATMs; and if that happens and ATM fees increase, then banks will close branches and profits will skyrocket.

20. If corporate welfare continues, then taxpayer interests will be ignored and billions of tax dollars will go to giant corporations; and if the latter occurs, then there will not be anything left for the poor and the budget will not be balanced.

iLrn **III.** Determine which of the following are *not* well-formed formulas.

1. $(S \cdot \sim T) \lor (\sim U \cdot W)$
2. $\sim(K \lor L) \cdot (\supset G \lor H)$
3. $(E \sim F) \lor (W \equiv X)$
4. $(B \supset \sim T) \equiv \sim(\sim C \supset U)$
5. $(F \equiv \sim Q) \cdot (A \supset E \lor T)$
6. $\sim D \lor \sim[(P \supset Q) \cdot (T \supset R)]$
7. $[(D \cdot \lor Q) \supset (P \lor E)] \lor [A \supset (\cdot H)]$
8. $M(N \supset Q) \lor (\sim C \cdot D)$
9. $\sim(F \lor \sim G) \supset [(A \equiv E) \cdot \sim H]$
10. $(R \equiv S \cdot T) \supset \sim(\sim W \cdot \sim X)$

6.2 Truth Functions

The truth value of a compound proposition expressed in terms of one or more logical operators is said to be a **function** of the truth values of its components. This means that the truth value of the compound proposition is completely determined by the truth values of its components. If the truth values of the components are known, then the truth value of the compound proposition can be calculated from the definitions of the logical operators. To point up the significance of this fact we need only note that many compound statements in ordinary language are not truth functional. For example, the statement "Mary believes that Paul is dishonest" is compound because it contains the statement "Paul is dishonest" as a component. Yet, the truth value of the compound statement is not determined by the truth value of the component, because Mary's beliefs about Paul are not compelled by any attribute that Paul may or may not possess.

The first part of this section presents the definitions of the five logical operators, the second part shows how they are used to compute the truth values of more complicated propositions, and the third examines further the degree to which symbolized expressions match the meaning of expressions in ordinary language.

Definitions of the Logical Operators

The definitions of the logical operators are presented in terms of **statement variables,** which are lower-case letters (p, q, r, s) that can stand for any statement. For example, the statement variable p could stand for the statements A, $A \supset B$, $B \lor C$, and so on.

Statement variables are used to construct **statement forms.** A statement form is an arrangement of statement variables and operators such that the uniform substitution of statements in place of the variables results in a statement. For example, $\sim p$ and $p \supset q$ are statement forms because substituting the statements A and B in place of p and q, respectively, results in the statements $\sim A$ and $A \supset B$. A compound statement is said to have a certain form if it can be produced by substituting statements in place of the letters in that form. Thus $\sim A$, $\sim(A \lor B)$, and $\sim[A \cdot (B \lor C)]$ are negations because they can be produced by substituting statements in place of p in the form $\sim p$.

Now let us consider the definition of the tilde operator (negation). This definition is given by a **truth table,** an arrangement of truth values that shows in every possible case how the truth value of a compound proposition is determined by the truth values of its simple components. The truth table for negation shows how any statement having the form of a negation ($\sim p$) is determined by the truth value of the statement that is negated (p):

Negation	p	$\sim p$
	T	F
	F	T

The truth table shows that $\sim p$ is false when p is true and that $\sim p$ is true when p is false. This is exactly what we would expect, because it perfectly matches ordinary English usage. Examples:

It is not the case that Haagen-Dazs makes ice cream. $\sim H$

It is not the case that Starbucks makes ice cream. $\sim S$

The first statement is false because H is true, and the second is true because S is false.

Let us now consider the definition of the dot operator (conjunction). The truth table that follows shows how any statement having the form of a conjunction ($p \cdot q$) is determined by the truth values of its conjuncts (p, q):

Conjunction	p	q	$p \cdot q$
	T	T	T
	T	F	F
	F	T	F
	F	F	F

This truth table shows that a conjunction is true when its two conjuncts are true and is false in all other cases. This definition reflects ordinary language usage almost as perfectly as negation. Consider the following conjunctive statements:

Ferrari and Maserati make sports cars. $F \cdot M$

Ferrari and GMC make sports cars. $F \cdot G$

GMC and Jeep make sports cars. $G \cdot J$

The first statement is true, because both conjuncts are true; but the second and third statements are false because at least one of their conjuncts is false.

Turning now to the definition of the wedge operator (disjunction), the truth table is as follows:

Disjunction	p	q	$p \lor q$
	T	T	T
	T	F	T
	F	T	T
	F	F	F

The truth table indicates that the disjunction is true when at least one of the disjuncts is true and that otherwise it is false. The truth-functional interpretation of "or" is that of *inclusive* disjunction: Cases in which the disjunction is true include the case when both disjuncts are true. This inclusive sense of "or" corresponds to many instances of ordinary usage, as the following examples illustrate:

Either Steven King or Jennifer Capriati is a novelist.	S v J
Either Steven King or Danielle Steel is a novelist.	S v D
Either Kobe Bryant or Tiger Woods is a novelist.	K v T

The first two statements are true, because in each case at least one of the disjuncts is true. The third is false, because both disjuncts are false.

The match between the truth-functional definition of disjunction and ordinary usage is not perfect, however. Sometimes the sense of a statement in ordinary language is that of *exclusive* disjunction. Examples:

The Orient Express is on either track A or track B.

You can have either soup or salad with this meal.

Tammy is either ten or eleven years old.

The sense of these statements excludes the possibility of both alternatives being true. Thus, if these statements were translated using the wedge, a portion of their ordinary meaning would be lost. If the exclusive aspect of these "either . . . or . . ." statements is essential, the symbolic equivalent of "but not both" can be attached to their translations. Thus the first statement could be translated $(A \lor B) \cdot \sim(A \cdot B)$.

Let us now consider the horseshoe operator (material implication). Its truth table is as follows:

Conditional
(material implication)

p	q	p ⊃ q
T	T	T
T	F	F
F	T	T
F	F	T

The truth table shows that a conditional statement is false when the antecedent is true and the consequent false and is true in all other cases. This truth functional interpretation of conditional statements conforms in part with the ordinary meaning of "if . . . then . . ." and in part it diverges. Consider the following examples:

If Kim Basinger is an actor, then so is Meryl Streep.	K ⊃ M
If Kim Basinger is an actor, then so is Aaron Brown.	K ⊃ A
If Aaron Brown is an actor, then so is Helen Hunt.	A ⊃ H
If Aaron Brown is an actor, then so is Larry King.	A ⊃ L

In these statements K, M, and H are true and A and L are false. Thus, according to the truth-functional interpretation, the first statement is true and the second false. This result conforms in large measure to our expectations. But the truth-functional interpretation of the last two statements is true. Although this result may not conflict with our expectations, it is not at all clear why these statements should be considered true.

For an intuitive approach to this problem, imagine that your logic instructor made the following statement: "If you get an A on the final exam, then you will get an A for the course." Under what conditions would you say that your instructor had lied to you? Clearly, if you got an A on the final exam but did not get an A for the course, you would say that she had lied. This outcome corresponds to a true antecedent and a false consequent. On the other hand, if you got an A on the final exam and also got an A for the course, you would say that she had told the truth (true antecedent, true consequent). But what if you failed to get an A on the final exam? Two alternatives are then possible: Either you got an A for the course anyway (false antecedent, true consequent) or you did not get an A for the course (false antecedent, false consequent). In neither case, though, would you say that your instructor had lied to you. Giving her the benefit of the doubt, you would say that she had told the truth.

Lastly, let us consider the definition of the triple bar operator (material equivalence, or biconditional). Its truth table is as follows:

Biconditional
(material equivalence)

p	q	$p \equiv q$
T	T	T
T	F	F
F	T	F
F	F	T

The truth table shows that the biconditional is true when its two components have the same truth value and that otherwise it is false. These results conform reasonably well with our expectations. However, given that $p \equiv q$ is simply a shorter way of writing $(p \supset q) \cdot (q \supset p)$, the truth table results are required by the definition of material implication. If p and q are either both true or both false, then $p \supset q$ and $q \supset p$ are both true, making their conjunction true. But if p is true and q is false, then $p \supset q$ is false, making the conjunction false. Similarly, if p is false and q is true, then $q \supset p$ is false, again making the conjunction false. Thus $p \equiv q$ is true when p and q have the same truth value and false when they have opposite truth values.

The truth table definition of the triple bar symbol conforms quite closely with ordinary usage, as the following examples illustrate:

Bill Maher is a show host if and only if Jay Leno is.	$B \equiv J$
Bill Maher is a show host if and only if Meg Ryan is.	$B \equiv M$
Meg Ryan is a show host if and only if Al Pacino is.	$M \equiv A$

In these statements, B and J are true and M and A false. Thus, from the truth-functional standpoint, the first is true and the second false. This is what we would ordinarily expect. The third statement, however, turns out to be true because both of its components are false. While this result may not be what we would expect, it does not violate our expectations either. Other biconditional statements having false components are more obviously true. Example:

Ralph Nader was elected president if and only if he received a majority vote from the electoral college.

This statement asserts what is required for any candidate to be elected or not elected, and so it is clearly true.

In summary, the definitions of the five logical operators conform reasonably well with ordinary linguistic usage. However, as the last part of this section shows, the match is less than perfect. Before considering this question, though, let us use the operator definitions to compute the truth values of more complicated statements.

Computing the Truth Value of Longer Propositions

To compute the truth value of a more complicated expression, use this procedure: Enter the truth values of the simple components directly beneath the letters. Then use these truth values to compute the truth values of the compound components. The truth value of a compound statement is written beneath the operator representing it. Let us suppose, for example, that we are told in advance that the simple propositions A, B, and C are true and D, E, and F are false. We may then compute the truth value of the following compound proposition:

$$(A \lor D) \supset E$$

First we write the truth values of the simple propositions immediately below the respective letters and bring the operators and parentheses down:

$$(A \lor D) \supset E$$
$$(T \lor F) \supset F$$

Next we compute the truth value of the proposition in parentheses and write it beneath the operator to which it pertains:

$$(A \lor D) \supset E$$
$$(T \lor F) \supset F$$
$$\quad T \quad \supset F$$

Finally, we use the last-completed line to obtain the truth value of the conditional, which is the "main operator" in the proposition:

$$(A \lor D) \supset E$$
$$(T \lor F) \supset F$$
$$\quad T \quad \supset F$$
$$\quad \quad \textcircled{F}$$

The final answer is circled. This is the truth value of the compound proposition given that A is true and D and E are false.

The general strategy is to build the truth values of the larger components from the truth values of the smaller ones. In general, the order to be followed in entering truth values is this:

1. Individual letters representing simple propositions
2. Tildes immediately preceding individual letters
3. Operators joining letters or negated letters
4. Tildes immediately preceding parentheses
5. And so on

Here are some additional examples. As above, let *A*, *B*, and *C* be true, *D*, *E*, and *F* false. Note that the computed truth values are written beneath the operators to which they pertain. The final answers, which are written beneath the main operators, are circled.

$(B \cdot C) \supset (E \supset A)$

$(T \cdot T) \supset (F \supset T)$

   T $\supset$ T

       Ⓣ

$\sim (C \vee \sim A) \supset \sim B$

$\sim (T \vee \sim T) \supset \sim T$

$\sim (T \vee F) \;\;\supset F$

$\sim \;\;\; T \;\;\;\supset F$

F $\supset$ F

      Ⓣ

$[\sim (D \vee F) \cdot (B \vee \sim A)] \supset \sim (F \supset \sim C)$

$[\sim (F \vee F) \cdot (T \vee \sim T)] \supset \sim (F \supset \sim T)$

$[\sim (F \vee F) \cdot (T \vee F \;)] \supset \sim (F \supset F \;\;)$

$[\sim \;\;\; F \;\; \cdot \;\; T \;\;\;] \supset \sim \;\;\; T$

$[T \;\;\;\;\;\;\; \cdot \;\; T \;\;\;] \supset F$

      T $\supset$ F

         Ⓕ

If preferred, the truth values of the compound components may be entered directly beneath the operators, without using the line-by-line approach illustrated in these examples. The following examples illustrate this second approach, which is used in the next section:

$[(D \equiv \sim A) \cdot \sim (C \cdot \sim B)] \equiv \sim [(A \supset \sim D) \vee (C \equiv E)]$

  F T F T TT TF F T ⒻF T T T F T TF F

$\sim \{[(C \cdot \sim E) \supset \sim (A \cdot \sim B)] \supset [\sim (B \vee D) \equiv (\sim C \vee E)]\}$

 Ⓕ   TTTF TT TFFT T F TTF T FTFF

Further Comparison with Ordinary Language

The first part of this section showed that the definitions of the five logical operators conform reasonably well with ordinary linguistic usage. This part further examines the extent of this match in meaning.

In regard to the dot operator, which is used to translate "and" and "but," the match is often good; but it fails, at least in part, when the meaning of a conjunctive statement depends on the order of the conjuncts. Consider the following statements:

She got married and had a baby.	$M \cdot B$
She had a baby and got married.	$B \cdot M$

The first statement implies that the marriage occurred first, and the baby came later, while the second statement implies that the baby came first. This implied meaning is lost in the truth-functional interpretation, because $M \cdot B$ is logically equivalent to $B \cdot M$.

For another example, consider the following:

This car is ugly, but it's economical to drive.	$U \cdot E$
This car is economical to drive, but it's ugly.	$E \cdot U$

If these statements are taken as single premises of separate arguments, they might suggest different conclusions. The first suggests "Therefore, we should buy this car," whereas the second suggests "Therefore, we shouldn't buy this car." Yet given that the word "but" is translated in the same way as "and," the two statements are logically equivalent when interpreted truth-functionally. When subtleties of expression are important in the interpretation of a statement, using logical operators to translate the statement may not be appropriate.

Another instance where the truth-functional interpretation of "and" differs from the ordinary linguistic meaning is offered by slang statements like this one:

You go for that gun, and you'll regret it.

The sense of this statement is not that you will in fact go for the gun but rather that, *if* you go for that gun, then ... Accordingly, if this statement were interpreted as a truth-functional conjunction, its meaning would be distorted.

In regard to the wedge operator, which is used to translate "or" and "unless," we saw that the wedge is defined as inclusive disjunction, but we observed that the English word "or" sometimes has the sense of exclusive disjunction. This same observation applies to "unless." In the following statements, "unless" has an inclusive sense:

You won't win the lottery unless you buy a ticket.

It will not rain unless there are clouds in the sky.

The meaning of the first statement includes the case of buying a ticket and not winning, and the meaning of the second includes the case of there being clouds and no rain. In statements like these, where "unless" has an inclusive sense, using the wedge symbol to translate "unless" results in no loss of meaning.

On the other hand, in the following statements "unless" is used in the exclusive sense:

Pork is not properly cooked unless the meat is white.

These logs will make a nice campfire unless they are wet.

The first statement suggests that the meat cannot be white and at the same time not be properly cooked, and the second suggests that the logs cannot be wet and at the same time be used to make a nice campfire. Thus, if these statements are translated using the wedge operator, part of the meaning will be left out. If this additional part is essential, it can be included by adding the symbolic equivalent of "but not both" to the translation.

In connection with the horseshoe operator, we saw that a question arose when the antecedent of a conditional statement turned out to be false. Why, under this circumstance, should the conditional statement be said to be true? For an example of some conditional statements that conform to the truth-functional interpretation, consider the following:

If the temperature rises above 32°F, then the snow will begin to melt.

If Figure A is a triangle, then Figure A has three sides.

If all *A* are *B* and all *B* are *C*, then all *A* are *C*.

In all three examples the statement remains true even though the antecedent might be false. In the first, even though the temperature does not rise above 32°F at any particular moment, the law that governs the melting point of snow holds true. In other words, the statement (which expresses this law) is true regardless of the truth value of the antecedent. In the second, the mere fact that Figure A might not be a triangle does not affect the fact that a triangle, by definition, has three sides. Thus, the statement (which expresses this fact) is true regardless of the truth value of the antecedent. The third statement expresses a logical relationship between statements. This logical relationship remains unchanged regardless of what the terms *A*, *B*, and *C* are taken to represent. Thus, if *A*, *B*, and *C* represent "dogs," "cats," and "birds," respectively, both antecedent and consequent turn out to be false, but the conditional statement remains true.

As these examples illustrate, the definition of the horseshoe operator matches the meaning of some conditional statements in ordinary language very well. However, in general, the match is far from perfect. The source of the mismatch stems from the fact that the horseshoe operator designates the *material* conditional, or *truth-functional* conditional. The material conditional is a kind of conditional statement whose truth value depends purely on the truth or falsity of the antecedent and consequent and not on any inferential connection *between* antecedent and consequent. Since many conditional statements in ordinary language express such an inferential connection, when the horseshoe operator is used to translate them, part of their meaning is left out. For example, compare the following two statements:

If Shakespeare wrote *Hamlet*, then the sun rises in the east.

If ice is lighter than water, then ice floats in water.

The first statement expresses no inferential connection between antecedent and consequent, so using the horseshoe operator to translate it results in no loss of meaning. However, the second statement does express such a connection. The fact that ice is lighter than water is the reason why it floats. Accordingly, when the horseshoe operator is used to translate the second statement, this special meaning is lost.

The fact that the material conditional ignores inferential connections between antecedent and consequent allows for conflicts between the truth-functional interpretation of a conditional statement and the ordinary interpretation. Consider, for example, the following:

If Barbara Boxer advocates the use of cocaine, then she is a good senator.

If Chicago is in Michigan, then Chicago is very close to Miami.

According to their ordinary language interpretation, both of these statements are false. Good senators do not advocate the use of cocaine, and Michigan is far from Miami. Yet, when these statements are interpreted as material conditionals, both turn out to be true, because their antecedents are false. In cases like these, when the truth-functional interpretation of a conditional statement conflicts with the ordinary language interpretation, using the horseshoe operator to translate it may not be appropriate.

While inferential relations between antecedent and consequent often play some role in conditionals expressed in the indicative mood (such as those we just considered), they play a dominant role in conditional statements expressed in the subjunctive mood. Consider, for example, the following:

> If I were Bill Gates, then I would be rich.
>
> If dolphins were fish, then they would be cold-blooded.
>
> If the Washington Monument were made of lead, then it would be lighter than air.
>
> If President Kennedy had committed suicide, then he would be alive today.

Subjunctive conditionals are often called counterfactual conditionals because their antecedents are typically false. As a result, the *only* way of determining their truth value in ordinary language is through some kind of inference. Thus, from our knowledge that Bill Gates is rich, we reason that if I were he, then I would be rich. Similarly, from our knowledge that all fish are cold-blooded, we conclude that if dolphins were fish, then they would be cold-blooded. On the other hand, we reason that the second two are false from our knowledge that lead is heavier than air and our knowledge that suicide results in death. Because the truth value of subjunctive conditionals is so closely tied to inferences like these and is so unrelated to the truth or falsity of the components, subjunctive conditionals are generally not considered to be truth functional at all, and the horseshoe operator is not used to translate them. But if they were interpreted truth-functionally, note that all four of these statements would turn out true, because they have false antecedents.

These observations about conditional statements apply equally to biconditionals. Just as the horseshoe operator expresses *material* implication, the triple bar operator expresses *material* equivalence. As such, it ignores any inferential connection between its component statements, and, as a result, conflicts can arise between the ordinary meaning of a biconditional and its truth-functional meaning. Here are two examples of biconditionals expressed in the indicative mood that illustrate such a conflict:

> Adolf Hitler was justified in killing millions of Jews if and only if he always confessed his sins to a priest.
>
> The Department of Defense building is a hexagon if and only if it has eight sides.

According to the ordinary interpretation, these statements are false. Confessing one's sins to a priest does not justify anything, and hexagons, by definition, have six sides, not eight. Yet, when these statements are interpreted as expressing material biconditionals, both are true, because in each case the component statements are false. In cases like these, when the ordinary meaning of a biconditional conflicts with the truth-functional meaning, using the triple bar operator to translate it may not be appropriate. Furthermore, as with subjunctive conditionals, subjunctive biconditionals are generally not considered to be truth-functional at all, so the triple bar operator is not used to translate them.

iLrn I. Identify the main operator in the following propositions:

★1. $\sim(A \lor M) \cdot \sim(C \supset E)$

2. $(G \cdot \sim P) \supset \sim(H \lor \sim W)$

3. $\sim[P \cdot (S \equiv K)]$

★4. $\sim(K \cdot \sim O) \equiv \sim(R \lor \sim B)$

5. $(M \cdot B) \lor \sim[E \equiv \sim(C \lor I)]$

6. $\sim[(P \cdot \sim R) \supset (\sim E \lor F)]$

★7. $\sim[(S \lor L) \cdot M] \supset (C \lor N)$

8. $[\sim F \lor (N \cdot U)] \equiv \sim H$

9. $E \cdot [(F \supset A) \equiv (\sim G \lor H)]$

★10. $\sim[(X \lor T) \cdot (N \lor F)] \lor (K \supset L)$

II. Write the following compound statements in symbolic form, then use your knowledge of the historical events referred to by the simple statements to determine the truth value of the compound statements.

★1. It is not the case that Hitler ran the Third Reich.

2. Nixon resigned the presidency and Lincoln wrote the Gettysburg Address.

3. Caesar conquered China, or Lindbergh crossed the Atlantic.

★4. Hitler ran the Third Reich and Nixon did not resign the presidency.

5. Edison invented the telephone, or Custer was killed by the Indians.

6. Alexander the Great civilized America if Napoleon ruled France.

★7. Washington was assassinated only if Edison invented the telephone.

8. Lincoln wrote the Gettysburg Address if and only if Caesar conquered China.

9. It is not the case that either Alexander the Great civilized America or Washington was assassinated.

★10. If Hitler ran the Third Reich, then either Custer was killed by the Indians or Einstein discovered aspirin.

11. Either Lindbergh crossed the Atlantic and Edison invented the telephone or both Nixon resigned the presidency and it is false that Edison invented the telephone.

12. Lincoln's having written the Gettysburg Address is a sufficient condition for Alexander the Great's having civilized America if and only if Washington's being assassinated is a necessary condition for Custer's having been killed by the Indians.

★13. Both Hitler ran the Third Reich and Lindbergh crossed the Atlantic if neither Einstein discovered aspirin nor Caesar conquered China.

14. It is not the case that Custer was killed by the Indians unless both Nixon resigned the presidency and Edison invented the telephone.

6

15. Custer was killed by the Indians, and Lincoln wrote the Gettysburg Address only if either Washington was assassinated or Alexander the Great civilized America.

iLrn III. Determine the truth values of the following symbolized statements. Let *A*, *B*, and *C* be true and *X*, *Y*, and *Z* be false. Circle your answer.

  ★1. $A \cdot X$

   2. $B \cdot \sim Y$

   3. $X \lor \sim Y$

  ★4. $\sim C \lor Z$

   5. $B \supset \sim Z$

   6. $Y \supset \sim A$

  ★7. $\sim X \supset Z$

   8. $B \equiv Y$

   9. $\sim C \equiv Z$

 ★10. $\sim (A \cdot \sim Z)$

  11. $\sim B \lor (Y \supset A)$

  12. $A \supset \sim (Z \lor \sim Y)$

 ★13. $(A \cdot Y) \lor (\sim Z \cdot C)$

  14. $\sim (X \lor \sim B) \cdot (\sim Y \lor A)$

  15. $(Y \supset C) \cdot \sim (B \supset \sim X)$

 ★16. $(C \equiv \sim A) \lor (Y \equiv Z)$

  17. $\sim (A \cdot \sim C) \supset (\sim X \supset B)$

  18. $\sim [(B \lor \sim C) \cdot \sim (X \lor \sim Z)]$

 ★19. $\sim [\sim (X \supset C) \equiv \sim (B \supset Z)]$

  20. $(X \supset Z) \supset [(B \equiv \sim X) \cdot \sim (C \lor \sim A)]$

  21. $[(\sim X \lor Z) \supset (\sim C \lor B)] \cdot [(\sim X \cdot A) \supset (\sim Y \cdot Z)]$

 ★22. $\sim [(A \equiv X) \lor (Z \equiv Y)] \lor [(\sim Y \supset B) \cdot (Z \supset C)]$

  23. $[(B \cdot \sim C) \lor (X \cdot \sim Y)] \supset \sim [(Y \cdot \sim X) \lor (A \cdot \sim Z)]$

  24. $\sim \{\sim [(C \lor \sim B) \cdot (Z \lor \sim A)] \cdot \sim [\sim (B \lor Y) \cdot (\sim X \lor Z)]\}$

 ★25. $(Z \supset C) \supset \{[(\sim X \supset B) \supset (C \supset Y)] \equiv [(Z \supset X) \supset (\ Y \supset Z)]\}$

iLrn IV. When possible, determine the truth values of the following symbolized statements. Let *A* and *B* be true, *Y* and *Z* false. *P* and *Q* have unknown truth value. If the truth value of the statement cannot be determined, write "undetermined."

  ★1. $A \lor P$

   2. $Q \lor Z$

   3. $Q \cdot Y$

  ★4. $Q \cdot A$

   5. $P \supset B$

   6. $Z \supset Q$

★7. $A \supset P$

8. $P \equiv \sim P$

9. $(P \supset A) \supset Z$

★10. $(P \supset A) \equiv (Q \supset B)$

11. $(Q \supset B) \supset (A \supset Y)$

12. $\sim (P \supset Y) \lor (Z \supset Q)$

★13. $\sim (Q \cdot Y) \equiv \sim (Q \lor A)$

14. $[(Z \supset P) \supset P] \supset P$

15. $[Q \supset (A \lor P)] \equiv [(Q \supset B) \supset Y]$

6.3   Truth Tables for Propositions

The previous section showed how the truth value of a compound proposition could be determined, given a *designated* truth value for each simple component. A truth table gives the truth value of a compound proposition for *every possible* truth value of its simple components. Each line in the truth table represents one such possible arrangement of truth values.

In constructing a truth table the first step is to determine the number of lines (or rows). Because each line represents one possible arrangement of truth values, the total number of lines is equal to the number of possible combinations of truth values for the simple propositions. Where L designates the number of lines and n the number of *different* simple propositions, the number of lines may be computed by the following formula:

$$L = 2^n$$

By means of this formula we obtain the following table:

Number of different simple propositions	Number of lines in truth table
1	2
2	4
3	8
4	16
5	32
6	64

Let us now construct a truth table for a compound proposition. We may begin with a fairly simple one:

$(A \lor \sim B) \supset B$

The number of different simple propositions is two. Thus the number of lines in the truth table is four. We draw these lines beneath the proposition as follows:

$(A \lor \sim B) \supset B$

_____
_____
_____
_____

The next step is to divide the number of lines in half. The result is 2. Then go to the first letter on the left (*A*) and enter T on the first two lines and F on the remaining two lines.

```
(A v ~ B) ⊃ B
T_____
T_____
F_____
F_____
```

Next we divide that number (two) in half and, since the result is one, write one T, one F, one T, and one F beneath the next letter (*B*):

```
(A v ~ B) ⊃ B
T____T_____
T____F_____
F____T_____
F____F_____
```

Inspection of the truth table at this stage reveals that every possible combination of truth and falsity has now been assigned to *A* and *B*. In other words, the truth table exhausts the entire range of possibilities. The next step is to duplicate the *B* column under the second *B*.

```
(A v ~ B) ⊃ B
T     T     T
T     F     F
F     T     T
F     F     F
```

This much has been automatic.

Now, using the principles developed in the previous section, we compute the remaining columns. First, the column under the tilde is computed from the column under *B*:

```
(A v ~ B) ⊃ B
T    F T     T
T    T F     F
F    F T     T
F    T F     F
```

Next, the column under the wedge is computed from the column under *A* and the column under the tilde:

```
(A v ~ B) ⊃ B
T T F T     T
T T T F     F
F F F T     T
F T T F     F
```

Last, the column under the horseshoe is computed from the column under the wedge and the column under *B*:

```
(A ∨ ~ B) ⊃ B
 T  T F T  │T│ T
 T  T T F  │F│ F
 F  F F T  │T│ T
 F  T T F  │F│ F
```

The column under the main operator is outlined to indicate that it represents the entire compound proposition. Inspecting the completed truth table, we see that the truth value of the compound proposition is true when *B* is true and false when *B* is false, regardless of the truth value of *A*.

Let us consider another example: $(C \cdot {\sim}D) \supset E$. The number of different letters is three, so the number of lines is eight. Under *C* we make half this number true, half false (that is, four true, four false). Then, under *D* we make half *this* number true, half false, and so on (two true, two false, two true, two false). Finally, under *E* the truth value alternates on every line. The truth table thus exhausts every possible arrangement of truth values:

```
(C  •  ~ D)  ⊃  E
 T      T        T
 T      T        F
 T      F        T
 T      F        F
 F      T        T
 F      T        F
 F      F        T
 F      F        F
```

Now we compute the truth values for the remaining columns—first for the tilde, then for the dot, and finally for the horseshoe:

```
(C  •  ~ D)  ⊃  E
 T F F  T   │T│  T
 T F F  T   │T│  F
 T T T  F   │T│  T
 T T T  F   │F│  F
 F F F  T   │T│  T
 F F F  T   │T│  F
 F F T  F   │T│  T
 F F T  F   │T│  F
```

Inspecting the completed truth table, we see that the compound proposition is false only when *C* is true and *D* and *E* are false.

An alternate method for constructing truth tables, which turns out to be faster for certain compound propositions, replicates the type of truth table used to define the meaning of the five logical operators in Section 6.2. Suppose, for example, that we are given this proposition: $[(A \vee B) \cdot (B \supset A)] \supset B$. We would begin by constructing columns for the simple propositions *A* and *B*. We write them to the left of the given proposition:

```
A  B │ [(A ∨ B) • (B ⊃ A)] ⊃ B
T  T │
T  F │
F  T │
F  F │
```

We then use the columns on the left to derive the truth values of the compound propositions. First we compute the truth values of the expressions in parentheses, then the dot, and finally the right-hand horseshoe:

A B	[(A v B)	•	(B ⊃ A)]	⊃ B
T T	T	T	T	T
T F	T	T	T	F
F T	T	F	F	T
F F	F	F	T	T

Classifying Statements

Truth tables may be used to determine whether the truth value of a compound statement depends solely on its form or whether it also depends on the specific truth values of its components. A compound statement is said to be **logically true** or **tautologous** if it is true regardless of the truth values of its components. It is said to be **logically false** or **self-contradictory** if it is false regardless of the truth values of its components. And it is said to be **contingent** if its truth value varies depending on the truth values of its components. By inspecting the column of truth values under the main operator, we can determine how the compound proposition should be classified:

Column under main operator	Statement classification
all true	tautologous (logically true)
all false	self-contradictory (logically false)
at least one true, at least one false	contingent

As the truth table we developed indicates, $(C • \sim D) \supset E$ is a contingent proposition. The column under the main operator contains at least one T and at least one F. In other words, the truth value of the compound proposition is "contingent" upon the truth values of its components. Sometimes it is true, sometimes false, depending on the truth values of the components.

On the other hand, consider the following truth tables:

[(G ⊃ H) • G] ⊃ H	(G v H) ≡ (~ G • ~ H)
T T T T T **T** T	T T T **F** F T F F T
T F F F T **T** F	T T F **F** F T F T F
F T T F F **T** T	F T T **F** T F F F T
F T F F F **T** F	F F F **F** T F T T F

The proposition on the left is tautologous (logically true or a tautology) because the column under the main operator is all true. The one on the right is self-contradictory (logically false) because the main operator column is all false. In neither case is the truth value of the compound proposition contingent upon the truth values of the components. The one on the left is true regardless of the truth values of its components—in other words, *necessarily* true. The one on the right is *necessarily* false.

If a proposition is either logically true or logically false, its truth value depends merely upon its form and has nothing to do with its content. As a result, such statements do not make any genuine assertions about things in the world. For example, the tautologous statement "It is either raining or it is not raining" provides no information about the weather. Similarly, the self-contradictory statement "It is raining and it is not raining" provides no information about the weather. On the other hand, the contingent statement "It is raining in the mountains" does provide information about the weather.

Comparing Statements

Truth tables may also be used to determine how two propositions are related to each other. Two propositions are said to be **logically equivalent** if they have the same truth value on each line under their main operators, and they are **contradictory** if they have opposite truth values on each line under their main operators. If neither of these relations hold, the propositions are either consistent or inconsistent. Two (or more) propositions are **consistent** if there is at least one line on which both (or all) of them turn out to be true, and they are **inconsistent** if there is no line on which both (or all) of them turn out to be true. By comparing the main operator columns, one can determine which is the case. However, because the first two relations are stronger than (and may overlap) the second two, the first two relations should be considered first.

Columns under main operators	Relation
same truth value on each line	logically equivalent
opposite truth value on each line	contradictory
there is at least one line on which the truth values are both true	consistent
there is no line on which the truth values are both true	inconsistent

For example, the following two propositions are logically equivalent. The main operator columns of their respective truth tables are identical. Note that for proper comparison the columns under K must be identical and the columns under L must be identical.

```
K ⊃ L              ~ L ⊃ ~ K
T T  T             F T  T  F T
T F  F             T F  F  F T          Logically equivalent
F T  T             F T  T  T F
F T  F             T F  T  T F
```

For any two propositions that are logically equivalent, the biconditional statement formed by joining them with a triple bar is tautologous. Thus, $(K \supset L) \equiv (\sim L \supset \sim K)$ is tautologous. This is easy to see because the columns under the main operators of $K \supset L$ and $\sim L \supset \sim K$ are identical.

The next two propositions are contradictory:

```
K ⊃ L              K • ~ L
T T  T             T F  F T
T F  F             T T  T F             Contradictory
F T  T             F F  F T
F T  F             F F  T F
```

The next two propositions are consistent. On the first line of each truth table the column under the main operator turns out true. This means that it is possible for both propositions to be true, which is the meaning of consistency:

```
 K v L          K · L
T[T]T          T[T]T
T[T]F          T[F]F        Consistent
F[T]T         ·F[F]T
F[F]F          F[F]F
```

Finally, the next two propositions are inconsistent. There is no line in the columns under the main operators where the truth values are both true:

```
 K ≡ L          K · ~ L
T[T]T          T[F]F T
T[F]F          T[T]T F       Inconsistent
F[F]T          F[F]F T
F[T]F          F[F]T F
```

Any pair of propositions is either consistent or inconsistent. Furthermore, some consistent propositions are also logically equivalent, and some inconsistent propositions are either contradictory or logically equivalent. Because of this partial overlap, pairs of propositions are usually first classified in terms of the stronger of these relations, which are logical equivalence and contradiction. If neither of these stronger relations applies, then the pair of propositions is classified in terms of the weaker relations, consistency and inconsistency.

Unlike logical equivalence and contradiction, which usually relate exactly two propositions, consistency and inconsistency often apply to larger groups of propositions. For consistency, the only requirement is that there be at least one line in the group of truth tables where all of the propositions are true, and for inconsistency the only requirement is that there be no such line. As a result of these requirements, the statement consisting of the conjunction of a group of inconsistent propositions will always be self-contradictory, whereas the statement consisting of the conjunction of a group of consistent propositions will never be self-contradictory.

Consistency and inconsistency are important because, among other things, they can be used to evaluate the overall rationality of a person's stated position on something. If the statements expressing such a position are consistent, then there is at least a possibility that the position makes sense. This is so because there will be at least one line in the group of truth tables where all of the person's statements are true. On the other hand, if the statements are inconsistent, then there is no possibility that the position makes sense. In this case there is no line in the truth tables where all of the statements are true. The group of statements, conjoined together, amounts to a self-contradiction.

The truth tables for consistency and logical equivalence also illustrate the important difference between two propositions being factually true and their being logically equivalent. For example, the statements "Water boils at 100° C" and "The current population of the United States is over 200 million" are both true in the present actual world. This real-world situation conforms to the one truth table line on which both statements are true. As a result of this line, the two statements are consistent. However, they are not logically equivalent because their truth values are not *necessarily* the same. The truth value of the second proposition might change in the future, while that of the first would remain the same. An analogous distinction, incidentally, holds between two statements having actually opposite truth values and their being contradictory.

iLrn I. Use truth tables to determine whether the following symbolized statements are tautologous, self-contradictory, or contingent:

★1. $N \supset (N \supset N)$

2. $(G \supset G) \supset G$

3. $(S \supset R) \cdot (S \cdot \sim R)$

★4. $[(E \supset F) \supset F] \supset E$

5. $(\sim K \supset H) \equiv \sim (H \vee K)$

6. $(M \supset P) \vee (P \supset M)$

★7. $[(Z \supset X) \cdot (X \vee Z)] \supset X$

8. $[(C \supset D) \cdot \sim C] \supset \sim D$

9. $[X \supset (R \supset F)] \equiv [(X \supset R) \supset F]$

★10. $[G \supset (N \supset \sim G)] \cdot [(N \equiv G) \cdot (N \vee G)]$

11. $[(Q \supset P) \cdot (\sim Q \supset R)] \cdot \sim (P \vee R)$

12. $[(H \supset N) \cdot (T \supset N)] \supset [(H \vee T) \supset N]$

★13. $[U \cdot (T \vee S)] \equiv [(\sim T \vee \sim U) \cdot (\sim S \vee \sim U)]$

14. $\{[(G \cdot N) \supset H] \cdot [(G \supset H) \supset P]\} \supset (N \supset P)$

15. $[(F \vee E) \cdot (G \vee H)] \equiv [(G \cdot E) \vee (F \cdot H)]$

iLrn II. Use truth tables to determine whether the following pairs of symbolized statements are logically equivalent, contradictory, consistent, or inconsistent. First determine whether the pairs of propositions are logically equivalent or contradictory; then, if these relations do not apply, determine if they are consistent or inconsistent.

★1. $\sim D \vee B$ $\sim (D \cdot \sim B)$

2. $F \cdot M$ $\sim (F \vee M)$

3. $\sim K \supset L$ $K \supset \sim L$

★4. $R \vee \sim S$ $S \cdot \sim R$

5. $\sim A \equiv X$ $(X \cdot \sim A) \vee (A \cdot \sim X)$

6. $H \equiv \sim G$ $(G \cdot H) \vee (\sim G \cdot \sim H)$

★7. $(E \supset C) \supset L$ $E \supset (C \supset L)$

8. $N \cdot (A \vee \sim E)$ $\sim A \cdot (E \vee \sim N)$

9. $M \supset (K \supset P)$ $(K \cdot M) \supset P$

★10. $W \equiv (B \cdot T)$ $W \cdot (T \supset \sim B)$

11. $G \cdot (E \vee P)$ $\sim (G \cdot E) \cdot \sim (G \cdot P)$

12. $R \cdot (Q \vee S)$ $(S \vee R) \cdot (Q \vee R)$

★13. $H \cdot (K \vee J)$ $(J \cdot H) \vee (H \cdot K)$

14. $Z \cdot (C \equiv P)$ $C \equiv (Z \cdot \sim P)$

15. $Q \supset \sim (K \vee F)$ $(K \cdot Q) \vee (F \cdot Q)$

III. Use truth tables to obtain the answers to the following exercises.

★1. Renowned economist Harold Carlson makes the following prediction: "The balance of payments will decrease if and only if interest rates remain steady; however, it is not the case that either interest rates will not remain steady or the balance of payments will decrease." What can we say about Carlson's prediction?

2. A high school principal made this statement to the school board: "Either music is not dropped from the curriculum or the students will become cultural philistines; furthermore, the students will not become cultural philistines if and only if music is dropped from the curriculum." Assuming the principal is correct, what has she told us about music and the students? (Hint: Construct a truth table for the principal's statement and examine the line on which the statement turns out true.)

3. Christina and Thomas are having a discussion about their plans for the evening. Christina: "If you don't love me, then I'm certainly not going to have sex with you." Thomas: "Well, that means that if I do love you, then you will have sex with me, right?" Is Thomas correct? (Hint: Construct a truth table for each statement and compare them.)

★4. Two astronomers are discussing supernovas. Dr. Frank says, "Research has established that if a supernova occurs within ten light years of the earth, then life on earth will be destroyed." Dr. Harris says, "Research has also established that either a supernova will not occur within ten light years of the earth or life on earth will not be destroyed." Is it possible that both astronomers are correct? If so, what can we determine about the occurrence of a supernova?

5. Antonia Martinez, who is running for the state senate, makes this statement: "Either a tax reduction is feasible only if both educational costs do not increase and the welfare program is abolished, or a tax reduction is feasible and either the welfare program will not be abolished or educational costs will increase." What has Martinez told us about taxes, educational costs, and welfare?

6. Automotive expert Frank Goodbody has this to say about Japanese imports: "If Mitsubishi is the sportiest, then both Toyota is the most trouble-free and Isuzu is not the lowest priced. If Isuzu is the lowest priced, then both Toyota is not the most trouble-free and Mitsubishi is the sportiest." Is it possible that Goodbody is correct in his assessment? If so, what may we conclude about Mitsubishi, Toyota, and Isuzu?

★7. Two stockbrokers are having a discussion. One claims that Netmark will introduce a new product if and only if both Datapro cuts its workforce and Compucel expands production. The other claims that Datapro will cut its workforce, and Compucel will expand production if and only if Netmark introduces a new product. Is it possible that both stockbrokers are right? If so, what have they told us about these companies?

8. Eric Carson sums up his beliefs about God as follows: "God exists if and only if either life is meaningful or the soul is not immortal. God exists and the soul is immortal. If God exists, then life is not meaningful." Is it possible that Eric's beliefs make sense?

9. Cindy, Jane, and Amanda witnessed a bank robbery. At trial, Cindy testified that Lefty did not enter the bank, and if Howard pulled a gun, then Conrad collected the money. Jane testified that if Howard did not pull a gun, then Lefty entered the bank. Amanda testified that if Conrad collected the money, then Howard pulled a gun. Is it possible that all three witnesses told the truth? If so, what can we conclude about Lefty, Howard, and Conrad?

★10. Nicole Evans expresses her philosophy as follows: "If the mind is identical to the brain, then personal freedom does not exist and humans are not responsible for their actions. If personal freedom does not exist, then the mind is identical to the brain. Either humans are responsible for their actions or the mind is not identical to the brain. If personal freedom exists, then humans are responsible for their actions." Is it possible that Nicole's philosophy makes sense? If so, what does it say about the mind, personal freedom, and responsibility?

6.4 Truth Tables for Arguments

Truth tables provide the standard technique for testing the validity of arguments in propositional logic. To construct a truth table for an argument, follow these steps:

1. Symbolize the arguments using letters to represent the simple propositions.
2. Write out the symbolized argument, placing a single slash between the premises and a double slash between the last premise and the conclusion.
3. Draw a truth table for the symbolized argument as if it were a proposition broken into parts, outlining the columns representing the premises and conclusion.
4. Look for a line in which all of the premises are true and the conclusion is false. If such a line exists, the argument is invalid; if not, it is valid.

For example, let us test the following argument for validity:

If juvenile killers are as responsible for their crimes as adults, then execution is a justifiable punishment.
Juvenile killers are not as responsible for their crimes as adults.
Therefore, execution is not a justifiable punishment.

The first step is to symbolize the argument:

$$J \supset E$$
$$\dfrac{\sim J}{\sim E}$$

Now a truth table may be constructed. Since the symbolized argument contains two different letters, the truth table has four lines. Make sure that identical letters have identical columns beneath them. Here are the columns for the individual letters:

J	⊃	E	/	~	J	//	~	E
T		T			T			T
T		F			T			F
F		T			F			T
F		F			F			F

The truth table is now completed, and the columns representing the premises and conclusion are outlined:

```
J ⊃ E /  ~ J //  ~ E
T [T] T   [F] T   [F] T
T [F] F   [F] T   [T] F
F (T) T   (T) F   (F) T
F [T] F   [T] F   [T] F
```

Inspection of the third line reveals that both of the premises are true and the conclusion is false. The argument is therefore invalid.

Another example:

> If insider trading occurs, then investors will not trust the securities markets. If investors do not trust the securities markets, then business in general will suffer. Therefore, if insider trading occurs, then business in general will suffer.

The completed truth table is:

```
O ⊃ ~ T /  ~ T ⊃ B //  O ⊃ B
T [F] F T   F T [T] T   T [T] T
T [F] F T   F T [T] F   T [F] F
T [T] T F   T F [T] T   T [T] T
T [T] T F   T F [F] F   T [F] F
F [T] F T   F T [T] T   F [T] T
F [T] F T   F T [T] F   F [T] F
F [T] T Γ   T F [T] T   Γ [T] T
F [T] T F   T F [F] F   F [T] F
```

Inspection of the truth table reveals that there is no line on which both premises are true and the conclusion is false. The argument is therefore valid.

The logic behind the method of truth tables is easy to understand. By definition, a valid argument is one in which it is not possible for the premises to be true and the conclusion false. A truth table presents every possible combination of truth values that the components of an argument may have. Therefore, if no line exists on which the premises are true and the conclusion false, then it is not possible for the premises to be true and the conclusion false, in which case the argument is valid. Conversely, if there *is* a line on which the premises are true and the conclusion false, then it *is* possible for the premises to be true and the conclusion false, and the argument is invalid. We therefore have the following rules for testing arguments by truth tables:

If there is no line on which all the premises are true and the conclusion false, the argument is valid.

If there is at least one line on which all the premises are true and the conclusion false, the argument is invalid.

Truth tables provide a convenient illustration of the fact that any argument having inconsistent premises is valid regardless of what its conclusion may be, and any argument having a tautologous conclusion is valid regardless of what its premises may be. Example:

> The sky is blue.
> The sky is not blue.
> Therefore, Paris is the capital of France.

S / ~ S // P

S	~ S	P
T	F T	T
T	F T	T
F	T F	T
F	T F	T

Since the premises of this argument are inconsistent, there is no line on which the premises are both true. Accordingly, there is no line on which the premises are both true and the conclusion false, so the argument is valid. Of course, the argument is unsound, because it has a false premise. Another example:

Bern is the capital of Switzerland. Therefore, it is either raining or it is not raining.

B // R v ~ R

B	R v ~ R
T	T T F T
T	F T T F
F	T T F T
F	F T T F

The conclusion of this argument is a tautology. Accordingly, there is no line on which the premise is true and the conclusion false, and so the argument is valid. Incidentally, it is also sound, because the premise is true.

The conditional statement having the conjunction of an argument's premises as its antecedent and the conclusion as its consequent is called the argument's **corresponding conditional**. For example, the corresponding conditional of the second argument tested in this section is $[(O \supset \sim T) \cdot (\sim T \supset B)] \supset (O \supset B)$. For any valid argument (such as this one), the corresponding conditional is a tautology. This is easy to see. In any valid argument, there is no line on which the premises are all true and the conclusion false. Thus, in the corresponding conditional, there is no line on which the antecedent is true and the consequent false, so the corresponding conditional is true on every line.

EXERCISE 6.4

iLrn I. Translate the following arguments into symbolic form. Then determine whether each is valid or invalid by constructing a truth table for each.

★1. If national elections deteriorate into TV popularity contests, then smooth-talking morons will get elected. Therefore, if national elections do not deteriorate into TV popularity contests, then smooth-talking morons will not get elected.

2. Brazil has a huge foreign debt. Therefore, either Brazil or Argentina has a huge foreign debt.

3. If fossil fuel combustion continues at its present rate, then a greenhouse effect will occur. If a greenhouse effect occurs, then world temperatures will rise. Therefore, if fossil fuel combustion continues at its present rate, then world temperatures will rise.

★4. If there are dried-up riverbeds on Mars, then water once flowed on the Martian surface. There are dried-up riverbeds on Mars. Therefore, water once flowed on the Martian surface.

5. If high school graduates are deficient in reading, they will not be able to compete in the modern world. If high school graduates are deficient in writing,

they will not be able to compete in the modern world. Therefore, if high school graduates are deficient in reading, then they are deficient in writing.

6. The disparity between rich and poor is increasing. Therefore, political control over economic equality will be achieved only if restructuring the economic system along socialist lines implies that political control over economic equality will be achieved.

★7. Einstein won the Nobel Prize either for explaining the photoelectric effect or for the special theory of relativity. But he did win the Nobel Prize for explaining the photoelectric effect. Therefore, Einstein did not win the Nobel Prize for the special theory of relativity.

8. If microchips are made from diamond wafers, then computers will generate less heat. Computers will not generate less heat and microchips will be made from diamond wafers. Therefore, synthetic diamonds will be used for jewelry.

9. Either the USS *Arizona* or the USS *Missouri* was not sunk in the attack on Pearl Harbor. Therefore, it is not the case that either the USS *Arizona* or the USS *Missouri* was sunk in the attack on Pearl Harbor.

★10. If racial quotas are adopted for promoting employees, then qualified employees will be passed over; but if racial quotas are not adopted, then prior discrimination will go unaddressed. Either racial quotas will or will not be adopted for promoting employees. Therefore, either qualified employees will be passed over or prior discrimination will go unaddressed.

iLrn II. Determine whether the following symbolized arguments are valid or invalid by constructing a truth table for each:

★1. $\dfrac{K \supset \sim K}{\sim K}$

2. $\dfrac{R \supset R}{R}$

3. $\dfrac{P \equiv \sim N}{N \lor P}$

★4. $\sim(G \cdot M)$
   $\dfrac{M \lor \sim G}{\sim G}$

5. $K \equiv \sim L$
   $\dfrac{\sim(L \cdot \sim K)}{K \supset L}$

6. $\dfrac{Z}{E \supset (Z \supset E)}$

★7. $\sim(W \cdot \sim X)$
   $\dfrac{\sim(X \cdot \sim W)}{X \lor W}$

8. $C \equiv D$
   $\dfrac{E \lor \sim D}{E \supset C}$

9. $A \equiv (B \lor C)$
   $\dfrac{\sim C \lor B}{A \supset B}$

★10. $J \supset (K \supset L)$
   $\dfrac{K \supset (J \supset L)}{(J \lor K) \supset L}$

11. $\sim(K \equiv S)$
   $\dfrac{S \supset \sim(R \lor K)}{R \lor \sim S}$

12. $E \supset (F \cdot G)$
   $\dfrac{F \supset (G \supset H)}{E \supset H}$

★13. $A \supset (N \lor Q)$
   $\dfrac{\sim(N \lor \sim A)}{A \supset Q}$

14. $G \supset H$
    $R \equiv G$
    $\dfrac{\sim H \vee G}{R \equiv H}$

15. $L \supset M$
    $M \supset N$
    $\dfrac{N \supset L}{L \vee N}$

★16. $S \supset T$
    $S \supset \sim T$
    $\dfrac{\sim T \supset S}{S \vee \sim T}$

17. $W \supset X$
    $X \supset W$
    $X \supset Y$
    $\dfrac{Y \supset X}{W \equiv Y}$

18. $K \equiv (L \vee M)$
    $L \supset M$
    $M \supset K$
    $\dfrac{K \vee L}{K \supset L}$

★19. $A \supset B$
    $(A \cdot B) \supset C$
    $\dfrac{A \supset (C \supset D)}{A \supset D}$

20. $\sim A \vee R$
    $\sim (N \cdot \sim C)$
    $R \supset C$
    $\dfrac{C \supset \sim N}{A \vee C}$

6.5   Indirect Truth Tables

Indirect truth tables provide a shorter and faster method for testing the validity of arguments than that provided by ordinary truth tables. This method is especially applicable to arguments that contain a large number of different simple propositions. For example, an argument containing five different simple propositions would require an ordinary truth table having thirty-two lines. The indirect truth table for such an argument, on the other hand, would usually require only a single line and could be constructed in a fraction of the time required for the ordinary truth table.

Indirect truth tables can also be used to test a series of statements for consistency. In Section 6.3 we showed how ordinary truth tables are used to test pairs of statements for consistency and we noted that consistency was a relation that applied to any group of propositions. In this section we use indirect truth tables to test groups of three, four, five, and six propositions for consistency. Given the abbreviated nature of indirect truth tables, this evaluation can usually be done much faster than it can with ordinary truth tables.

Testing Arguments for Validity

To construct an indirect truth table for an argument, we begin by assuming that the argument is invalid. That is, we assume that it is possible for the premises to be true and the conclusion false. Truth values corresponding to true premises and false conclusion are entered beneath the main operators for the premises and conclusion. Then, working backward, the truth values of the separate components are derived. If no contradiction is obtained in the process, this means that it is indeed possible for the premises to be true and the conclusion false, as originally assumed, so the argument is therefore invalid. If, however, the attempt to make the premises true and the conclusion false necessarily leads to a contradiction, it is not possible for the premises to be true and the conclusion false, in which case the argument is valid. Consider the following symbolized argument:

$$\sim A \supset (B \vee C)$$
$$\underline{\sim B}$$
$$C \supset A$$

We begin as before by writing the symbolized argument on a single line, placing a single slash between the premises and a double slash between the last premise and the conclusion. Then we assign T to the premises and F to the conclusion:

$$\sim A \supset (B \vee C) \, / \, \sim B \, // \, C \supset A$$
$$ T T F$$

We can now derive the truth values of B, C, and A, as follows:

$$\sim A \supset (B \vee C) \, / \, \sim B \, // \, C \supset A$$
$$ T \text{T F} \text{T F F}$$

These truth values are now transferred to the first premise:

$$\sim A \supset (B \vee C) \, / \, \sim B \, // \, C \supset A$$
$$\text{T F T} \text{F T T} \text{T F} \text{T F F}$$

We thus have a perfectly consistent assignment of truth values, which makes the premises true and the conclusion false. The argument is therefore invalid. If an ordinary truth table were constructed for this argument, it would be seen that the argument fails on the line on which *A* is false, *B* is false, and *C* is true. This is the exact arrangement presented in the indirect truth table above.

Here is another example. As always, we begin by assigning T to the premises and F to the conclusion:

$$A \supset (B \vee C) \, / \, B \supset D \, / \, A \, // \, \sim C \supset D$$
$$ T T T F$$

From the conclusion we can now derive the truth values of *C* and *D*, which are then transferred to the first two premises:

$$A \supset (B \vee C) \, / \, B \supset D \, / \, A \, // \, \sim C \supset D$$
$$ T F \text{T F} T \text{T F F F}$$

The truth value of *B* is now derived from the second premise and transferred, together with the truth value of *A*, to the first premise:

$$A \supset (B \vee C) \, / \, B \supset D \, / \, A \, // \, \sim C \supset D$$
$$\text{(T T} \text{F F) F} \text{F T F} T \text{T F F F}$$

A contradiction now appears in the truth values assigned to the first premise, since T ⊃ F is F. The inconsistent truth values are circled. Because every step was strictly necessitated by some prior step, we have have shown that it is impossible for the premises to be true and the conclusion false. The argument is therefore valid.

Sometimes a single row of truth values is not sufficient to prove an argument valid. Example:

$$\sim A \supset B \ / \ B \supset A \ / \ A \supset \sim B \ // \ A \cdot \sim B$$

$$\text{T} \qquad\qquad \text{T} \qquad\qquad \text{T} \qquad\qquad\qquad \text{F}$$

Since a conditional statement can be true in any one of three ways, and a conjunctive statement can be false in any one of three ways, merely assigning truth to the premises and falsity to the conclusion of this argument is not sufficient to obtain the truth values of any of the component statements. When faced with a situation such as this, we must list all of the possible ways that one of the premises can be true or the conclusion false, and proceed from there. If we list all of the possible ways the conclusion may be false, we obtain the following:

$$\sim A \supset B \ / \ B \supset A \ / \ A \supset \sim B \ // \ A \cdot \sim B$$

~ A ⊃ B	/	B ⊃ A	/	A ⊃ ~ B	//	A	•	~ B
T		T		T		T F	F	T
T		T		T		F F	T	F
T		T		T		F F	F	T

Extending the truth values of *A* and *B* to the premises, we obtain the following result:

$$\sim A \supset B \ / \ B \supset A \ / \ A \supset \sim B \ // \ A \cdot \sim B$$

~ A ⊃ B	/	B ⊃ A	/	A ⊃ ~ B	//	A	•	~ B
T		T		(T T F) T		T F	F	T
(T F T F)		T		T		F F	T	F
T		(T T F)		T		F F	F	T

Since each line necessarily leads to a contradiction, the argument is valid. If a contradiction had been avoided on some line, the argument would, of course, be invalid, because it would be possible for the premises to be true and the conclusion false. Note that in this argument it is not necessary to fill out all the truth values on any one line to be forced into a contradiction. On each line the contradiction is necessarily derived within the context of a single premise.

If an indirect truth table requires more than one line, the method to be followed is this. Either select one of the premises and compute all of the ways it can be made true, or select the conclusion and compute all of the ways it can be made false. This selection should be dictated by the requirement of simplicity. For example, if the conclusion can be made false in only two ways, while each of the premises can be made true in three ways, then select the conclusion. On the other hand, if one of the premises can be made true in only two ways while the conclusion can be made false in three ways, then select that premise. If neither of these situations prevails, then select the conclusion.

Having made your selection, proceed to compute the truth values of each line, beginning with the first. If no contradiction is derived on this line, stop! The argument has been proved invalid. If a contradiction *is* derived on the first line, proceed to the second line. If no contradiction is derived on this line, then, again, the argument has been proved invalid. If a contradiction *is* derived, proceed to the third line, and so on. Remember, the objective is to produce a line having no contradiction. Once such a line is produced, the argument has been proved invalid, and no further work need be done. If, on the other hand, each line necessarily leads to a contradiction, the argument is valid.

Three final points need to be made about indirect truth tables for arguments. First, if a contradiction is obtained in the assignment of truth values, it is essential that every step leading to it be logically implied by some prior step. In other words, the contra-

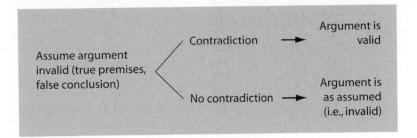

diction must be unavoidable. If a contradiction is obtained after truth values are assigned haphazardly or by guessing, then nothing has been proved. The objective is not to produce a contradiction but to *avoid* one (if possible).

For example, in the following indirect truth table a contradiction is apparent in the first premise:

$$A \supset B \ / \ C \supset B \ // \ A \supset C$$
$$\boxed{\text{T T F}} \quad \text{F T F} \quad \quad \text{T F F}$$

Yet the argument is invalid. The contradiction that appears is not *required* by the assignment of truth to the premises and falsity to the conclusion. The following indirect truth table, which is done correctly, proves the argument invalid:

$$A \supset B \ / \ C \supset B \ // \ A \supset C$$
$$\text{T T T} \quad \text{F T T} \quad \quad \text{T F F}$$

The second point is that for valid arguments the order in which the truth values are assigned may affect where the contradiction is obtained. That is, depending on the order of assignment, the contradiction may appear in the first premise, second premise, third premise, and so on. But, of course, the order of assignment does not affect the final determination of validity.

The last point is that it is essential that identical letters be assigned identical truth values. For example, if the letter A appears three times in a certain symbolized argument and the truth value T is assigned to it in one occurrence, then the same truth value must be assigned to it in the other occurrences as well. After the truth table has been completed, each letter should be rechecked to ensure that one and the same truth value has been assigned to its various occurrences.

Testing Statements for Consistency

The method for testing a series of statements for consistency is similar to the method for testing arguments. We begin by writing the statements on a line, separating each with a single slash mark. (Since we have no conclusion, we use no double slash marks.) Then we assume that the statements are consistent. We assign a T to the main operator of each, and we then compute the truth values of the components. If this computation leads necessarily to a contradiction, the statements are not as we assumed them to be. That is, they are inconsistent. But if no contradiction is reached, the statements are consistent. Here is an example:

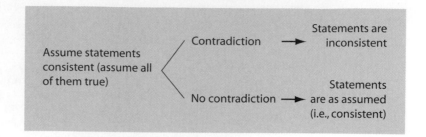

$A \lor B$
$B \supset (C \lor A)$
$C \supset \sim B$
$\sim A$

First, we write the statements on a single line separated by a single slash mark; we then assign T to each of the main operators:

```
A v B / B ⊃ (C v A) / C ⊃ ~ B / ~ A
  T       T           T         T
```

The next step is to compute the truth values of the components. First we compute the truth value of A. Next, we enter this truth value in the first statement and compute the truth value of B. Next, we enter the truth value of B in the second statement and compute the truth value of C. Finally, the truth values of C and B are carried to the third statement:

```
A v B / B ⊃ (C v A) / C ⊃ ~ B / ~ A
F T T   T T  T T F   (T T F) T   T F
```

Since this computation leads necessarily to a contradiction (third statement), the group of statements is inconsistent.

Here is another example. The statements are written on a single line, and a T is assigned to each of the main operators:

```
A ⊃ (B · C) / C ⊃ ~ A / B v A / B ⊃ C
  T              T         T       T
```

Since all of the statements can be true in three ways, we select one of them (the fourth) and figure all of the ways it can be true:

```
A ⊃ (B · C) / C ⊃ ~ A / B v A / B ⊃ C
  T              T         T     T T T
                                 F T T
                                 F T F
```

Filling out the first line leads to no contradiction, so the statements are consistent:

```
A ⊃ (B · C) / C ⊃ ~ A / B v A / B ⊃ C
F T  T T T    T T T F   T T F   T T T
                                F T T
                                F T F
```

As with testing arguments, the objective is to *avoid* a contradiction. As soon as no contradiction is reached, we stop. The statements are consistent. Only if all three lines had led to a contradiction would these statements be inconsistent.

Rule for all multiline indirect truth tables

Contradiction is derived ⟶ Go to next line (if there is one).

No contradiction is derived ⟶ Stop. Argument is invalid/
Statements are consistent.

EXERCISE 6.5

iLrn   I. Use indirect truth tables to determine whether the following arguments are valid or invalid:

★1. $B \supset C$
$\underline{\sim C}$
$\sim B$

2. $\sim E \vee F$
$\underline{\sim E}$
$\sim F$

3. $P \supset (Q \cdot R)$
$\underline{R \supset S}$
$P \supset S$

★4. $\sim(I \equiv J)$
$\overline{\sim(I \supset J)}$

5. $W \supset (X \supset Y)$
$\underline{X \supset (Y \supset Z)}$
$W \supset (X \supset Z)$

6. $A \supset (B \vee C)$
$C \supset (D \cdot E)$
$\underline{\sim B}$
$A \supset E$

★7. $G \supset H$
$H \supset I$
$\sim J \supset G$
$\underline{\sim I}$
J

8. $J \supset (\sim L \supset \sim K)$
$K \supset (\sim L \supset M)$
$\underline{(L \vee M) \supset N}$
$J \supset N$

9. $P \cdot (Q \vee R)$
$(P \cdot R) \supset \sim(S \vee T)$
$\underline{(\sim S \vee \sim T) \supset \sim(P \cdot Q)}$
$S \equiv T$

★10. $(M \vee N) \supset O$
$O \supset (N \vee P)$
$M \supset (\sim Q \supset N)$
$\underline{(Q \supset M) \supset \sim P}$
$N \equiv O$

11. $(A \vee B) \supset (C \cdot D)$
$\underline{(\sim A \vee \sim B) \supset E}$
$(\sim C \vee \sim D) \supset E$

12. $F \supset G$
$\sim H \vee I$
$(G \vee I) \supset J$
$\underline{\sim J}$
$\sim(F \vee H)$

★13. $(A \vee B) \supset (C \cdot D)$
$(X \vee \sim Y) \supset (\sim C \cdot \sim W)$
$\underline{(X \vee Z) \supset (A \cdot E)}$
$\sim X$

14. $\sim G \supset (\sim H \cdot \sim I)$
$J \supset H$
$K \supset (L \cdot M)$
$\underline{K \vee J}$
$L \cdot G$

15. $N \lor {\sim}O$
$P \lor O$
$P \supset Q$
$(N \lor Q) \supset (R \cdot S)$
$S \supset (R \supset T)$
$\underline{O \supset (T \supset U)}$
U

iLrn II. Use indirect truth tables to determine whether the following groups of statements are consistent or inconsistent.

★1. $K \equiv (R \lor M)$
$K \cdot {\sim}R$
$M \supset {\sim}K$

2. $F \equiv (A \cdot {\sim}P)$
$A \supset (P \cdot S)$
$S \supset {\sim}F$
$A \cdot {\sim}F$

3. $(G \lor {\sim}Q) \supset (F \lor B)$
${\sim}(F \lor Q)$
$B \supset N$
$(F \lor N) \supset Q$

★4. $(N \lor C) \equiv E$
$N \supset {\sim}(C \lor H)$
$H \supset E$
$C \supset H$

5. $P \lor {\sim}S$
$S \lor {\sim}T$
$T \lor {\sim}X$
$X \lor {\sim}J$
$J \lor {\sim}P$

6. $(Q \lor K) \supset C$
$(C \cdot F) \supset (N \lor L)$
$C \supset (F \cdot {\sim}L)$
$Q \cdot {\sim}N$

★7. $S \supset (R \equiv A)$
$A \supset (W \cdot {\sim}R)$
$R \equiv (W \lor T)$
$S \cdot U$
$U \supset T$

8. $(E \lor H) \supset (K \cdot D)$
$D \supset (M \cdot B)$
$B \supset {\sim}E$
${\sim}(H \lor K)$
$D \supset B$

9. $G \supset P$
$P \supset (A \cdot {\sim}G)$
$(R \lor T) \supset G$
$Y \supset R$
$B \supset T$
$Y \lor B$

★10. $A \lor Z$
$A \supset (T \cdot F)$
$Z \supset (M \cdot Q)$
$Q \supset {\sim}F$
$T \supset {\sim}M$
$M \supset A$

6.6 Argument Forms and Fallacies

Many of the arguments that occur in propositional logic have forms that bear specific names and can be immediately recognized as either valid or invalid. The first part of this section presents some of the more common ones and explains how they are recognized. The second part discusses ways of refuting two of these forms, constructive and destructive dilemmas. Finally, the third part applies to real-life arguments some of the principles developed in the first part.

Common Argument Forms

An **argument form** is an arrangement of statement variables and operators such that the uniform replacement of the variables by statements results in an argument. A *valid* argument form is any argument form that satisfies the truth table test.

The first valid argument form to consider is **disjunctive syllogism,** which is defined as follows:

disjunctive syllogism (DS):
$$p \lor q$$
$$\underline{\sim p}$$
$$q$$

The validity of this form can be easily checked by a truth table. Now, given that validity is purely a function of the form of an argument, any argument produced by uniformly substituting statements in place of the variables in this argument form is a valid argument. Such an argument is said to *have* the form of a disjunctive syllogism. The following argument was produced in this way and is therefore valid:

Either Harvard or Princeton is in New Jersey. $H \lor P$
Harvard is not in New Jersey. $\underline{\sim H}$
Therefore, Princeton is in New Jersey. P

The validity of a disjunctive syllogism arises from the fact that one of the premises presents two alternatives and the other premise eliminates one of those alternatives, leaving the other as the conclusion. This so-called "method of elimination" is essential to the validity of a disjunctive syllogism. If one premise should present two alternatives and the other premise should *affirm* one of those alternatives, the argument is invalid (unless the conclusion is a tautology). Example:

Either Harvard or Amherst is in Massachusetts. $H \lor A$
Harvard is in Massachusetts. H
Therefore, Amherst is not in Massachusetts. $\underline{\sim A}$

Since both Harvard and Amherst are in Massachusetts, the premises are true and the conclusion is false. Thus, the argument is invalid. Because the wedge symbol designates inclusive disjunction, the disjunctive premise includes the possibility of both disjuncts being true. Thus for the argument to be valid, the other premise must eliminate one of the disjuncts.

The next valid argument form we consider is **pure hypothetical syllogism.** It consists of two premises and one conclusion, all of which are hypothetical (conditional) statements, and is defined as follows:

pure hypothetical syllogism (HS):
$$p \supset q$$
$$\underline{q \supset r}$$
$$p \supset r$$

Any argument that has the form of a pure hypothetical syllogism (that is, any argument that can be produced by uniformly substituting statements in place of the variables in the form) is a valid argument. Example:

If world population continues to grow, then cities will become hopelessly overcrowded.	$W \supset C$
If cities become hopelessly overcrowded, then pollution will become intolerable.	$C \supset P$
Therefore, if world population continues to grow, then pollution will become intolerable.	$W \supset P$

The validity of a pure hypothetical syllogism is grounded in the fact that the premises link together like a chain. In the population argument, the consequent of the first premise is identical to the antecedent of the second. If the premises fail to link together in this way, the argument may be invalid. Example:

If Bill Gates is a man, then Bill Gates is a human being.	$M \supset H$
If Bill Gates is a woman, then Bill Gates is a human being.	$W \supset H$
Therefore, if Bill Gates is a man, then Bill Gates is a woman.	$M \supset W$

The premises of this argument are true, and the conclusion is false. Thus the argument is invalid.

Another important valid argument form is called modus ponens ("asserting mode"). It consists of a conditional premise, a second premise that asserts the antecedent of the conditional premise, and a conclusion that asserts the consequent:

modus ponens (MP):
$$p \supset q$$
$$p$$
$$\overline{q}$$

Any argument having the form of *modus ponens* is a valid argument. Example:

If twelve million children die yearly from starvation, then something is wrong with food distribution.	$T \supset S$
Twelve million children die yearly from starvation.	T
Therefore, something is wrong with food distribution.	S

Closely associated with *modus ponens* is **modus tollens** ("denying mode"). *Modus tollens* is a valid argument form consisting of one conditional premise, a second premise that denies the consequent of the conditional premise, and a conclusion that denies the antecedent. It is defined as follows:

modus tollens (MT):
$$p \supset q$$
$$\sim q$$
$$\overline{\sim p}$$

Modus tollens is a little harder to understand than *modus ponens*, but it can be understood by the following reasoning process: The conclusion states that we do not have p, because if we did have p, then (by the first premise) we would have q, and we do not have q (by the second premise). Any argument that has the form of *modus tollens* is a valid argument. Example:

If Japan cares about endangered species, then it has stopped killing whales.	$C \supset S$
Japan has not stopped killing whales.	$\sim S$
Therefore, Japan does not care about endangered species.	$\sim C$

Two invalid forms are closely associated with *modus ponens* and *modus tollens*. These are **affirming the consequent** and **denying the antecedent**. Affirming the consequent consists of one conditional premise, a second premise that asserts the consequent of the conditional, and a conclusion that asserts the antecedent:

affirming the consequent (AC): $p \supset q$

$\underline{q}$

p

Any argument that has the form of affirming the consequent is an invalid argument.* The following argument has this form and is therefore invalid:

If Napoleon was killed in a plane crash, then Napoleon is dead.	$K \supset D$
Napoleon is dead.	$\underline{D}$
Therefore, Napoleon was killed in a plane crash.	K

Given that this argument has true premises and a false conclusion, it is clearly invalid.

Denying the antecedent consists of a conditional premise, a second premise that denies the antecedent of the conditional, and a conclusion that denies the consequent:

denying the antecedent (DA): $p \supset q$

$\underline{\sim p}$

$\sim q$

Any argument that has the form of denying the antecedent is an invalid argument. Example:

If Napoleon was killed in a plane crash, then Napoleon is dead.	$K \supset D$
Napoleon was not killed in a plane crash.	$\underline{\sim K}$
Therefore, Napoleon is not dead.	$\sim D$

Again, this argument has true premises and a false conclusion, so it is clearly invalid.

A **constructive dilemma** is a valid argument form that consists of a conjunctive premise made up of two conditional statements, a disjunctive premise that asserts the antecedents in the conjunctive premise (like *modus ponens*), and a disjunctive conclusion that asserts the consequents of the conjunctive premise. It is defined as follows:

constructive dilemma (CD): $(p \supset q) \cdot (r \supset s)$

$\underline{p \vee r}$

$q \vee s$

Any argument that has the form of a constructive dilemma is a valid argument. Example:

If we choose nuclear power, then we increase the risk of a nuclear accident; but if we choose conventional power, then we add to the greenhouse effect.	$(N \supset I) \cdot (C \supset A)$
We must choose either nuclear power or conventional power.	$\underline{N \vee C}$
Therefore, we either increase the risk of nuclear accident or add to the greenhouse effect.	$I \vee A$

*See "Note on Invalid Forms" later in this section.

The **destructive dilemma** is also a valid argument form. It is similar to the constructive dilemma in that it includes a conjunctive premise made up of two conditional statements and a disjunctive premise. However, the disjunctive premise denies the consequents of the conditionals (like *modus tollens*), and the conclusion denies the antecedents:

destructive dilemma (DD): $(p \supset q) \cdot (r \supset s)$
$$\frac{\sim q \vee \sim s}{\sim p \vee \sim r}$$

Any argument that has the form of a destructive dilemma is a valid argument. Example:

If we are to reverse the greenhouse effect, then we must choose nuclear power; but if we are to lower the risk of a nuclear accident, then we must choose conventional power.	$(R \supset N) \cdot (L \supset C)$
We will either not choose nuclear power or not choose conventional power.	$\sim N \vee \sim C$
Therefore, we will either not reverse the greenhouse effect or not lower the risk of a nuclear accident.	$\sim R \vee \sim L$

Refuting Constructive and Destructive Dilemmas

Now that we are familiar with a number of argument forms in propositional logic, we may return for a closer look at two of them, constructive and destructive dilemmas. Arguments having these forms occur frequently in public debate, where they may be used by an arguer to trap an opponent. Since both forms are valid, the only direct mode of defense available to the opponent is to prove the dilemma unsound. This can be done by proving at least one of the premises false. If the conjunctive premise (otherwise called the "horns of the dilemma") is proven false, the opponent is said to have "grasped the dilemma by the horns." This, of course, may be done by proving either one of the conditional statements false. If, on the other hand, the disjunctive premise is proven false, the opponent is said to have "escaped between the horns of the dilemma." The latter strategy often involves finding a third alternative that excludes the two that are given in the disjunctive premise. If such a third alternative can be found, both of the given disjuncts will be proved false. Consider the following constructive dilemma:

If taxes increase, the economy will suffer, and if taxes decrease, needed governmental services will be curtailed. Since taxes must either increase or decrease, it follows that the economy will suffer or that needed governmental services will be curtailed.

It is easy to escape between the horns of this dilemma by arguing that taxes could be kept as they are, in which case they would neither increase nor decrease.

Some dilemmas, however, do not allow for the possibility of escaping between the horns. Consider the following constructive dilemma:

> If we encourage competition, we will have no peace, and if we do not encourage competition, we will make no progress. Since we must either encourage competition or not encourage it, we will either have no peace or make no progress.

Since the disjunctive premise of this dilemma is a tautology, it cannot be proven false. This leaves the strategy of grasping the dilemma by the horns, which may be done by proving either of the conditional statements in the conjunctive premise false. One debater might want to attack the first conditional and argue that competition and peace can coexist, while another might want to attack the second and argue that progress can be achieved through some means other than encouraging competition.

The strategy to be followed in refuting a dilemma is therefore this: Examine the disjunctive premise. If this premise is a tautology, attempt to grasp the dilemma by the horns by attacking one or the other of the conditional statements in the conjunctive premise. If the disjunctive premise is not a tautology, then either escape between the horns by, perhaps, finding a third alternative, or grasp the dilemma by the horns—whichever is easier.

A third, indirect strategy for refuting a dilemma involves constructing a counterdilemma. This is typically done by changing either the antecedents or the consequents of the conjunctive premise while leaving the disjunctive premise as it is, so as to obtain a different conclusion. If the dilemma in question is a constructive dilemma, the consequents of the conjunctive premise are changed. Here are possible counterdilemmas for the two dilemmas presented above:

> If taxes increase, needed governmental services will be extended, and if taxes decrease, the economy will improve. Since taxes must either increase or decrease, it follows that needed governmental services will be extended or the economy will improve.

> If we encourage competition, we will make progress, and if we do not encourage competition, we will have peace. Since we must either encourage competition or not encourage it, we will either make progress or have peace.

Constructing a counterdilemma falls short of a refutation of a given dilemma because it merely shows that a different approach can be taken to a certain problem. It does not cast any doubt on the soundness of the original dilemma. Yet, the strategy is often effective because it testifies to the cleverness of the debater who can accomplish it successfully. In the heat of debate the attending audience is often persuaded that the original argument has been thoroughly demolished.

Note on Invalid Forms

Throughout this book we have seen that any substitution instance of a valid argument form is a valid argument. For example, consider *modus ponens:*

$$p \supset q$$
$$\underline{p}$$
$$q$$

Literally any two statements uniformly substituted in the place of p and q will result in a valid argument. Thus, the following symbolized arguments both have the form of *modus ponens,* and are accordingly valid:

$$S \supset T \qquad\qquad (K \lor B) \supset (N \cdot R)$$
$$\underline{S} \qquad\qquad\qquad \underline{K \lor B}$$
$$T \qquad\qquad\qquad\quad N \cdot R$$

In the first argument S and T are uniformly substituted in the place of p and q, and in the second argument $K \lor B$ and $N \cdot R$ are uniformly substituted in the place of p and q.

However, this result does not extend to invalid argument forms. Consider, for example, affirming the consequent:

$$p \supset q$$
$$\underline{q}$$
$$p$$

Sometimes the uniform substitution of statements in the place of p and q results in an invalid argument, and sometimes it does not. Both of the following symbolized arguments are substitution instances of affirming the consequent, but the one on the left is invalid while the one on the right is valid:

$$G \supset N \qquad\qquad (F \lor D) \supset (F \cdot D)$$
$$\underline{N} \qquad\qquad\qquad \underline{F \cdot D}$$
$$G \qquad\qquad\qquad\quad F \lor D$$

To deal with this problem we adopt a convention about when an argument will be said to *have* an invalid form. We will say that an argument has an invalid form if it is a substitution instance of that form *and* it is not a substitution instance of any valid form. According to this convention only the argument on the left has the form of affirming the consequent. The argument on the right does not have this form because it is a substitution instance of the following valid form:

$$(p \lor q) \supset (p \cdot q)$$
$$\underline{p \cdot q}$$
$$p \lor q$$

The validity of this form results from the fact that the conclusion follows from the second premise alone, without any involvement of the first premise. This fact may be easily checked with a truth table.

Here is another invalid form:

$$p \supset q$$
$$\underline{r \supset q}$$
$$p \supset r$$

Both of the following symbolized arguments are substitution instances of this form, but only the one on the left is invalid:

$$K \supset L \qquad\qquad \sim C \supset A$$
$$\underline{R \supset L} \qquad\qquad \underline{(C \supset E) \supset A}$$
$$K \supset R \qquad\qquad \sim C \supset (C \supset E)$$

The argument on the right is valid because its conclusion is a tautology. Accordingly, only the argument on the left will be said to have the invalid form in question.

The point of this discussion is that when we attempt to determine the validity of arguments through mere inspection, we have to exert caution with invalid forms. The mere fact that an argument is a substitution instance of an invalid form does not guarantee that it is invalid. Before judging it invalid we must make sure that it is not valid for some other reason, such as its conclusion being a tautology. However, as concerns the exercises at the end of this section, all of the arguments that are substitution instances of invalid forms are invalid. In other words, none of them is like either of the right-hand examples considered in these paragraphs.

Summary and Application

Any argument having one of the following forms is valid:

$p \lor q$	disjunctive	$p \supset q$	pure hypothetical
$\underline{\sim p}$	syllogism	$\underline{q \supset r}$	syllogism (HS)
q	(DS)	$p \supset r$	
$p \supset q$	*modus ponens*	$p \supset q$	*modus tollens*
$\underline{p}$	(MP)	$\underline{\sim q}$	(MT)
q		$\sim p$	
$(p \supset q) \cdot (r \supset s)$	constructive	$(p \supset q) \cdot (r \supset s)$	destructive
$\underline{p \lor r}$	dilemma	$\underline{\sim q \lor \sim s}$	dilemma (DD)
$q \lor s$	(CD)	$\sim p \lor \sim r$	

Any argument having either of the following forms is invalid:

$p \supset q$	affirming the	$p \supset q$	denying the
$\underline{q}$	consequent (AC)	$\underline{\sim p}$	antecedent (DA)
p		$\sim q$	

In identifying arguments as having these argument forms, use the following procedure. First symbolize the argument, using upper-case letters for the simple propositions. Then see whether the symbolized argument fits the pattern of one of these forms. For example, the following symbolized argument has the form of *modus ponens,* and is therefore valid:

$$K \supset R$$
$$\underline{K}$$
$$R$$

If K and R are substituted respectively in place of p and q in the *modus ponens* form, we obtain the symbolized argument in question.

However, not every attempt at argument recognition is as simple as this. For more complicated cases it helps to keep two points in mind:

The order of the premises never affects the argument's form.
Negated letters can be substituted in place of the p, q, r, and s of an argument form just as can non-negated letters.

In regard to the first point, consider these symbolized arguments:

N	$\sim S$
$\underline{N \supset B}$	$\underline{S \lor F}$
B	F

The argument on the left is *modus ponens,* and the one on the right is a disjunctive syllogism. To see this more clearly, simply switch the order of the premises.

In regard to the second point (involving negated letters), consider these examples:

$\sim G \supset \sim H$	$\sim K \supset \sim M$
$\underline{\sim G}$	$\underline{\sim\sim M}$
$\sim H$	$\sim\sim K$

The argument on the left is *modus ponens,* and the one on the right is *modus tollens.* To produce the argument on the left, substitute $\sim$G in the place of p in the *modus ponens* form, and $\sim$H in the place of q. For the argument on the right, substitute $\sim K$ in the place of p in the *modus tollens* form, and $\sim M$ in the place of q.

Another problem that complicates the task of argument recognition arises from the fact that many arguments can be translated in alternate ways. Consider, for example, this argument:

Either the witness lied or Bob is guilty.
The witness told the truth.
Therefore, Bob is guilty.

If we select L to represent "The witness lied," then the argument can be translated into symbols as follows:

$L \lor B$
$\underline{\sim L}$
B

This symbolized argument is clearly an instance of disjunctive syllogism.

On the other hand, if we select T to represent "The witness told the truth," then we have this translation:

$\sim T \lor B$
$\underline{T}$
B

Technically this is not an instance of disjunctive syllogism because the second premise, T, is not preceded by a tilde. To avoid this kind of difficulty in connection with alternative translations, we introduce two rules. They should be obvious, but if there is any doubt about them they can be proved using truth tables. The rules are:

p is logically equivalent to ~~p.   (Double Negation)
p v q is logically equivalent to q v p.   (Commutativity)

According to the first rule, double tildes may be either inserted or deleted prior to any statement, and according to the second rule the order of the components in a disjunctive statement may be reversed. Applying the double negation rule to the second premise of the symbolized argument above, we have:

~T v B
~~T
___
B

After this change, the argument is now an instance of disjunctive syllogism.

For examples of how the commutativity rule is applied, consider these symbolized arguments:

M v E   (R ⊃ L) • (T ⊃ K)
~E   T v R
___   ___
M   L v K

Technically the argument on the left is not an instance of disjunctive syllogism because the letters in the first premise are in the wrong order, and the argument on the right is not an instance of constructive dilemma because the letters in the second premise are in the wrong order. We can reverse the order of these letters by applying the commutativity rule:

E v M   (R ⊃ L) • (T ⊃ K)
~E   R v T
___   ___
M   L v K

After these changes, the argument on the left is now clearly an instance of disjunctive syllogism, and the one on the right is an instance of constructive dilemma.

Here are some additional examples. In some cases the symbolized argument must be rewritten using double negation or commutativity before it fits the pattern of the argument form indicated.

~A ⊃ ~B   A ⊃ ~B
~B ⊃ C   HS—valid   B ⊃ ~C
___   ___
~A ⊃ C   A ⊃ ~C   invalid

~A ⊃ ~B   A ⊃ B
B   MT—valid   A   DA—invalid
___   ___
A   ~B

~A v ~B   ~A v B
A   DS—valid   ~A   invalid
___   ___
~B   B

(A ⊃ ~B) • (~C ⊃ D)   (~A ⊃ B) • (C ⊃ ~D)
A v ~C   CD—valid   B v ~D   invalid
___   ___
~B v D   A v ~C

$$A \lor \sim B$$
$$\underline{B}\qquad \text{DS—valid}$$
$$A$$

$$A \supset \sim B$$
$$\underline{\sim B}\qquad \text{AC—invalid}$$
$$A$$

$$A$$
$$\underline{A \supset B}\qquad \text{MP—valid}$$
$$B$$

$$A \lor C$$
$$\underline{(A \supset B) \cdot (C \supset D)}\qquad \text{CD—valid}$$
$$B \lor D$$

Let us now see how the argument forms presented in this section can be used to interpret the structure of some real-life arguments. Consider the following letter to the editor of a newspaper:

> If U.S. servicemen are indeed being held in Southeast Asia, what is the motivation of their captors? No government there has asked for anything in return, as might be expected if they were deliberately holding Americans.
>
> (Norm Oshrin)

This argument is enthymematic; in other words, it is missing certain parts. The author intends to prove that U.S. servicemen are not being held in Southeast Asia—because if they were, their captors would be demanding something for their return. The argument can thus be structured as a *modus tollens*:

> If U.S. servicemen are being held in Southeast Asia, then their captors have demanded something for their return.
> Their captors have not demanded something for their return.
> Therefore, U.S. servicemen are not being held in Southeast Asia.

Here is another example:

> In a time when an entire nation believes in Murphy's law (that if anything can go wrong, it surely will) and has witnessed serious accidents in the highly regulated, supposedly fail-safe nuclear industry, it's fascinating that people can persist in the fantasy that an error will not occur in the area of nuclear weaponry.
>
> (Burk Gossom, *Newsweek*)

Although this argument allows for more than one analysis, it is clear that the arguer presents two main reasons why we can expect an accident in the area of nuclear weaponry: "Murphy's law" (which everyone believes to be true) dictates it, and accidents have occurred in the area of nuclear power (which is presumed fail-safe). Thus, at the very least, we can extract two *modus ponens* arguments from this selection:

> If everyone believes Murphy's law, then we can expect accidents in nuclear weaponry.
> Everyone believes Murphy's law.
> Therefore, we can expect accidents in nuclear weaponry.

> If accidents have occurred in nuclear power, then we can expect accidents in nuclear weaponry.
> Accidents have occurred in nuclear power.
> Therefore, we can expect accidents in nuclear weaponry.

Many arguments that we encounter in ordinary life can be interpreted as instances of valid argument forms. After being so interpreted, however, not all will turn out sound. The invalid forms (denying the antecedent and affirming the consequent) should be reserved for the relatively few arguments that are clearly invalid as originally expressed.

iLrn I. Evalute the following symbolized arguments using the forms presented in this section. In some cases the argument may have to be rewritten using double negation or commutativity before it becomes an instance of one of these forms. Those without a named form are invalid.

★1. $N \supset C$
$\dfrac{\sim C}{\sim N}$

2. $S \supset F$
$\dfrac{F \supset \sim L}{S \supset \sim L}$

3. $A \vee \sim Z$
$\dfrac{\sim Z}{A}$

★4. $(S \supset \sim P) \cdot (\sim S \supset D)$
$\dfrac{S \vee \sim S}{\sim P \vee D}$

5. $\sim N$
$\dfrac{\sim N \supset T}{T}$

6. $M \vee \sim B$
$\dfrac{\sim M}{\sim B}$

★7. $(E \supset N) \cdot (\sim L \supset \sim K)$
$\dfrac{\sim N \vee K}{\sim E \vee L}$

8. $W \supset \sim M$
$\dfrac{\sim M}{W}$

9. $\sim B \supset \sim L$
$\dfrac{G \supset \sim B}{G \supset \sim L}$

★10. $F \supset O$
$\dfrac{\sim F}{\sim O}$

11. $(K \vee B) \cdot (N \vee Q)$
$\dfrac{K \vee N}{B \vee Q}$

12. X
$\dfrac{X \supset \sim E}{\sim E}$

★13. $P \vee \sim S$
$\dfrac{S}{P}$

14. $B \cdot T$
$\dfrac{T}{\sim B}$

15. $\sim R \vee \sim Q$
$\dfrac{(G \supset Q) \cdot (H \supset R)}{\sim G \vee \sim H}$

★16. $\sim G \supset H$
$\dfrac{H}{\sim G}$

17. $K \supset \sim C$
$\dfrac{C}{\sim K}$

18. $(I \supset M) \cdot (\sim O \supset A)$
$\dfrac{\sim O \vee I}{M \vee A}$

★19. $X \supset \sim F$
$\dfrac{W \supset \sim F}{W \supset X}$

20. $\sim L \supset U$
$\dfrac{L}{\sim U}$

II. Translate the following arguments into symbolic notation and then evaluate the symbolized arguments using the forms presented in this section. In some cases the argument may have to be rewritten using double negation or commutativity before it becomes an instance of one of these forms. Those without a named form are invalid.

★1. Future presidents will be allowed to serve a third term only if the Twenty-second Amendment is repealed. The Twenty-second Amendment will not be repealed. Therefore, future presidents will not be allowed to serve a third term.

2. If Michelangelo painted the ceiling of the Sistine Chapel, then he was familiar with stories from the Old Testament. Michelangelo was familiar with stories from the Old Testament. Therefore, Michelangelo painted the ceiling of the Sistine Chapel.

3. If you enter the teaching profession, you will have no money for vacations; and if you do not enter the teaching profession, you will have no time for vacations. Since you must either enter or not enter the teaching profession, it follows that either you will have no money or no time for vacations.

★4. Either the wealthiest people are the happiest, or it is not the case that money can buy everything. The wealthiest people are not the happiest. Therefore, money cannot buy everything.

5. Either tortured political prisoners in Turkey can openly complain of their mistreatment or Turkey is not a democracy. Tortured political prisoners in Turkey can openly complain of their mistreatment. Therefore, Turkey is a democracy.

6. If the sun is a variable star, then its energy will drop drastically at some point in the future. If the sun's energy drops drastically at some point in the future, then the earth will become a giant iceball. Therefore, if the sun is a variable star, then the earth will become a giant iceball.

★7. Twenty percent of America's children have never seen a dentist. But if that is so, health care in America is not properly distributed. Therefore, health care in America is not properly distributed.

8. If TV viewing provides genuine relaxation, then TV enhances the quality of life. But TV viewing does not provide genuine relaxation. Therefore, TV does not enhance the quality of life.

9. If high school clinics are to stem the tide of teenage pregnancy, then they must dispense birth control devices; but if they want to discourage illicit sex, then they must not dispense these devices. Since high school clinics must either dispense or not dispense birth control devices, either they will not stem the tide of teenage pregnancy, or they will not discourage illicit sex.

★10. If limits are imposed on medical malpractice suits, then patients will not be adequately compensated for their injuries; but if the cost of malpractice insurance continues to rise, then physicians will be forced out of business. Limits will not be imposed, and the cost of malpractice insurance will not continue to rise. Therefore, patients will be adequately compensated and physicians will not be forced out of business.

11. If Prohibition succeeded in the 1920s, then the war on drugs will succeed today. But Prohibition did not succeed in the 1920s. Therefore, the war on drugs will not succeed today.

12. If life is always better than death, then people do not commit suicide. People do commit suicide. Therefore, life is not always better than death.

★13. If we want to prevent foreign subsidies and dumping, then we must have tariffs and quotas; but if we want to avoid an international trade war, then we must have no tariffs or quotas. Since we must either have tariffs and quotas or not have them, we will either have foreign subsidies and dumping or an international trade war.

14. Either industrial pollutants will be more stringently controlled, or acid rain will continue to fall. Industrial pollutants will be more stringently controlled. Therefore, acid rain will not continue to fall.

15. Insurance companies contribute millions of dollars to political campaigns. But if that is so, then meaningful insurance reform is impossible. Therefore, meaningful insurance reform is impossible.

★16. If Mexico does not get its population growth under control, then its unemployment problem will never be solved. Mexico's unemployment problem will never be solved. Therefore, Mexico will not get its population growth under control.

17. Either the dinosaurs were not cold-blooded or they were not the ancestors of modern birds. The dinosaurs were the ancestors of modern birds. Therefore, the dinosaurs were not cold-blooded.

18. If coal burning continues, then heavy metals will be released into the atmosphere. If heavy metals are not released into the atmosphere, then nervous system damage will decrease. Therefore, if coal burning does not continue, then nervous system damage will decrease.

★19. If sea levels rise twenty feet worldwide, then coastal cities from New York to Sydney will be inundated. If the ice sheets on Antarctica slip into the sea, then sea levels will rise twenty feet worldwide. Therefore, if the ice sheets on Antarctica slip into the sea, then coastal cities from New York to Sydney will be inundated.

20. If tax credits are given for private education, then the government will be supporting religion; but if tax credits are not given for private education, then some parents will end up paying double tuition. Either tax credits will or will not be given for private education. Therefore, either the government will be supporting religion, or some parents will end up paying double tuition.

III. Identify the following dilemmas as either constructive or destructive. Then suggest a refutation for each by either escaping between the horns, grasping by the horns, or constructing a counterdilemma.

★1. If Melinda spends the night studying, she will miss the party; but if she does not spend the night studying, she will fail the test tomorrow. Melinda must either spend the night studying or not studying. Therefore, she will either miss the party or fail the test.

2. If we build our home in the valley, it will be struck by floods; and if we build it on the hilltop, it will be hit by lightning. Since we must either build it in the valley or on the hilltop, our home will either be struck by floods or hit by lightning.

3. If psychotherapists respect their clients' right to confidentiality, then they will not report child abusers to the authorities; but if they have any concern for

the welfare of children, then they will report them. Psychotherapists must either report or not report child abusers to the authorities. Therefore, psychotherapists either have no respect for their clients' right to confidentiality or no concern for the welfare of children.

★4. If corporations are to remain competitive, then they must not spend money to neutralize their toxic waste; but if the environment is to be preserved, then corporations must spend money to neutralize their toxic waste. Corporations either will or will not spend money to neutralize their toxic waste. Therefore, either they will not remain competitive, or the environment will be destroyed.

5. If physicians pull the plug on terminally ill patients, then they risk being charged with murder; but if they do not pull the plug, they prolong their patients' pain and suffering. Since physicians with terminally ill patients must do one or the other, either they risk being charged with murder or they prolong their patients' pain and suffering.

6. If the Mitchells get a divorce, they will live separately in poverty; but if they stay married, they will live together in misery. Since they must either get a divorce or stay married, they will either live separately in poverty or together in misery.

★7. If college students want courses that are interesting and rewarding, then they must major in liberal arts; but if they want a job when they graduate, then they must major in business. College students will either not major in liberal arts, or they will not major in business. Therefore, either they will not take courses that are interesting and rewarding, or they will not have a job when they graduate.

8. If merchants arrest suspected shoplifters, then they risk false imprisonment; but if they do not arrest them, they risk loss of merchandise. Merchants must either arrest or not arrest suspected shoplifters. Therefore, they will either risk false imprisonment or loss of merchandise.

9. If women threatened with rape want to avoid being maimed or killed, then they must not resist their assaulter; but if they want to ensure successful prosecution of the assailant, they must resist him. Since women threatened with rape must do one or the other, either they will risk being maimed or killed or they will jeopardize successful prosecution of the assailant.

★10. If we prosecute suspected terrorists, then we risk retaliation by other terrorists; but if we release them, then we encourage terrorism. Since we must either prosecute or release suspected terrorists, we either risk retaliation by other terrorists or we encourage terrorism.

IV. The following selections were taken from letters to the editor of newspapers. Each contains one or more arguments, but the exact form of the argument may be hidden or ambiguous. Use the argument forms presented in this section to structure the selections as specifically named arguments.

★1. Anyone who is wondering how well Oral Roberts receives messages from God will be interested in our experience. Two weeks after my mother died, a letter came from Oral Roberts saying God had told him to write to her that day and ask for money! It makes one wonder.

(Hazel Woodsmall)

2. OK, I've tried it for a week again this year, but I still don't like daylight-saving time. My grass is brown enough already—it doesn't need another hour of daylight each day. Let's turn the clocks back to the way God intended—standard time.

(Jim Orr)

3. The religious right, in its impassioned fervor to correct our alleged moral wrongs and protect the rights of our unborn "children," may one day realize its ultimate goal of a constitutional amendment banning abortion. And what will the punishment be for those caught performing or receiving an abortion? The death penalty, of course.

(David Fisher)

★4. Most educators believe math instructors ought to emphasize group problem solving. If *group* problem solving is so important (and I think it is), why do we place such emphasis on individual testing? The national math test is a mistake.

(Frederick C. Thayer)

5. If voluntary school prayer for our children is going to make them more moral, then just think what mandatory church attendance on Sunday could do for the rest of us.

(Roderick M. Boyes)

6. A country that replaces the diseased hearts of old white men but refuses to feed schoolchildren, pay women adequately, educate adolescents, or care for the elderly—that country is doomed. We are acting as if there is no tomorrow. Where is our shame?

(Robert Birch)

★7. We cannot afford to close the library at Central Juvenile Hall. These young people in particular need to have access to ideas, dreams, and alternative ways of living. It can make the difference for many students who might become interested in reading for the first time in their lives while in Juvenile Hall.

(Natalie S. Field)

8. If the death penalty deters one person from becoming a murderer, it is effective. There are also some other important reasons for having the death penalty. First, the families and friends of innocent victims have the right to see effective retribution. Second, terminating the life of a killer is more economical than keeping him in jail at the taxpayer's expense. Third, everyone will have greater respect for the judicial system when justice is carried out.

(Doug Kroker)

9. Regarding the bill to require parental consent for a minor's abortion, I would like to point out that the pious platitudes about parental authority quickly fall

by the wayside when the minor wants to keep the baby and the parents say, "Don't be silly! You have an abortion and finish your education." If the parents can veto a minor's abortion, shouldn't they also be able to require one? Better the choice, either pro or con, be left to the girl/woman herself.

(Jane Roberts)

★10. More than a million adult videocassettes are rented each week. Nor, as the propagandists would have you believe, does viewing such material lead to violent sex crimes. If it did, there would be over one million such crimes per week.

(Lybrand P. Smith)

Summary

Propositional logic is characterized by the fact that the fundamental units are whole statements. Simple statements, represented by capital letters, are combined through the use of logical operators to form compound statements. The five operators are the tilde, which is used to form negations; the dot, which forms conjunctions; the wedge, which forms disjunctions; the horseshoe, which forms conditional statements; and the triple bar, which forms biconditional statements. These operators roughly translate the English words "not," "and," "or," "if . . . then . . . ," and "if and only if," respectively.

The truth-functional meaning of the logical operators is defined in terms of truth tables. A truth table is an arrangement of truth values that shows in every possible case how the truth value of a compound statement is determined by the truth value of its simple components. The truth value of longer statements is computed by assigning truth values to the simple components and then working outward to the larger ones. The meaning of statements symbolized in terms of the logical operators conforms fairly closely to that of English statements, but it occasionally breaks down, especially with conditional and biconditional statements.

Truth tables can be used to classify individual compound statements and to compare one compound statement with another. A compound statement is tautologous if the truth values under the main operator are all true, it is self-contradictory if they are all false, and it is contingent if at least one is true and at least one is false. Two statements are logically equivalent if the truth values under the main operators are the same on each line, and they are contradictory if they are the opposite on each line. Two or more statements are consistent if there is at least one line under the main operators where all of the truth values are true, and they are inconsistent if there is no such line.

Arguments may be tested for validity using either ordinary truth tables or indirect truth tables. For the ordinary method, if there is a line on which the premises turn out true and the conclusion false, the argument is invalid; if not, the argument is valid. The indirect method begins by assuming the premises true and the conclusion false. If this assumption leads necessarily to a contradiction, the argument is valid; if not, it is invalid. To use the indirect method to test a series of statements for consistency, the statements are assumed to be true. If this assumption leads necessarily to a contradiction, the statements are inconsistent; if not, they are consistent.

Once an argument is symbolized, mere inspection will often determine whether it is valid or invalid. This determination is facilitated by a familiarity with a few common argument forms. Six such forms that are valid are disjunctive syllogism, pure hypothetical syllogism, *modus ponens, modus tollens,* constructive dilemma, and destructive dilemma. Two common invalid forms are affirming the consequent and denying the antecedent. A dilemma expressed in ordinary language may be refuted by proving it unsound. Two methods are grasping the dilemma by the horns and escaping between the horns. A third method, which falls short of strict refutation, is constructing a counterdilemma.

6

7

Natural Deduction in Propositional Logic

7.1 Rules of Implication I

Natural deduction is a method for establishing the validity of propositional type arguments that is both simpler and more enlightening than the method of truth tables. By means of this method, the conclusion of an argument is actually derived from the premises through a series of discrete steps. In this respect natural deduction resembles the method used in geometry to derive theorems relating to lines and figures; but whereas each step in a geometrical proof depends on some mathematical principle, each step in a logical proof depends on a **rule of inference.** Eighteen rules of inference will be set forth in this chapter. The first four should be familiar from the previous chapter:

1. *Modus ponens* (MP):

$p \supset q$

p

q

2. *Modus tollens* (MT):

$p \supset q$

$\sim q$

$\sim p$

3. Hypothetical syllogism (HS):

$p \supset q$

$q \supset r$

$p \supset r$

4. Disjunctive syllogism (DS):

$p \vee q$

$\sim p$

q

In constructing proofs, *modus ponens* allows us to assert the consequent of a conditional statement on a line by itself, and *modus tollens* allows us to assert the negation of the antecedent. Hypothetical syllogism is used to derive a conditional statement from two other conditionals, and disjunctive syllogism allows us to assert the right-hand disjunct of a disjunctive statement on a line by itself.

These four rules will be sufficient to derive the conclusion of many simple arguments in propositional logic. Further, once we are supplied with all eighteen rules together with conditional proof, the resulting system will be sufficient to derive the conclusion of any valid argument in propositional logic. Conversely, since each rule is a valid argument form unto itself, any conclusion derived from their correct use results in a valid argument. The method of natural deduction is thus equal in power to the truth table method as far as proving validity is concerned. However, since natural deduction cannot be used with any facility to prove invalidity, we still need the truth table method for that purpose.

A proof in natural deduction consists of a sequence of propositions, each of which is either a premise or is derived from preceding propositions by application of a rule of inference and the last of which is the conclusion of the original argument. For an example of how the rules of inference are used in constructing such a proof, consider the following argument:

> If the Astros win the playoff, then the Braves will lose the pennant. If the Astros do not win the playoff, then either Connolly or Davis will be fired. The Braves will not lose the pennant. Furthermore, Connolly will not be fired. Therefore, Davis will be fired.

The first step is to symbolize the argument, numbering the premises and writing the conclusion to the right of the last premise, separated by a slash mark:

1. $A \supset B$
2. $\sim A \supset (C \vee D)$
3. $\sim B$
4. $\sim C$ / D

The conclusion is now derived from the premises via steps 5 through 7. The justification for each line is written to the immediate right:

5. $\sim A$ 1, 3, MT
6. $C \vee D$ 2, 5, MP
7. D 4, 6, DS

Line 5 is obtained from lines 1 and 3 via *modus tollens*. In other words, when A and B in these lines are substituted respectively for the p and q of the *modus tollens* rule, line 5 follows as the conclusion. Then, when $\sim A$ and $C \vee D$ in lines 2 and 5 are substituted respectively for the p and q of the *modus ponens* rule, line 6 follows as the conclusion. Finally, when C and D in lines 4 and 6 are substituted respectively for the p and q of the disjunctive syllogism rule, line 7 follows as the final conclusion. These lines constitute a valid derivation of the conclusion from the premises because each line is a substitution instance of a valid argument form.

These arguments are all instances of ***modus ponens*** (MP)

$\sim F \supset (G \equiv H)$	$(A \vee B) \supset \sim(C \cdot D)$	$K \cdot L$
$\sim F$	$A \vee B$	$(K \cdot L) \supset [(R \supset S) \cdot (T \supset U)]$
$G \equiv H$	$\sim(C \cdot D)$	$(R \supset S) \cdot (T \supset U)$

Here is an example of another completed proof. The conclusion to be obtained is written to the right of the last premise (line 4). Lines 5 through 7 are used to derive the conclusion:

1. $F \supset G$
2. $F \lor H$
3. $\sim G$
4. $H \supset (G \supset I)$ / $F \supset I$
5. $\sim F$ 1, 3, MT
6. H 2, 5, DS
7. $G \supset I$ 4, 6, MP
8. $F \supset I$ 1, 7, HS

When the letters in lines 1 and 3 are substituted into the *modus tollens* rule, line 5 is obtained. Then, when the letters in lines 2 and 5 are substituted into the disjunctive syllogism rule, line 6 is obtained. Line 7 is obtained by substituting H and $G \supset I$ from lines 4 and 6 into the *modus ponens* rule. Finally, line 8 is obtained by substituting the letters in lines 1 and 7 into the hypothetical syllogism rule. Notice that the conclusion, stated to the right of line 4, is not (and never is) part of the proof. It merely indicates what the proof is supposed to yield in the end.

These arguments are all instances of ***modus tollens*** (MT)

$(D \lor F) \supset K$	$\sim G \supset \sim(M \lor N)$	$\sim T$
$\sim K$	$\sim\sim(M \lor N)$	$[(H \lor K) \cdot (L \lor N)] \supset T$
$\sim(D \lor F)$	$\sim\sim G$	$\sim[(H \lor K) \cdot (L \lor N)]$

The successful use of natural deduction to derive a conclusion from one or more premises depends on the ability of the reasoner to visualize more or less complex arrangements of simple propositions as instances of the basic rules of inference. Here is a slightly more complex example:

1. $\sim(A \cdot B) \lor [\sim(E \cdot F) \supset (C \supset D)]$
2. $\sim\sim(A \cdot B)$
3. $\sim(E \cdot F)$
4. $D \supset G$ / $C \supset G$
5. $\sim(E \cdot F) \supset (C \supset D)$ 1, 2, DS
6. $C \supset D$ 3, 5, MP
7. $C \supset G$ 4, 6, HS

Line 4 is the last premise. To obtain line 5, $\sim(A \cdot B)$ and $[\sim(E \cdot F) \supset (C \supset D)]$ are substituted respectively for the p and q of the disjunctive syllogism rule, yielding $[\sim(E \cdot F) \supset (C \supset D)]$ as the conclusion. Next, $\sim(E \cdot F)$ and $C \supset D$ are substituted respectively for the p and q of *modus ponens*, yielding $C \supset D$ on line 6. Finally, lines 6 and 4 are combined to yield line 7 via the hypothetical syllogism rule.

7

These arguments are all instances of pure *hypothetical syllogism* (HS)

$$A \supset (D \bullet F) \qquad \sim M \supset (R \supset S) \qquad (L \supset N) \supset [(S \vee T) \bullet K]$$
$$\underline{(D \bullet F) \supset \sim H} \qquad \underline{(C \vee K) \supset \sim M} \qquad \underline{(C \equiv F) \supset (L \supset N)}$$
$$A \supset \sim H \qquad (C \vee K) \supset (R \supset S) \qquad (C \equiv F) \supset [(S \vee T) \bullet K]$$

The proofs that we have investigated thus far have been presented in ready-made form. We turn now to the question of how the various lines are obtained, leading in the end to the conclusion. What strategy is used in deriving these lines? While the answer is somewhat complex, there are a few basic rules of thumb that should be followed. Always begin by looking at the conclusion and by then attempting to locate the conclusion in the premises. Let us suppose that the conclusion is a single letter L. We begin by looking for L in the premises. Let us suppose we find it in a premise that reads:

$$K \supset L$$

Immediately we see that we can obtain L via *modus ponens* if we first obtain K. We now begin searching for K. Let us suppose that we find K in another premise that reads

$$J \vee K$$

From this we see that we could obtain K via disjunctive syllogism if we first obtain $\sim J$. The process continues until we isolate the required statement on a line by itself. Let us suppose that we find $\sim J$ on a line by itself. The thought process is then complete, and the various steps may be written out in the reverse order in which they were obtained mentally. The proof would look like this:

1. $\sim J$
2. $J \vee K$
3. $K \supset L$ / L
4. K 1, 2, DS
5. L 3, 4, MP

These arguments are all instances of *disjunctive syllogism* (DS)

$$U \vee \sim (W \bullet X) \qquad \sim (E \vee F) \qquad \sim B \vee [(H \supset M) \bullet (S \supset T)]$$
$$\underline{\sim U} \qquad\qquad \underline{(E \vee F) \vee (N \supset K)} \qquad \underline{\sim \sim B}$$
$$\sim (W \bullet X) \qquad N \supset K \qquad (H \supset M) \bullet (S \supset T)$$

Turning now to a different example, let us suppose that the conclusion is the conditional statement $R \supset U$. We begin by attempting to locate $R \supset U$ in the premises. If we cannot find it, we look for its separate components, R and U. Let us suppose we find R in the antecedent of the conditional statement:

$$R \supset S$$

Furthermore, let us suppose we find U in the consequent of the conditional statement:

$T \supset U$

We then see that we can obtain $R \supset U$ via a series of hypothetical syllogism steps if we first obtain $S \supset T$. Let us suppose that we find $S \supset T$ on a line by itself. The proof has now been completely thought through and may be written out as follows:

1. $S \supset T$
2. $T \supset U$
3. $R \supset S$ / $R \supset U$
4. $R \supset T$ 1, 3, HS
5. $R \supset U$ 2, 4, HS

At this point a word of caution is in order about the meaning of a proposition being "obtained." Let us suppose that we are searching for E and we find it in a premise that reads $E \supset F$. The mere fact that we have located the letter E in this line does not mean that we have obtained E. $E \supset F$ means that *if* we have E, then we have F; it does *not* mean that we *have* either E or F. From such a line we could obtain F (via *modus ponens*) if we first obtain E, or we could obtain $\sim E$ (via *modus tollens*) if we first obtain $\sim F$. The proposition $E \supset F$ by itself gives us nothing, and even if we combine it with other lines, there is no way that we could ever obtain E from such a line.

Here is a sample argument:

1. $A \lor B$
2. $\sim C \supset \sim A$
3. $C \supset D$
4. $\sim D$ / B

We begin by searching for B in the premises. Finding it in line 1, we see that it can be obtained via disjunctive syllogism if we first obtain $\sim A$. This in turn can be gotten from line 2 via *modus ponens* if we first obtain $\sim C$, and this can be gotten from line 3 via *modus tollens* once $\sim D$ is obtained. Happily, the latter is stated by itself on line 4. The proof has now been completely thought through and can be written out as follows:

1. $A \lor B$
2. $\sim C \supset \sim A$
3. $C \supset D$
4. $\sim D$ / B
5. $\sim C$ 3, 4, MT
6. $\sim A$ 2, 5, MP
7. B 1, 6, DS

Another example:

1. $E \supset (K \supset L)$
2. $F \supset (L \supset M)$
3. $G \lor E$
4. $\sim G$
5. F / $K \supset M$

We begin by searching for $K \supset M$ in the premises. Not finding it, we search for the separate components, K and M, and locate them in lines 1 and 2. The fact that K appears in the antecedent of a conditional statement, and M in the consequent of another, immediately suggests hypothetical syllogism. But first we must obtain these conditional statements on lines by themselves. We can obtain $K \supset L$ via *modus ponens* if we first obtain E. This, in turn, we can obtain from line 3 via disjunctive syllogism if we first obtain $\sim G$. Since $\sim G$ appears by itself on line 4, the first part of the thought process is now complete. The second part requires that we obtain $L \supset M$. This we can get from line 2 via *modus ponens* if we can get F, and we do have F by itself on line 5. All of the steps leading to the conclusion have now been thought through, and the proof can be written out:

1. $E \supset (K \supset L)$
2. $F \supset (L \supset M)$
3. $G \vee E$
4. $\sim G$
5. F / $K \supset M$
6. E 3, 4, DS
7. $K \supset L$ 1, 6, MP
8. $L \supset M$ 2, 5, MP
9. $K \supset M$ 7, 8, HS

The thought process behind these proofs illustrates an important point about the construction of proofs by natural deduction. Ideally, we should never write down a line in a proof unless we know why we are doing it and where it leads. Typically, good proofs are not produced haphazardly or by luck; rather, they are produced by organized logical thinking. Occasionally, of course, we may be baffled by an especially difficult proof, and random deductive steps noted on the side may be useful. But we should not commence the actual writing out of the proof until we have used logical thinking to discover the path leading to the conclusion.

We end this section with some strategies for applying the first four rules of inference:

Strategy 1: Always begin by attempting to "find" the conclusion in the premises.

Strategy 2: If the conclusion contains a letter that appears in the consequent of a conditional statement in the premises, consider obtaining that letter via *modus ponens:*

1. $A \supset B$
2. $C \vee A$
3. A / B
4. B 1, 3, MP

Strategy 3: If the conclusion contains a negated letter that appears in the antecedent of a conditional statement in the premises, consider obtaining the negated letter via *modus tollens:*

1. $C \supset B$
2. $A \supset B$
3. $\sim B$ / $\sim A$
4. $\sim A$ 2, 3, MT

Strategy 4: If the conclusion is a conditional statement, consider obtaining it via hypothetical syllogism:

1. $B \supset C$
2. $C \supset A$
3. $A \supset B$ / $A \supset C$
4. $A \supset C$ 1, 3, HS

Strategy 5: If the conclusion contains a letter that appears in a disjunctive statement in the premises, consider obtaining that letter via disjunctive syllogism:

1. $A \supset B$
2. $A \vee C$
3. $\sim A$ / C
4. C   2, 3, DS

Of course, these strategies apply to obtaining any line prior to the conclusion, just as they apply to obtaining the conclusion.

EXERCISE 7.1

iLrn   I. For each of the following lists of premises, derive the conclusion and supply the justification for it. There is only one possible answer for each problem.

★(1) 1. $G \supset F$
     2. $\sim F$
     3. _G_   MT

(2) 1. S
     2. $S \supset M$
     3. _M_   MP

(3) 1. $R \supset D$
     2. $E \supset R$
     3. _E⊃D_   HS

★(4) 1. $B \vee C$
     2. $\sim B$
     3. _C_   DS

(5) 1. N
     2. $N \vee F$
     3. $N \supset K$
     4. _K_   MP

(6) 1. $\sim J \vee P$
     2. $\sim J$
     3. $S \supset J$
     4. _S_   DS

★(7) 1. $H \supset D$
     2. $F \supset T$
     3. $F \supset H$
     4. _F⊃D_   HS

(8) 1. $S \supset W$
     2. $\sim S$
     3. $S \vee N$
     4._N_   ___

(9) 1. $F \supset \sim A$
     2. $N \supset A$
     3. $\sim F$
     4. $\sim A$
     5. _____ ___

★(10) 1. $H \supset A$
     2. A
     3. $A \vee M$
     4. $G \supset H$
     5. _____ ___

(11) 1. $W \vee B$
     2. W
     3. $B \supset T$
     4. $W \supset A$
     5. _____ ___

(12) 1. $K \supset \sim R$
     2. $\sim R$
     3. $R \vee S$
     4. $R \supset T$
     5. _____ ___

★(13) 1. $\sim C \supset \sim F$
     2. $L \supset F$
     3. $\sim\sim F$
     4. $F \vee \sim L$
     5. _____ ___

(14) 1. $N \supset \sim E$
     2. $\sim\sim S$
     3. $\sim E \vee \sim S$
     4. $\sim S \vee N$
     5. _____ ___

(15) 1. ~R ⊃ ~T
    2. ~T ∨ B
    3. C ⊃ ~R
    4. ~C
    5. _____ ____

★(16) 1. ~K
    2. ~K ⊃ ~P
    3. ~K ∨ G
    4. G ⊃ Q
    5. _____ ____

(17) 1. F ∨ (A ⊃ C)
    2. A ∨ (C ⊃ F)
    3. A
    4. ~F
    5. _____ ____

(18) 1. (R ⊃ M) ⊃ D
    2. M ⊃ C
    3. D ⊃ (M ∨ E)
    4. ~M
    5. _____ ____

★(19) 1. (S ∨ C) ⊃ L
    2. ~S
    3. ~L
    4. S ⊃ (K ⊃ L)
    5. _____ ____

(20) 1. (A ∨ W) ⊃ (N ⊃ Q)
    2. Q ⊃ G
    3. ~A
    4. (Q ⊃ G) ⊃ (A ∨ N)
    5. _____ ____

II. The following symbolized arguments are missing a premise. Write the premise needed to derive the conclusion (last line), and supply the justification for the conclusion. Try to construct the simplest premise needed to derive the conclusion.

★(1) 1. B ∨ K
    2. _____
    3. K   ____

(2) 1. N ⊃ S
    2. _____
    3. S   ____

(3) 1. K ⊃ T
    2. _____
    3. ~K   ____

★(4) 1. C ⊃ H
    2. _____
    3. R ⊃ H   ____

(5) 1. F ⊃ N
    2. N ⊃ T
    3. _____
    4. ~F   ____

(6) 1. W ∨ T
    2. A ⊃ W
    3. _____
    4. A ⊃ T   ____

★(7) 1. M ⊃ B
    2. Q ⊃ M
    3. _____
    4. M   ____

(8) 1. C ∨ L
    2. L ⊃ T
    3. _____
    4. L   ____

(9) 1. E ⊃ N
    2. T ∨ ~E
    3. S ⊃ E
    4. _____
    5. E   ____

★(10) 1. H ⊃ A
    2. S ⊃ H
    3. ~M ∨ H
    4. _____
    5. ~H   ____

(11) 1. T ⊃ N
    2. G ⊃ T
    3. H ∨ T
    4. _____
    5. F ⊃ T   ____

(12) 1. G ⊃ C
    2. M ∨ G
    3. T ∨ ~G
    4. _____
    5. G   ____

★(13) 1. ~S ⊃ ~B
2. R v ~B
3. ~B ⊃ ~S
4. _____
5. ~~B   ____

(14) 1. ~R ⊃ D
2. ~J ⊃ ~R
3. N v ~R
4. _____
5. ~F ⊃ ~R   ____

(15) 1. ~S v ~P
2. ~K ⊃ P
3. ~P ⊃ F
4. _____
5. ~P   ____

★(16) 1. J ⊃ E
2. B v ~J
3. ~Z ⊃ J
4. _____
5. J   ____

(17) 1. (H ⊃ C) ⊃ A
2. N ⊃ (F ⊃ K)
3. (E • R) ⊃ K
4. _____
5. H ⊃ K   ____

(18) 1. (S ⊃ M) ⊃ G
2. S ⊃ (M • G)
3. G ⊃ (R ⊃ ~S)
4. _____
5. ~S   ____

★(19) 1. (W v ~F) ⊃ H
2. (H v G) ⊃ ~F
3. T ⊃ (F ⊃ G)
4. _____
5. ~F   ____

(20) 1. (H • A) v T
2. ~S ⊃ (P ⊃ T)
3. (N v T) ⊃ P
4. _____
5. T   ____

iLrn III. Use the first four rules of inference to derive the conclusions of the following symbolized arguments:

★(1) 1. ~C ⊃ (A ⊃ C)
2. ~C   / ~A

(2) 1. F v (D ⊃ T)
2. ~F
3. D   / T

(3) 1. (K • B) v (L ⊃ E)
2. ~(K • B)
3. ~E   / ~L

★(4) 1. P ⊃ (G ⊃ T)
2. Q ⊃ (T ⊃ E)
3. P
4. Q   / G ⊃ E

(5) 1. ~W ⊃ [~W ⊃ (X ⊃ W)]
2. ~W   / ~X

(6) 1. J ⊃ (K ⊃ L)
2. L v J
3. ~L   / ~K

★(7) 1. ~S ⊃ D
2. ~S v (~D ⊃ K)
3. ~D   / K

(8) 1. A ⊃ (E ⊃ ~F)
2. H v (~F ⊃ M)
3. A
4. ~H   / E ⊃ M

(9) 1. ~G ⊃ (G v ~A)
2. ~A ⊃ (C ⊃ A)
3. ~G   / ~C

★(10) 1. N ⊃ (J ⊃ P)
2. (J ⊃ P) ⊃ (N ⊃ J)
3. N   / P

(11) 1. G ⊃ [~O ⊃ (G ⊃ D)]
2. O v G
3. ~O   / D

(12) 1. ~M v (B v ~T)
2. B ⊃ W
3. ~~M
4. ~W   / ~T

★(13) 1. R ⊃ (G v ~A)
2. (G v ~A) ⊃ ~S
3. G ⊃ S
4. R   / ~A

(14) 1. $(L \equiv N) \supset C$
2. $(L \equiv N) \vee (P \supset \sim E)$
3. $\sim E \supset C$
4. $\sim C$ / $\sim P$

(15) 1. $\sim J \supset [\sim A \supset (D \supset A)]$
2. $J \vee \sim A$
3. $\sim J$ / $\sim D$

★(16) 1. $(B \supset \sim M) \supset (T \supset \sim S)$
2. $B \supset K$
3. $K \supset \sim M$
4. $\sim S \supset N$ / $T \supset N$

(17) 1. $H \vee (Q \vee F)$
2. $R \vee (Q \supset R)$
3. $R \vee \sim H$
4. $\sim R$ / F

(18) 1. $\sim A \supset (B \supset \sim C)$
2. $\sim D \supset (\sim C \supset A)$
3. $D \vee \sim A$
4. $\sim D$ / $\sim B$

★(19) 1. $\sim G \supset [G \vee (S \supset G)]$
2. $(S \vee L) \supset \sim G$
3. $S \vee L$ / L

(20) 1. $H \supset [\sim E \supset (C \supset \sim D)]$
2. $\sim D \supset E$
3. $E \vee H$
4. $\sim E$ / $\sim C$

(21) 1. $\sim B \supset [(A \supset K) \supset (B \vee \sim K)]$
2. $\sim J \supset K$
3. $A \supset \sim J$
4. $\sim B$ / $\sim A$

★(22) 1. $(C \supset M) \supset (N \supset P)$
2. $(C \supset N) \supset (N \supset M)$
3. $(C \supset P) \supset \sim M$
4. $C \supset N$ / $\sim C$

(23) 1. $(R \supset F) \supset [(R \supset \sim G) \supset (S \supset Q)]$
2. $(Q \supset F) \supset (R \supset Q)$
3. $\sim G \supset F$
4. $Q \supset \sim G$ / $S \supset F$

(24) 1. $\sim A \supset [A \vee (T \supset R)]$
2. $\sim R \supset [R \vee (A \supset R)]$
3. $(T \vee D) \supset \sim R$
4. $T \vee D$ / D

★(25) 1. $\sim N \supset [(B \supset D) \supset (N \vee \sim E)]$
2. $(B \supset E) \supset \sim N$
3. $B \supset D$
4. $D \supset E$ / $\sim D$

IV. Translate the following arguments into symbolic form and use the first four rules of inference to derive the conclusion of each. The letters to be used for the simple statements are given in parentheses after each exercise. Use these letters in the order in which they are listed.

★1. If the average child watches more than five hours of television per day, then either his power of imagination is improved or he becomes conditioned to expect constant excitement. The average child's power of imagination is not improved by watching television. Also, the average child does watch more than five hours of television per day. Therefore, the average child is conditioned to expect constant excitement. (W, P, C)

2. If a tenth planet exists, then its orbit is perpendicular to that of the other planets. Either a tenth planet is responsible for the death of the dinosaurs, or its orbit is not perpendicular to that of the other planets. A tenth planet is not responsible for the death of the dinosaurs. Therefore, a tenth planet does not exist. (E, O, R)

3. If quotas are imposed on textile imports only if jobs are not lost, then the domestic textile industry will modernize only if the domestic textile industry is

not destroyed. If quotas are imposed on textile imports, the domestic textile industry will modernize. The domestic textile industry will modernize only if jobs are not lost. Therefore, if quotas are imposed on textile imports, the domestic textile industry will not be destroyed. (Q, J, M, D)

★4. If teachers are allowed to conduct random drug searches on students only if teachers are acting *in loco parentis*, then if teachers are acting *in loco parentis*, then students have no Fourth Amendment protections. Either students have no Fourth Amendment protections or if teachers are allowed to conduct random drug searches on students, then teachers are acting *in loco parentis*. It is not the case that students have no Fourth Amendment protections. Therefore, teachers are not allowed to conduct random drug searches on students. (R, L, F)

5. Either funding for nuclear fusion will be cut or if sufficiently high temperatures are achieved in the laboratory, nuclear fusion will become a reality. Either the supply of hydrogen fuel is limited, or if nuclear fusion becomes a reality, the world's energy problems will be solved. Funding for nuclear fusion will not be cut. Furthermore, the supply of hydrogen fuel is not limited. Therefore, if sufficiently high temperatures are achieved in the laboratory, the world's energy problems will be solved. (C, H, R, S, E)

6. Either the continents are not subject to drift or if Antarctica was always located in the polar region, then it contains no fossils of plants from a temperate climate. If the continents are not subject to drift, then Antarctica contains no fossils of plants from a temperate climate. But it is not the case that Antarctica contains no fossils of plants from a temperate climate. Therefore, Antarctica was not always located in the polar region. (D, L, F)

★7. If terrorists take more hostages, then terrorist demands will be met if and only if the media give full coverage to terrorist acts. Either the media will voluntarily limit the flow of information or if the media will recognize they are being exploited by terrorists, they will voluntarily limit the flow of information. Either the media will recognize they are being exploited by terrorists or terrorists will take more hostages. The media will not voluntarily limit the flow of information. Therefore, terrorist demands will be met if and only if the media give full coverage to terrorist acts. (H, D, A, V, R)

8. Either we take recycling seriously or we will be buried in garbage. If we incinerate our garbage only if our health is jeopardized, then we do not take recycling seriously. If our landfills are becoming exhausted, then if we incinerate our garbage, then toxic ash will be produced. If toxic ash is produced, then our health is jeopardized. Our landfills are becoming exhausted. Therefore, we will be buried in garbage. (R, B, I, H, L, T)

9. If the drug interdiction program is strengthened only if cocaine becomes more readily available, then either the number of addicts is decreasing or the war on drugs is failing. If the drug interdiction program is strengthened, then smugglers will shift to more easily concealable drugs. If smugglers shift to more easily concealable drugs, then cocaine will become more readily available. Furthermore, the number of addicts is not decreasing. Therefore, the war on drugs is failing. (D, C, N, W, S)

★10. If the death penalty is not cruel and unusual punishment, then either it is cruel and unusual punishment or if society is justified in using it, then it will deter other criminals. If the death penalty is cruel and unusual punishment, then it is both cruel and unusual and its use degrades society as a whole. It is not the case that both the death penalty is cruel and unusual and its use degrades society as a whole. Furthermore, the death penalty will not deter other criminals. Therefore, society is not justified in using the death penalty. (C, J, D, U)

7.2 Rules of Implication II

Four additional rules of inference are listed below. Constructive dilemma should be familiar from Chapter 6. The other three are new.*

5. Constructive dilemma (CD):

$$(p \supset q) \cdot (r \supset s)$$
$$\underline{p \vee r}$$
$$q \vee s$$

6. Simplification (Simp):

$$\underline{p \cdot q}$$
$$p$$

7. Conjunction (Conj):

$$p$$
$$\underline{q}$$
$$p \cdot q$$

8. Addition (Add):

$$\underline{p}$$
$$p \vee q$$

Like the previous four rules, these four are fairly easy to understand, but if there is any doubt about them their validity may be proven by means of a truth table.

Constructive dilemma can be understood as involving two *modus ponens* steps. The first premise states that if we have p then we have q, and if we have r then we have s. But since, by the second premise, we do have either p or r, it follows by *modus ponens* that we have either q or s. Constructive dilemma is the only form of dilemma that will be included as a rule of inference. By the rule of transposition, which will be presented in Section 7.4, any argument that is a substitution instance of the destructive dilemma form can be easily converted into a substitution instance of constructive dilemma. Destructive dilemma, therefore, is not needed as a rule of inference.

These arguments are both instances of **constructive dilemma** (CD)

$\sim M \vee N$	$[(K \supset T) \supset (A \cdot B)] \cdot [(H \supset P) \supset (A \cdot C)]$
$(\sim M \supset S) \cdot (N \supset \sim T)$	$(K \supset T) \vee (H \supset P)$
$S \vee \sim T$	$(A \cdot B) \vee (A \cdot C)$

Simplification states that if two propositions are given as true on a single line, then each of them is true separately. According to the strict interpretation of the simplification rule, only the left-hand conjunct may be stated in the conclusion. Once the commutativity rule for conjunction has been presented, however (see Section 7.3), we will be justified in replacing a statement such as $H \cdot K$ with $K \cdot H$. Once we do this, the K will appear on the left, and the appropriate conclusion is K.

*Some texts include a rule called "absorption" by which the statement form $p \supset (q \cdot p)$ is deduced from $p \supset q$. This rule is necessary only if conditional proof is not presented. This text opts in favor of conditional proof.

These arguments are all instances of **simplification** (Simp)

$$\frac{\sim F \cdot (U \equiv E)}{\sim F} \qquad \frac{(M \vee T) \cdot (S \supset R)}{(M \vee T)} \qquad \frac{[(X \supset Z) \cdot M] \cdot (G \supset H)}{[(X \supset Z) \cdot M]}$$

Conjunction states that two propositions—for example, *H* and *K*—asserted separately on different lines may be conjoined on a single line. The two propositions may be conjoined in whatever order we choose (either *H* · *K* or *K* · *H*) without appeal to the commutativity rule for conjunction.

These arguments are all instances of **conjunction** (Conj)

$$\frac{\sim E}{\sim G} \qquad \frac{C \supset M}{D \supset N} \qquad \frac{R \supset (H \cdot T)}{K \supset (H \cdot O)}$$
$$\frac{}{\sim E \cdot \sim G} \qquad \frac{}{(C \supset M) \cdot (D \supset N)} \qquad \frac{}{[R \supset (H \cdot T)] \cdot [K \supset (H \cdot O)]}$$

Addition states that whenever a proposition is asserted on a line by itself it may be joined disjunctively with any proposition we choose. In other words, if *G* is asserted to be true by itself, it follows that *G* ∨ *H* is true. This may appear somewhat puzzling at first, but once one realizes that *G* ∨ *H* is a much weaker statement than *G* by itself, the puzzlement should disappear. The new proposition must, of course, always be joined disjunctively (not conjunctively) to the given proposition. If *G* is stated on a line by itself, we are *not* justified in writing *G* · *H* as a consequence of addition.

These arguments are all instances of **addition** (Add)

$$\frac{S}{S \vee \sim T} \qquad \frac{C \cdot D}{(C \cdot D) \vee (K \cdot \sim P)} \qquad \frac{W \equiv Z}{(W \equiv Z) \vee [A \supset (M \supset O)]}$$

The use of these four rules may now be illustrated. Consider the following argument form:

1. $A \supset B$
2. $(B \vee C) \supset (D \cdot E)$
3. A / D

As usual, we begin by looking for the conclusion in the premises. *D* appears in the consequent of the second premise, which we can obtain via simplification if we first obtain *B* ∨ C. This expression as such does not appear in the premises, but from lines 1 and 3 we see that we can obtain *B* by itself via *modus ponens*. Having obtained *B*, we can get *B* ∨ *C* via addition. The proof has now been thought through and can be written out as follows:

```
1.  A ⊃ B
2.  (B ∨ C) ⊃ (D • E)
3.  A                    / D
4.  B                    1, 3, MP
5.  B ∨ C                4, Add
6.  D • E                2, 5, MP
7.  D                    6, Simp
```

Another example:

```
1.  K ⊃ L
2.  (M ⊃ N) • S
3.  N ⊃ T
4.  K ∨ M                / L ∨ T
```

Seeing that *L* ∨ *T* does not appear as such in the premises, we look for the separate components. Finding *L* and *T* as the consequents of two distinct conditional statements causes us to think that the conclusion can be obtained via constructive dilemma. If a constructive dilemma can be set up, it will need a disjunctive statement as its second premise, and such a statement appears on line 4. Furthermore, each of the components of this statement, *K* and *M*, appears as the antecedent of a conditional statement, exactly as they should for a dilemma. The only statement that is missing now is *M* ⊃ *T*. Inspecting line 2 we see that we can obtain *M* ⊃ *N* via simplification, and putting this together with line 3 gives us *M* ⊃ *T* via hypothetical syllogism. The completed proof may now be written out:

```
1.  K ⊃ L
2.  (M ⊃ N) • S
3.  N ⊃ T
4.  K ∨ M                / L ∨ T
5.  M ⊃ N                2, Simp
6.  M ⊃ T                3, 5, HS
7.  (K ⊃ L) • (M ⊃ T)    1, 6, Conj
8.  L ∨ T                4, 7, CD
```

Another example:

```
1.  ~M • N
2.  P ⊃ M
3.  Q • R
4.  (~P • Q) ⊃ S         / S ∨ T
```

When we look for *S* ∨ *T* in the premises we find *S* in the consequent of line 4 but no *T* at all. This signals an important principle: Whenever the conclusion of an argument contains a letter not found in the premises, addition must be used to introduce the missing letter. Addition is the *only* rule of inference that can introduce new letters. To introduce *T* by addition, however, we must first obtain *S* on a line by itself. *S* can be obtained from line 4 via *modus ponens* if we first obtain ~*P* • *Q*. This, in turn, can be gotten via conjunction, but first ~*P* and *Q* must be obtained individually on separate lines. *Q* can be obtained from line 3 via simplification and ~*P* from line 2 via *modus tollens*, but the latter step requires that we first obtain ~*M* on a line by itself. Since this can be gotten from line 1 via simplification, the proof is now complete. It may be written out as follows:

```
1. ~M · N
2. P ⊃ M
3. Q · R
4. (~P · Q) ⊃ S          / S v T
5. ~M                    1, Simp
6. ~P                    2, 5, MT
7. Q                     3, Simp
8. ~P · Q                6, 7, Conj
9. S                     4, 8, MP
10. S v T                9, Add
```

Addition is used together with disjunctive syllogism to derive the conclusion of arguments having inconsistent premises. As we saw in Chapter 6, such arguments are always valid. The procedure is illustrated as follows:

```
1. S
2. ~S                    / T
3. S v T                 1, Add
4. T                     2, 3, DS
```

With arguments of this sort the conclusion is always introduced via addition and then separated via disjunctive syllogism. Since addition can be used to introduce any letter or arrangement of letters we choose, it should be clear from this example that inconsistent premises validly entail any conclusion whatever.

To complete this presentation of the eight rules of implication, let us consider some of the typical ways in which they are *misapplied*. Examples are as follows:

```
1. A ⊃ (B ⊃ C)
2. B
─────────────
3. C                     1, 2, MP (invalid—B ⊃ C must first be obtained on a line by itself)
```

```
1. P v (S · T)
─────────────
2. S                     1, Simp (invalid—S · T must first be obtained on a line by itself)
```

```
1. K
─────────────
2. K · L                 1, Add (invalid—the correct form of addition is "K v L")
```

```
1. M v N
─────────────
2. M                     1, Simp (invalid—simplification is possible only with a conjunctive premise; line 1 is a disjunction)
```

```
1. G ⊃ H
─────────────
2. G ⊃ (H v J)           1, Add (improper—J must be added to the whole line, not just to the consequent: (G ⊃ H) v J
```

```
1. (W ⊃ X) ⊃ Y
2. ~X
─────────────
3. ~W                    1, 2, MT (invalid—W ⊃ X must first be obtained on a line by itself)
```

```
1. L ⊃ M
2. L ⊃ N
─────────────
3. M · N                 1, 2, Conj (invalid—M and N must first be obtained on lines by themselves)
```

$$1.\ \sim(P \cdot Q)$$
$$\underline{2.\ \sim P}$$

1, Simp (invalid—parentheses must be removed first)

$$1.\ \sim(P \lor Q)$$
$$\underline{2.\ \sim P}$$
$$3.\ Q$$

1, 2, DS (invalid—parentheses must be removed first)

The use of addition in the $G \supset H$ example is called "improper" because the letter that is added is not added to the whole line. It turns out, however, that even though the addition rule is not correctly applied here, the inference is still valid. Hence, this inference is not called "invalid," as the others are. As for the last two examples, a rule will be presented in the next section (DeMorgan's Rule) that will allow us to remove parentheses preceded by negation signs. But even after the parentheses have been removed from these examples, the inferences remain invalid.

As with the previous section, we end this one with a few strategies for applying the last four rules of implication:

Strategy 6: If the conclusion contains a letter that appears in a conjunctive statement in the premises, consider obtaining that letter via simplification:

1. $A \supset B$
2. $C \cdot B$
3. $C \supset A$ / C
4. C 2, Simp

Strategy 7: If the conclusion is a conjunctive statement, consider obtaining it via conjunction by first obtaining the individual conjuncts:

1. $A \supset C$
2. B
3. $\sim C$ / $B \cdot \sim C$
4. $B \cdot \sim C$ 2, 3, Conj

Strategy 8: If the conclusion is a disjunctive statement, consider obtaining it via constructive dilemma or addition:

1. $(A \supset B) \cdot (C \supset D)$
2. $B \supset C$
3. $A \lor C$ / $B \lor D$
4. $B \lor D$ 1, 3, CD

1. $A \lor C$
2. B
3. $C \supset D$ / $B \lor D$
4. $B \lor D$ 2, Add

Strategy 9: If the conclusion contains a letter not found in the premises, addition *must* be used to introduce that letter. (See the second example under Strategy 8.)

EXERCISE 7.2

iLrn   I. For each of the following lists of premises, derive the indicated conclusion and complete the justification. In problems 4 and 8 you can add any statement you choose.

★(1) 1. S ∨ H
     2. B • E
     3. R ⊃ G
     4. _____ ____, Simp
 (2) 1. (N ⊃ T) • (F ⊃ Q)
     2. (N ⊃ R) ∨ (F ⊃ M)
     3. N ∨ F
     4. _____ ____, CD
 (3) 1. D
     2. W
     3. ____ ____, Conj
★(4) 1. H
     2. ____ ____, Add
 (5) 1. R • (N ∨ K)
     2. (G • T) ∨ S
     3. (Q • C) ⊃ (J • L)
     4. _____ ____, Simp
 (6) 1. ~R ∨ P
     2. (P ⊃ ~D) • (~R ⊃ S)
     3. (~R ⊃ A) • (P ⊃ ~N)
     4. _____ ____, CD
★(7) 1. (Q ∨ K) • ~B
     2. (M • R) ⊃ D
     3. (W • S) ∨ (G • F)
     4. _____ ____, Simp
 (8) 1. E • G
     2. _____ ____, Add
 (9) 1. ~B
     2. F ∨ N
     3. ____ ____, Conj
★(10) 1. S ∨ ~C
      2. (S ⊃ ~L) • (~C ⊃ M)
      3. (~N ⊃ S) • (F ⊃ ~C)
      4. _____ ____, CD

II. In the following symbolized arguments, derive the line needed to obtain the conclusion (last line), and supply the justification for both lines.

★(1) 1. G ⊃ N
     2. G • K
     3. _____ ____
     4. G ∨ T ____
 (2) 1. ~A
     2. A ∨ E
     3. _____ ____
     4. ~A • E ____

 (3) 1. B ⊃ N
     2. B ∨ K
     3. K ⊃ R
     4. _____ ____
     5. N ∨ R ____
★(4) 1. T
     2. T ⊃ G
     3. (T ∨ U) ⊃ H

4. _____ ____
5. H ____

(5) 1. $S \supset E$
2. $E \vee (S \cdot P)$
3. $\sim E$
4. _____ ____
5. S ____

(6) 1. N
2. $N \supset F$
3. $(N \supset A) \cdot (F \supset C)$
4. _____ ____
5. $A \vee C$ ____

★(7) 1. J
2. $\sim L$
3. $F \supset L$
4. _____ ____
5. $\sim F \cdot J$ ____

(8) 1. $(E \supset B) \cdot (Q \supset N)$
2. $K \supset E$
3. $B \supset K$
4. _____ ____
5. $E \supset K$ ____

(9) 1. $G \vee N$
2. $\sim G$
3. $\sim G \supset (H \cdot R)$
4. _____ ____
5. H ____

★(10) 1. M
2. $(M \cdot E) \supset D$
3. E
4. _____ ____
5. D ____

iLrn III. Use the first eight rules of inference to derive the conclusions of the following symbolized arguments:

★(1) 1. $\sim M \supset Q$
2. $R \supset \sim T$
3. $\sim M \vee R$ / $Q \vee \sim T$

(2) 1. $N \supset (D \cdot W)$
2. $D \supset K$
3. N / $N \cdot K$

(3) 1. $E \supset (A \cdot C)$
2. $A \supset (F \cdot E)$
3. E / F

★(4) 1. $(H \vee \sim B) \supset R$
2. $(H \vee \sim M) \supset P$
3. H / $R \cdot P$

(5) 1. $G \supset (S \cdot T)$
2. $(S \vee T) \supset J$
3. G / J

(6) 1. $(L \vee T) \supset (B \cdot G)$
2. $L \cdot (K \equiv R)$ / $L \cdot B$

★(7) 1. $(\sim F \vee X) \supset (P \vee T)$
2. $F \supset P$
3. $\sim P$ / T

(8) 1. $(N \supset B) \cdot (O \supset C)$
2. $Q \supset (N \vee O)$
3. Q / $B \vee C$

(9) 1. $(U \vee W) \supset (T \supset R)$
2. $U \cdot H$
3. $\sim R \cdot \sim J$ / $U \cdot \sim T$

★(10) 1. $(D \vee E) \supset (G \cdot H)$
2. $G \supset \sim D$
3. $D \cdot F$ / M

(11) 1. $(B \vee F) \supset (A \supset G)$
2. $(B \vee E) \supset (G \supset K)$
3. $B \cdot \sim H$ / $A \supset K$

(12) 1. $(P \supset R) \supset (M \supset P)$
2. $(P \vee M) \supset (P \supset R)$
3. $P \vee M$ / $R \vee P$

★(13) 1. $(C \supset N) \cdot E$
2. $D \vee (N \supset D)$
3. $\sim D$ / $\sim C \vee P$

(14) 1. $F \supset (\sim T \cdot A)$
2. $(\sim T \vee G) \supset (H \supset T)$
3. $F \cdot O$ / $\sim H \cdot \sim T$

(15) 1. $(S \vee B) \supset (S \vee K)$
2. $(K \vee \sim D) \supset (H \supset S)$
3. $\sim S \cdot W$ / $\sim H$

★(16) 1. $(C \vee \sim G) \supset (\sim P \cdot L)$
2. $(\sim P \cdot C) \supset (C \supset D)$
3. $C \cdot \sim R$ / $D \vee R$

(17) 1. $[A \lor (K \cdot J)] \supset (\sim E \cdot \sim F)$
2. $M \supset [A \cdot (P \lor R)]$
3. $M \cdot U$ / $\sim E \cdot A$

(18) 1. $\sim H \supset (\sim T \supset R)$
2. $H \lor (E \supset F)$
3. $\sim T \lor E$
4. $\sim H \cdot D$ / $R \lor F$

★(19) 1. $(U \cdot \sim\sim P) \supset Q$
2. $\sim O \supset U$
3. $\sim P \supset O$
4. $\sim O \cdot T$ / Q

(20) 1. $(M \lor N) \supset (F \supset G)$
2. $D \supset \sim C$
3. $\sim C \supset B$
4. $M \cdot H$
5. $D \lor F$ / $B \lor G$

(21) 1. $(F \cdot M) \supset (S \lor T)$
2. $(\sim S \lor A) \supset F$
3. $(\sim S \lor B) \supset M$
4. $\sim S \cdot G$ / T

★(22) 1. $(\sim K \cdot \sim N) \supset$
$[(\sim P \supset K) \cdot (\sim R \supset G)]$
2. $K \supset N$
3. $\sim N \cdot B$
4. $\sim P \lor \sim R$ / G

(23) 1. $(\sim A \lor D) \supset (B \supset F)$
2. $(B \lor C) \supset (A \supset E)$
3. $A \lor B$
4. $\sim A$ / $E \lor F$

(24) 1. $(J \supset K) \cdot (\sim O \supset \sim P)$
2. $(L \supset J) \cdot (\sim M \supset \sim O)$
3. $\sim K \supset (L \lor \sim M)$
4. $\sim K \cdot G$ / $\sim P$

★(25) 1. $(\sim M \cdot \sim N) \supset [(\sim M \lor H) \supset (K \cdot L)]$
2. $\sim M \cdot (C \supset D)$
3. $\sim N \cdot (F \equiv G)$ / $K \cdot \sim N$

(26) 1. $(P \lor S) \supset (E \supset F)$
2. $(P \lor T) \supset (G \supset H)$
3. $(P \lor U) \supset (E \lor G)$
4. P / $F \lor H$

(27) 1. $(S \supset Q) \cdot (Q \supset \sim S)$
3. $S \lor Q$
4. $\sim Q$ / $P \cdot R$

★(28) 1. $(D \supset B) \cdot (C \supset D)$
2. $(B \supset D) \cdot (E \supset C)$
3. $B \lor E$ / $D \lor B$

(29) 1. $(R \supset H) \cdot (S \supset I)$
2. $(\sim H \cdot \sim L) \supset (R \lor S)$
3. $\sim H \cdot (K \supset T)$
4. $H \lor \sim L$ / $I \lor M$

(30) 1. $(W \cdot X) \supset (Q \lor R)$
2. $(S \lor F) \supset (Q \lor W)$
3. $(S \lor G) \supset (\sim Q \supset X)$
4. $Q \lor S$
5. $\sim Q \cdot H$ / R

iLrn IV. Translate the following arguments into symbolic form and use the first eight rules of inference to derive the conclusion of each. Use the letters in the order in which they are listed.

★1. If topaz is harder than quartz, then it will scratch quartz and also feldspar. Topaz is harder than quartz and it is also harder than calcite. Therefore, either topaz will scratch quartz or it will scratch corundum. (*T, Q, F, C, O*)

2. If clearcutting continues in primary forests and the Endangered Species Act is not repealed, then either the Endangered Species Act will be repealed or thousands of animal species will become extinct. Clearcutting continues in primary forests. The Endangered Species Act will not be repealed. Therefore, thousands of animal species will become extinct. (*C, E, T*)

3. If the rate at which rubidium becomes strontium or the rate at which potassium becomes argon are accurate indicators of age, then rocks from Greenland

are 3.8 billion years old or rocks from the moon are 4.6 billion years old. The rate at which rubidium becomes strontium and the rate at which uranium becomes lead are accurate indicators of age. If rocks from Greenland are 3.8 billion years old, then the earth was formed more than 3.8 billion years ago; also, if rocks from the moon are 4.6 billion years old, then the earth was formed 4.6 billion years ago. If either the earth was formed more than 3.8 billion years ago or 4.6 billion years ago, then the Creationists are wrong. Therefore, the Creationists are wrong. (*R, P, G, M, U, E, F, C*)

★4. Either animals are mere mechanisms or they feel pain. If either animals feel pain or they have souls, then they have a right not to be subjected to needless pain and humans have a duty not to inflict needless pain on them. It is not the case that animals are mere mechanisms. Therefore, animals have a right not to be subjected to needless pain. (*M, P, S, R, D*)

5. If half the nation suffers from depression, then if either the insurance companies have their way or the psychiatrists have their way, then everyone will be taking antidepressant drugs. If either half the nation suffers from depression or sufferers want a real cure, then it is not the case that everyone will be taking antidepressant drugs. Half the nation suffers from depression. Therefore, it is not the case that either the insurance companies or the psychiatrists will have their way. (*H, I, P, E, W*)

6. If either parents get involved in their children's education or the school year is lengthened, then if the children learn phonics, their reading will improve and if they are introduced to abstract concepts earlier, their math will improve. If either parents get involved in their children's education or nebulous subjects are dropped from the curriculum, then either the children will learn phonics or they will be introduced to abstract concepts earlier. Parents will get involved in their children's education, and writing lessons will be integrated with other subjects. Therefore, either the children's reading or their math will improve. (*P, S, L, R, I, M, N, W*)

★7. If either manufacturers will not concentrate on producing a superior product or they will not market their product abroad, then if they will not concentrate on producing a superior product, then the trade deficit will worsen. Either manufacturers will concentrate on producing a superior product or the trade deficit will not worsen. Manufacturers will not concentrate on producing a superior product. Therefore, today's business managers lack imagination. (*C, M, T, B*)

8. If either medical fees or malpractice awards escape restrictions, then health care costs will soar and millions of poor will go uninsured. If the lawyers get their way, then malpractice awards will escape restrictions. If the doctors get their way, then medical fees will escape restrictions. Either the doctors or the lawyers will get their way, and insurance companies will resist reform. Therefore, health care costs will soar. (*F, A, H, P, L, D, I*)

9. If we are less than certain the human fetus is a person, then we must give it the benefit of the doubt. If we are certain the human fetus is a person, then we must accord it the right to live. If either we must give the fetus the benefit of the doubt or accord it the right to live, then we are not less than certain the

fetus is human and it is not merely a part of the mother's body. Either we are less than certain the human fetus is a person or we are certain about it. If we are certain the human fetus is a person, then abortion is immoral. Therefore, abortion is immoral. (*L, G, C, A, M, I*)

★10. If the assassination of terrorist leaders violates civilized values and also is not effective in the long run, then if it prevents terrorist atrocities, then it is effective in the long run. If the assassination of terrorist leaders violates civilized values, then it is not effective in the long run. The assassination of terrorist leaders violates civilized values and is also illegal. If the assassination of terrorist leaders is not effective in the long run, then either it prevents terrorist atrocities or it justifies acts of revenge by terrorists. Therefore, the assassination of terrorist leaders justifies acts of revenge by terrorists and also is not effective in the long run. (*V, E, P, I, J*)

7.3 Rules of Replacement I

The ten rules of replacement are stated in the form of logical equivalences. For this purpose, a new symbol, called a **double colon** (::), will be used to designate logical equivalence. This symbol is a *metalogical* symbol in that it makes an assertion not about things but about symbolized statements: It asserts that the expressions on either side of it have the same truth value regardless of the truth values of their components. Underlying the use of the rules of replacement is an **axiom of replacement,** which asserts that within the context of a proof, logically equivalent expressions may replace one another. The first five rules of replacement are as follows:

9. DeMorgan's Rule (DM):

    $\sim(p \cdot q) :: (\sim p \lor \sim q)$
    $\sim(p \lor q) :: (\sim p \cdot \sim q)$

10. Commutativity (Com):

    $(p \lor q) :: (q \lor p)$
    $(p \cdot q) :: (q \cdot p)$

11. Associativity (Assoc):

    $[p \lor (q \lor r)] :: [(p \lor q) \lor r]$
    $[p \cdot (q \cdot r)] :: [(p \cdot q) \cdot r]$

12. Distribution (Dist):

    $[p \cdot (q \lor r)] :: [(p \cdot q) \lor (p \cdot r)]$
    $[p \lor (q \cdot r)] :: [(p \lor q) \cdot (p \lor r)]$

13. Double negation (DN):

    $p :: \sim\sim p$

DeMorgan's Rule (named after the nineteenth-century logician Augustus DeMorgan) was discussed in Section 6.1 in connection with translation. There it was pointed out that "Not both *p* and *q*" is logically equivalent to "Not *p* or not *q*," and that "Not either *p* or *q*" is logically equivalent to "Not *p* and not *q*." When applying DeMorgan's

Rule, one should keep in mind that it holds only for conjunctive and disjunctive statements (not for conditionals or biconditionals). The rule may be summarized as follows: When moving a tilde inside or outside a set of parentheses, a dot switches with a wedge and vice versa.

Commutativity asserts that the truth value of a conjunction or disjunction is unaffected by the order in which the components are listed. In other words, the component statements may be commuted, or switched for one another, without affecting the truth value. The validity of this rule should be immediately apparent. You may recall from arithmetic that the commutativity rule also applies to addition and multiplication and asserts, for example, that 3 + 5 equals 5 + 3, and that 2 × 3 equals 3 × 2. However, it does *not* apply to division; 2 ÷ 4 does not equal 4 ÷ 2. A similar lesson applies in logic: The commutativity rule applies only to conjunction and disjunction; it does *not* apply to implication.

Associativity states that the truth value of a conjunctive or disjunctive statement is unaffected by the placement of parentheses when the same operator is used throughout. In other words, the way in which the component propositions are grouped, or associated with one another, can be changed without affecting the truth value. The validity of this rule is quite easy to see, but if there is any doubt about it, it may be readily checked by means of a truth table. You may recall that the associativity rule also applies to addition and multiplication and asserts, for example, that 3 + (5 + 7) equals (3 + 5) + 7, and that 2 × (3 × 4) equals (2 × 3) × 4. But it does *not* apply to division; (8 ÷ 4) ÷ 2 does not equal 8 ÷ (4 ÷ 2). Analogously, in logic, the associativity rule applies only to conjunctive and disjunctive statements; it does *not* apply to conditional statements. Also note, when applying this rule, that the order of the letters remains unchanged; only the placement of the parentheses changes.

Distribution, like DeMorgan's Rule, applies only to conjunctive and disjunctive statements. When a proposition is conjoined to a disjunctive statement in parentheses or disjoined to a conjunctive statement in parentheses, the rule allows us to put that proposition together with each of the components inside the parentheses, and also to go in the reverse direction. In the first form of the rule, a statement is distributed through a disjunction, and in the second form, through a conjunction. While the rule may not be immediately obvious, it is easy to remember: The operator that is at first outside the parentheses goes inside, and the operator that is at first inside the parentheses goes outside. Note also how distribution differs from commutativity and associativity. The latter two rules apply only when the *same* operator (either a dot or a wedge) is used throughout a statement. Distribution applies when a dot and a wedge appear *together* in a statement.

Double negation is fairly obvious and needs little explanation. The rule states simply that pairs of tildes immediately adjacent to one another may be either deleted or introduced without affecting the truth value of the statement.

There is an important difference between the rules of implication, treated in the first two sections of this chapter, and the rules of replacement. The **rules of implication** derive their name from the fact that each is a simple argument form in which the premises imply the conclusion. To be applicable in natural deduction, certain lines in a proof must be interpreted as substitution instances of the argument form in question. Stated another way, the rules of implication are applicable only to *whole lines* in a proof. For example, step 3 in the following proof is not a legitimate application of *modus ponens*, because the first premise in the *modus ponens* rule is applied to only a *part* of line 1.

1. $A \supset (B \supset C)$
2. B
3. C 1, 2, MP (incorrect)

The **rules of replacement,** on the other hand, are not rules of implication but rules of logical equivalence. Since, by the axiom of replacement, logically equivalent statement forms can always replace one another in a proof sequence, the rules of replacement can be applied either to a whole line or to any part of a line. Step 2 in the following proof is a quite legitimate application of DeMorgan's Rule, even though the rule is applied only to the consequent of line 1:

1. $S \supset {\sim}(T \cdot U)$
2. $S \supset ({\sim}T \lor {\sim}U)$ 1, DM (valid)

Another way of viewing this distinction is that the rules of implication are "one-way" rules, whereas the rules of replacement are "two-way" rules. The rules of implication allow us to proceed only from the premise lines of a rule to the conclusion line, but the rules of replacement allow us to replace either side of an equivalence expression with the other side.

Application of the first five rules of replacement may now be illustrated. Consider the following argument:

1. $A \supset {\sim}(B \cdot C)$
2. $A \cdot C$ / ${\sim}B$

Examining the premises, we find B in the consequent of line 1. This leads us to suspect that the conclusion can be obtained via *modus ponens*. If this is correct, the tilde would then have to be taken inside the parentheses via DeMorgan's Rule and the resulting ${\sim}C$ eliminated by disjunctive syllogism. The following completed proof indicates that this strategy yields the anticipated result:

1. $A \supset {\sim}(B \cdot C)$
2. $A \cdot C$ / ${\sim}B$
3. A 2, Simp
4. ${\sim}(B \cdot C)$ 1, 3, MP
5. ${\sim}B \lor {\sim}C$ 4, DM
6. $C \cdot A$ 2, Com
7. C 6, Simp
8. ${\sim}{\sim}C$ 7, DN
9. ${\sim}C \lor {\sim}B$ 5, Com
10. ${\sim}B$ 8, 9, DS

The rationale for line 6 is to get C on the left side so that it can be separated via simplification. Similarly, the rationale for line 9 is to get ${\sim}C$ on the left side so that it can be eliminated via disjunctive syllogism. Line 8 is required because, strictly speaking, the negation of ${\sim}C$ is ${\sim}{\sim}C$—not simply C. Thus, C must be replaced with ${\sim}{\sim}C$ to set up the disjunctive syllogism. If your instructor permits it, you can combine commutativity and double negation with other inferences on a single line, as the following shortened proof illustrates. However, we will avoid this practice throughout the remainder of the book.

1. $A \supset \sim(B \cdot C)$
2. $A \cdot C$ / $\sim B$
3. A 2, Simp
4. $\sim(B \cdot C)$ 1, 3, MP
5. $\sim B \vee \sim C$ 4, DM
6. C 2, Com, Simp
7. $\sim B$ 5, 6, Com, DN, DS

Another example:

1. $D \cdot (E \vee F)$
2. $\sim D \vee \sim F$ / $D \cdot E$

The conclusion requires that we get D and E together. Inspection of the first premise suggests distribution as the first step in achieving this. The completed proof is as follows:

1. $D \cdot (E \vee F)$
2. $\sim D \vee \sim F$ / $D \cdot E$
3. $(D \cdot E) \vee (D \cdot F)$ 1, Dist
4. $(D \cdot F) \vee (D \cdot E)$ 3, Com
5. $\sim(D \cdot F)$ 2, DM
6. $D \cdot E$ 4, 5, DS

Some proofs require that we use distribution in the reverse manner. Consider this argument:

1. $(G \cdot H) \vee (G \cdot J)$
2. $(G \vee K) \supset L$ / L

The conclusion can be obtained from line 2 via *modus ponens* if we first obtain $G \vee K$ on a line by itself. Since K does not occur in the first premise at all, it must be introduced by addition. Doing this requires in turn that we obtain G on a line by itself. Distribution applied to line 1 provides the solution:

1. $(G \cdot H) \vee (G \cdot J)$
2. $(G \vee K) \supset L$ / L
3. $G \cdot (H \vee J)$ 1, Dist
4. G 3, Simp
5. $G \vee K$ 4, Add
6. L 2, 5, MP

Application of the associativity rule is illustrated in the next proof:

1. $M \vee (N \vee O)$
2. $\sim O$ / $M \vee N$
3. $(M \vee N) \vee O$ 1, Assoc
4. $O \vee (M \vee N)$ 3, Com
5. $M \vee N$ 2, 4, DS

Before O can be eliminated via disjunctive syllogism from line 1, it must be moved over to the left side. Associativity and commutativity together accomplish this objective.

In some arguments the attempt to "find" the conclusion in the premises is not immediately successful. When confronted with such an argument, it is often best to begin by "deconstructing" the conclusion using the rules of replacement. In other words, one should first apply the rules of replacement to the conclusion to see how it is put together. After this is done it may be evident how the premises entail the conclusion. This procedure is justified by the fact that the rules of replacement are two-way rules. As a result, after the conclusion is deconstructed, it can be derived by using the same rules in the reverse order. Here is an example of such an argument:

1. $K \supset (F \lor B)$
2. $G \cdot K$ $/ (F \cdot G) \lor (B \cdot G)$

If immediate inspection does not reveal how the conclusion should be derived, we may begin by applying the rules of replacement to the conclusion. The form of the conclusion suggests the distribution rule, but first we must use commutativity to move the Gs to the left-hand side. The deconstruction proceeds as follows:

$(F \cdot G) \lor (B \cdot G)$	
$(G \cdot F) \lor (B \cdot G)$	Com
$(G \cdot F) \lor (G \cdot B)$	Com
$G \cdot (F \lor B)$	Dist

Now we see that if we can obtain G on a line by itself, and $F \lor B$ on a line by itself, we can combine them on a single line via the conjunction rule. We can then obtain the conclusion via distribution and commutativity. Inspection of the premises reveals that G can be obtained from line 2 of the premises by simplification, and $F \lor B$ can be obtained from line 1 by *modus ponens*. The completed proof is as follows:

1. $K \supset (F \lor B)$	
2. $G \cdot K$	$/ (F \cdot G) \lor (B \cdot G)$
3. G	2, Simp
4. $K \cdot G$	2, Com
5. K	4, Simp
6. $F \lor B$	1, 5, MP
7. $G \cdot (F \lor B)$	3, 6, Conj
8. $(G \cdot F) \lor (G \cdot B)$	7, Dist
9. $(F \cdot G) \lor (G \cdot B)$	8, Com
10. $(F \cdot G) \lor (B \cdot G)$	9, Com

Here are some strategies for applying the first five rules of replacement. Most of them show how these rules may be used together with other rules.

Strategy 10: Conjunction can be used to set up DeMorgan's Rule:

1. $\sim A$	
2. $\sim B$	
3. $\sim A \cdot \sim B$	1, 2, Conj
4. $\sim (A \lor B)$	3, DM

Strategy 11: Constructive dilemma can be used to set up DeMorgan's Rule:

1. $(A \supset \sim B) \cdot (C \supset \sim D)$	
2. $A \lor C$	
3. $\sim B \lor \sim D$	1, 2, CD
4. $\sim (B \cdot D)$	3, DM

Strategy 12: Addition can be used to set up DeMorgan's Rule:

1. ~A
2. ~A v ~B   1, Add
3. ~(A • B)   2, DM

Strategy 13: Distribution can be used in two ways to set up disjunctive syllogism:

1. (A v B) • (A v C)
2. ~A
3. A v (B • C)   1, Dist
4. B • C   2, 3, DS

1. A • (B v C)
2. ~(A • B)
3. (A • B) v (A • C)   1, Dist
4. A • C   2, 3, DS

Strategy 14: Distribution can be used in two ways to set up simplification:

1. A v (B • C)
2. (A v B) • (A v C)   1, Dist
3. A v B   2, Simp

1. (A • B) v (A • C)
2. A • (B v C)   1, Dist
3. A   2, Simp

Strategy 15: If inspection of the premises does not reveal how the conclusion should be derived, consider using the rules of replacement to deconstruct the conclusion. (See the previous example.)

EXERCISE 7.3

iLrn   I. For each of the following lists of premises, derive the indicated conclusion and complete the justification. For double negation, avoid the occurrence of triple tildes.

★(1) 1. ~(E ⊃ H)
      2. ~(N v G)
      3. ~A v D
      4. _____ ____, DM

 (2) 1. G ⊃ (N ⊃ K)
      2. R v (D ⊃ F)
      3. S • (T v U)
      4. _____ ____, Dist

 (3) 1. M v (G v T)
      2. P • (S ⊃ N)
      3. D • (R v K)
      4. _____ ____, Assoc

★(4) 1. B ⊃ W
      2. G ≡ F
      3. S • A
      4. _____ ____, Com

(5) 1. $\sim\sim R \lor T$
2. $\sim N \lor \sim B$
3. $\sim A \supset \sim H$
4. _____ ____, DN

(6) 1. $(F \lor N) \lor (K \cdot D)$
2. $(H \cdot Z) \lor (H \cdot W)$
3. $(P \supset H) \lor (P \supset N)$
4. _____ ____, Dist

★(7) 1. $\sim(G \cdot \sim Q)$
2. $\sim(K \equiv \sim B)$
3. $\sim T \supset \sim F$
4. _____ ____, DM

(8) 1. $G \supset (\sim L \supset T)$
2. $L \equiv (\sim R \supset \sim C)$
3. $J \supset (S \lor \sim N)$
4. _____ ____, Com

(9) 1. $S \supset (M \supset D)$
2. $(K \cdot G) \lor B$
3. $(E \cdot H) \cdot Q$
4. _____ ____, Assoc

★(10) 1. $\sim R \lor \sim P$
2. $\sim F \supset \sim W$
3. $G \cdot \sim A$
4. _____ ____, DM

(11) 1. $\sim B \lor E$
2. $\sim E \cdot \sim A$
3. $\sim C \supset \sim R$
4. _____ ____, DN

(12) 1. $\sim G \cdot (S \supset A)$
2. $\sim S \supset (B \cdot K)$
3. $\sim Q \lor (T \cdot R)$
4. _____ ____, Dist

★(13) 1. $F \supset (\sim S \lor M)$
2. $H \supset (\sim L \cdot \sim D)$
3. $N \supset (\sim G \supset \sim C)$
4. _____ ____, DM

(14) 1. $F \supset (P \supset \sim E)$
2. $C \lor (S \cdot \sim B)$
3. $M \cdot (R \cdot \sim T)$
4. _____ ____, Assoc

(15) 1. $(D \lor \sim K) \cdot (D \lor \sim W)$
2. $(S \lor \sim Z) \lor (P \lor \sim T)$
3. $(Q \supset \sim N) \cdot (Q \supset \sim F)$
4. _____ ____, Dist

II. In the following symbolized arguments, derive the line needed to obtain the conclusion (last line), and supply the justification for both lines:

★(1) 1. K v C
      2. ~C
      3. _____ ___
      4. K   ___

(2)   1. G ⊃ (R v N)
      2. ~R • ~N
      3. _____ ___
      4. ~G   ___

(3)   1. H • T
      2. _____ ___
      3. T   ___

★(4) 1. (L • S) • F
      2. _____ ___
      3. L   ___

(5)   1. ~B v K
      2. _____ ___
      3. ~(B • ~K) ___

(6)   1. C ⊃ ~A
      2. A
      3. _____ ___
      4. ~C   ___

★(7) 1. (D • M) v (D • N)
      2. _____ ___
      3. D   ___

(8)   1. (U v T) ⊃ R
      2. T v U
      3. _____ ___
      4. R   ___

(9)   1. ~L v M
      2. L
      3. _____ ___
      4. M   ___

★(10) 1. D v (N • H)
      2. _____ ___
      3. D v N   ___

(11) 1. (K v E) • (K v G)
      2. ~K
      3. _____ ___
      4. E • G   ___

(12) 1. (N ⊃ T) • (F ⊃ Q)
      2. F v N
      3. _____ ___
      4. T v Q   ___

★(13) 1. (M v G) v T
      2. ~M
      3. _____ ___
      4. G v T   ___

(14) 1. (~A ⊃ T) • (~S ⊃ K)
      2. ~(A • S)
      3. _____ ___
      4. T v K   ___

(15) 1. ~R
      2. _____ ___
      3. ~(R • T) ___

iLrn III. Use the first thirteen rules of inference to derive the conclusions of the following symbolized arguments:

★(1) 1. (~M ⊃ P) • (~N ⊃ Q)
      2. ~(M • N)   / P v Q

(2)   1. ~S   / ~(F • S)

(3)   1. J v (K • L)
      2. ~K   / J

★(4) 1. ~(N • T)
      2. T   / ~N

(5)   1. H ⊃ ~A
      2. A   / ~(H v ~A)

(6)   1. R ⊃ ~B
      2. D v R
      3. B   / D

★(7) 1. T ⊃ (B v E)
      2. ~E • T   / B

(8)   1. (O v M) ⊃ S
      2. ~S   / ~M

(9)   1. Q v (L v C)
      2. ~C   / L v Q

★(10) 1. $(K \cdot H) \lor (K \cdot L)$
2. $\sim L$ / H

(11) 1. $\sim(\sim E \cdot \sim N) \supset T$
2. $G \supset (N \lor E)$ / $G \supset T$

(12) 1. $H \cdot (C \cdot T)$
2. $\sim(\sim F \cdot T)$ / F

★(13) 1. $(E \cdot I) \lor (M \cdot U)$
2. $\sim E$ / $\sim(E \lor \sim M)$

(14) 1. $\sim(J \lor K)$
2. $B \supset K$
3. $S \supset B$ / $\sim S \cdot \sim J$

(15) 1. $(G \cdot H) \lor (M \cdot G)$
2. $G \supset (T \cdot A)$ / A

★(16) 1. $(Q \cdot N) \lor (N \cdot T)$
2. $(Q \lor C) \supset \sim N$ / T

(17) 1. $\sim(U \lor R)$
2. $(\sim R \lor N) \supset (P \cdot H)$
3. $Q \supset \sim H$ / $\sim Q$

(18) 1. $\sim(F \cdot A)$
2. $\sim(L \lor \sim A)$
3. $D \supset (F \lor L)$ / $\sim D$

★(19) 1. $[(I \lor M) \lor G] \supset \sim G$
2. $M \lor G$ / M

(20) 1. $E \supset \sim B$
2. $U \supset \sim C$
3. $\sim(\sim E \cdot \sim U)$ / $\sim(B \cdot C)$

(21) 1. $\sim(K \lor F)$
2. $\sim F \supset (K \lor C)$
3. $(G \lor C) \supset \sim H$ / $\sim(K \lor H)$

★(22) 1. $S \lor (I \cdot \sim J)$
2. $S \supset \sim R$
3. $\sim J \supset \sim Q$ / $\sim(R \cdot Q)$

(23) 1. $(J \lor F) \lor M$
2. $(J \lor M) \supset \sim P$
3. $\sim F$ / $\sim(F \lor P)$

(24) 1. $(K \cdot P) \lor (K \cdot Q)$
2. $P \supset \sim K$ / $Q \lor T$

★(25) 1. $E \lor \sim(D \lor C)$
2. $(E \lor \sim D) \supset C$ / E

(26) 1. $A \cdot (F \cdot L)$
2. $A \supset (U \lor W)$
3. $F \supset (U \lor X)$ / $U \lor (W \cdot X)$

(27) 1. $(T \cdot R) \supset P$
2. $(\sim P \cdot R) \cdot G$
3. $(\sim T \lor N) \supset H$ / H

★(28) 1. $P \lor (I \cdot L)$
2. $(P \lor I) \supset \sim(L \lor C)$
3. $(P \cdot \sim C) \supset (E \cdot F)$ / $F \lor D$

(29) 1. $B \lor (S \cdot N)$
2. $B \supset \sim S$
3. $S \supset \sim N$ / $B \lor W$

(30) 1. $(\sim M \lor E) \supset (S \supset U)$
2. $(\sim Q \lor E) \supset (U \supset H)$
3. $\sim(M \lor Q)$ / $S \supset H$

★(31) 1. $(\sim R \lor D) \supset \sim(F \cdot G)$
2. $(F \cdot R) \supset S$
3. $F \cdot \sim S$ / $\sim(S \lor G)$

(32) 1. $\sim Q \supset (C \cdot B)$
2. $\sim T \supset (B \cdot H)$
3. $\sim(Q \cdot T)$ / B

(33) 1. $\sim(A \cdot G)$
2. $\sim(A \cdot E)$
3. $G \lor E$ / $\sim(A \cdot F)$

★(34) 1. $(M \cdot N) \lor (O \cdot P)$
2. $(N \lor O) \supset \sim P$ / N

(35) 1. $(T \cdot K) \lor (C \cdot E)$
2. $K \supset \sim E$
3. $E \supset \sim C$ / $T \cdot K$

iLrn IV. Translate the following arguments into symbolic form and use the first thirteen rules of inference to derive the conclusion of each. Use the translation letters in the order in which they are listed.

★1. Either health care costs are skyrocketing and they are attributable to greedy doctors, or health care costs are skyrocketing and they are attributable to greedy hospitals. If health care costs are skyrocketing, then both the government should intercede and health care may have to be rationed. Therefore, health care costs are skyrocketing and health care may have to be rationed. (*S, D, H, I, R*)

7

2. Either the ancient Etruscans were experienced city planners and they invented the art of writing or they were highly skilled engineers and they invented the art of writing. If the ancient Etruscans were bloodthirsty numskulls (as scholars once thought), they did not invent the art of writing. Therefore, the ancient Etruscans were not bloodthirsty numskulls (as scholars once thought). (*C, I, H, B*)

3. It is not the case that either the earth's molten core is stationary or that it contains no iron. If it is not the case that both the earth's molten core is stationary and has a regular topography, then either the earth's core contains no iron or the direction of the earth's magnetic field is subject to change. Therefore, the direction of the earth's magnetic field is subject to change. (*S, C, R, D*)

★4. Either mosquito genes can be cloned or mosquitoes will become resistant to all insecticides and the incidence of encephalitis will increase. If either mosquito genes can be cloned or the incidence of encephalitis increases, then mosquitoes will not become resistant to all insecticides. Therefore, either mosquito genes can be cloned or mosquitoes will multiply out of control. (*G, R, E, M*)

5. Protein engineering will prove to be as successful as genetic engineering, and new enzymes will be developed for producing food and breaking down industrial wastes. If protein engineering proves to be as successful as genetic engineering and new enzymes are developed for breaking down industrial wastes, then it is not the case that new enzymes will be developed for producing food but not medicines. Therefore, protein engineering will prove to be as successful as genetic engineering and new enzymes will be developed for producing medicines. (*E, P, B, M*)

6. If workers have a fundamental right to a job, then unemployment will be virtually nonexistent but job redundancy will become a problem. If workers have no fundamental right to a job, then production efficiency will be maximized but job security will be jeopardized. Workers either have or do not have a fundamental right to a job. Therefore, either unemployment will be virtually nonexistent or production efficiency will be maximized. (*F, U, R, P, S*)

★7. If Japan is to reduce its huge trade surplus, then it must either convince its citizens to spend more or it must move its manufacturing facilities to other countries. It is not the case that Japan will either increase its imports or convince its citizens to spend more. Furthermore, it is not the case that Japan will either allow foreign construction companies to compete on an equal footing or move its manufacturing facilities to other countries. Therefore, Japan will not reduce its huge trade surplus. (*R, C, M, I, A*)

8. If women are by nature either passive or uncompetitive, then it is not the case that there are lawyers who are women. If men are by nature either insensitive or without the ability to nurture, then it is not the case that there are kindergarten teachers who are men. There are lawyers who are women and kindergarten teachers who are men. Therefore, it is not the case that either women by nature are uncompetitive or men by nature are without the ability to nurture. (*P, U, L, I, W, K*)

9. It is not the case that either the sun's interior rotates faster than its surface or Einstein's general theory of relativity is wrong. If the sun's interior does not

rotate faster than its surface and eccentricities in the orbit of Mercury can be explained by solar gravitation, then Einstein's general theory of relativity is wrong. Therefore, eccentricities in the orbit of Mercury cannot be explained by solar gravitation. (*S*, *E*, *M*)

★10. Either school dropout programs are not as effective as they could be, or they provide basic thinking skills and psychological counseling to their students. Either school dropout programs are not as effective as they could be, or they adequately prepare their students for getting a job and working effectively with others. Either school dropout programs do not provide psychological counseling to their students or they do not provide adequate preparation for working effectively with others. Therefore, school dropout programs are not as effective as they could be. (*E*, *B*, *P*, *G*, *W*)

7.4   Rules of Replacement II

The remaining five rules of replacement are as follows:

14. Transposition (Trans):
$(p \supset q) :: (\sim q \supset \sim p)$

15. Material implication (Impl):
$(p \supset q) :: (\sim p \lor q)$

16. Material equivalence (Equiv):
$(p \equiv q) :: [(p \supset q) \cdot (q \supset p)]$
$(p \equiv q) :: [(p \cdot q) \lor (\sim p \cdot \sim q)]$

17. Exportation (Exp):
$[(p \cdot q) \supset r] :: [p \supset (q \supset r)]$

18. Tautology (Taut):
$p :: (p \lor p)$
$p :: (p \cdot p)$

Transposition asserts that the antecedent and consequent of a conditional statement may switch places if and only if tildes are inserted before both or tildes are removed from both. The rule is fairly easy to understand and is easily proved by a truth table.

Material implication is less obvious than transposition, but it can be illustrated by substituting actual statements in place of the letters. For example, the statement "If you bother me, then I'll punch you in the nose" ($B \supset P$) is logically equivalent to "Either you stop bothering me or I'll punch you in the nose" ($\sim B \lor P$). The rule states that a horseshoe may be replaced by a wedge sign if the left-hand component is negated, and the reverse replacement is allowed if a tilde is deleted from the left-hand component.

Material equivalence has two formulations. The first is the same as the definition of material equivalence given in Section 6.1. The second formulation is easy to remember through recalling the two ways in which $p \equiv q$ may be true. Either p and q are both true or p and q are both false. This, of course, is the meaning of $[(p \cdot q) \lor (\sim p \cdot \sim q)]$.

Exportation is also fairly easy to understand. It asserts that the statement "If we have p, then if we have q we have r" is logically equivalent to "If we have both p and q, we have r." As an illustration of this rule, the statement "If Bob told the truth, then if Sue told the truth, then Jim is guilty" is logically equivalent to "If Bob and Sue told the truth, then Jim is guilty."

Tautology, the last rule introduced in this section, is obvious. Its effect is to eliminate redundancy in disjunctions and conjunctions.

The following proofs illustrate the use of these five rules.

   1. ~A   / A⊃B

In this argument the conclusion contains a letter not found in the premise. Obviously, addition must be used to introduce the B. The material implication rule completes the proof:

   1. ~A   / A⊃B
   2. ~A ∨ B   1, Add
   3. A⊃B   2, Impl

Here is another example:

   1. F⊃G
   2. F ∨ G   / G

To derive the conclusion of this argument, some method must be found to link the two premises together and eliminate the F. Hypothetical syllogism provides the solution, but first the second premise must be converted into a conditional. Here is the proof:

   1. F⊃G
   2. F ∨ G   / G
   3. ~~F ∨ G   2, DN
   4. ~F⊃G   3, Impl
   5. ~F⊃~~G   4, DN
   6. ~G⊃F   5, Trans
   7. ~G⊃G   1, 6, HS
   8. ~~G ∨ G   7, Impl
   9. G ∨ G   8, DN
  10. G   9, Taut

Another example:

   1. J⊃(K⊃L)   / K⊃(J⊃L)

The conclusion can be obtained by simply rearranging the components of the single premise. Exportation provides the simplest method:

   1. J⊃(K⊃L)   / K⊃(J⊃L)
   2. (J•K)⊃L   1, Exp
   3. (K•J)⊃L   2, Com
   4. K⊃(J⊃L)   3, Exp

Another example:

   1. M⊃N
   2. M⊃O   / M⊃(N•O)

As with the second example above, some method must be found to link the two premises together. In this case, however, hypothetical syllogism will not work. The solution lies in setting up a distribution step:

   1. M⊃N
   2. M⊃O   / M⊃(N•O)
   3. ~M ∨ N   1, Impl
   4. ~M ∨ O   2, Impl

5. $(\sim M \vee N) \cdot (\sim M \vee O)$ 3, 4, Conj
6. $\sim M \vee (N \cdot O)$ 5, Dist
7. $M \supset (N \cdot O)$ 6, Impl

Another example:

1. $P \supset Q$
2. $R \supset (S \cdot T)$
3. $\sim R \supset \sim Q$
4. $S \supset (T \supset P)$ / $P \equiv R$

The conclusion is a biconditional, and there are only two ways that a biconditional can be obtained from such premises—namely, via the two formulations of the material equivalence rule. The fact that the premises are all conditional statements suggests the first formulation of this rule. Accordingly, we must try to obtain $P \supset R$ and $R \supset P$. Again, the fact that the premises are themselves conditionals suggests hypothetical syllogism to accomplish this. Premises 1 and 3 can be used to set up one hypothetical syllogism; premises 2 and 4 provide the other. Here is the proof:

1. $P \supset Q$
2. $R \supset (S \cdot T)$
3. $\sim R \supset \sim Q$
4. $S \supset (T \supset P)$ / $P \equiv R$
5. $Q \supset R$ 3, Trans
6. $P \supset R$ 1, 5, HS
7. $(S \cdot T) \supset P$ 4, Exp
8. $R \supset P$ 2, 7, HS
9. $(P \supset R) \cdot (R \supset P)$ 6, 8, Conj
10. $P \equiv R$ 9, Equiv

As we showed in Section 7.3, if it is not readily apparent how the conclusion should be derived, we can use the rules of replacement to deconstruct the conclusion. This will usually provide insight on how best to proceed. Again, this technique is justified because the rules of replacement are two-way rules. As a result, they can be applied in reverse order in the completed proof. Here is an example:

1. $\sim S \supset K$
2. $S \supset (R \vee M)$ / $\sim R \supset (\sim M \supset K)$

In deconstructing the conclusion, the form of the conclusion suggests exportation, and the result of this step suggests DeMorgan's rule. For further insight, we apply transposition to the latter step. Each step follows from the one preceding it:

$\sim R \supset (\sim M \supset K)$
$(\sim R \cdot \sim M) \supset K$ Exp
$\sim (R \vee M) \supset K$ DM
$\sim K \supset \sim\sim (R \vee M)$ Trans
$\sim K \supset (R \vee M)$ DN

Now, examining the premises in light of the deconstruction suggests that we begin by setting up a hypothetical syllogism. This will give us the last step in the deconstruction. We can then obtain the conclusion by repeating the deconstruction steps in reverse order. The completed proof is as follows:

1. $\sim S \supset K$
2. $S \supset (R \lor M)$ / $\sim R \supset (\sim M \supset K)$
3. $\sim K \supset \sim\sim S$ 1, Trans
4. $\sim K \supset S$ 3, DN
5. $\sim K \supset (R \lor M)$ 2, 4, HS
6. $\sim(R \lor M) \supset \sim\sim K$ 5, Trans
7. $\sim(R \lor M) \supset K$ 6, DN
8. $(\sim R \cdot \sim M) \supset K$ 7, DM
9. $\sim R \supset (\sim M \supset K)$ 8, Exp

Here is another example:

1. $K \supset M$
2. $L \supset M$ / $(K \lor L) \supset M$

In deconstructing the conclusion, the form of the premises suggests that we use some procedure that will combine M separately with K and L. This, in turn, suggests distribution; but before we can use distribution, we must eliminate the horseshoe via implication. The deconstruction is as follows:

$(K \lor L) \supset M$	
$\sim(K \lor L) \lor M$	Impl
$(\sim K \cdot \sim L) \lor M$	DM
$M \lor (\sim K \cdot \sim L)$	Com
$(M \lor \sim K) \cdot (M \lor \sim L)$	Dist
$(\sim K \lor M) \cdot (M \lor \sim L)$	Com
$(\sim K \lor M) \cdot (\sim L \lor M)$	Com
$(K \supset M) \cdot (\sim L \lor M)$	Impl
$(K \supset M) \cdot (L \supset M)$	Impl

Now, examining the premises in light of the last line of the deconstruction suggests that we begin by joining the premises together via the conjunction rule. The conclusion can then be obtained by reversing the steps of the deconstruction:

1. $K \supset M$
2. $L \supset M$ / $(K \lor L) \supset M$
3. $(K \supset M) \cdot (L \supset M)$ 1, 2, Conj
4. $(\sim K \lor M) \cdot (L \supset M)$ 3, Impl
5. $(\sim K \lor M) \cdot (\sim L \lor M)$ 4, Impl
6. $(M \lor \sim K) \cdot (\sim L \lor M)$ 5, Com
7. $(M \lor \sim K) \cdot (M \lor \sim L)$ 6, Com
8. $M \lor (\sim K \cdot \sim L)$ 7, Dist
9. $(\sim K \cdot \sim L) \lor M$ 8, Com
10. $\sim(K \lor L) \lor M$ 9, DM
11. $(K \lor L) \supset M$ 10, Impl

It is important to realize that whenever we use this strategy of working backward from the conclusion, the rules of replacement are the *only* rules we may use. We may not use the rules of implication, because these rules are one-way rules.

We end this section with some strategies that show how the last five rules of replacement can be used together with various other rules.

Strategy 16: Material implication can be used to set up hypothetical syllogism:

1. ~A ∨ B
2. ~B ∨ C
3. A ⊃ B   1, Impl
4. B ⊃ C   2, Impl
5. A ⊃ C   3, 4, HS

Strategy 17: Exportation can be used to set up *modus ponens:*

1. (A • B) ⊃ C
2. A
3. A ⊃ (B ⊃ C)   1, Exp
4. B ⊃ C   2, 3, MP

Strategy 18: Exportation can be used to set up *modus tollens:*

1. A ⊃ (B ⊃ C)
2. ~C
3. (A • B) ⊃ C   1, Exp
4. ~(A • B)   2, 3, MT

Strategy 19: Addition can be used to set up material implication:

1. A
2. A ∨ ~B   1, Add
3. ~B ∨ A   2, Com
4. B ⊃ A   3, Impl

Strategy 20: Transposition can be used to set up hypothetical syllogism:

1. A ⊃ B
2. ~C ⊃ ~B
3. B ⊃ C   2, Trans
4. A ⊃ C   1, 3, HS

Strategy 21: Transposition can be used to set up constructive dilemma:

1. (A ⊃ B) • (C ⊃ D)
2. ~B ∨ ~D
3. (~B ⊃ ~A) • (C ⊃ D)   1, Trans
4. (~B ⊃ ~A) • (~D ⊃ ~C)   3, Trans
5. ~A ∨ ~C   2, 4, CD

Strategy 22: Constructive dilemma can be used to set up tautology:

1. (A ⊃ C) • (B ⊃ C)
2. A ∨ B
3. C ∨ C   1, 2, CD
4. C   3, Taut

Strategy 23: Material implication can be used to set up tautology:

1. A ⊃ ~A
2. ~A ∨ ~A   1, Impl
3. ~A   2, Taut

Strategy 24: Material implication can be used to set up distribution:

1. $A \supset (B \cdot C)$
2. $\sim A \lor (B \cdot C)$ 1, Impl
3. $(\sim A \lor B) \cdot (\sim A \lor C)$ 2, Dist

iLrn

EXERCISE 7.4

I. For each of the following lists of premises, derive the indicated conclusion and complete the justification:

★(1) 1. $H \lor F$
    2. $N \lor \sim S$
    3. $\sim G \lor Q$
    4. _____ ____, Impl

(2) 1. $R \supset (S \supset N)$
    2. $T \supset (U \lor M)$
    3. $K \cdot (L \supset W)$
    4. _____ ____, Exp

(3) 1. $G \equiv R$
    2. $H \supset P$
    3. $\sim F \lor T$
    4. _____ ____, Trans

★(4) 1. $(B \supset N) \cdot (N \supset B)$
    2. $(R \lor F) \cdot (F \lor R)$
    3. $(K \supset C) \lor (C \supset K)$
    4. _____ ____, Equiv

(5) 1. $E \lor \sim E$
    2. $A \lor A$
    3. $G \cdot \sim G$
    4. _____ ____, Taut

(6) 1. $S \lor \sim M$
    2. $\sim N \cdot \sim T$
    3. $\sim L \supset Q$
    4. _____ ____, Trans

★(7) 1. $\sim C \supset \sim F$
    2. $D \lor \sim P$
    3. $\sim R \cdot Q$
    4. _____ ____, Impl

(8) 1. $E \supset (R \cdot Q)$
    2. $(G \cdot N) \supset Z$
    3. $(S \supset M) \supset P$
    4. _____ ____, Exp

7

(9) 1. $(D \cdot H) \lor (\sim D \cdot \sim H)$
  2. $(F \supset J) \cdot (\sim F \supset \sim J)$
  3. $(N \lor T) \cdot (\sim N \lor \sim T)$
  4. _____ ____, Equiv

★(10) 1. $L \supset (A \supset A)$
  2. $K \supset (R \lor \sim R)$
  3. $S \supset (G \cdot G)$
  4. _____ ____, Taut

(11) 1. $K \cdot (S \lor B)$
  2. $\sim F \supset \sim J$
  3. $\sim E \lor \sim M$
  4. _____ ____, Trans

(12) 1. $H \supset (K \cdot J)$
  2. $(N \lor E) \supset B$
  3. $C \supset (H \supset A)$
  4. _____ ____, Exp

★(13) 1. $(A \supset \sim C) \cdot (C \supset \sim A)$
  2. $(W \supset \sim T) \cdot (\sim T \supset W)$
  3. $(M \supset \sim E) \cdot (\sim M \supset E)$
  4. _____ ____, Equiv

(14) 1. $(\sim K \lor M) \equiv S$
  2. $T \lor (F \cdot G)$
  3. $R \equiv (N \cdot \sim H)$
  4. _____ ____, Impl

(15) 1. $(S \lor S) \supset D$
  2. $K \supset (T \cdot \sim T)$
  3. $(Q \supset Q) \supset M$
  4. _____ ____, Taut

II. In the following symbolized arguments, derive the line needed to obtain the conclusion (last line), and supply the justification for both lines:

★(1) 1. $\sim J \lor M$
  2. $M \supset B$
  3. _____ ____
  4. $J \supset B$ ____

(2) 1. $(J \cdot F) \supset N$
  2. J
  3. _____ ____
  4. $F \supset N$ ____

(3) 1. $C \supset A$
  2. $A \supset C$
  3. _____ ____
  4. $C \equiv A$ ____

★(4) 1. $(G \supset K) \cdot (T \supset K)$
  2. $G \lor T$
  3. _____ ____
  4. K ____

(5) 1. $(G \supset B) \cdot (\sim C \supset \sim H)$
  2. $G \lor H$
  3. _____ ____
  4. $B \lor C$ ____

(6) 1. $J \supset (M \supset Q)$
  2. $J \cdot M$
  3. _____ ____
  4. Q ____

★(7) 1. $H \supset (\sim C \vee R)$
    2. _____ ____
    3. $(H \cdot C) \supset R$ ____

(8) 1. $\sim G \supset \sim T$
    2. $G \supset N$
    3. _____ ____
    4. $T \supset N$ ____

(9) 1. $K \supset (A \supset F)$
    2. $\sim F$
    3. _____ ____
    4. $\sim (K \cdot A)$ ____

★(10) 1. $H \supset \sim H$
    2. _____ ____
    3. $\sim H$ ____

(11) 1. $\sim S$
    2. _____ ____
    3. $S \supset K$ ____

(12) 1. $M \supset (M \supset D)$
    2. _____ ____
    3. $M \supset D$ ____

★(13) 1. $(N \supset A) \cdot (\sim N \supset \sim A)$
    2. _____ ____
    3. $N \equiv A$ ____

(14) 1. $E \cdot R$
    2. _____ ____
    3. $E \equiv R$ ____

(15) 1. $Q \supset (\sim W \supset \sim G)$
    2. _____ ____
    3. $(Q \cdot G) \supset W$ ____

iLrn III. Use the eighteen rules of inference to derive the conclusions of the following symbolized arguments:

★(1) 1. $(S \cdot K) \supset R$
    2. K / $S \supset R$

(2) 1. $T \supset (F \vee F)$
    2. $\sim (F \cdot F)$ / $\sim T$

(3) 1. $G \supset E$
    2. $H \supset \sim E$ / $G \supset \sim H$

★(4) 1. $S \equiv Q$
    2. $\sim S$ / $\sim Q$

(5) 1. $\sim N \vee P$
    2. $(N \supset P) \supset T$ / T

(6) 1. $F \supset B$
    2. $B \supset (B \supset J)$ / $F \supset J$

★(7) 1. $(B \supset M) \cdot (D \supset M)$
    2. $B \vee D$ / M

(8) 1. $Q \supset (F \supset A)$
    2. $R \supset (A \supset F)$
    3. $Q \cdot R$ / $F \equiv A$

(9) 1. $T \supset (\sim T \vee G)$
    2. $\sim G$ / $\sim T$

★(10) 1. $(B \supset G) \cdot (F \supset N)$
    2. $\sim (G \cdot N)$ / $\sim (B \cdot F)$

(11) 1. $(J \cdot R) \supset H$
    2. $(R \supset H) \supset M$
    3. $\sim (P \vee \sim J)$ / $M \cdot \sim P$

(12) 1. T / $S \supset T$

★(13) 1. $K \supset (B \supset \sim M)$
       2. $D \supset (K \cdot M)$ / $D \supset \sim B$

(14) 1. $(O \supset C) \cdot (\sim S \supset \sim D)$
       2. $(E \supset D) \cdot (\sim E \supset \sim C)$ / $O \supset S$

(15) 1. $\sim (U \cdot W) \supset X$
       2. $U \supset \sim U$ / $\sim (U \vee \sim X)$

★(16) 1. $T \supset R$
       2. $T \supset \sim R$ / $\sim T$

(17) 1. $S \vee \sim N$
       2. $\sim S \vee Q$ / $N \supset Q$

(18) 1. $M \supset (U \supset H)$
       2. $(H \vee \sim U) \supset F$ / $M \supset F$

★(19) 1. $\sim R \vee P$
       2. $R \vee \sim P$ / $R \equiv P$

(20) 1. $\sim H \supset B$
       2. $\sim H \supset D$
       3. $\sim (B \cdot D)$ / H

(21) 1. $J \supset (G \supset L)$ / $G \supset (J \supset L)$

★(22) 1. $S \supset (L \cdot M)$
       2. $M \supset (L \supset R)$ / $S \supset R$

(23) 1. $F \supset (A \cdot K)$
       2. $G \supset (\sim A \cdot \sim K)$
       3. $F \vee G$ / $A \equiv K$

(24) 1. $(I \supset E) \supset C$
       2. $C \supset \sim C$ / I

★(25) 1. $T \supset G$
       2. $S \supset G$ / $(T \vee S) \supset G$

(26) 1. $H \supset U$ / $H \supset (U \vee T)$

(27) 1. $Q \supset (W \cdot D)$ / $Q \supset W$

★(28) 1. $P \supset (\sim E \supset B)$
       2. $\sim (B \vee E)$ / $\sim P$

(29) 1. $(G \supset J) \supset (H \supset Q)$
       2. $J \cdot \sim Q$ / $\sim H$

(30) 1. $I \vee (N \cdot F)$
       2. $I \supset F$ / F

★(31) 1. $K \equiv R$
       2. $K \supset (R \supset P)$
       3. $\sim P$ / $\sim R$

(32) 1. $C \supset (\sim L \supset Q)$
       2. $L \supset \sim C$
       3. $\sim Q$ / $\sim C$

(33) 1. $(E \supset A) \cdot (F \supset A)$
2. $E \vee G$
3. $F \vee \sim G$ / A

★(34) 1. $(F \cdot H) \supset N$
2. $F \vee S$
3. H / $N \vee S$

(35) 1. $T \supset (H \cdot J)$
2. $(H \vee N) \supset T$ / $T \equiv H$

(36) 1. $T \supset \sim(A \supset N)$
2. $T \vee N$ / $T = \sim N$

★(37) 1. $(D \supset E) \supset (E \supset D)$
2. $(D \equiv E) \supset \sim(G \cdot \sim H)$
3. $E \cdot G$ / $G \cdot H$

(38) 1. $(O \supset R) \supset S$
2. $(P \supset R) \supset \sim S$ / $\sim R$

(39) 1. $(L \vee P) \supset U$
2. $(M \supset U) \supset I$
3. P / I

★(40) 1. $A \equiv W$
2. $\sim A \vee \sim W$
3. $R \supset A$ / $\sim(W \vee R)$

(41) 1. $(S \vee T) \supset (S \supset \sim T)$
2. $(S \supset \sim T) \supset (T \supset K)$
3. $S \vee T$ / $S \vee K$

(42) 1. $G \equiv M$
2. $G \vee M$
3. $G \supset (M \supset T)$ / T

★(43) 1. $O \supset (Q \cdot N)$
2. $(N \vee E) \supset S$ / $O \supset S$

(44) 1. $H \equiv I$
2. $H \supset (I \supset F)$
3. $\sim(H \vee I) \supset F$ / F

★(45) 1. $P \supset A$
2. $Q \supset B$ / $(P \vee Q) \supset (A \vee B)$

iLrn IV. Translate the following arguments into symbolic form and use the eighteen rules of inference to derive the conclusion of each. Use the translation letters in the order in which they are listed.

★1. If sports shoe manufacturers decline to use kangaroo hides in their products, then Australian hunters will cease killing millions of kangaroos yearly. It is not the case that both Australian hunters will cease killing millions of kangaroos yearly and the kangaroo not be saved from extinction. Therefore, if sports shoe manufacturers decline to use kangaroo hides in their products, then the kangaroo will be saved from extinction. (D, C, S)

2. If there is a direct correlation between what a nation spends for health care and the health of its citizens, then America has the lowest incidence of disease and the lowest mortality rates of any nation on earth. But America does not have the lowest mortality rates of any nation on earth. Therefore, there is not a direct correlation between what a nation spends for health care and the health of its citizens. (C, D, M)

3. It is not the case that strict controls exist on either the manufacture or the sale of handguns. Therefore, if strict controls exist on the sale of handguns, then the use of handguns in the commission of crimes has decreased. (M, S, U)

★4. If birth control devices are made available in high school clinics, then the incidence of teenage pregnancy will decrease. Therefore, if both birth control information and birth control devices are made available in high school clinics, then the incidence of teenage pregnancy will decrease. (D, P, I)

5. If Congress enacts a law that either establishes a religion or prohibits the free exercise of religion, then that law is unconstitutional. Therefore, if Congress enacts a law that establishes a religion, then that law is unconstitutional. (E, P, U)

6. If cigarette smokers are warned of the hazards of smoking and they continue to smoke, then they cannot sue tobacco companies for any resulting lung cancer or emphysema. Cigarette smokers are warned of the hazards of smoking. Therefore, if cigarette smokers continue to smoke, they cannot sue tobacco companies for any resulting lung cancer or emphysema. (W, C, S)

★7. If grade-school children are assigned daily homework, then their achievement level will increase dramatically. But if grade-school children are assigned daily homework, then their love for learning may be dampened. Therefore, if grade-school children are assigned daily homework, then their achievement level will increase dramatically but their love for learning may be dampened. (G, A, L)

8. If a superconducting particle collider is built, then the data yielded will benefit scientists of all nations and it deserves international funding. Either a superconducting particle collider will be built, or the ultimate nature of matter will remain hidden and the data yielded will benefit scientists of all nations. Therefore, the data yielded by a superconducting particle collider will benefit scientists of all nations. (S, D, I, U)

9. If parents are told that their unborn child has Tay-Sachs disease, then if they go ahead with the birth, then they are responsible for their child's pain and suffering. Therefore, if parents are not responsible for their child's pain and suffering, then if they go ahead with the birth, then they were not told that their unborn child had Tay-Sachs disease. (T, G, R)

★10. Vitamin E is an antioxidant and a useless food supplement if and only if it does not reduce heart disease. It is not the case either that vitamin E does not reduce heart disease or is not an antioxidant. Therefore, vitamin E is not a useless food supplement. (A, U, R)

Conditional Proof

Conditional proof is a method for obtaining a line in a proof sequence (either the conclusion or some intermediate line) that frequently offers the advantage of being both shorter and simpler to use than the direct method. Moreover, there are a number of arguments having conclusions that cannot be derived by the direct method, so some form of conditional proof must be used on them. While in theory the method of conditional proof can be used to derive any line in a proof sequence, in practice it is usually reserved for obtaining lines that are expressed in the form of conditional statements. The method consists of assuming the antecedent of the required conditional statement on one line, deriving the consequent on a subsequent line, and then "discharging" this sequence of lines in a conditional statement that exactly replicates the one that was to be obtained.

Any argument whose conclusion is a conditional statement is an immediate candidate for conditional proof. Consider the following example:

1. $A \supset (B \cdot C)$
2. $(B \lor D) \supset E$ $/ A \supset E$

Using the direct method to derive the conclusion of this argument would require a proof having at least twelve lines, and the precise strategy to be followed in constructing it might not be immediately obvious. Nevertheless, we need only give cursory inspection to the argument to see that the conclusion does indeed follow from the premises. The conclusion states that if we have A, we then have E. Let us suppose, for a moment, that we do have A. We could then obtain $B \cdot C$ from the first premise via *modus ponens*. Simplifying this expression we could obtain B, and from this we could get $B \lor D$ via addition. E would then follow from the second premise via *modus ponens*. In other words, if we assume that we have A, we can get E. But this is exactly what the conclusion says. Thus, we have just proved that the conclusion follows from the premises.

The method of conditional proof consists of incorporating this simple thought process into the body of a proof sequence. A conditional proof for this argument requires only eight lines and is substantially simpler than a direct proof:

1. $A \supset (B \cdot C)$
2. $(B \lor D) \supset E$ $/ A \supset E$
> 3. A ACP
> 4. $B \cdot C$ 1, 3, MP
> 5. B 4, Simp
> 6. $B \lor D$ 5, Add
> 7. E 2, 6, MP
8. $A \supset E$ 3–7, CP

Lines 3 through 7 are indented to indicate their hypothetical character: they all depend on the assumption introduced in line 3 via "ACP" (assumption for conditional proof). These lines, which constitute the conditional proof sequence, tell us that if we assume A (line 3), we can obtain E (line 7). In line 8 the conditional sequence is discharged in the conditional statement $A \supset E$, which simply reiterates the result of the conditional sequence. Since line 8 is not hypothetical, it is written adjacent to the original margin, under lines 1 and 2. A vertical line is added to the conditional sequence to emphasize the indentation.

The first step in constructing a conditional proof is to decide what should be assumed on the first line of the conditional sequence. While any statement whatsoever *can* be assumed on this line, only the right statement will lead to the desired result. The clue is always provided by the conditional statement to be obtained in the end. The antecedent of this statement is what must be assumed. For example, if the statement to be obtained is $(K \cdot L) \supset M$, then $K \cdot L$ should be assumed on the first line. This line is always indented and tagged with the designation "ACP." Once the initial assumption has been made, the second step is to obtain the consequent of the desired conditional statement at the end of the conditional sequence. To do this, we simply apply the ordinary rules of inference to any previous line in the proof (including the assumed line), writing the result directly below the assumed line. The third and final step is to discharge the conditional sequence in a conditional statement. The antecedent of this conditional statement is whatever appears on the first line of the conditional sequence, and the consequent is whatever appears on the last line. For example, if $A \vee B$ is on the first line and $C \cdot D$ is on the last, the sequence is discharged by $(A \vee B) \supset (C \cdot D)$. This discharging line is always written adjacent to the original margin and is tagged with the designation "CP" (conditional proof) together with the numerals corresponding to the first and last lines of the sequence.

It was suggested earlier that conditional proof can be used to obtain a line other than the conclusion of an argument. The following proof, which illustrates this fact, incorporates two conditional sequences one after the other within the scope of a single direct proof:

1. $G \supset (H \cdot I)$
2. $J \supset (K \cdot L)$
3. $G \vee J$ / $H \vee K$
    4. G ACP
    5. $H \cdot I$ 1, 4, MP
    6. H 5, Simp
7. $G \supset H$ 4–6, CP
    8. J ACP
    9. $K \cdot L$ 2, 8, MP
    10. K 9, Simp
11. $J \supset K$ 8–10, CP
12. $(G \supset H) \cdot (J \supset K)$ 7, 11, Conj
13. $H \vee K$ 3, 12, CD

The first conditional proof sequence gives us $G \supset H$, and the second $J \supset K$. These two lines are then conjoined and used together with line 3 to set up a constructive dilemma, from which the conclusion is obtained.

This proof sequence provides a convenient opportunity to introduce an important rule governing conditional proof. The rule states that after a conditional proof sequence has been discharged, no line in the sequence may be used as a justification for a subsequent line in the proof. If, for example, line 5 in the above proof were used as a justification for line 9 or line 12, this rule would be violated, and the corresponding inference would be invalid. Once the conditional sequence is discharged, it is sealed off from the remaining part of the proof. The logic behind this rule is easy to understand. The lines in a conditional sequence are hypothetical in that they depend on the assumption stated in the first line. Because no mere assumption can provide any genuine support for anything, neither can any line that depends on such an assumption. When a conditional sequence is discharged, the assumption upon which it rests is expressed as the antecedent of a conditional statement. This conditional statement *can* be used to support subsequent lines because it makes no claim that its antecedent is true. The conditional statement merely asserts that *if* its antecedent is true, then its consequent is true, and this, of course, is what has been established by the conditional sequence from which it is obtained.

Just as a conditional sequence can be used within the scope of a direct proof to obtain a desired statement, one conditional sequence can be used within the scope of another to obtain a desired statement. The following proof provides an example:

1. $L \supset [M \supset (N \lor O)]$	
2. $M \supset \sim N$	/ $L \supset (\sim M \lor O)$
3. L	ACP
4. $M \supset (N \lor O)$	1, 3, MP
5. M	ACP
6. $N \lor O$	4, 5, MP
7. $\sim N$	2, 5, MP
8. O	6, 7, DS
9. $M \supset O$	5–8, CP
10. $\sim M \lor O$	9, Impl
11. $L \supset (\sim M \lor O)$	3–10, CP

The rule introduced in connection with the previous example applies unchanged to examples of this sort. No line in the sequence 5–8 could be used to support any line subsequent to line 9, and no line in the sequence 3–10 could be used to support any line subsequent to line 11. Lines 3 or 4 could, of course, be used to support any line in the sequence 5–8.

One final reminder regarding conditional proof is that every conditional proof must be discharged. It is absolutely improper to end a proof on an indented line. If this rule is ignored, any conclusion one chooses can be derived from any set of premises. The following invalid proof illustrates this mistake:

1. P	/ $Q \supset R$
2. $\sim Q$	ACP
3. $\sim Q \lor R$	2, Add
4. $Q \supset R$	2, Impl

EXERCISE 7.5

iLrn I. Use conditional proof and the eighteen rules of inference to derive the conclusions of the following symbolized arguments. Having done so, attempt to derive the conclusions without using conditional proof.

   ★(1) 1. $N \supset O$
        2. $N \supset P$ / $N \supset (O \cdot P)$

(2) 1. $F \supset E$
    2. $(F \cdot E) \supset R$ / $F \supset R$

(3) 1. $G \supset T$
    2. $(T \lor S) \supset K$ / $G \supset K$

★(4) 1. $(G \lor H) \supset (S \cdot T)$
     2. $(T \lor U) \supset (C \cdot D)$ / $G \supset C$

(5) 1. $A \supset {\sim}(A \lor E)$ / $A \supset F$

(6) 1. $J \supset (K \supset L)$
    2. $J \supset (M \supset L)$
    3. ${\sim}L$ / $J \supset {\sim}(K \lor M)$

★(7) 1. $M \lor (N \cdot O)$ / ${\sim}N \supset M$

(8) 1. $P \supset (Q \lor R)$
    2. $(P \supset R) \supset (S \cdot T)$
    3. $Q \supset R$ / T

(9) 1. $H \supset (I \supset N)$
    2. $(H \supset {\sim}I) \supset (M \lor N)$
    3. ${\sim}N$ / M

★(10) 1. $C \supset (A \cdot D)$
      2. $B \supset (A \cdot E)$ / $(C \lor B) \supset A$

(11) 1. $M \supset (K \supset L)$
     2. $(L \lor N) \supset J$ / $M \supset (K \supset J)$

(12) 1. $F \supset (G \cdot H)$ / $(A \supset F) \supset (A \supset H)$

★(13) 1. $R \supset B$
      2. $R \supset (B \supset F)$
      3. $B \supset (F \supset H)$ / $R \supset H$

(14) 1. $(F \cdot G) \equiv H$
     2. $F \supset G$ / $F \equiv H$

(15) 1. $C \supset (D \lor {\sim}E)$
     2. $E \supset (D \supset F)$ / $C \supset (E \supset F)$

★(16) 1. $Q \supset (R \supset S)$
      2. $Q \supset (T \supset {\sim}U)$
      3. $U \supset (R \lor T)$ / $Q \supset (U \supset S)$

(17) 1. $N \supset (O \cdot P)$
     2. $Q \supset (R \cdot S)$ / $(P \supset Q) \supset (N \supset S)$

(18) 1. $E \supset (F \supset G)$
     2. $H \supset (G \supset I)$
     3. $(F \supset I) \supset (J \lor {\sim}H)$ / $(E \cdot H) \supset J$

★(19) 1. $P \supset [(L \lor M) \supset (N \cdot O)]$
      2. $(O \lor T) \supset W$ / $P \supset (M \supset W)$

(20) 1. $A \supset [B \supset (C \cdot {\sim}D)]$
     2. $(B \lor E) \supset (D \lor E)$ / $(A \cdot B) \supset (C \cdot E)$

II. Translate the following arguments into symbolic form, using the letters in the order in which they are listed. Then use conditional proof and the eighteen rules of inference to derive the conclusion of each. Having done so, attempt to derive the conclusion without using conditional proof.

★1. If high-tech products are exported to Russia, then domestic industries will benefit. If the Russians can effectively utilize high-tech products, then their standard of living will improve. Therefore, if high-tech products are exported to Russia and the Russians can effectively utilize them, then their standard of living will improve and domestic industries will benefit. (*H, D, U, S*)

2. If the police take you into custody, then if they inform you that you have the right to remain silent, then whatever you say will be used against you. If the police inform you that you have the right to remain silent, then if whatever you say will be used against you, then you should not say anything. Therefore, if the police take you into custody, then if they inform you that you have the right to remain silent, then you should not say anything. (*P, I, W, S*)

3. A doctor must disconnect a dying patient from a respirator if and only if the fact that patients are self-determining implies that the doctor must follow the patient's orders. If a dying patient refuses treatment, then the doctor must disconnect the patient from a respirator and the patient will die peacefully. Patients are self-determining. Therefore, if a dying patient refuses treatment, then the doctor must follow the patient's orders. (*D, S, F, R, P*)

★4. If jails are overcrowded, then dangerous suspects will be released on their own recognizance. If jails are overcrowded and dangerous suspects are released on their own recognizance, then crime will increase. If no new jails are built and crime increases, then innocent victims will pay the price of increased crime. Therefore, if jails are overcrowded, then if no new jails are built, then innocent victims will pay the price of increased crime. (*J, D, C, N, I*)

5. If astronauts attempt interplanetary space travel, then heavy shielding will be required to protect them from solar radiation. If massive amounts of either fuel or water are carried, then the spacecraft must be very large. Therefore, if heavy shielding is required to protect the astronauts from solar radiation only if massive amounts of fuel are carried, then if astronauts attempt interplanetary space travel, then the spacecraft must be very large. (*A, H, F, W, L*)

7.6   Indirect Proof

Indirect proof is a technique similar to conditional proof that can be used on any argument to derive either the conclusion or some intermediate line leading to the conclusion. It consists of assuming the negation of the statement form to be obtained, using this assumption to derive a contradiction, and then concluding that the original assumption is false. This last step, of course, establishes the truth of the statement form to be obtained. The following proof sequence uses indirect proof to derive the conclusion:

```
 1. (A ∨ B) ⊃ (C • D)
 2. C ⊃ ~D                / ~A
      3. A                 AIP
      4. A ∨ B             3, Add
      5. C • D             1, 4, MP
      6. C                 5, Simp
      7. ~D                2, 6, MP
      8. D • C             5, Com
      9. D                 8, Simp
     10. D • ~D            7, 9, Conj
 11. ~A                    3–10, IP
```

The indirect proof sequence (lines 3–10) begins by assuming the negation of the conclusion. Since the conclusion is a negated statement, it shortens the proof to assume A instead of ~~A. This assumption, which is tagged "AIP" (assumption for indirect proof), leads to a contradiction in line 10. Since any assumption that leads to a contradiction is false, the indirect sequence is discharged (line 11) by asserting the negation of the assumption made in line 3. This line is then tagged with the designation "IP" (indirect proof) together with the numerals indicating the scope of the indirect sequence from which it is obtained.

Indirect proof can also be used to derive an intermediate line leading to the conclusion. Example:

```
 1. E ⊃ [(F ∨ G) ⊃ (H • J)]
 2. E • ~(J ∨ K)          / ~(F ∨ K)
 3. E                     2, Simp
 4. (F ∨ G) ⊃ (H • J)     1, 3, MP
 5. ~(J ∨ K) • E          2, Com
 6. ~(J ∨ K)              5, Simp
 7. ~J • ~K               6, DM
      8. F                AIP
      9. F ∨ G            8, Add
     10. H • J            4, 9, MP
     11. J • H            10, Com
     12. J                11, Simp
     13. ~J               7, Simp
     14. J • ~J           12, 13, Conj
15. ~F                    8–14, IP
16. ~K • ~J               7, Com
17. ~K                    16, Simp
18. ~F • ~K               15, 17, Conj
19. ~(F ∨ K)              18, DM
```

The indirect proof sequence begins with the assumption of F (line 8), leads to a contradiction (line 14), and is discharged (line 15) by asserting the negation of the assumption. One should consider indirect proof whenever a line in a proof appears difficult to obtain.

As with conditional proof, when an indirect proof sequence is discharged, no line in the sequence may be used as a justification for a subsequent line in the proof. In reference to the above proof, this means that none of the lines 8–14 could be used as a justification for any of the lines 16–19. Occasionally, this rule requires certain priorities in the derivation of lines. For example, for the purpose of deriving the contradiction, lines 6 and 7 could have been included as part of the indirect sequence. But this would not have been advisable because line 7 is needed as a justification for line 16, which lies outside the indirect sequence. If lines 6 and 7 had been included within the indirect sequence, they would have had to be repeated after the sequence had been discharged to allow ~K to be obtained on a line outside the sequence.

Just as a conditional sequence may be constructed within the scope of another conditional sequence, so a conditional sequence can be constructed within the scope of an indirect sequence, and, conversely, an indirect sequence may be constructed within the scope of either a conditional sequence or another indirect sequence. The next example illustrates the use of an indirect sequence within the scope of a conditional sequence:

1. $L \supset [\sim M \supset (N \cdot O)]$		
2. $\sim N \cdot P$		/ $L \supset (M \cdot P)$
3. L		ACP
4. $\sim M \supset (N \cdot O)$		1, 3, MP
5. $\sim M$		AIP
6. $N \cdot O$		4, 5, MP
7. N		6, Simp
8. $\sim N$		2, Simp
9. $N \cdot \sim N$		7, 8, Conj
10. $\sim\sim M$		5–9, IP
11. M		10, DN
12. $P \cdot \sim N$		2, Com
13. P		12, Simp
14. $M \cdot P$		11, 13, Conj
15. $L \supset (M \cdot P)$		3–14, CP

The indirect sequence (lines 5–9) is discharged (line 10) by asserting the negation of the assumption made in line 5. The conditional sequence (lines 3–14) is discharged (line 15) in the conditional statement that has the first line of the sequence as its antecedent and the last line as its consequent.

Indirect proof provides a convenient way for proving the validity of an argument having a tautology for its conclusion. In fact, the only way in which the conclusion of many such arguments can be derived is through either conditional or indirect proof.

For the following argument, indirect proof is the easier of the two:

1. S	/ $T \vee \sim T$
2. $\sim(T \vee \sim T)$	AIP
3. $\sim T \cdot \sim\sim T$	2, DM
4. $\sim\sim(T \vee \sim T)$	2–3, IP
5. $T \vee \sim T$	4, DN

Here is another example of an argument having a tautology as its conclusion. In this case, since the conclusion is a conditional statement, conditional proof is the easier alternative:

1. S	/ $T \supset T$
2. T	ACP
3. $T \vee T$	2, Add
4. T	3, Taut
5. $T \supset T$	2–4, CP

The similarity of indirect proof to conditional proof may be illustrated by returning to the first example presented in this section. In the proof that follows, conditional proof—not indirect proof—is used to obtain the conclusion:

```
1. (A v B) ⊃ (C • D)
2. C ⊃ ~D                    / ~A
    3. A                     ACP
    4. A v B                 3, Add
    5. C • D                 1, 4, MP
    6. C                     5, Simp
    7. ~D                    2, 6, MP
    8. D • C                 5, Com
    9. D                     8, Simp
   10. D v ~A                9, Add
   11. ~A                    7, 10, DS
12. A ⊃ ~A                   3–11, CP
13. ~A v ~A                  12, Impl
14. ~A                       13, Taut
```

This example illustrates how a conditional proof can be used to derive the conclusion of *any* argument, whether or not the conclusion is a conditional statement. Simply begin by assuming the negation of the conclusion, derive contradictory statements on separate lines, and use these lines to set up a disjunctive syllogism yielding the negation of the assumption as the last line of the conditional sequence. Then, discharge the sequence and use tautology to obtain the negation of the assumption outside the sequence.

Indirect proof can be viewed as a variety of conditional proof in that it amounts to a modification of the way in which the indented sequence is discharged, resulting in an overall shortening of the proof for many arguments. The indirect proof for the argument above is repeated below, with the requisite changes noted in the margin:

```
1. (A v B) ⊃ (C • D)
2. C ⊃ ~D                    / ~A
    3. A                     AIP
    4. A v B                 3, Add
    5. C • D                 1, 4, MP
    6. C                     5, Simp
    7. ~D                    2, 6, MP
    8. D • C                 5, Com
    9. D                     8, Simp
   10. D • ~D                7, 9, Conj ⎫
11. ~A                       3–10, IP   ⎬——— changed
                                        ⎭
```

The reminder at the end of the previous section regarding conditional proof pertains to indirect proof as well: It is essential that every indirect proof be discharged. No proof can be ended on an indented line. If this rule is ignored, indirect proof, like conditional proof, can produce any conclusion whatsoever. The following invalid proof illustrates such a mistake:

```
1. P                         / Q
    2. Q                     AIP
    3. Q v Q                 2, Add
    4. Q                     3, Taut
```

iLrn I. Use either indirect proof or conditional proof (or both) and the eighteen rules of inference to derive the conclusions of the following symbolized arguments. Having done so, attempt to derive the conclusions without using indirect proof or conditional proof.

★(1) 1. $(S \lor T) \supset \sim S$ / $\sim S$

(2) 1. $(K \supset K) \supset R$
     2. $(R \lor M) \supset N$ / N

(3) 1. $(C \cdot D) \supset E$
     2. $(D \cdot E) \supset F$ / $(C \cdot D) \supset F$

★(4) 1. $H \supset (L \supset K)$
      2. $L \supset (K \supset \sim L)$ / $\sim H \lor \sim L$

(5) 1. $S \supset (T \lor \sim U)$
     2. $U \supset (\sim T \lor R)$
     3. $(S \cdot U) \supset \sim R$ / $\sim S \lor \sim U$

(6) 1. $\sim A \supset (B \cdot C)$
     2. $D \supset \sim C$ / $D \supset A$

★(7) 1. $(E \lor F) \supset (C \cdot D)$
      2. $(D \lor G) \supset H$
      3. $E \lor G$ / H

(8) 1. $\sim M \supset (N \cdot O)$
     2. $N \supset P$
     3. $O \supset \sim P$ / M

(9) 1. $(R \lor S) \supset T$
     2. $(P \lor Q) \supset T$
     3. $R \lor P$ / T

★(10) 1. K / $S \supset (T \supset S)$

(11) 1. $(A \lor B) \supset C$
      2. $(\sim A \lor D) \supset E$ / $C \lor E$

(12) 1. $(K \lor L) \supset (M \cdot N)$
      2. $(N \lor O) \supset (P \cdot \sim K)$ / $\sim K$

★(13) 1. $[C \supset (D \supset C)] \supset E$ / E

(14) 1. F / $(G \supset H) \lor (\sim G \supset J)$

(15) 1. $B \supset (K \cdot M)$
      2. $(B \cdot M) \supset (P \equiv \sim P)$ / $\sim B$

★(16) 1. $(N \lor O) \supset (C \cdot D)$
       2. $(D \lor K) \supset (P \lor \sim C)$
       3. $(P \lor G) \supset \sim (N \cdot D)$ / $\sim N$

(17) 1. $(R \cdot S) \equiv (G \cdot H)$
      2. $R \supset S$
      3. $H \supset G$ / $R \equiv H$

(18) 1. $K \supset [(M \lor N) \supset (P \cdot Q)]$
    2. $L \supset [(Q \lor R) \supset (S \cdot \sim N)]$ / $(K \cdot L) \supset \sim N$

★(19) 1. $A \supset [(N \lor \sim N) \supset (S \lor T)]$
    2. $T \supset \sim (F \lor \sim F)$ / $A \supset S$

(20) 1. $F \supset [(C \supset C) \supset G]$
    2. $G \supset \{[H \supset (E \supset H)] \supset (K \cdot \sim K)\}$ / $\sim F$

iLrn II. Translate the following arguments into symbolic form, using the letters in the order in which they are listed. Then use indirect proof and the eighteen rules of inference to derive the conclusion of each. Having done so, attempt to derive the conclusion without using indirect proof.

★1. If government deficits continue at their present rate and a recession sets in, then interest on the national debt will become unbearable and the government will default on its loans. If a recession sets in, then the government will not default on its loans. Therefore, either government deficits will not continue at their present rate or a recession will not set in. (*C, R, I, D*)

2. If either the sea turtle population continues to decrease or rescue efforts are commenced to save the sea turtle from extinction, then nesting sanctuaries will be created and the indiscriminate slaughter of these animals will be halted. If either nesting sanctuaries are created or poachers are arrested, then if the indiscriminate slaughter of these animals is halted, then the sea turtle population will not continue to decrease. Therefore, the sea turtle population will not continue to decrease. (*C, R, N, I, P*)

3. If asbestos workers sue their employers, then if punitive damages are awarded, then their employers will declare bankruptcy. If asbestos workers sue their employers, then punitive damages will be awarded. If asbestos workers contract asbestosis, then either they will sue their employers or their employers will declare bankruptcy. Therefore, either asbestos workers will not contract asbestosis or their employers will declare bankruptcy. (*S, P, B, C*)

★4. If astronauts spend long periods in zero gravity only if calcium is resorbed in their bodies, then astronauts on a Mars voyage will arrive with brittle bones. If astronauts attempt a voyage to Mars only if they spend long periods in zero gravity, then astronauts on a Mars voyage will arrive with brittle bones. Therefore, astronauts on a Mars voyage will arrive with brittle bones. (*Z, C, B, V*)

5. Either deposits should be required on beer and soft drink containers, or these containers will be discarded along highways and the countryside will look like a dump. If these containers will be discarded either in parks or along highways, then deposits should be required on soft drink containers. Therefore, deposits should be required on soft drink containers. (*B, S, H, C, P*)

7.7   Proving Logical Truths

Both conditional and indirect proof can be used to establish the truth of a tautology (logical truth). Tautological statements can be treated as if they were the conclusions of arguments having no premises. Such a procedure is suggested by the fact that any argument having a tautology for its conclusion is valid regardless of what its premises are. As we saw in the previous section, the proof for such an argument does not use the premises at all but derives the conclusion as the exclusive consequence of either a conditional or an indirect sequence. Using this strategy for logical truths, we write the statement to be proved as if it were the conclusion of an argument, and we indent the first line in the proof and tag it as being the beginning of either a conditional or an indirect sequence. In the end, this sequence is appropriately discharged to yield the desired statement form.

Tautologies expressed in the form of conditional statements are most easily proved via a conditional sequence. The following example utilizes two such sequences, one within the scope of the other:

$$/ \ P \supset (Q \supset P)$$

1. P		ACP
	2. Q	ACP
	3. $P \lor P$	1, Add
	4. P	3, Taut
5. $Q \supset P$		2–4, CP
6. $P \supset (Q \supset P)$		1–5, CP

Notice that line 6 restores the proof to the original margin—the first line is indented because it introduces the conditional sequence.

Here is a proof of the same statement using an indirect proof. The indirect sequence begins, as usual, with the negation of the statement to be proved:

$$/ \ P \supset (Q \supset P)$$

1. $\sim[P \supset (Q \supset P)]$	AIP
2. $\sim[\sim P \lor (Q \supset P)]$	1, Impl
3. $\sim[\sim P \lor (\sim Q \lor P)]$	2, Impl
4. $\sim\sim P \cdot \sim(\sim Q \lor P)$	3, DM
5. $P \cdot \sim(\sim Q \lor P)$	4, DN
6. $P \cdot (\sim\sim Q \cdot \sim P)$	5, DM
7. $P \cdot (\sim P \cdot \sim\sim Q)$	6, Com
8. $(P \cdot \sim P) \cdot \sim\sim Q$	7, Assoc
9. $P \cdot \sim P$	8, Simp
10. $\sim\sim[P \supset (Q \supset P)]$	1–9, IP
11. $P \supset (Q \supset P)$	10, DN

More complex conditional statements are proved by merely extending the technique used in the first proof above. In the proof that follows, notice how each conditional sequence begins by asserting the antecedent of the conditional statement to be obtained:

$$/ \ [P \supset (Q \supset R)] \supset [(P \supset Q) \supset (P \supset R)]$$

1. $P \supset (Q \supset R)$			ACP
	2. $P \supset Q$		ACP
		3. P	ACP
		4. $Q \supset R$	1, 3, MP
		5. Q	2, 3, MP
		6. R	4, 5, MP
	7. $P \supset R$		3–6, CP
8. $(P \supset Q) \supset (P \supset R)$			2–7, CP
9. $[P \supset (Q \supset R)] \supset [(P \supset Q) \supset (P \supset R)]$			1–8, CP

Tautologies expressed as equivalences are usually proved using two conditional sequences, one after the other. Example:

/ $P \equiv [P \cdot (Q \supset P)]$

1. P	ACP
2. $P \vee \sim Q$	1, Add
3. $\sim Q \vee P$	2, Com
4. $Q \supset P$	3, Impl
5. $P \cdot (Q \supset P)$	1, 4, Conj
6. $P \supset [P \cdot (Q \supset P)]$	1–5, CP
7. $P \cdot (Q \supset P)$	ACP
8. P	7, Simp
9. $[P \cdot (Q \supset P)] \supset P$	7–8, CP
10. {line 6} $\cdot$ {line 9}	6, 9, Conj
11. $P \equiv [P \cdot (Q \supset P)]$	10, Equiv

EXERCISE 7.7

iLrn Use conditional proof or indirect proof and the eighteen rules of inference to establish the truth of the following tautologies:

★1. $P \supset [(P \supset Q) \supset Q]$

2. $(\sim P \supset Q) \vee (P \supset R)$

3. $P \equiv [P \vee (Q \cdot P)]$

★4. $(P \supset Q) \supset [(P \cdot R) \supset (Q \cdot R)]$

5. $(P \vee \sim Q) \supset [(\sim P \vee R) \supset (Q \supset R)]$

6. $P \equiv [P \cdot (Q \vee \sim Q)]$

★7. $(P \supset Q) \vee (\sim Q \supset P)$

8. $(P \supset Q) \equiv [P \supset (P \cdot Q)]$

9. $[(P \supset Q) \cdot (P \supset R)] \supset [P \supset (Q \cdot R)]$

★10. $[\sim(P \cdot \sim Q) \cdot \sim Q] \supset \sim P$

11. $(P \supset Q) \vee (Q \supset P)$

12. $[P \supset (Q \supset R)] \equiv [Q \supset (P \supset R)]$

★13. $(P \supset Q) \supset [(P \supset \sim Q) \supset \sim P]$

14. $[(P \supset Q) \supset R] \supset [(R \supset \sim R) \supset P]$

15. $(\sim P \vee Q) \supset [(P \vee \sim Q) \supset (P \equiv Q)]$

★16. $\sim[(P \supset \sim P) \cdot (\sim P \supset P)]$

17. $P \supset [(Q \cdot \sim Q) \supset R]$

18. $[(P \cdot Q) \vee R] \supset [(\sim R \vee Q) \supset (P \supset Q)]$

★19. $P \equiv [P \vee (Q \cdot \sim Q)]$

20. $P \supset [Q \equiv (P \supset Q)]$

Summary

Natural deduction is a method for establishing the validity of arguments symbolized in terms of the five logical operators. The method consists in applying one or more rules of inference to the premises and deriving the conclusion as the last line in a sequence of lines. By studying such a derivation, one can see exactly how the premises imply the conclusion. Success in using the rules of inference depends on an intimate familiarity with the rules themselves and a working knowledge of how one rule can be used in conjunction with other rules.

The eight rules of implication are "one-way" rules because the premises of each rule can be used to derive the conclusion, but the conclusion cannot be used to derive the premises. On the other hand, the ten rules of replacement are "two-way" rules. These rules are expressed as logical equivalences, and the axiom of replacement states that logically equivalent expressions may replace each other in a proof. Thus, if one of these rules is used to derive a conclusion, the process can be reversed, and the rule can be used to derive the premise. This fact allows us to use the rules of replacement to "deconstruct" the conclusion for insight into how best to derive it in a proof sequence.

Conditional proof is a simple procedure for deriving a line in a proof sequence—either the conclusion or some other line. The procedure consists in assuming a certain statement as the first line in a conditional sequence, using that line to derive one or more additional lines, and then discharging the conditional sequence in a conditional statement having the first line of that sequence as antecedent and the last line as consequent. The procedure expresses the basic idea that if the antecedent of a true conditional statement is true, then so is the consequent.

Indirect proof is another simple procedure for deriving a line in a proof sequence. It consists in assuming the negation of the line to be obtained as the first line in an indirect sequence, using that line to derive a contradiction, and then discharging the indirect sequence in a statement that is the negation of the first line in that sequence. The procedure expresses the idea that any assumption that necessarily leads to a contradiction is false.

Natural deduction can also be used to prove logical truths. The technique employs conditional proof and indirect proof. Conditional proof is often used for logical truths expressed as conditionals. The antecedent of the logical truth is assumed as the first line of a conditional sequence, the consequent is derived, and the sequence is then discharged in a statement that expresses the logical truth to be proved. Indirect proof can be used for proving any logical truth. The negation of the logical truth is assumed as the first line of an indirect sequence, a contradiction is derived, and the sequence is then discharged in a statement consisting of the negation of the first line in that sequence.

7

Predicate Logic

8.1 Symbols and Translation

Techniques were developed in earlier chapters for evaluating two basically different kinds of arguments. The chapter on categorical syllogisms dealt with arguments such as the following:

> All student hookups are quickie sexual encounters.
> No quickie sexual encounters are committed relationships.
> Therefore, no student hookups are committed relationships.

In such arguments the fundamental components are *terms*, and the validity of the argument depends on the arrangement of the terms within the premises and conclusion.

The chapter on propositional logic, on the other hand, dealt with arguments such as this:

> If chronic stress is reduced, then relaxation increases and health improves.
> If health improves, then people live longer.
> Therefore, if chronic stress is reduced, then people live longer.

In such arguments the fundamental components are not terms but *statements*. The validity of these arguments depends not on the arrangement of the terms within the statements but on the arrangement of the statements themselves as simple units.

Not all arguments, however, can be assigned to one or the other of these two groups. There is a third type that is a kind of hybrid, sharing features with both categorical syllogisms and propositional arguments. Consider, for example, the following:

> Julia Roberts is rich and beautiful.
> If a woman is either rich or famous, she is happy.
> Therefore, Julia Roberts is happy.

The validity of this argument depends both on the arrangement of the terms and on the arrangement of the statements. Accordingly, neither syllogistic logic nor propositional logic alone is sufficient to establish its validity. What is needed is a third kind of logic that combines the distinctive features of syllogistic logic and propositional logic. This third kind is called **predicate logic.**

The fundamental component in predicate logic is the **predicate,** symbolized by upper-case letters (A, B, C, . . . X, Y, Z). Here are some examples of bare predicates:

English predicate	Symbolic predicate
___ is a rabbit	R___
___ is gigantic	G___
___ is a doctor	D___
___ is helpless	H___

The blank space immediately following the predicate letter is not part of the predicate; rather, it indicates the place for some lower-case letter that will represent the subject of the statement. Depending on what lower-case letter is used, and on the additional symbolism involved, symbolic predicates may be used to translate three distinct kinds of statements: singular statements, universal statements, and particular statements.

A **singular statement,** you may recall from Section 4.7, is a statement that makes an assertion about a specifically named person, place, thing, or time. Translating a singular statement involves writing a lower-case letter corresponding to the subject of the statement to the immediate right of the upper-case letter corresponding to the predicate. The letters that are allocated to serve as names of individuals are the first twenty-three letters of the alphabet (a, b, c, . . . u, v, w). These letters are called **individual constants.** Here are some examples of translated statements:

Statement	Symbolic translation
Socrates is mortal.	Ms
Tokyo is populous.	Pt
The *Sun-Times* is a newspaper.	Ns
King Lear is not a fairy tale.	$\sim Fk$
Berlioz was not a German.	$\sim Gb$

Compound arrangements of singular statements may be translated by using the familiar connectives of propositional logic. Here are some examples:

Statement	Symbolic translation
If Paris is beautiful, then Andre told the truth.	$B \supset Ta$
Irene is either a doctor or a lawyer.	$Di \lor Li$
Senator Wilkins will be elected only if he campaigns.	$Ew \supset Cw$
General Motors will prosper if either Nissan is crippled by a strike or Subaru declares bankruptcy.	$(Cn \lor Ds) \supset Pg$
Indianapolis gets rain if and only if Chicago and Milwaukee get snow.	$Ri \equiv (Sc \cdot Sm)$

A **universal statement** is a statement that makes an assertion about every member of its subject class. Such statements are either affirmative or negative, depending on whether the statement affirms or denies that the members of the subject class are members of the predicate class. The key to translating universal statements is provided by the Boolean interpretation of these statements (see Section 4.3):

Statement form	Boolean interpretation
All S are P.	If anything is an S, then it is a P.
No S are P.	If anything is an S, then it is not a P.

According to the Boolean interpretation, universal statements are translated as conditionals. Now that we have a symbol (the horseshoe "⊃") to translate conditional statements, we may use it to translate universal statements. What is still needed, however, is a symbol to indicate that universal statements make an assertion about *every* member of the S class. This symbol, which we introduce now, is called the **universal quantifier.** It is formed by placing a lower-case letter in parentheses, (x), and is translated as "for any x." The letters that are allocated for forming the universal quantifier are the last three letters of the alphabet (x, y, z). These letters are called **individual variables.**

The horseshoe operator and the universal quantifier are combined to translate universal statements as follows:

Statement form	Symbolic translation	Verbal meaning
All S are P.	$(x)(Sx \supset Px)$	For any x, if x is an S, then x is a P.
No S are P.	$(x)(Sx \supset {\sim}Px)$	For any x, if x is an S, then x is not a P.

An individual variable differs from an individual constant in that it can stand for any item at random in the universe. Accordingly, the expression $(x)(Sx \supset Px)$ means "If anything is an S, then it is a P," and $(x)(Sx \supset {\sim}Px)$ means "If anything is an S, then it is not a P." The fact that these expressions are equivalent to the Boolean interpretation of universal statements may be seen by recalling how the Boolean interpretation is represented by Venn diagrams (see Section 4.3). The Venn diagrams corresponding to the two universal statement forms are as follows:

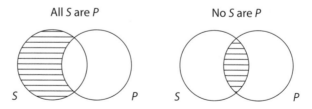

Where shading designates emptiness, the diagram on the left asserts that if anything is in the S circle, it is also in the P circle, and the one on the right asserts that if anything is in the S circle, it is not in the P circle. This is exactly what is asserted by the symbolic expressions above. These symbolic expressions may therefore be taken as being exactly synonymous with the Boolean interpretation of universal statements.

A possible source of confusion at this point concerns the fact that both S and P in the symbolic expressions are predicates, whereas in the original statement forms S is the subject and P is the predicate. Any problem in this regard vanishes, however, once one understands what happens when universal statements are converted into conditionals. When so converted, S becomes the predicate of the antecedent and P becomes the predicate of the consequent. In other words, in the conditional "If anything is an S, then it is a P," both S and P are predicates. Thus, using predicate symbolism to translate universal statements leads to no difficulties. When translating these statements, the point to remember is simply this: The subject of the original statement is represented by a capital letter in the antecedent, and the predicate by a capital letter in the consequent. Here are some examples:

Statement	Symbolic translation
All skyscrapers are tall.	$(x)(Sx \supset Tx)$
No frogs are birds.	$(x)(Fx \supset {\sim}Bx)$
All ambassadors are statesmen.	$(x)(Ax \supset Sx)$
No diamonds are rubies.	$(x)(Dx \supset {\sim}Rx)$

In these examples, the expressions $Sx \supset Tx$, $Fx \supset {\sim}Bx$, and so on are called **statement functions.** A statement function is a mere pattern for a statement. It makes no definite assertion about anything in the universe, has no truth value, and cannot be translated as a statement. The variables that occur in statement functions are called **free variables** because they are not bound by any quantifier. In contrast, the variables that occur in statements are called **bound variables.**

In using quantifiers to translate statements, we adopt a convention similar to the one adopted for the tilde operator. That is, the quantifier governs only the expression immediately following it. For example, in the statement $(x)(Ax \supset Bx)$ the universal quantifier governs the entire statement function in parentheses—namely, $Ax \supset Bx$. But in the expression $(x)Ax \supset Bx$, the universal quantifier governs only the statement function Ax. The same convention is adopted for the existential quantifier, which will be introduced presently.

Particular statements are statements that make an assertion about one or more unnamed members of the subject class. As with universal statements, particular statements are either affirmative or negative, depending on whether the statement affirms or denies that members of the subject class are members of the predicate class. Also, as with universal statements, the key to translating particular statements is provided by the Boolean interpretation:

Statement form	Boolean interpretation
Some S are P.	At least one thing is an S and it is also a P.
Some S are not P.	At least one thing is an S and it is not a P.

In other words, particular statements are translated as conjunctions. Since we are already familiar with the symbol for conjunction (the dot), the only additional symbol that we need in order to translate these statements is a symbol for existence. This is provided by the **existential quantifier,** formed by placing a variable to the right of a backward E in parentheses, thus: $(\exists x)$. This symbol is translated "there exists an x such that." The existential quantifier is combined with the dot operator to translate particular statements as follows:

Statement form	Symbolic translation	Verbal meaning
Some S are P.	$(\exists x)(Sx \cdot Px)$	There exists an x such that x is an S and x is a P.
Some S are not P.	$(\exists x)(Sx \cdot \sim Px)$	There exists an x such that x is an S and x is not a P.

As in the symbolic expression of universal statements, the letter x is an individual variable, which can stand for any item in the universe. Accordingly, the expression $(\exists x)(Sx \cdot Px)$ means "Something exists that is both an S and a P," and $(\exists x)(Sx \cdot \sim Px)$ means "Something exists that is an S and not a P." To see the equivalence of these expressions with the Boolean (and Aristotelian) interpretation of particular statements, it is again useful to recall how these statements are represented by Venn diagrams:

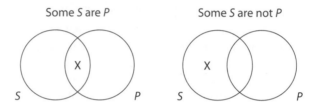

Where the X designates at least one existing item, the diagram on the left asserts that something exists that is both an S and a P, and the one on the right asserts that something exists that is an S and not a P. In other words, these diagrams assert exactly the same thing as the symbolic expressions above. These symbolic expressions, therefore, exactly express the Boolean (and Aristotelian) interpretation of particular statements. Here are some examples:

Statement	Symbolic translation
Some men are paupers.	$(\exists x)(Mx \cdot Px)$
Some diseases are not contagious.	$(\exists x)(Dx \cdot \sim Cx)$
Some jobs are boring.	$(\exists x)(Jx \cdot Bx)$
Some vehicles are not motorcycles.	$(\exists x)(Vx \cdot \sim Mx)$

The general rule to follow in translating statements in predicate logic is always to make an effort to understand the meaning of the statement to be translated. If the statement makes an assertion about every member of its subject class, a universal quantifier should be used to translate it; but if it makes an assertion about only one or more members of this class, an existential quantifier should be used.

Many of the principles developed in syllogistic logic (see Section 4.7) may be carried over into predicate logic. Specifically, it should be understood that statements beginning with the words *only* and *none but* are exclusive propositions. When these statements are translated, the term occurring first in the original statement becomes the consequent in the symbolic expression, and the term occurring second becomes the antecedent. One of the few differences in this respect between predicate logic and syllogistic logic concerns singular statements. In syllogistic logic singular statements are translated as universals, while in predicate logic, as we have seen, they are translated in a unique way. Here are some examples of a variety of statements:

Statement	Symbolic translation
There are happy marriages.	$(\exists x)(Mx \cdot Hx)$
Every pediatrician loses sleep.	$(x)(Px \supset Lx)$
Animals exist.	$(\exists x)Ax$
Unicorns do not exist.	$\sim(\exists x)Ux$
Anything is conceivable	$(x)Cx$
Sea lions are mammals.	$(x)(Sx \supset Mx)$
Sea lions live in these caves.	$(\exists x)(Sx \cdot Lx)$
Egomaniacs are not pleasant companions.	$(x)(Ex \supset \sim Px)$
A few egomaniacs did not arrive on time.	$(\exists x)(Fx \cdot \sim Ax)$
Only close friends were invited to the wedding.	$(x)(Ix \supset Cx)$
None but citizens are eligible to vote.	$(x)(Ex \supset Cx)$
It is not the case that every Girl Scout sells cookies.	$\sim(x)(Gx \supset Sx)$ or $(\exists x)(Gx \cdot \sim Sx)$
Not a single psychologist attended the convention.	$\sim(\exists x)(Px \cdot Ax)$ or $(x)(Px \supset \sim Ax)$

As these examples illustrate, the general procedure in translating statements in predicate logic is to render universal statements as conditionals preceded by a universal quantifier, and particular statements as conjunctions preceded by an existential quantifier. However, as the third and fifth examples indicate, there are exceptions to this procedure. A statement that makes an assertion about literally everything in the universe is translated in terms of a single predicate preceded by a universal quantifier, and a statement that asserts that some class of things simply exists is translated in terms of a single predicate preceded by an existential quantifier. The last two examples illustrate the fact that a particular statement is equivalent to a negated universal, and vice versa. The first of these is equivalent to "Some Girl Scouts do not sell cookies" and the second to "No psychologists attended the convention." Actually, any quantified statement can be translated using either a universal or an existential quantifier, provided that one of them is negated. The equivalence of these two forms of expression will be analyzed further in Section 8.3.

More complex statements may be translated by following the basic rules just presented. Examples:

Statement	Symbolic translation
1. Only snakes and lizards thrive in the desert.	$(x)[Tx \supset (Sx \lor Lx)]$
2. Oranges and lemons are citrus fruits.	$(x)[(Ox \lor Lx) \supset Cx]$
3. Ripe apples are crunchy and delicious.	$(x)[(Rx \cdot Ax) \supset (Cx \cdot Dx)]$
4. Azaleas bloom if and only if they are fertilized.	$(x)[Ax \supset (Bx \equiv Fx)]$
5. Peaches are edible unless they are rotten.	$(x)[Px \supset (\sim Rx \supset Ex)]$ or $(x)[Px \supset (Ex \lor Rx)]$
6. Cats and dogs bite if they are frightened or harassed.	$(x)\{(Cx \lor Dx) \supset [(Fx \lor Hx) \supset Bx]\}$

Notice that the first example is translated in terms of the disjunction $Sx \lor Lx$ even though the English statement reads "snakes *and* lizards." If the translation were rendered as $(x)[Tx \supset (Sx \cdot Lx)]$ it would mean that anything that thrives in the desert is both a snake and a lizard (at the same time). And this is surely *not* what is meant. For the same reason, the second example is translated in terms of the disjunction $Ox \lor Lx$ even though the English reads "oranges *and* lemons." If the statement were translated $(x)[(Ox \cdot Lx) \supset Cx]$, it would mean that anything that is simultaneously an orange and a lemon (and there are none of these) is a citrus fruit. The same principle is used in translating the sixth example, which, incidentally, reads "If anything is a cat or a dog, then if it is frightened or harassed, it bites." The third example employs the conjunction $Rx \cdot Ax$ to translate ripe apples. This, of course, is correct, because such a thing is both ripe and an apple at the same time. The fifth example illustrates the fact that "unless" may be translated as either "if not" or "or."

The operators of propositional logic can be used to form compound arrangements of universal and particular statements, just as they can be used to form compound arrangements of singular statements. Here are some examples:

Statement	Symbolic translation
If Elizabeth is a historian, then some women are historians.	$He \supset (\exists x)(Wx \cdot Hx)$
If some cellists are music directors, then some orchestras are properly led.	$(\exists x)(Cx \cdot Mx) \supset (\exists x)(Ox \cdot Px)$

Statement	Symbolic translation
Either everything is alive or Bergson's theory is not correct.	$(x)Ax \lor {\sim}Cb$
All novels are interesting if and only if some Steinbeck novels are not romances.	$(x)(Nx \supset Ix) \equiv (\exists x)[(Nx \cdot Sx) \cdot {\sim}Rx)]$
Green avocados are never purchased unless all the ripe ones are expensive.	$(x)[(Gx \cdot Ax) \supset {\sim}Px] \lor (x)[(Rx \cdot Ax) \supset Ex]$

We have seen that the general procedure is to translate universal statements as conditionals preceded by a universal quantifier, and to translate particular statements as conjunctions preceded by an existential quantifier. Let us see what happens to these translations when they are preceded by the wrong quantifier. Consider the false statement "No cats are animals." This is correctly translated $(x)(Cx \supset {\sim}Ax)$. If, however, it were translated $(\exists x)(Cx \supset {\sim}Ax)$, the symbolic statement would turn out to be true. This may be seen as follows. $(\exists x)(Cx \supset {\sim}Ax)$ is equivalent via material implication to $(\exists x)({\sim}Cx \lor {\sim}Ax)$, which in turn is equivalent via DeMorgan's Rule to $(\exists x){\sim}(Cx \cdot Ax)$. The latter statement, however, merely asserts that something exists that is not both a cat and an animal—for example, a dog—which is true. Again, consider the true statement "Some cats are animals." This is correctly translated $(\exists x)(Cx \cdot Ax)$. If, however, it were translated $(x)(Cx \cdot Ax)$, the symbolic statement would assert that everything in the universe is both a cat and an animal, which is clearly false. Thus, as these examples illustrate, it is imperative that the two quantifiers not be confused with each other.

One final observation needs to be made. It was mentioned earlier that the letters x, y, and z are reserved for use as variables for translating universal and particular statements. In accord with this convention, the other twenty-three lower-case letters (a, b, c, ... u, v, w) may be used as names for translating singular statements. Thus, for example, "Albert is a scientist" is translated Sa. But a question naturally arises with statements such as "Xerxes was a king." Should this statement be translated Kx? The answer is no. Some other letter, for example the second letter in the name, should be selected instead of x. Maintaining this alphabetical convention will help us avoid mistakes in the next section when we use natural deduction to derive the conclusions of arguments.

EXERCISE 8.1

iLrn Translate the following statements into symbolic form. Avoid negation signs preceding quantifiers. The predicate letters are given in parentheses.

★ 1. Elaine is a chemist. (C) Ce

2. Nancy is not a sales clerk. (S) ${\sim}SN$

3. Neither Wordsworth nor Shelley was Irish. (I) ${\sim}(Iw \supset Is)$

★ 4. Rachel is either a journalist or a newscaster. (J, N) $Jr \lor Nr$

5. Intel designs a faster chip only if Micron does. (D)

6. Belgium and France subsidize the arts only if Austria or Germany expand museum holdings. (S, E)

★ 7. All maples are trees. (*M*, *T*) $(x)(Mx \supset Tx)$

8. Some grapes are sour. (*G*, *S*)

9. No novels are biographies. (*N*, *B*)

★ 10. Some holidays are not relaxing. (*H*, *R*) $(\exists x)(Hx \cdot \sim Rx)$

11. If Gertrude is correct, then the Taj Mahal is made of marble. (*C*, *M*)

12. Gertrude is not correct only if the Taj Mahal is made of granite. (*C*, *G*)

★ 13. Tigers exist. (*T*) $(\exists x) Tx$

14. Anything that leads to violence is wrong. (*L*, *W*)

15. There are pornographic art works. (*A*, *P*)

★ 16. Not every smile is genuine. (*S*, *G*) $(\exists x)(Sx \cdot \sim Gx)$

17. Every penguin loves ice. (*P*, *L*)

18. There is trouble in River City. (*T*, *R*)

★ 19. Whoever is a socialite is vain. (*S*, *V*) $(\exists x)(Sx \cdot Vx)$

20. Any caring mother is vigilant and nurturing. (*C*, *M*, *V*, *N*)

21. Terrorists are neither rational nor empathic. (*T*, *R*, *E*)

★ 22. Nobody consumed by jealousy is happy. (*C*, *H*)

23. Everything is imaginable. (*I*)

24. Ghosts do not exist. (*G*)

★ 25. A thoroughbred is a horse. (*T*, *H*) $(x)(Tx \supset Hx)$

26. A thoroughbred won the race. (*T*, *W*)

27. Not all mushrooms are edible. (*M*, *E*)

★ 28. Not any horse chestnuts are edible. (*H*, *E*) $(\exists x)(Hx \cdot \sim Ex)$

29. A few guests arrived late. (*G*, *A*)

30. None but gentlemen prefer blondes. (*G*, *P*)

★ 31. A few cities are neither safe nor beautiful. (*C*, *S*, *B*) $(\exists x)(Cx \supset \sim (Sx \supset Bx))$

32. There are no circular triangles. (*C*, *T*)

33. Snakes are harmless unless they have fangs. (*S*, *H*, *F*)

★ 34. Some dogs bite if and only if they are teased. (*D*, *B*, *T*) $(\exists x)[(Dx \cdot Bx) \equiv Ty]$

35. An airliner is safe if and only if it is properly maintained. (*A*, *S*, *P*)

36. Some companies go bankrupt if sales decline. (*C*, *B*, *S*)

★ 37. Some children act up only if they are tired. (*C*, *A*, *T*) $(\exists x)[(Cx \cdot Ax) \lor Tx]$

38. The only musicians that are available are trombonists. (*M*, *A*, *T*)

39. Only talented musicians perform in the symphony. (*T*, *M*, *P*)

★ 40. Any well-made car runs smoothly. (*W*, *C*, *R*) $(x)((Wx \cdot Cr) \supset Rx)$

41. Not every foreign car runs smoothly. (*F*, *C*, *R*)

42. A good violin is rare and expensive. (*G*, *V*, *R*, *E*)

★ 43. Violins and cellos are stringed instruments. (*V*, *C*, *S*, *I*) $(x)[(Vx \lor Cx) \supset (Sx \cdot Ix)]$

44. A room with a view is available. (*R*, *V*, *A*)

8

45. A room with a view is expensive. (*R, V, E*)

★ 46. Some French restaurants are exclusive. (*F, R, E*)

47. Some French cafés are not recommended. (*F, C, R*)

48. Hurricanes and earthquakes are violent and destructive. (*H, E, V, D*)

★ 49. Taylor is guilty if and only if all the witnesses committed perjury. (*G, W, C*)

50. If any witnesses told the truth, then either Parsons or Harris is guilty. (*W, T, G*)

51. If all mysteries are interesting, then *Rebecca* is interesting. (*M, I*)

★ 52. If there are any interesting mysteries, then *Rebecca* is interesting. (*M, I*)

53. Skaters and dancers are energetic individuals. (*S, D, E, I*)

54. Swiss watches are not expensive unless they are made of gold. (*S, W, E, M*)

★ 55. If all the buildings in Manhattan are skyscrapers, then the Chrysler building is a skyscraper. (*B, M, S*)

56. Experienced mechanics are well paid only if all the inexperienced ones are lazy. (*E, M, W, L*)

57. Balcony seats are never chosen unless all the orchestra seats are taken. (*B, S, C, O, T*)

★ 58. Some employees will get raises if and only if some managers are overly generous. (*E, R, M, O*)

59. The physicists and astronomers at the symposium are listed in the program if they either chair a meeting or read a paper. (*P, A, S, L, C, R*)

60. If the scientists and technicians are conscientious and exacting, then some of the mission directors will be either pleased or delighted. (*S, T, C, E, M, P, D*)

8.2   Using the Rules of Inference

The chief reason for using truth-functional operators (the dot, wedge, horseshoe, and so on) in translating statements into the symbolism of predicate logic is to allow for the application of the eighteen rules of inference to derive the conclusion of arguments via natural deduction. Since, however, the first eight of these rules are applicable only to whole lines in an argument, as long as the quantifier is attached to a line these rules of inference cannot be applied—at least not to the kind of arguments we are about to consider. To provide for their application, four additional rules are required to remove quantifiers at the beginning of a proof sequence and to introduce them, when needed, at the end of the sequence. These four rules are called universal instantiation, universal generalization, existential instantiation, and existential generalization. The first two are used to remove and introduce universal quantifiers, respectively, and the second two to remove and introduce existential quantifiers.

Let us first consider **universal instantiation.** As an illustration of the need for this rule, consider the following argument:

All economists are social scientists. $(x)(Ex \supset Sx)$
Milton Friedman is an economist. Em / Sm
Therefore, Milton Friedman is a social scientist.

This argument, which is clearly valid, is symbolized as follows:

1. (x)(Ex ⊃ Sx)
2. Em   / Sm

As the argument now stands, none of the first eight rules of inference can be applied; as a result, there is no way in which the two premises can be combined to obtain the conclusion. However, if the first premise could be used to obtain a line that reads *Em ⊃ Sm*, this statement could be combined with the second premise to yield the conclusion via *modus ponens*. Universal instantiation serves exactly this purpose.

The first premise states that for any item *x* in the universe, if that item is an *E*, then it is an *S*. But since Milton Friedman is himself an item in the universe, the first premise implies that if Milton Friedman is an *E*, then Milton Friedman is an *S*. A line stating exactly this can be obtained by universal instantiation (UI). In other words, universal instantiation provides us with an *instance* of the universal statement (x)(Ex ⊃ Sx). In the completed proof, which follows, the *m* in line 3 is called the **instantial letter**:

1. (x)(Ex ⊃ Sx)
2. Em   / Sm
3. Em ⊃ Sm   1, UI
4. Sm   2, 3, MP

At this point the question might arise as to why *modus ponens* is applicable to lines 2 and 3. In Chapter 7 we applied *modus ponens* to lines of the form *p ⊃ q*, but are we justified in applying it to a line that reads *Em ⊃ Sm*? The answer is yes, because *Em* and *Sm* are simply alternate ways of symbolizing simple statements. As so understood, these symbols do not differ in any material way from the *p* and *q* of propositional logic.

We may now give a general definition of instantiation. Instantiation is an operation that consists in deleting a quantifier and replacing every variable bound by that quantifier with the same instantial letter. For an example of an operation that violates the rule expressed in this definition, consider line 3 of the foregoing proof. If this line were instantiated as *Em ⊃ Sx*, it would not be correct because the *x* in *Sx* was not replaced with the instantial letter *m*.

Let us now consider **universal generalization.** The need for this rule may be illustrated through reference to the following argument:

All psychiatrists are doctors.   (x)(Px ⊃ Dx)
All doctors are college graduates.   (x)(Dx ⊃ Gx)
Therefore, all psychiatrists are college graduates.
                                        (x)(Px ⊃ Cx)

This valid argument is symbolized as follows:

1. (x)(Px ⊃ Dx)
2. (x)(Dx ⊃ Cx)   / (x)(Px ⊃ Cx)

Once universal instantiation is applied to the two premises, we will have lines that can be used to set up a hypothetical syllogism. But then we will have to reintroduce a universal quantifier to obtain the conclusion as written. This final step is obtained by universal generalization (UG). The justification for such a step lies in the fact that both premises are universal statements. The first states that if *anything* is a *P*, then it is a *D*, and the second states that if *anything* is a *D*, then it is a *C*. We may therefore conclude that if *anything* is a *P*, then it is a *C*. But because of the complete generality of this reasoning process, there is a special way in which we must perform the universal instantiation step. Instead of selecting a *specifically named* instance, as we did in the previous example, we must select a *variable* that can range over every instance in the universe. The variables at our disposal, you may recall from the previous section, are *x*, *y*, and *z*. Let us select *y*. The completed proof is as follows:

1. $(x)(Px \supset Dx)$
2. $(x)(Dx \supset Cx)$ / $(x)(Px \supset Cx)$
3. $Py \supset Dy$ 1, UI
4. $Dy \supset Cy$ 2, UI
5. $Py \supset Cy$ 3, 4, HS
6. $(x)(Px \supset Cx)$ 5, UG

(handwritten:)
3. $Pm \supset Dm$ 1, UI
4. $Dm \supset Cm$ 2, UI
5. $Pm \supset Cm$ 3, 4 HS
6. $(x)(Px \supset Cx)$ 5, UG

As noted earlier, the expressions in lines 3, 4, and 5 are called *statement functions*. As such, they are mere patterns for statements; they have no truth value and cannot be translated as statements. Yet if we take certain liberties, we might characterize line 5 as saying "If *it* is a *P*, then *it* is a *C*, where "it" designates any item at random in the universe. Line 6 can then be seen as reexpressing this sense of line 5.

As the two previous examples illustrate, we have two ways of performing universal instantiation. On the one hand, we may instantiate with respect to a *constant*, such as *a* or *b*, and on the other, with respect to a *variable*, such as *x* or *y*. The exact way in which this operation is to be performed depends on the kind of result intended. If we want some part of a universal statement to match a singular statement on another line, as in the first example, we instantiate with respect to a constant. But if, at the end of the proof, we want to perform universal generalization over some part of the statement we are instantiating, then we *must* instantiate by using a variable. This latter point leads to an important restriction governing universal generalization—namely, that we cannot perform this operation when the instantial letter is a constant. Consider the following *erroneous* proof sequence:

1. *Ta*
2. $(x)Tx$ 1, UG (invalid)

If *Ta* means "Albert is a thief," then on the basis of this information, we have concluded (line 2) that everything in the universe is a thief. Clearly, such an inference is invalid. This illustrates the fact that universal generalization can be performed only when the instantial letter (in this case *a*) is a variable.

Let us now consider **existential generalization.** The need for this operation is illustrated through the following argument:

All tenors are singers.
Placido Domingo is a tenor.
Therefore, there is at least one singer.

(handwritten:) $(x)(Tx \supset Sx)$
   Tp / $(\exists x)(Sx)$

This argument is symbolized as follows:

1. $(x)(Tx \supset Sx)$
2. Tp / $(\exists x)Sx$

If we instantiate the first line with respect to p, we can obtain Sp via *modus ponens*. But if it is true that Placido Domingo is a tenor, then it certainly follows that there is at least one singer (namely, Placido Domingo). This last step is accomplished by existential generalization (EG). The proof is as follows:

1. $(x)(Tx \supset Sx)$
2. Tp / $(\exists x)Sx$
3. $Tp \supset Sp$ 1, UI
4. Sp 2, 3, MP
5. $(\exists x)Sx$ 4, EG

There are no restrictions on existential generalization, and the operation can be performed when the instantial letter is either a constant (as above) or a variable. As an instance of the latter, consider the following sequence:

1. $(x)(Px \supset Qx)$
2. $(x)Px$ / $(\exists x)Qx$
3. $Py \supset Qy$ 1, UI
4. Py 2, UI
5. Qy 3, 4, MP
6. $(\exists x)Qx$ 5, EG

Line 5 states in effect that everything in the universe is a Q. From this, the much weaker conclusion follows (line 6) that *something* is a Q. If you should wonder how an existential conclusion can be drawn from universal premises, the answer is that predicate logic assumes that at least one thing exists in the universe. Hence, line 2, which asserts that everything in the universe is a P, entails that at least one thing is a P. Without this assumption, universal instantiation in line 4 would not be possible.

We may now give a definition of generalization that covers both varieties. Generalization is an operation that consists in (1) introducing a quantifier immediately prior to a statement, a statement function, or another quantifier, and (2) replacing one or more occurrences of a certain instantial letter in the statement or statement function with the same variable that appears in the quantifier. For universal generalization, *all* occurrences of the instantial letter must be replaced with the variable in the quantifier, and for existential generalization, *at least one* of the instantial letters must be replaced with the variable in the quantifier. Thus, both of the following cases of existential generalization are valid (although the one on the left is by far the more common version):

1. $Fa \cdot Ga$
2. $(\exists x)(Fx \cdot Gx)$ 1, EG

1. $Fa \cdot Ga$
2. $(\exists x)(Fx \cdot Ga)$ 1, EG

On the other hand, only one of the following cases of universal generalization is valid:

1. $Fx \supset Gx$
2. $(y)(Fy \supset Gy)$ 1, UG

1. $Fx \supset Gx$
2. $(y)(Fy \supset Gx)$ 1, UG (invalid)

The inference on the right is invalid because the x in Gx was not replaced with the variable in the quantifier (that is, y).

Of course, it may happen that the instantial letter is the same as the variable that appears in the quantifier. Thus, the operation "Gx, therefore $(x)Gx$" counts as a gener-

8

alization. Cases of generalization where a quantifier is introduced prior to another quantifier will be presented in Section 8.6.

The need for **existential instantiation** can be illustrated through the following argument:

All attorneys are college graduates.
Some attorneys are golfers.
Therefore, some golfers are college graduates.

The symbolic formulation is as follows:

1. $(x)(Ax \supset Cx)$
2. $(\exists x)(Ax \cdot Gx)$ $/ (\exists x)(Gx \cdot Cx)$

[Handwritten annotations:]
$(x)(Ax \supset Cx)$
$(\exists x)(Ax \cdot Gx) \quad / \quad (\exists x)(Gx \cdot Cx)$
③ $Ad \cdot Gd \quad 2, EI$
④ $Ad \supset Cd \quad 1, UI$
⑤ $Ad \quad\quad 3\ Simp$
⑥ $Cd \quad\quad 4,5\ Simp\ MP$

If both quantifiers can be removed, the conclusion can be obtained via simplification, *modus ponens*, and conjunction. The universal quantifier can be removed by universal instantiation, but to remove the existential quantifier we need existential instantiation (EI). Line 2 states that there is *something* that is both an *A* and a *G*. Existential instantiation consists in giving this something a *name*, for example, "David." We will call this name an "existential name" because it is obtained through existential instantiation. The completed proof is as follows:

1. $(x)(Ax \supset Cx)$
2. $(\exists x)(Ax \cdot Gx)$ $/ (\exists x)(Gx \cdot Cx)$
3. $Ad \cdot Gd$ 2, EI
4. $Ad \supset Cd$ 1, UI
5. Ad 3, Simp
6. Cd 4, 5, MP
7. $Gd \cdot Ad$ 3, Com
8. Gd 7, Simp
9. $Gd \cdot Cd$ 6, 8, Conj
10. $(\exists x)(Gx \cdot Cx)$ 9, EG

Examination of this proof reveals an immediate restriction that must be placed on existential instantiation. The name that we have assigned to the particular something in line 2 that is both an *A* and a *G* is a hypothetical name. It would be a mistake to conclude that this something really has that name. Accordingly, we must introduce a restriction that prevents us from ending the proof with some line that includes the letter *d*. If, for example, the proof were ended at line 9, we would be concluding that the something that is a *G* and a *C* really does have the name *d*. This, of course, would not be legitimate, because *d* is an arbitrary name introduced into the proof for mere convenience. To prevent such a mistake, we require that the name selected for existential instantiation not appear to the right of the slanted line adjacent to the last premise that indicates the conclusion to be obtained. Since the last line in the proof must be identical to this line, such a restriction prevents us from ending the proof with a line that contains the existential name.

Further examination of this proof indicates another important restriction on existential instantiation. Notice that the line involving existential instantiation is listed before the line involving universal instantiation. There is a reason for this. If the order were reversed, the existential instantiation step would rest upon the illicit assumption that the something that is both an *A* and a *G* has the *same* name as the name used in the earlier universal instantiation step. In other words, it would involve the assumption that the something that is both an *A* and a *G* is the very same something named in the line *Ad* ⊃ *Cd*. Of course, no such assumption is legitimate. To keep this mistake from happening, we introduce the restriction that the name introduced by existential instantiation be a new name not occurring earlier in the proof sequence. The following defective proof illustrates what can happen if this restriction is violated:

1. (∃x)(Fx • Ax)
2. (∃x)(Fx • Ox)   / (∃x)(Ax • Ox)
3. Fb • Ab   1, EI
4. Fb • Ob   2, EI (invalid)
5. Ab • Fb   3, Com
6. Ab   5, Simp
7. Ob • Fb   4, Com
8. Ob   7, Simp
9. Ab • Ob   6, 8, Conj
10. (∃x)(Ax • Ox)   9, EG

To see that this proof is indeed defective, let *F* stand for fruits, *A* for apples, and *O* for oranges. The argument that results is:

Some fruits are apples.
Some fruits are oranges.
Therefore, some apples are oranges.

Since the premises are true and the conclusion false, the argument is clearly invalid. The defect in the proof occurs on line 4. This line asserts that the something that is both an *F* and an *O* is the very same something that is both an *F* and an *A*. In other words, the restriction that the name introduced by existential instantiation be a new name not occurring earlier in the proof is violated.

The first restriction on existential instantiation requires that the existential name not occur in the line that indicates the conclusion to be obtained, and the second restriction requires that this name be a new name that has not occurred earlier in the proof. These two restrictions can easily be combined into a single restriction that requires that the name introduced by existential instantiation be a new name that has not occurred in *any* previous line, including the line adjacent to the last premise that indicates the conclusion to be obtained.

One further restriction that affects all four of these rules of inference requires that the rules be applied only to *whole lines* in a proof. The following sequence illustrates a violation of this restriction:

1. (x)Px ⊃ (x)Qx
2. Py ⊃ Qy   1, UI (invalid)

In line 2 universal instantiation is applied to both the antecedent and consequent of the first line. To obtain line 2 validly the first line would have to read (x)(Px ⊃ Qx). With this final restriction in mind, the four new rules of inference may now be summarized. In the formulation that follows, the symbols 𝓕x and 𝓕y represent any **statement function**—that is, any symbolic arrangement containing individual variables, such as $Ax \supset Bx$, $Cy \supset (Dy \vee Ey)$, or $Gz \cdot Hz$. And the symbol $\mathscr{F}a$ represents any **statement**; that is, any symbolic arrangement containing individual constants (or names), such as $Ac \supset Bc$, $Cm \supset (Dm \vee Em)$, or $Gw \cdot Hw$:

1. Universal instantiation (UI):

$$\frac{(x)\mathscr{F}x}{\mathscr{F}y} \qquad \frac{(x)\mathscr{F}x}{\mathscr{F}a}$$

2. Universal generalization (UG):

$$\frac{\mathscr{F}y}{(x)\mathscr{F}x} \qquad \text{not} \atop \text{allowed:} \qquad \frac{\mathscr{F}a}{(x)\mathscr{F}x}$$

3. Existential instantiation (EI):

$$\frac{(\exists x)\mathscr{F}x}{\mathscr{F}a} \qquad \text{not} \atop \text{allowed} \qquad \frac{(\exists x)\mathscr{F}x}{\mathscr{F}y}$$

Restriction: The existential name a must be a new name that has not occurred in any previous line.

4. Existential generalization (EG):

$$\frac{\mathscr{F}a}{(\exists x)\mathscr{F}x} \qquad \frac{\mathscr{F}y}{(\exists x)\mathscr{F}x}$$

The *not allowed* version of universal generalization recalls the already familiar fact that generalization is not possible when the instantial letter is a constant. In other words, the mere fact that the individual a is an $\mathscr{F}$ is not sufficient to allow us to conclude that everything in the universe is an $\mathscr{F}$. At present this is the only restriction needed for universal generalization. In Sections 8.4 and 8.6, however, two additional restrictions will be introduced. The *not allowed* version of existential instantiation merely recalls the fact that this operation is a naming process. Because variables (x, y, and z) are not names, they cannot be used as instantial letters in existential instantiation.

Let us now investigate some applications of these rules. Consider the following proof:

1. $(x)(Hx \supset Ix)$
2. $(x)(Ix \supset Hx)$ / $(x)(Hx \equiv Ix)$
3. $Hx \supset Ix$ 1, UI
4. $Ix \supset Hx$ 2, UI
5. $(Hx \supset Ix) \cdot (Ix \supset Hx)$ 3, 4, Conj
6. $Hx \equiv Ix$ 5, Equiv
7. $(x)(Hx \equiv Ix)$ 6, UG

Because we want to perform universal generalization on the last line of the proof, we instantiate lines 1 and 2 using a variable, not a constant. Notice that the variable selected for lines 3 and 4 is the same letter that occurs in lines 1 and 2. While a new letter (y or z) *could* have been selected, this is never necessary in such a step. It *is* necessary, however, since we want to combine lines 3 and 4, that the *same* variable be selected in obtaining these lines. Another example:

1. $(x)[(Ax \lor Bx) \supset Cx]$
2. $(\exists x)Ax$ / $(\exists x)Cx$
3. Am 2, EI
4. $(Am \lor Bm) \supset Cm$ 1, UI
5. $Am \lor Bm$ 3, Add
6. Cm 4, 5, MP
7. $(\exists x)Cx$ 6, EG

In conformity with the restriction on existential instantiation, the EI step is performed *before* the UI step. The same letter is then selected in the UI step as was used in the EI step. In line 5, *Bm* is joined disjunctively via addition to *Am*. This rule applies in predicate logic in basically the same way that it does in propositional logic. Any statement or statement function we choose can be joined disjunctively to a given line.

Another example:

1. $(\exists x)Kx \supset (x)(Lx \supset Mx)$
2. $Kc \cdot Lc$ / Mc
3. Kc 2, Simp
4. $(\exists x)Kx$ 3, EG
5. $(x)(Lx \supset Mx)$ 1, 4, MP
6. $Lc \supset Mc$ 5, UI
7. $Lc \cdot Kc$ 2, Com
8. Lc 7, Simp
9. Mc 6, 8, MP

Since the instantiation (and generalization) rules must be applied to whole lines, it is impossible to instantiate line 1. The only strategy that can be followed is to use some other line to obtain the antecedent of this line and then obtain the consequent via *modus ponens*. Once the consequent is obtained (line 5), it is instantiated using the same letter that appears in line 2.

The next example incorporates all four of the instantiation and generalization rules:

1. $(x)(Px \supset Qx) \supset (\exists x)(Rx \cdot Sx)$
2. $(x)(Px \supset Sx) \cdot (x)(Sx \supset Qx)$ / $(\exists x)Sx$
3. $(x)(Px \supset Sx)$ 2, Simp
4. $(x)(Sx \supset Qx) \cdot (x)(Px \supset Sx)$ 2, Com
5. $(x)(Sx \supset Qx)$ 4, Simp
6. $Py \supset Sy$ 3, UI
7. $Sy \supset Qy$ 5, UI
8. $Py \supset Qy$ 6, 7, HS
9. $(x)(Px \supset Qx)$ 8, UG
10. $(\exists x)(Rx \cdot Sx)$ 1, 9, MP
11. $Ra \cdot Sa$ 10, EI
12. $Sa \cdot Ra$ 11, Com
13. Sa 12, Simp
14. $(\exists x)Sx$ 13, EG

As with the previous example, line 1 cannot be instantiated. To instantiate the two conjuncts in line 2, they must first be separated (lines 3 and 5). Because UG is to be used in line 9, lines 3 and 5 are instantiated using a variable. On the other hand, a constant is used to instantiate line 10 because the statement in question is a particular statement.

Another example:

```
1.  [(∃x)Ax • (∃x)Bx] ⊃ Cj
2.  (∃x)(Ax • Dx)
3.  (∃x)(Bx • Ex)                    / Cj
4.  Am • Dm                          2, EI
5.  Bn • En                          3, EI
6.  Am                               4, Simp
7.  Bn                               5, Simp
8.  (∃x)Ax                           6, EG
9.  (∃x)Bx                           7, EG
10. (∃x)Ax • (∃x)Bx                  8, 9, Conj
11. Cj                               1, 10, MP
```

When line 2 is instantiated (line 4), a letter other than *j*, which appears in line 1, is selected. Then, when line 3 is instantiated (line 5), another new letter is selected. The conclusion is obtained, as in earlier examples, via *modus ponens* by obtaining the antecedent of line 1.

The following examples illustrate *invalid* or *improper* applications of the instantiation and generalization rules:

```
1.  Fy ⊃ Gy
─────────────
2.  (x)(Fx ⊃ Gy)      1, UG   (invalid—every instance of y must be
                              replaced with x)

1.  (x)Fx ⊃ Ga
─────────────
2.  Fx ⊃ Ga           1, UI   (invalid—instantiation can be applied
                              only to whole lines)

1.  (x)Fx ⊃ (x)Gx     1, UI   (invalid—instantiation can be applied
─────────────                 only to whole lines)
2.  Fx ⊃ Gx

1.  Fc
2.  (∃x)Gx
─────────────
3.  Gc                2, EI   (invalid—c appears in line 1)

1.  Fm ⊃ Gm
─────────────
2.  (x)(Fx ⊃ Gx)      1, UG   (invalid—the instantial letter must be a
                              variable; m is a constant)

1.  (∃x)Fx
2.  (∃x)Gx
─────────────
3.  Fe                1, EI
4.  Ge                2, EI   (invalid—e appears in line 3)

1.  Fs • Gs
─────────────
2.  (∃x)Fx • Gs       1, EG   (improper—generalization can be
                              applied only to whole lines)

1.  ~(x)Fx
─────────────
2.  ~Fy               1, UI   (invalid—lines involving negated
                              quantifiers cannot be instantiated;
                              see Section 8.3)
```

EXERCISE 8.2

iLrn I. Use the eighteen rules of inference to derive the conclusions of the following symbolized arguments. Do not use either conditional proof or indirect proof.

★ (1) 1. $(x)(Ax \supset Bx)$
      2. $(x)(Bx \supset Cx)$ / $(x)(Ax \supset Cx)$

  (2) 1. $(x)(Bx \supset Cx)$
      2. $(\exists x)(Ax \cdot Bx)$ / $(\exists x)(Ax \cdot Cx)$

  (3) 1. $(x)(Ax \supset Bx)$
      2. $\sim Bm$ / $(\exists x)\sim Ax$

★ (4) 1. $(x)[Ax \supset (Bx \lor Cx)]$
      2. $Ag \cdot \sim Bg$ / Cg

  (5) 1. $(x)[(Ax \lor Bx) \supset Cx]$
      2. $(\exists y)(Ay \cdot Dy)$ / $(\exists y)Cy$

  (6) 1. $(x)[Jx \supset (Kx \cdot Lx)]$
      2. $(\exists y)\sim Ky$ / $(\exists z)\sim Jz$

★ (7) 1. $(x)[Ax \supset (Bx \lor Cx)]$
      2. $(\exists x)(Ax \cdot \sim Cx)$ / $(\exists x)Bx$

  (8) 1. $(x)(Ax \supset Bx)$
      2. $Am \cdot An$ / $Bm \cdot Bn$

  (9) 1. $(x)(Ax \supset Bx)$
      2. $Am \lor An$ / $Bm \lor Bn$

★ (10) 1. $(x)(Bx \lor Ax)$
       2. $(x)(Bx \supset Ax)$ / $(x)Ax$

  (11) 1. $(x)[(Ax \cdot Bx) \supset Cx]$
       2. $(\exists x)(Bx \cdot \sim Cx)$ / $(\exists x)\sim Ax$

  (12) 1. $(\exists x)Ax \supset (x)(Bx \supset Cx)$
       2. $Am \cdot Bm$ / Cm

★ (13) 1. $(\exists x)Ax \supset (x)Bx$
       2. $(\exists x)Cx \supset (\exists x)Dx$
       3. $An \cdot Cn$ / $(\exists x)(Bx \cdot Dx)$

  (14) 1. $(\exists x)Ax \supset (x)(Cx \supset Bx)$
       2. $(\exists x)(Ax \lor Bx)$
       3. $(x)(Bx \supset Ax)$ / $(x)(Cx \supset Ax)$

  (15) 1. $(\exists x)Ax \supset (x)(Bx \supset Cx)$
       2. $(\exists x)Dx \supset (\exists x)\sim Cx$
       3. $(\exists x)(Ax \cdot Dx)$ / $(\exists x)\sim Bx$

iLrn II. Translate the following arguments into symbolic form. Then use the eighteen rules of inference to derive the conclusion of each. Do not use conditional or indirect proof.

★ 1. Oranges are sweet. Also, oranges are fragrant. Therefore, oranges are sweet and fragrant. (O, S, F)

  2. Tomatoes are vegetables. Therefore, the tomatoes in the garden are vegetables. (T, V, G)

  3. Apples and pears grow on trees. Therefore, apples grow on trees. (A, P, G)

★ 4. Carrots are vegetables and peaches are fruit. Furthermore, there are carrots and peaches in the garden. Therefore, there are vegetables and fruit in the garden. (*C, V, P, F, G*)

5. Beans and peas are legumes. There are no legumes in the garden. Therefore, there are no beans in the garden. (*B, P, L, G*)

6. There are some cucumbers in the garden. If there are any cucumbers, there are some pumpkins in the garden. All pumpkins are vegetables. Therefore, there are some vegetables in the garden. (*C, G, P, V*)

★ 7. All gardeners are industrious persons. Furthermore, any person who is industrious is respected. Therefore, since Arthur and Catherine are gardeners, it follows that they are respected. (*G, I, P, R*)

8. Some huckleberries are ripe. Furthermore, some boysenberries are sweet. If there are any huckleberries, then the boysenberries are edible if they are sweet. Therefore, some boysenberries are edible. (*H, R, B, S, E*)

9. If there are any ripe watermelons, then the caretakers performed well. Furthermore, if there are any large watermelons, then whoever performed well will get a bonus. There are some large, ripe watermelons. Therefore, the caretakers will get a bonus. (*R, W, C, P, L, B*)

★ 10. If the artichokes in the kitchen are ripe, then the guests will be surprised. Furthermore, if the artichokes in the kitchen are flavorful, then the guests will be pleased. The artichokes in the kitchen are ripe and flavorful. Therefore, the guests will be surprised and pleased. (*A, K, R, G, S, F, P*)

8.3 Change of Quantifier Rule

The rules of inference developed thus far are not sufficient to derive the conclusion of every argument in predicate logic. For instance, consider the following:

$$\frac{\begin{array}{l} \sim(\exists x)(Px \cdot \sim Qx) \\ \sim(x)(\sim Rx \vee Qx) \end{array}}{(\exists x)\sim Px}$$

Both premises have negation signs preceding the quantifiers. As long as these negation signs remain, neither statement can be instantiated; and if these statements cannot be instantiated, the conclusion cannot be derived. What is needed is a rule that will allow us to remove the negation signs. This rule, which we will proceed to develop now, is called the **change of quantifier rule.**

As a basis for developing the change of quantifier rule, consider the following statements:

Everything is beautiful.
It is not the case that everything is beautiful.
Something is beautiful.
It is not the case that something is beautiful.

You should be able to see that these statements are equivalent in meaning to the following statements, respectively:

It is not the case that something is not beautiful.
Something is not beautiful.
It is not the case that everything is not beautiful.
Everything is not beautiful.

If we generalize these English equivalencies symbolically, we obtain:

$$(x)\mathscr{F}x \;::\; \sim(\exists x)\sim\mathscr{F}x$$
$$\sim(x)\mathscr{F}x \;::\; (\exists x)\sim\mathscr{F}x$$
$$(\exists x)\mathscr{F}x \;::\; \sim(x)\sim\mathscr{F}x$$
$$\sim(\exists x)\mathscr{F}x \;::\; (x)\sim\mathscr{F}x$$

These four expressions constitute the change of quantifier rule (CQ). Since they are stated as logical equivalences, they apply to parts of lines as well as to whole lines. They can be summarized as follows:

One type of quantifier can be replaced by the other type if and only if immediately before and after the new quantifier:
1. Tilde operators that were originally present are deleted.
2. Tilde operators that were not originally present are inserted.

To see how the change of quantifier rule is applied, let us return to the argument at the beginning of this section. The proof is as follows:

1.	$\sim(\exists x)(Px \cdot \sim Qx)$	
2.	$\sim(x)(\sim Rx \lor Qx)$	$/ (\exists x)\sim Px$
3.	$(x)\sim(Px \cdot \sim Qx)$	1, CQ
4.	$(\exists x)\sim(\sim Rx \lor Qx)$	2, CQ
5.	$\sim(\sim Ra \lor Qa)$	4, EI
6.	$\sim(Pa \cdot \sim Qa)$	3, UI
7.	$\sim\sim Ra \cdot \sim Qa$	5, DM
8.	$Ra \cdot \sim Qa$	7, DN
9.	$\sim Pa \lor \sim\sim Qa$	6, DM
10.	$\sim Pa \lor Qa$	9, DN
11.	$\sim Qa \cdot Ra$	8, Com
12.	$\sim Qa$	11, Simp
13.	$Qa \lor \sim Pa$	10, Com
14.	$\sim Pa$	12, 13, DS
15.	$(\exists x)\sim Px$	14, EG

Before either line 1 or line 2 can be instantiated, the tilde operators preceding the quantifiers must be removed. In accordance with the change of quantifier rule, tilde operators are introduced immediately after the new quantifiers in the expressions on lines 3 and 4.

Another example:

1.	$(\exists x)(Hx \cdot Gx) \supset (x)Ix$	
2.	$\sim Im$	$/ (x)(Hx \supset \sim Gx)$
3.	$(\exists x)\sim Ix$	2, EG

4. ~(x)Ix   3, CQ
5. ~(∃x)(Hx • Gx)   1, 4, MT
6. (x)~(Hx • Gx)   5, CQ
7. (x)(~Hx ∨ ~Gx)   6, DM
8. (x)(Hx ⊃ ~Gx)   7, Impl

The statement that *m* is not an *I* (line 2) intuitively implies that not everything is an *I* (line 4); but existential generalization and change of quantifier are needed to get the desired result. Notice that lines 7 and 8 are obtained via DeMorgan's Rule and material implication, even though the quantifier is still attached. Since these rules are rules of replacement, they apply to parts of lines as well as to whole lines. The following example illustrates the same point with respect to the change of quantifier rule:

1. (∃x)Jx ⊃ ~(∃x)Kx
2. (x)~Kx ⊃ (x)~Lx   / (∃x)Jx ⊃ ~(∃x)Lx
3. (∃x)Jx ⊃ (x)~Kx   1, CQ
4. (∃x)Jx ⊃ (x)~Lx   2, 3, HS
5. (∃x)Jx ⊃ ~(∃x)Lx   4, CQ

The change of quantifier rule is applied to only the consequent of line 1, yielding line 3. Similarly, the change of quantifier rule is then applied to only the consequent of line 4, yielding line 5.

EXERCISE 8.3

iLrn I. Use the change of quantifier rule together with the eighteen rules of inference to derive the conclusions of the following symbolized arguments. Do not use either conditional proof or indirect proof.

★ (1) 1. (x)Ax ⊃ (∃x)Bx
       2. (x)~Bx   / (∃x)~Ax

  (2) 1. (∃x)~Ax ∨ (∃x)~Bx
       2. (x)Bx   / ~(x)Ax

  (3) 1. ~(∃x)Ax   / (x)(Ax ⊃ Bx)

★ (4) 1. (∃x)Ax ∨ (∃x)(Bx • Cx)
       2. ~(∃x)Bx   / (∃x)Ax

  (5) 1. (x)(Ax • Bx) ∨ (x)(Cx • Dx)
       2. ~(x)Dx   / (x)Bx

  (6) 1. (∃x)~Ax ⊃ (x)(Bx ⊃ Cx)
       2. ~(x)(Ax ∨ Cx)   / ~(x)Bx

★ (7) 1. (x)(Ax ⊃ Bx)
       2. ~(x)Cx ∨ (x)Ax
       3. (x)Bx   / (∃x)~Cx

  (8) 1. (x)Ax ⊃ (∃x)~Bx
       2. ~(x)Bx ⊃ (∃x)~Cx   / (x)Cx ⊃ (∃x)~Ax

  (9) 1. (∃x)(Ax ∨ Bx) ⊃ (x)Cx
       2. (∃x)~Cx   / ~(∃x)Ax

8

★ (10) 1. ~(∃x)(Ax • ~Bx)
    2. ~(∃x)(Bx • ~Cx)   / (x)(Ax ⊃ Cx)

(11) 1. ~(∃x)(Ax • ~Bx)
    2. ~(∃x)(Ax • ~Cx)   / (x)[Ax ⊃ (Bx • Cx)]

(12) 1. (x)[(Ax • Bx) ⊃ Cx]
    2. ~(x)(Ax ⊃ Cx)   / ~(x)Bx

★ (13) 1. (x)(Ax • ~Bx) ⊃ (∃x)Cx
    2. ~(∃x)(Cx ∨ Bx)   / ~(x)Ax

(14) 1. (∃x)~Ax ⊃ (x)~Bx
    2. (∃x)~Ax ⊃ (∃x)Bx
    3. (x)(Ax ⊃ Cx)   / (x)Cx

(15) 1. ~(∃x)(Ax ∨ Bx)
    2. (∃x)Cx ⊃ (∃x)Ax
    3. (∃x)Dx ⊃ (∃x)Bx   / ~(∃x)(Cx ∨ Dx)

II. Translate the following arguments into symbolic form. Then use the change of quantifier rules and the eighteen rules of inference to derive the conclusion of each. Do not use either conditional proof or indirect proof.

★ 1. If all the physicians are either hematologists or neurologists, then there are no cardiologists. But Dr. Frank is a cardiologist. Therefore, some physicians are not neurologists. (P, H, N, C)

2. Either Dr. Adams is an internist or all the pathologists are internists. But it is not the case that there are any internists. Therefore, Dr. Adams is not a pathologist. (I, P)

3. If some surgeons are allergists, then some psychiatrists are radiologists. But no psychiatrists are radiologists. Therefore, no surgeons are allergists. (S, A, P, R)

★ 4. Either some general practitioners are pediatricians or some surgeons are endocrinologists. But it is not the case that there are any endocrinologists. Therefore, there are some pediatricians. (G, P, S, E)

5. All physicians who did not attend medical school are incompetent. It is not the case, however, that some physicians are incompetent. Therefore, all physicians have attended medical school. (P, A, I)

6. It is not the case that some internists are not physicians. Furthermore, it is not the case that some physicians are not doctors of medicine. Therefore, all internists are doctors of medicine. (I, P, D)

★ 7. All pathologists are specialists and all internists are generalists. Therefore, since it is not the case that some specialists are generalists, it is not the case that some pathologists are internists. (P, S, I, G)

8. If some obstetricians are not gynecologists, then some hematologists are radiologists. But it is not the case that there are any hematologists or gynecologists. Therefore, it is not the case that there are any obstetricians. (O, G, H, R)

9. All poorly trained allergists and dermatologists are untrustworthy specialists. It is not the case, however, that some specialists are untrustworthy. Therefore, it is not the case that some dermatologists are poorly trained. (P, A, D, U, S)

★ 10. It is not the case that some physicians are either on the golf course or in the hospital. All of the neurologists are physicians in the hospital. Either some physicians are cardiologists or some physicians are neurologists. Therefore, some cardiologists are not on the golf course. (*P, G, H, N, C*)

8.4   Conditional and Indirect Proof

Many arguments with conclusions that are either difficult or impossible to derive by the conventional method can be handled with ease by using either conditional or indirect proof. The use of these techniques on arguments in predicate logic is basically the same as it is on arguments in propositional logic. Arguments having conclusions expressed in the form of conditional statements or disjunctions (which can be derived from conditional statements) are immediate candidates for conditional proof. For these arguments, the usual strategy is to put the antecedent of the conditional statement to be obtained in the first line of an indented sequence, to derive the consequent as the last line, and to discharge the conditional sequence in a conditional statement that exactly matches the one to be obtained. Here is an example of such a proof:

1. $(x)(Hx \supset Ix)$	/ $(\exists x)Hx \supset (\exists x)Ix$
2. $(\exists x)Hx$	ACP
3. Ha	2, EI
4. $Ha \supset Ia$	1, UI
5. Ia	3, 4, MP
6. $(\exists x)Ix$	5, EG
7. $(\exists x)Hx \supset (\exists x)Ix$	2–6, CP

In this argument the antecedent of the conclusion is a complete statement consisting of a statement function, *Hx*, preceded by a quantifier. This complete statement is assumed as the first line in the conditional sequence. The instantiation and generalization rules are used within an indented sequence (both conditional and indirect) in basically the same way as they are in a conventional sequence. When the consequent of the conclusion is obtained, the conditional sequence is completed, and it is then discharged in a conditional statement having the first line of the sequence as its antecedent and the last line as its consequent.

The next example differs from the previous one in that the antecedent of the conclusion is a statement function, not a complete statement. With arguments such as this, only the statement function is assumed as the first line in the conditional sequence. The quantifier is added after the sequence is discharged.

1. $(x)[(Ax \vee Bx) \supset Cx]$	/ $(x)(Ax \supset Cx)$
2. Ax	ACP
3. $Ax \vee Bx$	2, Add
4. $(Ax \vee Bx) \supset Cx$	1, UI
5. Cx	3, 4, MP
6. $Ax \supset Cx$	2–5, CP
7. $(x)(Ax \supset Cx)$	6, UG

This example leads to an important restriction on the use of universal generalization. You may recall that the *x* in line 2 of this proof is said to occur *free* because it is not governed by any quantifier. (In contrast, the *x*'s in lines 1 and 7 are said to occur *bound*.) The restriction is as follows:

UG: $\dfrac{\mathcal{F}y}{(x)\mathcal{F}x}$ *Restriction:* UG must not be used within the scope of an indented sequence if the instantial variable occurs free in the first line of that sequence.

The above proof does not violate this restriction because UG is not used within the scope of the indented sequence at all. It is used only after the sequence has been discharged, which is perfectly acceptable. If, on the other hand, UG had been applied to line 5 to produce a statement reading $(x)Cx$, the restriction would have been violated because the instantial variable x occurs free in the first line of the sequence.

To understand why this restriction is necessary, consider the following *defective* proof:

1. $(x)Rx \supset (x)Sx$ / $(x)(Rx \supset Sx)$
  | 2. Rx ACP
  | 3. $(x)Rx$ 2, UG (invalid)
  | 4. $(x)Sx$ 1, 3, MP
  | 5. Sx 4, UI
6. $Rx \supset Sx$ 2–5, CP
7. $(x)(Rx \supset Sx)$ 6, UG

If Rx means "x is a rabbit" and Sx means "x is a snake," then the premise translates "If everything in the universe is a rabbit, then everything in the universe is a snake." This statement is *true* because the antecedent is false; that is, it is *not* the case that everything in the universe is a rabbit. The conclusion, on the other hand, is *false*, because it asserts that all rabbits are snakes. The argument is therefore invalid. If the restriction on UG had been obeyed, UG would not have been used on line 3 and, as a result, the illicit conclusion would not have been obtained.

It is interesting to see what happens when the premise and the conclusion of this defective argument are switched. The proof, which is perfectly legitimate, is as follows:

1. $(x)(Rx \supset Sx)$ / $(x)Rx \supset (x)Sx$
  | 2. $(x)Rx$ ACP
  | 3. Rx 2, UI
  | 4. $Rx \supset Sx$ 1, UI
  | 5. Sx 3, 4, MP
  | 6. $(x)Sx$ 5, UG
7. $(x)Rx \supset (x)Sx$ 2–6, CP

Notice in this proof that UG *is* used within the scope of a conditional sequence, but the restriction is not violated because the instantial variable x does not occur free in the first line of the sequence.

Let us now consider some examples of *indirect* proof. We begin an indirect sequence by assuming the negation of the statement to be obtained. When a contradiction is derived, the indirect sequence is discharged by asserting the denial of the original assumption. In the examples that follow, the negation of the conclusion is assumed as the first line of the sequence, and the change of quantifier rule is then used to eliminate the negation sign. When the resulting statement is then instantiated, a new letter, *m*, is selected that has not appeared anywhere in a previous line. The same letter is then selected for the universal instantiation of line 1:

1. $(x)[(Px \supset Px) \supset (Qx \supset Rx)]$ / $(x)(Qx \supset Rx)$
    2. ~ $(x)(Qx \supset Rx)$ AIP
    3. $(\exists x)\sim(Qx \supset Rx)$ 2, CQ
    4. $\sim(Qm \supset Rm)$ 3, EI
    5. $(Pm \supset Pm) \supset (Qm \supset Rm)$ 1, UI
    6. $\sim(Pm \supset Pm)$ 4, 5, MT
    7. $\sim(\sim Pm \lor Pm)$ 6, Impl
    8. $\sim\sim Pm \cdot \sim Pm$ 7, DM
    9. $Pm \cdot \sim Pm$ 8, DN
10. $\sim\sim(x)(Qx \supset Rx)$ 2–9, IP
11. $(x)(Qx \supset Rx)$ 10, DN

The next example has a particular statement for its conclusion:

1. $(\exists x)Ax \lor (\exists x)Fx$
2. $(x)(Ax \supset Fx)$ / $(\exists x)Fx$
    3. $\sim(\exists x)Fx$ AIP
    4. $(\exists x)Fx \lor (\exists x)Ax$ 1, Com
    5. $(\exists x)Ax$ 3, 4, DS
    6. Ac 5, FI
    7. $Ac \supset Fc$ 2, UI
    8. Fc 6, 7, MP
    9. $(x)\sim Fx$ 3, CQ
   10. $\sim Fc$ 9, UI
   11. $Fc \cdot \sim Fc$ 8, 10, Conj
12. $\sim\sim(\exists x)Fx$ 3–11, IP
13. $(\exists x)Fx$ 12, DN

Since indirect proof sequences are indented, they are subject to the same restriction on universal generalization as conditional sequences. The following proof, which is similar to the previous one, violates this restriction because the instantial variable *x* occurs free in the first line of the sequence. The violation (line 4) allows a universal statement to be drawn for the conclusion, whereas only a particular statement (as above) is legitimate:

1. $(\exists x)Ax \lor (\exists x)Fx$
2. $(x)(Ax \supset Fx)$ / $(x)Fx$
    3. $\sim Fx$ AIP
    4. $(x)\sim Fx$ 3, UG (invalid)
    5. $\sim(\exists x)Fx$ 4, CQ
    6. $(\exists x)Fx \lor (\exists x)Ax$ 1, Com
    7. $(\exists x)Ax$ 5, 6, DS
    8. Ac 7, EI
    9. $Ac \supset Fc$ 2, UI
   10. Fc 8, 9, MP
   11. $\sim Fc$ 4, UI
   12. $Fc \cdot \sim Fc$ 10, 11, Conj
13. $\sim\sim Fx$ 3–12, IP
14. Fx 13, DN
15. $(x)Fx$ 14, UG

To see that this argument is indeed invalid, let *Ax* stand for "*x* is an apple" and *Fx* for "*x* is a fruit." The first premise then reads "Either an apple exists or a fruit exists" (which is true), and the second premise reads "All apples are fruits" (which is also true). The conclusion, however, reads "Everything in the universe is a fruit," and this, of course, is false.

As in propositional logic, conditional and indirect sequences in predicate logic may include each other. The following proof uses an indirect sequence within the scope of a conditional sequence.

1. $(x)[(Px \lor Qx) \supset (Rx \cdot Sx)]$		/ $(\exists x)(Px \lor Sx) \supset (\exists x)Sx$
2. $(\exists x)(Px \lor Sx)$		ACP
3. $\sim(\exists x)Sx$		AIP
4. $(x)\sim Sx$		3, CQ
5. $Pa \lor Sa$		2, EI
6. $\sim Sa$		4, UI
7. $Sa \lor Pa$		5, Com
8. Pa		6, 7, DS
9. $Pa \lor Qa$		8, Add
10. $(Pa \lor Qa) \supset (Ra \cdot Sa)$		1, UI
11. $Ra \cdot Sa$		9, 10, MP
12. $Sa \cdot Ra$		11, Com
13. Sa		12, Simp
14. $Sa \cdot \sim Sa$		6, 13, Conj
15. $\sim\sim(\exists x)Sx$		3–14, IP
16. $(\exists x)Sx$		15, DN
17. $(\exists x)(Px \lor Sx) \supset (\exists x)Sx$		2–16, CP

The conditional sequence begins, as usual, by assuming the antecedent of the conditional statement to be obtained. The objective, then, is to obtain the consequent. This is accomplished by the indirect sequence, which begins with the negation of the consequent and ends (line 14) with a contradiction.

EXERCISE 8.4

iLrn I. Use either indirect proof or conditional proof to derive the conclusions of the following symbolized arguments:

★ (1) 1. $(x)(Ax \supset Bx)$
　　　 2. $(x)(Ax \supset Cx)$　　/ $(x)[Ax \supset (Bx \cdot Cx)]$

　 (2) 1. $(\exists x)Ax \supset (\exists x)(Bx \cdot Cx)$
　　　 2. $(\exists x)(Cx \lor Dx) \supset (x)Ex$　　/ $(x)(Ax \supset Ex)$

　 (3) 1. $(\exists x)Ax \supset (\exists x)(Bx \cdot Cx)$
　　　 2. $\sim(\exists x)Cx$　　/ $(x)\sim Ax$

★ (4) 1. $(x)(Ax \supset Cx)$
　　　 2. $(\exists x)Cx \supset (\exists x)(Bx \cdot Dx)$　　/ $(\exists x)Ax \supset (\exists x)Bx$

　 (5) 1. $(x)(Ax \supset Bx)$
　　　 2. $(x)[(Ax \cdot Bx) \supset Cx]$　　/ $(x)(Ax \supset Cx)$

　 (6) 1. $(\exists x)Ax \supset (x)Bx$
　　　 2. $An \supset \sim Bn$　　/ $\sim An$

★ (7) 1. $(x)[(Ax \lor Bx) \supset Cx]$
　　2. $(x)[(Cx \lor Dx) \supset Ex]$　　/ $(x)(Ax \supset Ex)$

(8) 1. $(\exists x)(Ax \lor Bx) \supset {\sim}(\exists x)Ax$　　/ $(x){\sim}Ax$

(9) 1. $(x)(Ax \supset Bx)$
　　2. $(x)(Cx \supset Dx)$　　/ $(\exists x)(Ax \lor Cx) \supset (\exists x)(Bx \lor Dx)$

★ (10) 1. $(x)(Ax \supset Bx)$
　　2. $Am \lor An$　　/ $(\exists x)Bx$

(11) 1. $(x)[(Ax \lor Bx) \supset Cx]$
　　2. $(x)[(Cx \lor Dx) \supset {\sim}Ax]$　　/ $(x){\sim}Ax$

(12) 1. $(\exists x)Ax \supset (x)(Bx \supset Cx)$
　　2. $(\exists x)Dx \supset (x){\sim}Cx$　　/ $(x)[(Ax \cdot Dx) \supset {\sim}Bx]$

★ (13) 1. $(\exists x)Ax \supset (x)(Bx \supset Cx)$
　　2. $(\exists x)Dx \supset (\exists x)Bx$　　/ $(\exists x)(Ax \cdot Dx) \supset (\exists x)Cx$

(14) 1. $(\exists x)Ax \lor (\exists x)(Bx \cdot Cx)$
　　2. $(x)(Ax \supset Cx)$　　/ $(\exists x)Cx$

(15) 1. $(\exists x)Ax \supset (\exists x)(Bx \cdot Cx)$
　　2. $(\exists x)Cx \supset (x)(Dx \cdot Ex)$　　/ $(x)(Ax \supset Ex)$

★ (16) 1. $(x)[(Ax \lor Bx) \supset Cx]$
　　2. $(\exists x)({\sim}Ax \lor Dx) \supset (x)Ex$　　/ $(x)Cx \lor (x)Ex$

(17) 1. $(x)Ax \equiv (\exists x)(Bx \cdot Cx)$
　　2. $(x)(Cx \supset Bx)$　　/ $(x)Ax \equiv (\exists x)Cx$

(18) 1. $(x)(Ax \equiv Bx)$
　　2. $(x)[Ax \supset (Bx \supset Cx)]$
　　3. $(\exists x)Ax \lor (\exists x)Bx$　　/ $(\exists x)Cx$

★ (19) 1. $(x)[Bx \supset (Cx \cdot Dx)]$　　/ $(x)(Ax \supset Bx) \supset (x)(Ax \supset Dx)$

(20) 1. $(x)[Ax \supset (Bx \cdot Cx)]$
　　2. $(x)[Dx \supset (Ex \cdot Fx)]$　　/ $(x)(Cx \supset Dx) \supset (x)(Ax \supset Fx)$

(21) 1. $(\exists x)(Ax \lor Bx)$
　　2. $(\exists x)Ax \supset (x)(Cx \supset Bx)$
　　3. $(\exists x)Cx$　　/ $(\exists x)Bx$

iLrn II. Translate the following arguments into symbolic form. Then use conditional or indirect proof to derive the conclusion of each.

★ 1. All ambassadors are wealthy. Furthermore, all Republicans are clever. Therefore, all Republican ambassadors are clever and wealthy. (*A, W, R, C*)

2. All senators are well liked. Also, if there are any well-liked senators, then O'Brien is a voter. Therefore, if there are any senators, then O'Brien is a voter. (*S, W, V*)

3. If all judges are wise, then some attorneys are rewarded. Furthermore, if there are any judges who are not wise, then some attorneys are rewarded. Therefore, some attorneys are rewarded. (*J, W, A, R*)

★ 4. All secretaries and undersecretaries are intelligent and cautious. All those who are cautious or vigilant are restrained and austere. Therefore, all secretaries are austere. (*S, U, I, C, V, R, A*)

5. All ambassadors are diplomats. Furthermore, all experienced ambassadors are cautious, and all cautious diplomats have foresight. Therefore, all experienced ambassadors have foresight. (*A*, *D*, *E*, *C*, *F*)

6. If there are any senators, then some employees are well paid. If there is anyone who is either an employee or a volunteer, then there are some legislative assistants. Either there are some volunteers or there are some senators. Therefore, there are some legislative assistants. (*S*, *E*, *W*, *V*, *L*)

★ 7. If there are any consuls, then all ambassadors are satisfied diplomats. If no consuls are ambassadors, then some diplomats are satisfied. Therefore, some diplomats are satisfied. (*C*, *A*, *S*, *D*)

8. If there are any voters, then all politicians are astute. If there are any politicians, then whoever is astute is clever. Therefore, if there are any voters, then all politicians are clever. (*V*, *P*, *A*, *C*)

9. Either no senators are present or no representatives are present. Furthermore, either some senators are present or no women are present. Therefore, none of the representatives who are present are women. (*S*, *P*, *R*, *W*)

★ 10. Either some governors are present or some ambassadors are present. If anyone is present, then some ambassadors are clever diplomats. Therefore, some diplomats are clever. (*G*, *P*, *A*, *C*, *D*)

8.5 Proving Invalidity

In the previous chapter we saw that natural deduction could not be used with any facility to prove invalidity in propositional logic. The same thing can be said about natural deduction in predicate logic. But in predicate logic there is no simple and automatic technique such as truth tables or Venn diagrams to fall back on. However, there are two methods for proving invalidity in predicate logic that are just as effective as these other techniques, even though they may not be as convenient. One is the method used in Chapter 1 to prove the invalidity of various kinds of syllogisms—namely, the counterexample method. The other is what we will call the finite universe method. Both appeal to the basic idea underlying most proofs of invalidity: Any argument is proved invalid if it is shown that it is possible for it to have true premises and a false conclusion. Both methods are aimed at disclosing a situation that fulfills this requirement.

Counterexample Method

Application of the **counterexample method** consists in finding a substitution instance of a given invalid argument form (or, equally well, a given invalid symbolized argument) that has actually true premises and a false conclusion. For an example of its use, consider the following invalid symbolized argument:

$(\exists x)(Ax \cdot {\sim}Bx)$
$(x)(Cx \supset Bx)$ / $(\exists x)(Cx \cdot {\sim}Ax)$

In creating a substitution instance it is often easiest to begin with the conclusion. The conclusion is translated as "Some *C* are not *A*." Thus, to make this statement false, we need to find an example of a class (for *C*) that is included in another class (for *A*).

Cats and animals will serve this purpose. A little ingenuity provides us with the following substitution instance:

> Some animals are not mammals.
> All cats are mammals.
> Therefore, some cats are not animals.

In producing such a substitution instance it is important that the premises turn out to be indisputably true in the actual world, and the conclusion indisputably false. Statements involving the names of animal classes are convenient for this purpose, because everyone agrees about cats, dogs, mammals, fish, and so on. Also, it should be noted that several different substitution instances can usually be produced that suffice to prove the argument invalid. Finally, it goes without saying that any substitution instance that results in true premises and a true conclusion (or any arrangement other than true premises and false conclusion) proves nothing.

Here is an example of an invalid symbolized argument that includes a singular statement:

$(x)(Ax \supset Bx)$
$\sim Ac \qquad / \sim Bc$

This argument form commits the fallacy of denying the antecedent. Producing a substitution instance is easy:

> All cats are animals.
> Lassie is not a cat.
> Therefore, Lassie is not an animal.

In selecting the name of an individual for the second premise, it is again necessary to pick something that everyone agrees on. Since everyone knows that Lassie is a dog, this name serves our purpose. But if we had selected some other name, such as Trixie or Ajax, this would hardly suffice, because there is no general agreement as to what these names denote.

Here is a slightly more complex example:

$(x)[Ax \supset (Bx \lor Cx)]$
$(x)[Bx \supset (Cx \cdot Dx)] \qquad / (x)(Ax \supset Dx)$

A little ingenuity produces the following substitution instance:

> All dogs are either sharks or animals.
> All sharks are animals that are fish.
> Therefore, all dogs are fish.

The counterexample method is effective with most fairly simple invalid arguments in predicate logic. Since its application depends on the ingenuity of the user, however, it is not very well suited for complex arguments. For those, the finite universe method is probably a better choice.

Finite Universe Method

The **finite universe method** can be used to establish the invalidity of any invalid argument expressed in terms of a single variable. It depends on the idea that a valid argument remains valid no matter how things in the actual universe might be altered.

Accordingly, if we are given a valid argument, then that argument remains valid if it should happen that the universe is contracted so that it contains only a single member. On the other hand, if it should turn out that an argument has true premises and false conclusion in a universe consisting of only one or a few members, then that argument has been proved invalid.

To see how this method works, it is important to understand what happens to the meaning of universal and particular statements when the universe is shrunk in size. Accordingly, let us imagine that the universe contains only one thing instead of the billions of things that it actually contains. Let us name that one thing "Abigail." The statement "Everything in the universe is perfect" is then equivalent to "Abigail is perfect" (because Abigail is all that there is), and the statement "Something in the universe is perfect" is also equivalent to "Abigail is perfect" (because Abigail is that "something").

To represent this equivalence symbolically, we need a new metalogical symbol that asserts that the expressions on either side of it necessarily have the same truth value given a universe of a designated size. Although this equivalence bears a close resemblance to logical equivalence, it is not identical to it because logical equivalence holds independently of any alterations in the universe. The concept that we need to represent is a kind of conditional logical equivalence. Accordingly, we will select the double colon superscribed with a "c" (for "conditional"). For our purpose here, $\overset{c}{::}$ has the same effect as ::. Using the former symbol, we have for a universe consisting of one member:

$$(x)Px \overset{c}{::} Pa$$
$$(\exists x)Px \overset{c}{::} Pa$$

Proceeding, if we imagine that the universe contains exactly two things—let us name them "Abigail" and "Beatrice"—the statement "Everything in the universe is perfect" is equivalent to "Abigail is perfect *and* Beatrice is perfect." On the other hand, the statement "Something in the universe is perfect" is equivalent to "Abigail is perfect *or* Beatrice is perfect" (because "some" means at least one). In other words, the universal statement is equivalent to a *conjunction* of singular statements, and the particular statement is equivalent to a *disjunction* of singular statements. In symbols:

$$(x)Px \overset{c}{::} (Pa \cdot Pb)$$
$$(\exists x)Px \overset{c}{::} (Pa \lor Pb)$$

If the universe is increased to three—let us call the new member "Charmaine"—we have:

$$(x)Px \overset{c}{::} (Pa \cdot Pb \cdot Pc)$$
$$(\exists x)Px \overset{c}{::} (Pa \lor Pb \lor Pc)$$

This equivalence continues indefinitely as more and more members are added to the universe.

Extending this treatment to the more typical kinds of universal and particular statements, we have, for a universe of three:

$$(x)(Px \supset Qx) \overset{c}{::} [(Pa \supset Qa) \cdot (Pb \supset Qb) \cdot (Pc \supset Qc)]$$
$$(\exists x)(Px \cdot Qx) \overset{c}{::} [(Pa \cdot Qa) \lor (Pb \cdot Qb) \lor (Pc \cdot Qc)]$$

For expressions involving combinations of quantified statements, each of the component statements is translated separately and the resulting statement groups are linked together by means of the connective appearing in the original statement. Here are two examples for a universe of three:

$$[(x)Px \supset (\exists x)Qx] \overset{\varsigma}{::} [(Pa \cdot Pb \cdot Pc) \supset (Qa \vee Qb \vee Qc)]$$
$$[(x)(Px \supset Qx) \vee (\exists x)(Rx \cdot Sx)] \overset{\varsigma}{::} \{[(Pa \supset Qa) \cdot (Pb \supset Qb) \cdot (Pc \supset Qc)]$$
$$\vee [(Ra \cdot Sa) \vee (Rb \cdot Sb) \vee (Rc \cdot Sc)]\}$$

The method for proving an argument invalid consists in translating the premises and conclusion into singular statements, as per the above examples, and then testing the result with an indirect truth table (see Section 6.5). First a universe of one is tried. If it is possible for the premises to be true and the conclusion false in this universe, the argument is immediately identified as invalid. If, on the other hand, a contradiction results from this assumption, a universe of two is then tried. If, in this second universe, it is possible for the premises to be true and the conclusion false, the argument is invalid. If not, a universe of three is tried, and so on.

Consider the following symbolized argument:

$$(x)(Gx \supset Hx)$$
$$(\exists x)Hx \quad / \ (\exists x)Gx$$

For a universe having one member—call this member "Abigail"—the argument translates into:

$$Ga \supset Ha$$
$$Ha \quad / \ Ga$$

Testing with an indirect truth table, we have

$$\begin{array}{cccccc} Ga & \supset & Ha & / & Ha & / & / & Ga \\ F & T & T & & T & & & F \end{array}$$

Because it is possible for the premises to be true and the conclusion false, the argument is invalid. Another example:

$$(x)(Jx \supset Kx)$$
$$(\exists x)Jx \quad / \ (x)Kx$$

For a universe having one member, the indirect truth table is as follows:

$$\begin{array}{cccccc} Ja & \supset & Ka & / & Ja & / & / & Ka \\ \boxed{T \ T \ F} & & & & T & & & F \end{array}$$

Since it is impossible for the premises to be true and the conclusion false for this universe, we try a universe having two members, a and b:

$$\begin{array}{c} (Ja \supset Ka) \cdot (Jb \supset Kb) \ / \ Ja \vee Jb \ / \ / \ Ka \cdot Kb \\ \ \ T \ \ T \ \ T \ \ T \ \ F \ \ T \ \ F \quad\ \ T \ T \ F \quad\ \ T \ F \ F \end{array}$$

Since it is possible for the premises to be true and the conclusion false for this universe, the argument is invalid.

Here is an example involving compound statements:

$$(\exists x)Hx \supset (x)(Fx \supset Gx)$$
$$(\exists x)Fx \quad /(\exists x)Hx \supset (x)Gx$$

The indirect truth table for a universe having one member is as follows:

$$Ha \supset (Fa \supset Ga) \quad / \; Fa \quad / / \; Ha \supset Ga$$
$$\boxed{T \quad T \quad T \quad F} \quad F \qquad T \qquad T \; F \; F$$

A contradiction results, so we try a universe having two members. The resulting indirect truth table proves the argument invalid:

$$(Ha \lor Hb) \supset [(Fa \supset Ga) \cdot (Fb \supset Gb)] \quad / \; Fa \lor Fb \quad / / \; (Ha \lor Hb) \supset (Ga \cdot Gb)$$
$$\quad T \qquad T \quad T \; T \; T \; T \; F \; T \; F \qquad T \; T \; F \qquad\qquad T \qquad F \; T \; F \; F$$

The next example involves singular statements:

$$(\exists x)Mx \cdot (\exists x)Nx$$
$$Md \quad / \; Nd$$

The second premise asserts that something named *d* is an *M*. For this argument, the assumption that the universe contains only one member entails that this one member is named *d*. Here is the indirect truth table for such a universe:

$$Md \cdot Nd \quad / \; Md \quad / / \; Nd$$
$$\boxed{T \; T \; F} \qquad T \qquad F$$

When the universe is expanded to include two members, we are free to give any name we wish to the second member. Let us call it *e*. The resulting indirect truth table, which follows, shows that the argument is invalid. Notice that the second premise and the conclusion remain the same:

$$(Md \lor Me) \cdot (Nd \lor Ne) \quad / \; Md \quad / / \; Nd$$
$$\quad T \; T \qquad T \; F \; T \; T \qquad T \qquad F$$

The basic concept behind this method of proving invalidity rests on the fact that a valid argument is valid in all possible universes. Consequently, if an argument fails in a universe consisting of one, two, or any number of members, it is invalid.

While this method is primarily intended for proving arguments invalid, theoretically it can also be used to prove arguments valid. Several years ago a theorem was proved to the effect that an argument that does not fail in a universe of 2^n members, where *n* designates the number of different predicates, is valid.* According to this theorem, establishing the validity of an argument containing two different predicates requires a universe having four members, establishing the validity of an argument containing three different predicates requires a universe having eight members, and so on. For most arguments, however, a universe having four members is unwieldy at best, and a universe having eight members approaches the impossible (although a computer could handle it easily). Thus, while this method is usually quite convenient for proving invalidity, its usefulness in establishing validity is impeded by certain practical limitations.

EXERCISE 8.5

I. Use the counterexample method to prove that the following symbolized arguments are invalid.

---

*See Wilhelm Ackermann, *Solvable Cases of the Decision Problem* (Amsterdam: North-Holland Publishing Co., 1954), Chapter 4. This theorem, incidentally, holds only for monadic predicates.

★ (1) 1. $(x)(Ax \supset Bx)$
        2. $(x)(Ax \supset \sim Cx)$ / $(x)(Cx \supset Bx)$

  (2) 1. $(\exists x)(Ax \cdot Bx)$
       2. $(x)(Cx \supset Ax)$ / $(\exists x)(Cx \cdot Bx)$

  (3) 1. $(x)(Ax \supset Bx)$
       2. Bc / Ac

★ (4) 1. $(\exists x)(Ax \cdot Bx)$
        2. $(\exists x)(Ax \cdot Cx)$ / $(\exists x)[Ax \cdot (Bx \cdot Cx)]$

  (5) 1. $(x)[Ax \vee (Bx \vee Cx)]$ / $(x)Ax \vee [(x)Bx \vee (x)Cx]$

  (6) 1. $(x)[Ax \supset (Bx \vee Cx)]$
       2. $(x)[(Bx \cdot Cx) \supset Dx]$ / $(x)(Ax \supset Dx)$

★ (7) 1. $(\exists x)Ax$
        2. $(\exists x)Bx$
        3. $(x)(Ax \supset \sim Cx)$ / $(\exists x)(Bx \cdot \sim Cx)$

  (8) 1. $(x)[(Ax \vee Bx) \supset Cx]$
       2. $(x)[(Cx \cdot Dx) \supset Ex]$ / $(x)(Ax \supset Ex)$

  (9) 1. $(x)[(Ax \cdot Bx) \supset Cx]$
       2. $(x)[(Ax \cdot Cx) \supset Dx]$ / $(x)[(Ax \cdot Dx) \supset Cx]$

★ (10) 1. $(\exists x)(Ax \cdot Bx)$
         2. $(\exists x)(Cx \cdot \sim Bx)$
         3. $(x)(Ax \supset Cx)$ / $(\exists x)[(Cx \cdot Bx) \cdot \sim Ax]$

iLrn II. Use the finite universe method to prove that the following symbolized arguments are invalid.

  ★ (1) 1. $(x)(Ax \supset Bx)$
          2. $(x)(Ax \supset Cx)$ / $(x)(Bx \supset Cx)$

   (2) 1. $(x)(Ax \vee Bx)$
        2. $\sim An$ / $(x)Bx$

   (3) 1. $(\exists x)Ax \vee (\exists x)Bx$
        2. $(\exists x)Ax$ / $(\exists x)Bx$

  ★ (4) 1. $(x)(Ax \supset Bx)$
          2. $(\exists x)Ax$ / $(x)Bx$

   (5) 1. $(x)[Ax \supset (Bx \vee Cx)]$
        2. $(\exists x)Ax$ / $(\exists x)Bx$

   (6) 1. $(\exists x)Ax$
        2. $(\exists x)Bx$ / $(\exists x)(Ax \cdot Bx)$

  ★ (7) 1. $(x)(Ax \supset Bx)$
          2. $(\exists x)Bx \supset (\exists x)Cx$ / $(x)(Ax \supset Cx)$

   (8) 1. $(\exists x)(Ax \cdot Bx) \equiv (\exists x)Cx$
        2. $(x)(Ax \supset Bx)$ / $(x)Ax \equiv (\exists x)Cx$

   (9) 1. $(\exists x)(Ax \cdot \sim Bx)$
        2. $(\exists x)(Bx \cdot \sim Ax)$ / $(x)(Ax \vee Bx)$

★ (10) 1. $(\exists x)(Ax \cdot Bx)$
      2. $(\exists x)(\sim Ax \cdot \sim Bx)$ / $(x)(Ax \equiv Bx)$

III. Translate the following arguments into symbolic form. Then use either the counterexample method or the finite universe method to prove that each is invalid.

★ 1. Violinists who play well are accomplished musicians. There are some violinists in the orchestra. Therefore, some musicians are accomplished. (*V, P, A, M, O*)

2. Pianists and harpsichordists are meticulous. Alfred Brendel is a pianist. Therefore, everyone is meticulous. (*P, H, M*)

3. If there are any oboists, there are some bassoonists. If there are any clarinetists, there are some flutists. Amelia is both an oboist and a clarinetist. Therefore, some bassoonists are flutists. (*O, B, C, F*)

★ 4. All tympanists are haughty. If some tympanists are haughty, then some percussionists are overbearing. Therefore, all tympanists are overbearing. (*T, H, P, O*)

5. All cellists and violinists are members of the string section. Some violinists are not cellists. Also, some cellists are not violinists. Therefore, everyone is a member of the string section. (*C, V, M*)

8.6   Relational Predicates and Overlapping Quantifiers

Even the logical machinery developed thus far is not adequate for deriving the conclusions of a number of arguments. Consider, for example, the following:

> All dogs are animals. Therefore, whoever owns a dog owns an animal.

> If there are any butterflies, then if all butterflies are free, they are free. There are butterflies in the garden. Therefore, if all butterflies are free, something in the garden is free.

The first argument involves a relation—the relation of ownership—and we have yet to see how relations can be dealt with. The second argument, while not involving any relations, involves a quantifier that overlaps another quantifier. In this section the apparatus of predicate logic will be extended to cover examples such as these.

The predicates we have used thus far are called **monadic predicates,** or one-place predicates, because they are used to assign an attribute to individual things. A **relational predicate** (or relation) is a predicate that is used to establish a connection *between* or *among* individuals.

Relations occur in varying degrees of complexity, depending on the number of individuals related. The simplest, called *binary* (or *dyadic*) relations, establish a connection between two individuals. Some examples are the relation of being taller than, as expressed in the statement "Steve is taller than David," and the relation of being a friend, as expressed in "Sylvia is a friend of Olivia." *Trinary* (or *triadic*) relations establish a connection among three individuals. For example, the relation of being between, as in "St. Louis is between Chicago and New Orleans," and the relation of reading something to someone, as in "George read *Othello* to Madeline." *Quaternary* (or *tetradic*) relations link four individuals together—for example, the relation of reading something to someone at a certain time, as in "George read *Othello* to Madeline on Thursday." The complexity increases until we have what are called *n-ary* (or *n-adic*) relations, which link *n* things together. In this section we will restrict our attention to binary relations.

Translating Relational Statements

Relations are symbolized like other predicates except that two lower-case letters, representing the two related individuals, are written to the immediate right of the upper-case letter representing the relation. Here are some examples of relational statements involving specifically named individuals:

Statement	Symbolic translation
Anthony is married to Cynthia.	*Mac*
Deborah loves physics.	*Ldp*
The Sears Tower is taller than the Empire State Building.	*Tse*
Donald is the father of Jim.	*Fdj*

Notice that the order in which the lower-case letters are listed often makes a difference. If the third statement were translated *Tes*, the symbolic statement would read "The Empire State Building is taller than the Sears Tower," which is false. Quantifiers are attached to relational predicates in the same way they are to monadic predicates. Some examples of relational statements involving quantifiers are as follows:

Statement	Symbolic translation
Thomas knows everything.	$(x)Ktx$
Thomas knows something.	$(\exists x)Ktx$
Everything is different from everything.	$(x)(y)Dxy$
Something is different from something.	$(\exists x)(\exists y)Dxy$
Everything is different from something (or other).	$(x)(\exists y)Dxy$
Something is different from everything.	$(\exists x)(y)Dxy$

The last four statements involve **overlapping quantifiers.** We may read these symbols as follows:

$(x)(y)$	For all *x* and for all *y* . . .
$(\exists x)(\exists y)$	There exists an *x* such that there exists a *y* such that . . .
$(x)(\exists y)$	For all *x* there exists a *y* such that . . .
$(\exists x)(y)$	There exists an *x* such that for all *y* . . .

Applying this phraseology to the last statement above, for example, we have "There exists an *x* such that for all *y*, *x* is different from *y*"—which is simply another way of saying "Something is different from everything."

When two quantifiers of the same sort appear adjacent to each other, the order in which they are listed is not significant. In other words, the statement $(x)(y)Dxy$ is logically equivalent to $(y)(x)Dxy$, and $(\exists x)(\exists y)Dxy$ is logically equivalent to $(\exists y)(\exists x)Dxy$. A little reflection on the meaning of these statements should justify this equivalence. But when different quantifiers appear adjacent to each other, the order *does* make a difference, sometimes even when the statement function is nonrelational. Accordingly, $(x)(\exists y)Dxy$ is not logically equivalent to $(\exists y)(x)Dxy$. This fact can be seen more clearly in terms of a different example. If Lxy means "x loves y" and we imagine the universe restricted to persons, then $(x)(\exists y)Lxy$ means "Everyone loves someone (or other)," while $(\exists y)(x)Lxy$ means "There is someone whom everyone loves." Clearly these two statements are not equivalent.

Relational predicates can be combined with ordinary predicates to translate statements having varying degrees of complexity. In the examples that follow, Px means "x is a person." The meaning of the other predicates should be clear from the context:

1. Any heavyweight can defeat any lightweight.
   $(x)[Hx \supset (y)(Ly \supset Dxy)]$

2. Some heavyweights can defeat any lightweight.
   $(\exists x)[Hx \cdot (y)(Ly \supset Dxy)]$

3. No heavyweight can defeat every lightweight.
   $(x)[Hx \supset (\exists y)(Ly \cdot \sim Dxy)]$
   or
   $\sim(\exists x)[Hx \cdot (y)(Ly \supset Dxy)]$

4. Everyone cares for someone (or other).
   $(x)[Px \supset (\exists y)(Py \cdot Cxy)]$

5. Someone does not care for anyone.
   $(\exists x)[Px \cdot (y)(Py \supset \sim Cxy)]$

6. Anyone who cares for someone is cared for himself.
   $(x)\{[Px \cdot (\exists y)(Py \cdot Cxy)] \supset (\exists z)(Pz \cdot Czx)\}$

7. Not everyone respects himself.
   $(\exists x)(Px \cdot \sim Rxx)$
   or
   $\sim(x)(Px \supset Rxx)$

8. Anyone who does not respect himself is not respected by anyone.
   $(x)[(Px \cdot \sim Rxx) \supset (y)(Py \supset \sim Ryx)]$

The same general rule applies in translating these statements as applies in translating any other statement in predicate logic: Universal quantifiers go with implications and existential quantifiers go with conjunctions. Every one of the symbolic expressions above follows this rule. For example, in the first statement, both quantifiers are universal and both operators are horseshoes. In the second statement, the main quantifier is existential and the subordinate quantifier universal; accordingly, the main operator is a dot and the subordinate operator is a horseshoe. Among these statements, number 6 is the most complex. The symbolic translation of this statement reads, "For all x, if x is a person and there exists a y such that y is a person and x cares for y, then there exists a *z* such that *z* is a person and *z* cares for *x*." Upon reflection it should be clear that this is simply another way of expressing the original English statement.

Another important rule to keep in mind when translating statements of this kind is that every variable must be bound by some quantifier. If a variable is left dangling outside the scope of its intended quantifier, the translation is defective. For example, if the second statement were translated $(\exists x)Hx \cdot (y)(Ly \supset Dxy)$, then the *x* in *Dxy* would not be bound by the existential quantifier. As a result, the translation would be defective. To correct it, brackets must be inserted that provide for the existential quantifier to range over *Dxy*.

The same techniques used to translate these eight statements are also used to translate certain statements involving monadic predicates throughout. Consider the following:

If anything is good and all good things are safe, then it is safe.

$(x)\{[Gx \cdot (y)(Gy \supset Sy)] \supset Sx\}$

If anything is good and some good things are dangerous, then it is dangerous.

$(x)\{[Gx \cdot (\exists y)(Gy \cdot Dy)] \supset Dx\}$

Since the "it" at the end of these statements refers to one of the "good" things mentioned at the beginning, the quantifier that binds the *x* in *Gx* must also bind the *x* in *Sx* and *Dx*. The set of braces in the symbolic expressions ensures this.

Another point to notice regarding statements such as these is that the quantified expression inside the brackets is expressed in terms of a *new* variable. This procedure is essential to avoid ambiguity. If instead of *y*, *x* had been used, the variable in this expression would appear to be bound by two different quantifiers at the same time.

In other statements, the one or more individuals mentioned at the end are *not* necessarily the same ones mentioned at the beginning. In such cases the quantifier that binds the individuals at the beginning should *not* bind those at the end. Compare the next pair of statements with those we have just considered.

If anything is good and all good things are safe, then something is safe.

$[(\exists x)Gx \cdot (y)(Gy \supset Sy)] \supset (\exists z)Sz$

If anything is good and some good things are dangerous, then something is dangerous.

$[(\exists x)Gx \cdot (\exists y)(Gy \cdot Dy)] \supset (\exists z)Dz$

In these cases the "something" at the end is not necessarily one of the "good" things mentioned at the beginning. Accordingly, the quantifier that binds the *x* in *Gx* does *not* range all the way to the end of the statement. Furthermore, the quantifier in question is now an *existential* quantifier. In the previous pair of statements the quantifier had to be universal because it ranged over the main operator, which was a horseshoe. In the new pair, however, no quantifier ranges over the implication symbol. As a result, the sense of these statements has shifted to mean "If *something* is good . . ."

Note that, although a different variable is used to express each of the three different components in the pair of statements above, this is not required. Because in this case no quantifier ranges over any other quantifier, it would be perfectly appropriate to use the same variable throughout.

8

The next pair of statements involve relational predicates. As in the previous pair, no single quantifier ranges over the entire statement because the individuals mentioned at the end are not necessarily the same ones mentioned at the beginning:

If everyone helps himself, then everyone will be helped.

$(x)(Px \supset Hxx) \supset (x)[(Px \supset (\exists y)Hyx)]$

If someone helps himself, then someone will be helped.

$(\exists x)(Px \cdot Hxx) \supset (\exists x)(\exists y)(Px \cdot Hyx)$

This completes our explanation of how to translate statements involving relational predicates and overlapping quantifiers. You may, if you wish, proceed directly to Exercise 8.6 Part I before completing the remainder of this section.

Using the Rules of Inference

Let us first see how the various quantifier rules apply to overlapping quantifiers. The change of quantifier rule is applied in basically the same way as it is with single quantifiers. The following short sequence illustrates its application:

1. $\sim(x)(\exists y)Pxy$
2. $(\exists x)\sim(\exists y)Pxy$ 1, CQ
3. $(\exists x)(y)\sim Pxy$ 2, CQ

As the tilde operator is moved past a quantifier, the quantifier in question is switched for its correlative. With the exception of a restriction on universal generalization, which we will introduce presently, the instantiation and generalization rules are also used in basically the same way as they are with single quantifiers. Example:

1. $(\exists x)(\exists y)Pxy$
2. $(\exists y)Pay$ 1, EI
3. Pab 2, EI
4. $(\exists x)Pxb$ 3, EG
5. $(\exists y)(\exists x)Pxy$ 4, EG

With each successive instantiation the outermost quantifier drops off. Generalization restores the quantifiers in the reverse order.

This proof demonstrates our earlier observation that the order of the quantifiers is not significant when the same kind of quantifier is used throughout. We also observed that the order does make a difference when different quantifiers appear together. Accordingly, the statement $(x)(\exists y)Pxy$ is not logically equivalent to $(\exists y)(x)Pxy$. As the instantiation and generalization rules now stand, however, it is quite possible, with a proof similar to the one above, to establish the logical equivalence of these two expressions. Therefore, to keep this from happening we now introduce a new restriction on universal generalization:

UG: $\dfrac{\mathscr{F}y}{(x)\mathscr{F}x}$ *Restriction:*   UG must not be used if $\mathscr{F}y$ contains an existential name and y is free in the line where that name is introduced.

To see how this restriction applies, let us attempt to deduce $(\exists y)(x)Pxy$ from $(x)(\exists y)Pxy$:

```
1. (x)(∃y)Pxy
2. (∃y)Pxy          1, UI
3. Pxa              2, EI
4. (x)Pxa           3, UG (invalid)
5. (∃y)(x)Pxy       4, EG
```

The proof fails on line 4 because $\mathscr{F}y$ (that is, *Pxa*) contains a name introduced by existential instantiation (namely, *a*), and *x* is free in line 3 where that name is introduced. Our new restriction is required precisely to prevent this kind of proof sequence from occurring. The reasonableness of the restriction may be seen once it is realized what happens in this proof. Line 1 asserts that for every *x* in the universe there exists some *y* that has relation *P* to it. This does not mean that there is one *single* thing that is so related to every *x* but that each *x* has, perhaps, a *different* thing so related to it. On line 2 we select one of these *x*'s at random, and on line 3 we give the name *a* to the thing so related to it. Then on line 4 we draw the conclusion that everything in the universe has relation *P* to *a*. But this, as we just saw, is precisely what line 1 does *not* say. Line 4, therefore, is fallacious.

In summary, we now have two restrictions on universal generalization. The first concerns only conditional and indirect sequences and prevents UG from occurring within the scope of such a sequence when the instantial variable is free in the first line. The second restriction concerns only arguments involving overlapping quantifiers. With these two restrictions in hand, we may now proceed to illustrate the use of natural deduction in arguments involving relational predicates and overlapping quantifiers. The example that follows does not include any relational predicates, but it does involve overlapping quantifiers:

```
1. (∃x)Ax ⊃ (∃x)Bx      / (∃y)(x)(Ax ⊃ By)
   2. Ax                 ACP
   3. (∃x)Ax             2, EG
   4. (∃x)Bx             1, 3, MP
   5. Bc                 4, EI
6. Ax ⊃ Bc              2–5, CP
7. (x)(Ax ⊃ Bc)         6, UG
8. (∃y)(x)(Ax ⊃ By)     7, EG
```

Conditional and indirect proof are used in the same way with relational predicates and overlapping quantifiers as they are with monadic predicates and nonoverlapping quantifiers. The conditional proof above begins, as usual, by assuming the antecedent of the conclusion. When line 7 is reached, we must be careful that neither of the restrictions against universal generalization is violated. While the instantial variable *x* is free in the first line of the conditional sequence, line 7 does not lie within that sequence, so the first restriction is obeyed. And while line 7 does include the existential name *c*, *x* is not free in line 5 where that name is introduced. Thus, the second restriction is obeyed as well.

The next proof involves a relational predicate. The proof shows that while (x)(∃y) *Dxy* is not logically equivalent to (∃y)(x)*Dxy*, it can be deduced from that statement:

```
1. (∃y)(x)Dxy          / (x)(∃y)Dxy
2. (x)Dxm              1, EI
```

3. *Dxm*	2, UI
4. *(∃y)Dxy*	3, EG
5. *(x)(∃y)Dxy*	4, UG

The next example concludes with a line in which an individual is related to itself. Since there are no restrictions on universal instantiation, the procedure leading up to this line is perfectly legitimate. Notice in line 4 that tautology is used with relational predicates in the same way that it is with monadic predicates:

1. *(∃y)(x)(Exy ∨ Eyx)*	/ *(∃z)Ezz*
2. *(x)(Exa ∨ Eax)*	1, EI
3. *Eaa ∨ Eaa*	2, UI
4. *Eaa*	3, Taut
5. *(∃z)Ezz*	4, EG

Sometimes the order in which instantiation steps are performed is critical. The following proof provides an example:

1. *(x)(∃y)(Fxy ⊃ Gxy)*	
2. *(∃x)(y)Fxy*	/ *(∃x)(∃y)Gxy*
3. *(y)Fmy*	2, EI
4. *(∃y)(Fmy ⊃ Gmy)*	1, UI
5. *Fmo ⊃ Gmo*	4, EI
6. *Fmo*	3, UI
7. *Gmo*	5, 6, MP
8. *(∃y)Gmy*	7, EG
9. *(∃x)(∃y)Gxy*	8, EG

Line 2 must be instantiated before line 1 because the step introduces a new existential name. For the same reason, line 4 must be instantiated before line 3.

The next proof involves an indirect sequence. Such sequences often make use of the change of quantifier rule, as this proof illustrates:

1. *(∃x)(∃y)(Jxy ∨ Kxy) ⊃ (∃x)Lx*	
2. *(x)(y)(Lx ⊃ ~Ly)*	/ *(x)(y)~Jxy*
3. *~(x)(y)~Jxy*	AIP
4. *(∃x)~(y)~Jxy*	3, CQ
5. *(∃x)(∃y)~~Jxy*	4, CQ
6. *(∃x)(∃y)Jxy*	5, DN
7. *(∃y)Jmy*	6, EI
8. *Jmn*	7, EI
9. *Jmn ∨ Kmn*	8, Add
10. *(∃y)(Jmy ∨ Kmy)*	9, EG
11. *(∃x)(∃y)(Jxy ∨ Kxy)*	10, EG
12. *(∃x)Lx*	1, 11, MP
13. *Lo*	12, EI
14. *(y)(Lo ⊃ ~Ly)*	2, UI
15. *Lo ⊃ ~Lo*	14, UI
16. *~Lo*	13, 15, MP
17. *Lo • ~Lo*	13, 16, Conj
18. *~~(x)(y)~Jxy*	3–17, IP
19. *(x)(y)~Jxy*	18, DN

Because line 1 cannot be instantiated, the only strategy is to obtain the antecedent of the conditional with the aim of obtaining the consequent via *modus ponens*. This is accomplished on line 11 via indirect proof. Notice on line 9 that addition is used with relational predicates in the same way that it is with monadic predicates.

A final word of caution is called for regarding universal instantiation and the two generalization rules. First, when UI is used to introduce variables into a proof, it is important that these variables end up free and that they not be captured in the process by other quantifiers. The following examples illustrate both correct and incorrect applications of this rule:

1. $(x)(\exists y)Pxy$
2. $(\exists y)Pyy$ 1, UI   (invalid—the instantial variable *y* has been captured by the existential quantifier)

1. $(x)(\exists y)Pxy$
2. $(\exists y)Pxy$ 1, UI   (valid—the instantial variable *x* is free)

1. $(x)(\exists y)Pxy$
2. $(\exists y)Pzy$ 1, UI   (valid—the instantial variable *z* is free)

An analogous caution applies to the two generalization rules. When UG and EG are used, it is important that the instantial letter be replaced by a variable that is captured by no previously introduced quantifier and that no other variables be captured by the newly introduced quantifier. The following examples illustrate both correct and incorrect applications of this rule:

1. $(\exists x)Pxy$
2. $(x)(\exists x)Pxx$ 1, UG   (invalid—the new *x* has been captured by the existential quantifier)

1. $(\exists x)Pxy$
2. $(\exists x)(\exists x)Pxx$ 1, EG   (invalid—the new *x* has been captured by the old existential quantifier)

1. $(\exists x)Pxy$
2. $(\exists y)(\exists x)Pxy$ 1, EG   (valid)

1. $(x)(\exists y)Lxy$
2. $(\exists y)Lxy$ 1, UI
3. Lxa 2, EI
4. $(\exists x)Lxx$ 3, EG   (invalid—the quantifier has captured the *x* immediately adjacent to the *L*)

1. $(x)(\exists y)Lxy$
2. $(\exists y)Lxy$ 1, UI
3. Lxa 2, EI
4. $(\exists z)Lxz$ 3, EG   (valid—the *x* remains free)

1. $(x)(y)Kxy$
2. $(y)Kxy$ 1, UI
3. Kxx 2, UI
4. $(x)Kxx$ 3, UG   (valid)

To see that the fourth example is indeed invalid, let *Lxy* stand for "*x* is larger than *y*," and let the variables range over the real numbers. The statement $(x)(\exists y)Lxy$ then means that there is no smallest number—which is true. But the statement $(\exists x)Lxx$ means that there is a number that is larger than itself—which is false.

EXERCISE 8.6

iLrn I. Translate the following statements into symbolic form:

★ 1. Charmaine read *Paradise Lost*. (*Rxy: x* read *y*)

2. Whoever reads *Paradise Lost* is educated. (*Rxy: x* reads *y; Ex: x* is educated)

3. James is a friend of either Ellen or Connie. (*Fxy: x* is a friend of *y*)

★ 4. If James has any friends, then Marlene is one of them. (*Fxy: x* is a friend of *y*)

5. Dr. Jordan teaches only geniuses. (*Txy: x* teaches *y; Gx: x* is a genius)

6. Dr. Nelson teaches a few morons. (*Txy: x* teaches *y; Mx: x* is a moron)

★ 7. Every person can sell something or other. (*Px: x* is a person; *Sxy: x* can sell *y*)

8. Some people cannot sell anything.

9. No person can sell everything.

★ 10. Some people can sell anything.

11. The Royal Hotel serves only good drinks. (*Sxy: x* serves *y; Gx: x* is good; *Dx: x* is a drink)

12. The Clark Corporation advertises everything it produces. (*Axy: x* advertises *y; Pxy: x* produces *y*)

★ 13. Peterson can drive some of the cars in the lot. (*Dxy: x* can drive *y; Cx: x* is a car; *Lx: x* is in the lot)

14. Jones can drive any car in the lot.

15. Sylvia invited only her friends. (*Ixy: x* invited *y; Fxy: x* is a friend of *y*)

★ 16. Christopher invited some of his friends.

17. Some people break everything they touch. (*Px: x* is a person; *Bxy: x* breaks *y; Txy: x* touches *y*)

18. Some people speak to whoever speaks to them. (*Px: x* is a person; *Sxy: x* speaks to *y*)

★ 19. Every person admires some people he or she meets. (*Px: x* is a person; *Axy: x* admires *y; Mxy: x* meets *y*)

20. Some people admire every person they meet.

21. Some policemen arrest only traffic violators. (*Px: x* is a policeman; *Axy: x* arrests *y; Tx: x* is a traffic violator)

★ 22. Some policemen arrest every traffic violator they see. (*Px: x* is a policeman; *Axy: x* arrests *y; Tx: x* is a traffic violator; *Sxy: x* sees *y*)

23. If there are cheaters, then some cheaters will be punished. (*Cx: x* is a cheater; *Px: x* will be punished)

24. If there are any cheaters, then if all the referees are vigilant they will be punished. (*Cx: x* is a cheater; *Rx: x* is a referee; *Vx: x* is vigilant; *Px: x* will be punished)

★ 25. Every lawyer will represent a wealthy client. (*Lx: x* is a lawyer; *Rxy: x* will represent *y*; *Wx: x* is wealthy; *Cx: x* is a client)

26. Some lawyers will represent any person who will not represent himself. (*Lx: x* is a lawyer; *Px: x* is a person; *Rxy: x* represents *y*)

27. Some children in the third grade can read any of the books in the library. (*Cx: x* is a child; *Tx: x* is in the third grade; *Rxy: x* can read *y*; *Bx: x* is a book; *Lx: x* is in the library)

★ 28. All children in the fourth grade can read any of the books in the library.

29. If there are any safe drivers, then if none of the trucks break down they will be hired. (*Sx: x* is safe; *Dx: x* is a driver; *Tx: x* is a truck; *Bx: x* breaks down; *Hx: x* will be hired)

30. If there are any safe drivers, then some safe drivers will be hired.

iLrn II. Derive the conclusion of the following symbolized arguments. Use conditional proof or indirect proof as needed.

★ (1) 1. $(x)[Ax \supset (y)Bxy]$
    2. Am / $(y)Bmy$

(2) 1. $(x)[Ax \supset (y)(By \supset Cxy)]$
    2. $Am \cdot Bn$ / Cmn

(3) 1. $(\exists x)[Ax \cdot (y)(By \supset Cxy)]$
    2. $(\exists x)Ax \supset Bj$ / $(\exists x)Cxj$

★ (4) 1. $(x)(\exists y)(Ax \supset By)$ / $(x)Ax \supset (\exists y)By$

(5) 1. $(\exists x)Ax \supset (\exists y)By$ / $(\exists y)(x)(Ax \supset By)$

(6) 1. $(x)(y)(Ax \supset By)$
    2. $(x)(\exists y)(Ax \supset Cy)$ / $(x)(\exists y)[Ax \supset (By \cdot Cy)]$

★ (7) 1. $(\exists x)[Ax \cdot (y)(Ay \supset Bxy)]$ / $(\exists x)Bxx$

(8) 1. $(\exists x)[Ax \cdot (y)(By \supset Cxy)]$
    2. $(x)(\exists y)(Ax \supset By)$ / $(\exists x)(\exists y)Cxy$

(9) 1. $(\exists x)(y)(Axy \supset Bxy)$
    2. $(x)(\exists y)\sim Bxy$ / $\sim(x)(y)Axy$

★ (10) 1. $(x)(\exists y)Axy \supset (x)(\exists y)Bxy$
    2. $(\exists x)(y)\sim Bxy$ / $(\exists x)(y)\sim Axy$

(11) 1. $(\exists x)\{Ax \cdot [(\exists y)By \supset Cx]\}$
    2. $(x)(Ax \supset Bx)$ / $(\exists x)Cx$

(12) 1. $(\exists x)(y)[(Ay \cdot By) \supset Cxy]$
    2. $(y)(Ay \supset By)$ / $(y)[Ay \supset (\exists x)Cxy]$

★ (13) 1. $(\exists x)\{Ax \cdot (y)[(By \lor Cy) \supset Dxy]\}$
    2. $(\exists x)Ax \supset (\exists y)By$ / $(\exists x)(\exists y)Dxy$

(14) 1. $(x)\{Ax \supset [(\exists y)(By \cdot Cy) \supset Dx]\}$
    2. $(x)(Bx \supset Cx)$ / $(x)[Ax \supset (Bx \supset Dx)]$

(15) 1. $(\exists x)(y)(Ayx \supset \sim Axy)$ / $\sim(x)Axx$

★ (16) 1. $(x)(\exists y)(Ax \cdot By)$ / $(\exists y)(x)(Ax \cdot By)$

8

(17) **1.** $(x)(\exists y)(Ax \lor By)$ / $(\exists y)(x)(Ax \lor By)$

(18) **1.** $(x)[Ax \supset (\exists y)(By \cdot Cxy)]$
2. $(\exists x)[Ax \cdot (y)(By \supset Dxy)]$ / $(\exists x)(\exists y)(Cxy \cdot Dxy)$

★ (19) **1.** $(x)(\exists y)Axy \lor (x)(y)Bxy$
2. $(x)(\exists y)(Cx \supset \sim Bxy)$ / $(x)(\exists y)(Cx \supset Axy)$

(20) **1.** $(x)(y)[Axy \supset (Bx \cdot Cy)]$
2. $(x)(y)[(Bx \lor Dy) \supset \sim Axy]$ / $\sim(\exists x)(\exists y)Axy$

iLrn **III.** Translate the following arguments into symbolic form. Then derive the conclusion of each, using conditional proof or indirect proof when needed.

★ 1. Any professional can outplay any amateur. Jones is a professional but he cannot outplay Meyers. Therefore, Meyers is not an amateur. (*Px: x* is a professional; *Ax: x* is an amateur; *Oxy: x* can outplay *y*)

2. Whoever is a friend of either Michael or Paul will receive a gift. If Michael has any friends, then Eileen is one of them. Therefore, if Ann is a friend of Michael, then Eileen will receive a gift. (*Fxy: x* is a friend of *y*; *Rx: x* will receive a gift)

3. A horse is an animal. Therefore, whoever owns a horse owns an animal. (*Hx: x* is a horse; *Ax: x* is an animal; *Oxy: x* owns *y*)

★ 4. O'Brien is a person. Furthermore, O'Brien is smarter than any person in the class. Since no person is smarter than himself, it follows that O'Brien is not in the class. (*Px: x* is a person; *Sxy: x* is smarter than *y*; *Cx: x* is in the class)

5. If there are any honest politicians, then if all the ballots are counted they will be reelected. Some honest politicians will not be reelected. Therefore, some ballots will not be counted. (*Hx: x* is honest; *Px: x* is a politician; *Bx: x* is a ballot; *Cx: x* is counted; *Rx: x* will be reelected)

6. Dr. Rogers can cure any person who cannot cure himself. Dr. Rogers is a person. Therefore, Dr. Rogers can cure himself. (*Px: x* is a person; *Cxy: x* can cure *y*)

★ 7. Some people are friends of every person they know. Every person knows someone (or other). Therefore, at least one person is a friend of someone. (*Px: x* is a person; *Fxy: x* is a friend of *y*; *Kxy: x* knows *y*)

8. If there are any policemen, then if there are any robbers, then they will arrest them. If any robbers are arrested by policemen, they will go to jail. There are some policemen and Macky is a robber. Therefore, Macky will go to jail. (*Px: x* is a policeman; *Rx: x* is a robber; *Axy: x* arrests *y*; *Jx: x* will go to jail)

9. If anything is missing, then some person stole it. If anything is damaged, then some person broke it. Something is either missing or damaged. Therefore, some person either stole something or broke something. (*Mx: x* is missing; *Px: x* is a person; *Sxy: x* stole *y*; *Dx: x* is damaged; *Bxy: x* broke *y*)

★ 10. If there are any instructors, then if at least one classroom is available they will be effective. If there are either any textbooks or workbooks, there will be instructors and classrooms. Furthermore, if there are any classrooms, they will be available. Therefore, if there are any textbooks, then some instructors will be effective. (*Ix: x* is an instructor; *Cx: x* is a classroom; *Ax: x* is available; *Ex: x* is effective; *Tx: x* is a textbook; *Wx: x* is a workbook)

8

8.7 Identity

Many arguments in ordinary language involve a special relation called *identity*, and translating this relation requires special treatment. Consider, for example, the following argument:

> The only friend I have is Elizabeth. Elizabeth is not Nancy. Nancy is a Canadian. Therefore, there is a Canadian who is not my friend.

The peculiar feature of this argument is that it involves special statements about individuals. To translate such statements, we adopt a symbol from arithmetic, the equal sign ($=$), to represent the identity relation. We can use this symbol to translate a large variety of statements, including simple identity statements, existential assertions about individuals, statements involving "only," "the only," "no . . . except," and "all except," and statements involving superlatives, numerical claims, and definite descriptions. After seeing how the identity relation is used to translate such statements, we will see how natural deduction is used to derive the conclusions of arguments involving identity.

Simple Identity Statements

The simplest statements involving identity are those asserting that a named individual is identical to another named individual. Here are some examples:

Samuel Clemens is Mark Twain.	$c = t$
Woody Allen is Allen Konigsberg.	$a = k$
Dr. Jekyll is Mr. Hyde.	$j = h$

The first statement asserts that Samuel Clemens is identically the same person as Mark Twain, the second that Woody Allen is the same person as Allen Konigsberg, and the third that Dr. Jekyll is the same person as Mr. Hyde. In other words, the statements claim that the names "Samuel Clemens" and "Mark Twain" designate the same person, "Woody Allen" and "Allen Konigsberg" designate the same person, and so on.

To translate a negated identity statement, we simply draw a slash through the identity symbol. Thus "Beethoven is not Mozart" is translated $b \neq m$. The expression $b \neq m$ is just an abbreviated way of writing $\sim(b = m)$. Here are some additional examples:

William Wordsworth is not John Keats.	$w \neq k$
Jodie Foster is not Meryl Streep.	$f \neq s$
Peter Jennings is not Aaron Brown.	$j \neq b$

The kinds of statements we will consider next are more complicated, and to facilitate their translation a set of conventions governing conjunctions, disjunctions, and simple identity statements will now be introduced. Many of our translations will involve lengthy strings of conjunctions, such as $Pm \cdot Km \cdot Pn \cdot Kn$. Instead of introducing parentheses and brackets into these expressions, we may simply write them as a string of conjuncts. Lengthy disjunctions may be treated the same way. In simple identity statements, the identity symbol controls only the letters to its immediate left and right. Accordingly, instead of writing $(c = n) \cdot (e = p) \cdot (s = t)$, we may write $c = n \cdot e = p \cdot s = t$, and instead of writing $P \supset (a = m)$, we may write $P \supset a = m$. Let us now use these conventions to translate some special kinds of statements involving identity.

"Only," "The Only," and "No ... Except"

Section 4.7 explained that the words "only," "the only," and "no ... except" signal an ordinary categorical proposition when the word that follows is a plural noun or pronoun. For example, the statement "Only relatives are invited" means simply "All invited persons are relatives," and "The only animals in this canyon are skunks" means "All animals in this canyon are skunks." However, when the word that follows "only," "the only," or "no ... except" designates an individual, something more is intended. Thus the statement "Only Nixon resigned the presidency" means (1) that Nixon resigned the presidency and (2) that if anyone resigned the presidency, that person is Nixon. Thus the general form of such statements is that a designated individual has a stated attribute and anything having that attribute is identical to the designated individual. Here are some examples:

Only Nolan Ryan has struck out 5000 batters.	$Sn \cdot (x)(Sx \supset x = n)$
The only opera written by Beethoven is *Fidelio*.	$Of \cdot Bf \cdot (x)[(Ox \cdot Bx) \supset x = f]$
No nation except Australia is a continent.	$Na \cdot Ca \cdot (x)[(Nx \cdot Cx) \supset x = a]$
The only presidents who were Whigs were Taylor and Fillmore.	$Pt \cdot Wt \cdot Pf \cdot Wf \cdot (x)[(Px \cdot Wx) \supset (x = t \lor x = f)]$

The first translation may be read as "Nolan Ryan has struck out 5,000 batters, and if anyone has struck out 5,000 batters, then he is identical to Nolan Ryan." The last part of the translation ensures that no other person has struck out 5,000 batters. The second translation may be read as "*Fidelio* is an opera, and *Fidelio* was written by Beethoven, and if anything is an opera written by Beethoven, then it is identical to *Fidelio*." Analogous remarks pertain to the other two statements. The third statement is equivalent to "The only nation that is a continent is Australia."

"All Except"

Statements beginning with "all except" are similar to those beginning with "the only" in that they, too, assert something about a designated individual (or individuals). For example, the statement "All presidents except Washington had a predecessor" means that Washington did not have a predecessor but all other presidents did. Thus the general form of such statements is that a designated individual lacks a stated attribute and anything not identical to the designated individual has the stated attribute. Examples:

All painters except Jackson Pollock make sense.	$Pj \cdot {\sim}Mj \cdot (x)[(Px \cdot x \neq j) \supset Mx]$
All continents except Antarctica are heavily populated.	$Ca \cdot {\sim}Ha \cdot (x)[(Cx \cdot x \neq a) \supset Hx]$
All states except Alaska and Hawaii are contiguous with their sister states.	$Sa \cdot {\sim}Ca \cdot Sh \cdot {\sim}Ch \cdot (x)[(Sx \cdot x \neq a \cdot x \neq h) \supset Cx]$

The first translation may be read as "Jackson Pollock is a painter who does not make sense, and every painter not identical to Jackson Pollock makes sense."

Superlatives

Statements containing superlative adjectives are yet another kind of statement that can be translated by using the identity relation. These are statements asserting that, of all the members of a class, something is the largest, tallest, smallest, heaviest, lightest, and so on. To translate these statements, first give the designated item the class attribute, and then say that, if anything else has that attribute, it is somehow exceeded by the designated item. Here are some examples:

The largest planet is Jupiter.	$Pj \cdot (x)[(Px \cdot x \neq j) \supset Ljx]$
The deepest lake is Ozero Baykal.	$Lo \cdot (x)[(Lx \cdot x \neq o) \supset Dox]$
The highest peak in North America is Mt. McKinley.	$Pm \cdot Nm \cdot (x)[(Px \cdot Nx \cdot x \neq m) \supset Hmx]$

The first translation may be read as "Jupiter is a planet, and if anything is a planet and not identical to Jupiter, then Jupiter is larger than it." The second may be read as "Ozero Baykal is a lake, and if anything is a lake and not identical to Ozero Baykal, then Ozero Baykal is deeper than it."

Numerical Statements

One of the more interesting uses of the identity symbol is to translate certain kinds of numerical statements, such as "There are three people in this room." In particular, the identity symbol allows us to translate such statements without the use of numerals. There are three types of numerical statements: those that assert a property of *at most n* items, those that assert a property of *at least n* items, and those that assert a property of *exactly n* items.

The first group does not assert that there actually are any items that have the stated property but only that, if there are any with the stated property, then the maximum number is *n*. Accordingly, for "at most" statements we use universal quantifiers. Here are some examples:

There is at most one god.	$(x)(y)[(Gx \cdot Gy) \supset x = y]$
There is at most one U.S. Representative from Alaska.	$(x)(y)[(Ux \cdot Ax \cdot Uy \cdot Ay) \supset x = y]$
There are at most two superpowers.	$(x)(y)(z)[(Sx \cdot Sy \cdot Sz) \supset (x = y \lor x = z \lor y = z)]$
There are at most two cities in Kuwait.	$(x)(y)(z)[Cx \cdot Kx \cdot Cy \cdot Ky \cdot Cz \cdot Kz) \supset (x = y \lor x = z \lor y = z)]$

It can be seen from these examples that to translate "at most *n*" is to say that, if there are *n* + 1 items that have the stated property, then at least one of them is identical to at least one of the "others." The result is to limit the number of such items to *n*. Thus, to translate "at most one," we need two quantifiers; to translate "at most two," we need three quantifiers; and so on. We could use this procedure to translate statements about any number of items, but because such translations become rather lengthy, this discussion is limited to statements about at most one or two items.

Unlike "at most" statements, statements that assert something about *at least n* items do claim that the items actually exist. Thus to translate "at least" statements we need to use existential quantifiers. The number of quantifiers must be equal to the number of items asserted. Examples:

There is at least one city in Monaco.	$(\exists x)(Cx \cdot Mx)$
There are at least two women in *Hamlet*.	$(\exists x)(\exists y)(Wx \cdot Hx \cdot Wy \cdot Hy \cdot x \neq y)$
There are at least three satellites of Neptune.	$(\exists x)(\exists y)(\exists z)(Sx \cdot Sy \cdot Sz \cdot x \neq y \cdot x \neq z \cdot y \neq z)$

The first of these examples merely asserts that some city is in Monaco. Thus it is translated without any inclusion of the identity relation. When the stated number is greater than one, however, the translation must incorporate one or more negative identity statements to ensure that the items referred to are distinct. Thus in the second statement, if x and y should be identical, then there would actually be only one woman (at least) in *Hamlet*. To ensure that there are at least two distinct women, we must conjoin the assertion that x and y are not identical. Similarly, when we assert something about at least three items, we must conjoin the assertion that none of them is identical to either of the other two.

A statement about *exactly n* items can be seen to be the conjunction of a statement about at least *n* items and a statement about at most *n* items. For example, the statement "There are exactly three cars in the lot" means that there are at least three cars in the lot and at most three cars in the lot. Thus a statement about exactly *n* items requires *n* existential quantifiers to ensure the existence of the items, one or more negated identity statements to ensure their distinctness (assuming *n* is greater than 1), and a universally quantified statement to limit the group to at most *n* items. Here are some examples:

There is exactly one city in Grenada.	$(\exists x)\{Cx \cdot Gx \cdot (y)[(Cy \cdot Gy) \supset x = y]\}$
There are exactly two houses of Congress.	$(\exists x)(\exists y)\{Hx \cdot Hy \cdot x \neq y \cdot$ $(z)[Hz \supset (z = x \lor z = y)]\}$
There are exactly two sopranos in *La Boheme*.	$(\exists x)(\exists y)\{Sx \cdot Lx \cdot Sy \cdot Ly \cdot x \neq y \cdot$ $(z)[(Sz \cdot Lz) \supset (z = x \lor z = y)]\}$

Definite Descriptions

The last form of phraseology considered here is the definite description. A definite description is a group of words of the form "The such-and-such" that identifies an individual person, place, or thing. Here are some examples:

The author of *Evangeline*
The capital of Nebraska
The mother of John F. Kennedy

The first designates Henry Wadsworth Longfellow, the second the city of Lincoln, and the third Rose Fitzgerald Kennedy. Definite descriptions are like names in that they identify only one thing, but unlike names they do so by describing a situation or relationship that only that one thing satisfies.

Statements incorporating definite descriptions have given rise to disputes in logic, because alternate interpretations of such statements can lead to conflicts in truth value. Suppose, for example, we are given the statement "The queen of the United States is a woman." Should we consider this statement to be true, because every queen is a woman, or should we consider it to be false, because there is no queen of the United States? In response to this question, most logicians today accept an interpretation of definite descriptions originally proposed by Bertrand Russell. According to this interpretation, a statement that incorporates a definite description asserts three things: an item of a certain sort exists, there is only one such item, and that item has the attribute assigned to it by the statement. If we accept this interpretation, the statement about the queen of the United States is false, because no such person exists.

Here are some additional examples with their translations:

The inventor of the phonograph was an American.	$(\exists x)[Ixp \cdot (y)(Iyp \supset y = x) \cdot Ax]$
The author of *Middlemarch* was a Victorian freethinker.	$(\exists x)[Wxm \cdot (y)(Wym \supset y = x) \cdot Vx \cdot Fx]$
The painter of *The Starry Night* was Van Gogh.	$(\exists x)[Pxs \cdot (y)(Pys \supset y = x) \cdot x = v]$

The first translation may be read as "There is someone who invented the phonograph, and if anyone invented the phonograph, then that person is identical to the first, and the first person is an American." The second may be read as "There is someone who wrote *Middlemarch*, and if anyone wrote *Middlemarch*, then that person is identical to the first, and the first person is a Victorian freethinker." The third may be read as "There is someone who painted *The Starry Night*, and if anyone painted *The Starry Night*, then that person is identical to the first, and the first person is identical to Van Gogh."

This completes our explanation of how to translate statements involving the identity relation. At this point, you may, if you wish, proceed to Exercise 8.7 Part I before completing the remainder of this section.

Using the Rules of Inference

Now that we have seen how to translate statements involving the identity relation, let us use natural deduction to derive the conclusions of arguments that include statements of this sort. Before doing so, however, some special rules governing the identity relation must be introduced. These rules, which are collectively designated "Id," are as follows:

ID: (1) $\dfrac{\text{Prem.}}{a = a}$ (2) $a = b :: b = a$ (3) $\dfrac{\begin{array}{l}\mathcal{F}a \\ a = b\end{array}}{\mathcal{F}b}$

(a, b are any individual constants)

The first rule expresses the idea that anything is identical to itself; it asserts what is called the reflexive property of the identity relation. The rule allows us to insert a self-identity statement after any premise (that is, on any line in a proof).

The second rule is a rule of replacement; it expresses what is called the symmetric property of the identity relation. It states, very simply, that the letters on either side of the equal sign can be switched. An immediate use of this rule is to prove that $a \neq b$ is logically equivalent to $b \neq a$. Recall that $a \neq b$ is simply an abbreviation for $\sim(a = b)$. If we apply the rule to the latter expression, we obtain $\sim(b = a)$, which, in its abbreviated form, is $b \neq a$.

The third rule expresses the intuitively obvious idea that, if something is true of x and x is identical to y, then that something is true of y. This rule is the basis of what is called the transitive property of identity, which allows us to infer from $a = b$ and $b = c$ that $a = c$. If we suppose that the $\mathcal{F}$ in this rule stands for the expression "$a =$", that α is b, and that β is c, then the first line of the rule reads $a = b$, the second line reads $b = c$, and the conclusion is $a = c$. This inference is used often in the derivation of the conclusions of arguments.

In general, the rules of inference used earlier apply to arguments containing identity statements in the same way they apply to any other arguments. Also, conditional proof and indirect proof are used in the same way. We need only note that because α and β in these rules represent only individual constants ($a, b, \ldots v, w$) they cannot be applied to variables (x, y, z).

The following argument illustrates the first expression of the rule for identity.

No biologists are identical to Isabel. Therefore, Isabel is not a biologist.

If we use Bx to translate "x is a biologist," and i for Isabel, this argument becomes:

1. $(x)(Bx \supset x \neq i)$ / $\sim Bi$

The fact that the conclusion contains i suggests that we instantiate line 1 with respect to that letter. The proof is as follows:

1. $(x)(Bx \supset x \neq i)$ / $\sim Bi$
2. $Bi \supset i \neq i$ 1, UI
3. $i = i$ Id
4. $\sim(i \neq i)$ 3, DN
5. $\sim Bi$ 2, 4, MT

Line 3 comes merely from the first expression of the identity rule, which allows us to insert any self-identity statement after any premise. Thus, no numeral is included in the justification for that line. Also note that line 4 is simply another way of writing $\sim\sim(i = i)$.

Now let us return to the argument given at the beginning of this section:

The only friend I have is Elizabeth. Elizabeth is not Nancy. Nancy is a Canadian. Therefore, there is a Canadian who is not my friend.

If we use Fx to translate "x is my friend" and Cx to translate "x is a Canadian," this argument may be translated as follows:

1. $Fe \cdot (x)(Fx \supset x = e)$
2. $e \neq n$
3. Cn / $(\exists x)(Cx \cdot \sim Fx)$

Inspecting the second line, we see a negated identity statement involving *e* and *n*. This suggests that we instantiate the universal statement in the first line with respect to *n*. The proof is as follows:

1. $Fe \cdot (x)(Fx \supset x = e)$
2. $e \neq n$
3. Cn / $(\exists x)(Cx \cdot \sim Fx)$
4. $(x)(Fx \supset x = e) \cdot Fe$ 1, Com
5. $(x)(Fx \supset x = e)$ 4, Simp
6. $Fn \supset n = e$ 5, UI
7. $n \neq e$ 2, Id
8. $\sim Fn$ 6, 7, MT
9. $Cn \cdot \sim Fn$ 3, 8, Conj
10. $(\exists x)(Cx \cdot \sim Fx)$ 9, EG

Line 7 is justified by the second rule for identity. Also, since $n \neq e$ is simply an abbreviation for $\sim(n = e)$, line 8 follows directly from lines 6 and 7.

Here is another example:

> The only person who invested is Ms. Snyder. Cathy is one of the persons who lost money. Some persons who invested did not lose money. Therefore, Cathy is not Ms. Snyder.

The translation is as follows:

1. $Ps \cdot Is \cdot (x)[(Px \cdot Ix) \supset x = s]$
2. $Pc \cdot Lc$
3. $(\exists x)(Px \cdot Ix \cdot \sim Lx)$ / $c \neq s$

Cursory inspection reveals no easy way to obtain the conclusion. This suggests indirect proof:

1. $Ps \cdot Is \cdot (x)[(Px \cdot Ix) \supset x = s]$
2. $Pc \cdot Lc$
3. $(\exists x)(Px \cdot Ix \cdot \sim Lx)$ / $c \neq s$
4. $c = s$ AIP
5. $Pa \cdot Ia \cdot \sim La$ 3, EI
6. $(x)[(Px \cdot Ix) \supset x = s] \cdot Ps \cdot Is$ 1, Com
7. $(x)[(Px \cdot Ix) \supset x = s]$ 6, Simp
8. $Pa \cdot Ia \supset a = s$ 7, UI
9. $Pa \cdot Ia$ 5, Simp
10. $a = s$ 8, 9, MP
11. $s = c$ 4, Id
12. $a = c$ 10, 11, Id
13. $\sim La \cdot Pa \cdot Ia$ 5, Com
14. $\sim La$ 13, Simp
15. $\sim Lc$ 12, 14, Id
16. $Lc \cdot Pc$ 2, Com
17. Lc 16, Simp
18. $Lc \cdot \sim Lc$ 15, 17, Conj
19. $c \neq s$ 4–18, IP

As usual, the existential statement is instantiated first, then the universal. Line 11 is obtained by commuting line 4 by the second rule of identity, and line 12 is obtained from lines 10 and 11 by applying the third rule of identity. Line 15 is obtained by substituting *c* in the place of *a* in line 14 according to the third rule of identity. The indirect sequence is discharged in line 19 in the normal way.

In arguments involving identity, especially more complicated ones, it is often difficult or impossible to see by mere inspection how to obtain the conclusion. A good general procedure is to begin with instantiation. Always instantiate the existential statements first, then the universals. When instantiating the universal statements, normally pick the letter (or one of the letters) used to instantiate the existential statement(s). If there are no existential statements, pick one of the letters appearing in the singular statements. If the conclusion is still not apparent, try indirect proof. In general, whenever the conclusion is a complicated statement, it is best to start out with indirect proof. Developing facility in proving arguments involving identity requires a little practice, but adequate skill should not take too long to acquire.

Translation hints

Only *i* is *F*.	$Fi \cdot (x)[Fx \supset x = i]$
The only *F* that is *G* is *i*.	$Fi \cdot Gi \cdot (x)[(Fx \cdot Gx) \supset x = i]$
No *F* except *i* is *G*.	$Fi \cdot Gi \cdot (x)[(Fx \cdot Gx) \supset x = i]$
All *F* except *i* are *G*.	$Fi \cdot {\sim}Gi \cdot (x)[(Fx \cdot x \neq i) \supset Gx]$
i is the *F* that is most so-and-so.	$Fi \cdot (x)[(Fx \cdot x \neq i) \supset i$ is more so-and-so than $x]$
There is at most one *F*.	$(x)(y)[(Fx \cdot Fy) \supset x = y]$
There are at least two *F*s.	$(\exists x)(\exists y)[Fx \cdot Fy \cdot x \neq y]$
There are exactly two *F*s.	$(\exists x)(\exists y)\{Fx \cdot Fy \cdot x \neq y \cdot (z)[Fz \supset (z = x \lor z = y)]\}$
The *F* is *G*.	$(\exists x)[Fx \cdot (y)(Fy \supset y = x) \cdot Gx]$

EXERCISE 8.7

iLrn   I. Translate the following:

Simple identity statements
★ 1. Dr. Seuss is Theodore Geisel. (*s, g*)
  2. Auguste Renoir is not Claude Monet. (*r, m*)
  3. Marilyn Monroe is Norma Jean Baker. (*m, b*)
★ 4. Hermann Hesse is not André Gide. (*h, g*)

Statements involving "only," "the only," and "no . . . except"
★ 5. Only Linus Pauling has won two Nobel prizes. (*Wx: x* has won two Nobel prizes; *p:* Linus Pauling)
  6. Only Don Larsen has pitched a perfect World Series game. (*Px: x* has pitched a perfect World Series game; *l:* Don Larsen)

7. The only national park in Maine is Acadia. (*Nx: x* is a national park; *Mx: x* is in Maine; *a:* Acadia)

★ 8. The only nation having a maple leaf flag is Canada. (*Nx: x* is a nation; *Mx: x* has a maple leaf flag; *c:* Canada)

9. The only U.S. presidents who were Federalists were Washington and Adams. (*Ux: x* is a U.S. president; *Fx: x* is a Federalist; *w:* Washington; *a:* Adams)

10. No state except Hawaii is surrounded by water. (*Sx: x* is a state; *Wx: x* is surrounded by water; *h:* Hawaii)

★ 11. No sport except hockey uses a puck. (*Sx: x* is a sport; *Px: x* uses a puck; *h:* hockey)

Superlative statements

★ 12. Hydrogen is the lightest element. (*Ex: x* is an element; *Lxy: x* is lighter than *y*; *h:* hydrogen)

13. The smallest planet in our solar system is Pluto. (*Px: x* is a planet in our solar system; *Sxy: x* is smaller than *y*; *p:* Pluto)

14. Harvard is the oldest American university. (*Ax: x* is American; *Ux: x* is a university; *Oxy: x* is older than *y*; *h:* Harvard)

★ 15. Death Valley is the lowest region in North America. (*Rx: x* is a region; *Nx: x* is in North America; *Lyx: x* is lower than *y*; *d:* Death Valley)

Statements involving "all except"

★ 16. All actors except Peter Lorre speak normally. (*Ax: x* is an actor; *Sx: x* speaks normally; *l:* Peter Lorre)

17. Every U.S. President except Ford won a national election. (*Ux: x* is a U.S. president; *Wx: x* won a national election; *f:* Ford)

18. All metals except mercury are solids at room temperature. (*Mx: x* is a metal; *Sx: x* is a solid at room temperature; *m:* mercury)

★ 19. Every pitcher except Cy Young has won fewer than 500 games. (*Px: x* is a pitcher; *Wx: x* has won fewer than 500 games; *c:* Cy Young)

Numerical statements

★ 20. There is at most one city in Belize. (*Cx: x* is a city; *Bx: x* is in Belize)

21. There are at most two national parks in South Dakota. (*Nx: x* is a national park; *Sx: x* is in South Dakota)

22. There is at most one national holiday in July. (*Nx: x* is a national holiday; *Jx: x* is in July)

★ 23. There are at most two cities in Malta. (*Cx: x* is a city; *Mx: x* is in Malta)

24. There is at least one quarterback on a football team. (*Qx: x* is a quarterback; *Fx: x* is on a football team)

25. There are at least two atoms in a water molecule. (*Ax: x* is an atom; *Wx: x* is in a water molecule)

★ 26. There are at least three carbon allotropes. (*Cx: x* is a carbon allotrope)

27. There is exactly one U.S. Supreme Court. (*Ux: x* is a U.S. Supreme Court)

8

28. There is exactly one natural satellite of the earth. (*Sx: x* is a satellite of the earth; *Nx: x* is natural)

★ 29. There are exactly two bright stars in Gemini. (*Sx: x* is a star; *Bx: x* is bright; *Gx: x* is in Gemini)

Statements containing definite descriptions

★ 30. The author of *Vanity Fair* was born in India. (*Wxy: x* wrote *y*; *Bx: x* was born in India; *v: Vanity Fair*)

31. The wife of Othello is Desdemona. (*Wxy: x* is the wife of *y*; *o: Othello*; *d: Desdemona*)

32. The man who composed *The Nutcracker* was Russian. (*Mx: x* is a man; *Cxy: x* composed *y*; *Rx: x* was Russian; *n: The Nutcracker*)

★ 33. The artist who painted the *Allegory of Spring* was Botticelli. (*Ax: x* is an artist; *Pxy: x* painted *y*; *a:* the *Allegory of Spring*; *b: Botticelli*)

34. The capital of Georgia is not Savannah. (*Cxy: x* is the capital of *y*, *g: Georgia*; *s: Savannah*)

Assorted statements

★ 35. The smallest state is Rhode Island. (*Sx: x* is a state; *Sxy: x* is smaller than *y*; *r: Rhode Island*)

36. There is at least one newspaper in St. Louis. (*Nx: x* is a newspaper; *Sx: x* is in St. Louis)

37. Cat Stevens is Yusuf Islam. (*s: Cat Stevens*; *i: Yusuf Islam*)

★ 38. The only American president elected to a fourth term was Franklin D. Roosevelt. (*Ax: x* is an American president; *Ex: x* was elected to a fourth term; *r: Franklin D. Roosevelt*)

39. There are at least two cities in Qatar. (*Cx: x* is a city; *Qx: x* is in Qatar)

40. Only George Blanda has played 340 professional football games. (*Px: x* has played 340 professional football games; *b: George Blanda*)

★ 41. Hamlet had at most one sister. (*Sxy: x* is a sister of *y*; *h: Hamlet*)

42. No major league baseball player has hit 73 home runs except Barry Bonds. (*Mx: x* is a major league baseball player; *Hx: x* has hit 73 home runs; *b: Barry Bonds*)

43. There are at most two Senators from New Hampshire. (*Sx: x* is a Senator; *Nx: x* is from New Hampshire)

★ 44. Gustav Mahler is not Anton Bruckner. (*m: Gustav Mahler*; *b: Anton Bruckner*)

45. The explorer who discovered the North Pole was Admiral Peary. (*Ex: x* is an explorer; *Dxy: x* discovered *y*; *n:* the North Pole; *a: Admiral Peary*)

46. Hinduism is the oldest religion. (*Rx: x* is a religion; *Oxy: x* is older than *y*; *h: Hinduism*)

★ 47. There are exactly two tenors in *Carmen*. (*Tx: x* is a tenor; *Cx: x* is in *Carmen*)

48. Every recent pope except John Paul II was Italian. (*Px: x* is a pope; *Rx: x* is recent; *Ix: x* is Italian; *j: John Paul II*)

49. The person who discovered relativity theory was an employee in the Swiss patent office. (*Px:* *x* is a person; *Dxy:* *x* discovered *y*; *Ex:* *x* is an employee in the Swiss patent office; *r:* relativity theory)

★ **50.** There are at least three stars in Orion. (*Sx:* *x* is a star; *Ox:* *x* is in Orion)

iLrn II. Derive the conclusion of the following symbolized arguments. Use conditional proof or indirect proof as needed.

★ (1) 1. $(x)(x = a)$
    2. $(\exists x)Rx$ / Ra

(2) 1. Ke
    2. $\sim Kn$ / $e \neq n$

(3) 1. $(x)(x = c \supset Nx)$ / Nc

★ (4) 1. $(\exists x)(x = g)$
    2. $(x)(x = i)$ / $g = i$

(5) 1. $(x)(Gx \supset x = a)$
    2. $(\exists x)(Gx \cdot Hx)$ / Ha

(6) 1. $(x)(Ax \supset Bx)$
    2. $Ac \cdot \sim Bi$ / $c \neq i$

★ (7) 1. $(x)(x = a)$
    2. Fa / $Fm \cdot Fn$

(8) 1. $(x)(x = r)$
    2. $Hr \cdot Kn$ / $Hn \cdot Kr$

(9) 1. $(x)(Lx \supset x = e)$
    2. $(x)(Sx \supset x = i)$
    3. $(\exists x)(Lx \cdot Sx)$ / $i = e$

★ (10) 1. $(x)(Px \supset x = a)$
    2. $(x)(x = c \supset Qx)$
    3. $a = c$ / $(x)(Px \supset Qx)$

(11) 1. $(x)(y)(Txy \supset x = e)$
    2. $(\exists x)Txi$ / Tei

(12) 1. $(x)[Rx \supset (Hx \cdot x = m)]$ / $Rc \supset Hm$

★ (13) 1. $(x)(Ba \supset x \neq a)$
    2. Bc / $a \neq c$

(14) 1. $(\exists x)Gx \supset (\exists x)(Kx \cdot x = i)$ / $Gn \supset Ki$

(15) 1. $(x)(Rax \supset \sim Rxc)$
    2. $(x)Rxx$ / $c \neq a$

★ (16) 1. $(x)[Nx \supset (Px \cdot x = m)]$
    2. $\sim Pm$ / $\sim Ne$

(17) 1. $(x)(Fx \supset x = e)$
    2. $(\exists x)(Fx \cdot x = a)$ / $a = e$

(18) 1. $(x)[Ex \supset (Hp \cdot x = e)]$
    2. $(\exists x)(Ex \cdot x = p)$ / He

★ (19) 1. $(x)(\exists y)(Cxy \supset x = y)$
   2. $(\exists x)(y)(Cxy \cdot x = a)$ / Caa

(20) 1. $(x)[Fx \supset (Gx \cdot x = n)]$
   2. $Gn \supset (\exists x)(Hx \cdot x = e)$ / $Fm \supset He$

iLrn III. Derive the conclusion of the following arguments. Use conditional proof or indirect proof as needed.

★ 1. Some of Jane Collier's novels are interesting. The only novel Jane Collier wrote is *The Cry*. Therefore, *The Cry* is interesting. (*Nx: x* is a novel; *Wxy: x* wrote *y*; *Ix: x* is interesting; *j:* Jane Collier; *c: The Cry*)

2. Ronald Reagan was the oldest U.S. president. Woodrow Wilson was a U.S. president. Woodrow Wilson is not Ronald Reagan. Therefore, Ronald Reagan was older than Woodrow Wilson. (*Ux: x* is a U.S. president; *Oxy: x* is older than *y; r:* Ronald Reagan; *w:* Woodrow Wilson)

3. The artist who painted the *Mona Lisa* was a Florentine. Leonardo is the artist who painted the *Mona Lisa*. Therefore, Leonardo was a Florentine. (*Ax: x* is an artist; *Pxy: x* painted *y; Fx: x* was a Florentine; *m:* the *Mona Lisa; l:* Leonardo)

★ 4. The novel on the table was written by Margaret Mitchell. The only novel Margaret Mitchell wrote is *Gone with the Wind*. Therefore, the novel on the table is *Gone with the Wind*. (*Nx: x* is a novel; *Tx: x* is on the table; *Wxy: x* wrote *y; m:* Margaret Mitchell; *g: Gone with the Wind*)

5. The author of *King Lear* was an English actor. John Milton was English but not an actor. Therefore, John Milton is not the author of *King Lear*. (*Wxy: x* wrote *y; Ex: x* is English; *Ax: x* is an actor; *k: King Lear; m:* John Milton)

6. The dog that bit the letter carrier is a large terrier. Ajax is a small dog. Therefore, Ajax did not bite the letter carrier. (*Dx: x* is a dog; *Bx: x* bit the letter carrier; *Lx: x* is large; *Tx: x* is a terrier; *a:* Ajax)

★ 7. Every member except Ellen sang a song. Every member except Nancy gave a speech. Ellen is not Nancy. Therefore, Ellen gave a speech and Nancy sang a song. (*Mx: x* is a member; *Sx: x* sang a song; *Gx: x* gave a speech; *e:* Ellen; *n:* Nancy)

8. The only person who ordered fish is Astrid. The only person who suffered indigestion is Ms. Wilson. Some person who ordered fish also suffered indigestion. Therefore, Astrid is Ms. Wilson. (*Px: x* is a person; *Ox: x* ordered fish; *Sx: x* suffered indigestion; *a:* Astrid; *w:* Ms. Wilson)

9. The highest mountain is in Tibet. Therefore, there is a mountain in Tibet that is higher than any mountain not in Tibet. (*Mx: x* is a mountain; *Hxy: x* is higher than *y; Tx: x* is in Tibet)

★ 10. The tallest building in North America is the Sears Tower. The tallest building in North America is located in Chicago. If one thing is taller than another, then the latter is not taller than the former. Therefore, the Sears Tower is located in Chicago. (*Bx: x* is a building in North America; *Txy: x* is taller than *y; Cx: x* is located in Chicago; *s:* the Sears Tower)

11. There are at least two philosophers in the library. Robert is the only French philosopher in the library. Therefore, there is a philosopher in the library who

is not French. (*Px: x* is a philosopher; *Lx: x* is in the library; *Fx: x* is French; *r:* Robert)

12. The only dogs that barked were Fido and Pluto. Fido is not Pluto. Every dog except Fido ran on the beach. Therefore, exactly one barking dog ran on the beach. (*Dx: x* is a dog; *Bx: x* barked; *Rx: x* ran on the beach; *f:* Fido; *p:* Pluto)

★ 13. There are at least two attorneys in the office. All attorneys are professionals. There are at most two professionals in the office. Therefore, there are exactly two professionals in the office. (*Ax: x* is an attorney; *Ox: x* is in the office; *Px: x* is a professional)

14. There are at most two scientists in the laboratory. At least two scientists in the laboratory are Russians. No Russians are Chinese. Therefore, if Norene is a Chinese scientist, then she is not in the laboratory. (*Sx: x* is a scientist; *Lx: x* is in the laboratory; *Rx: x* is Russian; *Cx: x* is Chinese; *n:* Norene)

15. Every candidate except Mary was elected. The only candidate who was elected is Ralph. Mary is not Ralph. Therefore, there were exactly two candidates. (*Cx: x* is a candidate; *Ex: x* was elected; *m:* Mary; *r:* Ralph)

★ 16. Every student except Charles and Norman passed the course. The only student who was dismissed was Norman. Every student retook the course if and only if he/she was not dismissed and did not pass. Charles is not Norman. Therefore, exactly one student retook the course. (*Sx: x* is a student; *Px: x* passed the course; *Dx: x* was dismissed; *Rx: x* retook the course; *c:* Charles; *n:* Norman)

Summary

Predicate logic combines the five operators of propositional logic with symbols for predicates and quantifiers to produce a more powerful symbolic system for representing the content of ordinary language statements and arguments. Once an argument is translated into the symbols of predicate logic, natural deduction can be used to derive its conclusion.

Predicates, represented by capital letters, are combined with individual constants (*a, b, c . . . u, v, w*) to translate singular statements. Thus, "Abigail is a Canadian" is translated *Ca*. The universal and existential quantifiers (*x*) and (∃*x*) are combined with predicate symbols and individual variables (*x, y, z*) to translate universal and particular statements. Universal statements are normally rendered as conditionals, and particular statements as conjunctions. Thus, "All Canadians are patriotic" is translated (*x*)(*Cx* ⊃ *Px*), and "Some Canadians are women" is translated (∃*x*)(*Cx* • *Wx*).

Rules for removing and introducing quantifiers are introduced to allow the application of the rules of inference. Universal instantiation and universal generalization remove and introduce universal quantifiers, respectively, and existential instantiation and existential generalization remove and introduce existential quantifiers.

The change of quantifier rule allows a universal quantifier to be replaced by an existential quantifier, and vice versa, provided that tildes preceding quantifiers be either deleted or introduced. By deleting tildes, these rules allow for the application of the instantiation rules. Conditional and indirect proof are used in predicate logic in basi-

8

cally the same way as they are in propositional logic, but certain restrictions apply to the use of universal generalization within such sequences.

The counterexample method, introduced in Chapter 1, is adapted to proving the invalidity of invalid arguments. The method consists in finding a substitution instance of a symbolized argument that has indisputably true premises and an indisputably false conclusion. The finite universe method is used for the same purpose; it consists in showing that an invalid argument is susceptible to having true premises and a false conclusion when the universe is contracted to a finite number of members.

Relational predicates, symbolized by upper-case letters followed by spaces for two or more lower-case letters, are used to translate statements expressing relations. For example, "Peter is taller than Cynthia" is translated Tpc. Relational predicates are combined with overlapping quantifiers to translate complex statements involving relations. Thus, "Some man is taller than every woman" is translated $(\exists x)[Mx \cdot (y)(Wy \supset Txy)]$.

The identity relation, represented by an equal sign (=), is used to translate statements claiming that one person or thing is identical to another. It is also used to translate statements involving "only," "the only," "no . . . except," and "all except" when these expressions are used with individuals, and to translate superlative statements, numerical statements, and definite descriptions. A special rule of inference for identity is introduced to allow the application of the other rules.

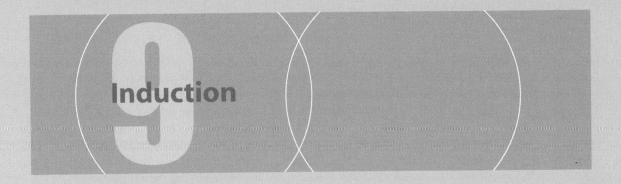

9 Induction

Unlike deductive logic, the logic of induction offers no neat, harmonious system of ideas agreed upon by all logicians. Rather, it consists of several independently developed areas of thought about which there is little agreement. The sections in this chapter touch upon six such areas. The first section deals with analogy and its relation to legal and moral reasoning, the second deals with causality and John Stuart Mill's methods for discovering causal connections, and the third with probability. The fourth section deals with statistical methods of reasoning, the fifth with hypothetical and scientific reasoning, and the sixth with the difference between science and superstition. Except for Section 9.6, which depends in part on Section 9.5, these six sections are basically independent of one another, so they can be read in any order. Furthermore, the material presented is only slightly dependent on ideas developed earlier in this book. In addition to material from Chapter 1, which is presupposed by all six sections, Sections 9.2 and 9.3 presuppose only a few ideas from Chapter 6, and Section 9.4 extends the material developed in Chapter 3.

9.1   Analogy and Legal and Moral Reasoning

Analogical reasoning may be the most fundamental and the most common of all rational processes. It stands at the basis of many ordinary decisions in life. For example, a woman wanting to buy a can of soup might deliberate between Campbell's and Brand X and, after recalling that other varieties of Campbell's were good, decide in favor of that brand. A man contemplating a haircut might recall that a friend got an especially good cut at the Golden Touch and as a result decide to go there himself. A woman selecting a plant for her garden might observe that gardenias grow well at the house next door and conclude that gardenias would grow well at her house, too. A man thinking of reading a novel by Stephen King might recall that King's last three novels were thrilling and conclude that his latest novel is also thrilling.

Analogical reasoning is reasoning that depends on a comparison of instances. If the instances are sufficiently similar, the decision reached in the end is usually a good one; but if they are not sufficiently similar, the decision may not be good. When such a reasoning process is expressed in words, the result is an **argument from analogy**. Simple arguments from analogy have the following structure:

Entity A has attributes $a, b, c,$ and z.
Entity B has attributes a, b, c.
Therefore, entity B probably has attribute z also.

If the attributes a, b, and c are connected in some important way to z (that is, are relevant to z), the argument is usually strong. If they are not so connected (that is, are irrelevant to z), the argument is usually weak.

Analogical arguments are closely related to generalizations. In a generalization, the arguer begins with one or more instances and proceeds to draw a conclusion about all the members of a class. The arguer may then apply the generalization to one or more members of this class that were not noted earlier. The first stage of such an inference is inductive, and the second stage is deductive. For example, the man thinking of reading a Stephen King novel might argue that because the last three novels by King were thrilling, all King novels are thrilling (inductive argument). Applying this generalization to the latest novel, he might then conclude that it too is thrilling (deductive argument). In an argument from analogy, on the other hand, the arguer proceeds directly from one or more individual instances to a conclusion about another individual instance without appealing to any intermediate generalization. Such an argument is purely inductive. Thus the arguer might conclude directly from reading three earlier King novels that the latest one is thrilling.

In any argument from analogy, the items that are compared are called *analogues*. Thus if one should argue that Britney Spears's latest CD is probably good because her two previous CDs were good, the three CDs are the analogues. The two earlier CDs are called the *primary analogues*, and the latest CD is called the *secondary analogue*. With these definitions in mind, we may now examine a set of principles that are useful for evaluating most arguments from analogy. They include (1) the relevance of the similarities shared by the primary and secondary analogues, (2) the number of similarities, (3) the nature and degree of disanalogy, (4) the number of primary analogues, (5) the diversity among the primary analogues, and (6) the specificity of the conclusion.

1. *Relevance of the similarities.* Suppose a certain person—let us call her Lucy—is contemplating the purchase of a new car. She decides in favor of a Chevrolet because she wants good gas mileage and her friend Tom's new Chevy gets good gas mileage. To support her decision, Lucy argues that both cars have a padded steering wheel, tachometer, vinyl upholstery, tinted windows, CD player, and white paint. Lucy's argument is weak because these similarities are irrelevant to gas mileage. On the other hand, if Lucy bases her conclusion on the fact that both cars have the same size engine, her argument is relatively strong, because engine size is relevant to gas mileage.

2. *Number of similarities.* Suppose, in addition to the same-size engine, Lucy notes further similarities between the car she intends to buy and Tom's car: curb weight, aerodynamic body, gear ratio, and tires. These additional similarities, all of which are relevant to gas mileage, tend to strengthen Lucy's argument. If, in

addition, Lucy notes that she and Tom both drive about half on city streets and half on freeways, her argument is strengthened even further.

3. *Nature and degree of disanalogy.* On the other hand, if Lucy's car is equipped with a turbocharger, if Lucy loves to make jackrabbit starts and screeching stops, if Tom's car has overdrive but Lucy's does not, and if Lucy constantly drives on congested freeways while Tom drives on relatively clear freeways, Lucy's argument is weakened. These differences are called *disanalogies*. Depending on how they relate to the conclusion, disanalogies can either weaken or strengthen an argument. If we suppose instead that Tom's car has the turbocharger, that Tom loves jackrabbit starts, and so on, then Lucy's argument is strengthened, because these disanalogies tend to reduce Tom's gas mileage.

4. *Number of primary analogues.* Thus far, Lucy has based her conclusion on the similarity between the car she intends to buy and only one other car—Tom's. Now suppose that Lucy has three additional friends, that all of them drive cars of the same model and year as Tom's, and that all of them get good gas mileage. These additional primary analogues strengthen Lucy's argument because they lessen the likelihood that Tom's good gas mileage is a freak incident. On the other hand, suppose that two of these additional friends get the same good gas mileage as Tom but that the third gets poor mileage. As before, the first two cases tend to strengthen Lucy's argument, but the third now tends to weaken it. This third case is called a *counteranalogy* because it supports a conclusion opposed to that of the original analogy.

5. *Diversity among the primary analogues.* Suppose now that Lucy's four friends (all of whom get good mileage) all buy their gas at the same station, have their cars tuned up regularly by the same mechanic, put the same friction-reducing additive in their oil, inflate their tires to the same pressure, and do their city driving on uncongested, level streets at a fuel-maximizing 28 miles per hour. Such factors would tend to reduce the probability of Lucy's conclusion, because it is possible that one or a combination of them is responsible for the good mileage and that this factor (or combination of them) is absent in Lucy's case. On the other hand, if Lucy's friends buy their gas at different stations, have their cars tuned up at different intervals by different mechanics, inflate their tires to different pressures, drive at different speeds on different grades, and have different attitudes toward using the oil additive, then it is less likely that the good gas mileage they enjoy is attributable to any factor other than the model and year of their car.

6. *Specificity of the conclusion.* Lucy's conclusion is simply that her car will get "good" mileage. If she now changes her conclusion to state that her car will get gas mileage "at least as good" as Tom's, then her argument is weakened. Such a conclusion is more specific than the earlier conclusion and is easier to falsify. Thus if her mileage were only one-tenth of a mile per gallon less than Tom's, her conclusion would turn out to be false. Now suppose that Lucy changes her conclusion to state that her car will get exactly the same gas mileage as Tom's. This conclusion is even more specific than the "at least as good" conclusion, and it is

easier still to falsify. Thus such a conclusion renders Lucy's argument much weaker than her original argument.

Let us now use these six principles to evaluate an argument from analogy. Suppose that you want to shade a bedroom window from the intense western sun. To accomplish this purpose, you decide to plant some trees, but the trees must be narrow ones that will grow approximately 25 feet tall. Recalling that a friend has some Italian cypresses that are almost exactly 25 feet tall, you conclude that this variety of tree will do the job. Thus far, your argument is based on a single similarity, the species of the tree. Because this similarity is very relevant to height, your argument is fairly strong. Now if, in addition, it turns out that your friend lives in the same city and has the same kind of soil as you have, your argument is strengthened. However, if it happens that your friend has a knack for growing trees while you have a knack for killing them, your argument is weakened.

To this set of facts, suppose we add the observation that four of your neighbors have Italian cypresses and that all of their trees are approximately 25 feet tall. This fact tends to strengthen your argument. Also, if all four neighbors planted their trees in different years, use different kinds of fertilizers on them, and give them different amounts of water, your argument is further strengthened. Finally, should you broaden your conclusion to state that your trees will grow to between 22 and 28 feet, your argument is strengthened even further. But if you narrow your conclusion to state that your trees will grow to between $24\frac{1}{2}$ and $25\frac{1}{2}$ feet, your argument is weakened.

Legal Reasoning

Many of the arguments used by lawyers in the United States and Canada to support a case at trial are analogical arguments. The reason is that the legal systems of these countries were derived many years ago from the English system, and an essential feature of the English system is its dependence on precedent. According to the requirement of precedent, similar cases must be decided similarly. Thus, in arguing a case, a lawyer will often attempt to show that the case is analogous to some earlier case that was decided in a favorable way. Sometimes, even today, these precedents go back to early English law.

For example, suppose that you own a factory and one of your machines, a drill press, breaks down, causing the entire operation to come to a halt. Urgently you call a repair company and explain the whole situation. The spokesperson for the company promises to have the drill press back in operation within two days. Unfortunately, however, there are delays, and two weeks elapse before the drill press is repaired. In the meantime your company loses an additional $10,000 in profits. Because you relied on the spokesperson's assurance that the drill press would be fixed in two days, you demand that the repair company reimburse you for the additional lost profits. When the repair company refuses your demand, you file suit.

The lawyer who argues your case will probably make reference to a much earlier case, *Hadley v. Baxendale*, decided in Gloucester, England in 1854. In that case the operation of a mill was halted because of a broken crankshaft, and the owner of the mill (Hadley) employed a shipping company (Baxendale) to return the crankshaft to the manufacturer. Hadley informed Baxendale that the broken crankshaft had interrupted the operation of the mill, and Baxendale replied that the broken crankshaft would be in the hands of the manufacturer within one day. As it turned out, however, the shipment was delayed by several days, and Hadley incurred lost profits from the additional time the mill was shut down. Hadley demanded reimbursement from Baxendale, and when Baxendale refused, Hadley filed suit. The court ruled that Baxendale should pay only if he foresaw when he agreed to do the work that delays would result in lost profits for Hadley.

Applying this result to the drill press case, your lawyer will argue that because the repair company was informed that delays in repairing the drill press would result in lost profits, it should reimburse you for the losses incurred.

In the early days, much of English law was the direct result of judges rendering decisions in particular cases. This judge-made law is otherwise called common law. However, today many of our laws are not the direct product of judges but rather of legislative bodies. These laws, called *statutes*, are codified in books that are periodically revised. Can it be said that precedent plays a central role in decisions involving statutory law in the same way that it does in decisions involving common law? The answer is a definite yes. Statutory laws are invariably phrased in relatively general language, and precedent is required to determine how the statutes should be interpreted and applied.

Consider, for example, a "law" that we are all familiar with, the First Amendment to the U.S. Constitution, which provides for freedom of speech and religious expression. Suppose that you decide, in reliance on the First Amendment, to pass out religious pamphlets on a downtown street corner. Suppose further that most of the people you hand your pamphlets to merely glance at them and then throw them on the street and that the gathering litter makes the area look like a garbage dump. To prevent the litter, the police tell you that you can hand out your pamphlets only in the vicinity of public garbage cans, so that those who do not want the pamphlets can properly dispose of them. You object that such a restriction violates your First Amendment rights, and you take the issue to court.

In presenting your case, your lawyer will argue that the case is analogous to a number of other cases where the state attempted to limit not the content of religious expression, but the time, place, and manner of its expression. Next, your lawyer will note that in such cases the state is allowed to restrict the expression only if the restriction is "narrowly tailored" to serve a "significant government interest." Finally, your lawyer will attempt to show that your case is analogous to cases in which the government failed to prove that the restriction was so tailored.

As these examples illustrate, many of the arguments that occur in law are arguments from analogy, and the principles developed at the beginning of this section can be used to evaluate them. The first principle, which deals with the relevance of the similarities, has an obvious application to legal arguments. Suppose, for example, that two cases are similar in that each involves a burning building, the building in each case is located in Chicago, and in each case ten people died. The comparison is pointless if the issue in the first case is whether an insurance company is liable to pay damages while the issue in the second is whether somebody is guilty of arson.

The second and third principles, which deal with the number of similarities and the nature and degree of disanalogy, are also applicable. If a preceding case resembles the case at hand in virtually all important details, then the preceding case is said to be "on point" and, given certain other requirements (discussed shortly), will dictate the outcome of the case to be decided. As for the nature and degree of disanalogy, if a preceding case deals with fraud by a stockbroker while the case to be decided deals with fraud by a real estate broker, the precedent may be more or less controlling, depending on such circumstances as applicable statutory law.

As applied to legal analogies, the fourth principle (number of primary analogues) usually determines how well established a legal precedent is. If fifty previous courts have followed a certain rule, the precedent is stronger (everything else being equal) than if only two courts have followed that rule. The fifth principle (diversity of primary analogues) is also applicable. If a certain rule turns up in a broad range of cases, it provides a stronger precedent (other things being equal) than a rule that turns up in a narrow range of cases. For example, the principle underlying the inadmissibility of hearsay testimony is well established because it appears in a broad cross section of cases.

Finally, the sixth principle states that the more specific a conclusion is, the weaker the argument becomes. Suppose, in an earlier case, a person is awarded half a million dollars for injuries inflicted by a surgeon who, during an appendix operation, left a stethoscope in the body opening. The argument that another person injured in the same way by another doctor should be awarded *exactly* the same amount of money is relatively weak in comparison with the argument that the person should be awarded *approximately* the same amount of money.

Analogical arguments that occur in law differ from the fairly simple analogies considered earlier in at least two important ways. In the analogy dealing with gas mileage, the modes of similarity that linked the analogues (number of engine cylinders, curb weight, and the like) were clearly defined by conventional thinking, and their relevance to the conclusion has been established by scientific principles. In law, however, clarity of this sort is seldom to be found. Modes of similarity between cases are often the result of highly creative thinking by lawyers and judges, and the relevance of these similarities to the proposed conclusion is nearly always debatable. These differences render analogical arguments in law considerably more elusive than those dealing with subjects such as gas mileage.

The other difference between simple analogical arguments and those found in law is that the primary analogues in law (earlier cases) do not all have equal weight. The reason is that our courts operate in different jurisdictions. The system of federal courts is totally separate from the system of state courts. As a result, a case that might have considerable weight as a precedent in one system might have little or no weight in the other. In addition, within these systems there are different circuits, and a case that is controlling in one circuit may not be in another. Lastly, within these systems, the courts exist on different levels. For example, within the federal system there are the district courts, courts of appeals, and the U.S. Supreme Court. A case that is binding on a lower court may not be binding on a higher court.

Let us now illustrate the process of legal reasoning with a hypothetical example. Suppose a certain vagrant—let us call him Blake—attempted to earn some pocket change by breaking into a cigarette vending machine and stealing the cash. The police apprehended Blake in the act, and the district attorney charged him with burglary. Blake had one prior conviction for breaking into a cigarette machine.

The first thing that any lawyer would do with this case is to recall the definition of "burglary." According to the traditional definition, "burglary" means "the trespassory breaking and entering of a dwelling house of another at night with the intent to commit a felony therein." Under many modern statutes, "dwelling house" has been replaced by "structure" and "at night" has been deleted.

There is little doubt that Blake has broken into a structure. The question is, is a cigarette machine the kind of structure intended by the statute? A second question is, did Blake intend to commit a felony when he broke into the cigarette machine? To answer these questions a lawyer would consult additional statutes and relevant cases. Let us suppose that our jurisdiction has a statute that defines felony theft as theft of $400 or more. Also, let us suppose that the cash box of this particular machine contained $450 but most similar machines can hold no more than $350.

As for cases, let us suppose that our jurisdiction has two controlling precedents. In *People v. Harris*, Harris broke into a warehouse with the intent of stealing its contents. The warehouse contained microwave ovens valued at $10,000, and Harris was found guilty of burglary. In *People v. Sawyer*, Sawyer broke into a newspaper vending machine with the intent to steal the cash in the cash box. The maximum capacity of the cash box was $20, and Sawyer was found not guilty of burglary.

Relying on these facts and preceding cases, the district attorney might present the following argument to the judge (or jury):

> In breaking into the cigarette machine, Blake is guilty of burglary for the following reasons. In *People v. Harris*, the defendant was found guilty of burglary for breaking into a warehouse. A cigarette vending machine is like a warehouse in that it contains goods stored for resale. Furthermore, like a warehouse, people's livelihoods depend on the goods stored therein. Also, the vending machine contained over $400, and Blake intended to steal this money. Stealing over $400 is a felony. Therefore, Blake intended to commit a felony when he broke into the machine. Also, by placing his hand into the machine, he "entered" it. A cigarette machine differs from a newspaper machine in that it can hold goods valued much more than a stack of newspapers. Thus all the requirements are met for conviction.

Defense counsel, on the other hand, might argue as follows:

> In breaking into the cigarette machine, Blake is not guilty of burglary for the following reasons. The original crime of burglary extended only to dwelling houses because people live in dwelling houses and it is important that their lives be protected. Modern law has extended the kind of structure requisite for burglary to include warehouses because people work and live in them. A cigarette machine is unlike a warehouse in that a person is not capable of working and living in it. Also, for the crime of burglary to be committed, the burglar must enter the structure. A cigarette machine differs from a warehouse in that a person is not capable of entering it with his whole body.
>
> On the contrary, a cigarette vending machine is very similar to a newspaper vending machine in that it contains relatively small quantities of products for resale. In *People v. Sawyer*, the defendant was found not guilty of burglary in breaking into a newspaper vending machine. Finally, Blake was familiar with cigarette machines (he broke into one once before), and he therefore knew that their cash boxes are usually limited to holding

less than $400. Therefore, when he broke into this particular machine, Blake intended to steal less than $400, and therefore he did not intend to commit a felony.

In deciding whether Blake is guilty, the judge or jury will have to evaluate these analogical arguments by determining which analogies are the strongest.

Sometimes lawyers and judges are confronted with cases for which there is no clear precedent. Such cases are called cases of first impression, and the attempt to deal with them by appeal to analogous instances involves even more creativity than does the attempt to deal with ordinary cases. In deciding cases of first impression, judges often resort to moral reasoning, and they grope for any analogy that can shed light on the issue. The reasoning process in such a decision often involves a sequence of analogies followed by disanalogies and counteranalogies. These analogies present the issue in a continually shifting light, and the experience of coming to grips with them expands the outlook of the reasoner. New perspectives are created, attitudes are changed, and world views are altered.

Moral Reasoning

As in law, arguments from analogy are also useful in deciding moral questions. Such arguments often occur in the context of a dialogue. As an example of a dialogue that includes a number of arguments from analogy, consider the following one between two fictional characters, Jason and Deirdre. The dialogue deals with the morality and legality of fetal abuse.

"Jason, I read an article in this morning's newspaper about fetal abuse—you know, expectant mothers who take drugs or drink alcohol during pregnancy and cause damage to their fetus. The article said that 11 percent of all babies currently born in this country have traces of alcohol or illegal drugs in their blood. I think such women should be shot!"

"I can see that you're pretty worked up about this, Deirdre, but don't you think you're being a bit prudish? After all, what's so bad about a little alcohol or a few drugs?"

"I can't believe you said that!" Deirdre scolds. "The alcohol and drugs cause permanent brain damage to the fetus and leave the child maimed for life. Many of these kids will grow up retarded, and many will become criminals and end up in jail. The burden on society will be incredible! Women who treat their unborn child in this way are utterly immoral, and they ought to be sent to jail."

"Let's take these claims one at a time," Jason responds. "First, why do you think feeding alcohol or drugs to a fetus is immoral, Deirdre?"

"Because I think the fetus has rights."

"But wait a minute," counters Jason. "According to *Roe v. Wade*, the mother can abort the fetus. That must mean the fetus has no right to life; and if it has no right to life, surely it has no rights at all."

Deirdre scratches her head. "It seems to me you're overlooking something," she says. "When a mother intends to abort her fetus, it's one thing. But when she intends to bring it to term, it's quite another thing. It's almost as if she has extended a contract to the fetus. Look, suppose I tell a house painter, 'You paint my house, and I'll pay you $1000.' If the painter fulfills his end of the bargain but I refuse to pay, clearly I am doing something wrong. In the same way, the mother who intends to bear her child in effect tells the fetus, 'You agree to grow and develop in a normal way, and I'll provide you with a healthy environment.' If the fetus grows and develops normally and then the mother feeds it drugs, she welshes on the deal."

Mom has a contract with her fetus.

"I agree with you about the house painter," Jason answers. "But it seems to me that you can only enter into contracts with human beings. You don't enter into contracts with dogs and cats, and you don't enter into contracts with fetuses either."

"A fetus is very much like a complete human being, though," Deirdre replies. "It's made up of human flesh and blood, it has the same genetic code as a human being, and as it develops, it has the same organization of internal organs as a human being and it even looks like a human being. Isn't this enough?"

"And because of these similarities you think the fetus has rights?"

"Yes, I do."

"Well, I think your analogy is nice," Jason replies, "but I don't think the similarities you cite are relevant to your conclusion. The reason human beings have rights and can enter into contracts is because they are rational and have the power of speech. They demonstrate these powers by proving theorems in geometry and engaging in conversations. I've never seen a fetus do either of these things."

"No," replies Deirdre, "but neither do people when they're asleep. Do you think a sleeping person is not human? Would you take a sleeping person and sweep him out the door like a clump of dust because he wasn't at that moment demonstrating rational powers?"

"Of course not," Jason replies. "But unlike a sleeping person, a fetus has *never* demonstrated rational powers."

When does a fetus become human?

"But neither has a newborn baby," Deirdre argues. "When do you think a newborn baby becomes human? Does it happen at the moment it's born? Was it not a human being one hour before birth? Isn't a tomato growing on a vine as much a tomato one day before it ripens as it is when it's ripe? Isn't an apple growing on a tree as much an apple when it's green as it is after it turns red?"

"That's a good analogy," says Jason.

"Also, even if a fetus can't be proved beyond any uncertainty to be fully human, don't you think it should be given the benefit of the doubt? When a person falls through the ice on a frozen lake, don't the rescuers who pull the person out rush him to a hospital even though no signs of life remain? Isn't the person, whether dead or alive, treated as if he were still alive? Similarly, shouldn't a fetus, who shows no signs of rationality, be treated as if it had rationality?"

"Perhaps," Jason answers, "but I have trouble attributing humanity or personhood to a mere lump of flesh. This wart on the back of my hand is made of human flesh and blood, and its cells carry the same genetic code as I do. Of course it's not shaped like a human being, but neither is a fetus in the early stages of development. Does this mean that I should consider this wart to be human or a person?"

"So what you're saying," Deirdre replies, "is that the fetus is just a part of its mother's body, like that wart is part of yours?"

"Exactly," he says. "And that means the fetus can have no rights or interests distinct from those of the mother, any more than someone's liver can have rights distinct from the person who has the liver. When an alcoholic abuses his liver by excessive alcohol consumption, we don't say that he is immoral and incarcerate him for liver abuse. Similarly, we don't say that smokers are immoral for abusing their lungs and put them in jail for lung abuse. Accordingly, we shouldn't call pregnant women immoral and put them in jail for fetal abuse."

"Your analogy has one fatal flaw," Deirdre answers with a smile. "If the fetus is merely part of its mother's body, then it would have exactly the same genetic code as the mother.

A fetus has its own genes.

Every ordinary body part—heart, liver, lungs, and so on—carries the same genes as the host organism. But the fetus has its own unique genetic code. Also, it's meant to develop and separate from the body of its host, unlike a liver or a lung. Therefore, a fetus is not merely a part of the mother's body."

"Well, perhaps you're right," Jason says. "But I have a better analogy. The fetus is like a seed planted in the ground or a group of cells growing in a petri dish. Imagine you were walking down the street and a little seed shouted up at you, 'Help! Get me out of this soil! It's too acidic!' What would you do? Would you reach down, lift the seedling up, and transplant it elsewhere? Of course not. You'd say to the seed, 'Be quiet! It's lucky you found any soil at all to grow in.' Isn't that what you'd say?"

"Maybe I would," she says, "but not if I expected the seed to grow into a human being. And incidentally, don't ever accuse me of anthropomorphizing! I think a far better analogy is that of someone who perpetrates a battery on another person. I was reading about a famous case where a man approached a woman in her sleep and gave her a kiss on the cheek. The man was someone the woman despised, and when she woke up and found out what had happened, she was so furious that she sued the man for battery—and she won. A battery, you know, is any intentionally produced harmful or offensive contact. The case establishes the principle that the target of a battery need not be aware of it at the time it happens. Now if a kiss can be a battery, how much more so is being drowned in drugs and booze. The fetus might not be able to sue till after it's born, but the battery was nevertheless committed before birth."

"Very clever," Jason responds. "However, I don't think you can say someone's asleep if that person has never been awake. A fetus has never been awake."

"I see you're still harping on whether the fetus has human thought processes," replies Deirdre. "Well, consider this. After the child is born, everyone agrees it's a full-fledged human being. When that child enters the world with drugs in its body, we can appropriately ask where those drugs came from. The answer, of course, is the mother. Thus the mother has given drugs not to a mere fetus but to a real child. The situation would be exactly the same as if a common drug dealer had given drugs to the kid. Thus the mother should be treated the same way as any drug dealer."

"I think you've got me there," Jason admits. "But your analogy holds only for kids who are actually born with drugs or alcohol in their system. What about fetuses who are fed drugs or alcohol weeks before birth but who are delivered without any trace of them?"

"Suppose," replies Deirdre, "a doctor who is treating a pregnant woman periodically injects cocaine into the fetus using a long hypodermic needle. Not only would everyone consider the doctor fiendish and immoral, but the doctor would be liable for civil and criminal sanctions. Is the mother who feeds cocaine to her fetus any different from this doctor?"

"Interesting point," says Jason. "I expect, however, that the doctor would be subject to liability for acting without the mother's consent—not for acting without the fetus's consent."

"I hope you're wrong," says Deirdre. "But you know how I feel about these fetal abusers? I see a child in a playpen near a window. Outside the window other kids are playing on the grass. The child in the playpen is excited and happy when it sees them and can't wait until it's big enough to go out and join them. Then one day the mother comes in with a baseball bat and smashes the child's legs, and the child is never able to walk from that day on. That's what fetal abuse does, as far as I'm concerned."

"Getting a little emotional, aren't we, Deirdre?"

"Maybe. But I don't think morality is something devoid of feeling. Morality concerns life and life is feeling, and the two can't be separated."

"Well, even if I agreed with you that fetal abuse is immoral, that doesn't mean I think it should be made illegal. I know our criminal laws are closely tied to public morality, but that's true only up to a point. I think making fetal abuse a crime might be going too far."

"Why is that?" asks Deirdre.

"Because it's so invasive," Jason responds. "Like a rapist, the state would be invading the most private aspects of a woman's life. Also, it would be patronizing. The state would be treating the pregnant woman like an errant, recalcitrant child who's done something wrong and needs to be punished."

"But there is a long history of state intervention in the lives of people who are a danger to themselves or others," Deirdre observes. "For example, people who attempt suicide are sometimes institutionalized to prevent them from killing themselves. Also, mental deviants are often committed to mental institutions for their own benefit. The theory is that, if these people were in their right minds, they would want the state to do exactly that. Women who abuse their fetuses are very similar to mental deviants. If these women were in their right minds, they would want the state to intercede and prevent them from injuring their fetuses."

The state protects citizens from deviants.

"Still," replies Jason, "I think a law criminalizing fetal abuse would be unenforceable. It would be just like the law against alcohol during prohibition. That law was eventually repealed because, among other things, it was impossible to enforce. A law against fetal abuse would suffer the same fate. It would require that police officers snoop into the homes and bedrooms of every pregnant woman reasonably suspected of abusing her fetus. Such action would violate one of our most cherished values, the right to privacy, and it would require massive additions to our police force."

"Yes," answers Deirdre, "but the problem is so significant that I think something must be done. You can look at the whole of society as a single human body grown large. Women who abuse their unborn children are like spiders who inject venom into the body of society. This venom creates a sore that lasts for seventy years or more. Now I ask you, what person threatened by such a spider would not go to any lengths to prevent its bite? What rational person would stand idle, let the spider inject its venom, and then tolerate the resulting canker for seventy years?"

"Yes," agrees Jason, "but unfortunately, getting rid of fetal abuse is harder than simply brushing off a spider. I think the solution is to stress educational programs and provide prenatal care for every expectant mother. After all, you catch more flies with honey than you do with vinegar. Such programs might reduce the problem of fetal abuse to a point where it becomes tolerable."

Honey catches more flies than vinegar.

"I think any amount of fetal abuse is intolerable," Deirdre replies.

"Society is like a water supply," Jason says. "Public health officials test it for contaminants and find microscopic amounts of this and microscopic amounts of that. If these amounts are within acceptable limits, they pronounce the water supply potable. Yes, the thought of any fetal abuse is disturbing, but we can never eliminate it entirely. The best we can hope for is to reduce it to a point where it won't cripple society as a whole."

"Perhaps you're right," concludes Deirdre, "but the thought of that child in the playpen still bothers me."

This dialogue contains numerous analogies and counteranalogies. The modes of similarity between the many primary analogues and the secondary analogues (the fetus, women who commit fetal abuse, laws against fetal abuse, and so on) are never relevant beyond dispute, and the nature and degree of disanalogy rarely has undisputed consequences. However, the dialogue serves to illustrate the subtle effect that analogies have on our thought processes and the power they have to alter our attitudes and perspectives.

EXERCISE 9.1

I. Evaluate the arguments from analogy contained in the dialogue between Jason and Deirdre. First identify the primary and secondary analogues in each analogy and counteranalogy. Next list the similarities between the primary and secondary analogues and note their relevance to the conclusion. Add any additional similarities you can think of. Finally, identify the disanalogies associated with each analogy or counteranalogy, and evaluate their effectiveness in destroying the original analogy.

iLrn II. Work the following problems.

★1. Jessica has long admired Rachel's near perfect body, and she notes that Rachel works out on a Roboflex exercise machine. Jessica concludes that if she buys a Roboflex for herself, she will be able to duplicate Rachel's results. How do the following facts bear on Jessica's argument?

    a. Roboflex recently changed its corporate headquarters from Ohio to Illinois.

    b. Jessica and Rachel are siblings.

    c. Rachel is 25 years old, but Jessica is 32.

    d. Jessica is 40 pounds overweight.

    e. Whenever Jessica makes up her mind to do something, she always sticks with it.

    f. Jessica knows of five other women who work out on a Roboflex, and these women all look as good as Rachel.

    g. These women are all between the ages of 24 and 26.

    h. Jessica discovers four additional women between the ages of 31 and 33 who work out on a Roboflex, and these women look nearly as good as Rachel.

    i. Jessica changes her conclusion to state that she will look almost as good as Rachel.

    j. Jessica changes her conclusion to state that she will look better than Rachel.

2. Harold needs to have his rugs cleaned, and his friend Veronica reports that Ajax Carpet Service did an excellent job on her rugs. From this, Harold concludes that Ajax will do an equally good job on his rugs. How do the following facts bear on Harold's argument?

    a. Veronica hired Ajax several times, and Ajax always did an excellent job.

    b. Veronica's rugs are wool, whereas Harold's are nylon.

    c. Veronica's carpets never had any stains on them before they were cleaned, but Harold's have several large stains.

    d. Veronica always had her rugs cleaned in mid-October, whereas Harold wants his done just a week before Easter.

    e. Harold knows of six additional people who have had their carpets cleaned by Ajax, and all six have been very pleased.

    f. All six own rugs made of different material.

    g. All six were born in Massachusetts.

    h. Ajax has recently undergone a change in management.

    i. The Environmental Protection Agency recently banned the cleaning solution Ajax has used for many years.

    j. Harold changes his conclusion to state that Ajax will get his carpets approximately as clean as it has gotten Veronica's.

3. Kristin is president of a corporation that operates a chain of clothing stores, and she faces the task of hiring a manager for one of the stores to replace a man who retired. The former manager increased sales by 15 percent every year for the past five years. Kristin concludes that Roger Benson, a recent graduate of Wharton School of Business, will duplicate the former manager's performance. How do the following facts bear on Kristin's argument?

   a. The manager who retired was a graduate of Wharton.

   b. The manager who retired liked tennis and drove a Jaguar, whereas Benson dislikes tennis and drives a BMW.

   c. Unlike the manager who retired, Benson formerly managed a shoe store, where he increased sales 20 percent for each of the two years he was there.

   d. A labor dispute has recently erupted in the store Benson will manage.

   e. The manager who retired was an alcoholic, whereas Benson is a moderate drinker.

   f. The government has approved a 10 percent increase in federal income taxes that takes effect at the beginning of the year.

   g. Three additional stores owned by Kristin's company are managed by recent Wharton graduates, and all three managers have increased sales by 18 percent for each of the past three years.

   h. These three stores are located in the city's three wealthiest suburbs.

   i. The store Benson will manage is located in a neighborhood that has recently begun to decline.

   j. Kristin changes her conclusion to state that Benson will increase sales by at least 10 percent for the first year.

★4. Sam has planned a one-day fishing trip in Alaska. He intends to fish off Rocky Point, where he fished last year. Because he caught five fish in a one-day outing last year, Sam concludes that he will catch five fish this year. How do the following facts bear on Sam's argument?

   a. Last year Sam used a wooden boat, but this year he will use a fiberglass boat.

   b. Sam used herring for bait last year, but this year he will use anchovies.

   c. Sam fished with four friends last year, and each of them caught more than five fish on that day.

   d. This year Sam will fish on July 15, but last year he fished on August 1.

   e. Last year these four friends caught an average of five fish per day from July 15 to August 1.

   f. These four friends are women.

   g. These four friends used various kinds of bait—herring, squid, anchovies, and artificial lures.

   h. It is now July 12. Yesterday, ten people fished off Rocky Point, and none caught any fish.

     i. A fleet of commercial fishing boats has been fishing the area near Rocky Point for the first time.

     j. Sam changes his conclusion to state that he will catch at least one fish.

5. Susan is considering a job as public relations specialist with the Chamber of Commerce. Her friend Terry took such a job one year ago, and within nine months her annual salary was $50,000. Susan argues that if she takes this job, then her annual salary will be at least $50,000 within nine months. How do the following facts bear on Susan's argument?

     a. Susan is beautiful and outgoing, whereas Terry is average looking and introverted.

     b. Susan is a Democrat, but Terry is a Republican.

     c. Like Terry, Susan is 5 feet 4 inches tall and has blonde hair.

     d. Susan's parents are elementary school teachers, but Terry's parents are prominent businesspeople.

     e. One year ago, Cindy, April, Elizabeth, and Jackie accepted jobs as public relations specialists with the Chamber of Commerce, and today all are earning $44,000.

     f. April is a Republican, Cindy is a Democrat, Elizabeth is a Libertarian, and Jackie is a member of the Peace and Freedom Party.

     g. Cindy, April, Elizabeth, and Jackie are beautiful and outgoing.

     h. Susan has five years experience as a public relations specialist, whereas Terry, when she was hired, had only two years experience in that area.

     i. There is a shortage of public relations specialists in the local job pool.

     j. Susan changes her conclusion to state that after nine months she will be earning at least $47,000.

6. Paul is searching for a puppy that will grow up to be friendly with his children. His friend Barbara has an Airedale that is good with her children. From this, Paul concludes that an Airedale puppy would make a good choice. How do the following facts bear on Paul's argument?

     a. Barbara's dog is a female, but Paul plans to get a male.

     b. Tim, Ed, and Irene have male Airedales that are friendly with their children.

     c. Tim's, Ed's, and Irene's dogs all came from the same litter.

     d. Fran, Penny, and Bob have Airedales that snap at their children.

     e. Fran's, Penny's and Bob's Airedales all came from different litters.

     f. The puppy that Paul plans to get was born in June, just as Barbara's was.

     g. The puppy that Paul plans to get is of the same subspecies as Barbara's dog.

     h. The puppy that Paul plans to get had a littermate that was vicious and had to be destroyed. Barbara's dog had no such littermates.

     i. Paul plans to give his dog special training, but Barbara's dog received no such training.

     j. Paul changes his conclusion to state that if he gets an Airedale puppy, it will grow up at least to tolerate children.

★7. Laura is considering taking Calculus I from Professor Rogers. Her friend Gina took Professor Rogers for this class and got an A. Laura concludes that she, too, will get an A from Professor Rogers. How do the following facts bear on Laura's argument?

a. Gina earned straight A's in high school math, whereas Laura got B's.

b. Laura took pre-calculus in high school, but Gina took no precalculus class.

c. Laura is a Buddhist, whereas Gina is a Protestant.

d. Kevin, Toni, and Samantha took precalculus in high school, and all of them received A's in Professor Rogers's Calculus I class.

e. Kevin, Toni, and Samantha all have different majors.

f. Kevin, Toni, and Samantha attended Franklin High School.

g. Laura attended Roosevelt High School.

h. Kevin, Toni, and Samantha took precalculus from different instructors.

i. Laura and Gina earned equal scores on the college math entrance exam.

j. Laura changes her conclusion to state that she will receive an "A+" in Professor Rogers's class.

8. Andrew is thinking about buying stock in E-Tron, a new company that sells electronic equipment over the Internet. Six months ago, he bought shares in E-Boot, a new company that sells shoes over the Internet, and the price of the stock doubled in two months. Andrew argues that if he buys E-Tron, the stock will double in two months. How do the following facts bear on Andrew's argument?

a. Stocks in Internet companies have been in a steep decline for the past two weeks, whereas they were rising six months ago.

b. E-Tron will be run by the same management team that runs E-Boot.

c. During the past year, the stock of five other new companies that sell over the Internet doubled within two months of their initial offering.

d. These five companies market Swiss chocolates, tires, appliances, furniture, and luggage.

e. A survey was taken of E-Boot customers, and 90 percent said they would not consider buying electronic equipment over the Internet.

f. Two other companies that market jewelry and lingerie over the Internet have done poorly.

g. America Online, the most widely used Net service provider, just increased its monthly service charge by 50 percent.

h. E-Boot is incorporated in New Jersey, whereas E-Tron is incorporated in Delaware.

i. E-Boot introduced its products with a major ad campaign, whereas E-Tron plans no such campaign.

j. Andrew changes his conclusion to state that E-Tron stock will triple within the next two months.

9. According to the doctrine of adverse possession, a person occupying a piece of land in a way that is open, notorious, and hostile to the owner's rights can

claim ownership of the land after a certain number of years of continuous occupancy. In this connection, Dr. Wacko, a mad scientist, hauled telescopes and radio antennas to the top of Mica Peak every night for twenty years to detect extraterrestrial life. At the end of the period he petitioned the court for a decree stating that he owned Mica Peak under the theory of adverse possession. Tom Bell, the owner of Mica Peak, attempts to defeat Dr. Wacko's petition.

Construct two arguments, one supporting Dr. Wacko's position, the other supporting Tom Bell's position. The statutory period for adverse possession in this jurisdiction is twenty years, and there are two controlling cases:

Crick v. Hoskins: Crick occupied a house in Centerville that was owned by Hoskins. She lived in the house continuously, mowed the lawn weekly, and parked her car in front. After twenty years she petitioned the court for a decree stating that she owned the property under the theory of adverse possession, and the court granted the decree against the objections of Hoskins.

Raymond v. McBride: Raymond set up a large tent on a piece of rural property owned by McBride and lived in it for nine months each year. During the remaining three months, heavy snow made the property inaccessible. After twenty years Raymond petitioned the court for a decree stating that he owned the property under the theory of adverse possession, and the court denied Raymond's petition.

10. The Fourth Amendment to the U.S. Constitution prohibits unreasonable searches and seizures. A "search" is defined as a "violation of a person's reasonable expectation of privacy by the police." Legal issues dealing with searches usually turn on the question of whether the person who was searched had a reasonable expectation of privacy at the time and place the search was conducted. In this connection, consider the following set of facts. Maxie was lining up drug contacts from his cell phone while he was driving on the freeway. Without obtaining a search warrant, federal agents intercepted one of his messages and used it to locate Maxie's car and arrest Maxie. Maxie argues that the federal agents violated his reasonable expectation of privacy, and the government denies it.

Your task is to construct two arguments, one supporting Maxie's position, the other supporting the position of the federal agents. There are three controlling cases in this jurisdiction:

U.S. v. Taylor: Federal agents suspected Taylor of illegal distribution of firearms. Without obtaining a search warrant, they planted a listening device on the phone in Taylor's home and used the evidence obtained to arrest Taylor. The court ruled that their action violated Taylor's reasonable expectation of privacy and disallowed the evidence.

U.S. v. Weber: Without obtaining a search warrant, federal agents operating inside U.S. borders intercepted a radio transmission from a plane flying over Mexico. The message mentioned drugs, and it disclosed the location of a landing strip inside the United States. Using this information, the agents met the plane and arrested its pilot for drug smuggling. The court ruled that their action did not violate the pilot's reasonable expectation of privacy.

U.S. v. Robinson: Federal agents were using a telescope to conduct surveillance on the resident of a distant apartment building. Inadvertently they noticed some teenagers smoking crack in a car parked in the lot near the building, and they proceeded to arrest them. The court ruled that their action did not violate the teenagers' reasonable expectation of privacy.

11. The First Amendment to the U.S. Constitution states that Congress shall make no law abridging the freedom of speech or the right to peaceable assembly. This "law" applies to states (and cities) as a result of the adoption of the Fourteenth Amendment. In reliance on the First Amendment, a group of gays and lesbians apply for a permit to march on Gay Freedom day. Similar parades in other cities have been calm and orderly, but the police chief denies a parade permit to this group.

Construct two arguments, one supporting the position of the group, the other supporting the position of the police chief. There are three controlling cases in this jurisdiction:

Lester v. City: Police seized an art collection displayed in a public park because it depicted heterosexuals in nude poses. The court ruled that the display was protected by the First Amendment.

Byron v. City: Police denied a parade permit to a Nazi group that wanted to march on Hitler's birthday. The court ruled that the denial violated the group's rights under the First Amendment.

Stone v. City: Police closed down a theater showing an erotic gay film because they claimed that the film promoted the spread of AIDS. The court ruled that the action of the police was allowed under the First Amendment.

12. Constructive eviction is a legal doctrine by which a landlord who substantially interferes with a tenant's use and enjoyment of the premises will be considered to have evicted the tenant. Such a landlord cannot collect rent from the tenant. In this connection, Isabel signed a lease for an apartment owned by Carolyn. A clause in the lease stated that all tenants must keep noise to a minimum during evening hours. After moving in, Isabel found that another tenant played his stereo all night long at ear-splitting levels. Carolyn declined to enforce the noise clause in the lease. After one week without sleep, Isabel moved out, and Carolyn now sues Isabel for rent.

Construct two arguments, one supporting Isabel's position, the other supporting Carolyn's. There are two controlling cases in this jurisdiction:

Garvin v. Linder: Linder rented an apartment from Garvin, and the lease stated that Garvin would provide heat during the winter. When winter arrived, Garvin provided heat for only one hour per day, and the inside temperature sometimes dropped to 50°F. Linder moved out, and Garvin sued Linder for rent. The court ruled in favor of Linder.

Quincy v. Fulton: Fulton rented a tenth-floor apartment from Quincy. Shortly thereafter Quincy decided to have repairs made on the elevator, causing it to be shut down for a month. Because Fulton had arthritis, he had great difficulty climbing ten flights of stairs. Fulton moved out, and Quincy sued Fulton for rent. The court ruled in favor of Quincy.

13. A negligent person who causes an injury to another person is liable for the latter's injuries. Because it is sometimes very difficult to determine the causal extent of a negligent action, courts have developed the theory of proximate cause, which limits the scope of liability. In this connection, Liz Shaffer negligently failed to maintain the brakes on her car, and as a result her car crashed into one driven by Mary Vassar. Mary was taken to the hospital for bumps and bruises, but while she was there, doctors mistakenly amputated her perfectly healthy leg. Mary sues Liz for loss of her leg.

    Construct two arguments, one supporting Mary's position, the other supporting Liz's position. The only issue is whether Liz proximately caused the loss of the leg. There are two controlling cases in this jurisdiction:

    Sacco v. Lane: Lane negligently used gasoline to light his barbecue in a strong wind. The flames from the barbecue ignited nearby trees and then spread to ten houses in the neighborhood, burning them to the ground. The court ruled that Lane was liable for damage to the houses.

    Hunt v. Gomez: Hunt was a passenger in a taxi driven by Gomez. Gomez was drunk and negligently let Hunt out at the wrong corner. While Hunt was walking home, a worker dropped a brick from a building that was under construction, injuring Hunt. Hunt sued Gomez for injury resulting from the falling brick. The court ruled in favor of Gomez.

14. Lynn Dodd, age twenty, has become a member of New Age Enlightenment, a religious cult group. The group has convinced Lynn to sell all her worldly possessions and give the proceeds to the group. The group forbids any contact between Lynn and her relatives and friends. On one occasion Lynn's parents encountered Lynn on a street corner, and they tried to persuade her to leave the group and return home, but she refused. The parents fear that some form of mind control is being used to keep Lynn in the group, and they plan a rescue operation.

    Write a dialogue, similar to the dialogue in the text, examining the morality and legality of such an operation. Include in your dialogue analogies between the proposed rescue operation and the following: rescuing an adult who has been hypnotized by captors, kidnapping someone against his or her will, rescuing a child who has been kidnapped, spiriting away a novice who has joined a Jesuit seminary or Franciscan convent, coercing an alcoholic to enter a detoxification center, forcing a child to attend a certain school, preventing someone from committing suicide, forcing a child to attend a certain church, rescuing an eighteen-year-old from a Nazi youth group, removing one's daughter from the Girl Scouts, and any other pertinent analogy that comes to mind.

15. During fifteen years of marriage, James and Leslie Knox had not succeeded in having a baby. As a last resort, they tried in vitro fertilization. Doctors surgi-

cally removed nine eggs from Leslie and fertilized them with James's sperm. The embryos were then placed in a freezer until the proper time for them to be implanted in Leslie's womb. In the meantime, James and Leslie came to realize that their marriage was going nowhere, and they decided to get a divorce. The couple has had no trouble arriving at a settlement concerning the house, cars, bank accounts, and other possessions, but they cannot agree on the disposition of the frozen embryos. James is adamant about not wanting to have any children by Leslie, and he wants the embryos destroyed. Leslie, on the other hand, realizing that she is getting older, thinks that the frozen embryos offer her the best chance of having a baby, and she wants them implanted.

Write a dialogue, similar to the one in the text, examining the moral and/or legal ramifications of this dispute. Include in your dialogue analogies between this situation and the following: killing a fetus, killing a baby, forcing your wife to have an abortion, having an abortion against the wishes of your husband, owning a dog or cat, owning a child, determining custody of a child upon divorce, dividing a bank account, determining ownership of a unique and valuable painting produced jointly by two people, implanting an embryo in a surrogate mother, and any other analogies that come to mind, including analogies that show that the embryos have or do not have rights and analogies that illustrate the investment that James and Leslie have in the embryos.

9.2   Causality and Mill's Methods

A knowledge of causal connections plays a prominent role in our effort to control the environment in which we live. We insulate our homes because we know insulation will prevent heat loss, we vaccinate our children because we know vaccination will protect them from polio and diphtheria, we practice the piano and violin because we know that by doing so we may become proficient on these instruments, and we cook our meat and fish because we know that doing so will make them edible.

When the word "cause" is used in ordinary English, however, it is seriously affected by ambiguity. For example, when we say that sprinkling water on the flowers will cause them to grow, we mean that water is required for growth, not that water alone will do the job—sunshine and the proper soil are also required. On the other hand, when we say that taking a swim on a hot summer day will cause us to cool off, we mean that the dip by itself *will* do the job, but we understand that other things will work just as well, such as taking a cold shower, entering an air-conditioned room, and so on.

To clear up this ambiguity affecting the meaning of "cause," it is useful to adopt the language of sufficient and necessary conditions. When we say that electrocution is a cause of death, we mean "cause" in the sense of *sufficient* condition. Electrocution is sufficient to produce death, but there are other methods equally effective, such as poisoning, drowning, and shooting. On the other hand, when we say that the presence of clouds is a cause of rain, we mean "cause" in the sense of *necessary* condition. Without clouds, rain cannot occur, but clouds alone are not sufficient. Certain combinations of pressure and temperature are also required.

Sometimes "cause" is used in the sense of necessary *and* sufficient condition, as when we say that the action of a force causes a body to accelerate or that an increase in voltage causes an increase in electrical current. For a body to accelerate, nothing more and nothing less is required than for it to be acted on by a net force; and for an electrical current to increase through a resistive circuit, nothing more and nothing less is required than an increase in voltage.

Thus, as these examples illustrate, the word "cause" can have any one of three different meanings:

1. Sufficient condition
2. Necessary condition
3. Sufficient and necessary condition

Sometimes the context provides an immediate clue to the sense in which "cause" is being used. If we are trying to *prevent* a certain phenomenon from happening, we usually search for a cause that is a necessary condition, and if we are trying to *produce* a certain phenomenon we usually search for a cause that is a sufficient condition. For example, in attempting to prevent the occurrence of smog around cities, scientists try to isolate a necessary condition or group of necessary conditions that, if removed, will eliminate the smog. And in their effort to produce an abundant harvest, farmers search for a sufficient condition that, given sunshine and rainfall, will increase crop growth.

Another point that should be understood is that whenever an event occurs, at least *one* sufficient condition is present and *all* the necessary conditions are present. The conjunction of the necessary conditions *is* the sufficient condition that actually produces the event. For example, the necessary conditions for lighting a match are heat (produced by striking) and oxygen. Combining these two necessary conditions gives the sufficient condition. In other words, striking the match in the presence of oxygen is sufficient to ignite it. In cases where the sufficient condition is also a necessary condition, there is only one necessary condition, which is identical with the sufficient condition.

We can now summarize the meaning of cause in the sense of a sufficient condition and a necessary condition:

> A is a sufficient condition for B: A's occurrence requires B's occurrence.
> A is a necessary condition for B: B's occurrence requires A's occurrence.

According to these statements, if A occurs and B does not occur, then A is not a sufficient condition for B, and if B occurs and A does not occur, then A is not a necessary condition for B. Thus:

> A is not a sufficient condition for B: A is present when B is absent.
> A is not a necessary condition for B: A is absent when B is present.

These results will serve as important rules in the material that follows.

In his *System of Logic,* the nineteenth-century philosopher John Stuart Mill compiled five methods for identifying causal connections between events. These he called the method of agreement, the method of difference, the joint method of agreement and difference, the method of residues, and the method of concomitant variation. In the years that have elapsed since the publication of Mill's *Logic,* the five methods have received a good deal of philosophical criticism. Today most logicians agree that the methods fall short of the claims made for them by Mill, but the fact remains that the methods function implicitly in many of the inductive inferences we make in ordinary life.

In addition to criticizing these methods, modern logicians have introduced many variations that have multiplied their number beyond the original five. Some of these variations have resulted from the fact that Mill himself failed to distinguish causes that are sufficient conditions from causes that are necessary conditions. The account that follows introduces this distinction into the first three methods, but apart from that, it remains faithful to Mill's own presentation.

Method of Agreement

Suppose that five people eat dinner in a certain restaurant, and a short while later all five become sick. Suppose further that these people ordered an assortment of items from the menu, but the only food that all of them ordered was vanilla ice cream for dessert. In other words, all of the dinners were in agreement only as to the ice cream. Such a situation suggests that the ice cream caused the sickness. The **method of agreement** consists in a systematic effort to find a single factor (such as the ice cream) that is common to a number of occurrences for the purpose of identifying that factor as the cause of a phenomenon present in the occurrences (such as the sickness).

The method of agreement identifies a cause in the sense of a necessary condition. To see how this method works, let us develop the restaurant example a bit further.

> Five people eat dinner in a restaurant. Jack has salad, French fries, a hamburger, ice cream, and mixed vegetables; Bob has salad, French fries, soup, ice cream, fish, and mixed vegetables; Mary has a hamburger, soup, and ice cream; Tim has fish, mixed vegetables, ice cream, salad, and soup; and Gail has mixed vegetables, fish, ice cream, French fries, and salad. Afterwards all of them became sick from something they ate. What food caused the sickness?

If we let occurrences 1 through 5 stand for Jack, Bob, Mary, Tim, and Gail, respectively, and let A through G represent salad, soup, French fries, a hamburger, fish, ice cream, and mixed vegetables, respectively, we can construct a table that reflects what these five people ate. In this table an asterisk means that a certain food was eaten, and a dash means that it was not eaten.

Table 9.1

| Occurrence | Possible necessary conditions | | | | | | | Phenomenon (sickness) |
	A	B	C	D	E	F	G	
1	*	-	*	*	-	*	*	*
2	*	*	*	-	*	*	*	*
3	-	*	-	*	-	*	-	*
4	*	*	-	-	*	*	*	*
5	*	-	*	-	*	*	*	*

Now, since the method of agreement identifies a cause in the sense of a necessary condition, we begin by eliminating from this table the conditions that are not necessary for the occurrence of the phenomenon. In doing so, we use the rule that a condition is not necessary for the occurrence of a phenomenon if that condition is absent when the phenomenon is present. Thus, occurrence 1 eliminates condition *B* and condition *E*; occurrence 2 eliminates *D*; occurrence 3 eliminates *A, C, E* (again), and *G*; occurrence 4 eliminates *C* (again) and *D* (again), and occurrence 5 eliminates *B* (again) and *D* (again). This leaves only *F* (the ice cream) as a possible necessary condition. The conclusion is therefore warranted that the ice cream caused the sickness of the diners.

This conclusion follows only probably for two reasons. First, it is quite possible that some condition was overlooked in compiling conditions *A* through *G*. For example, if the ice cream was served with contaminated spoons, then the sickness of the diners could have been caused by that condition and not by the ice cream. Second, if more than one of the foods were contaminated (for example, both soup and French fries), then the sickness could have been caused by this combination of foods and not by the ice cream. Thus, the strength of the argument depends on the nonoccurrence of these two possibilities.

It is also important to realize that the conclusion yielded by Table 9.1 applies directly only to the five diners represented in the five occurrences, and not to everyone who may have eaten in the restaurant. Thus, if some food other than those listed in the table—for example, spaghetti—were contaminated, then only if they avoided both spaghetti and ice cream could the other diners be assured of not getting sick. But if, among all the foods in the restaurant, only the ice cream was contaminated, the conclusion would extend to the other patrons as well. This last point illustrates the fact that a conclusion reached by the method of agreement has limited generality. It applies directly only to those occurrences listed, and only indirectly, through a second inductive inference, to others.

Furthermore, because the conclusion yields a cause in the sense of a necessary condition, it does not assert that anyone who ate the ice cream would get sick. Many people have a natural immunity to food poisoning. What the conclusion says is that patrons who did not eat the ice cream would not get sick—at least not from the food. Thus, the method of agreement has a certain limited use. Basically what it says, in reference to the above example, is that the ice cream is a highly suspect factor in the sickness of the patrons, and if investigators want to track down the cause of the sickness, this is where they should begin.

An example of an actual use of the method of agreement is provided by the discovery of the beneficial effects of fluoride on teeth. It was noticed several decades ago that people in certain communities were favored with especially healthy teeth. In researching the various factors these communities shared in common, scientists discovered that all had a high level of natural fluoride in their water supply. The scientists concluded from this evidence that fluoride causes teeth to be healthy and free of cavities.

Method of Difference

For an example of how this method works, let us modify our earlier case of people becoming sick from eating food in a restaurant. Instead of five people, suppose that identical twins, who have identical susceptibilities to food poisoning, go to that restaurant for dinner. They both order identical meals except that one orders ice cream for dessert while the other does not. The ice cream is the only way that the two meals differ. Later the twin who ordered the ice cream gets sick, whereas the other twin does not. The natural conclusion is that the ice cream caused the sickness.

The **method of difference** consists in a systematic effort to identify a single factor that is present in an occurrence in which the phenomenon in question is present, and absent from an occurrence in which the phenomenon is absent. The method is confined to investigating exactly two occurrences, and it identifies a cause in the sense of a sufficient condition. For a clearer illustration of how this method works, let us add a few details to the twin example:

> A pair of twins, Jane and Jan, have dinner in a restaurant. The twins have identical susceptibilities to food poisoning. Jane orders soup, salad, chicken, carrots, rice, and ice cream. Jan orders soup, salad, chicken, carrots, rice, and no ice cream. Later, Jane gets sick from something she ate, but Jan does not. What food caused Jan's sickness?

If we let Jane and Jan stand for occurrences 1 and 2, respectively, and let A stand for the specific susceptibility to food poisoning shared by Jane and Jan, and B through G stand for soup, salad, chicken, carrots, rice, and ice cream, respectively, we can produce the following table. Again, an asterisk indicates that a certain condition is present, and a dash indicates it is absent:

Table 9.2

Occurrence	Possible sufficient conditions							Phenomenon (sickness)
	A	B	C	D	E	F	G	
1	*	*	*	*	*	*	*	*
2	*	*	*	*	*	*	-	-

As with the method of agreement, we proceed to eliminate certain conditions, but in this case we use the rule that a condition is not sufficient for the occurrence of a phenomenon if it is present when the phenomenon is absent. Accordingly, occurrence 2 eliminates A, B, C, D, E, and F. This leaves only G as the sufficient condition for the phenomenon. Thus, G (ice cream) is the cause of Jan's sickness.

Since the result yielded by the method of difference applies to only the one occurrence in which the phenomenon is present (in this case, Jane), it is often less susceptible to generalization than the method of agreement, which usually applies to several occurrences. Thus, the mere fact that the ice cream may have caused Jane to become sick does not mean that it caused other patrons who ate ice cream to get sick. Perhaps these other people have a higher resistance to food poisoning than Jane or Jan. But given that the others are similar to Jane and Jan in relevant respects, the result can often be generalized to cover these others as well. At the very least, if others in the restaurant became sick, the fact that the ice cream is what made Jane sick suggests that this is where investigators should begin when they try to explain what made the others sick.

The conclusion yielded by the method of difference is only probable, however, even for the one occurrence to which it directly applies. The problem is that it is impossible for two occurrences to be literally identical in every respect but one. The mere fact that two occurrences occupy different regions of space, that one is closer to the wall than the other, amounts to a difference. Such differences may be insignificant, but therein lies the possibility for error. It is not at all obvious how insignificant differences should be distinguished from significant ones. Furthermore, it is impossible to make an exhaustive list of all the possible conditions; but without such a list there is no assurance that significant conditions have not been overlooked.

The objective of the method of difference is to identify a sufficient condition among those that are *present* in a specific occurrence. Sometimes, however, the *absence* of a factor can count as something positive that must be taken into account. Suppose, for example, that both of the twins who dined in the restaurant are allergic to dairy products, but they can avoid an allergic reaction by taking Lactaid tablets. Suppose further that both twins ordered ice cream for dessert, but only Jan took the tablets. After the meal, Jane got sick. We can attribute Jane's sickness to the absence of the Lactaid.

We can illustrate this situation by modifying Table 9.2 as follows. Let A stand for the allergy to dairy products, let B through G stand for the same foods as before, and let H stand for Lactaid tablets. Then $\sim H$ will stand for the *absence* of Lactaid (the symbol $\sim$ means "not"). As before, let occurrence 1 stand for Jane, and occurrence 2 for Jan. The modified table is as follows.

Table 9.3

Occurrence	Possible sufficient conditions								Phenomenon (sickness)
	A	B	C	D	E	F	G	$\sim H$	
1	*	*	*	*	*	*	*	*	*
2	*	*	*	*	*	*	*	–	–

Using the same rule for elimination as with Table 9.2, we see that occurrence 2 eliminates A through G as sufficient conditions. This leaves $\sim H$ (the absence of Lactaid) as the cause of Jane's sickness. In this case, the ice cream is not identified as the cause because Jan (occurrence 2) ate ice cream (G) but did not get sick.

The method of difference has a wide range of applicability. For example, a farmer might fertilize one part of a field but not the other part to test the benefit of using fertilizer. If the fertilized part of the crop turns out to be fuller and healthier than the nonfertilized part, then the farmer can conclude that the improvement was caused by the fertilizer. On the other hand, a cook might leave some ingredient out of a batch of biscuits to determine the importance of that ingredient. If the biscuits turn out dry and crunchy, the cook can attribute the difference to the absence of that ingredient.

Joint Method of Agreement and Difference

To illustrate the joint method, we can once again modify the example of the diners who got sick by eating food in a restaurant. In place of the original five diners and the pair of twins, suppose that six people eat dinner in the restaurant. Among the first three, suppose that a variety of meals are eaten but that only ice cream is consumed by all, and later all three get sick. And among the other three, suppose that a variety of meals are eaten but that none of these diners eats any ice cream, and later none of them gets sick. The conclusion is warranted that the ice cream is what made the first three diners sick.

The **joint method of agreement and difference** consists of a systematic effort to identify a single condition that is present in two or more occurrences in which the phenomenon in question is present and that is absent from two or more occurrences in which the phenomenon is absent. This condition is then taken to be the cause of the phenomenon in the sense of a necessary and sufficient condition. To see more clearly how this method works, let us add some details to the example:

> Six people eat dinner in a restaurant. Liz has soup, a hamburger, ice cream, French fries, and mixed vegetables. Tom has salad, soup, fish, mixed vegetables, and ice cream. Andy has salad, a hamburger, French fries, and ice cream. Sue has French fries, a hamburger, and salad. Meg has fish and mixed vegetables. Bill has French fries, a hamburger, and soup. Later Liz, Tom, and Andy get sick from something they ate, but Sue, Meg, and Bill do not. What food made the first three diners sick?

Let occurrences 1 through 6 stand for Liz, Tom, Andy, Sue, Meg, and Bill, respectively. And let *A* through *G* stand for salad, soup, a hamburger, fish, ice cream, French fries, and mixed vegetables. The finished table is as follows:

Table 9.4

| Occurrence | Possible necessary or sufficient conditions | | | | | | | Phenomenon (sickness) |
	A	*B*	*C*	*D*	*E*	*F*	*G*	
1	-	*	*	-	*	*	*	*
2	*	*	-	*	*	-	*	*
3	*	-	*	-	*	*	-	*
4	x	-	x	-	-	*	-	-
5	-	-	-	*	-	-	*	-
6	-	*	*	-	-	*	-	-

In the first three occurrences the phenomenon is present, so we proceed by eliminating possible necessary conditions. Using the rule that a condition is not necessary if it is absent when the phenomenon is present, occurrence 1 eliminates *A* and *D*, occurrence 2 eliminates *C* and *F*, and occurrence 3 eliminates *B*, *D* (again), and *G*. This leaves only *E* as the necessary condition. Next, in the last three occurrences the phenomenon is absent, so we use the rule that a condition is not sufficient if it is present when the phenomenon is absent. Occurrence 4 eliminates *A*, *C*, and *F*; occurrence 5 eliminates *D* and *G*; and occurrence 6 eliminates *B*, *C* (again), and *F* (again). This leaves only *E* as the sufficient condition. Thus, condition *E* (ice cream) is the cause in the sense of both a necessary and sufficient condition of the sickness of the first three diners.

Since the joint method yields a cause in the sense of both a necessary and sufficient condition, it is usually thought to be stronger than either the method of agreement by itself, which yields a cause in the sense of a necessary condition, or the method of difference by itself, which yields a cause in the sense of a sufficient condition. However, when any of these methods is used as a basis for a subsequent inductive generalization, the strength of the conclusion is proportional to the number of occurrences that are included. Thus, an application of the method of agreement that included, say, one hundred occurrences might offer stronger results than an application of the joint method that included, say, only six occurrences. By similar reasoning, multiple applications of the method of difference might offer stronger results than a single application of the joint method.

As with the other methods, the conclusion yielded by the joint method is only probable because some relevant condition may have been overlooked in producing the table. If, for example, both salad and soup were contaminated, then the ice cream could not be identified as a necessary condition for the sickness, and if one of the last three diners was naturally immune, then the ice cream could not be identified as a sufficient condition. Obviously the attempt to extend the results of this example to other patrons of the restaurant who may have gotten sick is fraught with other difficulties.

Lastly, we note that even though the name of the joint method suggests that it results from a mere combination of the method of agreement with the method of difference, this is not the case—at least not as Mill presented it. Such a combination would consist of one occurrence in which the phenomenon is present, one occurrence in which the phenomenon is absent and which differs from the former occurrence as to only one condition, and one occurrence in which the phenomenon is present and which agrees with the first occurrence in only one condition. However, according to Mill, the joint method requires "two or more" occurrences in which the phenomenon is present, and "two or more" occurrences in which the phenomenon is absent.* His further description of the method accords with the foregoing account.

Method of Residues

This method and the one that follows are used to identify a causal connection between two conditions without regard for the specific kind of connection. Both methods may be used to identify conditions that are sufficient, necessary, or both sufficient and necessary. The **method of residues** consists of separating from a group of causally connected conditions and phenomena those strands of causal connection that are already known, leaving the required causal connection as the "residue." Here is an example:

> After occupying his new house Mr. Smith found it drafty. He traced the source of the draft to three conditions: a broken window in the garage, a crack under the front door, and a broken damper in the fireplace. When the window was replaced he noticed an improvement, and a further improvement when weather stripping was installed on the door. He concluded that the draft that remained was caused by the broken damper in the fireplace.

The method of residues as illustrated in this example may be diagramed as follows:

*A System of Logic, Book III, Chapter VIII, Sect. 4, Third Canon.

$$(A \ B \ C) \text{ causes } (a \ b \ c.)$$

A causes a.

B causes b.

Therefore, C causes c.

In reference to the draft example, $(A \ B \ C)$ is the combination of possible conditions producing $(a \ b \ c)$, the total draft. When A (the broken window) is separated out, it is found to cause a (a portion of the draft). When B (the crack) is separated out, it is found to cause b (another portion of the draft). The conclusion is that C (the broken damper) causes c (the remaining portion of the draft). The conclusion follows only probably because it is quite possible that a fourth source of the draft was overlooked. Here is another example:

> After realizing a loss of $100,000 a department store's chief accountant could suggest only three causes: an excessive number of clerks, increases in utility rates, and damage to merchandise caused by a flood. These expenses were estimated at $25,000, $30,000, and $10,000, respectively. Since no other ordinary sources could be found, the accountant attributed the remaining $35,000 to shoplifting.

In this case $(A \ B \ C \ D)$ is the combination of conditions consisting of the number of clerks, the utility rate increases, the flood, and shoplifting; and $(a \ b \ c \ d)$ is the total loss of $100,000. After A, B, and C are separated out, the conclusion is that D (shoplifting) caused d (the remaining loss). Because the estimates might have been incorrect and because additional sources of financial loss might have been overlooked, the conclusion is only probable.

Some procedures that, at least on the face of it, appear to utilize the method of residues come closer to being deductive than inductive. A case in point is the procedure used to determine the weight of the cargo carried by a truck. First, the empty truck is put on a scale and the weight recorded. Then the truck is loaded and the truck together with the cargo is put on the same scale. The weight of the cargo is the difference between the two weights. If, to this procedure, we add the rather unproblematic assumptions that weight is an additive property, that the scale is accurate, that the scale operator reads the indicator properly, that the truck is not altered in the loading process, and a few others, the conclusion about the weight of the cargo follows deductively.

To distinguish deductive from inductive uses of the method of residues, one must take into account such factors as the role of mathematics. If the conclusion depends on a purely arithmetical computation, the argument is probably best characterized as deductive. If not, then it is probably inductive.

Method of Concomitant Variation

The **method of concomitant variation** identifies a causal connection between two conditions by matching variations in one condition with variations in another. According to one formulation, increases are matched with increases and decreases with decreases. Example:

> In attempting to diagnose Mrs. Thompson's high blood pressure, a cardiologist noticed a correlation between fluctuations in blood pressure and certain brain waves. As the blood pressure increased, so did the intensity of the brain waves, and as the blood pressure decreased, the intensity of the brain waves decreased. The cardiologist concluded that the two conditions were causally related.

The method of concomitant variation as illustrated in this example may be diagramed as follows:

$$\boxed{A\ B\ C}\ \text{is coincident with}\ \boxed{X\ Y\ Z.}$$
$$\boxed{A\ B+\ C}\ \text{is coincident with}\ \boxed{X\ Y+\ Z}$$
$$\boxed{A\ B-\ C}\ \text{is coincident with}\ \boxed{X\ Y-\ Z}$$

Therefore, *B* is causally connected to *Y*.

Here, $\boxed{A\ B\ C}$ is a set of observable conditions such as cholesterol level, liver function, basal metabolism, etc., with *B* representing blood pressure; and $\boxed{X\ Y\ Z}$ is another set of observable conditions with *Y* representing certain brain waves. In the second and third rows, $B+$ and $B-$ represent increases and decreases in blood pressure, and $Y+$ and $Y-$ represent increases and decreases in the intensity of the brain waves. The conclusion asserts that either *B* causes *Y*, *Y* causes *B*, or *B* and *Y* have a common cause. Determining which is the case requires further investigation; but of course if *B* occurs earlier in time than *Y*, then *Y* does not cause *B*, and if *Y* occurs earlier in time than *B*, then *B* does not cause *Y*.

The blood pressure example matches increases in one condition with increases in another. For an example that matches increases in one condition with decreases in another consider the following:

> A sociologist studying divorce noticed a correlation between changes in the national divorce rate and fluctuations in the gross domestic product. As the GDP increases, the divorce rate decreases, and when the GDP sags, the divorce rate goes up. The sociologist concluded that the two phenomena are causally connected.

This second version of the method of concomitant variation may be diagramed as follows:

$$\boxed{A\ B\ C}\ \text{is coincident with}\ \boxed{X\ Y\ Z.}$$
$$\boxed{A\ B+\ C}\ \text{is coincident with}\ \boxed{X\ Y-\ Z}$$
$$\boxed{A\ B-\ C}\ \text{is coincident with}\ \boxed{X\ Y+\ Z}$$

Therefore, *B* is causally connected to *Y*.

In this example $\boxed{A\ B\ C}$ is a set of economic conditions such as stock exchange indexes, interest rates, commodity prices, etc., with *B* representing gross domestic product; and $\boxed{X\ Y\ Z}$ is a set of social conditions such as birth rates, employment rates, immigration numbers, etc., with *Y* representing the national divorce rate. The conclusion is that *B* is somehow causally connected to *Y*. However, in this example an even

stronger conclusion could probably be drawn—namely, that decreases in the GDP cause increases in the divorce rate, and not conversely. That changes in economic prosperity (which is indicated by GDP) should affect the divorce rate is quite plausible, but the converse is less so.

At this point we should note that the existence of a mere correlation between two phenomena is never sufficient to identify a causal connection. In addition, the causal connection suggested by the correlation must at least make sense. Consider the following example:

> After an in-depth study researchers discovered a correlation between the price of pork belly futures on the Chicago Mercantile Exchange and earthquake activity in Japan. As the number and intensity of the quakes increased, the future prices also increased, and vice versa. The researchers concluded that the two phenomena were causally connected.

The argument is clearly weak. Because it is virtually inconceivable that either phenomenon could cause a change in the other, or that changes in both could have a common cause, it is most likely that the correlation is purely coincidental.

The method of concomitant variation is useful when it is impossible for a condition to be either wholly present or wholly absent, as was required for the use of the first three of Mill's methods. Many conditions are of this sort—for example, the temperature of the ocean, the price of gold, the incidence of crime, the size of a mountain glacier, a person's cholesterol level, and so on. If some kind of correlation can be detected between variations in conditions such as these, the method of concomitant variation asserts that the two are causally connected. The method has been used successfully in the past to help establish the existence of causal connections between smoking and lung cancer, nuclear radiation and leukemia, and alcohol consumption and cirrhosis of the liver.

Mill's Methods and Science

Mill's methods closely resemble certain scientific methods that are intended to establish causal connections and correlations. For example, the method of difference is virtually identical to the method of controlled experiment employed in such fields as biology, pharmacology, and psychology. A controlled experiment is one that involves two groups of subjects, an experimental group and a control group. The experimental group includes the subjects that receive a certain treatment, and the control group includes the subjects that do not receive the treatment but are otherwise subjected to the same conditions as members of the experimental group.

The simplest type of controlled experiment involves an experimental group and a control group each consisting of just one member. Example:

> Two mice were used in a controlled experiment to determine whether a certain substance was carcinogenic. The two mice had identical genes, were the same age, were placed in identical cages in the same location, were subjected to the same environmental conditions, and were fed the same food, over the same period of time. One mouse was injected with the suspected carcinogen, and the other was not. After two months, the injected mouse developed cancerous tumors, but the other mouse did not.

To summarize the results of this experiment we can construct a table just like the one for the method of difference. If we let occurrence 1 represent the injected mouse and occurrence 2 the mouse that was not injected, and let *A* through *F* represent the conditions common to the two mice (genes, age, cage, etc.) and *G* represent the injection, we have:

Table 9.5

	Possible sufficient conditions							Phenomenon (tumors)
Occurrence	A	B	C	D	E	F	G	
1	*	*	*	*	*	*	*	*
2	*	*	*	*	*	*	-	-

Using the rule that a condition is not sufficient if it is present when the phenomenon is absent, occurrence 2 eliminates *A* through *F*, leaving *G* (the suspected carcinogen) as the cause of the phenomenon.

The principal drawback of this experiment is that the suspected carcinogen was given to only one mouse. As a result, the experiment offers relatively weak evidence that *any* mouse injected with this substance would develop tumors. Perhaps the injected mouse had some hidden defect that would have caused tumors even without the injection. Scientists address this problem by increasing the size of the experimental group and the control group. Thus, suppose the same experiment were performed on one hundred mice, of which fifty were injected and fifty were not. Suppose that after two months all fifty injected mice developed tumors and none of the control subjects did. Such a result would constitute much stronger evidence that the injected substance was carcinogenic.

This expanded experiment can be considered to be a case of multiple uses of Mill's method of difference. Since the method of difference always involves just two occurrences, mouse #1 could be matched with mouse #51 for one use of the method, mouse #2 with mouse #52 for a second use of the method, and so on. Although this expanded experiment might look like a case of the joint method, it is not (at least not a successful one). Any successful application of the joint method includes occurrences in which certain conditions are absent when the phenomenon is present. Those conditions are then eliminated as possible necessary conditions. The expanded experiment with the mice includes no such occurrences.

This fact points up an important difference between Mill's joint method and his method of difference. The purpose of the method of difference is to determine whether a *preselected* condition is the cause of a phenomenon. This preselected condition is present in one of the two occurrences and absent from the other. On the other hand, the purpose of the joint method is to determine which condition, among a selected *class* of conditions, is a cause of a phenomenon. The joint method applies rules for sufficient conditions and necessary conditions to (one hopes) reduce the class of conditions to just one.

Returning to the expanded experiment with the mice, let us suppose that only forty of the mice in the experimental group developed tumors, and none of those in the control group did. From Mill's standpoint, this would be equivalent to forty uses of the method of difference yielding positive results and ten yielding negative results. On

the basis of such an outcome, the experimenter might conclude that the likelihood of the suspected carcinogen producing tumors in mice was 80 percent (40÷50).

Controlled experiments such as the one involving a hundred mice are often conducted on humans, but with humans it is never possible to control the circumstances to the degree that it is with mice. Humans cannot be put in cages, fed exactly the same food for any length of time, are not genetically identical to other humans, etc. Also, humans react to their environment in ways that cannot be anticipated or controlled. To correct this deficiency, statistical methods are applied to the results to enable the drawing of a conclusion.

For example, an experiment could be conducted to test the effectiveness of some new drug on children with attention-deficit/hyperactivity disorder (ADHD). Fifty children with ADHD could be selected, with twenty-five being placed at random in the experimental group and twenty-five in the control group. The children in the experimental group would be given the drug, probably in a classroom situation, and the children in the control group would be given a placebo (sugar pill). This could be done on a "double blind" basis, so that neither the children nor the persons conducting the experiment would know in advance who was getting the drug. The objective is to control the conditions as much as possible. Then the negative behavior of each of the fifty children would be recorded over a period, say, of an hour. Each time a child was out of his/her seat, disturbed others, fidgeted, failed to follow instructions, etc., the incident would be noted.

The results of such an experiment would be expected to follow what is called a normal probability distribution (bell-shaped curve). (Further discussion of normal probability distribution is presented in Section 9.4.) One curve would represent the experimental group, another curve the control group. Assuming the drug is effective, the two curves would be displaced from one another; but they would probably overlap in part, as indicated in Figure 1. This means that certain children in the experimental group exhibited more negative behaviors than certain children in the control group, but most of the children in the experimental group exhibited fewer negative behaviors than most of the children in the control group. Then statistical methods would be applied to the two curves to determine the effectiveness of the drug. Such an experiment is similar to Mill's method of difference except that instead of the phenomenon (negative behavior) being wholly present in some occurrences, it is present in varying degrees. In this sense, the experiment resembles the method of concomitant variation.

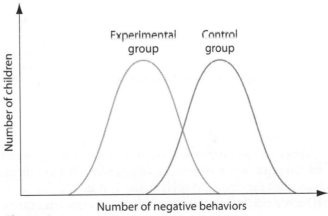

Figure 1

In some kinds of scientific research on humans, it is nearly impossible to control the circumstances to any significant degree. Such research includes investigations that cover a long period of time or investigations in which the health of the subjects is at issue and legal or moral restrictions come into play. Example:

> A nutritionist wanted to determine the effect of fifteen vitamin and mineral supplements on atherosclerosis (artery disease). Because the effect was expected to require several years to develop, the nutritionist ran an ad in a health publication for individuals who had ingested these substances on a regular basis for five years. Eighty people answered the ad and reported which substances they had taken and how much of each. These people were then examined. Some showed no evidence of the disease, while others manifested the disease in varying degrees. After analyzing the data, the nutritionist concluded that certain vitamins and minerals offer protection against atherosclerosis.

The procedure followed by the nutritionist is very similar to Mill's joint method of agreement and difference. The objective is to identify a cause among a preselected class of possible conditions, some of which are accompanied by the phenomenon (atherosclerosis), and some of which are not. The major difference between the nutritionist's procedure and Mill's joint method is that the nutritionist took account of varying degrees in which the conditions and the phenomenon were present in the eighty occurrences. In this sense, again, the nutritionist's procedure was similar to Mill's method of concomitant variation. However, the nutritionist may also have taken into account various combinations of conditions, a consideration that lies beyond the power of the joint method by itself.

The procedure illustrated in this example is not an experiment but a study. More precisely, it is a *retrospective study* because it examines subjects who have already fulfilled the requirements of the examination—as opposed to a *prospective study,* where the subjects are expected to fulfill the requirements in the future. For a prospective study, the nutritionist could select a group of subjects and follow their vitamin and mineral intake for five years into the future. Such a study, however, would be more costly, and if the nutritionist instructed the subjects to ingest certain vitamins and minerals and avoid others, the study could involve legal or moral implications.

Another kind of study found widely in the social sciences uses what is called the *correlational method,* which closely replicates Mill's method of concomitant variation. Example:

> A psychology professor was interested in the relationship between IQ scores and grade point average. The professor randomly selected one hundred graduating seniors, obtained their GPAs from the registrar, and asked them to take an IQ test. All of them complied. Then the professor compared the scores of each student with his/her GPA. The professor found that in general higher IQ scores corresponded with higher GPAs.

The results of this study indicate a positive correlation between IQ score and GPA. If the study showed that students with higher IQs had, in general, lower GPAs, this would indicate a negative correlation. Once a study of this sort is done, the next step is to compute the *correlation coefficient,* which is a number between +1.00 and −1.00 that expresses the degree of correlation. If it turned out that the student with the highest IQ score also had the highest GPA, the student with the next highest IQ score had proportionately the next highest GPA, and so on, so that the IQ-GPA graph was a straight line, then the correlation coefficient would be +1.00. This would reflect a perfect positive correlation.

On the other hand, if it turned out that the student with the highest IQ score had the lowest GPA, the student with the next highest IQ score had proportionately the next lowest GPA, and so on, so that, once again, the IQ-GPA graph was a straight line, then the correlation coefficient would be −1.00. This would reflect a perfect negative correlation. A correlation coefficient of 0.00 would mean that no correlation exists, which would be the case if the IQ scores corresponded randomly with the GPAs. A correlation coefficient of, say, +0.60 would mean that in general higher IQ scores corresponded positively with higher GPAs.

The outcome of this study can also be indicated graphically, with IQ score representing one coordinate on a graph, and GPA the other coordinate. The result for each student would then correspond to a point on the graph, such as the one in Figure 2. The graph of all the points is called a scatter diagram. A line that "best fits" the data can then be drawn through the scatter diagram. This line is called the *regression line*, and it can be used to produce a linear equation, $y = bx + a$, that describes the approximate relation between IQ score (x) and GPA (y). This equation can then be used to predict future GPAs. For example, suppose that an entering freshman student has an IQ of 116. This student's future GPA could be predicted to be approximately $116b + a$.

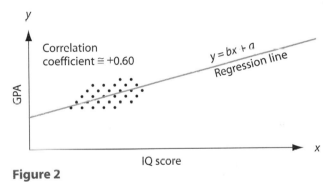

Figure 2

Hundreds of studies such as this one have been conducted to detect correlations between such factors as TV violence and aggression in children, self-esteem and intelligence, motivation and learning time, exposure to classical music and retention ability, and marijuana use and memory. However, such studies often fall short of establishing a causal connection between the two factors. For example, a positive correlation between exposure to TV violence and aggression in children does not necessarily mean that exposure to TV violence causes aggression. It might be the case that children who tend to be violent are naturally attracted to violent TV shows. Or perhaps a third factor is the cause of both. But a positive correlation can at least suggest a causal connection.

Once a correlation is established, a controlled experiment can often be designed that will identify a causal connection. For example, in the case of TV violence, a group of children could be randomly divided into an experimental group and a control group. The experimental group could then be exposed to violent TV shows for a certain period of time, and the control group would be exposed to nonviolent shows for the same period. Later, the behavior of the children in both groups could be observed, with every act of aggression noted. If the experimental group displayed more acts of aggression than the control group, the conclusion might be drawn that TV violence causes aggression.

Experimental procedures resembling Mill's method of concomitant variation have also been used in the physical sciences to identify causal connections. For example, in the early part of the nineteenth century, Hans Christian Oerstead noticed that a wire carrying a current of electricity could deflect a nearby compass needle. As the current was increased, the amount of deflection increased, and as the current was decreased, the amount of deflection decreased. Also, if the current were reversed, the deflection would be reversed. Oerstead concluded that a current of electricity flowing through a wire causes a magnetic field to be produced around the wire.

Other applications of the method of concomitant variation have been used not so much to detect the existence of a causal connection (which may have already been known) as to determine the precise nature of a causal law. For example, in the latter part of the sixteenth century Galileo performed experiments involving spheres rolling down inclined planes. As the plane was incrementally lifted upward, the sphere covered greater and greater distances in a unit of time. Recognizing that the downward force on the sphere is proportional to the pitch of the plane, Galileo derived the law that the acceleration imparted to a body is directly proportional to the force acting on it. Galileo also noticed that whatever the angle of the plane, the distance covered by the ball increased exponentially with the time in which it was allowed to roll. For example, if the time was doubled, the distance was quadrupled. From this correlation he derived the law that the distance traveled by a falling body is proportional to the square of the time that it falls.

In the seventeenth century, Robert Boyle conducted experiments involving the pressure and volume of gases. Boyle constructed an apparatus that allowed him to compute the volume of a gas as he varied the pressure. He noted that as the pressure increased, the volume decreased, and as the pressure decreased, the volume increased. From this correlation he derived the law that the volume of a gas is inversely proportional to its pressure. A century later, Jacques Alexandre Charles observed a correlation between the temperature of a gas and its volume. As the temperature increased, the volume increased, and vice versa. This correlation provided the basis for Charles's law for gases.

Detecting correlations has also been important in astronomy. Early in the twentieth century, Henrietta Swan Leavitt recognized a correlation between the average brightness of certain variable stars, called Cepheids (pronounced sef'-ee-ids), and their periods of variation. Cepheids fluctuate in brightness over periods ranging from a day to several months, and Leavitt discovered that longer periods correspond with greater average brightness, and shorter periods with lesser average brightness. Once the distance of a few nearby Cepheids was determined, the distance of any Cepheid could then be computed from its average brightness and its period of variation. This correlation provided the first method available to astronomers for measuring the distance between our planet and galaxies other than our own.

iLrn I. Identify the kind of causality intended by the following statements. Is the cause a sufficient condition, necessary condition, or both sufficient and necessary condition?

★1. Throwing a brick through a window will cause the window to break.

2. Heating an iron rod causes it to expand.

3. Slashing an inflated automobile tire with a knife will cause it to go flat.

★4. Releasing the shutter of a camera causes an image to appear on the film.

5. Pulling the trigger of a gun causes it to fire.

6. Wetting litmus paper with an acid causes it to turn red.

★7. Pouring water on a wood fire will cause it to be extinguished.

8. Eating contaminated food will cause one to become ill.

9. Stretching a spring causes it to exert an opposing force.

★10. Flipping the wall switch to the "up" position causes the overhead lights to go on.

iLrn II. The following problems pertain to Mill's methods.

★1. To determine the effectiveness of an oil additive, a testing firm purchased two cars of the same make, year, and model, and drove each a distance of 30,000 miles using the same kind of gasoline, the same kind of oil, the same driver, under the same road conditions. The oil in one engine included the additive, whereas the oil in the other engine did not. At the end of the test, the engines of both cars were dismantled, and it was found that the engine that contained the additive had less wear. The testing firm concluded that the oil additive caused the reduced wear. Construct a table that supports this conclusion. Which one of Mill's methods did the testing firm use? What sense of causality is involved in the conclusion?

2. An eighth-grade teacher had five pupils who read very well. These pupils were distinguished by the following features. Tom came from a large family, had professional parents who were not wealthy, had training in phonics, read novels, lived close to a library, and watched educational TV. Andy came from a family that was not large, had wealthy professional parents, watched educational TV, did not live close to a library, did not read novels, and had training in phonics. Cindy did not read novels, lived close to a library, had training in phonics, had wealthy professional parents, came from a large family, and did not watch educational TV. April had training in phonics, read novels, lived close to a library, watched educational TV, came from a large family, and had wealthy parents who were not professionals. Joe read novels, did not live close to a library, had professional parents who were not wealthy, had training in phonics, watched educational TV, and came from a large family. What can the teacher conclude caused these children to be good readers? Construct a table that supports this conclusion. Which one of Mill's methods did the teacher use? What sense of causality is involved in the conclusion?

3. An administrator for the Internal Revenue Service noticed that tax revenues for a certain year were down by 14 percent. Of this amount, the administrator attributed 6 percent to an economic slowdown that year, 3 percent to higher interest rates that led to higher write-offs, and 2 percent to changes in the tax code. Unable to attribute the remaining 3 percent to any lawful factor, the administrator concluded that it resulted from increased cheating by the taxpayers. Which one of Mill's methods did the administrator use?

★4. The repair manager for a manufacturer of home computers noticed that a large number of units were being returned for repairs. The manager selected a sample of seven returned units and noticed that these units were distinguished by the following characteristics. Units 1 and 3 had type X circuitry and were shipped to coastal regions. Units 2 and 7 were sold to business customers, were manufactured in the Kansas City plant, and were shipped to coastal regions. Units 4 and 5 were used to play computer games and were manufactured in the Kansas City plant. Units 6 and 7 were shipped to large cities and had Type X circuitry. Unit 4 was shipped to a large coastal city. Units 2 and 3 were shipped to large cities. Unit 5 was shipped to a coastal region and had type X circuitry. Unit 3 was sold to a business customer who used it to play computer games. Unit 1 was used to play computer games and was manufactured in the Kansas City plant. Finally, Unit 6 was sold to a business customer in a coastal region. Among these six distinguishing characteristics the manager concluded that salty air caused the computers to break down. Construct a table that supports this conclusion. Which one of Mill's methods did the manufacturer use? What sense of causality is involved in the conclusion?

5. A manufacturer of fishing equipment conducted a test of its products by giving them to eight fishermen who used them with the following results. Ed and Flo used a Hot Spot lure and caught no fish. Dan and Amy used a Trusty rod with a Husky reel, and Amy caught fish but Dan did not. Jake used a Sure Catch lure, a Best Bet rod, a Spiffy reel, and caught fish. Bill and Tim used a Husky reel, but only Bill caught fish. Kat used a Best Bet rod with a Husky reel and caught fish. Amy and Kat used a Sure Catch lure, but only Kat used monofilament line. Bill used a Trusty rod, monofilament line, and a Sure Catch lure. Flo and Tim used Best Bet rods, and both Tim and Dan used Dynamite lures. Finally, Flo used a Husky reel, Jake and Dan used monofilament line, and Ed used a Spiffy reel on a Trusty rod. What conclusion can the manufacturer draw about the power of this equipment to catch fish? Construct a table that supports this conclusion. Which one of Mill's methods did the manufacturer use? What sense of causality is involved in the conclusion?

6. Nancy was contemplating the purchase of a new oven for her kitchen, but she could not decide between an electric or a gas unit. Thus, she decided to conduct an experiment using the ovens, one gas, one electric, of two friends who live in adjoining apartments. She mixed up two identical batches of brownies under identical conditions of relative humidity and identical altitudes, put them into identical baking dishes, and cooked them at the same temperature

for exactly the same time. The brownies cooked in the electric oven came out moist, while the brownies cooked in the gas oven came out relatively dry. Nancy concluded that baking in the electric oven caused the brownies to be moist. Construct a table that supports this conclusion. Which one of Mill's methods did Nancy use? What sense of causality is involved in the conclusion?

★7. Mrs. Wilkins sometimes has trouble sleeping. In order to determine the cause, she decided to take note of her pre-bedtime behavior over the course of a week. On Monday she drank camomile tea, had a late dinner, took a hot bath, read from a book, took a walk, and she slept well. On Tuesday she had a late dinner, read from a book, and slept poorly. On Wednesday she drank a glass of wine, got a massage, took a walk, and slept poorly. On Thursday she had a late dinner, drank a glass of wine, read from a book, took a hot bath, got a massage, and slept well. On Friday she read from a book, drank camomile tea, got a massage, had a late dinner, took a walk, and slept well. On Saturday she drank a glass of wine, got a massage, took a walk, drank camomile tea, took a hot bath, and slept well. On Sunday she read from a book, took a hot bath, drank camomile tea, and slept poorly. What can Mrs. Wilkins conclude is the cause of sleeping well? Construct a table that supports this conclusion. Which one of Mill's methods did Mrs. Wilkins use? What sense of causality is involved in the conclusion?

8. From a comparison of statistics a criminologist detected what he thought was a correlation between fluctuations in the employment rate and crimes of theft. For every 2 percent increase in the employment rate, the rate of theft decreased by 1 percent, and for every 2 percent decrease in the employment rate, the theft rate increased by 1 percent. The criminologist concluded that unemployment causes crimes of theft. Which one of Mill's methods did the criminologist use?

9. A man developed an allergic reaction to an unknown food. His doctor asked him about a number of foods that often cause allergies, and the man replied that he had eaten coconut, chocolate, nuts, milk products, shellfish, peppers, eggs, and wheat products prior to suffering the reaction. The doctor told him to eliminate all of these foods from his diet, and when he had done so, the reaction disappeared. The doctor then told him to introduce each of these foods back into his diet, one at a time. The man did so, and the reaction reappeared only when he ate milk products. The doctor concluded that milk products caused the allergic reaction. Construct a table that supports this conclusion. Which one of Mill's methods did the doctor use? What sense of causality is involved in the conclusion?

★10. A psychiatrist had six adult women patients who suffered blurred ego boundaries. These patients were distinguished by the following characteristics. Meg and Sue had been subjected to corporal punishment as children and both had siblings. Dot and Jane were adopted, had a male parent figure, and experienced sexual abuse. Lynn and Flo had siblings and a male parent figure, but only Flo had a domineering mother. Also, Lynn and Meg had experienced sexual abuse and were adopted, but only Meg had a domineering mother. Jane and Dot were uprooted often as children. Flo and Sue had experienced sexual abuse, but only Sue was raised in day-care centers. Jane and Dot each had a domineering mother, and each had been subjected to corporal punishment. Flo was uprooted often as a child and had been subjected to corporal punishment. Dot and Lynn were raised in day-care centers, Sue had a male parent figure, and Jane had siblings. What can the psychiatrist conclude is the cause of the blurred ego boundaries of these women? Construct a table that supports this conclusion. Which one of Mill's methods did the psychiatrist use? What sense of causality is involved in the conclusion?

11. A metallurgist added eight substances in various combinations to seven samples of molten aluminum for the purpose of producing aluminum alloys. The metallurgist was interested in producing an alloy that had a special resistance to corrosion. The samples were distinguished by the following characteristics. Samples 1, 2, and 3 contained both tin and copper, but only samples 1 and 2 were resistant. Samples 6 and 7 contained both silver and iron, but only Sample 7 was resistant. Samples 4 and 5 contained sodium, but only sample 5 was resistant. In addition, samples 1 and 7 contained zinc, silicon, and nickel. Sample 2 contained sodium, iron, and silicon, and Sample 5 contained silicon and copper. Finally, Sample 3 contained nickel, and Sample 4 contained zinc. Assuming no interaction occurs among these eight additives, what conclusion can the metallurgist draw about these additives? Construct a table that supports this conclusion. Which one of Mill's methods did the metallurgist use? What sense of causality is involved in the conclusion?

12. A doctor has five patients who suffer from an unusual form of cancer. The patients are distinguished by the following living conditions. Davis, Jones, and Ellis live in a smoggy area near high-tension power lines, and Smith and Frank smoke cigarettes and live downwind from a company that produces chemical defoliants for the military. Frank also lives near the nuclear power plant. Davis, Smith, and Ellis eat red meat every day and live near the nuclear power plant. Jones smokes cigarettes and lives downwind from the chemical defoliant company. Smith lives in a smoggy area, and Davis and Ellis live downwind from the defoliant company. What can the doctor conclude is the cause of the cancer? Construct a table that supports this conclusion. Which one of Mill's methods did the doctor use? What sense of causality is involved in the conclusion?

★13. Two of Mr. Andrews's rose bushes became infected with aphids. Mr. Andrews proceeded to spray one of the bushes with malathion insecticide but left the other bush untouched. The two bushes are both American Beauty, are five years old, have virtually identical locations, receive the same amount of water and sunlight, are planted in the same kind of soil, and receive the same degree of cultivation and the same amount of Bandini rose food. Within three days the aphids disappeared from the bush that was sprayed, but they continued to thrive on the other bush. Mr. Andrews concluded that the malathion killed the aphids on the bush that was sprayed. Construct a table that supports Mr.

Andrews's conclusion. Which one of Mill's methods did Mr. Andrews use? What sense of causality is involved in the conclusion?

14. A sociologist conducted a study to determine if a correlation exists between grade point average at the time of graduation and income ten years after graduation. The sociologist visited the alumni office of a local university and obtained the names and addresses of those who had graduated ten years earlier. The sociologist then contacted these graduates and asked them to disclose their income and give permission for the university to disclose their graduating GPAs. Two hundred students replied to this inquiry. The sociologist then applied statistical methods to compute the correlation coefficient, which turned out to be +0.2. How does this study relate to Mill's methods? What does a correlation coefficient of +0.2 say about the correlation between GPA and income? Is such a study called a prospective study or a retrospective study? How do the two differ?

15. A cosmetics manufacturer tested a new cleansing cream on forty rabbits. The rabbits were virtually the same genetically and were the same age. Twenty of the rabbits were randomly placed in the experimental group and the other twenty were placed in the control group. A patch containing the cream was applied to the skin of each rabbit in the experimental group, and an identical patch containing a harmless substance was applied to the skin of each rabbit in the control group. Then, all forty rabbits were kept in the same room, at the same temperature, under the same lighting conditions, and fed the same food. After five days, two of the rabbits in the experimental group developed a rash where the patch was applied, but none of the other rabbits did. The manufacturer concluded that there is a 10 percent likelihood that the cleansing cream will cause a rash on the skin of rabbits. How does this experiment relate to Mill's methods? What sense of causality is involved in the conclusion?

iLrn III. Identify the cause suggested by the information presented in the following tables. Is the cause a sufficient condition, a necessary condition, or both a sufficient and necessary condition? What method is used?

★1.

Occurrence	Possible conditions					Phenomenon
	A	**B**	**C**	**D**	**E**	
1	*	-	*	*	*	*
2	*	*	*	*	-	*
3	*	-	*	*	*	*
4	*	*	-	*	*	*
5	-	*	*	*	-	*

2.

Occurrence	Possible conditions					Phenomenon
	A	**B**	**C**	**D**	**E**	
1	*	*	*	*	*	*
2	*	-	*	*	*	-

3.

Occurrence	Possible conditions						Phenomenon
	A	B	C	D	E	F	
1	*	-	-	*	-	-	-
2	-	*	*	*	-	-	*
3	*	-	*	*	*	-	*
4	-	*	-	-	-	*	-
5	*	-	-	-	*	-	-
6	*	*	*	-	*	-	*

★4.

Occurrence	Possible conditions					Phenomenon
	A	B	C	D	E	
1	*	*	*	*	-	*
2	-	-	*	-	*	*
3	*	-	-	-	*	-
4	-	*	-	*	*	*
5	*	*	-	-	-	-
6	-	*	*	-	-	-

5.

Occurrence	Possible conditions					Phenomenon
	A	B	C	D	E	
1	-	-	*	-	*	-
2	-	*	*	-	*	*
3	*	*	-	*	*	*
4	-	*	-	-	*	-
5	*	-	*	*	-	-
6	*	*	*	-	-	*

9.3   Probability

Probability is a topic that is central to the question of induction, but like causality, it has different meanings. Consider the following statements:

> The probability of picking a spade from a full deck of cards is one-fourth.
> The probability that a twenty-year-old man will live to age seventy-five is .63.
> There is a high probability that Margaret and Peter will get married.

In each statement the word "probability" is used in a different sense. This difference stems from the fact that a different procedure is used in each case to determine or estimate the probability. To determine the probability of picking a spade from a deck of cards, a purely mathematical procedure is used. Given that there are fifty-two cards in a deck and thirteen are spades, thirteen is divided by fifty-two to obtain one-fourth. A different procedure is used to determine the probability that a twenty-year-old man will live to age seventy-five. For this, one must sample a large number of twenty-year-old men and count the number that live fifty-five more years. Yet a different procedure is used to determine the probability that Margaret and Peter will get married. This probability can only be estimated roughly, and doing so requires that we become acquainted with Margaret and Peter and with how they feel toward each other and toward marriage. These three procedures give rise to three distinct theories about probability: the classical theory, the relative frequency theory, and the subjectivist theory.

The **classical theory** traces its origin to the work of the seventeenth-century mathematicians Blaise Pascal and Pierre de Fermat in determining the betting odds for a game of chance. The theory is otherwise called the *a priori theory of probability* because the computations are made independently of any sensory observation of actual events. According to the classical theory, the probability of an event A is given by the formula

$$P(A) = \frac{f}{n}$$

where f is the number of favorable outcomes and n is the number of possible outcomes. For example, in computing the probability of drawing an ace from a poker deck, the number of favorable outcomes is four (because there are four aces) and the number of possible outcomes is fifty-two (because there are fifty-two cards in the deck). Thus, the probability of that event is 4/52 or 1/13 (or .077).

It is important not to confuse the probability of an event's happening with the betting odds of its happening. For events governed by the classical theory, the fair betting odds that an event A will happen is given by the formula

$$\text{odds}(A) = f{:}u$$

where f is the number of favorable outcomes, and u is the number of unfavorable outcomes. For example, the fair betting odds of drawing an ace from a poker deck is 4 to 48, or 1 to 12, since there are four aces and 48 cards that are not aces. Or suppose that five horses are running a race; three are yours, two are your friend's, and there is an equal chance of any of the horses winning. The fair betting odds that one of your horses will win is 3 to 2, whereas the probability that one of your horses will win is 3/5.

Given that you and your friend accept these betting odds, if you bet $3 that one of your horses wins, and you win the bet, your friend must pay you $2. On the other hand, the odds that one of your friend's horses will win is 2 to 3, so if your friend bets $2 that one of her horses wins, and she wins the bet, then you must pay her $3.

Two assumptions are involved in computing probabilities and betting odds according to the classical theory: (1) that all possible outcomes are taken into account and (2) that all possible outcomes are equally probable. In the card example the first assumption entails that only the fifty-two ordinary outcomes are possible. In other words, it is assumed that the deck has not been altered, that the cards will not suddenly self-destruct or reproduce, and so on. In the racing example, the first assumption entails that no other horses are running in the race, and that none of the horses will simply vanish.

The second assumption, which is otherwise called the **principle of indifference,** entails for the card example that there is an equal likelihood of selecting any card. In other words, it is assumed that the cards are stacked evenly, that no two are glued together, and so on. For the horse race example, the second principle entails that each of the horses has an equal chance of winning.

Whenever these two assumptions can be made about the occurrence of an event, the classical theory can be used to compute its probability or the odds of its happening. Here are some additional examples:

P(a fair coin turning up heads) = 1/2	odds = 1:1
P(drawing a face card) = 12/52 = 3/13	odds = 12:40 = 3:10
P(a single die coming up "3") = 1/6	odds = 1:5
P(a single die coming up even) = 3/6 = 1/2	odds = 1:1

Strictly speaking, of course, the two assumptions underlying the classical theory are never perfectly reflected in any actual situation. Every coin is slightly off balance, as is every pair of dice. As a result, the probabilities of the various outcomes are never exactly equal. Similarly, the outcomes are never strictly confined to the normal ones entailed by the first assumption. When tossing a coin, there is always the possibility that the coin will land on edge, and in rolling dice there is the analogous possibility that one of them might break in half. These outcomes may not be possible in the *practical* sense, but they are *logically* possible in that they do not involve any contradiction. Because these outcomes are so unusual, however, it is reasonable to think that for all practical purposes the two assumptions hold and that therefore the classical theory is applicable.

There are many events, however, for which the two assumptions required by the classical theory obviously do not hold. For example, in attempting to determine the probability of a sixty-year-old woman dying of a heart attack within ten years, it would be virtually impossible to take account of all the possible outcomes. She might die of cancer, pneumonia, or an especially virulent case of the flu. She might be incapacitated by a car accident, or she might move to Florida and buy a house on the beach. Furthermore, none of these outcomes is equally probable in comparison with the others. To compute the probability of events such as these we need the relative frequency theory of probability.

The **relative frequency theory** originated with the use of mortality tables by life insurance companies in the eighteenth century. In contrast with the classical theory, which rests upon a priori computations, the relative frequency theory depends on actual observations of the frequency with which certain events happen. The probability of an event A is given by the formula

$$P(A) = \frac{f_o}{n_o}$$

where f_o is the number of *observed* favorable outcomes and n_o is the total number of *observed* outcomes. For example, to determine the probability that a fifty-year-old man will live five more years, a sample of 1,000 fifty-year-old men could be observed. If 968 were alive five years later, the probability that the man in question will live an additional five years is 968/1000 or .968.

Similarly, if one wanted to determine the probability that a certain irregularly shaped pyramid with different colored sides would, when rolled, come to rest with the green side down, the pyramid could be rolled 1,000 times. If it came to rest with its green side down 327 times, the probability of this event happening would be computed to be .327.

The relative frequency method can also be used to compute the probability of the kinds of events that conform to the requirements of the classical theory. For example, the probability of a coin coming up heads could be determined by tossing the coin 100 times and counting the heads. If, after this many tosses, 46 heads have been recorded, one might assign a probability of .46 to this event. This leads us to an important point about the relative frequency theory: the results hold true only in the long run. It might be necessary to toss the coin 1,000 or even 10,000 times to get a close approximation. After 10,000 tosses one would expect to count close to 5,000 heads. If in fact only 4,623 heads have been recorded, one would probably be justified in concluding that the coin is off balance or that something was irregular in the way it had been tossed.

Strictly speaking, neither the classical method nor the relative frequency method can assign a probability to individual events. From the standpoint of these approaches only certain *kinds* or *classes* of events have probabilities. But many events in the actual world are unique, one-of-a-kind happenings—for example, Margaret's marrying Peter or Native Prancer's winning the fourth race at Churchill Downs. To interpret the probability of these events we turn to the subjectivist theory.

The **subjectivist theory** interprets the meaning of probability in terms of the beliefs of individual people. Although such beliefs are vague and nebulous, they may be given quantitative interpretation through the odds that a person would accept on a bet. For example, if a person believes that a certain horse will win a race and he or she is willing to give 7 to 4 odds on that event happening, this means that he or she has assigned a probability of 7/(7+4) or 7/11 to that event. This procedure is unproblematic as long as the person is consistent in giving odds on the same event *not* happening. If, for example, 7 to 4 odds are given that an event will happen and 5 to 4 odds that it will not happen, the individual who gives these odds will inevitably lose. If 7 to 4 odds are given that an event *will* happen, no better than 4 to 7 odds can be given that the same event will *not* happen.

One of the difficulties surrounding the subjectivist theory is that one and the same event can be said to have different probabilities, depending on the willingness of different people to give different odds. If probabilities are taken to be genuine attributes of events, this would seem to be a serious problem. The problem might be avoided, though, either by interpreting probabilities as attributes of beliefs or by taking the average of the various individual probabilities as *the* probability of the event.

The three theories discussed thus far—the classical theory, the relative frequency theory, and the subjectivist theory—provide separate procedures for assigning a probability to an event (or class of events). Sometimes one theory is more readily applicable, sometimes another. But once individual events have been given a probability, the groundwork has been laid for computing the probabilities of compound arrangements of events. This is done by means of what is called the **probability calculus.** In this respect the probability calculus functions analogously to the set of truth-functional rules in propositional logic. Just as the truth-functional rules allow us to compute the truth values of compound propositions from the individual truth values of the simple components, the rules of the probability calculus allow us to compute the probability of compound events from the individual probabilities of the simple events.

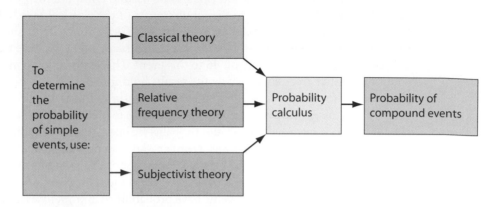

Two preliminary rules of the probability calculus are (1) the probability of an event that must necessarily happen is taken to be 1, and (2) the probability of an event that necessarily cannot happen is taken to be 0. For example, the event consisting of it either raining or not raining (at the same time and place) has probability 1, and the event consisting of it both raining and not raining (at the same time and place) has probability of 0. These events correspond to statements that are tautological and self-contradictory, respectively. Contingent events, on the other hand, have probabilities greater than 0 but less than 1. For example, the probability that the Dow Jones Industrial Average will end a certain week at least five points higher than the previous week would usually be around 1/2, the probability that the polar ice cap will melt next year is very close to 0, and the probability that a traffic accident will occur somewhere tomorrow is very close to 1. Let us now consider six additional rules of the probability calculus.

1. Restricted Conjunction Rule

The **restricted conjunction rule** is used to compute the probability of two events occurring together when the events are *independent* of each other. Two events are said to be independent when the occurrence of one has no effect on the probability of the other one occurring. Examples include getting two heads from two tosses of a coin, drawing two hearts from a deck when the first is replaced before the second is drawn, and playing two sequential games of poker or roulette. The probability of two such events A and B occurring together is given by the formula

$$P(A \text{ and } B) = P(A) \times P(B)$$

For example, the probability of tossing two heads on a single throw of two coins is

$$P(H_1 \text{ and } H_2) = 1/2 \times 1/2 = 1/4$$

This result may be checked very easily by listing all the possible outcomes and comparing that number with the number of favorable outcomes:

Coin 1	Coin 2
H	H
H	T
T	H
T	T

Only one of the four possible outcomes shows both coins turning up heads.

Similarly, we may compute the probability of rolling two sixes with a pair of dice:

$$P(S_1 \text{ and } S_2) = 1/6 \times 1/6 = 1/36$$

Again, we may check the results by listing all the possible outcomes:

1-1	2-1	3-1	4-1	5-1	6-1
1-2	2-2	3-2	4-2	5-2	6-2
1-3	2-3	3-3	4-3	5-3	6-3
1-4	2-4	3-4	4-4	5-4	6-4
1-5	2-5	3-5	4-5	5-5	6-5
1-6	2-6	3-6	4-6	5-6	6-6

Since only one of the thirty-six possible outcomes shows two sixes together, the probability of this event is 1/36.

2. General Conjunction Rule

The **general conjunction rule** is used to compute the probability of two events occurring together whether or not the events are independent. When the events are independent, the general conjunction rule reduces to the restricted conjunction rule. Some examples of events that are not independent (that is, that are *dependent*) are drawing two spades from a deck on two draws when the first card drawn is not replaced, and selecting two or more window seats on an airplane. After the first card is drawn, the number of cards available for the second draw is reduced, and after one of the seats is taken on the plane, the number of seats remaining for subsequent choices is reduced. In other words, in both cases the second event is dependent on the first. The formula for computing the probability of two such events occurring together is

$$P(A \text{ and } B) = P(A) \times P(B \text{ given } A)$$

The expression $P(B \text{ given } A)$ is the probability that B will occur on the assumption that A has already occurred. Let us suppose, for example, that A and B designate the events of drawing two kings from a deck when the first card is not replaced before the second is drawn. If event A occurs, then only three kings remain, and the deck is also reduced to fifty-one cards. Thus, $P(B \text{ given } A)$ is 3/51. Since the probability of event A is 4/52, the probability of both events happening is the product of these two fractions, or 12/2652 (= 1/221).

For another illustration, consider an urn containing five red balls, six green balls, and seven yellow balls. The probability of drawing two red balls (without replacement) is computed as follows:

$$P(R_1 \text{ and } R_2) = 5/18 \times 4/17 = 20/306 = 10/153$$

If a red ball is selected on the first draw, this leaves four red balls from a total of seventeen. Thus, the probability of drawing a second red ball if one has already been drawn is 4/17.

For another example, consider the same urn with the same contents, but let us compute the probability of drawing first a green ball and then a yellow ball (without replacement):

$$P(G \text{ and } Y) = 6/18 \times 7/17 = 42/306 = 7/51$$

If a green ball is selected on the first draw, this affects the selection of a yellow ball on the second draw only to the extent of reducing the total number of balls to seventeen.

3. Restricted Disjunction Rule

The **restricted disjunction rule** is used to compute the probability of either of two events occurring when the events are *mutually exclusive*—that is, when they cannot both occur. Examples of such events include picking either an ace or a king from a deck of cards on a single draw or rolling either a six or a one on a single roll of a die. The probability is given by the formula

$$P(A \text{ or } B) = P(A) + P(B)$$

For example, the probability of drawing either a king or a queen (of any suit) from a deck of cards on a single draw is

$$P(K \text{ or } Q) = 4/52 + 4/52 = 8/52 = 2/13$$

For another example, consider an urn containing six black balls, four white balls, and two red balls. The probability of selecting either a black or red ball on a single draw is

$$P(B \text{ or } R) = 6/12 + 2/12 = 8/12 = 2/3$$

When the event in question is one that must *necessarily* occur, the probability is, of course, 1. Thus, the probability of obtaining either heads or tails on a single toss of a coin is

$$P(H \text{ or } T) = 1/2 + 1/2 = 1$$

The restricted disjunction rule may be combined with the restricted conjunction rule to compute the probability of getting either a five or a six on each of two consecutive rolls of a single die:

$$\begin{aligned} P[(F \text{ or } S)_1 \text{ and } (F \text{ or } S)_2] &= P(F \text{ or } S)_1 \times P(F \text{ or } S)_2 \\ &= (1/6 + 1/6) \times (1/6 + 1/6) \\ &= 1/3 \times 1/3 \\ &= 1/9 \end{aligned}$$

Since getting a five and getting a six on a single die are mutually exclusive events, $P(F \text{ or } S)_1$ is evaluated using the restricted disjunction rule. The same is true of $P(F$ or

$S)_2$. Then, since two rolls of a die are independent events, the conjunction of the two disjunctive events is evaluated by the restricted conjunction rule.

4. General Disjunction Rule

The **general disjunction rule** is used to compute the probability of either of two events whether or not they are mutually exclusive. The rule holds for any two events, but since its application is simplified when the events are independent, we will confine our attention to events of this kind. Examples of independent events that are not mutually exclusive include obtaining at least one head on two tosses of a coin, drawing at least one king from a deck on two draws when the first card is replaced before the second card is drawn, and getting at least one six when rolling a pair of dice. The formula for computing the probability of either of two such events is

$$P(A \text{ or } B) = P(A) + P(B) - P(A \text{ and } B)$$

If the events are independent, $P(A \text{ and } B)$ is computed using the restricted conjunction rule, and the general disjunction formula reduces to

$$P(A \text{ or } B) = P(A) + P(B) - [P(A) \times P(B)]$$

The general disjunction rule may be proved as follows. When A and B are nonexclusive, A occurs either with or without B, and B occurs either with or without A. Thus

$$P(A) = P(A \text{ and } B) + P(A \text{ and not-}B)$$
$$P(B) = P(B \text{ and } A) + P(B \text{ and not-}A)$$

But A or B occurs in exactly three possible ways: A and not-B, B and not-A, and A and B. Thus

$$P(A \text{ or } B) = P(A \text{ and not-}B) + P(B \text{ and not-}A) + P(A \text{ and } B)$$

Thus, when $P(A \text{ and } B)$ is subtracted from $P(A) + P(B)$, the difference is equal to $P(A \text{ or } B)$. [Note: $P(A \text{ and } B) = P(B \text{ and } A)$.]

For an example of the use of the general disjunction rule let us consider the probability of getting heads on either of two tosses of a coin. We have

$$P(H_1 \text{ or } H_2) = 1/2 + 1/2 - (1/2 \times 1/2)$$
$$= 1 - 1/4$$
$$= 3/4$$

For another example, consider the probability of getting at least one six when rolling a pair of dice. The computation is

$$P(S_1 \text{ or } S_2) = 1/6 + 1/6 - (1/6 \times 1/6)$$
$$= 2/6 - 1/36$$
$$= 11/36$$

The general disjunction rule may be combined with the restricted disjunction rule to compute the probability of getting either a three or a five when rolling a pair of dice. This is the probability of getting either a three or a five on the first die or either a three or a five on the second:

$$P[(T \text{ or } F)_1 \text{ or } (T \text{ or } F)_2] = P(T \text{ or } F)_1 + P(T \text{ or } F)_2 - [P(T \text{ or } F)_1 \times P(T \text{ or } F)_2]$$
$$= (1/6 + 1/6) + (1/6 + 1/6) - [(1/6 + 1/6) \times (1/6 + 1/6)]$$
$$= 2/6 + 2/6 - 4/36$$
$$= 20/36$$
$$= 5/9$$

Since getting a three or getting a five on a single throw are mutually exclusive events, $P(T \text{ or } F)_1$ is equal to the sum of the separate probabilities. The same is true for $P(T \text{ or } F)_2$.

The general disjunction rule may be combined with the general conjunction rule to compute the probability of drawing first a red ball and then a black ball on pairs of draws from either of two urns (without replacement). Suppose that the first urn contains two red balls, two black balls, and one green ball, and that the second urn contains three red balls, one black ball, and one white ball. The probability, giving two draws per urn, is

$$P[(R \text{ and } B)_1 \text{ or } (R \text{ and } B)_2]$$
$$= P(R \text{ and } B)_1 + P(R \text{ and } B)_2 - [P(R \text{ and } B)_1 \times P(R \text{ and } B)_2]$$
$$= (2/5 \times 2/4) + (3/5 \times 1/4) - [(2/5 \times 2/4) \times (3/5 \times 1/4)]$$
$$= 4/20 + 3/20 - (4/20 \times 3/20)$$
$$= 7/20 - 12/400$$
$$= 8/25$$

5. Negation Rule

The **negation rule** is useful for computing the probability of an event when the probability of the event *not* happening is either known or easily computed. The formula is as follows:

$$P(A) = 1 - P(\text{not-}A)$$

The formula can be proved very easily. By the restricted disjunction rule the probability of A or not-A is

$$P(A \text{ or not-}A) = P(A) + P(\text{not-}A)$$

But since *A* or not-*A* happens necessarily, $P(A \text{ or not-}A) = 1$. Thus

$$1 = P(A) + P(\text{not-}A)$$

Rearranging the terms in this equation gives us the negation rule. For an example of the use of this rule, consider the probability of getting heads at least once on two tosses of a coin. The probability of the event *not* happening, which is the probability of getting tails on both tosses, is immediately computed by the restricted conjunction rule to be 1/4. Then, applying the negation rule

$$P(H_1 \text{ or } H_2) = 1 - 1/4$$
$$= 3/4$$

The negation rule may also be used to compute the probabilities of disjunctive events that are *dependent*. In presenting the general disjunction rule we confined our attention to *independent* events. Let us suppose we are given an urn containing two black balls and three white balls. To compute the probability of getting at least one black ball on two draws (without replacement), we first compute the probability of the event not happening. This event consists in drawing two white balls, which, by the general conjunction rule, has the probability

$$P(W_1 \text{ and } W_2) = 3/5 \times 2/4 = 6/20$$

Now, applying the negation rule, the probability of getting at least one black ball on two draws is

$$P(B_1 \text{ or } B_2) = 1 - 6/20$$
$$= 14/20$$
$$= 7/10$$

For an example that is only slightly more complex, consider an urn containing two white, two black, and two red balls. To compute the probability of getting either a white or black ball on two draws (without replacement) we first compute the probability of the event not happening. This is the probability of getting red balls on both draws, which is

$$P(R_1 \text{ and } R_2) = 2/6 \times 1/5 = 2/30 = 1/15$$

Now, by the negation rule the probability of drawing either a white or black ball is

$$P(W \text{ or } B) = 1 - 1/15$$
$$= 14/15$$

6. Bayes's Theorem

Bayes's Theorem, named after the eighteenth-century English clergyman Thomas Bayes, is a useful rule for evaluating the conditional probability of two or more mutually exclusive and jointly exhaustive events. The conditional probability of an event is the probability of that event happening given that another event has already happened, and it is expressed $P(A \text{ given } B)$. You may recall that an expression of this form occurred in the formulation of the general conjunction rule. When the number of mutually exclusive and jointly exhaustive events is limited to two, which we will designate A_1 and A_2, Bayes's Theorem is expressed as follows:

$$P(A_1 \text{ given } B) = \frac{P(A_1) \times P(B \text{ given } A_1)}{[P(A_1 \times P(B \text{ given } A_1)] + [P(A_2) \times P(B \text{ given } A_2)]}$$

This limited formulation of Bayes's theorem may be proved as follows. Applying the general conjunction rule to the events A_1 and B, we have

$$P(A_1 \text{ and } B) = P(A_1) \times P(B \text{ given } A_1)$$

Applying the same rule to the same events written in the reverse order, we have

$$P(B \text{ and } A_1) = P(B) \times P(A_1 \text{ given } B)$$

Now, since $P(A_1 \text{ and } B)$ is equal to $P(B \text{ and } A_1)$, we may set the right-hand side of these two equations equal to each other:

$$P(B) \times P(A_1 \text{ given } B) = P(A_1) \times P(B \text{ given } A_1)$$

Dividing both sides of this equation by $P(B)$, we have

$$P(A_1 \text{ given } B) = \frac{P(A_1) \times P(B \text{ given } A_1)}{P(B)} \tag{*}$$

Now, it can be easily proved using a truth table that B is logically equivalent to the expression $[(A_1$ and $B)$ or (not-A_1 and $B)]$. Furthermore, since A_1 and A_2 are mutually exclusive and jointly exhaustive, one and only one of them will happen. Thus, A_2 is simply another way of writing not-A_1. Accordingly, the former expression in brackets can be written $[(A_1$ and $B)$ or $(A_2$ and $B)]$, and since this expression is logically equivalent to B,

$$P(B) = P[(A_1 \text{ and } B) \text{ or } (A_2 \text{ and } B)]$$

Now, applying the general conjunction rule and the restricted disjunction rule to the right-hand side of this equation, we have

$$P(B) = [P(A_1) \times P(B \text{ given } A_1)] + [P(A_2) \times P(B \text{ given } A_2)]$$

Finally, substituting the right-hand side of this equation in place of $P(B)$ in equation (*) above, we have Bayes's Theorem:

$$P(A_1 \text{ given } B) = \frac{P(A_1) \times P(B \text{ given } A_1)}{[P(A_1) \times P(B \text{ given } A_1)] + [P(A_2) \times P(B \text{ given } A_2)]}$$

For an illustration of the use of Bayes's Theorem, suppose we are given one beige urn and four gray urns in a dimly lit room, so we cannot distinguish one color from the other. The beige urn contains eight red and two white balls, and each of the gray urns contains three red and seven white balls. Suppose that a red ball is drawn from one of these five urns. What is the probability that the urn was beige? In other words, we want to know the probability that the urn was beige given that a red ball was drawn. The events A_1 and A_2 in Bayes's Theorem correspond to drawing a ball from either a beige urn or a gray urn. Substituting B and G for A_1 and A_2, respectively, we have

$$P(B \text{ given } R) = \frac{P(B) \times P(R \text{ given } B)}{[P(B) \times P(R \text{ given } B)] + [P(G) \times P(R \text{ given } G)]}$$

Now, since there are a total of five urns, the probability of randomly selecting the beige urn is 1/5, and the probability of randomly selecting one of the gray urns is 4/5. Finally, since each urn contains ten balls, the probability of drawing a red ball from the beige urn is 8/10, and the probability of drawing a red ball from the gray urn is 3/10. Thus, we have

$$P(B \text{ given } R) = \frac{1/5 \times 8/10}{(1/5 \times 8/10) + (4/5 \times 3/10)}$$
$$= \frac{8/50}{8/50 + 12/50} = \frac{8/50}{20/50} = 8/20 = .40$$

Bayes's Theorem is highly useful in practical affairs because it allows us to change our probability estimates of ordinary events as new information is acquired. For an example of how Bayes's Theorem is used for this purpose, consider the following example:

> Mr. Jones became seriously ill from ingesting defectively manufactured tablets of the painkiller novaprine. He intends to file a lawsuit against the most probable manufacturer of the tablets. After a brief investigation, he finds that 70 percent of the novaprine

sold in this country is manufactured by Alpha Pharmaceuticals, and 30 percent is manufactured by Beta Pharmaceuticals.

From this information the probability that Alpha Pharmaceuticals manufactured the tablets is .70, in comparison with .30 for Beta Pharmaceuticals. Thus, Mr. Jones tentatively decides to file his lawsuit against Alpha. However, upon further investigation Mr. Jones discovers the following:

Of the novaprine manufactured by Alpha, 10 percent is sold on the east coast and 90 percent on the west coast, while 80 percent of Beta's novaprine is sold on the east coast and 20 percent on the west coast. Furthermore, Mr. Jones recalls that he purchased his novaprine on the east coast.

Clearly this new information affects Mr. Jones's original probability estimate. We use Bayes's Theorem to recompute the probability that Alpha manufactured the defective tablets given that the tablets were purchased on the east coast as follows:

$$P(A \text{ given } E) = \frac{P(A) \times P(E \text{ given } A)}{[P(A) \times P(E \text{ given } A)] + [P(B) \times P(E \text{ given } B)]}$$

For $P(A)$ and $P(B)$ we use the original probabilities of .70 and .30, respectively. The probability that the tablets were purchased on the east coast given that they were manufactured by Alpha is .10, and the probability that they were purchased on the east coast given that they were manufactured by Beta is .80. Thus, we have

$$P(A \text{ given } E) = \frac{.70 \times .10}{(.70 \times .10) + (.30 \times .80)} = \frac{.07}{.07 + .24} = .07/.31 = .23$$

The new information that Mr. Jones acquired has significantly affected the probability that Alpha manufactured the defective tablets. The probability has dropped from .70 to .23. With this new information, it is more likely that Beta manufactured the tablets, so Mr. Jones should now file his lawsuit against Beta. The probability for Beta is $1 - .23$, or .77.

The earlier probability for Alpha (.70) is called the *prior* probability, and the later figure (.23) is called the *posterior* probability. If Mr. Jones should acquire even more information, the posterior probability becomes a new prior, and it is used as the value for $P(A)$ in a subsequent application of Bayes's Theorem.

Additional Applications

Most of the examples considered thus far have used the classical theory to determine the probability of the component events. But as was mentioned earlier, the probability calculus can also be used in conjunction with the relative frequency theory and the subjectivist theory. If we apply the relative frequency theory to the mortality tables used by insurance companies, we find that the probability of a twenty-five-year-old man living an additional forty years is .82, and the probability of a twenty-five-year old woman living the same number of years is .88. To compute the probability of such a man and woman both living that long, we use the restricted conjunction rule and obtain $.82 \times .88 = .72$. For the probability that either of these people would live that long, we use the general disjunction rule and obtain

$$.82 + .88 - (.82 \times .88) = .98$$

Let us suppose that these two people are married and both would give 9 to 1 odds on their staying married for forty years. This translates into a probability of $9/(9 + 1)$ or .90. Using the restricted conjunction rule, the probability of this event happening is the product of the latter figure and the probability of their both living that long, or .65.

For an example involving the subjectivist theory, if the Philadelphia Eagles are given 7 to 5 odds of winning the NFC championship, and the New England Patriots are given 3 to 2 odds of winning the AFC championship, the probability that at least one of these teams will win is computed using the general disjunction rule. The odds translate respectively into probabilities of 7/12 and 3/5, and so the probability of the disjunction is $7/12 + 3/5 - (7/12 \times 3/5) = 5/6$. The probability that the two teams will meet in the Super Bowl (that both will win their conference championship) is, by the restricted conjunction rule, $7/12 \times 3/5 = 21/60$, or 7/20. The probability that neither will play in the Super Bowl is, by the negation rule, $1 - 5/6 = 1/6$.

The probability calculus can also be used to evaluate the strength of inductive arguments. Consider the following argument:

> The Philadelphia Eagles are given 7 to 5 odds of winning the NFC championship. The New England Patriots are given 3 to 2 odds of winning the AFC championship. Therefore, the Eagles and the Patriots will meet in the Super Bowl.

On the assumption that the premises are true, that is, on the assumption that the odds are reported correctly, the conclusion follows with a probability of 7/20 or .35. Thus, the argument is not particularly strong. But if the odds given in the premises should increase, the strength of the argument would increase proportionately. The premises of the following argument give different odds:

> The Philadelphia Eagles are given 7 to 2 odds of winning the NFC championship. The New England Patriots are given 8 to 3 odds of winning the AFC championship. Therefore, the Eagles and the Patriots will meet in the Super Bowl.

In this argument, if the premises are assumed true, the conclusion follows with probability $7/9 \times 8/11 = 56/99$, or .57. Thus, the argument is at least moderately strong.

Lest this procedure be misinterpreted, however, it is important to recall a point raised in Chapter 1. The strength of an inductive argument depends not merely upon whether the conclusion is probably true but upon whether the conclusion follows probably from the premises. As a result, to evaluate the strength of an inductive argument it is not sufficient merely to know the probability of the conclusion on the assumption that the premises are true. One must also know whether the probability of the conclusion rests upon the evidence given in the premises. If the probability of the conclusion does not rest on this evidence, the argument is weak regardless of whether the conclusion is probably true. The following argument is a case in point:

> All dogs are animals. Therefore, probably a traffic accident will occur somewhere tomorrow.

The conclusion of this argument is probably true independently of the premises, so the argument is weak.

In this connection the analogy between deductive and inductive arguments breaks down. As we saw in Chapter 6, any argument having a conclusion that is necessarily true is deductively valid regardless of the content of its premises. But any inductive argument having a probably true conclusion is not strong unless the probability of the conclusion rests upon the evidence given in the premises.

A final comment is in order about the material covered in this section. Probability is one of those subjects about which there is little agreement in philosophical circles. There are philosophers who defend each of the theories we have discussed as providing the only acceptable approach, and there are numerous views regarding the fine points of each. In addition, some philosophers argue that there are certain uses of "probability" that none of these theories can interpret. The statement "There is high probability that Einstein's theory of relativity is correct" may be a case in point. In any event, the various theories about the meaning of probability, as well as the details of the probability calculus, are highly complex subjects, and the brief account given here has done little more than scratch the surface.

EXERCISE 9.3

iLrn I. Compute probabilities or odds for the following simple events:

★1. What is the probability of rolling a five on a single roll of a die? What are the odds for this event?

2. From a sample of 9,750 Ajax trucks, 273 developed transmission problems within the first two years of operation. What is the probability that an Ajax truck will develop transmission problems within the first two years?

3. If the standard odds are 8 to 5 that the Chargers will beat the Lions, what is the probability that this event will happen?

★4. From a sample of 7,335 seventy-five-year-old women, 6,260 lived an additional five years. What is the probability that a seventy-five-year-old woman will live to age eighty?

5. What is the probability of picking a black jack from a poker deck (without jokers) on a single draw?

6. If the probability of the Red Sox beating the Tigers is 6/17, what are the odds for this event?

★7. Given an urn containing three red balls, four green balls, and five yellow balls, what is the probability of drawing a red ball on a single draw?

8. If the odds of the Broncos beating the Dolphins is 5 to 4, and you bet $10 on the Broncos, how much do you stand to win?

9. Given an urn containing four red balls, three green balls, and five yellow balls, what are the odds of drawing a red ball on a single draw?

★10. Suppose you give 1:6 odds that you can roll a "1" with a single fair die. If someone accepts your bet, how much could you expect to win after 100 rolls if you bet $1 on each roll?

iLrn II. Compute probabilities for the following compound events:

★1. What is the probability of getting either a six or a one from a single roll of a die?

2. What is the probability of getting heads on three successive tosses of a coin?

3. What is the probability of drawing either a king or a queen from a poker deck (no jokers) on a single draw?

★4. What is the probability of drawing two aces from a poker deck in two draws:
   a. If the first card is replaced before the second is drawn?
   b. If the first card is not replaced before the second is drawn?

5. What is the probability of drawing at least one ace from a poker deck on two draws if the first card is replaced before the second is drawn?

6. What is the probability of getting at least one head on three tosses of a coin?

★7. What is the probability of getting at least one six on three rolls of a die?

8. If a pair of dice are rolled, what is the probability that the points add up to:
   a. 5?
   b. 6?
   c. 7?

9. Given two urns, one containing two red, three green, and four yellow balls, the other containing four red, two green, and three yellow balls, if a single ball is drawn from each urn, what is the probability that:
   a. Both are red?
   b. At least one is green?
   c. One is red, the other yellow?
   d. At least one is either red or yellow?
   e. Both are the same color?

★10. Given an urn containing three red, four green, and five yellow balls, if two balls are drawn from the urn (without replacement), what is the probability that:
   a. Both are red?
   b. One is green, the other yellow?
   c. One is either red or green?
   d. At least one is green?
   e. Both have the same color?

11. What is the probability of drawing either an ace or a king (or both) on three draws (without replacement) from a poker deck? (Hint: Use the negation rule.)

12. What is the probability of drawing an ace and a king on three draws (without replacement) from a poker deck? (Hint: Use the negation rule.)

★13. The probability of a twenty-year-old man living to age seventy is .74, and the probability of a twenty-year-old woman living to the same age is .82. If a recently married couple, both age twenty, give 8 to 1 odds on their staying married for fifty years, what is the probability that:
   a. At least one will live to age seventy?
   b. They will celebrate their golden wedding anniversary?

14. Assign a numerical value to the strength of the following argument: The odds are 5 to 3 that the Indians will win the American League pennant and 7 to 5

that the Cardinals will win the National League pennant. Therefore, the Indians and the Cardinals will meet in the World Series.

15. Assign a numerical value to the strength of the following argument: The Wilson family has four children. Therefore, at least two of the children were born on the same day of the week.

★16. We are given three new urns each containing seven red, five green, and three white balls, and two old urns each containing five red, three green, and seven white balls. The urns are identical except for an old or new date stamped beneath the base. If a single red ball is randomly drawn from one of these urns, was it most probably drawn from an old urn or a new urn? (Hint: For this exercise and the ones that follow, use Bayes's Theorem.)

17. Knowing that your friend Angella studies for her tests only 40 percent of the time, you place an even bet with a third party that Angella will not study for her upcoming test. Later, you just happen to hear that Angella passed the test. Should you retract your bet? Assume that Angella passes nine out of ten tests when she studies, and three out of ten when she does not.

18. A physician has diagnosed a patient as having either hepatitis or liver cancer (but not both). Statistics reveal that hepatitis occurs in the general population twice as frequently as liver cancer. Thus, the physician tentatively concludes that the patient probably has hepatitis. Later the physician conducts a test on the patient that turns out positive. On this test, nine out of ten cases of liver cancer trigger a positive outcome, and one out of six cases of hepatitis trigger a positive outcome. What is the new probability that the patient has liver cancer?

★19. Ms. Jones, a bookstore owner, wishes to send out an advertisement to potential customers. She estimates that 20 percent of the town's residents are recreational readers, and she knows that all of the residents are either recreational readers or TV addicts (but not both). Also, a TV repair person has told her that two of ten TV addicts are newspaper subscribers, and from a survey of her own customers she has learned that seven of ten recreational readers are newspaper subscribers. If Ms. Jones places an ad in the local newspaper, how effective will the ad be? (That is, what is the probability that a newspaper subscriber is a recreational reader?)

20. Mr. Andrews, a grape merchant, inquires about a certain wine that he tastes at a party. The host tells him that from a total of ten bottles of that wine, six came from the north vineyard and four came from the south vineyard. From this information, the merchant concludes that he should visit the north vineyard for a sample of the grapes. Later, he discovers that the wine in question came from a bottle labeled Classic Reserve, and 30 of 100 barrels of north vineyard wine were bottled with that label, while 130 of 200 barrels of south vineyard wine were bottled with that label. Now, with this new information, what is the probability that the wine came from the north vineyard?

9.4 Statistical Reasoning

In our day-to-day experience all of us encounter arguments that rest on statistical evidence. An especially prolific source of such arguments is the advertising industry. We are constantly told that we ought to smoke a certain brand of cigarettes because it has 20 percent less tar, buy a certain kind of car because it gets 5 percent better gas mileage, and use a certain cold remedy because it is recommended by four out of five physicians. But the advertising industry is not the only source. We often read in the newspapers that some union is asking an increase in pay because its members earn less than the average or that a certain region is threatened with floods because rainfall has been more than the average.

To evaluate such arguments, we must be able to interpret the statistics upon which they rest, but doing so is not always easy. Statements expressing averages and percentages are often ambiguous and can mean any number of things, depending on how the average or percentage is computed. These difficulties are compounded by the fact that statistics provide a highly convenient way for people to deceive one another. Such deceptions can be effective even though they fall short of being outright lies. Thus, to evaluate arguments based on statistics one must be familiar not only with the ambiguities that occur in the language but with the devices that unscrupulous individuals use to deceive others.

This section touches on five areas that are frequent sources of such ambiguity and deception: problems in sampling, the meaning of "average," the importance of dispersion in a sample, the use of graphs and pictograms, and the use of percentages for the purpose of comparison. By becoming acquainted with these topics and with some of the misuses that occur, we are better able to determine whether a conclusion follows probably from a set of statistical premises.

Samples

Much of the statistical evidence presented in support of inductively drawn conclusions is gathered from analyzing samples. When a sample is found to possess a certain characteristic, it is argued that the group as a whole (the population) possesses that characteristic. For example, if we wanted to know the opinion of the student body at a certain university about whether to adopt an academic honor code, we could take a poll of 10 percent of the students. If the results of the poll showed that 80 percent of those sampled favored the code, we might draw the conclusion that 80 percent of the entire student body favored it. Such an argument would be classified as an inductive generalization.

The problem that arises with the use of samples has to do with whether the sample is representative of the population. Samples that are not representative are said to be **biased.** Depending on what the population consists of, whether machine parts or human beings, different considerations enter into determining whether a sample is biased. These considerations include (1) whether the sample is randomly selected, (2) the size of the sample, and (3) psychological factors.

A sample is **random** if and only if every member of the population has an equal chance of being selected. The requirement that a sample be randomly selected applies to practically all samples, but sometimes it can be taken for granted. For example, when a physician draws a blood sample to test for blood sugar, there is no need to take a little bit from the finger, a little from the arm, and a little from the leg. Because blood is a circulating fluid, it can be assumed that it is homogenous in regard to blood sugar.

The randomness requirement must be given more attention when the population consists of discrete units. Suppose, for example, that a quality control engineer for a manufacturing firm needed to determine whether the components on a certain conveyor belt were within specifications. To do so, let us suppose the engineer removed every tenth component for measurement. The sample obtained by such a procedure would not be random if the components were not randomly arranged on the conveyor belt. As a result of some malfunction in the manufacturing process it is quite possible that every tenth component turned out perfect and the rest imperfect. If the engineer happened to select only the perfect ones, the sample would be biased. A selection procedure that would be more likely to ensure a random sample would be to roll a pair of dice and remove every component corresponding to a roll of ten. Since the outcome of a roll of dice is a random event, the selection would also be random. Such a procedure would be more likely to include defective components that turn up at regular intervals.

The randomness requirement presents even greater problems when the population consists of human beings. Suppose, for example, that a public opinion poll is to be conducted on the question of excessive corporate profits. It would hardly do to ask such a question randomly of the people encountered on Wall Street in New York City. Such a sample would almost certainly be biased in favor of the corporations. A less biased sample could be obtained by randomly selecting phone numbers from the telephone directory, but even this procedure would not yield a completely random sample. Among other things, the time of day in which a call is placed influences the kind of responses obtained. Most people who are employed full time are not available during the day, and even if calls are made at night, a large percentage of the population have unlisted numbers.

A poll conducted by mail based on the addresses listed in the city directory would also yield a fairly random sample, but this method, too, has shortcomings. Many apartment dwellers are not listed, and others move before the directory is printed. Furthermore, none of those who live in rural areas are listed. In short, it is both difficult and expensive to conduct a large-scale public opinion poll that succeeds in obtaining responses from anything approximating a random sample of individuals.

A classic case of a poll that turned out to be biased in spite of a good deal of effort and expense was conducted by *Literary Digest* magazine to predict the outcome of the 1936 presidential election. The sample consisted of a large number of the magazine's subscribers together with a number of others selected from the telephone directory. Because four similar polls had picked the winner in previous years, the results of this poll were highly respected. As it turned out, however, the Republican candidate, Alf Landon, got a significant majority in the poll, but Franklin D. Roosevelt won the election by a landslide. The incorrect prediction is explained by the fact that the 1936 election occurred in the middle of the Depression, at a time when many people could afford neither a telephone nor a subscription to the *Digest*. These were the people who were overlooked in the poll, and they were also the ones who voted for Roosevelt.

Size is also an important factor in determining whether a sample is representative. Given that a sample is randomly selected, the larger the sample, the more closely it replicates the population. In statistics, this degree of closeness is expressed in terms of **sampling error.** The sampling error is the difference between the relative frequency with which some characteristic occurs in the sample and the relative frequency with which the same characteristic occurs in the population. If, for example, a poll were taken of a labor union and 60 percent of the members sampled expressed their intention to vote for Smith for president but in fact only 55 percent of the whole union intended to vote for Smith, the sampling error would be 5 percent. If a larger sample were taken, the error would be less.

Just how large a sample should be is a function of the size of the population and of the degree of sampling error that can be tolerated. For a sampling error of, say, 5 percent, a population of 10,000 would require a larger sample than would a population of 100. However, the ratio is not linear. The sample for the larger population need not be 100 times as large as the one for the smaller population to obtain the same precision. When the population is very large, the size of the sample needed to ensure a certain precision levels off to a constant figure. Studies based on the Gallup poll show that a random sample of 400 will yield results of plus or minus 6 percent whether the population is 100,000 or 100 million. Additional figures for large populations are given in Table 9.6:

Table 9.6 Sample Size and Sampling Error*

Numbers of interviews	Margin of error (in percentage points)
4,000	±2
1,500	±3
1,000	±4
750	±4
600	±5
400	±6
200	±8
100	±11

As the table indicates, reducing the sampling error below 5 percent requires rather substantial increases in the size of the sample. The cost of obtaining large samples may not justify an increase in precision. The table also points up the importance of randomness. The sample in the 1936 *Literary Digest* poll was based on 2 million responses, yet the sampling error was huge because the sample was not randomly selected.

Statements of sampling error are often conspicuously absent from surveys used to support advertising claims. Marketers of products such as patent medicines have been known to take a number of rather small samples until they obtain one that gives the

*From Charles W. Roll Jr. and Albert H. Cantril, *Polls: Their Use and Misuse in Politics* (New York: Basic Books, 1972), p. 72.

"right" result. For example, twenty polls of twenty-five people might be taken inquiring about the preferred brand of aspirin. Even though the samples might be randomly selected, one will eventually be found in which twenty of the twenty-five respondents indicate their preference for Alpha brand aspirin. Having found such a sample, the marketing firm proceeds to promote this brand as the one preferred by four out of five of those sampled. The results of the other samples are, of course, discarded, and no mention is made of sampling error.

Psychological factors can also have a bearing on whether the sample is representative. When the population consists of inanimate objects, such as cans of soup or machine parts, psychological factors are usually irrelevant, but they can play a significant role when the population consists of human beings. If the people composing the sample think that they will gain or lose something by the kind of answer they give, it is to be expected that their involvement will affect the outcome. For example, if the residents of a neighborhood were to be surveyed for annual income with the purpose of determining whether the neighborhood should be ranked among the fashionable areas in the city, it would be expected that the residents would exaggerate their answers. But if the purpose of the study were to determine whether the neighborhood could afford a special levy that would increase property taxes, one might expect the incomes to be underestimated.

The kind of question asked can also have a psychological bearing. Questions such as "How often do you brush your teeth?" and "How many books do you read in a year?" can be expected to generate responses that overestimate the truth, while "How many times have you been intoxicated?" and "How many extramarital affairs have you had?" would probably receive answers that underestimate the truth. Similar exaggerations can result from the way a question is phrased. For example, "Do you favor a reduction in welfare benefits as a response to rampant cheating?" would be expected to receive more affirmative answers than simply "Do you favor a reduction in welfare benefits?"

Another source of psychological influence is the personal interaction between the surveyor and the respondent. Suppose, for example, that a door-to-door survey were taken to determine how many people believe in God or attend church on Sunday. If the survey were conducted by priests and ministers dressed in clerical garb, one might expect a larger number of affirmative answers than if the survey were taken by nonclerics. The simple fact is that many people like to give answers that please the questioner.

To prevent this kind of interaction from affecting the outcome, scientific studies are often conducted under "double blind" conditions in which neither the surveyor nor the respondent knows what the "right" answer is. For example, in a double blind study to determine the effectiveness of a drug, bottles containing the drug would be mixed with other bottles containing a placebo (sugar tablet). The contents of each bottle would be matched with a code number on the label, and neither the person distributing the bottles nor the person recording the responses would know what the code is. Under these conditions the persons conducting the study would not be able to influence, by some smile or gesture, the response of the persons to whom the drugs are given.

Most of the statistical evidence encountered in ordinary experience contains no reference to such factors as randomness, sampling error, or the conditions under which the sample was taken. In the absence of such information, the person faced with evaluating the evidence must use his or her best judgment. If either the organization conducting the study or the persons composing the sample have something to gain by the kind of answer that is given, the results of the survey should be regarded as suspect. And if the questions that are asked concern topics that would naturally elicit distorted answers, the results should probably be rejected. In either event, the mere fact that a study *appears* scientific or is expressed in mathematical language should never intimidate a person into accepting the results. Numbers and scientific terminology are no substitute for an unbiased sample.

The Meaning of "Average"

In statistics the word "average" is used in three different senses: mean, median, and mode. In evaluating arguments and inferences that rest upon averages, it is often important to know in precisely what sense the word is being used.

The **mean** value of a set of data is the arithmetical average. It is computed by dividing the sum of the individual values by the number of data in the set. Suppose, for example, that we are given Table 9.7 listing the ages of a group of people:

Table 9.7

Number of People	Age
1	16
4	17
1	18
2	19
3	23

To compute the mean age, we divide the sum of the individual ages by the number of people:

$$\text{mean age} = \frac{(1 \times 16) + (4 \times 17) + (1 \times 18) + (2 \times 19) + (3 \times 23)}{11} = 19$$

The **median** of a set of data is the middle point when the data are arranged in ascending order. In other words, the median is the point at which there are an equal number of data above and below. In Table 9.7 the median age is 18 because there are five people above this age and five below.

The **mode** is the value that occurs with the greatest frequency. Here the mode is 17, because there are four people with that age and fewer people with any other age.

In this example, the mean, median, and mode, while different from one another, are all fairly close together. The problem for induction occurs when there is a great disparity between these values. This sometimes occurs in the case of salaries. Consider, for example, Table 9.8, which reports the salaries of a hypothetical architectural firm:

Table 9.8

Capacity	Number of Personnel	Salary
president	1	$275,000
senior architect	2	150,000
junior architect	2	80,000
senior engineer	1	65,000 ←mean
junior engineer	4	55,000
senior draftsman	1	45,000 ←median
junior draftsman	10	30,000 ←mode

Since there are twenty-one employees and a total of $1,365,000 is paid in salaries, the mean salary is $1,365,000/21, or $65,000. The median salary is $45,000 because ten employees earn less than this and ten earn more, and the mode, which is the salary that occurs most frequently, is $30,000. Each of these figures represents the "average" salary of the firm, but in different senses. Depending on the purpose for which the average is used, different figures might be cited as the basis for an argument.

For example, if the senior engineer were to request a raise in salary, the president could respond that his or her salary is already well above the average (in the sense of median and mode) and that therefore that person does not deserve a raise. If the junior draftsmen were to make the same request, the president could respond that they are presently earning the firm's average salary (in the sense of mode), and that for draftsmen to be earning the average salary is excellent. Finally, if someone from outside the firm were to make the allegation that the firm pays subsistence-level wages, the president could respond that the average salary of the firm is a hefty $65,000. All of the president's responses would be true, but if the reader or listener is not sophisticated enough to distinguish the various senses of "average," he or she might be persuaded by the arguments.

In some situations, the mode is the most useful average. Suppose, for example, that you are in the market for a three-bedroom house. Suppose further that a real estate agent assures you that the houses in a certain complex have an average of three bedrooms and that therefore you will certainly want to see them. If the salesman has used "average" in the sense of mean, it is possible that half the houses in the complex are four-bedroom, the other half are two-bedroom, and there are no three-bedroom houses at all. A similar result is possible if the salesman has used average in the sense of median. The only sense of average that would be useful for your purposes is mode: If the modal average is three bedrooms, there are more three-bedroom houses than any other kind.

On other occasions a mean average is the most useful. Suppose, for example, that you have taken a job as a pilot on a plane that has nine passenger seats and a maximum carrying capacity of 1,350 pounds (in addition to yourself). Suppose further that you have arranged to fly a group of nine passengers over the Grand Canyon and that you must determine whether their combined weight is within the required limit.

If a representative of the group tells you that the average weight of the passengers is 150 pounds, this by itself tells you nothing. If he means average in the sense of median, it could be the case that the four heavier passengers weigh 200 pounds and the four lighter ones weigh 145, for a combined weight of 1,530 pounds. Similarly, if the passenger representative means average in the sense of mode, it could be that two passengers weigh 150 pounds and that the others have varying weights in excess of 200 pounds, for a combined weight of over 1,700 pounds. Only if the representative means average in the sense of mean do you know that the combined weight of the passengers is 9×150 or 1,350 pounds.

Finally, sometimes a median average is the most meaningful. Suppose, for example, that you are a manufacturer of a product that appeals to an age group under thirty-five. To increase sales you decide to run an ad in a national magazine, but you want some assurance that the ad will be read by the right age group. If the advertising director of a magazine tells you that the average age of the magazine's readers is 35, you know virtually nothing. If the director means average in the sense of mean, it could be that 90 percent of the readership is over 35 and that the remaining 10 percent bring the average down to 35. Similarly, if the director means average in the sense of mode, it could be that 3 percent of the readership are exactly 35 and that the remaining 97 percent have ages ranging from 35 to 85. Only if the director means average in the sense of median do you know that half the readership is 35 or less.

Dispersion

Although averages often yield important information about a set of data, there are many cases in which merely knowing the average, in any sense of the term, tells us very little. The reason for this is that the average says nothing about how the data are distributed. For this, we need to know something about **dispersion**, which refers to how spread out the data are in regard to numerical value. Three important measures of dispersion are *range*, *variance*, and *standard deviation*.

Let us first consider the **range** of a set of data, which is the difference between the largest and the smallest values. For an example of the importance of this parameter, suppose that after living for many years in an intemperate climate, you decide to relocate in an area that has a more ideal mean temperature. Upon discovering that the annual mean temperature of Oklahoma City is 60°F you decide to move there, only to find that you roast in the summer and freeze in the winter. Unfortunately, you had ignored the fact that Oklahoma City has a temperature *range* of 130°, extending from a record low of −17° to a record high of 113°. In contrast, San Nicholas Island, off the coast of California, has a mean temperature of 61° but a range of only 40 degrees, extending from 47° in the winter to 87° in the summer. The temperature ranges for these two locations are approximated in Figure 1.

Even granting the importance of the range of the data in this example, however, range really tells us relatively little because it comprehends only two data points, the maximum and minimum. It says nothing about how the other data points are distributed. For this we need to know the **variance**, or the **standard deviation**, which measure how every data point varies or deviates from the mean.

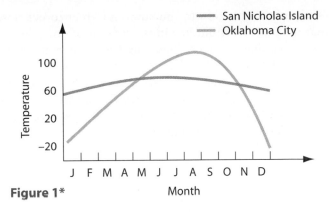

Figure 1*

Month

*This example is taken from Darrell Huff, *How to Lie with Statistics* (New York: W. W. Norton, 1954), p. 52.

For an example of the importance of these two parameters in describing a set of data, suppose you have a four-year-old child and you are looking for a day-care center that will provide plenty of possible playmates about the same age as your child. After calling several centers on the phone, you narrow the search down to two: the Rumpus Center and the Bumpus Center. Both report that they regularly care for nine children, that the mean and median age of the children is four, and that the range in ages of the children is six. Unable to decide between these two centers, you decide to pay them a visit. Once having done so, it is obvious that the Rumpus Center will meet your needs better than the Bumpus Center. The reason is that the ages of the children in the two centers are distributed differently.

The ages of the children in the two centers are as follows:

Rumpus Center: 1, 3, 3, 4, 4, 4, 5, 5, 7
Bumpus Center: 1, 1, 2, 2, 4, 6, 6, 7, 7

To illustrate the differences in distribution, these ages can be plotted on a certain kind of bar graph, called a *histogram*, as shown in Figures 2a and 2b.

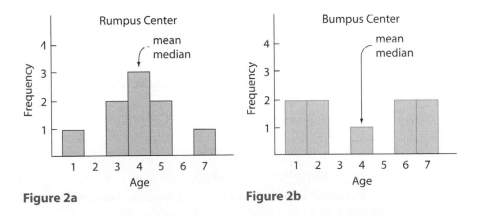

Figure 2a   **Figure 2b**

Obviously the reason why the Rumpus Center comes closer to meeting your needs is that it has seven children within one year of your own child, whereas the Bumpus Center has only one such child. This difference in distribution is measured by the variance and the standard deviation. Computing the value of these parameters for the two centers is quite easy, but first we must introduce some symbols. The standard deviation is represented in statistics by the Greek letter σ (sigma), and the variance, which is the square of the standard deviation, is represented by σ^2. We compute the variance first, which is defined as follows:

$$\sigma^2 = \frac{\Sigma (x - \mu)^2}{n}$$

In this expression (which looks far more complicated than it is), Σ (upper-case sigma) means the sum of, x is a variable that ranges over the ages of the children, the Greek letter μ (mu) is the mean age, (4), and n is the number of children (9). Thus, to compute the variance, we take each of the ages of the children, subtract the mean age (4) from each, square the result of each, add up the squares, and then divide the sum by the number of children (9). The first three steps of this procedure for the Rumpus Center are reported in Table 9.9:

Table 9.9

x	$(x - \mu)$	$(x - \mu)^2$
1	−3	9
3	−1	1
3	−1	1
4	0	0
4	0	0
4	0	0
5	+1	1
5	+1	1
7	+3	9
		Total = 22

First, the column for x (the children's ages) is entered, next the column for $(x - \mu)$, and last the column for $(x - \mu)^2$. After adding up the figures in the final column, we obtain the variance by dividing the sum (22) by n (9):

$$\text{Variance} = \sigma^2 = \frac{22}{9} = 2.44$$

Finally, to obtain the standard deviation, we take the square root of the variance:

$$\text{Standard deviation} = \sigma = \sqrt{2.44} = 1.56$$

Next, we can perform the same operation on the ages of the children in the Bumpus Center. The figures are expressed in Table 9.10.

Table 9.10

x	(x − μ)	(x − μ)²
1	−3	9
1	−3	9
2	−2	4
2	−2	4
4	0	0
6	+2	4
6	+2	4
7	+3	9
7	+3	9
		Total = 52

Now, for the variance, we have

$$\sigma^2 = \frac{52}{9} = 5.78$$

And for the standard deviation, we have

$$\sigma = \sqrt{5.78} = 2.40$$

These figures for the variance and standard deviation reflect the difference in distribution shown in the two histograms. In the histogram for the Rumpus Center, the ages of most of the children are clumped around the mean age (4). In other words, they vary or deviate relatively slightly from the mean, and this fact is reflected in relatively small figures for the variance (2.44) and the standard deviation (1.56). On the other hand, in the histogram for the Bumpus center, the ages of most of the children vary or deviate relatively greatly from the mean, so the variance (5.78) and the standard deviation (2.40) are larger.

One of the more important kinds of distribution used in statistics is called the **normal distribution,** which expresses the distribution of random phenomena in a population. Such phenomena include (approximately) the heights of adult men or women in a city, the useful life of a certain kind of tire or light bulb, and the daily sales figures of a certain grocery store. To illustrate this concept, suppose that a certain college has 2000 female students. The heights of these students range from 57 inches to 73 inches. If we divide these heights into one-inch intervals and express them in terms of a histogram, the resulting graph would probably look like the one in Figure 3a.

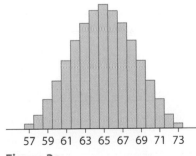

57 59 61 63 65 67 69 71 73

Figure 3a

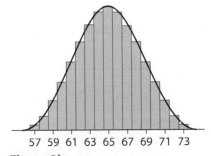

57 59 61 63 65 67 69 71 73

Figure 3b

This histogram has the shape of a bell. When a continuous curve is superimposed on top of this histogram, the result appears in Figure 3b. This curve is called a normal curve, and it represents a normal distribution. The heights of all of the students fit under the curve, and each vertical slice under the curve represents a certain subset of these heights. The number of heights trails off toward a zero at the extreme left and right ends of the curve, and it reaches a maximum in the center. The peak of the curve reflects the average height in the sense of mean, median, and mode.

The parameters of variance and standard deviation apply to normal distributions in basically the same way as they do for the histograms relating to the day-care centers. Normal curves with a relatively small standard deviation tend to be relatively narrow and pointy, with most of the population clustered close to the mean, while curves with a relatively large standard deviation tend to be relatively flattened and stretched out, with most of the population distributed some distance from the mean. This idea is expressed in Figure 4. As usual, σ represents the standard deviation, and μ represents the mean.

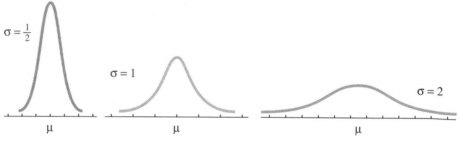

Figure 4

For a final example that illustrates the importance of dispersion, suppose that you decide to put your life savings into a business that designs and manufactures women's dresses. As corporation president you decide to save money by restricting production to dresses that fit the average woman. Because the average size in the sense of mean, median, and mode is 12, you decide to make only size 12 dresses. Unfortunately, you later discover that while size 12 is indeed the average, 95 percent of women fall outside this interval, as Figure 5 shows:

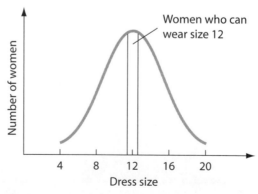

Figure 5

The problem is that you failed to take into account the standard deviation. If the standard deviation were relatively small, then most of the dress sizes would be clustered about the mean (size 12). But in fact the standard deviation is relatively large, so most of the dress sizes fall outside this interval.

Graphs and Pictograms

Graphs provide a highly convenient and informative way to represent statistical data, but they are also susceptible to misuse and misinterpretation. Here we will confine our attention to some of the typical ways in which graphs are misused.

First of all, if a graph is to represent an actual situation, it is essential that both the vertical and horizontal axes be scaled. Suppose, for example, that the profit level of a corporation is represented by a graph such as Figure 6. Such a graph is practically meaningless because it fails to show how much the profits increased over what period of time. If the curve represents a 10 percent increase over twenty years, then, of course, the picture is not very bright. Although they convey practically no information, graphs of this kind are used quite often in advertising. A manufacturer of vitamins, for example, might print such a graph on the label of the bottle to suggest that a person's energy level is supposed to increase dramatically after taking the tablets. Such ads frequently make an impression because they look scientific, and the viewer rarely bothers to check whether the axes are scaled or precisely what the curve is supposed to signify.

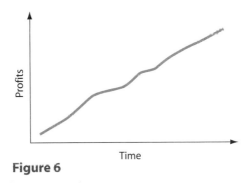

Figure 6

A graph that more appropriately represents corporate profits is given in Figure 7 (the corporation is fictitious):

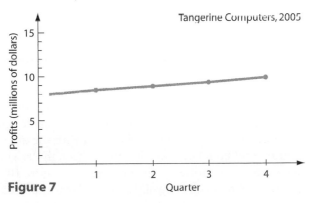

Figure 7

Inspection of the graph reveals that between January and December profits rose from $8 to $10 million, which represents a respectable 25 percent increase. This increase can be made to *appear* even more impressive by chopping off the bottom of the graph and altering the scale on the vertical axis while leaving the horizontal scale as is:

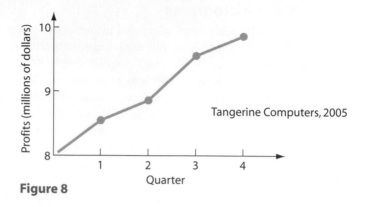

Figure 8

Again, strictly speaking, the graph accurately represents the facts, but if the viewer fails to notice what has been done to the vertical scale, he or she is liable to derive the impression that the profits have increased by something like a hundred percent or more.

The same strategy can be used with bar graphs. The graphs in Figure 9 compare sales volume for two consecutive years, but the one on the right conveys the message more dramatically:

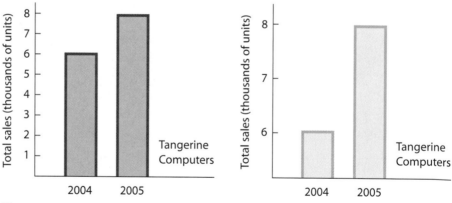

Figure 9

Of course, if the sales volume has decreased, the corporate directors would probably want to minimize the difference, in which case the design on the left is preferable.

An even greater illusion can be created with the use of pictograms. A **pictogram** is a diagram that compares two situations through drawings that differ either in size or in the number of entities depicted. Consider Figure 10, which illustrates the increase in production of an oil company between 2000 and 2005.

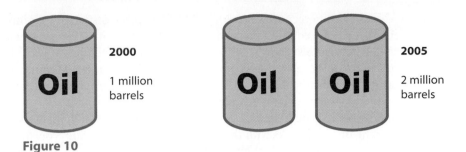

Figure 10

This pictogram accurately represents the increase because it unequivocally shows that the amount doubled between the years represented. But the effect is not especially dramatic. The increase in production can be exaggerated by representing the 2005 level with an oil barrel twice as tall:

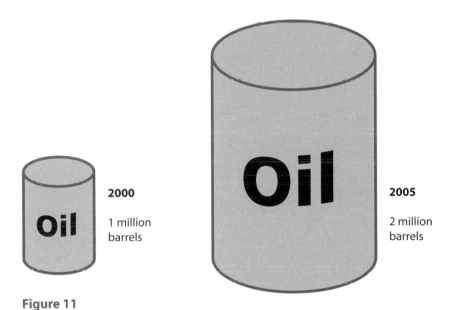

Figure 11

Even though the actual production is stated adjacent to each drawing, this pictogram creates the illusion that production has much more than doubled. While the drawing on the right is exactly twice as high as the one on the left, it is also twice as wide. Thus, it occupies four times as much room on the page. Furthermore, when the viewer's three-dimensional judgment is called into play, the barrel on the right is perceived as having eight times the volume of the one on the left. Thus, when the third dimension is taken into account, the increase in consumption is exaggerated by 600 percent.

Percentages

The use of percentages to compare two or more situations or quantities is another source of illusion in statistics. A favorite of advertisers is to make claims such as "Zesty

Cola has 20 percent fewer calories" or "The price of the new Computrick computer has been reduced by 15 percent." These claims are virtually meaningless. The question is, 20 percent less than *what*, and 15 percent reduced from *what*? If the basis of the comparison or reduction is not mentioned, the claim tells us nothing. Yet such claims are often effective because they leave us with the impression that the product is in some way superior or less expensive.

Another strategy sometimes used by governments and businesses involves playing sleight-of-hand tricks with the base of the percentages. Suppose, for example, that you are a university president involved with a funding drive to increase the university's endowment. Suppose further that the endowment currently stands at $15 million and that the objective is to increase it to $20 million. To guarantee the success of the drive, you engage the services of a professional fund-raising organization. At the end of the allotted time the organization has increased the endowment to $16 million. They justify their effort by stating that, since $16 million of the $20 million has been raised, the drive was 80 percent successful ($16/20 \times 100\%$).

In fact, of course, the drive was nowhere near that successful. The objective was not to raise $20 million but only $5 million, and of that amount only $1 million has actually been raised. Thus, at best the drive was only 20 percent successful. Even this figure is probably exaggerated, though, because $1 million might have been raised without any special drive. The trick played by the fund-raising organization consisted in switching the numbers by which the percentage was to be computed.

This same trick, incidentally, was allegedly used by Joseph Stalin to justify the success of his first five-year plan.[*] Among other things, the original plan called for an increase in steel output from 4.2 million tons to 10.3 million. After five years the actual output rose to 5.9 million, whereupon Stalin announced that the plan was 57 percent successful ($5.9/10.3 \times 100\%$). The correct percentage, of course, is much less. The plan called for an increase of 6.1 million tons and the actual increase was only 1.7 million. Thus, at best, the plan was only 28 percent successful.

Similar devices have been used by employers on their unsuspecting employees. When business is bad, an employer may argue that salaries must be reduced by 20 percent. Later, when business improves, salaries will be raised by 20 percent, thus restoring them to their original level. Such an argument, of course, is fallacious. If a person earns $10 per hour and that person's salary is reduced by 20 percent, the adjusted salary is $8. If that figure is later increased by 20 percent, the final salary is $9.60. The problem, of course, stems from the fact that a different base is used for the two percentages. The fallacy committed by such arguments is a variety of equivocation. Percentages are relative terms, and they mean different things in different contexts.

A different kind of fallacy occurs when a person attempts to add percentages as if they were cardinal numbers. Suppose, for example, that a baker increases the price of a loaf of bread by 50 percent. To justify the increase the baker argues that it was necessitated by rising costs: the price of flour increased by 10 percent, the cost of labor by 20 percent,

[*]Stephen K. Campbell, *Flaws and Fallacies in Statistical Thinking* (Englewood Cliffs, N.J.: Prentice-Hall, 1974), p. 8. The original reference is to Eugene Lyons's *Workers' Paradise Lost.*

utility rates went up 10 percent, and the cost of the lease on the building increased 10 percent. This adds up to a 50 percent increase. Again, the argument is fallacious. If *everything* had increased by 20 percent, this would justify only a 20 percent increase in the price of bread. As it is, the justified increase is less than that. The fallacy committed by such arguments would probably be best classified as a case of missing the point (*ignoratio elenchi*). The arguer has failed to grasp the significance of his own premises.

Statistical variations of the suppressed evidence fallacy are also quite common. One variety consists in drawing a conclusion from a comparison of two different things or situations. For example, persons running for political office sometimes cite figures indicating that crime in the community has increased by, let us say, 20 percent during the past three or four years. What is needed, they conclude, is an all-out war on crime. But they fail to mention the fact that the population in the community has also increased by 20 percent during the same period. The number of crimes per capita, therefore, has not changed. Another example of the same fallacy is provided by the ridiculous argument that 90 percent more traffic accidents occur in clear weather than in foggy weather and that therefore it is 90 percent more dangerous to drive in clear than in foggy weather. The arguer ignores the fact that the vast percentage of vehicle miles are driven in clear weather, which accounts for the greater number of accidents.

A similar misuse of percentages is committed by businesses and corporations that, for whatever reason, want to make it appear that they have earned less profit than they actually have. The technique consists of expressing profit as a percentage of sales volume instead of as a percentage of investment. For example, during a certain year a corporation might have a total sales volume of $100 million, a total investment of $10 million, and a profit of $5 million. If profits are expressed as a percentage of investment, they amount to a hefty 50 percent; but as a percentage of sales they are only 5 percent. To appreciate the fallacy in this procedure, consider the case of the jewelry merchant who buys one piece of jewelry each morning for $9 and sells it in the evening for $10. At the end of the year the total sales volume is $3650, the total investment $9, and the total profit $365. Profits as a percentage of sales amount to only 10 percent, but as a percentage of investment they exceed 4000 percent.

EXERCISE 9.4

I. Criticize the following arguments in light of the material presented in this section:

★1. To test the algae content in a lake, a biologist took a sample of the water at one end. The algae in the sample registered 5 micrograms per liter. Therefore, the algae in the lake at that time registered 5 micrograms per liter.

2. To estimate public support for a new municipality-funded convention center, researchers surveyed 100 homeowners in one of the city's fashionable neighborhoods. They found that 89 percent of those sampled were enthusiastic about the project. Therefore, we may conclude that 89 percent of the city's residents favor the convention center.

3. A quality-control inspector for a food-processing firm needed assurance that the cans of fruit in a production run were filled to capacity. He opened every tenth box in the warehouse and removed the can in the left front corner of

each box. He found that all of these cans were filled to capacity. Therefore, it is probable that all of the cans in the production run were filled to capacity.

★4. When a random sample of 600 voters was taken on the eve of the presidential election, it was found that 51 percent of those sampled intended to vote for the Democrat and 49 percent for the Republican. Therefore, the Democrat will probably win.

5. To determine the public's attitude toward TV soap operas, 1,000 people were contacted by telephone between 8 A.M. and 5 P.M. on week days. The numbers were selected randomly from the phone directories of cities across the nation. The researchers reported that 43 percent of the respondents said that they were avid viewers. From this we may conclude that 43 percent of the public watches TV soap operas.

6. To predict the results of a U.S. Senate race in New York State, two polls were taken. One was based on a random sample of 750 voters, the other on a random sample of 1,500 voters. Since the second sample was twice as large as the first, the results of the second poll were twice as accurate as the first.

★7. In a survey conducted by the manufacturers of Ultrasheen toothpaste, 65 percent of the dentists randomly sampled preferred that brand over all others. Clearly Ultrasheen is the brand preferred by most dentists.

8. To determine the percentage of adult Americans who have never read the U.S. Constitution, surveyors put this question to a random sample of 1,500 adults. Only 13 percent gave negative answers. Therefore, since the sampling error for such a sample is 3 percent, we may conclude that no more than 16 percent of American adults have not read the Constitution.

9. To determine the percentage of patients who follow the advice of their personal physician, researchers asked 200 randomly chosen physicians to put the question to their patients. Of the 4,000 patients surveyed, 98 percent replied that they did indeed follow their doctor's advice. We may therefore conclude that at least 95 percent of the patients across the nation follow the advice of their personal physician.

★10. Janet Ryan can afford to pay no more than $15 for a birthday gift for her eight-year-old daughter. Since the average price of a toy at General Toy Company is $15, Janet can expect to find an excellent selection of toys within her price range at that store.

11. Anthony Valardi, who owns a fish market, pays $2 per pound to fishermen for silver salmon. A certain fisherman certifies that the average size of the salmon in his catch of the day is 10 pounds, and that the catch numbers 100 salmon. Mr. Valardi is therefore justified in paying the fisherman $2,000 for the whole catch.

12. Pamela intends to go shopping for a new pair of shoes. She wears size 8. Since the average size of the shoes carried by the Bon Marche is size 8, Pamela can expect to find an excellent selection of shoes in her size at that store.

★13. Tim Cassidy, who works for a construction company, is told to load a pile of rocks onto a truck. The rocks are randomly sized, and the average piece weighs 50 pounds. Thus, Tim should have no trouble loading the rocks by hand.

14. The average IQ (in the sense of mean, median, and mode) of the students in Dr. Jacob's symbolic logic class is 120. Thus, none of the students should have any trouble mastering the subject matter.

15. An insecticide manufacturer prints the following graph on the side of its spray cans:

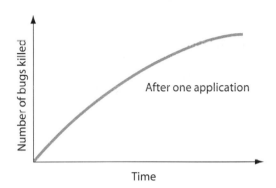

Obviously, the insecticide is highly effective at killing bugs, and it keeps working for a long time.

★16. A corporation's sales for two consecutive years are represented in a bar graph. Since the bar for the later year is twice as high as the one for the previous year, it follows that sales for the later year were double those for the previous year.

17. Forced to make cutbacks, the president of a manufacturing firm reduced certain costs as follows: advertising by 4 percent, transportation by 5 percent, materials by 2 percent, and employee benefits by 3 percent. The president thus succeeded in reducing total costs by 14 percent.

18. During a certain year, a grocery store chain had total sales of $100 million and profits of $10 million. The profits thus amounted to a modest 10 percent for that year.

★19. There were 20 percent more traffic accidents in 2005 than there were in 1980. Therefore, it was 20 percent more dangerous to drive a car in 2005 than it was in 1980.

20. An efficiency expert was hired to increase the productivity of a manufacturing firm and was given three months to accomplish the task. At the end of the period the productivity had increased from 1,500 units per week to 1,700. Since the goal was 2,000 units per week, the effort of the efficiency expert was 85 percent successful (1,700/2,000).

II. Compute the answers to the following questions.

★1. Given the following group of people together with their weights, what is the average weight in the sense of mean, median, and mode?

Number of People	Weight
2	150
4	160
3	170
1	180
1	190
1	200
1	220
2	230

2. Given the following group of people together with their salaries, what is the average salary in the sense of mean, median, and mode?

Number of People	Salary
1	$95,000
2	85,000
1	70,000
3	40,000
1	30,000
2	20,000
5	15,000

3. A small company has five employees who missed work during a certain month. The number of days missed were: 1, 1, 2, 4, 7. What is the mean number of days missed? What is the variance and standard deviation of this set of data?

★4. A day-care center cares for 10 children. Their ages are 1, 1, 2, 2, 2, 3, 3, 4, 6, 6. Construct a histogram that represents the distribution of ages. What is the mean age? What is the variance and standard deviation of these ages?

5. An instructor gave a ten-question multiple choice quiz to twelve students. The scores were 10, 10, 9, 9, 8, 8, 8, 7, 7, 7, 7, 6. What is the mean score? What is the variance and standard deviation of these scores?

III. Answer "true" or "false" to the following statements:

★1. If a sample is very large, it need not be randomly selected.

2. If a population is randomly arranged, a sample obtained by selecting every tenth member would be a random sample.

3. If a sample is randomly selected, the larger the sample is, the more closely it replicates the population.

★4. To ensure the same precision, a population of 1 million would require a much larger random sample than would a population of 100,000.

5. In general, if sample A is twice as large as sample B, then the sampling error for A is one-half that for B.

6. When a sample consists of human beings, the purpose for which the sample is taken can affect the outcome.

★7. The personal interaction between a surveyor and a respondent can affect the outcome of a survey.

8. The mean value of a set of data is the value that occurs with the greatest frequency.

9. The median value of a set of data is the middle point when the data are arranged in ascending order.

★10. The modal value of a set of data is the arithmetical average.

11. If one needed to know whether a sizable portion of a group were above or below a certain level, the most useful sense of average would be mode.

12. Data reflecting the results of a random sample conform fairly closely to the normal probability distribution.

★13. If a set of data conform to the normal probability distribution, then the mean, median, and mode have the same value.

14. The range, variance, and standard deviation are measurements of dispersion.

15. Statements about averages often present an incomplete picture without information about the dispersion.

★16. Data reflecting the size of full-grown horses would exhibit greater dispersion than data reflecting the size of full-grown dogs.

17. The visual impression made by graphs can be exaggerated by changing one of the scales while leaving the other unchanged.

18. Data reflecting a 100 percent increase in housing construction could be accurately represented by a pictogram of two houses, one twice as high as the other.

★19. If a certain quantity is increased by 10 percent and later decreased by 10 percent, the quantity is restored to what it was originally.

20. Expressing profits as a percentage of sales volume presents an honest picture of the earnings of a corporation.

9.5   Hypothetical/Scientific Reasoning

Hypothetical reasoning is most immediately applied to the production of explanations. You will recall from Chapter 1 of this book that an explanation is a kind of expression that purports to shed light on some event. Many explanations are grounded in direct observation and memory. For example, suppose that you happen to be wearing a cast on your arm. You know from direct observation that you broke your arm while playing football a week earlier. Suppose somebody asks you about the cast, and you reply, "I am wearing the cast because I broke my arm playing football." This is an explanation. Or suppose that your mathematics instructor asks you why you failed the calculus test. You reply, "I failed the test because I didn't study the night before." No hypothetical reasoning is used to produce explanations of this sort.

However, it often happens that the needed explanation cannot be produced from direct observation. Suppose that you get into your car one morning, turn the key in the ignition, and the engine cranks but fails to start. Why it fails to start is a complete mystery. After all, it started perfectly well the day before. Because it is impossible for you to peer into the inner workings of the engine to furnish the needed explanation, you begin by producing conjectures about why the car will not start. Perhaps the spark plugs are dirty, or the ignition coil is shorted, or the fuel pump is broken. Or perhaps someone sabotaged the car overnight. These conjectures are **hypotheses,** and the reasoning used to produce them is **hypothetical reasoning.** The hypotheses make up for the lack of direct observation in producing the needed explanation.

As a follow-up, you decide to remove one of the spark plugs and inspect its condition. You do so and find it covered with carbon deposits. Now you think you have the answer: The car fails to start because the spark plugs are dirty. But of course this explanation could be wrong. The correct explanation could be something else, but this is the nature of all inductive reasoning. The outcome is only probable. However, having produced this explanation, you can now convert it into an inductive argument. Suppose a friend comes up and says, "I see you ran out of gas." You reply, "No, the spark plugs are dirty, so if I replace them, the car should start." Now you are trying to prove something to your friend, and the kind of argument used is a causal inference.

Hypothetical reasoning is used by nearly all of us in our day-to-day experience. The television repairman constructs hypotheses to determine why the picture appears unclear after all the ordinary solutions have been tried without success, the motorist on the freeway or turnpike reasons hypothetically to determine why the traffic is backed up bumper-to-bumper even though it is not yet rush hour, the physician hypothesizes about the cause of a disease prior to prescribing medicine, the teacher hypothesizes about the best way to present a complicated subject in the classroom, and the prosecuting attorney suggests hypotheses to the jury in arguing about the motive for a crime. In all of these cases the evidence is not sufficient to indicate exactly what is going on, what lies behind the scene, or what approach to take, so hypotheses are constructed to make sense of the situation and to direct future action.

Hypothetical reasoning is used most explicitly in philosophical and scientific inquiry. Every scientific theory can be viewed as a hypothesis for unifying and rationalizing events in nature. The Ptolemaic and Copernican theories about the sun and planets, Dalton's atomic theory, Darwin's theory of evolution, and Einstein's theory of relativity are all hypotheses for making sense of the data of observation. The problem for the scientist is that the underlying structure of nature is hidden from view, and the data of observation by themselves are not sufficient to reveal this structure. In response, the scientist constructs hypotheses that provide ways of conceptualizing the data and that suggest specific questions to be answered through the design of controlled experiments.

Analogously, every philosophical system can be viewed as a grand hypothesis for interpreting the content of experience. Plato's theory of forms, Aristotle's theory of substance, Leibniz's monads, and Kant's theory about the mind are all hypotheses aimed at illuminating various aspects of experience. Just as the structure of nature is hidden from the scientist, the meaning of experience is hidden from the philosopher, and ordinary common sense will not provide the answer. In response, the philosopher constructs hypotheses that can be used to shed light on the content of experience and to provide suggestions for further analysis.

Whether it is applied in philosophy, science, or ordinary life, the hypothetical method involves four basic stages:

1. Occurrence of a problem
2. Formulating a hypothesis
3. Drawing implications from the hypothesis
4. Testing the implications

These four stages may be illustrated through the procedure used by a detective in solving a crime. Suppose that a woman has been murdered in her apartment. Initially, everything in the apartment is a potential clue: the empty wine glasses in the sink, the small container of cocaine on the coffee table, the automobile key found on the carpet, the strand of blonde hair removed from the couch, and so on. To introduce an element of rationality into the situation, the detective formulates a hypothesis—let us say the hypothesis that the key found on the carpet fits the murderer's car.

From this hypothesis a number of implications can be drawn. Suppose that the key is the kind that fits only late-model Cadillacs. It follows that the murderer drives a late-model Cadillac. Furthermore, if the key is the only one the murderer owns, it follows that the car may be parked nearby. A third implication is that the murderer's name may be on record at the local Cadillac dealership. To test these implications, the detective conducts a search of the streets in the vicinity and contacts the local Cadillac dealer for the names of recent buyers.

This example illustrates three additional points about hypotheses. The first is that a hypothesis is not *derived* from the evidence to which it pertains but rather is *added* to the evidence by the investigator. A hypothesis is a free creation of the mind used to structure the evidence and unveil the pattern that lies beneath the surface. It may be that the detective's hypothesis is completely false. Perhaps the key fits a car that was lent to the victim for the weekend. Any number of other possibilities are conceivable.

The second point is that a hypothesis directs the search for evidence. Without a hypothesis for guidance, all facts are equally relevant. The mineral content of moon rocks and the temperature in the Sahara would be as relevant as the cars parked on the street outside the apartment. The hypothesis tells the investigator what to look for and what to ignore.

The third point concerns the proof of hypotheses. Let us suppose that the detective finds a late-model Cadillac parked outside the apartment building and that the key fits the ignition. Such a discovery might lend credibility to the hypothesis, but it would not in any sense prove it. Concluding that a hypothesis is proven true by the discovery that one of its implications is true amounts to committing the fallacy of affirming the consequent (see Section 6.6). Where H stands for a hypothesis and I for an implication, such an argument has the invalid form

If H, then I

$$\frac{I}{H}$$

Let us suppose, on the other hand, that the murderer turns himself or herself in to the police and that the only car the murderer owns or drives is a Ford. Such a fact would prove the hypothesis false because it would falsify the implication that the murderer drives a Cadillac. The argument form involved in such an inference is *modus tollens*:

$$
\begin{array}{l}
\text{If } H, \text{ then } I \\
\text{not } I \\
\hline
\text{not } H
\end{array}
$$

For the hypothesis to be proved true, the car that the key fits would have to be found and the owner would have to confess to the crime.

Some of the clearest illustrations of the hypothetical method of reasoning can be found in scientific discoveries. Four examples are the discovery of radium by Pierre and Marie Curie; the discovery of the planet Neptune by Adams, Leverrier, and Galle; the discovery of atmospheric pressure by Torricelli; and Pasteur's research concerning the spontaneous generation of life. Following is a consideration of each of these examples with special attention to the four stages of hypothetical inquiry.

Radium

In 1896 the French physicist Henri Becquerel discovered that crystals containing uranium had the power to expose photographic plates. He found that when these crystals were placed on top of an unexposed plate and left for a certain time, dark blotches appeared in their place when the plate was developed. Becquerel concluded that the crystals emitted certain rays that penetrated the opaque covering of the plates and reacted with the photosensitive material underneath. Further investigation showed that these rays were not as strong as x-rays, which could be used to photograph bone structure, and so Becquerel's interest in them lapsed.

A year later Marie Curie revived the question when she adopted it as the topic of her doctoral research at the University of Paris. In place of Becquerel's photographic plates she substituted an electrometer, which was better suited to measuring the intensity of the rays, and she proceeded to conduct various experiments with pure uranium to determine the source of the rays that the metal emitted. When none of these experiments proved fruitful, she shifted her attention to the question of whether other metals or minerals emitted the same kind of rays as uranium. She tested hundreds of metals, compounds, and ores, but the only one that proved interesting was pitchblende, a certain ore of uranium. Because pitchblende contained uranium, she anticipated that it would emit rays; but because it also contained a number of impurities, she expected the rays to be weaker than they were for pure uranium. Instead, they turned out to be stronger. This problem caught Madame Curie's attention and provided the focus for her research in the months ahead.

In response to the problem, Madame Curie formulated the hypothesis that the impurities in the pitchblende somehow triggered the uranium to increase the emission of rays. One implication of this hypothesis was that mixing pure uranium with the kinds of impurities found in pitchblende would cause an increase in the emission of rays. To test this implication, Curie diluted pure uranium with various elements and measured the strength of the rays. The results were always the same: the emissions were always less than they were for pure uranium. Because of these results, she abandoned the hypothesis.

Madame Curie then formulated a second hypothesis: The intensified emissions were caused directly by some impurity in the pitchblende. The only other element besides uranium that was known to emit rays, however, was thorium, and the pitchblende that had been tested contained no thorium. Thus, an immediate implication of the hypothesis was that the increased rays were caused by an unknown element. A second implication was that this element could be separated from the pitchblende through a process of refinement. At this point Marie Curie was joined by her husband, Pierre, and they began a combined effort to isolate the unknown element.

Because the element was present in only the most minute quantities, separating a measurable amount from the other impurities required a great deal of effort. The Curies began by grinding up some pitchblende and dissolving it in acid. Finally, after numerous stages of filtration and the addition of other chemicals, they obtained a pinch of white powder. By weight, this material was found to be 900 times more radioactive than pure uranium, but since the primary component in the powder was barium, the unknown element still had not been isolated.

Rather than continue with additional stages of refinement, the Curies decided to attempt a spectrographic analysis of the powder. Such analysis, they hoped, would reveal the characteristic spectrum line of the unknown element. This proposal, which amounted to a third implication of the hypothesis, was put to the test. When the powder was burned in a spectrometer, a line appeared in the ultraviolet range that was different from that for any other element. From the combined evidence of the spectrum line and the intense radiation the Curies announced in 1898 the discovery of a new element, which they called radium. After more processing and refinement, enough of the material was finally obtained to determine the atomic weight.

Neptune

In 1781 the planet Uranus was discovered by William Herschel, but the production of a table giving the motion of the new planet had to wait until the gravitational interaction between Uranus, Jupiter, and Saturn had been worked out mathematically. The latter task was accomplished by Pierre Laplace in his *Mechanique Celeste*, and in 1820 Alexis Bouvard used this work to construct tables for all three planets. These tables predicted the orbital motions of Jupiter and Saturn very accurately, but within a few years Uranus was found to have deviated from its predicted path. A problem thus emerged: Why did the tables work for Jupiter and Saturn but not for Uranus?

In response to this problem a number of astronomers entertained the hypothesis that an eighth planet existed beyond the orbit of Uranus and that the gravitational interaction between these two planets caused Uranus to deviate from its predicted position. It was not until 1843, however, that John Couch Adams, a recent graduate of Cambridge, undertook the task of working out the mathematical implications of this hypothesis. After two years' work Adams produced a table of motions and orbital elements that predicted the location of the hypothetical planet, and his computations were so accurate that if anyone with a telescope had bothered to look, they would have found the new planet within two degrees of its predicted position. Unfortunately, no one looked for it.

At about the same time that Adams completed his work on the problem, the French astronomer U. J. J. Leverrier, working independently of Adams, reported a similar set of motions and orbital elements to the French Academy of Science. The close agreement between Adams's and Leverrier's predictions prompted a search for the planet; but because a rather broad section of sky was swept, the planet was missed.

Finally, Leverrier sent a copy of his figures to Johann Galle at the Berlin Observatory, where a set of star charts was being prepared. It was suggested that the region corresponding to Leverrier's computations be observed and the results matched against the charts. This was done, and a small starlike object was found that was not on the charts. The next night the same object was sighted, and it was found to have moved. The new planet was thus identified. It was named Neptune after most astronomers outside France objected to the original suggestion that it be called Leverrier.

Atmospheric Pressure

The principle that nature abhors a vacuum, originated by Aristotle, was used for centuries to explain the fact that in emptying a keg of wine an opening had to be made at the top as well as at the bottom. Because nature would not allow a vacuum to be created inside the keg, the wine would not drain from the bottom until air was let in at the top. It was thought that this principle held universally for all applications involving a vacuum, but in the sixteenth century it was found that suction pumps used to drain water from mine shafts would not work if the pump was situated over 30 feet above the water level. This caused people to wonder whether nature's abhorrence of a vacuum, while holding true for kegs of wine, had certain limits for pumps.

In 1630 Giovanni Baliani of Genoa discovered a similar limitation in regard to siphons. When he attempted to siphon water from a reservoir over a 60-foot hill, he found that the siphon would not work. When the siphon was completely filled with water and the stoppers were removed from both ends, a vacuum seemed to be created in the uppermost parts of the pipe.

These findings were communicated to Gasparo Berti in Rome, who, around 1641, attempted to determine more scientifically whether a vacuum could actually be created. Berti designed an apparatus consisting of a spherical glass vessel attached to a pipe about 40 feet long. The apparatus was affixed upright to the side of a tower, and after the valve at the lower end of the pipe was closed, water was poured through the upper opening in the glass vessel. When both the pipe and the glass vessel were completely filled, the opening in the vessel was sealed and the valve at the lower end of the pipe was opened. Immediately water rushed from the bottom of the pipe, creating a vacuum in the glass vessel. This experiment crystallized a problem that had been developing for a number of years: If nature abhorred a vacuum, how did it happen that it tolerated the creation of one in the glass vessel? Furthermore, why did it happen, when the experiment was repeated, that the water always descended to the same level in the pipe?

The results of Berti's experiment were communicated to Evangelista Torricelli in Florence, who was at that time Galileo's assistant. Galileo himself thought that the water was supported in the pipe by the power of the vacuum, but after Galileo's death in 1642, Torricelli formulated his own hypothesis: The water was supported in the pipe by the pressure of the atmosphere. Torricelli reasoned that we live "at the bottom of an ocean of air" and that the pressure of the air pushing against the bottom of the pipe supported the water at a certain height in the pipe. A point of equilibrium was reached, he thought, when the weight of the water remaining in the pipe equalled the weight of the air pushing down from above.

From this hypothesis Torricelli derived several implications. One was that the pressure of the atmosphere would support a column of mercury about 29 inches high in a tube sealed at the top. This followed from the fact that the atmosphere supports a column of water 33 feet high, that mercury is 13.6 times as dense as water, and that $33/13.6 \times 12$ inches = 29 inches. A second implication was that such a tube filled with mercury could be used to measure fluctuations in atmospheric pressure. This second implication won Torricelli the credit for formulating the theory of the barometer. Finally, Torricelli reasoned that if such a device were conveyed to a place where the air was more rarefied, such as on a mountaintop, the column of mercury would descend.

The first of these implications was tested by Torricelli's associate, Vincenzo Viviani. Viviani obtained a 4-foot section of glass tube sealed at one end, enough mercury to completely fill it, and a dish to hold more mercury. After pouring the mercury into the tube Viviani placed his thumb over the open end, inverted the tube, and placed the open end in the dish of mercury. After he released his thumb he watched the column of mercury descend to about 29 inches above the level of mercury in the dish. Thus was created the first barometer. Its successful use in measuring atmospheric pressure came later.

The test of Torricelli's third implication was taken up in 1647 by the French philosopher Blaise Pascal. Having received word of Torricelli's experiments with the barometer, Pascal constructed one for himself. He readily became convinced of the correctness of Torricelli's hypothesis, and to demonstrate its correctness in opposition to the vacuum principle, he requested that his brother-in-law, F. Perier, convey a barometer to the top of the Puy de Dôme, one of the highest mountains in Auvergne. A year later Perier was able to fulfill this request. He began the experiment by setting up two barometers in the monastery at the foot of the mountain. After noting that both columns of mercury rose to an identical height, he disassembled one of the barometers and instructed one of the friars to check the mercury level in the other throughout the day. Then Perier, accompanied by a group of witnesses, set off up the mountain with the other barometer. Upon reaching the summit, he assembled the second barometer and discovered to the amazement of all that the mercury level was more than 3 inches lower than it had been at the foot of the mountain. As a double check the barometer was taken apart and reassembled at five different spots on the summit. Each time the results were the same.

At the midpoint of his descent Perier reassembled the barometer once again. He found that the mercury level was about midway between where it was at the bottom and at the top of the mountain. Finally, upon returning to the monastery, the friar who had been watching the barometer there was questioned about what he had observed. He reported that the mercury level had not changed since early that morning when the group had departed. Pascal announced the results of this experiment to the educated world, and the announcement succeeded in abolishing the principle that nature abhors a vacuum.

Spontaneous Generation

The theory of spontaneous generation holds that living beings arise spontaneously from lifeless matter. The roots of the theory extend into ancient times. Aristotle held that worms, the larvae of bees and wasps, ticks, fireflies, and other insects developed continually from the morning dew and from dry wood and hair. He also held that crabs and various molluscs developed from moist soil and decaying slime. Extensions of this theory prevailed throughout the Middle Ages and well into modern times. In the seventeenth century it was widely held that frogs were produced from the slime of marshes and eels from river water, and the physician Van Helmont thought that mice were produced from the action of human sweat on kernels of wheat. All one needed to do, according to Van Helmont, was toss a dirty shirt into a container of wheat, and in 21 days the container would be teeming with mice. Even Descartes and Newton accepted the theory of spontaneous generation. Descartes held that various plants and insects originated in moist earth exposed to sunlight, and Newton thought that plants were produced from emanations from the tails of comets.

The first systematic effort to abolish the belief in spontaneous generation was made by the Italian physician Francesco Redi. In response to the commonly held idea that worms were spontaneously generated in rotting meat, Redi hypothesized that the worms were caused by flies. An immediate implication was that if flies were kept away from the meat, the worms would not develop. To test this hypothesis Redi cut up a piece of meat and put part of it in sealed glass flasks and the other part in flasks open to the air. Flies were attracted to the open flasks, and in a short time worms appeared; but no worms developed in the flasks that were sealed.

When Redi published his findings in 1668, they had an immediate impact on the theory of spontaneous generation. Within a few years, though, the microscope came into common use, and it was discovered that even though meat sealed in glass containers produced no worms, it did produce countless microorganisms. The theory of spontaneous generation was thus reawakened on the microbial level.

By the middle of the nineteenth century the theory had received considerable refinement. It was thought that spontaneous generation resulted from the direct action of oxygen on lifeless organic nutrients. Oxygen was thought to be essential to the process because the technique of canning fruits and vegetables had come into practice, and it was known that boiling fruits and vegetables and sealing them in the absence of oxygen would cause them to be preserved. If they were left exposed to the air, however, microbes would develop in a short time.

One of the defenders of spontaneous generation at that time was the Englishman John Needham, an amateur biologist. Needham conducted an experiment in which flagons containing oxygen and a vegetable solution were buried in hot coals. The coals would have been expected to kill any life in the solution, but several days later the flagons were opened and the contents were found to be alive with microbes. Needham concluded that the oxygen acting alone on the nutrient solution caused the generation of the microbes. In response to this experiment, Lazzaro Spallanzani, an Italian physiologist, conducted a similar experiment. To ensure that the nutrient solution was lifeless he boiled it for an hour. Later no microbes could be found. To this Needham objected that in boiling the solution for a full hour Spallanzani had destroyed its "vegetative force." In addition, Needham argued, he had polluted the small amount of oxygen in the containers by the fumes and heat. Thus, it was no wonder that microbes were not spontaneously generated.

To settle the issue once and for all, the French Academy of Science offered a prize for an experimental endeavor that would shed light on the question of spontaneous generation. This challenge succeeded in drawing Louis Pasteur into the controversy. Spontaneous generation presented a special problem for Pasteur because of his previous work with fermentation. He had discovered that fermentations, such as those involved in the production of wine and beer, required yeast; and yeast, as he also discovered, was a living organism. In view of these findings Pasteur adopted the hypothesis that life comes only from life. An immediate implication was that for life forms to develop in a sterile nutrient solution, they must first be introduced into the solution from the outside.

It was well known that life forms did indeed develop in sterile nutrient solutions exposed to the air. To account for this Pasteur adopted the second hypothesis that life forms are carried by dust particles in the air. To test this second hypothesis Pasteur took a wad of cotton and drew air through it, trapping dust particles in the fibers. Then he washed the cotton in a mixture of alcohol and examined drops of the fluid under a microscope. He discovered microbes in the fluid.

Returning to his first hypothesis, Pasteur prepared a nutrient solution and boiled it in a narrow-necked flask. As the solution boiled, the air in the neck of the flask was forced out by water vapor, and as it cooled the water vapor was slowly replaced by sterilized air drawn through a heated platinum tube. The neck of the flask was then closed off with a flame and blowpipe. The contents of the flask thus consisted of a sterilized nutrient solution and unpolluted sterilized air—all that was supposedly needed for the production of life. With the passage of time, however, no life developed in the flask. This experiment posed a serious threat to the theory of spontaneous generation.

Pasteur now posed the hypothesis that sterile nutrient solutions exposed to the air normally developed life forms precisely because these forms were deposited by dust particles. To test this third hypothesis Pasteur reopened the flask containing the nutrient solution, and, using a special arrangement of tubes that ensured that only sterilized air would contact the solution, he deposited a piece of cotton in which dust particles had been trapped. The flask was then resealed, and in due course microbes developed in the solution. This experiment proved not only that dust particles were responsible for the life but that the "vegetative force" of the nutrient solution had not been destroyed by boiling, as Needham was prone to claim.

Pasteur anticipated one further objection from the proponents of spontaneous generation: Perhaps the capacity of oxygen to generate life was destroyed by drawing it through a heated tube. To dispel any such notions Pasteur devised yet another experiment. He boiled a nutrient solution in a flask with a long, narrow gooseneck. As the solution boiled, the air was forced out, and as it cooled, the air returned very slowly through the long neck, trapping the dust particles on the moist inside surface. No microbes developed in the solution. Then, after a prolonged wait, Pasteur sealed the flask and shook it vigorously, dislodging the particles that had settled in the neck. In a short time the solution was alive with microbes.

When Pasteur reported these experiments to the Academy of Science in 1860, he was awarded the prize that had been offered a year earlier. The experiments dealt a mortal blow to the theory of spontaneous generation, and although the theory was not abandoned immediately, by 1900 it had very little support.

The Proof of Hypotheses

The four instances of hypothetical reasoning in science that we have investigated illustrate the use of two different kinds of hypotheses. The hypotheses involved in the discovery of Neptune and radium are sometimes called **empirical hypotheses,** and those relating to atmospheric pressure and spontaneous generation are sometimes called **theoretical hypotheses.** Empirical hypotheses concern the production of some thing or the occurrence of some event that can be observed. When radium had finally been obtained as a pure metal it was something that could be seen directly, and when Neptune was finally sighted through the telescope, it, too, had been observed. Theoretical hypotheses, on the other hand, concern how something should be conceptualized. When Galileo observed the water level rising in a suction pump, he conceived it as being *sucked* up by the vacuum. When Torricelli observed it, however, he conceived it as being *pushed* up by the atmosphere. Similarly, when Needham observed life emerging in a sterile nutrient solution, he conceived it as being spontaneously generated by the action of oxygen. But when Pasteur observed it, he conceived it as being implanted there by dust particles in the air.

The distinction between empirical and theoretical hypotheses has certain difficulties, which we will turn to shortly, but it sheds some light on the problem of the verification or confirmation of hypotheses. Empirical hypotheses are for all practical purposes *proved* when the thing or event hypothesized is observed. Today practically all of us would agree that the hypotheses relating to radium and Neptune have been established. Theoretical hypotheses, on the other hand, are never proved but are only *confirmed* to varying degrees. The greater the number of implications that are found to be correct, the more certain we can be of the hypothesis. If an implication is found to be incorrect, however, a theoretical hypothesis can be *disproved*. For example, if it should happen some day that life is produced in a test tube from inorganic materials, Pasteur's hypothesis that life comes only from life might be considered to be disproved.

The problem with the distinction between empirical and theoretical hypotheses is that observation is theory-dependent. Consider, for example, a man and a woman watching a sunrise. The man happens to believe that the sun travels around the earth, as Ptolemy held, and the woman that the earth travels around the sun, as Copernicus and Galileo contended. As the sun rises, the man thinks that he sees the sun moving upward, while the woman thinks she sees the earth turning. The point is that all of us have a tendency to see what we think is out there to be seen. As a result, it is sometimes difficult to say when something has or has not been observed.

In regard to the discovery of Neptune, the unknown planet was observed two times in 1795 by J. J. Lalande, fifty-one years before it was "discovered" by Adams, Leverrier, and Galle. Lalande noted that his observations of the position of the small starlike object were discordant, so he rejected one as erroneous. But he thought he was observing a *star*, so he received no credit for discovering a *planet*. Analogous remarks extend to Galle's observations of the *planet* Neptune in 1846. If Leverrier's computations had been erroneous, Galle might have seen what was really a comet. Thus, if we can never be sure that we really see what we think we see, is it ever possible for a hypothesis to be actually proved? Perhaps it is better to interpret the proof of empirical hypotheses as a high degree of confirmation.

Conversely, with theoretical hypotheses, would we want to say that Torricelli's hypothesis relating to atmospheric pressure has *not* been proved? Granted, we cannot observe atmospheric pressure directly, but might we not say that we observe it *instrumentally*? If barometers can be regarded as extensions of our sense organs, Torricelli's hypothesis has been proved. Another example is provided by Copernicus's hypothesis that the earth and planets move around the sun, instead of the sun and planets around the earth, as Ptolemy hypothesized. Can we consider this theoretical hypothesis to be proved? If a motion picture camera were sent outside the solar system and pictures were taken supporting the Copernican hypothesis, would we say that these pictures constituted proof? We probably would. Thus, while the distinction between theoretical and empirical hypotheses is useful, it is more a distinction in degree than in kind.

The Tentative Acceptance of Hypotheses

A certain amount of time is required for a hypothesis to be proved or disproved. The hypotheses relating to the discovery of radium and Neptune required more than a year to prove. Theoretical hypotheses in science often take much longer, and theoretical hypotheses in philosophy may never be confirmed to the satisfaction of the majority of philosophers. During the period that intervenes between the proposal of a hypothesis and its proof, confirmation, or disproof, the question arises as to its tentative acceptability. Four criteria that bear upon this question are (1) adequacy, (2) internal coherence, (3) external consistency, and (4) fruitfulness.

A hypothesis is **adequate** to the extent that it fits the facts it is intended to unify or explain. A hypothesis is said to "fit" the facts when each fact can be interpreted as an instance of some idea or term in the hypothesis. For example, before the Neptune hypothesis was confirmed, every fluctuation in the position of Uranus could be interpreted as an instance of gravitational interaction with an unknown planet. Similarly, before Torricelli's hypothesis was confirmed, the fact that water would rise only 30 feet in suction pumps and siphons could be interpreted as an instance of equilibrium between the pressure of the water and the pressure of the atmosphere.

A hypothesis is inadequate to the extent that facts exist that the hypothesis cannot account for. The principle that nature abhors a vacuum was inadequate to explain the fact that water would rise no more than 30 feet in suction pumps and siphons. Nothing in the hypothesis could account for this fact. Similarly, Needham's hypothesis that life is generated by the direct action of oxygen on nutrient solutions was inadequate to account for the fact that life would not develop in Pasteur's flask containing a sterilized nutrient solution and sterilized oxygen.

In scientific hypotheses a second kind of adequacy is the *accuracy* with which a hypothesis accounts for the data. If one hypothesis accounts for a set of data with greater accuracy than another, then that hypothesis is more adequate than the other. For example, Kepler's hypothesis that the orbits of the planets were ellipses rather than circles, as Copernicus had hypothesized, accounted for the position of the planets with greater accuracy than the Copernican hypothesis. Similarly, Einstein's theory of relativity accounted for the precise time of certain eclipses with greater accuracy than Newton's theory. For these reasons Kepler's and Einstein's theories were more adequate than the competing theories.

A hypothesis is **internally coherent** to the extent that its component ideas are rationally interconnected. The purpose of a hypothesis is to unify and interconnect a set of data and by so doing to *explain* the data. Obviously, if the hypothesis itself is not internally connected, there is no way that it can interconnect the data. After the mathematical details of the Neptune hypothesis had been worked out by Adams and Leverrier, it exhibited a great deal of internal coherence. The hypothesis showed how all the fluctuations in the position of Uranus could be rationally linked in terms of the gravitational interaction of an eighth planet. Similarly, Torricelli's hypothesis showed how the various fluid levels could be rationally interconnected in terms of the equilibrium of pressures. Internal coherence is responsible for the features of elegance and simplicity that often attract scientists to a hypothesis.

An example of incoherence in science is provided by the theoretical interpretation of light, electricity, and magnetism that prevailed during the first half of the nineteenth century. During that period each of these phenomena was understood separately, but the interconnections between them were unknown. Toward the end of the century the English physicist James Clerk Maxwell showed how these three phenomena were interconnected in terms of his theory of the electromagnetic field. Maxwell's theory was thus more coherent than the ones that preceded it.

Similarly, in philosophy, Spinoza's metaphysical theory is more internally coherent than Descartes's. Descartes postulated the existence of two kinds of substance to account for the data of experience. He introduced extended, material substance to explain the data of the visible world, and nonextended, immaterial substance to explain the phenomena of the invisible world, including the existence and activity of the human soul. But Descartes failed to show how the two kinds of substance were interconnected. In the wake of this disconnection there arose the famous mind-body problem, according to which no account could be given of how the human body acted on the mind through the process of sensation or how the mind acted on the body through the exercise of free choice. Spinoza, on the other hand, postulated only one substance to account for everything. Spinoza's theory is thus more internally coherent than Descartes's.

A hypothesis is **externally consistent** when it does not disagree with other, well-confirmed hypotheses. Adams's and Leverrier's hypothesis of an eighth planet was perfectly consistent with the nineteenth-century theory of the solar system, and it was rendered even more attractive by the fact that the seventh planet, Uranus, had been discovered only a few years earlier. Similarly, Marie Curie's hypothesis of the existence of a new element was consistent with Mendeleev's periodic table and with the general hypothesis that elements could emit penetrating rays. In 1890 Mendeleev's table had certain gaps that were expected to be filled in by the discovery of new elements, and two ray-emitting elements, thorium and uranium, had already been discovered.

The fact that a hypothesis is inconsistent with other, well-confirmed hypotheses does not, however, immediately condemn it to obscurity. It often happens that a new hypothesis arises in the face of another, well-confirmed hypothesis and that the two hypotheses compete for acceptance in the future. Which hypothesis will win is determined by an appeal to the other three criteria. For example, Torricelli's hypothesis was inconsistent with the ancient hypothesis that nature abhors a vacuum, and Pasteur's hypothesis was inconsistent with the equally ancient hypothesis of spontaneous generation. In the end, the newer hypotheses won out because they were more adequate, coherent, or fruitful than their competitors. For the same reason the Copernican hypothesis eventually triumphed over the Ptolemaic, the theory of oxidation won out over the old phlogiston theory, and Einstein's theory of relativity won out over Newton's theory.

A hypothesis is **fruitful** to the extent that it suggests new ideas for future analysis and confirmation. Torricelli's hypothesis suggested the design of an instrument for measuring fluctuations in the pressure of the atmosphere. Similarly, Pasteur's hypothesis suggested changes in the procedures used to maintain sterile conditions in hospitals. After these changes were implemented, the death rate from surgical operations decreased dramatically. The procedure of pasteurization, used to preserve milk, was another outgrowth of the hypothesis that life comes only from life.

Newton's theory of universal gravitation is an example of a hypothesis that proved especially fruitful. It was originated to solve the problem of falling bodies, but it also explained such things as the ebb and flow of the tides, the orbital motion of the moon and planets, and the fluctuations in planetary motion caused by a planet's interaction with other planets. Einstein's theory of relativity is another example. It was originated to account for certain features of Maxwell's theory of electricity and magnetism, but it succeeded, forty years later, in ushering in the atomic age.

The factors of coherence and fruitfulness together account for the overall rationality and explanatory power of a hypothesis. Suppose, for example, that someone formulated the hypothesis that the water level in suction devices is maintained by the action of demons instead of by atmospheric pressure. Such a hypothesis would be neither coherent nor fruitful. It would not be coherent because it would not explain why the maximum water level in these devices is consistently about 30 feet, why the mercury level in barometers is much less, and why the mercury level in a barometer decreases when the instrument is carried to the top of a mountain. Do the demons decide to maintain these levels by free choice or according to some plan? Because there is no answer to this question, the hypothesis exhibits internal disconnectedness, which leaves it open to the charge of being irrational. As for the fourth criterion, the demon hypothesis is unfruitful because it suggests no new ideas that experimenters can put to the test. The hypothesis that nature abhors a vacuum is hardly any more fruitful, which accounts in part for why it was so suddenly abandoned in favor of Torricelli's hypothesis—it simply did not lead anywhere.

In summary, for any hypothesis to receive tentative acceptance it must cover the facts it is intended to interpret and it must rationally interconnect these facts—in other words, it must be adequate and coherent. After that, it helps if the hypothesis does not conflict with other, well-confirmed hypotheses. Finally, it is important that a hypothesis capture the imagination of the community to which it is posed. This it does by being fruitful—by suggesting interesting ideas and experiments to which members of the community can direct their attention in the years ahead.

EXERCISE 9.5

I. For each of the following situations, invent at least three hypotheses aimed at explaining what went wrong or at solving the problem. Then, for each hypothesis, describe one or more experiments or inquiries that would confirm or disconfirm the hypothesis.

1. Someone you have been dating has a birthday coming up, so you call a florist and order flowers for the occasion. Two days later the person is cold and distant.

2. After settling in a new location you buy some seeds for a flower garden. When the flowers come up, they are stunted and of poor quality.

3. After mailing your paycheck to the bank, you write a check to pay your rent. The rent check bounces.

4. On a windy day you pick up the phone to call a friend, but you find that the line is dead. You live in a house and share phone expenses with a housemate.

5. After driving for miles on a dusty road, you park your car near the bank of a river and take a hike through the woods. Soon you become lost. In one direction you see a small stream, and in the other, a trail.

6. A close friend calls you on the phone and confides a personal secret. That night you write the secret in your diary. A few days later your friend is furious with you because the friend overheard someone on campus talking about the secret.

7. On a rainy evening you return to your ground-floor apartment and discover that you have been burglarized. You can't believe it, because you are certain you locked the door when you went out. You share the apartment with a roommate.

8. You are a philosophy professor at a university, and while reading a set of term papers you discover that two of them are identical. Those two papers are also extremely well written.

9. You are a manager of a department store, and, although business has been brisk lately, your chief accountant informs you that the store is losing money.

10. A short time before final exams you lose your class notes. You recall having seen them four days ago. Use your own personal activities and movements during the past four days as the basis for formulating your hypotheses as to the whereabouts of the notes.

II. For the four scientific discoveries presented in this section identify the problem, the hypotheses that were formulated, the implications that were drawn, and the test procedure that was used.

III. The following article was written by a physician in the emergency room of a hospital.* The article describes the difficulty that the author and other physicians faced in diagnosing the nature of a patient's illness. Identify the problem, the hypotheses suggested, the implications drawn, and the tests conducted to confirm or disconfirm the hypotheses. You should be able to find fifteen hypotheses. Try to distinguish the tests and observations made to narrow down the problem from the tests and observations made to confirm or disconfirm the hypotheses.

---

*Discover magazine, October 1994, pp. 28–31. © 1994 The Walt Disney Co., reprinted with permission of the author.

An Unreasonable Sleep
by Elisabeth Rosenthal

The emergency room was unusually quiet early that Thursday morning, and rounds promised to be brief. "You have only one patient," said the doctor I was relieving. "He's a real winner, though. He's basically unresponsive, but I can't find anything wrong." "Well, you know," I said dryly, "when a patient's in a coma, there is usually a problem." "Look, I know it sounds weird, but all the tests are coming back normal. I'm beginning to think the guy's faking. Well, not faking exactly. But I'm beginning to think the problem's psychiatric. Hey, if you find something else, more power to you—you're a better doc than I am." And with that, he was out the door.

When I stopped by Mr. Gerard's room, I found a handsome blond man in his early thirties lying motionless in bed. His eyes were closed and perfectly still; his arms lay crooked at his sides. When I pulled down his sheet I was slightly surprised to find his feet crossed at the ankles. Maybe the nurse's aide had left him that way when she had put on his hospital gown.

He looked so perfectly peaceful, so perfectly asleep, that I suspected this coma business was some kind of practical joke. I tapped his arm and whispered to try to wake him up.

"Mr. Gerard."

No stirring.

"Mr. Gerard!"—this time with a little nudge.

No reply.

"MR. GERARD!!" I took both his shoulders and shook as hard as I could. But again, no response. When I let go of his torso, he slumped back on the pillow. The only movement I could detect was the perfectly rhythmic rise and fall of his chest 12 times a minute, the most normal of normal respiratory rates.

The chart at the foot of the bed recorded 14 hours of the most stable vital signs an ER doctor could ever hope to see. And my brief neurological exam suggested that every major brain pathway was intact: With his eyelids propped open, his pupils reacted normally to light. When I tapped on his knees and tickled his feet, his reflexes performed on cue. A man so profoundly unresponsive, with nothing obviously wrong? I retreated to the nurses' station to pore over his chart.

Mr. Gerard had been brought in the previous evening by an ambulance his sister had summoned. He was a well-respected estate lawyer in a large city halfway across the country, she said, and had just made partner two years before. He had no real medical problems and, as far as she knew, had never seen a psychiatrist or had any mental illness. She was fairly certain that he didn't drink or take drugs. But she confessed to the social worker that she and her brother had become close only in the past year, during his tumultuous breakup with a longtime girlfriend; before that they had done little more than exchange birthday cards.

Mr. Gerard had finished a major project the week before and had called her Friday night saying he had no plans for the Fourth of July and might he join her family for the week? He seemed fine for the first three days of his visit, even organizing a picnic in the park and a trip to a ballgame, she said. But on Wednesday he seemed depressed, and he retired to his room early because he didn't feel well. On Thursday he hadn't emerged by the time she left for work. When she got home at 6 P.M. the door was still closed, so she went in and found him, as she put it, "looking dead." She called an ambulance and frantically searched her brother's suitcase for clues. All she found were books and clothes—no pill bottles, liquor, or drug paraphernalia.

En route to the ER, Mr. Gerard had received the standard treatment for patients who are unresponsive. First the paramedics gave him a shot of Narcan—which reverses the effects of heroin and other narcotics by blocking opiate receptors in the brain. Then they gave him a shot of dextrose, which brings around patients who are comatose because of low blood sugar. But neither had helped. The ER staff was faced with a man who appeared absolutely healthy yet profoundly unresponsive.

The ER team
got nowhere.

There are only a handful of reasons for a coma in a young person: a drug overdose or poisoning, a massive hemorrhage in the head because of trauma or a premature stroke, a seizure, a metabolic abnormality, a brain tumor or abscess, or a rare overwhelming infection. By the time I arrived, the night staff had methodically tested Mr. Gerard and found no trace of these conditions.

Although overdoses are the most common cause of comas in young people, they almost always produce some other symptoms. With heroin, the pupils shrink. With Valium, the respiratory rate dips slightly. With many antidepressants, the heart races. But aside from Mr. Gerard's absolute failure to respond to voices or even pain, his exam showed nothing wrong.

Just to be sure, the night doctors had put a tube down his throat and pumped out his stomach looking for pills. They had drawn blood to test for poisons and drugs. They had sent Mr. Gerard up for an emergency CT scan of the brain to rule out hemorrhage or a stroke. Still, they had come up empty-handed. At 5 A.M. they called a neurologist to see if she had any ideas.

Dr. Green wasn't too pleased about being dragged out of bed, and she was immediately suspicious of this motionless body with an apparently normal neurological exam. She began a series of standard neurological tests designed to elicit signs of consciousness.

Patient not
responsive to pain.

She started by shaking his shoulders but quickly adopted more aggressive tactics to see if she could get him to react. She pressed the handle of her reflex hammer against his toenail with all her might. No response. She then pushed down hard on his breastbone. This move, the so-called sternal rub, is so unpleasant that it evokes at least a grimace from patients in pretty deep comas. But there was not a twitch from Mr. Gerard.

She even went so far as to squirt ice water into his ear, a technique neurologists use to find out if the brainstem—the primitive region of the brain that regulates basic brain function—is working. If it is intact, the eyes jiggle reflexively. And if the patient is conscious, he becomes dizzy and sick to his stomach. Dr. Green saw Mr. Gerard's eyes jiggle. And she thought she saw him begin to retch. Her hunch was that he was awake.

She then tried to find out whether Mr. Gerard was capable of voluntary movement. Without giving any warning, she sprinkled ice water on his face. He seemed to wince slightly and sink back into his trance. She resorted to a neurologist's ploy to distinguish the conscious from the comatose: she took his limp arm by the hand and raised it a foot above his face, then let it drop. Patients in true comas have no choice but to smack themselves, hard, in the face or chest. Every time she tried this, however, Mr. Gerard's hand somehow veered right and glanced off his cheek.

Based on her observations and Mr. Gerard's normal CT scan, Dr. Green pronounced that there was nothing neurologically wrong with the patient. Her note concluded: "Catatonia, of psychiatric origin. No evidence of neurological dysfunction."

I agreed with her, but I had to admit the diagnosis made me nervous. True, catatonia can befall patients with psychiatric illnesses, producing movements that are frenzied, bizarre, or slowed to the point of complete stupor. And if left untreated, the stupor can be deadly because the patient cannot eat or drink. But catatonia in someone with no previous psychiatric history was extremely rare—yet what else could explain this condition?

I called the psychiatrist at the mental hospital to which we would refer Mr. Gerard, described the case, and tentatively suggested that he be admitted. The doctor, as I suspected, wouldn't readily agree.

"I don't know if we can take him," he began, and then he proceeded to echo my own worst fears. "Are you sure he's not an overdose? Maybe he's taken something weird that's not on our drug screen. Can you guarantee he's not seizing? You know not all seizures involve obvious twitching. Will you write on the record that you're positive he hasn't had a stroke? They don't always show up on the scan right away."

"Look, I can't promise you anything right now—come see him and we'll talk. But it would be weird for a guy with an overdose or a stroke or a seizure to be so rock stable for over 12 hours."

Within 20 minutes the psychiatrist was in the ER. He spent some time talking with Mr. Gerard's relatives—some at the hospital, and some at their homes—and unearthed still more clues. What they had dismissed as eccentricity began to seem more like serious mental illness.

When he called Mr. Gerard's mother, who lived on the opposite coast, she told him that her son's behavior had been so erratic that she had been urging him to see a therapist for several years. In the past six months, however, she had stopped because her son had started accusing her of tapping his phone conversations and monitoring his mail—and she worried about feeding his escalating paranoia. A younger brother said he had been called to pick up Mr. Gerard at a hospital three months before. He had been brought there by the police after a security guard had found him in his office at 5 A.M. dressed in swim trunks. Although the ER doctors had thought he needed psychiatric help, Mr. Gerard had insisted on leaving without any care.

"I'm beginning to think he is a little nuts," the psychiatrist said, as he relayed his new findings. "But I'm still not sure. You can torture the guy and he doesn't react. How about a rush order on the drug tests that haven't come back yet? And maybe an EEG and a better CT scan."

Inside I groaned. That would be another six hours' worth of tests and another $2,000. I called to arrange for an EEG to monitor the electrical patterns deep in his brain, which would guarantee 1,000 percent that he was not having a seizure. I also asked for a CT scan enhanced with a dye that might reveal some odd tumor or infection. And I left a message at the toxicology lab begging for the remaining results as soon as possible.

After much coaxing and cajoling, Mr. Gerard got his EEG and second CT scan. As I suspected, both tests were normal. But when the chief lab technician returned my call, it was bad news. "No way for today," he said. "We sent the screen out to another state."

By now, though, the evidence was all pointing in one direction. When I looked in on Mr. Gerard one last time, his feet were again crossed—and hadn't they been crossed the other way before?

I called the psychiatrist. "He's yours," I began, mentioning the latest results to assuage his fears. "The tox screen won't be back until tomorrow, but he's been lying here rock stable for almost 24 hours and there's no overdose that can explain it."

My colleague started in with another round of questions. His temperature? Normal. His chest x-ray? Totally clear. His blood counts? Perfect. Had they been repeated? Yes, perfect again. His urine output?

I faltered. I tried to picture Mr. Gerard's bed. I didn't recall a urine bag hanging by its side, and he certainly hadn't gotten up to use the men's room. "I'll have to check."

I rummaged through the nursing charts trying to calculate how much fluid Mr. Gerard had gotten through his IV line—and how much he'd put out. With renewed trepidation I realized that there was no sign that he'd urinated at all. I looked around his stretcher for a urine bag that had not been emptied. Nothing there.

Evidently Mr. Gerard had gone almost 24 hours without urinating. How could I have missed this potentially critical clue? Were his kidneys failing? Was his bladder paralyzed by an unusual overdose that had left him in a coma? Or was he holding back voluntarily? I drew down his sheet to see if I could feel the outline of a bloated bladder under his skin—indeed, I thought I could. But as I pressed, there it was again: that slight grimace of a man who is awake and feeling pain.

Clearly, we needed one more test. I asked the nurse to accompany me, explaining, "Let's stick a catheter in his bladder to see what's in there."

Working in an ER, you get in the habit of talking to unconscious patients because you never know what they may feel or understand. So as the nurse draped a sterile sheet across his pelvis, she said exactly what she would say to any patient:

"Mr. Gerard, you haven't urinated in a while, so I'm going to put a tube in through your penis and up into your bladder to see if there's any backup there." By now she had cleansed the area with disinfectant, put on sterile gloves, and unwrapped the thin rubber catheter connected to a urine collection bag.

"Okay, Mr. Gerard," she said, picking up the catheter and taking aim. "It's going in." As if those three small words had broken some deep trance, suddenly the sheets began to stir and the carefully cleaned equipment tumbled to the floor.

The patient suddenly revives.

The nurse and I were speechless as Mr. Gerard sat bolt upright and said, "Excuse me, if you give me a urinal and close the curtains, I can handle this myself." Stunned, not knowing what else to do or say, we granted his request and left.

What a way to clinch a diagnosis. We were finally certain that Mr. Gerard's problem was not caused by some undetected neurological injury. "I should have known," I said to the nurse, "that to a man, the threat of a catheter is the most noxious stimulus of all."

When we returned to the room several minutes later, Mr. Gerard was once again lying on his stretcher, limp and silent, unresponsive to commands. But now we all agreed where he should spend the night.

Over the next week, as Mr. Gerard went in and out of his stupor, doctors at the psychiatric hospital garnered a bit more information from him. Mr. Gerard was basically lucid, they said, but paranoid, and his thought patterns did not always follow normal logic. They suspected that he had a mild form of schizophrenia and started him on a low dose of an antipsychotic drug to treat that disease.

As the drug brought Mr. Gerard's symptoms under control, however, a clearer picture of his condition began to emerge. In retrospect, it was obvious that Mr. Gerard had been suffering for months from mood swings, and his odd behavior more closely matched the symptoms of bipolar disorder, or what used to be called manic-depressive illness. Patients with this psychiatric disorder, which tends to run in families, suffer alternating bouts of hyperactivity and depression.

It had taken a catatonic episode to force Mr. Gerard into treatment for his illness, but his prognosis was good. Fortunately, treatment with lithium can prevent the destructive mood swings and permit the patient to lead a normal life. Not long after he was admitted, Mr. Gerard was walking, talking—even gregarious, the psychiatrists said. Just two weeks later he was able to return home and resume his practice.

IV. Write a short paper (3–5 pages) on one of the following scientific events. Discuss the problem, one or more hypotheses that were formulated, the implications that were drawn, and the test procedures that were used. Then evaluate the hypothesis in terms of adequacy, internal coherence, external consistency, and fruitfulness.

1. Isaac Newton: corpuscular theory of light
2. Christian Huygens: wave theory of light
3. Johannes Kepler: orbit of Mars
4. Nicolaus Copernicus: theory of the solar system

5. Count von Rumford: theory of heat
6. Charles Darwin: theory of natural selection
7. John Dalton: theory of atoms
8. William Harvey: circulation of the blood
9. Louis Pasteur: theory of vaccination
10. J. J. Thomson: discovery of the electron
11. Andre Marie Ampere: discovery of the electromagnet
12. Niels Bohr: structure of the atom
13. Alexander Fleming: discovery of penicillin
14. Henri Becquerel: radioactivity of uranium
15. Dmitri Mendeleev and Clemens Winkler: discovery of germanium
16. Amedeo Avogadro: Avogadro's law
17. Johann Balmer: theory of the spectrograph
18. Alfred Wegener: theory of continental drift
19. James Watson and Francis Crick: structure of the DNA molecule
20. John Bardeen: theory of superconductivity
21. Albert Einstein: theory of Brownian motion
22. Edwin Hubble: recession of the galaxies
23. Jean Baptiste Lamarck: inheritance of acquired characteristics

V. Write a short paper (2–3 pages) analyzing one or more of the hypotheses formulated by Sherlock Holmes in one of the stories by Arthur Conan Doyle. Include a discussion of the problem, the hypothesis, the implications that were drawn, and the test procedures.

VI. Answer "true" or "false" to the following statements:

★1. Hypothetical reasoning is useful when the evidence by itself does not provide the solution to the problem.

2. Hypotheses are derived directly from the evidence.

3. Hypotheses serve the purpose of directing the search for additional evidence.

★4. If the implications of a hypothesis are true, then we may conclude that the hypothesis is true.

5. If an implication of a hypothesis is false, then we may conclude that the hypothesis is false, at least in part.

6. In the episode pertaining to the discovery of radium, all of the hypotheses turned out to be true.

★7. In the Neptune episode, Adams and Leverrier deserve the credit for working out the implications of the hypothesis.

8. Torricelli's hypothesis was consistent with the hypothesis that nature abhors a vacuum.

9. In Pasteur's day, the theory of spontaneous generation held that life was produced by the direct action of oxygen on organic nutrients.

★10. The hypotheses relating to the discoveries of radium and Neptune may be classified as empirical hypotheses.

11. Torricelli's and Pasteur's hypotheses may be classified as theoretical hypotheses.

12. Theoretical hypotheses concern how something should be conceptualized.

★13. The problem with the distinction between empirical and theoretical hypotheses is that observation is dependent on theory.

14. The adequacy of a hypothesis has to do with how well the ideas or terms in the hypothesis are rationally interconnected.

15. The coherence of a hypothesis has to do with how well the hypothesis fits the facts.

★16. If a hypothesis is not externally consistent, then it must be discarded.

17. A hypothesis is fruitful to the extent that it suggests new ideas for future analysis and confirmation.

18. If a theory is incoherent, it is deficient in rationality.

★19. The theoretical interpretations of light, electricity, and magnetism during the first part of the nineteenth century illustrate a condition of inadequacy.

20. If a hypothesis gives rise to contradictory implications, it is incoherent.

9.6   Science and Superstition

The idea that the human mind is capable of operating on different levels in its effort to comprehend reality is as old as philosophy itself. Twenty-four centuries ago Plato drew a distinction between what he called opinion and knowledge. Opinion, he said, is a kind of awareness that is uncertain, confined to the particular, inexact, and subject to change, whereas knowledge is certain, universal, exact, and eternally true. Every human being starts out in life by operating on the level of opinion, and only through great struggle and effort can he or she escape it and rise to the level of knowledge. This struggle is called education, and it opens the eye of the mind to realities that cannot even be imagined from the standpoint of opinion.

Today's distinction between science and superstition is a modern equivalent of Plato's distinction between knowledge and opinion. Everyone recognizes that science has revealed wonderful truths about the world of nature. It has put men on the moon, wiped out life-threatening diseases, and ushered in the computer age. Also, almost everyone recognizes that superstition is little better than foolishness. It leads people to fear walking under ladders, breaking mirrors, and spilling salt. Practically everyone agrees that if some claim is grounded in science, then it is probably worthy of belief, while if it is grounded in superstition, then it is probably not worthy of belief. Where people do not agree, however, is in what constitutes science and what constitutes superstition. What one person calls science another calls superstitious nonsense.

Both science and superstition involve hypotheses, so the four criteria developed in Section 9.5 for evaluating hypotheses are relevant to the distinction between science and superstition. These criteria are adequacy, internal coherence, external consistency, and fruitfulness. But the distinction between science and superstition also involves psychological and volitional elements. It involves such factors as how the observer's subjective states influence how he sees the world, and how his needs and desires play a role in the formation of his beliefs. Accordingly, to explore the distinction between science and superstition, we must introduce criteria that include these psychological and volitional elements. The criteria we suggest are evidentiary support, objectivity, and integrity. The following account of evidentiary support encompasses adequacy and fruitfulness, and the account of integrity encompasses adequacy, internal coherence, and external consistency.

Science and superstition are, in large measure, polar opposites. Where scientific activity recognizes the importance of evidentiary support, objectivity, and integrity, superstition ignores them. Accordingly, these criteria can be used as a kind of measuring stick for sizing up the various beliefs people have about the world. To the extent that those beliefs are supported by evidence, are objective, and arise from research that reflects integrity, the closer they come to the ideal of science, and the more justified they are. Conversely, to the extent that our beliefs do not share in these characteristics, the closer they come to the "ideal" of superstition, and the less justified they are.

We note, however, that to say a belief is justified is not to say it is true in any absolute sense. As we saw in Section 9.5, all beliefs that arise from science are tentative at best. But such beliefs are the best ones we can have for now. Also, to say that a belief is not justified is not to say it is absolutely false. It is quite possible that a belief grounded in superstition today could tomorrow be grounded in science. But such a belief is not worthy of assent today. An analogy can be found in rolling dice. No sensible person would bet even money that a pair of dice will come up "snake eyes" on the next roll, even though he realizes that tomorrow it might be discovered that the dice were loaded in favor of this outcome.

Evidentiary Support

In the preceding section of this chapter we saw that hypotheses in themselves are mere conjectures, and before they are believed they should be supported by evidence. This rule applies equally to the hypotheses that underlie science and to those that underlie superstition. This rule is strictly obeyed in science, but it is often ignored in the realm of superstition. For example, in the sixteenth century Copernicus formulated the hypothesis that the sun is the center of our planetary system and that the earth revolves around the sun—in opposition to the prevailing Ptolemaic hypothesis, which put the earth at the center. In the years that followed, the telescope was invented, and thousands of observations were made that confirmed the Copernican hypothesis and disconfirmed the Ptolemaic hypothesis. Without these observations, the Copernican hypothesis would never have been adopted.

In contrast, consider the superstition that allowing a black cat to cross one's path will bring bad luck. No evidence has ever been collected in support of this hypothesis. No tests have been conducted and no experiments performed. Possibly on one occasion or other someone did allow a black cat to cross his or her path and later lost money on the stock exchange or was injured in a car accident, but surely it would be unreasonable to believe that allowing a black cat to cross one's path caused the loss or the accident. Such reasoning constitutes a classic case of the *post hoc ergo propter hoc* (false cause) fallacy. But in spite of the lack of evidence, many people believe the black cat hypothesis.

Before inquiring further into the need for evidence, however, we must first investigate what counts as evidence. Does the testimony of authorities count as evidence? What about ancient authorities? Does the Bible count as evidence? The answer is that scientific hypotheses are about the natural world, so only observations of the natural world count as evidence. Every scientific experiment is a question the experimenter asks of the world, and the result of that experiment is nature's reply. The problem with the testimony of authority is that we have no certain knowledge that the authority is correct in his or her assessment. The same holds true of the Bible. We have no way of knowing whether what the Bible says about the natural world is true. If someone should reply that the Bible is divinely inspired, then the obvious reply is, How do we know that? Do we have any observational evidence for it? Appeals to authority figures and the Bible amount to passing the explanatory buck.

Does the Bible count as evidence?

Another kind of evidence that is considered unreliable is anecdotal evidence. Suppose that you have cancer and a friend advises you that eating garlic can cure it. You decide to take this advice, and after eating a clove of garlic every day for a year, the cancer goes into remission. Did the garlic cure the cancer? Evidence of this sort is called anecdotal, and it is usually rejected by science. The trouble with anecdotal evidence is that it is too isolated to establish any causal connection. Thus, the garlic evidence ignores the thousands of people with cancer who have eaten garlic and have not been cured, and it ignores the thousands of people who have experienced spontaneous remission of cancer and have not eaten any garlic. Also, there is no way to turn the clock back and try the experiment again.

One of the key features of scientific evidence gathering is that an experiment be replicable under controlled conditions. This means that the experiment must be repeatable by different scientists at different times and places. Replicability helps ensure that the outcome of the experiment did not result from anything peculiar to one certain experimenter operating at a single place and time. Also, the controlled conditions are designed to eliminate the influence of extraneous factors. Perhaps, in reference to the garlic example, the cure was effected not by the garlic but by something else that was eaten, or by any one of a thousand other factors that occurred during this time, or by any combination of these factors.

Scientific experiments must be replicable.

The evidence offered in support of superstitious hypotheses is rarely replicable, and when it is, the outcome almost always fails to support the hypothesis. For example, the belief in ghosts is usually supported by what one or more individuals claim to have seen on some unique occasion. This occasion can never be repeated. And the belief in psychic phenomena such as extrasensory perception is sometimes claimed to be supported by experiments involving Zener cards: cards imprinted with crosses, circles, wavy lines, stars, and squares whose image an observer might "transmit" to a psychic receiver. But when these experiments have been repeated under carefully controlled conditions, the outcome has never been other than what would have been expected to occur through mere chance.

Another defect found in superstitious hypotheses is that they are often framed so vaguely that it is virtually impossible to provide any kind of unequivocal confirmation. For example, according to *feng shui* (pronounced fung-shway), an ancient Chinese system of magic, bad luck travels in straight lines, whereas good luck does not. As a result, one invites bad luck by living in a house or apartment that has two (or, what is worse, three) doors lined up in a row. But what, exactly, is the meaning of bad luck? What is interpreted as bad luck today may turn out to be good luck tomorrow. If a person loses $1000 in the stock market today, that may lead him to be more cautious in the future, and that increased caution may save $10,000 later on.

In contrast, the hypotheses of science are often framed in the language of mathematics, or they can at least be translated into some mathematical expression. This fact provides for extremely accurate confirmations and is largely responsible for the extraordinary success science has enjoyed during the past 500 years. For example, in 1802 the French chemist Joseph Louis Gay-Lussac formulated the hypothesis that if the temperature is raised one degree Celsius on a closed container of gas—any gas—the pressure of the gas will increase by .3663 percent. The hypothesis has been tested thousands of times by chemists and students in chemistry labs, and it has been found to be correct.

Scientific hypotheses are phrased precisely.

Closely related to the problem of vagueness is the breadth with which a hypothesis is framed. If a hypothesis is framed so broadly and comprehensively that even contradictory evidence serves to confirm it, then the hypothesis is not really confirmed by anything. Suppose, for example, that a health care practitioner should invent a hypothesis involving diet. Practicing this diet is guaranteed to make you feel great, but before it has this effect it may make you feel either rotten or the same as usual. After following this diet for six months you report that you feel the same as before. The practitioner replies that your experience confirms the hypothesis, because this is what the diet is supposed to do. On the other hand, suppose that after six months you feel great, or perhaps rotten. Again the practitioner will report that your experience confirms the hypothesis. Hypotheses of this sort are not genuinely scientific.

In 1919 the philosopher Karl Popper discovered this very problem concerning hypotheses. In response, he argued that any genuinely scientific hypothesis must be framed narrowly enough so that it forbids certain things from happening. In other words, the hypothesis must be falsifiable. In the years following its announcement, many philosophers criticized Popper's falsifiability criterion because, strictly speaking, hypotheses are rarely susceptible of being disproved. But, as we saw in Section 9.5, hypotheses can be disconfirmed (or rendered less plausible). Thus, we can retain Popper's basic insight by requiring that any genuinely scientific hypothesis be disconfirmable. This means that the hypothesis must be framed narrowly enough so that it is possible for evidence to count against it. Newton's gravitational hypothesis, for example, satisfies this criterion because the discovery of two large bodies that failed to attract one another would tend to disconfirm the hypothesis. But the dietary hypothesis we just mentioned fails the disconfirmability criterion because no outcome could ever count against it.

A problem closely associated with excessively broad hypotheses arises in connection with what are called *ad hoc* modifications of hypotheses. For an example, suppose that you are a sociologist conducting research into alcoholism. You formulate a hypothesis that alcoholism is caused by cultural factors that present alcohol consumption in a favorable light. When you gather evidence to support this hypothesis, however, you find that relatively few people who come from such cultures are alcoholics. Thus, you modify the hypothesis to say that alcoholism is caused by cultural factors but only when a genetic predisposition exists. But then you find that many alcoholics drink to ease the pain of depression and other psychological problems. Thus, you modify the hypothesis once again to take this fact into account. Further research shows that parental drinking patterns play a role, so you add another modification. These changes are called ad hoc ("to this") modifications because they are introduced purely to cover some problem or anomaly that was not recognized when the hypothesis was first framed.

The problem with ad hoc modifications is that their purpose is to shore up a failure of evidentiary support in the original hypothesis. As more and more modifications are added, the hypothesis becomes self-supporting; it becomes a mere description of the phenomenon it is supposed to explain. For example, suppose that we introduce a certain hypothesis h to explain the occurrence of a certain phenomenon x among a group of entities A, B, C, D, E. As ad hoc modifications are added, we find that A has x because of some unique attribute a, B has x because of b, and so on. In the end our hypothesis states that anyone who has attributes a, b, c, d, e exhibits x. But the set of attributes a, b, c, d, e is simply a description of A, B, C, D, E. If we should ask *why* entity A has x, the answer is that A has x because of a, where a is just a unique something that A has. Applying this analysis to the alcoholism hypothesis, if we ask why a certain person (let us call him Smith) is an alcoholic, the answer is that Smith is an alcoholic because he has a certain attribute s that causes him to be an alcoholic. The explanation is vacuous.

Another problem with ad hoc modifications is that they result in hypotheses that are so complicated that it becomes difficult to apply them. Science has always favored simplicity over complexity. Given two hypotheses that explain the same phenomenon, the simpler of the two is always the preferable one. In part this preference is aesthetic. The simpler hypothesis is more "beautiful" than the more complex one. But the preference for simplicity also results from the application of what has been called "Ockham's razor." This is a principle, introduced by the fourteenth-century philosopher William of Ockham, that holds that theoretical entities are not to be multiplied needlessly. Why settle for a complicated theory when a simpler one works equally well? Besides, the simpler one is easier to apply.

Returning to the question of evidentiary support, one of the surest ways to know that our hypotheses are supported by evidence is that they lead to predictions that turn out to be true. Each true prediction represents a pillar of support for the hypothesis. But some predictions are better than others, and the best ones are those that reveal ways of viewing the world that would never have been dreamed of apart from the hypothesis. If a hypothesis leads to predictions of this sort, and if those predictions are confirmed by evidence, then the hypothesis has earned a very special kind of support. Such a hypothesis reveals hidden truths about nature that would never have been recognized without it.

A classic example of a prediction of this kind resulted from the hypothesis underlying Einstein's general theory of relativity. One of the consequences predicted by this hypothesis is that light is affected by gravity. In particular, the hypothesis predicted that a light ray coming from a star and passing by the sun would be bent in the direction of the sun. As a result, the position of the star with respect to other stars would appear to be different from what it was usually observed to be. Of course, testing such a prediction under normal circumstances would be impossible, because the light of the sun is so bright that it completely blocks out the light from stars. But it could be tested during a solar eclipse. Such an opportunity arose on May 29, 1919, and scientists took advantage of it. The prediction turned out to be true, and as a result Einstein's theory was quickly adopted. Within a few years the theory led to the discovery of atomic energy.

Science is progressive, superstition is not.

Hypotheses that yield striking, novel predictions are largely responsible for progress in science. And it is precisely these kinds of predictions, argues philosopher Imre Lakatos, that distinguish science from pseudoscience. Of course, not every scientific hypothesis leads to such startling predictions as Einstein's, but they may at least be integrally connected to broader, umbrella hypotheses that have led to such predictions. In contrast, the hypotheses underlying astrology have been around for twenty-seven centuries, and they have produced not a single startling prediction that has been verified and not a single new insight into the course of human events. They have produced no master plan for future civilization and no hint about future discoveries in physics or medicine. This lack of progress over centuries is one reason that philosopher Paul Thagard concluded that astrology is a pseudoscience.

Objectivity

Our beliefs about the world are objective to the extent that they are unaffected by conditions peculiar to the experiencing subject. Such conditions can be either motivational or observational. For example, a belief that is motivated by the emotions of the experiencing subject and that exists for the primary purpose of satisfying those emotions tends to lack objectivity. Also, a belief that is grounded in observations peculiar to the experiencing subject, such as visual hallucinations, lacks objectivity. Even though objectivity is an ideal that can never be completely attained, practically everyone would agree that beliefs are more trustworthy if their content is not distorted by the experiencing subject. The scientist constantly strives to avoid such distortions, but the superstitious mind either revels in them or, in the more tragic cases, succumbs to them.

Superstitions exist to satisfy emotional needs.

All superstitions exist at least in part to satisfy the emotional needs of the experiencing subject. The chief emotions that give rise to superstitious beliefs are fear and anxiety, and they are often reinforced by a disposition to fantasy and mental laziness. Much of the fear and anxiety is generated by the fact that everyone dies. Death can come suddenly, as in a freeway accident, a fall from a roof, or an avalanche, or it can come as a result of cancer, heart failure, or stroke. Short of death, everyone is subject to injury with its attendant pain, and most people at some time experience the mental suffering that accompanies rejection, loneliness, and failure.

People have little control over these facts of life, and to relieve the anxiety they produce, many resort to charms and amulets, the rosary beads dangling from the rear view mirror or the scapular or medal worn around the neck. If nothing else will protect us from the terrors of life, perhaps these objects will. After all, science has failed to conquer disease and death, and it offers to the believer nothing but tentative truths that may change tomorrow. To the person facing an uncertain future, dejection, or loneliness, it may seem more reasonable to dial up the Psychic Friends Network and buy a bit of immediate consolation.

A second element in the human condition that generates anxiety is freedom and the responsibility freedom entails. The idea that you, and you only, are in charge of your destiny can be an extremely frightening idea. Many people recoil from the thought and seek refuge in a leader or guru. They turn all their power of critical thinking over to this leader and blindly follow his or her instructions to the last detail. When the leader orders them to believe any form of nonsense, no matter how silly, they do so. The belief or practice ordered by the leader, they are told, is essential to their protection. And when the leader orders them to send a check for fifty dollars to help restore the television tower or complete the mansion on the hill, they do so. To refuse means they will have to face their own freedom. Sometimes, following such orders can lead to tragedy, as it did in the Jonestown massacre in 1978 and the Heaven's Gate suicides in 1997.

A disposition to magical ways of thinking and mental laziness greatly facilitates the flight to superstition. Many people, if not most, are fascinated by the mysterious, the arcane, and the occult, and some would rather believe an explanation clothed in magic than they would a scientifically grounded one. Psychologists Barry F. Singer and Victor A. Benassi performed a series of experiments on their students in which they had a magician pose as a "psychic" and perform demonstrations of psychic feats. Before the demonstrations began, the students were told repeatedly in the clearest language that the magician was only pretending to be a psychic, and that what they were about to witness was really a series of conjurer's tricks. Nevertheless, in spite of these warnings, a majority of students concluded, in one experiment after another, that the magician was really a psychic. Furthermore, many concluded that the magician was an agent of Satan.

People are fascinated by the mysterious.

The disposition toward the magical and the fantastic is greatly reinforced by the media, particularly television and motion pictures. The media are slavishly subservient to the entertainment desires of their audience, so, given a widespread fascination with the magical, the media issue a constant stream of movies, miniseries, and "news" stories devoted to that subject. These programs touch everything from vampires and disembodied spirits to irrational conspiracies and the intervention of angels. This persistent attention to the fantastical increases the public's acceptance of superstitious explanations whenever realistic ones are not readily available, or even in the face of realistic explanations.

A disposition to mental laziness also assists in the formation of superstitious beliefs. It is, in fact, extremely difficult to ensure that one's beliefs are supported by evidence and that they pass the test of internal coherence. Sloppy logic is so easy it is no wonder people resort to it. Most of the informal fallacies treated in Chapter 3 can arise from sloppy thinking. After old Mrs. Chadwicke hobbled past the church, lightning struck the steeple and burned the church to the ground. Obviously old Mrs. Chadwicke is a witch (false cause). Furthermore, old Mrs. Chadwicke wears a black cape and a black hood. It must be the case that all witches wear such clothing (hasty generalization). And of course witches exist because everybody in the village believes in them (appeal to the people).

Superstitions are supported by sloppy thinking.

Another kind of sloppy thinking involves an appeal to what might be called false coherence. A farmer discovers that one of his cows has been slain. At the same time the farmer happens to read a story in a local tabloid saying that a satanic cult is operating in the vicinity. The cult practices its rites on the thirteenth day of each month. The cow was slain on the thirteenth. Thus, the farmer concludes that the cow was slain by Satan worshippers. This line of thinking involves many loose ends, but that rarely deters people from drawing a conclusion. Becoming a clear, critical thinker is one of the primary goals of education, but unfortunately becoming educated is no less of a struggle for students today than it was for students in Plato's day.

Thus far we have focused on emotions and dispositions in the experiencing subject that lead to superstitious beliefs. We now turn to some of the many ways that our observation of the world can be distorted. Such distortions constitute avenues in which conditions peculiar to the experiencing subject enter into the content of observation. When such distorted observations are combined with the emotions and dispositions mentioned earlier, superstitious beliefs are likely to arise. The distorted observations can occur in the same person who has the emotions and dispositions or they can be conveyed second hand. In either case, the combination leads to superstition.

One well-documented phenomenon that influences our observation of our own bodily states is the so-called placebo effect. A placebo is any kind of "medicine" or procedure that provides no medicinal or therapeutic benefit by itself but that can effect a cure when the patient is told that it has such benefit. For example, patients with knee pain have been told that an operation will cure them, and after they undergo a minor incision that, by itself, has no therapeutic effect, the pain often disappears. Also, patients who suffer from nervous tension or depression have been told that a little colored pill (which consists of nothing but sugar) will cure them, and after they take the pill, the tension or depression disappears. Obviously in these cases it is not the placebo alone that effects the cure but the placebo together with the suggestion implanted in the patients' minds by their doctors.

Placebos can masquerade as cures.

Another well-documented effect that influences our observation of the world around us is called pareidolia. This is the effect by which we can look at clouds, smoke, or the textured coatings on walls and ceilings and see animals, faces, trees, and so on. We project the visual images we are familiar with onto vague, relatively formless sensory stimuli and "see" that image as if it were really there. Pareidolia is responsible for a good deal of religious superstition. For example, in February, 1999, volunteers working in the Episcopalian Church of the Good Shepherd in Wareham, Massachusetts, saw the image of Jesus in the wood grains of a door they were staining. They concluded that the image was a miraculous appearance of Jesus. After all, one of them observed, Jesus was a carpenter. Hundreds of incidents like this have been reported in the media, but it never happens that someone who was raised a Buddhist or Hindu sees an image of Jesus.

Closely related to pareidolia is the concept of the perceptual set, where "set" refers to our tendency to perceive events and objects in a way that our prior experience has led us to expect. The idea of perceptual set is a product of *Gestalt* psychology, according to which perceiving is a kind of problem solving. When we are confronted with a problem, such as finding the solution to a riddle or puzzle, we enter into a state of mental incubation in which potential solutions are turned

We perceive what we expect to perceive.

over in our minds. This state is followed by a flash of insight (assuming we are able to solve the puzzle), after which the solution seems obvious. When we consider the puzzle at a later time, the solution leaps into our minds. Such a solution is called a *Gestalt*, which, in German, means form or configuration. Analogously, every act of perception involves solving the puzzle of organizing sensory stimuli into meaningful patterns. Each such pattern is a perceptual *Gestalt*, or set, and once such a set is formed, it serves to guide the processing of future perceptions. As a result, we perceive what we expect to perceive.

Can you see the white triangle?
Is the white triangle really "there"?
(Taken from Kanizsa, 1979, 74.)

In 1949 psychologists Jerome S. Bruner and Leo J. Postman performed a famous experiment in which subjects were shown replicas of ordinary playing cards—but some of the cards had been altered by reversing their color. For example, in some groups of cards, the three of hearts was black and the six of spades was red. Of twenty-eight subjects, twenty-seven initially saw the altered cards as normal ones. One subject identified the black three of hearts as a three of spades on forty-four successive showings. This experiment clearly shows that we perceive what we expect to perceive and, indeed, this fact is familiar to everyone. For example, we expect to receive a phone call, and while taking a shower we think we hear the phone ringing, only to be told by someone in the other room that the phone did not ring. Or, while driving, we might approach a red octagonal sign that reads ST_P (our view of the sign being partly blocked by a tree branch between the S and the P). However, we bring the car to a stop, because we perceived the sign to read STOP. In fact, what our sense of vision received was three consonants (S, T, P), meaningless until processed through perception.

Yet another factor that influences our sense of vision is the autokinetic effect. According to this effect a small, stationary light surrounded by darkness will often be seen to move. One can prove the existence of this effect for oneself by looking at a bright star on a dark night, or by observing a small stationary point of light in a dark room. The lighted object will often appear to move. Psychologists speculate that the autokinetic effect results from small, involuntary motions of the eyeball of the observer, and they have shown that the effect is enhanced by the reports of other observers. If someone standing nearby says that she just saw the object move, others will often confirm this report. The autokinetic effect is thought to be responsible for many claims of UFO sightings.

Hallucinations of various sorts can also distort the content of perception. Two kinds of hallucination that affect many people in the drowsy moments between sleep and wakefulness are hypnagogic and hypnopompic hallucinations (Hines, 1988, 61–62). The former occur just before drifting off to sleep, when the brain's alpha waves are switching to theta waves, and the latter occur just before awakening. During these moments the subject may experience extremely vivid, emotionally charged images that seem to be very real. These hallucinations are thought to be responsible for the ghosts and other appearances that people sometimes see in bedrooms.

Hallucinations distort perception.

Collective hallucinations are another kind of perceptual distortion that can occur in large crowds of people. Before such hallucinations can happen, the crowd must be brought to a heightened emotional state, which may be brought on by the expectation of seeing something important or miraculous. An occurrence of this sort may have happened on October 13, 1917, when some 70,000 people gathered in the village of Fatima in Portugal expecting to see a miraculous sign from heaven. At midday, one of the children who was supposedly in contact with the Virgin Mary cried out to the people to look at the sun. They did so, whereupon thousands saw the sun swirl amid the clouds and plunge toward the earth. Of course, if the sun had actually moved, it would have triggered seismograph readings all over the globe. Also, many of the people there did not see anything unusual, but their reports were discounted. Nevertheless, even to this day many of the faithful take this observation of the swirling sun as evidence of a miracle.

Finally, the operation of memory can distort the way we recall our observations. Human memory is not like the process whereby a computer recalls information from its hard drive with total accuracy. Rather, it is a creative process susceptible to many influences. When images are recalled from human memory, they are retrieved in bits and pieces. The brain then fills in the gaps through a process called confabulation. The brain naturally and unconsciously tries to produce a coherent account of what happened, but precisely how the gaps are filled in depends on such things as one's feelings at the time of recall, other people's suggestions about the event recalled, and one's own successive reports of what happened. Given that memory recall is selective to begin with and that many details are inevitably left out, the final picture recalled may range anywhere from a fairly accurate representation to a total fabrication.

Confabulation produces false recollections.

These effects represent only a few of the ways that human observation and memory can be influenced by the subjective state of the observer. To avoid such distortions, scientific inquiry restricts human observation to circumstances in which known aberrations of perception and recall are least likely to occur. In the natural sciences, much if not most observation occurs through instruments, such as volt meters, Geiger counters, and telescopes, the behavior of which is well known and highly predictable. The results are then recorded on relatively permanent media such as photographic paper, magnetic tape, or computer discs. In the social sciences, techniques such as double-blind sampling and statistical analysis of data insulate the observer from the outcome of the experiment. Such procedures provide considerable assurance that the data are not distorted by the subjective state of the experimenter.

Integrity

Our efforts to understand the world in which we live have integrity to the extent that they involve honesty in gathering and presenting evidence and honest, logical thinking in responding to theoretical problems that develop along the way. Most forms of superstition involve elements of dishonesty in gathering evidence or a failure of logic in responding to theoretical problems. Such failures of logic can be found in the lack of response by the community of practitioners to problems involving the adequacy, coherence, or external consistency of the hypotheses related to their practices.

The most severe lack of integrity arises when the evidence is faked. One of the more striking examples of faked evidence is found in the case of the Israeli entertainer Uri Geller. Beginning in the early 1970s, Geller presented himself in numerous venues

Practitioners of superstition fake the evidence. throughout the world as a psychic who could perform marvelous feats such as bending spoons, keys, nails, and other metal objects through the sheer power of his mind. Such objects would appear to bend when he merely stroked them with his finger, or even without his touching them at all. Scientists were called in to witness these feats, and many came away convinced of their authenticity. But in fact Geller was just a clever trickster who duped his audiences into thinking that he had psychic powers. Geller's trickery was exposed in large measure by the magician James Randi.

After watching videotapes of Geller's performances, Randi discovered how Geller performed his tricks, and in no time he was able to perform every one of them himself. Sometimes Geller would prepare a spoon or key beforehand by bending it back and forth several times to the point where it was nearly ready to break. Later, by merely stroking it gently, he could cause it to double over. On other occasions Geller, or his accomplices, would use sleight of hand maneuvers to substitute bent objects in the place of straight ones. In yet another trick, Geller claimed to be able to deflect a compass needle by merely concentrating his attention on it. As he would wave his hands over the compass, the needle would spin—and his hands had been thoroughly examined earlier for hidden magnets. But Geller had concealed a powerful magnet in his mouth, and as he bent over the compass, the needle would spin in tune with his head gyrations.

Donald Singleton, reporter for the *New York Daily News,* was familiar with Uri Geller's alleged psychic ability to bend spoons and keys and identify hand-made drawings that had been sealed inside two envelopes, one inside the other. He suspected that the latter trick was performed by holding the envelopes up to a strong light while the subject's attention was diverted. Prior to writing a story on Geller, Singleton performed the following test:

> I went to a locksmith and got a duplicate of the strongest, thickest key on my key ring. I tried with all my might and I couldn't bend it, even by pressing it against the corner of a steel desk. Then I made a simple drawing (of an eye), wrapped it in aluminum foil and put it into two envelopes.
>
> I went to see Geller the next afternoon.
>
> He tried for more than an hour, with me keeping the envelope in my sight every second, to get the drawing. And he failed.
>
> Then he made an effort to bend the key, again with me keeping it in view every second. Again, nothing happened. Uri said that he was terribly disappointed, that this simply had been an all-around bad day for him (Quoted in Randi, 1982, 29).

For another example of faked evidence, let us look at fire-walking. Practitioners of this art claim that their self-help seminars can alter a person's body chemistry so as to allow him or her to walk barefoot over a bed of glowing coals without being burned. One of the leading gurus of this business is Tony Robbins of the Robbins Research Institute. Robbins uses what he calls "neurolinguistic programming" to cure all sorts of physical and psychological ailments, from irrational fears and impotence to drug addiction and tumors. As proof of the efficacy of this technique, he invites those who have taken his seminar to engage in a fire-walk. By merely believing they will avoid burning their feet, he tells them, they will survive the ordeal unharmed.

The truth is that anyone, whether or not he has taken the seminar and regardless of what he believes, can, under controlled conditions, walk across burning coals and escape unharmed. Physicist Bernard J. Leikind proved this, at least to his own satisfaction, when he showed up at a Robbins seminar in the fall of 1984 (Frazier, 1991, 182–193). Even though he had not attended the sessions and he declined to think cool thoughts as per the instructions of the attendants, he found that he could perform the fire-walk without even getting singed. He explained his success by noting certain basic laws of physics. In spite of their high temperature, wood coals contain a very low quantity of heat, and they conduct heat very poorly. Also, the foot is in contact with the coals for only a second at a time, thus allowing only a small quantity of heat energy to flow to the foot. As a result, the feet of fire-walkers rarely sustain injury (or at least serious injury).

For a third example of faked evidence we need look no further than the thousands of fortune tellers, palm readers, and mentalists who use the art of "cold reading" to divine all sorts of amazing truths about their clients' lives. Most people who engage the services of these "readers" do so because they have problems concerning love, health, or finances. The reader knows this and often begins the reading with a flattering spiel that is tailored to fit practically everybody. This recital is intended to put the client at ease and condition him or her to open up to the reader. All the while the reader is taking in every detail: the client's age, sex, weight, posture, speech patterns, grammar, eye contact, build, hands, clothing (style, age, neatness, and cost), hair style, jewelry, and whatever the client might be holding or carrying (books, car keys, etc.). All

Cold readers deceive their clients.

of these provide clues to the personality, intelligence, line of work, socioeconomic status, religion, education, and political affiliation of the client.

The reader uses this information to formulate hypotheses that are then presented to the client in the form of subtle questions. Depending on the client's reactions—facial expression, eye motion, pupil dilation, gestures—the reader can often tell if she is on the right track. Once the reader hits on something close to home, the client will usually react in amazement and begin revealing more details about himself. After appropriate intervals, the reader will then rephrase this information in a different sequence and feed it back to the client, to the client's ever-increasing amazement. The client then provides even more details, which the reader weaves together with everything else she has learned. The use of a crystal ball, satin cape, or tarot cards combined with a polished sense of confidence convey to the client that the reader can literally read the client's mind.

Psychologist Ray Hyman, who, as a teenager, read palms to supplement his income, has studied the art of cold reading in some depth. He relates a story about a young lady who visited a mind reader during the 1930s:

> She was wearing expensive jewelry, a wedding band, and a black dress of cheap material. The observant reader noticed that she was wearing shoes that were currently being advertised for people with foot trouble. He assumed that this client came to see him, as did most of his female customers, because of a love or financial problem. The black dress and the wedding band led him to reason that her husband had died recently. The expensive jewelry suggested that she had been financially comfortable during marriage, but the cheap dress indicated that her husband's death had left her penniless. The therapeutic shoes signified that she was now standing on her feet more than she used to, implying that she was working to support herself since her husband's death.
>
> The reader's shrewdness led him to the following conclusion—which turned out to be correct: The lady had met a man who had proposed to her. She wanted to marry the man to end her economic hardship. But she felt guilty about marrying so soon after her husband's death. The reader told her what she had come to hear— that it was all right to marry without further delay (Frazier, 1981, 85–86).

If the deceptive techniques of the magician who pretends to be a psychic, the neurolinguistic programmer, and the cold reader are accepted at face value, they appear to constitute evidence that really supports the hypotheses underlying these activities. But faking the evidence is not the only way in which the practitioners of superstition lack integrity. The other way concerns the reaction of the community of practitioners to problems that arise in connection with the adequacy, coherence, and external consistency of those hypotheses.

Such problems arise in connection with scientific hypotheses no less often than they do with superstitious ones. When they arise in science, the community of scientists shifts to what philosopher Thomas Kuhn calls a puzzle-solving mode, and scientists work on them with great persistence until the problems

Scientists are puzzle-solvers.

are solved. This puzzle-solving activity occupies the attention of the vast majority of scientists for the greatest part of their careers, and it constitutes what Kuhn calls "normal science." Furthermore, it is precisely this puzzle-solving character of normal science, Kuhn argues, that distinguishes science from pseudoscience.

For example, after the Copernican hypothesis was introduced, a problem turned up in connection with what is called stellar parallax. If, as the hypothesis held, the earth travels around the sun, then, in the course of its orbit, the farthest stars should appear to shift in position with respect to the nearer ones. An analogous phenomenon can be observed as you change your position in a room. The distant lamp, which originally appeared to the left of the chair in the foreground, now appears to the right of it. In the case of the stars, however, no parallax could be observed. The explanation given at the time was that the stars were too far away for any parallax to be detectable. Nevertheless, stellar parallax constituted an adequacy problem that the community of astronomers regarded as a puzzle, and they worked on it for 300 years. Eventually more powerful telescopes were produced that did indeed detect a change in position of the stars as the earth orbited the sun.

In contrast, when an astrological prediction fails to materialize, the community of astrologers never sets to work to figure out what went wrong. Astrologers never recheck the location and birth time of the client or the exact position of the planets at the time of his birth. They merely charge forward and issue more predictions. Similarly, when the bumps on a person's head fail to indicate essential features of that person's personality, or when the lines on his palm fail to reveal features of his life, the community of phrenologists and the community of palm readers never try to account for the failures. They just ignore them and move on to the next batch of clients. Such a response reveals a lack of integrity on the part of these practitioners toward their respective hypotheses. Something is clearly wrong with the hypotheses or with the measurements, but no one cares enough to do anything about it.

A similar response occurs in connection with coherence problems. Most superstitions involve serious incoherencies, many of which arise from the lack of known causal connections. For example, if astrology claims that the planets influence our lives, then there must be some causal connection between the planets and individual humans. But what could this connection be? Is it gravity? If so, then astrologers need to show how infinitesimally small gravitational fluctuations can affect people's lives. On the other hand, if some other causal influence is at work, the astrologers need to pin it down. What kind of laws govern it? Is it an inverse square law, like the law of gravity, or some other kind of law? Analogously, if the lines on a person's palms indicate something about the person's life, then what form of causality is at work here? Do the lines influence the life, or is it the other way around? And what laws does this form of causality obey?

Any absence of a causal connection is a defect in coherence, because it signals the lack of a connection between ideas functioning in a hypothesis. However, such a lack of coherence need not be fatal to a hypothesis. Physicians from the time of Hippocrates knew that willow leaves, which contain the essential ingredient of aspirin, had the power to relieve pain, but they failed to understand the causal connection until recently. But what distinguishes the biomedical community from the community of astrologers lies in their respective reactions to such problems. The members of the biomedical community recognized the aspirin problem as a puzzle, and they worked on it until they found the solution, but members of the astrological community are unconcerned with identifying the causal mechanism by which the planets influence human lives. Similarly, members of the community of palm readers and members of the community of phrenologists care nothing about identifying the essential causal connections implied by their respective hypotheses.

An even more serious problem is posed by hypotheses that are inconsistent with established theories or laws. A case in point may be found in claims made by promoters of the Transcendental Meditation movement. The practice of TM was popularized in the 1960s by the Maharishi Mahesh Yogi, and since then it has attracted thousands of adherents. It consists in the silent repetition of a mantra, which induces a mental state similar to self-hypnosis. For many who have tried it, the benefits are mental and physical relaxation leading to a sense of rejuvenation. But with further instruction in TM (at considerable cost to the student), longer and deeper trances can be induced that, the Maharishi claims, allow the meditator to levitate—to hover in the air without any physical support. Thousands of disciples, he claims, have learned how to do this, and he has released photographs that purport to verify this claim. But of course if levitation actually occurs, it constitutes a violation of, or a suspension of, the law of gravity.

> Levitation is a puzzle no one wants to solve.

The inconsistency of the Maharishi hypothesis with such a well-confirmed theory as the law of gravity is probably sufficient reason to assign it to the category of superstition. But the reaction of the community of TM practitioners to this inconsistency leaves little room for doubt. In 1971 the Maharishi bought the grounds and buildings of what was formerly Parsons College in Fairfield, Iowa, and he converted the site into Maharishi International University. The University then became the home of the International Center for Scientific Research, which, one would think, would be the perfect forum for investigating levitation. Given the availability of scores of alleged levitators, the "scientists" in residence could conduct in-depth studies into this phenomenon. Their findings could provide the basis for interplanetary space travel, to say nothing of what they might do for safer airplanes. However, from its inception, the International Center has conducted not a shred of research on levitation. No experiments have been performed and no scholarly papers have been written. This response is inconceivable for any bona fide center of scientific research.

Summary

Distinguishing science from superstition is no idle preoccupation of armchair philosophers, as some have suggested, but an issue vital to the future of civilization. In Stalinist Russia responsible scientists were shipped off to the gulag for refusing to knuckle under to the state's ideas as to what was scientific. And in America, court battles have been fought over what counts as science for curriculum reform in the public schools. Also, the attempt to distinguish science from superstition has long-standing roots in the history of philosophy. It can be taken as a modern equivalent of the same question Plato asked long ago; numerous philosophers since then have addressed the question from their own perspectives.

On the foregoing pages we have outlined some features that are characteristic of scientific inquiry and some contrasting features that are characteristic of superstition. The purpose of this exposition has not been to provide the sufficient and necessary conditions for an absolute demarcation line between science and superstition. Rather, the purpose has been the more modest one of setting forth a group of family resemblances that a fair-minded inquirer may use in rendering a judgment that a set of beliefs is more probably scientific or more probably superstitious.

Key terms introduced in this section

ad hoc modifications	Ockham's razor
anecdotal evidence	pareidolia
autokinetic effect	perceptual set
collective hallucination	placebo effect
confabulation	replicability
disconfirmability	scientific progress
hypnagogic hallucination	striking predictions
hypnopompic hallucination	vague hypotheses

To the extent that a set of beliefs rests on hypotheses that are coherent, precisely tailored, narrowly formulated, supported by genuine evidence, and productive of new insights, these beliefs can be considered scientifically grounded. This judgment is reinforced by the conscientious response of the scientific community to problems that develop concerning the adequacy, coherence, and external consistency of those hypotheses. But to the extent that a set of beliefs rests on hypotheses that are incoherent, inconsistent with well-established theories, vague, overly broad, motivated by emotional needs, supported by evidence that fails to be trustworthy, and that lead to no new insights, then those beliefs tend to be superstitious. Such a judgment is reinforced by a reaction of oblivious unconcern on the part of the community of practitioners to problems that arise in connection with the adequacy, coherence, and external consistency of those hypotheses.

Selected Readings

Best, John B. *Cognitive Psychology.* St. Paul: West Publishing Company, 1986.

Bruner, Jerome S., and Leo J. Postman. "On the Perception of Incongruity: A Paradigm." In *Beyond the Information Given,* by Jerome S. Bruner. New York: W. W. Norton and Company, 1973.

Feyerabend, Paul. *Against Method.* London: New Left Books, 1975.

Frazier, Kendrick (ed.). *Paranormal Borderlines of Science.* Buffalo, NY: Prometheus Books, 1981.

——— (ed.). *The Hundredth Monkey, and Other Paradigms of the Paranormal.* Buffalo, NY: Prometheus Books, 1991.

Gardner, Martin. *Fads and Fallacies in the Name of Science.* New York: Dover Publications, 1957.

Hines, Terence. *Pseudoscience and the Paranormal.* Amherst, NY: Prometheus Books, 1988.

Kanizsa, Gaetano. *Organization in Vision.* New York: Praeger Publishers, 1979.

Kitcher, Philip. *Abusing Science: The Case against Creationism.* Cambridge, MA: The MIT Press, 1982.

Kuhn, Thomas S. "Logic of Discovery or Psychology of Research." In *Criticism and the Growth of Knowledge,* ed. Imre Lakatos and Alan Musgrave. Cambridge: Cambridge University Press, 1970, 4–10.

———. *The Structure of Scientific Revolutions,* 2nd ed. Chicago: University of Chicago Press, 1970.

Lakatos, Imre. *Philosophical Papers,* Vol. 1. Cambridge: Cambridge University Press, 1977.

Popper, Karl. *Conjectures and Refutations.* London: Routledge and Kegan Paul, 1963.

Radner, Daisie, and Michael Radner. *Science and Unreason.* Belmont, CA: Wadsworth Publishing Company, 1982.

Randi, James. *Flim Flam.* Buffalo, NY: Prometheus Books, 1982.

———. *The Truth About Uri Geller.* Buffalo, NY: Prometheus Books, 1982.

Schick, Theodore, and Lewis Vaughn. *How to Think About Weird Things.* Mountain View, CA: Mayfield, 1995.

Singer, Bary, and Victor A. Benassi. "Fooling Some of the People All of the Time." In *The Skeptical Inquirer,* Winter, 1980–81, 17–24.

Thagard, Paul. "Why Astrology Is a Pseudoscience." In *Proceedings of the Philosophy of Science Association,* Vol. 1, 223–234.

EXERCISE 9.6

I. Discussion exercises

1. Discuss the evidentiary problems raised by the following questions.

   a. After drinking tea made from tarragon leaves every day for a year, your grandfather reports that his bunions cleared up. Does this prove that tarragon tea has the power to cure bunions?

   b. You go to a psychotherapist who diagnoses your emotional condition as resulting from suppressed Oedipal tendencies. When these tendencies rise to the surface they can cause outbursts of emotion, but when they are held in check your behavior may be either normal or overly placid. Is the psychotherapist's hypothesis a good one?

   c. Every time the star running back of your school's football team makes a touchdown, he kneels for a quick prayer in the end zone. Is God blessing this player's performance on the field?

   d. On March 11, 1999, the Federal Trade Commission filed a complaint against Rose Creek Health Products of Kettle Falls, Washington. The complaint alleges that the company took mere salt water, labeled it "Vitamin O," and sold it for $10 per ounce. A testimonial on the company's Web site stated, "Three days after starting the Vitamin O, I threw my cane away. In November we went to Arizona and I bought myself a bicycle." Another testimonial by a man who had suffered severe headaches for twenty years stated, "The day he began taking Vitamin O his headaches disappeared." Do these testimonials prove that the allegations of the FTC are false?

   e. Shortly before drifting off to sleep, your roommate reports that she heard someone call out her name in a loud, clear voice. Since no one else was in the room at that time, does this mean that the voice came from a ghost?

f. In 1978 a New Mexico housewife, while cooking tortillas, noticed that the burn marks on one of them looked like the face of Jesus with a crown of thorns. The tortilla was encased in glass, and thousands of pilgrims came to see it. Do these burn marks prove that Jesus is alive and dwelling among us?

2. Discuss the meaning of the following selections.

a. "The universe is a macrocosm of creative energy and power, and every man, woman, and child is the epitome of this totality of the cosmos. Within your individualized energy field, the microcosm called *you,* are twenty-two Causal Powers, or angels, that control your conscious behavior and govern the manifestation of all forms and experiences in your personal life." (John Randolph Price, *The Angels Within Us*)

b. "What is remarkable about the nervous system of the human species is that it can command this infinite organizing power through conscious intent. Intent in the human species is not fixed or locked into a rigid network of energy and information. It has infinite flexibility. In other words, as long as you do not violate the other laws of nature, through your intent you can literally command the laws of nature to fulfill your dreams and desires." (Deepak Chopra, *The Seven Spiritual Laws of Success*)

c. "Every plant has an aura, the invisible charge of energy that exists around all things. It is the refracted and reflected light from electrical impulses, heat, and vapor of the object. Or put another way, it is simply light dancing around, inside, and off all things." (Laurie Cabot, *The Power of the Witch*)

d. "The Pleiadians are back from the future to give us a broader perspective on 'the absurd times' we live in. They explain how we are fragmented and cut off from our connection to the whole of life. The crucial test for us will be to shift from lineal thinking to a multidimensional perspective and expand our understanding of the frequency of love—the gateway to freeing ourselves." (Advertisement for *Family of Light,* by Barbara Marciniak)

e. "When advice from your angel is incorrect, it ain't your angel. Messages that prove misleading or untrue are due to desire or fear that was not released before you began talking with your heavenly helper. You're aware, of course, that any situation has the likelihood of multiple outcomes." (Alma Daniel, Timothy Wyllie, and Andrew Ramer, *Ask Your Angels*)

3. Discuss the following reports from residents of Hong Kong (taken from "Hong Kong's *Feng Shui:* Popular Magic in a Modern Urban Setting," by Charles F. Emmons, *Journal of Popular Culture,* Summer, 1992):

a. I have a little restaurant in Aberdeen, a seafood place facing the sea. I used to be on the other side of the street and had very bad business. The *feng shui* man told me that it should face the sea. Now I have very good business.

b. I am a guard at a dockyard. The Westerners there believe in *feng shui.* They changed the entrance to the place because the old one was unlucky. They also put out a [shiny] wok to deflect the bad luck, and a *fok dzi* [the Chinese Script character for good luck] upside down to bring luck in rather than out. All the workers there feel a lot better now and are in better health.

c. There were a lot of car accidents on the slope we faced, and even a murder upstairs from there, so we put up a fork and mirror to eliminate the killing atmosphere. The mirror faced east and reflected the morning sun. A guy across from us came over and said he had been sick since we had put the mirror up, and asked us to take it down. We did, and then he said he had been well after that. But we moved to another place then.

d. *Feng shui* is what causes radios to work better facing one way than another.

4. One of the early creationist theories advanced in opposition to Darwin's theory of natural selection was put forward by the nineteenth-century naturalist Philip Gosse. According to this theory God created the world in about 4000 B.C., and he did so in exactly six days, as per the account in *Genesis*. To reconcile this story with indications that the world is much older, Gosse argued that God created the world with the appearance of a history. Adam was created with a navel, trees were created with rings, and fossils were implanted in geological formations and in sea beds. Is Gosse's theory plausible? Does his theory make God out to be a deceiver? Is a world with a fake history intrinsically better than one with no history? If we were to update Gosse's theory, we would have to add that God created the world complete with light rays that appear to have been emitted by distant galaxies more than 10 billion years ago, and with fossils having ratios of carbon-12 to carbon-14 that indicate (by carbon dating techniques) the fossils are millions of years old. Given these provisions, is there any way of disproving Gosse's theory? In other words, is the theory disconfirmable? If not, does this fact make the theory unscientific?

5. The modern creationist theory, called "scientific creationism," propounded by Duane Gish and Henry Morris, accounts for geological formations and fossils by appealing to the great flood of Noah. This flood allegedly killed countless mammals, birds, fish, and insects, and their carcasses settled in different strata amid the swirling waters, thus producing the fossils. But is it plausible that all the animals that populate the earth today were saved on Noah's ark? These would include 25,000 species of birds, 15,000 species of mammals, 2,500 species of amphibians, 6,000 species of reptiles, including dinosaurs, and one million species of insects. How large must the ark have been, in comparison, say, with the *Titanic,* to house these animals together with sufficient food for a 300-day voyage? Based on the number of human hours it took to build the *Titanic* (do some research on this), how long do you think it would have taken Noah, his wife, and three sons to build the ark? Assuming the ark was made of wood, approximately how many board feet of lumber would have been needed to build it (include enough wood for walls and floors between the animals)? How long would it have taken Noah and his family to collect and load the animals on the ark? How much time would it have taken to provide one meal for the animals? Is scientific creationism a plausible theory?

6. Suppose you are a fortune-teller. You have a small shop in Milwaukee complete with a crystal ball, beads hanging in the doorway, incense, and a shelf of books

devoted to the dark arts. At about 4 o'clock in the afternoon in early March a couple in their mid-thirties come into your shop. They are apparently healthy, and both are well dressed and wearing slightly worn gold wedding bands. They are obviously affectionate, and as they take a seat on your couch, the woman gives the man a quick kiss. You notice that their faces and arms are well tanned, and the man is holding a key ring with two keys. One is stamped with the word "Porsche." When you glance through the front window, you notice a small, two-seat sports car of that make parked on the street. You introduce yourself as a fortune-teller famous throughout the world, and as you gaze into your crystal ball, you say, "I see. . . ." (Do a cold reading of this couple.)

At about 10 o'clock the next morning a woman in her mid-forties comes through the front door. She looks tired, her make-up is slightly smeared, and behind dark glasses you notice that her eyes look puffy. Her clothing is rumpled, and you detect a slight scent of alcohol on her breath. As she takes a seat on your couch, you notice that she is agitated and nervous, and she fidgets with the wedding ring on her finger. In a subdued tone of voice she says that she wants her fortune told. You reply that she has come to the right place, and as you wave your hands over your crystal ball, you begin with the words "I see. . . ." (Do a cold reading of this woman.)

7. Psychic phenomena include psychokinesis, telepathy, clairvoyance, and precognition. Psychokinesis is the ability to move objects through the direct power of the mind; telepathy is the power to perceive the thoughts of others without the use of the senses; clairvoyance is the ability to perceive distant objects without the use of the senses; and precognition is the ability to see the future without the use of the senses.

Psychologist Terence Hines [Hines, 1988, p. 83] argues that gambling casinos and government-run lotteries provide a real-world test for the existence of psychic phenomena. Every roll of a pair of dice, every spin of a roulette wheel, every game of poker or blackjack, and every purchase of a lottery ticket is an opportunity for the operation of psychokinesis, telepathy, clairvoyance, or precognition. If these phenomena actually occurred, then one would expect that the earnings of casinos and lotteries would be affected. But in fact these earnings are exactly as the laws of chance predict. Does this fact provide a fair test for the existence of psychic phenomena? Some defenders of psychic phenomena argue that psychic powers cannot be used for personal gain. Does this argument amount to an ad hoc modification of the hypothesis underlying psychic phenomena? Is the argument plausible?

8. In 1975 James Randi offered $10,000 (later increased to $1,000,000) to any person who could perform a paranormal feat (including any demonstration of psychic power) in his presence under controlled conditions. (This offer was still open as of the printing of this book.) Since that time, hundreds of people have tried to win the prize, but not a single one has succeeded. Does the failure of such people to collect the prize constitute a fair test of the existence of psychic phenomena?

During the past hundred years, thousands of experiments have been performed to demonstrate unequivocally the existence of psychic phenomena, but thus far none has succeeded. To account for the negative results of some of these experiments Gertrude Schmeidler invented the "sheep-goat" hypothesis, according to which such experiments are influenced by the attitudes of the experimenters. If the experimenters doubt the existence of psychic phenomena, then the experiment is doomed to failure; but if the experimenters are believers, then the experiment will succeed. Is this hypothesis believable? Does it qualify as an ad hoc modification? How might the attitude of the experimenters affect the outcome of the experiment? Could James Randi's presence account for the inability of performers such as Uri Geller to demonstrate their alleged psychic powers? [G. R. Schmeidler, "Separating the Sheep from the Goats," *Journal of the American Society for Psychical Research,* 39, no. 1 (1945), 47–50.]

9. In 1970, physicist David Simpson and his colleague Norman Foxwell performed an experiment involving a group of UFO buffs in England. On a Saturday evening about thirty of these individuals had gathered on a remote hilltop where they thought there was a good chance of sighting a UFO. Simpson positioned himself on another hilltop, about three-quarters of a mile away, and he pointed a purple spotlight, connected to a 12-volt battery, in the direction of the group. At 11:00 P.M. he switched on the light for 5 seconds, and after a five-second pause he switched it on again for 25 seconds. Mr. Foxwell, Simpson's accomplice, was stationed among the observers, and to enhance the emotional effect, shortly after the purple light was sighted, Foxwell switched on a buzzer that was attached to a bogus magnetic field sensor. According to UFO lore, UFOs are supposed to generate intense magnetic fields, so the buzzer signaled to the crowd that a UFO was operating nearby. To further enhance the effect, Foxwell had loaded a camera with a roll of film, two frames of which had been doctored with a fake latent image of a UFO. Foxwell proceeded to take two additional snapshots in the general direction of the purple light (which by then had been turned off), and he then gave the film to one of the members of the group for processing.

When the film was developed, sure enough, a tiny image of what appeared to be a UFO was visible on two frames. But those two frames (which were taken a year earlier) also contained geographical features that were inconsistent with the other two (genuine) frames. These inconsistencies were so glaring that anyone who examined all four frames closely would detect that at least two of them had been faked. However, when the photographs were examined in the laboratory of the *Flying Saucer Review,* an international publication devoted to UFO sightings, the experts announced that the negatives were "genuine beyond all doubt." Later, the director of research at the Astrophysical Institute of the French National Centre for Scientific Research published a "tentative interpretation" of the photographs, stating "In my opinion there is no question of the object photographed being in any possible way the result of faking."

Four months after the sighting, a report of the incident was published in the *Flying Saucer Review.* As you read the following selection from the report, remember that the purple light was turned on for a total of 30 seconds, that it was absolutely stationary, and that it was located on the horizon, at zero degrees elevation from the observers:

At 11:02 P.M. an object was seen at an elevation of approximately 20 degrees in the eastern sky. The object appeared very suddenly as if it came through the clouds, and appeared to the eye as a very bright ovoid light—purple in colour with a periphery of white. Two members of my group who observed the object through binoculars both remarked they could see a crimson light in the centre; this was also attested to by witnesses with good vision.

The object remained stationary for approximately 30 seconds, during which time Mr. Foxwell was able to take the first of his photographs. The object then moved slowly to the right—towards the town—and lost a little altitude in the process. At one stage in the movement it dimmed considerably as though obscured by a low cloud. The object continued moving for approximately 20 to 30 seconds, and then stopped again. The light then increased considerably in intensity, though we could not be sure if the object was moving directly toward the observation point, or if it remained stationary. At this point the alarm of a detector sounded and a witness ran to switch it off. After 10 to 20 seconds the light dimmed and went out as though concealed by a cloud. However we were all certain that the object had not moved once more. The sighting had lasted for approximately one to one and a half minutes.

Why do you think the observers saw the purple light move? Was it because they associated the light with the faked UFO images (the second of which appeared slightly below and to the right of the first)? Why did the observers see the light as elevated 20 degrees off the horizon? (The faked UFO images appeared approximately on the horizon.) Do you think that the expectations of the observers affected what they reportedly saw? Do you think that confabulation played a role in the report? How about the autokinetic effect? Or perceptual sets? Why do you think the specialists who examined the photographs failed to detect the inconsistencies? Could emotions have played a role in this oversight? [Taken from "A Controlled UFO Hoax: Some Lessons," by David I. Simpson, in Frazier, 1981.]

10. On the basis of a person's natal chart (horoscope cast according to the person's date, time, and place of birth), astrologers claim to be able to analyze that person's character and personality and make predictions about his or her life course. To test the claims of astrology about character analysis, UCLA physicist Shawn Carlson conducted a study involving thirty American and European astrologers considered by their peers to be among the best in the field. To complete the study Carlson selected 116 "clients," who were then given the California Personality Inventory (CPI), a widely used and scientifically accepted test that measures personality traits. The results of the CPI were then used to compile a personality profile for each of the clients. The astrologers were informed about the nature of the CPI, and to prevent any anti-astrology bias, many of their suggestions were incorporated into the study.

The astrologers were then given each client's natal chart together with three personality profiles. One of the profiles matched the client in question, and the other two were chosen at random from a separate batch of personality profiles composed in the same way as the true one. No astrologer was able to confront any client face-to-face, and the study was done on a double blind basis so that neither the astrologer nor the experimenters knew which profile corresponded with which natal chart. The astrologers predicted that they would be able to match a chart with the correct profile at least 50 percent of the time. However, as it turned out, only one out of three matches was correct—exactly what would be expected by chance. The results of Carlson's study were published in the widely respected scientific journal *Nature*.

Do you think that Carlson's study tends to disprove the claim that astrology can analyze personality features? Do you think that if the astrologers were allowed to meet the clients face-to-face, the results would have been different? Why? [From "Double-Blind Test of Astrology..." in Frazier, 1991]

Astrologers also claim the ability to make predictions. In 1978, R. N. Hunter and J. S. Durr of the U.S. Geological Survey invited astrologers to submit predictions about earthquakes. Hunter and Durr analyzed 240 predictions made by 27 astrologers and found that their accuracy was worse than would have been the case had they simply guessed. Also, in 1985, G. Chatillon analyzed thirty predictions for North America made by Huguette Hirsig, one of Montreal's most famous astrologers. Only two were found to be correct. Do studies of this sort tend to disprove the claims that astrologers are able to make true predictions?

11. The first step in providing an astrological reading is to cast the chart. This is followed by an analysis of interacting chart factors, which in turn is followed by the astrologer's interpretation of these factors. In regard to the third step, D. Hamblin, former chairman of the United Kingdom Astrological Association, wrote:

> If I find a very meek and unaggressive person with five planets in Aries, this does not cause me to doubt that Aries means aggression. I may be able to point to his Pisces Ascendant, or to his Sun conjunct Saturn, or to his ruler in the twelfth house; and if none of these alibis are available, I can simply say that he has not yet fulfilled his Aries potential. Or I can argue (as I have heard argued) that, if a person has an *excess* of planets in a particular sign, he will tend to suppress the characteristics of that sign because he is scared that, if he reveals them, he will carry them to excess. But if on the next day I meet a very aggressive person who also has five planets in Aries, I will change my tune: I will say that he *had* to be like that because of his planets in Aries.

Does this statement indicate that the step involving chart interpretation is not subject to disconfirmation and is therefore unscientific? Is Hamblin saying here that the interpretation is not of the chart but of the face-to-face encounter with the client? [From "Does Astrology Need to be True?" by Geoffrey Dean, in Frazier, 1991.]

12. In 1955, psychologist N. D. Sundburg gave the Minnesota Multiphasic Personality Inventory, a commonly used personality test, to forty-four students, and he then had two highly experienced psychologists draw up personality sketches for each student based on the results of the test. He then presented the individualized personality sketch to each student together with a univer-

sal faked sketch. Fifty-nine percent of the students picked the faked sketch as describing their true personality. What do these findings imply about self-knowledge and the accuracy of personal validation? Are people prone to accept descriptions of themselves that are flattering? Do people tend to find some specific feature in their makeup that fits any generalization?

Specifically, Sundburg found that the following sketch was acceptable as describing the majority of college males:

You are a person who is very normal in his attitudes, behavior and relationships with people. You get along well without effort. People naturally like you, and you are not overly critical of them or yourself. You are neither overly conventional nor overly individualistic. Your prevailing mood is one of optimism and constructive effort, and you are not troubled by periods of depression, psychosomatic illness or nervous symptoms.

The following sketch was found to be acceptable as describing the majority of college females.

You appear to be a cheerful, well-balanced person. You may have some alternation of happy and unhappy moods, but they are not extreme now. You have few or no problems with your health. You are sociable and mix well with others. You are adaptable to social situations. You tend to be adventurous. Your interests are wide. You are fairly confident and usually think clearly.

Do you find that either of these descriptions fits you fairly well? If so, what implications does this have for the astrologer, the Tarot card reader, or the fortune-teller?

13. On June 24 and 26, 1981, six children in the little village of Medjugorje in Bosnia (former Yugoslavia) claimed to have had a vision of the Virgin Mary. In the days and weeks that followed, more alleged visions occurred, and reports began to attract visitors anxious for a vision of their own. From 1981 until mid-1998, approximately 26 million people, many from the United States, visited Medjugorje, and many reported that their hopes were fulfilled. By the time these visits began, claims of visions were popping up everywhere, to the obvious glee of the charismatic pastor of the local church. However, not everyone accepted the authenticity of these visions. Among the detractors was the local bishop, Pavao Zanic, who, on July 25, 1987, issued a declaration that included the following:

The Madonna, they say, started to appear on the Podbrdo [a hamlet] of the Mountain Crnica, but when the militia forbade going there, she came into homes, into forests, fields, vineyards and tobacco fields; she appeared in the church, on the altar, in the sacristy, in the choir loft, on the roof, on the church steeple, on the roads, on the way to Cerno, in a car, on buses, in classrooms, in several places in Mostar and Sarajevo, in monasteries in Zagreb, Verazdin, Switzerland, Italy, once again in the Podbrdo, atop Krizevac, in the parish, in the rectory, etc. It is certain that not even half of the alleged places where the apparitions have taken place have been mentioned....

In 1991, after a lengthy inquiry, the Yugoslavian Bishops Conference issued a statement that nothing miraculous had occurred at Medjugorje; nevertheless, thousands of pilgrims continue to stream into the village even to this day. Also, the original six visionaries continue to claim apparitions of the Virgin.

9

How do you think all these visions are best explained? Do you think they are evidence of miracles? Or, could collective hallucination be responsible? Do people see what they want to see? What is your estimate of the average annual economic benefit that 26 million visitors would bring to a small village over a span of seventeen years? Do you think that this benefit has anything to do with the motives of the original six visionaries? Do you think that the pilgrims to Medjugorje are prone to superstition?

Philosopher Paul Kurtz suggests that religion, with its emphasis on miracles and the supernatural, sensitizes people to belief in the superstitious and the paranormal. Do you think that Kurtz is correct in this assessment? Is there any essential difference between the miraculous and the superstitious? If so, is there any evidence to support this difference? [Paul Kurtz, "Reflections on the 'Transcendental Temptation,'" in Frazier, 1991, 13–16.]

II. Experiment exercises

1. Psychic phenomena include psychokinesis, telepathy, clairvoyance, and precognition (see Exercise I, 6). Design an experiment to test for the existence of one or more forms of these phenomena. The experiment might use Zener cards, dice, remote viewing tests, or Ganzfield (sensory deprivation) conditions. (For Ganzfield studies see Frazier, 1991, pp. 143–148.) Be sure to build sufficient precautions into the experiment to prevent cheating.

2. Iridology is a diagnostic procedure that depends on the hypothesis that each organ of the body is represented by a specific part of the iris. By examining the eyes of a patient, the iridologist is supposed to be able to detect disease. Design an experiment to test this hypothesis. Employ proper restrictions to prevent cheating.

3. Dowsing involves the use of a forked tree branch ("dowsing rod") to find underground water. Sometimes a pair of metal rods are used, and sometimes oil, minerals, and metal objects are claimed to have been found. When the dowser feels sudden jerks from the dowsing rod, he knows he is standing over a source of water (or oil, etc.). The practice depends on the hypothesis that water exerts some kind of magnetic influence over the rod, or engages the psychic abilities of the dowser (or both). Design an experiment to test for the existence of this phenomenon. (See the references to dowsing in Randi, 1982.)

4. Try your hand at cold reading. Have an assistant select some "clients" who are willing to come in for a reading. They should be told in advance that you have genuine abilities in this area. In preparation read Ray Hayman's article in Frazier, 1981, pp. 79–96.

5. Set up an experiment to test for the autokinetic effect. The experiment might involve a small point of light in a large, dark room, or a flashlight some distance away on a dark night. Select a small group of observers for this experiment, and include a test for the claim that one observer's insistence that the light is moving influences what the others see.

6. Design an experiment to test whether people are prone to believing fantastical explanations of things they do not understand (including conjurors'

tricks.) Consider repeating the experiment (described in the text) that was performed by Singer and Benassi.

7. Design an experiment to test the claims of astrology. You might begin by selecting ten "clients"; obtain the exact time and location of their births and have an astrologer do a reading for each. Then see if the clients can recognize which reading (out of, say, a total of five) pertains to them. Or, alternately, for each reading you might prepare a "reverse reading" in which the character description is the exact reverse of the "true" reading. Then give each client a copy of both readings (true and reverse) and see if he or she can distinguish the true one. (See Geoffrey Dean's two articles in Frazier, 1991, pp. 279–319.)

III. Essay exercises. After researching one of the following topics, write an essay of eight to ten pages evaluating the plausibility of the underlying hypothesis.

1. The existence of UFOs.
2. Extraterrestrial abductions.
3. Scientific creationism.
4. Darwin's theory of natural selection.
5. Biorhythms.
6. Phrenology.
7. Seances and channeling.

Summary

Inductive logic is not as developed as deductive logic, and at present it consists merely of several independent topical areas. This chapter considers six of them: analogy and its application to legal and moral reasoning, causality and Mill's methods, probability theory, statistical reasoning, hypothetical and scientific reasoning, and how science differs from superstition.

An argument from analogy is an inductive argument that rests on a similarity between two things. Because one of these things (the primary analogue) has a certain attribute, it is argued that the other (the secondary analogue) does also. Six factors that bear on the strength of an argument from analogy are the relevance of the similarities shared by the primary and secondary analogues, the number of similarities, the nature and degree of disanalogy, the number of primary analogues, the diversity among the primary analogues, and the specificity of the conclusion. Legal and moral reasoning provide a natural vehicle for studying the function of analogical arguments in real-life situations. The analogy between precedent cases and the case at hand may determine the outcome of a trial, and analogies are effective in characterizing elusive moral situations.

Causes can be described in terms of sufficient conditions, necessary conditions, and sufficient and necessary conditions. Mill's methods, named after the philosopher John Stuart Mill, are inductive techniques that allow us to identify causal connections. The method of agreement identifies necessary conditions, the method of difference identifies sufficient conditions present in a specific occurrence, and the joint method of agreement and difference identifies sufficient and necessary conditions. The method of residues and the method of concomitant variation identify causal connections without regard to the kind of causality involved. The methods of agreement, difference, and concomitant variation resemble certain methods used in the natural sciences and the social sciences to identify causal connections.

Probability theory is a branch of mathematics that assigns a numerical figure to the probability of certain occurrences. It comprises the classical theory, which rests on a priori calculations; the relative frequency theory, which depends on empirical experimentation; and the subjectivist theory, which rests on the subjective beliefs of individual people. Once these theories are used to assign a numerical figure to the probability of a simple event, the rules of the probability calculus can be used to calculate the probability of compound events. The conjunction rules compute the probability of two events occurring together, the disjunction rules compute the probability of either of two events occurring, the negation rule computes the probability of an event not happening, and Bayes's Theorem computes the conditional probability of two or more mutually exclusive and jointly exhaustive events.

Statistical reasoning includes any kind of argumentation based on statistical measurement. Such arguments can be misleading because of ambiguities in language, improper measuring techniques, hidden factors, and the skewed drawing of pictograms and graphs. Samples used to generate statistics must not be biased: They must be randomly selected, of the proper size, and unaffected by psychological factors. The word "average" can mean either the mean value of a set of data, the median value, or the mode. Statistical claims must specify the meaning intended. The dispersion of the data, expressed in terms of range, variance, and standard deviation, must also be acknowledged. Graphs and pictograms must be drawn so they avoid illusions, and percentages must state the base upon which the percentage is calculated and avoid various numerical fallacies.

Hypothetical reasoning is used to solve a problem when the solution is not apparent to undirected observation. The method consists of inventing a hypothesis that illuminates the situation, drawing implications from the hypothesis, and testing the implications. This method is not only applicable to many puzzling occurrences in ordinary life, but is also essential to the progress of science. Four examples from the history of science that clarify the hypothetical method are the discoveries of radium, the planet Neptune, atmospheric pressure, and the refutation of spontaneous generation. Scientific hypotheses may be either theoretical or empirical. Empirical hypotheses may be proved true or false, but theoretical hypotheses may only be confirmed in varying degrees. Criteria that bear on the tentative acceptance of hypotheses are adequacy, internal coherence, external consistency, and fruitfulness.

The final section introduces three general criteria for distinguishing science from superstition. These are evidentiary support, objectivity, and integrity. These criteria can be used as a kind of measuring stick for sizing up the beliefs people have about the world. To the extent that those beliefs are supported by evidence, are objective, and arise from research that reflects integrity, the closer those beliefs come to the ideal of science and the more justified they are. But to the extent that the beliefs do not share in these characteristics, the closer they come to the "ideal" of superstition, and the less justified they are.

Appendix: Logic and Standardized Tests

Fifty percent of the LSAT (Law School Admission Test) and a substantial part of the GMAT (Graduate Management Admission Test) relates to questions involving arguments. Of these questions, a large number ask that the test-taker do one of three things: (I) identify the conclusion implied by a set of premises; (II) identify a missing premise needed to draw a stated conclusion; or (III) identify a statement that either strengthens or weakens a given argument. These tasks are closely related to the primary subject matter of this textbook.

The questions* that follow have been taken from *Logic and Reading Review for the GRE, GMAT, LSAT, MCAT,* published by Thomson Peterson's. The book contains four complete practice tests and an extensive set of instructions on how to approach the various kinds of questions found in admissions tests for graduate school.

I Identify-the-Conclusion Questions

1. Five separate applications of the pesticide failed to rid the area of the mites. Only the most resistant of the mites survived each application. When the surviving mites reproduced, their offspring resisted the pesticide more effectively than did the parents.

   Which of the following conclusions can best be drawn from the statement above?

   *Answers are on the last page of this appendix.

(A) Normally, more pesticide-resistant mites tend to mate with less resistant mites.
(B) The mites that survived each exposure grew more pesticide resistant with each application.
(C) The pesticide applications did not coincide with the mating season of the mites.
(D) The pesticide was formulated to kill the mites in one application.
(E) Resistance to the pesticide is passed from parent to offspring.

2. Every year, the members of the school board PTA select a new Student Representative. If the school board PTA selects a senior as the Student Representative, then the PTA will give the high school money for a spring musical. However, the school board PTA has already given the school money for a spring musical.

   If all the statements in the above argument are true, which of the following conclusions must also be true?
(A) The PTA should not select a senior as the Student Representative.
(B) The PTA already has given enough money to the high school.
(C) The current Student Representative is a junior.
(D) If the PTA does not give any additional money to the high school, then the PTA must not have selected a senior as its Student Representative.
(E) If the PTA gives more money to the high school this year, then its Student Representative must be a senior.

3. Archaeologists at the University of South America have concluded that all species of dinosaurs that inhabited any parts of South America died at least 3 million years ago. The Southern Andes iguana is a species of animal that has existed continuously on the Earth for more than 5 million years. It is well established that South American dinosaurs and the

Southern Andes iguana never lived on the Earth at the same time.

Based on the results of the studies reported above, which of the following must be true?

(A) South American dinosaurs became extinct at least 5 million years ago.
(B) The conclusion of the archaeologists at the University of South America is incorrect.
(C) If South American dinosaurs and Southern Andes iguanas had lived together on the Earth, the dinosaurs would have eaten the iguanas.
(D) South American dinosaurs and Southern Andes iguanas may have existed together on the Earth but in different locations.
(E) Southern Andes iguanas have been extinct longer than South American dinosaurs have.

4. Any movie starring Robert Redford will win an Academy Award, but no movie starring Robert Redford will ever earn more than $5 million from ticket sales. Some movies that earn more than $5 million from ticket sales are directed by Steven Spielberg.

Which of the following conclusions must be true, based on the above statements?

(A) No movie directed by Steven Spielberg will win an Academy Award.
(B) Some movies directed by Steven Spielberg may star Robert Redford.
(C) Some movies earning more than $5 million in ticket sales may star Robert Redford.
(D) No movie starring Robert Redford will win an Academy Award.
(E) All movies directed by Steven Spielberg will win an Academy Award.

5. A philosopher makes the following statements: "I think, therefore I am. If I am not, then I think not. If I think, then life means nothing."

Applying the preceding argument, if life does not mean nothing, then what more can the philosopher conclude?

(A) I am.
(B) I think.
(C) I do not think.
(D) I think and I am.
(E) I think not and I am.

6. All blue cars have tailfins. Nothing that is blue has ever traveled to the bottom of the ocean.

Based on the above statements, which of the following may logically be concluded?

(A) Only things with tailfins have traveled to the bottom of the ocean.
(B) All things with tailfins are blue.
(C) Some cars have not traveled to the bottom of the ocean.

(D) All cars have tailfins.
(E) Some cars are not blue.

7. Whenever the national budget exceeds $8 trillion the government spends $2 billion on travel expenses. Whenever the government spends $2 billion or more on travel expenses, then the President's activities are too visual to the public, too many reports are released to the press, and the President gets impeached. Before 1998, no President had been impeached since 1865, which was 133 years ago.

Which of the following statements must be true?

(A) In 1865, the national budget was at least $8 trillion.
(B) The President will be impeached again in 2131, which is 133 years from now.
(C) The government needs to spend at least $2 billion on travel expenses each year.
(D) In 1980, the government may have spent more than $2 billion on travel expenses.
(E) The national budget in 1940 was less than or equal to $8 trillion.

8. *Advertisement:* Seven out of ten municipal employees choose Green Arrow Underwriters as their health insurance provider.

From the information provided in this advertisement, what further conclusion may be drawn?

(A) Green Arrow Underwriters has the cheapest premium rates of any insurance company available.
(B) All other health insurance providers, excluding Green Arrow Underwriters, provide services to less than 50 percent of the municipal employees.
(C) Municipal employees need less health insurance coverage than employees in other industries.
(D) Green Arrow Underwriters provides more valuable services and better customer assistance than any of its competitors.
(E) Except for Green Arrow Underwriters, the health insurance industry is suffering a decline in the rate of obtaining new customers.

9. The different types of speech therapy based on experience produce virtually the same rates of success. While practitioner proponents of each type of therapy assert that their procedure is different from the others, studies of the results achieved by every one of these treatments show no significant differences in effectiveness.

It can be best inferred from the statement above that

(A) there are few differences among the different types of speech therapies considered.
(B) the speech therapies discussed are less effective than other types of treatment.

(C) the differences among the various speech therapies considered are not causally relevant to their effectiveness.

(D) practitioner proponents differ substantially in their conceptions of therapeutic success.

(E) practitioner proponents ignore the connection between therapeutic experience and effectiveness.

10. In a game of Monopoly®, if a player owns a hotel on Boardwalk, he must own both Boardwalk and Park Place. If he owns a hotel in Marvin Gardens, he must own Marvin Gardens and either Boardwalk or Park Place. If he owns Park Place, he also owns Marvin Gardens.

   If the player described above does not own Park Place, which of the following conclusions may be drawn?

(A) The player owns a hotel on Boardwalk.

(B) The player owns a hotel in Marvin Gardens but does not own a hotel on Boardwalk.

(C) The player owns Marvin Gardens and Boardwalk but does not own a hotel on either property.

(D) The player does not own a hotel in Marvin Gardens.

(E) The player does not own a hotel on Boardwalk.

II Identify-the-Missing-Premise Questions

1. New electric heating elements that use the patented "coiled element system" save energy by requiring less electricity. Therefore, if homeowners use only heating elements with the "coiled element system," their electric bills will decrease.

   Which of the following represents a necessary assumption that is part of the preceding argument?

(A) Homeowners are always concerned with lowering their utility bills.

(B) By lowering electricity use, homeowners can help decrease pollution levels in their communities.

(C) Heating units with the "coiled element system" are less expensive than more standard heating units.

(D) Heating units with the "coiled element system" are as effective in providing heat as standard heating units.

(E) Heating units with the "coiled element system" have been shown to create less low-level radiation in the home, and people using them have fewer medical problems.

2. The belief in an organized religion is one of the indications of an advanced society. Anthropologists have recently discovered evidence that tribes of people living in Asia 7 million years ago buried people together with small statues of common animals and with certain tools and utensils. Therefore, these tribes can be considered the earliest advanced society to have existed.

   Which of the following assumptions is part of the above argument?

(A) Organized religion began in Asia.

(B) The ancient tribes in Asia worshiped common animals.

(C) Burying people together with tools and utensils is an indication of belief in an organized religion.

(D) Animals that existed in Asia 7 million years ago are now extinct.

(E) Only an advanced society would be able to create statues of animals.

3. A guard dog from Acme Dogs will assume an alert position and will begin barking every time she hears the footsteps of a person walking toward the owner's house. Therefore, anyone with a guard dog from Acme Dogs should feel very secure at home, because the dog will warn the owner if an intruder approaches.

   This conclusion makes which of the following assumptions?

(A) A dog from Acme Dogs would provide good protection after an intruder enters the house.

(B) A dog from Acme Dogs will hear any intruder who approaches.

(C) A dog from Acme Dogs has received special training as a guard dog.

(D) The speaker lives in a dangerous area.

(E) Some intruders may not be people.

4. Today is Tuesday and yesterday was Monday. Therefore, tomorrow will be Wednesday.

   This speaker's conclusion depends on which of the following assumptions?

(A) Wednesday is the day that precedes Thursday.

(B) Tuesday always follows Monday.

(C) If, in any given week, Tuesday follows Monday, then Wednesday will follow Tuesday.

(D) Every week consists of seven days arranged in a particular order.

(E) The speaker always schedules a certain meeting to occur on Wednesday.

5. More people are going out to eat than ever before. This must be true, since the number of Greek restaurants in major cities in the United States has increased in recent years.

   For the above conclusion to be correct, which of the following assumptions must be true?

(A) The increase in the number of Greek restaurants does not coincide with a decrease in other restaurants.

(B) The number of restaurants in any major city remains relatively constant.

(C) Greek restaurants are more popular nationwide than any other ethnic restaurant.

(D) Unemployment rates have declined, so more people can afford to go out to eat.

(E) New restaurants open only when existing restaurants are filled to their capacity.

6. In 1994, Tom bought a new foreign-import automobile. In 1996, the electrical system in Tom's car developed severe problems that required expensive repairs. Now Tom has concluded that the manufacturer of his automobile makes cars of inferior quality, and he refuses ever to buy another car from that manufacturer again.

Which of the following statements represents Tom's major assumption?

(A) Once a car's electrical system breaks down, it can never be repaired adequately so that it functions as well as it did before the problem occurred.

(B) Cars are not built as well in 1996 as they were in 1994.

(C) Domestic cars are more reliable than import cars.

(D) The problems that occurred to Tom's car are representative of what will happen with all cars from the same manufacturer.

(E) From one year to the next, manufacturers do not usually make complete changes in the electrical systems they put in the cars they make.

7. Fossil collections in various archaeological retrieval sites around the world have shown scientists that the first creatures resembling modern man originally appeared on earth between 3 million and 4 million years ago. The species called *Homo erectus* first appeared approximately 2 million years later and survived, scientists believe, until about 1 million years ago. It is easy to see, therefore, that the species identified as "Neanderthals" must have appeared sometime more than 1 million years ago.

Which of the following statements does the author of the above passage assume?

(A) Fossil collecting is the most efficient method for determining details about the history of the human species on Earth.

(B) Carbon dating is an effective and scientifically accurate method of measuring the age of human fossils.

(C) *Homo erectus* is an ancestor of the current human species of *Homo sapiens*.

(D) Neanderthals and *Homo erectus* are both ancestor species of today's common man.

(E) *Homo erectus* and the Neanderthals both lived on Earth at the same time.

8. Officials reviewing conditions of a local police station are considering whether major structural renovations are required. "The chances are good that a police officer will be killed or injured by a prisoner because of the cramped space and poor design of the holding cells," one official concluded. The official's conclusion is based most upon which of the following assumptions?

(A) In crowded conditions, dangerous criminals will have more access to weapons and closer contact with police officers.

(B) All criminals who are brought to this particular holding cell are violently dangerous and present a serious threat to safety.

(C) Storage of and access to police files will be more efficient if the planned renovations are accomplished.

(D) Police officers will be able to perform their public duties more effectively if they are provided with new office spaces.

(E) Holding prisoners in small, cramped holding cells is unconstitutional because it constitutes cruel and inhuman punishment.

9. The ethereal state of the Lotophagai of Greek history was thought to result from eating the narcotic in the lotus fruit. But modern research with rats has shown that the smell of the fruit produces the sleepy, dreamy condition that identified the lotus eaters.

This statement assumes that

(A) eating the narcotic in the lotus fruit has no effect on people.

(B) the fragrance of the lotus enhances the narcotic effect of the fruit.

(C) rats and humans are affected by the lotus fragrance in the same way.

(D) the effect produced by eating the lotus fruit is greater than that produced by smelling the fruit.

(E) it is the fragrance of the lotus fruit that is addictive rather than the narcotic.

10. Nursing home residents have the right to refuse treatment. Forcing a resident to take sedatives, unless that person threatens the well-being of others, is a clear affront to human dignity, an illegal invasion of privacy, and an intolerable violation of the individual's right to think and make decisions about one's own welfare.

A major assumption in this argument is that

(A) residents in nursing homes are no threat to the well-being of others.

(B) treatment in nursing homes is clearly harmful to residents.

(C) sedating drugs should not be used as a treatment in nursing homes.

(D) nursing home residents are capable of making decisions about their own welfare.

(E) the privacy rights of most residents of nursing homes are not protected.

III Strengthen/Weaken Questions

1. The psychological stress of telling a lie produces certain physiological changes. By using appropriate instruments, the physiological symptoms of lying can be measured and result in reliable lie detection.

   Which of the following, if true, most weakens the above argument?

   (A) Lie detectors are sensitive machines that require constant maintenance.

   (B) Lying is only moderately stress-inducing to some people.

   (C) Lie detector operators must be highly trained and careful.

   (D) Numerous kinds of psychological stress produce similar physiological symptoms.

   (E) Measurement instruments such as lie detectors can be misused and abused.

2. Two Congressmen were both elected in the same year. Since their election, Representative Smith has always voted exactly the same as Representative Brown on every issue. Representative Brown has just been recalled by his district and will be replaced by newly elected Representative Jones. Therefore, it is clear that Representative Smith should also be recalled and replaced.

   Which of the following statements, if true, would most strengthen the above argument?

   (A) Representative Smith has radical ideas that are very different from the views of the great majority of the voters in his district.

   (B) Representative Smith is a Republican, but Representative Brown is a Democrat.

   (C) Representative Smith and Representative Brown were both elected from the same district.

   (D) Representative Smith and Representative Brown were elected from different districts.

   (E) Representative Smith's age is closer to the average age of the voters in his district than Representative Brown's is to the age of the voters in his own district.

3. Of the students graduating from Governor Smith Academy, a private high school, 93 percent go on to college. From Eastern High, the public high school in the same city, only 74 percent go on to attend college. As a result, many parents with children about to enter high school believe that Governor Smith Academy gives students a better education than they can get at Eastern High School.

Which of the following statements, if true, would cast the most doubt on the conclusion about Governor Smith Academy?

(A) Until 1992, Governor Smith Academy was exclusively a girls' school, but Eastern High School has always been coeducational.

(B) Governor Smith Academy requires students to pass an admissions examination before entering, but Eastern High School admits all applicants who live in the city.

(C) Eastern High School has problems with severe student violence during school hours.

(D) Governor Smith Academy has a higher percentage of students attending Ivy League colleges than any other high school in the state.

(E) Eastern High School receives its funding from local property taxes, while Governor Smith Academy receives funding from tuition costs and from alumni donations.

4. While some job loss is inevitable in a changing American economy, the current phase of corporate "downsizing" has reached the level of becoming an epidemic. Many employees are being fired simply to enhance profits for top management and company shareholders. Even so, some economists see improvement in the fact that the total number of new jobs being created is increasing at a steady rate.

   Which of the following facts, if true, would show that the economists' view of improvement is incorrect?

   (A) The new jobs that are being created come as a result of governmental tax incentives to large corporations.

   (B) Corporate downsizing is not actually resulting in higher profits for shareholders as expected.

   (C) Many of the new jobs are low-paying entry-level positions that do not provide health-care or pension benefits.

   (D) A separate study of corporate shareholders reveals that many of them would be willing to forgo higher profits in order to increase hiring levels.

   (E) Other countries are experiencing similar increases in job creation.

5. Scientists have found through experimentation that baby female gorillas who were "nurtured" by inanimate mother substitutes that performed some parenting functions were unable to function as mothers when they had offspring. This teaches us that infants should not be placed in the care of babysitters and day-care centers but should only be raised by their natural mothers.

   The conclusion reached by the author would be strengthened by which of the following?

(A) The scientists found that the baby gorillas in the experiments were very dependent on each other.

(B) The gorilla babies in the experiments would only accept food from the scientists, not from the "surrogate" mothers.

(C) Baby gorillas that had brief but regular exposure to their natural mothers were able to function as mothers later.

(D) Baby gorillas raised by females other than their own mothers were unable to function as mothers when they had offspring.

(E) Mature female gorillas that were "raised" by the mother substitutes could be taught many mothering functions when they had offspring.

6. An effective resume, containing accurate information and clearly presented details about a person's education and business experience, is often the best method of obtaining a job in sales. Many job applicants, however, have the bad habit of sending a resume with no cover letter at all. As a result, their resumes are frequently discarded without being considered at all.

 Which of the following statements, if true, would most weaken the conclusion of the above statement?

(A) A survey of people in charge of hiring sales personnel reveals that most of them never read letters of introduction accompanying resumes.

(B) A career in a sales position is very limiting and affords the employee very little ability to grow or improve.

(C) A resume is not always required when applying for a job in a sales-related field.

(D) Many personnel offices prefer to meet applicants directly before considering their qualifications for employment.

(E) Some studies have shown that resumes copied onto colored paper result in higher rates of success than resumes copied onto plain white paper.

7. United Artists' most recent film is based on a best-selling novel and stars Brad Heartthrob. Therefore, the film is expected to do well at the box office.

 Which of the following statements most strengthens the argument?

(A) The film will only play in urban areas.

(B) The producers of the film have cast their next movie without Brad H.

(C) The film is not likely to win an Academy Award.

(D) The book upon which the film is based is a worldwide hit.

(E) Brad H.'s popularity ratings are at an all-time low.

8. High does of niacin in a person's diet have been shown to raise HDL levels, which doctors call the "good" cholesterol, and to lower levels of triglyc-erides and LDL, the so-called "bad" cholesterol. As a result of this study, some nutritionists are now recommending diets that are extremely high in niacin.

 Which of the following facts, if true, would most question the recommendations of the nutritionists?

(A) The original study was conducted on a sample of hospital patients who initially had dangerously high cholesterol levels.

(B) High doses of niacin have been shown to reduce the clotting factors in blood, thereby reducing a person's ability to heal after receiving minor injuries.

(C) When levels of triglycerides decrease, patients report higher levels of stamina and improved physical endurance.

(D) The doctors reporting the results of the study had once been discredited for falsifying the results of their research.

(E) Other studies have shown that the body eventually reaches a maximum plateau with regard to its LDL level.

9. Many states have recently passed versions of a law commonly referred to as "Megan's Law." This law requires individuals who have been convicted of sexual abuse of women or children to notify the local police and certain other agencies upon moving into a new community. As a result of this law, we can now expect repeat offenses of such sexual abuse to decrease significantly.

 Which of the following statements could proponents of "Megan's Law" use to reinforce the conclusion of this argument?

(A) Children do not usually fabricate reports of sexual abuse, so the conviction rate for identified suspects in this area is much higher than for other crimes.

(B) Sociologists have conducted studies that show that people generally prefer not to live in communities where they know that convicted criminals may be living.

(C) Experimental programs requiring people convicted of drunk driving to use special license plates identifying them have resulted in much lower rates of repeat drunk driving offenses.

(D) When members of a community are informed of the identity of someone convicted of sex-related crimes, those community members become more careful to protect their children and to avoid contact with that person.

(E) Nationally, the rate of child abuse has been steadily declining since the mid-1980s.

10. Unlike the more traditional energy sources of coal, gas, and nuclear energy, energy from the sun pro-

duces no major problems. It produces no pollution and requires no transportation from foreign lands. It threatens no one with radiation dangers and is not controlled by powerful corporations. Therefore, we should encourage people to use solar energy.

Which of the following statements, if true, most seriously weakens this argument?

(A) There have been very few studies of solar energy use by households.
(B) The cost of oil and gas could be regulated to make it less costly for home consumption.
(C) The cost of the equipment required to collect enough solar energy for a family of four equals the amount a family now pays for oil, gas, or nuclear energy in one year.
(D) Most critics of solar energy are connected to energy monopolies.
(E) An effective way for families to capture and store solar energy has not yet been developed.

Answers

Part I: 1-E, 2-D, 3-A, 4-B, 5-C, 6-C, 7-E, 8-B, 9-C, 10-E
Part II: 1-D, 2-C, 3-B, 4-C, 5-A, 6-D, 7-E, 8-A, 9-C, 10-D
Part III: 1-D, 2-C, 3-B, 4-C, 5-D, 6-A, 7-D, 8-B, 9-D, 10-E

Answers to Selected Exercises

Exercise 1.1

I.

1. P: Titanium combines readily with oxygen, nitrogen, and hydrogen, all of which have an adverse effect on its mechanical properties.

   C: Titanium must be processed in their absence.

4. P: When individuals voluntarily abandon property, they forfeit any expectation of privacy in it that they might have had.

   C: A warrantless search and seizure of abandoned property is not unreasonable under the Fourth Amendment.

7. P_1: After October 1963, when Hurricane Flora devastated the island and killed more than a thousand people, the Cuban government overhauled its civil defense system.

   P_2: It was so successful that when six powerful hurricanes thumped Cuba between 1996 and 2002 only 16 people died.

   P_3: And when Hurricane Ivan struck Cuba in 2004 there was not a single casualty, but the same storm killed at least 70 people in other Caribbean countries.

   C: Cuba's record on disaster prevention is impressive.

10. P_1: Punishment, when speedy and specific, may suppress undesirable behavior.

    P_2: Punishment cannot teach or encourage desirable alternatives.

    C: It is crucial to use positive techniques to model and reinforce appropriate behavior that the person can use in place of the unacceptable response that has to be suppressed.

13. P_1: Private property helps people define themselves.

    P_2: Private property frees people from mundane cares of daily subsistence.

    P_3: Private property is finite.

    C: No individual should accumulate so much property that others are prevented from accumulating the necessities of life.

16. P_1: The nations of planet earth have acquired nuclear weapons with an explosive power equal to more than a million Hiroshima bombs.

    P_2: Studies suggest that explosion of only half these weapons would produce enough soot, smoke, and dust to blanket the earth, block out the sun, and bring on a nuclear winter that would threaten the survival of the human race.

    C: Radioactive fallout isn't the only concern in the aftermath of nuclear explosions.

19. P_1: Antipoverty programs provide jobs for middle-class professionals in social work, penology, and public health.

    P_2: Such workers' future advancement is tied to the continued growth of bureaucracies dependent on the existence of poverty.

C: Poverty offers numerous benefits to the nonpoor.

22. P: Take the nurse who alleges that physicians enrich themselves in her hospital through unnecessary surgery; the engineer who discloses safety defects in the braking systems of a fleet of new rapid-transit vehicles; the Defense Department official who alerts Congress to military graft and overspending: all know that they pose a threat to those whom they denounce and that their own careers may be at risk.

C: The stakes in whistle-blowing are high.

25. P1: It is generally accepted that by constantly swimming with its mouth open, the shark is simply avoiding suffocation.

P2: This assures a continuous flow of oxygen-laden water into the shark's mouth, over its gills, and out through the gill slits.

C: Contrary to the tales of some scuba divers, the toothy, gaping grin on the mouth of an approaching shark is not necessarily anticipatory.

28. P1: Anyone familiar with our prison system knows that there are some inmates who behave little better than brute beasts.

P2: If the death penalty had been truly effective as a deterrent, such prisoners would long ago have vanished.

C: The very fact that these prisoners exist is a telling argument against the efficacy of capital punishment as a deterrent.

II.

1. College sports are as much driven by money as professional sports.

4. Business majors are robbing themselves of the true purpose of collegiate academics, a sacrifice that outweighs the future salary checks.

7. The religious intolerance of television preachers must not be tolerated.

10. Protecting the environment requires that we limit population growth.

Exercise 1.2

I.

1. Nonargument; explanation.

4. Nonargument; illustration.

7. Argument (conclusion: If stem-cell research is restricted, then people will die prematurely).

10. Nonargument; report.

13. Nonargument; report.

16. Nonargument; piece of advice.

19. Argument (conclusion: For organisms at the sea surface, sinking into deep water usually means death).

22. Argument (conclusion: Atoms can combine to form molecules whose properties generally are very different from those of the constituent atoms).

25. Nonargument; explanation.

28. Argument (conclusion: A person never becomes truly self-reliant).

31. This passage could be both an argument and an explanation (conclusion: In areas where rats are a problem, it is very difficult to exterminate them with bait poison).

34. Nonargument; loosely associated statements.

II.

1. Nonargument.

4. Nonargument.

7. Argument (conclusion: The poor quality of parenting and the lack in continuity of adult care provided to many U.S. children contribute to a passivity and a sense of helplessness that hobbles individuals for the remainder of their lives).

10. Nonargument.

VI.

1. Sufficient: If something is a tiger, then it is an animal.
4. Necessary: If a person has no racket, then he/she cannot play tennis. *Or,* If a person plays tennis, then he/she has a racket.
7. Sufficient: If leaves burn, then smoke is produced.
10. Necessary: If a person does not open the door, then he/she cannot cross the threshold. *Or,* If a person crosses the threshold, then he/she has opened the door.

Exercise 1.3

I.

1. Deductive (argument based on mathematics; also, conclusion follows necessarily from the premises).
4. Deductive (categorical syllogism; also, conclusion follows necessarily from the premises).
7. Inductive (causal inference; also, conclusion follows only probably from the premise).
10. Inductive (argument from analogy; also, conclusion follows only probably from the premise).
13. Inductive (argument from authority; also, conclusion follows only probably from the premise).
16. Deductive (conclusion follows necessarily from the premise).
19. Inductive (causal inference; also, conclusion follows only probably from the premises).
22. Deductive (conclusion follows necessarily from the premise; this example might also be interpreted as an argument from definition—the definition of "refraction").
25. Inductive (causal inference: The dog's familiarity with the visitor caused the dog to be silent).
28. Inductive (causal inference; also, the word "may" suggests a probabilistic inference).

Exercise 1.4

I.

1. Valid, unsound; false premises, false conclusion.
4. Valid, sound; true premises, true conclusion.
7. Invalid, unsound; true premise, true conclusion.
10. Valid, unsound; false premise, false conclusion.
13. Invalid, unsound; true premises, true conclusion.

II.

1. Strong, cogent; true premise, probably true conclusion.
4. Weak, uncogent; true premise, probably false conclusion.
7. Strong, uncogent; false premise, probably true conclusion.
10. Strong, cogent; true premise, probably true conclusion.
13. Weak, uncogent; true premises, probably false conclusion.

III.

1. Deductive, valid.	7. Inductive, weak.	13. Inductive, weak.
4. Deductive, valid.	10. Deductive, invalid.	16. Deductive, invalid.
		19. Inductive, strong.

Exercise 1.5

I.

1. All *G* are *S*.   All cats are animals. (T)
   All *Q* are *S*.   All dogs are animals. (T)
   All *G* are *Q*.   All cats are dogs. (F)

4. No *I* are *P*.
Some *I* are not *F*.
Some *F* are not *P*.

No fish are mammals. (T)
Some fish are not cats. (T)
Some cats are not mammals. (F)

7. No *P* are *H*.
No *C* are *H*.
No *P* are *C*.

No dogs are fish. (T)
No mammals are fish. (T)
No dogs are mammals. (F)

10. Some *S* are not *O*.
Some *G* are not *O*.
Some *S* are not *G*.

Some dogs are not fish. (T)
Some animals are not fish. (T)
Some dogs are not animals. (F)

II.

1. If *A* then *E*.
Not *A*.
Not *E*.

If George Washington was assassinated, then
George Washington is dead. (T)
George Washington was not assassinated. (T)
George Washington is not dead. (F)

4. If *E*, then either *D* or *C*.
If *D*, then *I*.
If *E*, then *I*.

If Tom Cruise is a man, then he is either
a mouse or a human. (T)
If Tom Cruise is a mouse, then he has a tail. (T)
If Tom Cruise is a man, then he has a tail. (F)

7. All *C* with *L* are either
S or *I*.
All *C* are *I*.

All cats with fur are either mammals or dogs. (T)
All cats are dogs. (F)

10. All *R* that are *F* are either
L or *H*.
All *R* are *H*.
All *F* are *L*.

All cats that are mammals are either
dogs or animals. (T)
All cats are animals. (T)
All mammals are dogs. (F)

Exercise 1.6

I.

1.
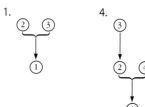

4.

7.
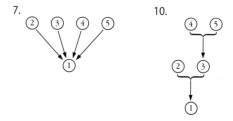

10.

II.

1.

4.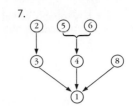

7.

10.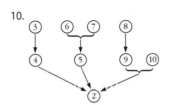

Note: Possible variations exist for ⑤, ⑥, and ⑦.

13.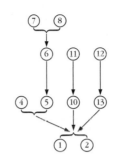

Exercise 2.1

II.

1. In dog sled races the dogs are tortured.
   Torturing animals is morally wrong.
   Therefore, dog sled races are morally wrong.

4. Free ownership of guns is as noble as belief in God and intestinal fortitude.
   Belief in God and intestinal fortitude made our country great and free.
   Continued belief in God and intestinal fortitude are necessary to keep our country the way it is.
   Free ownership of guns is no less important than God and intestinal fortitude.
   Therefore, gun control is wrong.

7. The celebration of cultural diversity causes social fragmentation.
   The celebration of cultural diversity is symptomatic of a split personality.
   The people who set this country up framed one nation, indivisible.
   The celebration of cultural diversity works against the intention of these people.
   The celebration of cultural diversity erodes national identity.
   Therefore, the celebration of cultural diversity is wrong.

10. Liberalism has excessively enlarged the welfare system.
    Liberalism has made welfare recipients indolent and irresponsible.
    The liberals refuse to acknowledge or correct the defects in this system.
    Liberalism has made the criminal justice system too sensitive to the criminal and too insensitive to the victim of crime.
    Liberalism has given more rights to the criminal than to the ordinary citizen.
    Liberalism has promoted sex and violence in the school system.
    Liberals have opposed prayer in the schools.
    Therefore, liberalism is bad.

2

III.

1. Probably verbal; ambiguity. Does "sound" designate a subjective perception or an objective disturbance of the air (or some other medium)?

4. Probably verbal; ambiguity. By "violence" do we mean intentional hostility exerted by one human against another, or the operation of blind physical forces? Possibly a combination of verbal and factual. Is human violence caused by the operation of physical forces just as other physical events are?

7. Factual. Did Paul go to Knoxville or Nashville?

10. Factual. When was the Battle of Trafalgar fought, and when did Nelson die?

13. Probably a combination of verbal (ambiguity) and factual. First, does "freedom" mean the absence of external constraint only, or the absence of both internal and external constraint? Second, given the former, is it appropriate to punish the perpetrator of evil acts even though those acts might be internally compelled?

16. Verbal; vagueness. What is the meaning of "overpaid"?

19. Verbal; vagueness. What is the meaning of "poverty"?

Exercise 2.2

I.

4a. Plant, tree, conifer, spruce, Sitka spruce.

Exercise 2.3

I.

1. Precising definition.
4. Lexical definition.
7. Persuasive definition.

10. Theoretical definition.
13. Stipulative definition.
16. Persuasive definition.

19. Lexical definition.
22. Precising definition.
25. Stipulative definition.

Exercise 2.4

I.

1. Definition by subclass.
4. Enumerative definition.
7. Demonstrative definition.
10. Operational definition.
13. Definition by genus and difference.

16. Etymological definition.
19. Enumerative definition.
22. Synonymous definition.
25. Definition by subclass.
28. Definition by genus and difference.

II.

1a. "Skyscraper" means the Empire State Building, Chrysler Building, Sears Tower, and so on. Nonsynonymous term: building.

3a. "Animal" means a horse, bear, lion, and so on. Nonsynonymous term: mammal.

5a. "Intersection" means crossing.

6a. A person is a "genius" if and only if that person can earn a score of 140 on an IQ test.

7a. "Drake" means a male duck.

8a. "Morphology" is derived from the Greek words *morphe*, meaning "form," and *logos*, meaning reason, speech, or account. The morphology of something (such as an animal or a plant) gives an account or explanation of the form or structure of that thing.

Exercise 2.5

1. Rule 3: too narrow; the definiens excludes images made of bronze, wood, plaster, and so on.
4. Rule 6: figurative language.
7. Rule 5: negative.

10. Rule 7: affective terminology.

13. Rule 1: improper grammar.

16. Rule 4: circular.

19. Rule 6: vague.

22. Rule 1: improper grammar; Rule 6: vague; Rule 3: too broad (the definiens also includes ketches, sloops, and yawls).

25. Rule 3: too broad (the definiens also describes violins, violas, and string basses).

28. Rule 2: fails to convey the essential meaning; the definition says nothing about the purpose of a clock, which is to tell the time; also too narrow: the definiens excludes 24-hour clocks and clocks without 12 numerals on their face.

31. Rule 7: affective terminology.

34. Rule 3: both too narrow and too broad; the definiens excludes instruments used for writing on canvas, glass, metal, plastic, and so on, and it includes pencils, crayons, and so on.

Exercise 3.1

1. Formal fallacy.

4. Informal fallacy.

7. Informal fallacy.

10. Formal fallacy.

Exercise 3.2

I.

1. Appeal to pity.

4. Accident.

7. Appeal to force.

10. *Tu quoque* (you, too).

13. Red herring.

16. *Ad hominem* (argument against the person) circumstantial.

19. Straw man.

22. Appeal to the people, indirect variety.

25. Missing the point.

Exercise 3.3

I.

1. Hasty generalization (converse accident).

4. Slippery slope.

7. Appeal to ignorance.

10. Appeal to unqualified authority.

13. Weak analogy.

III.

1. Hasty generalization.

4. *Ad hominem* (argument against the person) circumstantial.

7. False cause (gambler's fallacy).

10. Straw man.

13. Red herring.

16. Missing the point.

19. Weak analogy.

22. No fallacy.

25. Appeal to ignorance.

28. False cause.

Exercise 3.4

I.

1. False dichotomy.

4. Amphiboly.

7. Begging the question.

10. Equivocation.

13. Composition.

16. Suppressed evidence.

19. Division.

22. Complex question.

25. Begging the question.

III.

1. *Ad hominem* (argument against the person) circumstantial.
4. Equivocation.
7. Begging the question.
10. Division.
13. False cause (oversimplified cause).
16. Appeal to unqualified authority.
19. Composition.
22. Weak analogy.
25. Straw man.
28. Accident.
31. Red herring.
34. Amphiboly.
37. False cause (gambler's fallacy).
40. Begging the question.
43. Missing the point or suppressed evidence.
46. Hasty generalization.
49. Composition.

Exercise 3.5

I.

1. Missing the point or begging the question.
4. Composition.
7. No fallacy? Weak analogy?
10. Appeal to unqualified authority. The statement "Only a fool . . ." involves an *ad hominem* abusive.
13. False cause, suppressed evidence, begging the question. There is little or no evidence of any causal connection between malpractice suits and the decision of some obstetricians to leave the field. An unmentioned factor is the inconvenience of being on call twenty-four hours per day waiting for patients to deliver. There is also little or no evidence of any genuine "lawsuit crisis."
16. Begging the question? (Strange argument!)
19. Slippery slope.
22. False cause? No fallacy?
25. False cause.
28. Suppressed evidence? Begging the question? No fallacy? The Commerce Clause of the U.S. Constitution and pertinent federal legislation prohibit unfair trade practices between states. No equivalent regulations exist for international trade.
31. Appeal to the people (direct variety). Also appeal to pity?
34. Appeal to the people (direct variety)?
37. False dichotomy? No fallacy?
40. Appeal to unqualified authority, slippery slope.
43. Several cases of weak analogy. Also, a possible case of *ad hominem* abusive.
46. Begging the question; straw man.
49. Appeal to unqualified authority. The last paragraph suggests a hasty generalization.
52. Hasty generalization. *Ad hominem* abusive? Also, begging the question or red herring?
55. Weak analogy.
58. Weak analogy? No fallacy?

Exercise 4.1

1. *Quantifier:* some; *subject term:* airport screeners; *copula:* are; *predicate term:* officials who harass frail grandmothers.
4. *Quantifier:* some; *subject term:* preachers who are intolerant of others' beliefs; *copula:* are not; *predicate term:* television evangelists.
7. *Quantifier:* no; *subject term:* sex education courses that are taught competently; *copula:* are; *predicate term:* programs that are currently eroding public morals.

Exercise 4.2

I.
1. E proposition, universal, negative, subject and predicate terms are distributed.
4. O proposition, particular, negative, subject term undistributed, predicate term distributed.
7. I proposition, particular, affirmative, subject and predicate terms undistributed.

II.
1. No drunk drivers are threats to others on the highway.
4. Some CIA operatives are champions of human rights.

III.
1. Some owners of pit bull terriers are persons who can expect expensive lawsuits.
4. No residents of Manhattan are people who can afford to live there.

IV.
1. Some oil spills are not events catastrophic to the environment.
4. All corporate lawyers are persons with a social conscience.

Exercise 4.3

I.

1.
   L   H

4.
   R   F

7.
   H   C

II.
1. Invalid
4. Valid
7. Invalid
10. Valid
13. Invalid

III.
1. No S are B.

S   B

All S are B.
(invalid)

S   B

4. All M are C.

M   C

False: Some M are
not C.
(valid)

M   C

7. No F are S.

F   S

False: All F are S.
(invalid,
existential fallacy)

F   S

10. No V are A.

V   A

False: Some V are A.
(valid)

V   A

13. False: Some *S* are not *O*.

Some *S* are *O*.
(invalid,
existential fallacy)

Exercise 4.4

I.

1. No non-*B* are *A*. (true)
4. All non-*B* are *A*. (false)
7. Contraposition. (undetermined)
10. Obversion. (false)

II.

1a. All storms intensified by global warming are hurricanes. (not logically equivalent)
2a. No radically egalitarian societies are societies that preserve individual liberties. (logically equivalent)
3a. All physicians eligible to practice are physicians with valid licenses. (logically equivalent)

III.

1. Invalid (illicit conversion).
7. Valid.
13. Invalid (illicit conversion).
19. Valid.

4. Invalid (illicit contraposition).
10. Valid.
16. Invalid (illicit contraposition).

Exercise 4.5

I.

1. (a) false, (b) true, (c) false.
4. (a) undetermined, (b) true, (c) undetermined.
7. (a) false, (b) undetermined, (c) undetermined.

II.

1. Valid.
7. Invalid (illicit contrary).
13. Invalid (existential fallacy).

4. Invalid (existential fallacy).
10. Invalid (illicit subcontrary).

III.

1. All non-*B* are *A*. (true)
7. No non-*A* are *B*. (false)
13. Obversion. (false)
19. Contrary. (undetermined)

4. Some non-*A* are *B*. (undetermined)
10. Some non-*A* are not non-*B*. (true)
16. Contradiction. (true)

IV.

1. Valid.
7. Valid.
13. Invalid (illicit subcontrary).

4. Invalid (illicit contraposition).
10. Invalid (illicit contrary).

V.

1. All *I* are *C*.
   Some *I* are *C*. (subalternation)
   Some *C* are *I*. (conversion)
4. All *E* are *A*.
   False: No *E* are *A*. (contrary)
   False: No *A* are *E*. (conversion)
   False: All *A* are non-*E*. (obversion)

7. Some *P* are not non-*S*.
   Some *P* are *S*. (obversion)
   Some *S* are *P*. (conversion)
   False: No *S* are *P*. (contradiction)
10. False: Some *F* are not *A*.
    False: No *F* are *A*. (subalternation)
    False: No *A* are *F*. (conversion)
    False: All *A* are non-*F*. (obversion)

Exercise 4.6

I.

1. Some *A* are not *B*.

A   B

No *A* are *B*.
(invalid)

A   B

4. All *A* are *B*.

A   B

False: No *A* are *B*.
(invalid, Boolean;
conditionally valid,
Aristotelian)

A   B

7. False: Some *A* are *B*.

A   B

No *A* are *B*.
(valid, Boolean)

A   B

10. No *A* are *B*.

A   B

Some *A* are not *B*.
(invalid, Boolean;
conditionally valid,
Aristotelian)

A   B

II.

1. No *S* are *B*.

S   B

False: Some *S* are *B*.
(valid, Boolean)

S   B

4. False: Some *D* are *A*.

D   A

Some *D* are not *A*.
(invalid, Boolean; valid,
Aristotelian; existential
fallacy, Boolean)

D   A

7. All *P* are *F*.

P   F

False: No *P* are *F*.
(invalid; existential
fallacy, Boolean and
Aristotelian)

P   F

10. False: Some *T* are *Q*.

T   Q

All *T* are *Q*.
(invalid)

T   Q

13. False: Some *P* are T.

False: All *P* are *T.*
(invalid, Boolean;
valid; Aristotelian;
existential fallacy,
Boolean)

Exercise 4.7

I.
1. All banks that make too many risky loans are banks that will fail.
4. All substances identical to bromine are substances extractable from seawater.
7. No halogens are chemically inert elements.
10. All ships that fly the Jolly Roger are pirate ships.
13. All bachelors are unmarried men.
16. Some organic silicones are things used as lubricants.
19. Some giant stars are things in the Tarantula Nebula. *Or* All things identical to the Tarantula Nebula are things that contain a giant star.
22. All persons who believe Noah's ark lies beneath the snows of Ararat are persons given to flights of fancy.
25. All cities identical to Berlin are cities that were the setting for the 1936 Olympic Games.
   Or All events identical to the 1936 Olympic Games are events that took place in Berlin.
28. All places there is smoke are places there is fire.
31. All ores identical to pitchblende are radioactive ores.
34. All novels written by John Grisham are are novels about lawyers.
37. All times a rainbow occurs are times the sun is shining.
40. Some corporate raiders are persons known for their integrity, and some corporate raiders are not persons known for their integrity.
43. All persons identical to me are persons who like strawberries. *Or* All things identical to strawberries are things I like.
46. All places Cynthia wants to travel are places Cynthia travels.
49. No physicists are persons who understand the operation of superconductors.
52. All measures that increase efficiency are measures that improve profitability.
55. Some picnics are events entirely free of ants, and some picnics are not events entirely free of ants.
58. All Net surfers are computer buffs.

II.
1. Some third-generation computers are machines that take dictation.
4. No downhill skiers who suffer from altitude sickness are effective competitors.
7. No matadors are performers who succumb easily to fear.
10. All hungry crocodiles are dangerous animals.

Exercise 5.1

I.

1. *Major term:* things that produce intense gravity.
   Minor term: extremely dense objects.
   Middle term: neutron stars.
   Mood, figure: **AAA**-3; invalid.

4. *Major term:* good witnesses.
   Minor term: hypnotized persons.
   Middle term: persons who mix fact with fantasy.
   Mood, figure: **EIO**-1; valid, Boolean.

II.

1. All *B* are *D.*
   No *R* are *D.*
   No *R* are *B.*
   AEE-2
   valid, Boolean

4. No *M* are *F.*
   All *M* are *I.*
   Some *I* are not *F.*
   EAO-3
   invalid, Boolean;
   valid, Aristotelian

7. All *P* are *E.*
   All *L* are *P.*
   Some *L* are *E.*
   AAI-1
   invalid

10. Some *O* are not *C.*
    All *S* are *O.*
    Some *S* are *C.*
    OAI-1
    invalid

III.

1. Some *M* are not *P.*
   All *M* are *S.*
   No *S* are *P.*

4. Some *M* are *P.*
   All *S* are *M.*
   No *S* are *P.*

7. All *M* are *P.*
   All *S* are *M.*
   All *S* are *P.*

10. Some *P* are not *M.*
    No *M* are *S.*
    All *S* are *P.*

IV.

1. No dogmatists are scholars who encourage free thinking.
   Some theologians are scholars who encourage free thinking.
   Some theologians are not dogmatists.

4. Some viruses are not things capable of replicating by themselves.
   All viruses are structures that invade cells.
   Some structures that invade cells are not things capable of replicating by themselves.

Exercise 5.2

I.

1. All *C* are *U.*
   Some *U* are *I.*
   Some *I* are *C.*
   AII-4
   invalid

4. All *H* are *D.*
   Some *D* are not *P.*
   Some *P* are not *H.*
   AOO-4
   invalid

7. No *P* are *I*.
 All *F* are *I*.
 No *F* are *P*.
 EAE-2
 valid, Boolean

10. No *C* are *O*.
 Some *D* are not *O*.
 Some *D* are not *C*.
 EOO-2
 invalid

13. No *P* are *W*.
 All *D* are *P*.
 No *D* are *W*.
 EAE-1
 valid, Boolean

16. All *C* are *G*.
 All *G* are *E*.
 Some *E* are *C*.
 AAI-4
 invalid

19. No *S* are *I*.
 All *S* are *N*.
 Some *N* are not *I*.
 EAO-3
 invalid, Boolean;
 valid, Aristotelian

II.

1.

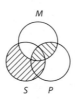

Conclusion: No *S* are *P*.

4.

Conclusion: Some *S* are not *P*.

7.

Conclusion: All *S* are *P*.

10.

Conclusion: None.

Exercise 5.3

I.

1. All *M* are *P*.
 All *M* are *S*.
 All *S* are *P*.
 invalid;
 illicit minor

4. All *P* are *M*.
 All *S* are *M*.
 Some *S* are *P*.
 invalid;
 undistributed middle

7. No *M* are *P*.
   All *S* are *M*.
   ___
   All *S* are *P*.
   invalid;
   drawing affirmative
   conclusion from
   negative premise

10. Some *M* are *P*.
   All *M* are *S*.
   ___
   Some *S* are not *P*.
   invalid;
   illicit major;
   drawing negative
   conclusion from
   affirmative premises

13. All *P* are *M*.
   No *M* are *S*.
   ___
   No *S* are *P*.
   valid, Boolean;
   no rules broken

16. No *M* are *P*.
   No *S* are *M*.
   ___
   No *S* are *P*.
   invalid;
   exclusive premises

19. All *P* are *M*.
   Some *S* are not *M*.
   ___
   Some *S* are not *P*.
   valid, Boolean;
   no rules broken

II.

1. Some *N* are *C*.
   Some *C* are *O*.
   ___
   Some *O* are *N*.
   invalid;
   undistributed middle

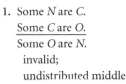

4. Some *C* are not *M*.
   No *C* are *I*.
   ___
   Some *I* are not *M*.
   invalid;
   exclusive premises

7. No *S* are *V*.
   Some *W* are *V*.
   ___
   Some *W* are not *S*.
   valid, Boolean
   no rules broken

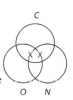

10. All *S* are *M*.
   All *M* are *P*.
   ___
   Some *P* are *S*.
   invalid, Boolean;
   valid, Aristotelian;
   existential fallacy,
   Boolean

Exercise 5.4

1. Some non-*T* are *M*. (convert, obvert)
   All non-*I* are non-*M*. (contrapose)
   ___
   Some *I* are *T*.

Some *M* are not *T*.
All *M* are *I*.
___
Some *I* are *T*.
   invalid; drawing affirmative conclusion
   from negative premise

4. Some *I* are *C*.   Some *I* are *C*.
   All *C* are non-*P*.   All *C* are non-*P*.
   Some non-*I* are not *P*. (contrapose)   Some non-*P* are not *I*.
                                           invalid; illicit major

7. All non-*M* are non-*E*. (contrapose)   All *E* are *M*.
   Some *P* are not *M*.   Some *P* are not *M*.
   Some *P* are non-*E*. (obvert)   Some *P* are not *E*.
                                           valid

10. Some *S* are non-*D*. (obvert)   Some *S* are not *D*.
    No *D* are *V*.   No *D* are *V*.
    Some non-*V* are *S*. (convert, obvert)   Some *S* are not *V*.
                                            invalid; exclusive premises

Exercise 5.5

1. All scientists who theorize about the nature of time are physicists.
   All persons identical to Stephen Hawking are scientists who theorize about the nature of time.
   All persons identical to Stephen Hawking are physicists.
       valid

4. All persons who wrote the Declaration of Independence are persons who had a big impact on civilization.
   All persons identical to Thomas Jefferson are persons who had a big impact on civilization.
   All persons identical to Thomas Jefferson are persons who wrote the Declaration of Independence.
       invalid, undistributed middle

7. Some songs Shania Twain sings are country songs.
   All songs Shania Twain wants to sing are songs Shania Twain sings.
   Some songs Shania Twain wants to sing are country songs.
       invalid, undistributed middle

10. All TV viewers who receive scrambled signals are viewers with a decoder.
    All persons who receive digital satellite signals are TV viewers who receive scrambled signals.
    All persons who receive digital satellite signals are viewers with a decoder.
        valid

13. All diseases carried by recessive genes are diseases that can be inherited by offspring of two carriers.
    All diseases identical to cystic fibrosis are diseases carried by recessive genes.
    All diseases identical to cystic fibrosis are diseases that can be inherited by offspring of two carriers.
        valid

Exercise 5.6

I.

1. Premise missing: Some police chiefs fix parking tickets.
4. Conclusion missing: A few fraternities have no legitimate role in campus life.
7. Conclusion missing: Some phone calls are not from friends.
10. Premise missing: Whenever the humpback whale is overhunted, the humpback whale population decreases.
13. Premise missing: No one who thinks that everything is governed by deterministic laws believes in free will.

II.

1. All persons who fix parking tickets are persons who undermine the evenhanded enforcement of the law.

   Some police chiefs are persons who fix parking tickets.
   _____
   Some police chiefs are persons who undermine the evenhanded enforcement of the law.

   valid

4. No groups that have dangerous initiation rites are groups that have a legitimate role in campus life.

   Some fraternities are groups that have dangerous initiation rites.
   _____
   Some fraternities are not groups that have a legitimate role in campus life.

   valid

7. All calls from friends are welcome calls.

   Some phone calls are not welcome calls.
   _____
   Some phone calls are not calls from friends.

   valid

10. All times the humpback whale is overhunted are times the humpback whale population decreases.

    All recent years are times the humpback whale is overhunted.
    _____
    All recent years are times the humpback whale population decreases.

    valid

13. No persons who think that everything is governed by deterministic laws are persons who believe in free will.

    All mechanistic materialists are persons who think everything is governed by deterministic laws.
    No mechanistic materialists are persons who believe in free will.

    valid

III.

1. No organizations that make alcohol readily available and acceptable are organizations that are serious about fighting alcohol abuse.

   All organizations identical to the Defense Department are organizations that make alcohol readily available and acceptable.
   _____
   No organizations identical to the Defense Department are organizations that are serious about fighting alcohol abuse.

4. All efforts to ban books are efforts that ensure those books will be read.

   All efforts by the fundamentalist families in Church Hill, Tennessee, to remove *Macbeth*, etc. from the libraries are efforts to ban books.
   _____
   All efforts by the fundamentalist families in Church Hill, Tennessee, to remove *Macbeth*, etc. from the libraries are efforts that ensure those books will be read.

7. All policies that promote more college graduates tomorrow are policies that result in higher tax revenues tomorrow.

   All policies that offer financial aid to college students today are policies that promote more college graduates tomorrow.
   _____
   All policies that offer financial aid to college students today are policies that result in higher tax revenues tomorrow.

   and

   All policies that result in higher tax revenues tomorrow are good investments in the future.

   All policies that offer financial aid to college students today are policies that result in higher tax revenues tomorrow.
   _____
   All policies that offer financial aid to college students today are good investments in the future.

10. All people who act in ways that decrease their chances of survival are people who will die out through natural selection.

All smokers who continue smoking are people who act in ways that decrease their chances of survival.

All smokers who continue smoking are people who will die out through natural selection.

and

All people who act in ways that increase their chances of survival are people who will survive through natural selection.

All smokers who quit are people who act in ways that increase their chances of survival.

All smokers who quit are people who will survive through natural selection.

Exercise 5.7

I.

1. All *A* are *B.*
   No *B* are *C.* } No *C* are *A.* }
   Some *D* are *C.* ⟶ }
   Some *D* are not *A.*
      valid

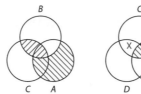

4. No *K* are *N.*
   Some *T* are *K.* } Some *T* are not *N.* }
   All *T* are *C.* ⟶ } Some *C* are not *N.* }
   Some *C* are *Q.* ⟶ }
   Some *Q* are not *N.*
      invalid

7. After contraposing the first premise, obverting the second premise and the conclusion, and rearranging the premises, we have:

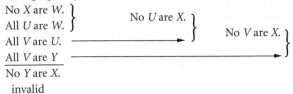

No *X* are *W.* ⎫
All *U* are *W.* ⎬ No *U* are *X.* ⎫
All *V* are *U.* ─────────────→ ⎬ No *V* are *X.* ⎫
All *V* are *Y* ──────────────────────────→ ⎬
No *Y* are *X.*
    invalid

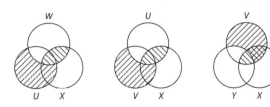

      W   *U*   *V*

   U   *X*   *V*   *X*   *Y*   *X*

10. After converting and obverting the second and fourth premises, obverting the third and fifth premises and the conclusion, and rearranging the premises, we have:

All *P* are *Q.* ⎫
All *Q* are *R.* ⎬ All *P* are *R.* ⎫
All *R* are *S,* ─────────────→ ⎬ All *P* are *S.* ⎫
No *T* are *S.* ──────────────────────────→ ⎬ No *P* are *T.* ⎫
All *T* are *V.* ──→ ⎬
No *V* are *P.*
    invalid

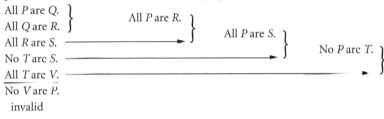

      Q   *R*   *S*   *T*

  P   *R*   *P*   *S*   *P*   *T*   *V*   *P*

II.

1. All things that produce oxygen are things that support human life.   All *O* are *S.*
     All rain forests are things that produce oxygen.   All *R* are *O.*
     No things that support human life are things that should be destroyed.   No *S* are *D.*
     No rain forests are things that should be destroyed.   No *R* are *D.*

After rearranging the premises, we have:

No *S* are *D.* ⎫
All *O* are *S.* ⎬ No *O* are *D.* ⎫
All *R* are *O.* ─────────────→ ⎬
No *R* are *D.*

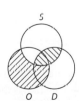

      S   *O*

   O   *D*   *R*   *D*

4. No brittle things are ductile things.   No B are D.
   All superconductors are ceramics.   All S are C.
   All things that can be pulled into wires are ductile things.   All P are D.
   All ceramics are brittle things.   All C are B.
   No superconductors are things that can be pulled into wires.   No S are P.

   After rearranging the premises, we have:

   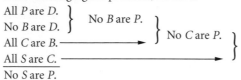

     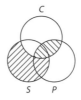

7. All persons who give birth to crack babies are persons who
   increase future crime rates.   All B are I.
   Some pregnant women are pregnant crack users.   Some P are U.
   All persons who increase future crime rates are criminals.   All I are C.
   No pregnant crack users are persons who fail to give birth to
   crack babies.   No U are non-B.
   Some pregnant women are criminals.   Some P are C.

   After obverting the fourth premise and rearranging the premises, we have:

   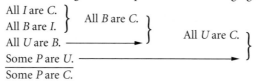

10. All things that promote skin cancer are things that cause death.   All S are C.
    All things that preserve the ozone layer are things that prevent the
    release of CFCs.   All O are non-R.
    No things that resist skin cancer are things that increase UV radiation. No non-S are U.
    All things that do not preserve the ozone layer are things that
    increase UV radiation.   All non-O are U.
    Some packaging materials are things that release CFCs.   Some M are R.
    No things that cause death are things that should be legal.   No C are L.
    Some packaging materials are things that should not be legal.   Some M are non-L.

After contraposing the second premise, converting and obverting the third premise, and obverting the conclusion, we have:

No *C* are *L.* ⎱
All *S* are *C.* ⎰ No *S* are *L.* ⎱
All *U* are *S.* ─────────→ ⎰ No *U* are *L.* ⎱
All non-*O* are *U.* ─────────────────→ ⎰ No non-*O* are *L.* ⎱
All *R* are non-*O.* ─────────────────────────→ ⎰ No *R* are *L.* ⎱
Some *M* are *R.* ─────────────────────────────────────→ ⎰
Some *M* are not *L.*

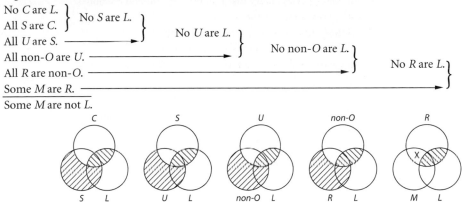

III.

1. No ducks are waltzers.   No *D* are *W.*
   No officers are non-waltzers.   No *O* are non-*W.*
   All poultry of mine are ducks.   All *P* are *D.*
   No poultry of mine are officers.   No *P* are *O.*

   After obverting the second premise and rearranging the premises, we have:

   All *O* are *W.* ⎱
   No *D* are *W.* ⎰ No *D* are *O.* ⎱
   All *P* are *D.* ─────────→ ⎰
   No *P* are *O.*

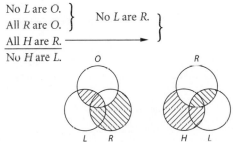

4. All hummingbirds are richly colored birds.   All *H* are *R.*
   No large birds are birds that live on honey.   No *L* are *O.*
   All birds that do not live on honey are birds that are dull in color.   All non-*O* are non-*R.*
   All hummingbirds are small birds.   All *H* are non-*L.*

   After contraposing the third premise, obverting the conclusion, and rearranging the premises, we have:

   No *L* are *O.* ⎱
   All *R* are *O.* ⎰ No *L* are *R.* ⎱
   All *H* are *R.* ─────────→ ⎰
   No *H* are *L.*

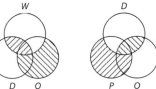

7. All books in this library that I do not recommend are books that are unhealthy in tone.
   All the bound books are well-written books.
   All the romances are books that are healthy in tone.
   All the unbound books are books in this library that I do not recommend.
   _____
   All the romances are well-written books.

   All non-*R* are non-*H*.
   All *B* are *W*.
   All *O* are *H*.

   All non-*B* are non-*R*.
   _____
   All *O* are *W*.

   After contraposing the first and fourth premises, we have:

   All *B* are *W*. ⎱ All *R* are *W*. ⎱
   All *R* are *B*. ⎰   ⎰ All *H* are *W*. ⎱
   All *H* are *R*. ──────────────→   All *H* are *W*. ⎱
   All *O* are *H*. ──────────────────────────────────→ ⎰
   _____
   All *O* are *W*.

   B

   R

   H

   R   W   H   W   O   W

10. All animals that belong to me are animals I trust.
    All dogs are animals that gnaw bones.
    All animals I admit to my study are animals that beg when told to do so.
    All the animals in the yard are animals that belong to me.
    All animals I trust are animals I admit into my study.
    All animals that are willing to beg when told to do so are dogs.
    _____
    All the animals in the yard are animals that gnaw bones.

    All *A* are *T*.
    All *D* are *G*.
    All *S* are *B*.
    All *Y* are *A*.
    All *T* are *S*.
    All *B* are *D*.
    _____
    All *Y* are *G*.

    After rearranging the premises, we have:

    All *D* are *G*. ⎱ All *B* are *G*. ⎱
    All *B* are *D*. ⎰   ⎰ All *S* are *G*. ⎱
    All *S* are *B*. ──────────→   All *S* are *G*. ⎱
    All *T* are *S*. ──────────────────→   All *T* are *G*. ⎱
    All *A* are *T*. ──────────────────────────────────→ ⎰ All *A* are *G*. ⎱
    All *Y* are *A*. ──→ ⎰
    _____
    All *Y* are *G*.

    D   B   S   T   A

    B   G   S   G   T   G   A   G   Y   G

Exercise 6.1

I.

1. ~C
4. F · U
7. M ≡ S
10. C ⊃ P
13. P · (H ∨ S)
16. ~H · ~A
19. ~(M ∨ P) or ~M · ~P
22. (C ⊃ M) ⊃ U
25. ~O ∨ (N ⊃ A)
28. (~H · ~T) ⊃ (P ∨ S)
31. (Y · K) ∨ (~B · ~Z)
34. ~M · [I ⊃ (D ∨ A)]
37. S ⊃ [D ⊃ (P · M)]
40. ~[(M ∨ B) · (T ∨ K)]
43. M ≡ C
46. ~[(C ⊃ G) · (T ⊃ N)]
49. [(G · A) ≡ O] ⊃ ~(N ∨ S)

II

1. R ∨ F
4. ~(H ∨ S)
7. S ⊃ G
10. A ⊃ (~N ⊃ M)
13. (C · K) ≡ P
16. [(T · L) ⊃ H] · (H ⊃ I)
19. (B ⊃ M) · [(M · I) ⊃ (C · P)]

Exercise 6.2

I.

1. Dot.   4. Triple bar.   7. Horseshoe.   10. Wedge.

II.

1. ~ H
   Ⓕ T

4. H · ~ N
   T Ⓕ F T

7. W ⊃ E
   F Ⓣ F

10. H ⊃ (C ∨ E)
    T Ⓣ T T F

13. ~ (E ∨ C) ⊃ (H · L)
    T F F F Ⓣ T T T

III.

1. $A \cdot X$
   T Ⓕ F

4. $\sim C \lor Z$
   F T Ⓕ F

7. $\sim X \supset Z$
   T F Ⓕ F

10. $\sim (A \cdot \sim Z)$
   Ⓕ T T T F

13. $(A \cdot Y) \lor (\sim Z \cdot C)$
   T F F Ⓣ T F T T

16. $(C \equiv \sim A) \lor (Y \equiv Z)$
   T F F T Ⓣ F T F

19. $\sim [\sim (X \supset C) \equiv \sim (B \supset Z)]$
   Ⓣ F F T T F T T F F

22. $\sim [(A \equiv X) \lor (Z \equiv Y)] \lor [(\sim Y \supset B) \cdot (Z \supset C)]$
   F T F F T F T F Ⓣ T F T T T F T T

25. $(Z \supset C) \supset \{[(\sim X \supset B) \supset (C \supset Y)] \equiv [(Z \supset X) \supset (\sim Y \supset Z)]\}$
   F T T Ⓣ T F T T F T F F T F T F F T F F F

IV.

1. $A \lor P$
   T Ⓣ ?

4. $Q \cdot A$
   ? Ⓣ T

   (? Ⓠ T)

7. $A \supset P$
   T Ⓟ ?

10. $(P \supset A) \equiv (Q \supset B)$
   ? T T Ⓣ ? T T

13. $\sim (Q \cdot Y) \equiv \sim (Q \lor A)$
   T ? F F Ⓕ F ? T T

Exercise 6.3

I.

1. $N \supset (N \supset N)$

T	[T]	T T T
F	[T]	F T F

   tautologous

4. $[(E \supset F) \supset F] \supset E$

T T T	T	T	[T]	T
T F F	T	F	[T]	T
F T T	T	T	[F]	F
F T F	F	F	[T]	F

   contingent

7. $[(Z \supset X) \cdot (X \lor Z)] \supset X$

T T T	T	T T T	[T]	T
T F F	F	F T T	[T]	F
F T T	T	T T F	[T]	T
F T F	F	F F F	[T]	F

   tautologous

10. [G ⊃ (N ⊃ ~ G)] • [(N ≡ G) • (N ∨ G)]

```
T F   T F F T   F   T T T   T   T T T
T T   F T F T   F   F F T   F   F T T
F T   T T T F   F   T F F   F   T T F
F T   F T T F   F   F T F   F   F F F
```
self-contradictory

13. [U • (T ∨ S)] ≡ [(~ T ∨ ~ U) • (~ S ∨ ~ U)]

```
T T T T T   F   F T F F T F   F T F F T
T T T T F   F   F T F F T F   T F T F T
T T F T T   F   T F T F T F   F T F F T
T F F F F   F   T F T F T T   T F T F T
F F T T T   F   F T T T F T   F T T T F
F F T T F   F   F T T T F T   T F T T F
F F F T T   F   T F T T F T   F T T T F
F F F F F   F   T F T T F T   T F T T F
```
self-contradictory

II.

1. ~ D ∨ B   ~ (D • ~ B)

```
F T T T        T   T F F T
F T F F        F   T T T F
T F T T        T   F F F T
T F T F        T   F F T F
```
logically equivalent

4. R ∨ ~ S   S • ~ R

```
T T F T        T F F T
T T T F        F F F T
F F F T        T T T F
F T T F        F F T F
```
contradictory

7. (E ⊃ C) ⊃ L   E ⊃ (C ⊃ L)

```
T T T T T        T T T T T
T T T F F        T F T F F
T F F T T        T T F T T
T F F T F        T T F T F
F T T T T        F T T T T
F T T F F        F T T F F
F T F T T        F T F T T
F T F F F        F T F T F
```
consistent

10. W ≡ (B • T)   W • (T ⊃ ~ B)

```
T T T T T        T F T F F T
T F T F F        T T F T F T
T F F F T        T T T T T F
T F F F F        T T F T T F
F F T T T        F F T F F T
F T T F F        F F F T F T
F T F F T        F F T T T F
F T F F F        F F F T T F
```
inconsistent

13. $H \cdot (K \lor J)$ $(J \cdot H) \lor (H \cdot K)$

```
H · (K ∨ J)          (J · H) ∨ (H · K)
T T  T T T           T T T  T  T T T
T T  T T F           F F T  T  T T T
T T  F T T           T T T  T  T F F
T F  F F F           F F T  F  T F F
F F  T T T           T F F  F  F F T
F F  T T F           F F F  F  F F T
F F  F T T           T F F  F  F F F
F F  F F F           F F F  F  F F F
```
logically equivalent

III.

1. Carlson's prediction is false (self-contradictory).

4. It is possible that both astronomers are correct. If they are, a supernova will not occur within 10 light years of the earth.

7. It is possible that both stockbrokers are correct. If they are, then Datapro will cut back its workforce. We can conclude nothing about Netmark and Compucel.

10. It is possible that Nicole's philosophy makes sense. If it does, then the mind is not identical to the brain, personal freedom exists, and humans are responsible for their actions.

Exercise 6.4

I.

1. $N \supset S$ // $\sim N \supset \sim S$
```
T T T    F T T F T
T F F    F T T T F
F T T    T F F F T
F T F    T F T T F
```
invalid

4. $D \supset W$ / D // W

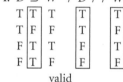
```
T T T    T    T
T F F    T    F
F T T    F    T
F T F    F    F
```
valid

7. Invalid (fails on first line).

10. Valid.

II.

1. Valid.

4. Valid.

7. Invalid (fails on fourth line).

10. Invalid (fails on fourth and sixth lines).

13. Valid.

16. Invalid (fails on third line).

19. Valid.

Exercise 6.5

Note: Truth values may vary depending on how the problem is done.

1. $B \supset C$ / $\sim C$ // $\sim B$
```
(T T F)  T F    F T
```
valid

4. $\sim (I \equiv J)$ // $\sim (I \supset J)$
```
T T F F   (F T F) F
T F F T    F F T T
```
invalid

7. $G \supset H$ / $H \supset I$ / $\sim J \supset G$ / $\sim I$ // J
```
T T T   T T T   T F T T   (T T)  F
```
valid

604   Answers to Selected Exercises

10. $(M \lor N) \supset O \ / \ O \supset (N \lor P) \ / \ M \supset (\sim Q \supset N) \ / \ (Q \supset M) \supset \sim P \ / / \ N \equiv O$

   (T T T F)   T   T   T   T F F

          T T   T T   F T T   F T   T F F T F T   F F T

   invalid

13. $(A \lor B) \supset (C \cdot D) \ / \ (X \lor \sim Y) \supset (\sim C \cdot \sim W) \ / \ (X \lor Z) \supset (A \cdot E) \ / / \ \sim X$

   T (T   T F F)   T T   T T F T T F   T T   T T T T   F T

   valid

II.

1. $K \equiv (R \lor M) \ / \ K \cdot \sim R \ / \ M \supset \sim K$

   T T F T T   T T T F   (T T F)T

   inconsistent

4. $(N \lor C) \equiv E \ / \ N \supset \sim (C \lor H) \ / \ H \supset E \ / \ C \supset H$

    F T T T T   F T F T T T   T T T   T T T

                                            F T T

                                          F T F

   consistent

7. $S \supset (R \equiv A) \ / \ A \supset (W \cdot \sim R) \ / \ R \equiv (W \lor T) \ / \ S \cdot U \ / \ U \supset T$

   T T (T T F)   F T   F F T   T T   T T   T T T   T T T

   inconsistent

10. $A \lor Z \ / \ A \supset (T \cdot F) \ / \ Z \supset (M \cdot Q) \ / \ Q \supset \sim F \ / \ T \supset \sim M \ / \ M \supset A$

   T T T   (T T F F)F   T T T T T   T T T F   F T F T   T T T

   T T F   T T T T T   F T F F F   F T F T   T T T F   F T T

                                                               F T F

   consistent

Exercise 6.6

I.

1. MT—valid   **7.** DD—valid   **13.** DS—valid   **19.** Invalid.

4. CD—valid   **10.** DA—invalid   **16.** AC—invalid

Numbers 7 and 13 must be rewritten:

7. $(E \supset N) \cdot (\sim L \supset \sim K)$ **13.** $\sim S \lor P$

   $\underline{\sim N \lor \sim\sim K \qquad\qquad}$ $\underline{\sim\sim S \qquad}$

   $\sim E \lor \sim\sim L$ P

II.

1. $F \supset T$

   $\underline{\sim T \qquad}$

   $\sim F$ MT—valid

4. $W \lor \sim M$

   $\underline{\sim W \qquad}$

   $\sim M$ DS—valid

7. T

   $\underline{T \supset \sim H}$

   $\sim H$ MP—valid

10. $(L \supset \sim A) \cdot (C \supset F)$

   $\underline{\sim L \cdot \sim C \qquad\qquad}$

   $A \cdot \sim F$ invalid

13. $(P \supset T) \cdot (A \supset \sim T)$

   $\underline{T \lor \sim T \qquad\qquad}$

   $\sim P \lor \sim A$

   rewritten:

   $(P \supset T) \cdot (A \supset \sim T)$

   $\underline{\sim T \lor \sim\sim T \qquad}$

   $\sim P \lor \sim A$ DD—valid

16. $\sim M \supset U$

   $\underline{U \qquad}$

   $\sim M$ AC—invalid

19. $S \supset C$

   $\underline{I \supset S}$

   $I \supset C$ HS—valid

6

III.

1. $(S \supset M) \cdot (\sim S \supset F)$

   $\underline{S \lor \sim S}$

   $M \lor F$ CD

   Since the second premise is a tautology, it is impossible to escape between the horns. The two available strategies are therefore grasping by the horns and constructing a counterdilemma. If Melinda adequately prepares for the test before the party, then she does not spend the party night studying and she does not fail the test. This would falsify the right-hand conjunct of the first premise, thus falsifying the entire premise. Here is a counterdilemma:

   > If Melinda spends the night studying, she will pass the test tomorrow; and, if she doesn't spend the night studying, she will go to the party. She will either spend the night studying or not studying. Therefore, she will either pass the test or go to the party.

4. $(C \supset \sim S) \cdot (E \supset S)$ rewritten: $(C \supset \sim S) \cdot (E \supset S)$

   $\underline{S \lor \sim S}$ $\underline{\sim\sim S \lor \sim S}$

   $\sim C \lor \sim E$ $\sim C \lor \sim E$ DD

   The second premise is a tautology, so it is impossible to escape between the horns. One could grasp the dilemma by the horns by arguing that corporations could share the cost of neutralizing toxic waste, thus preserving the competitive edge. Here is a constructive counterdilemma:

   > If corporations spend money to neutralize their toxic waste, then the environment will be preserved; but if corporations do not spend money to neutralize their toxic waste, then they will remain competitive. Corporations will do one or the other. Therefore, either the environment will be preserved or corporations will remain competitive.

7. $(C \supset L) \cdot (J \supset B)$

   $\underline{\sim L \lor \sim B}$

   $\sim C \lor \sim J$ DD

   Here the second premise is not a tautology, so it is possible to escape between the horns. Perhaps students could take a double major in liberal arts and business. One could also grasp the dilemma by the horns by arguing that students could major in a liberal arts field where a job *would* be available upon graduation. Here is a constructive counterdilemma:

   > If students major in liberal arts, then they will take courses that are interesting and rewarding; but if they major in business, then they will have a job when they graduate. Students will either major in liberal arts or business. Therefore, either they will take courses that are interesting and rewarding or they will have a job when they graduate.

10. $(P \supset R) \cdot (T \supset E)$

   $\underline{P \lor T}$

   $R \lor E$ CD

   The second premise is not a tautology, so it is at least possible to escape between the horns. If we instructed counter-terrorist squads to execute terrorists on the spot, we would neither prosecute them nor release them. Can you think of a way to grasp the dilemma by the horns? Here is a counterdilemma:

   > If we prosecute suspected terrorists, then we discourage terrorism; but if we release them, then we avoid the risk of retaliation by other terrorists. We must either prosecute or release suspected terrorists. Therefore, either we will discourage terrorism or we will avoid the risk of retaliation by other terrorists.

IV.

1. If Oral Roberts actually receives messages from God, then he would not have sent the letter. Oral Roberts did send the letter. Therefore, he does not actually receive messages from God. (MT)

4. If group problem solving is important, then we should not emphasize individual testing. Group problem solving is important. Therefore, we should not emphasize individual testing. (MP)

If we should not emphasize individual testing, then the national math test is a mistake. We should not emphasize individual testing. Therefore, the national math test is a mistake. (MP)

7. If we close the library at Central Juvenile Hall, then delinquents will be deprived of an opportunity to read. If delinquents are deprived of an opportunity to read, then they will not have access to ideas, dreams, and alternative ways of living. Therefore, if we close the library at Central Juvenile Hall, then delinquents will not have access to ideas, dreams, and alternative ways of living. (HS)

If we close the library at Central Juvenile Hall, then delinquents will not have access to ideas, dreams, and alternative ways of living. Delinquents must have access to ideas, dreams, and alternative ways of living. Therefore, we must not close the library at Central Juvenile Hall. (MT)

10. If viewing adult videocassettes led to violent sex crimes, then there would be over a million violent sex crimes per week. It is not the case that there are over a million violent sex crimes per week. Therefore, viewing adult videocassettes does not lead to violent sex crimes. (MT)

Exercise 7.1

I.

1. ~G	1, 2, MT		13. ~~C	1, 3, MT
4. C	1, 2, DS		16. ~P	1, 2, MP
7. F ⊃ D	1, 3, HS		19. ~(S ∨ C)	1, 3, MT
10. G ⊃ A	1, 4, HS			

II.

1. ~B			13. ~~S	
	1, 2, DS			3, 4, MT
4. R ⊃ C			16. ~Z	
	1, 2, HS			3, 4, MP
7. Q			19. H ∨ G	
	2, 3, MP			2, 4, MP
10. ~A				
	1, 4, MT			

III.

(1) 1. ~C ⊃ (A ⊃ C)
    2. ~C   / ~A
    3. A ⊃ C   1, 2, MP
    4. ~A   2, 3, MT

(4) 1. P ⊃ (G ⊃ T)
    2. Q ⊃ (T ⊃ E)
    3. P
    4. Q   / G ⊃ E
    5. G ⊃ T   1, 3, MP
    6. T ⊃ E   2, 4, MP
    7. G ⊃ E   5, 6, HS

(7) 1. ~S ⊃ D
    2. ~S ∨ (~D ⊃ K)
    3. ~D   / K
    4. ~~S   1, 3, MT
    5. ~D ⊃ K   2, 4, DS
    6. K   3, 5, MP

(10) 1. $N \supset (J \supset P)$
2. $(J \supset P) \supset (N \supset J)$
3. N / P
4. $J \supset P$ 1, 3, MP
5. $N \supset J$ 2, 4, MP
6. $N \supset P$ 4, 5, HS
7. P 3, 6, MP

(13) 1. $R \supset (G \vee \sim A)$
2. $(G \vee \sim A) \supset \sim S$
3. $G \supset S$
4. R / $\sim A$
5. $G \vee \sim A$ 1, 4, MP
6. $\sim S$ 2, 5, MP
7. $\sim G$ 3, 6, MT
8. $\sim A$ 5, 7, DS

(16) 1. $(B \supset \sim M) \supset (T \supset \sim S)$
2. $B \supset K$
3. $K \supset \sim M$
4. $\sim S \supset N$ / $T \supset N$
5. $B \supset \sim M$ 2, 3, HS
6. $T \supset \sim S$ 1, 5, MP
7. $T \supset N$ 4, 6, HS

(19) 1. $\sim G \supset [G \vee (S \supset G)]$
2. $(S \vee L) \supset \sim G$
3. $S \vee L$ / L
4. $\sim G$ 2, 3, MP
5. $G \vee (S \supset G)$ 1, 4, MP
6. $S \supset G$ 4, 5, DS
7. $\sim S$ 4, 6, MT
8. L 3, 7, DS

IV.

(1) 1. $W \supset (P \vee C)$
2. $\sim P$
3. W / C
4. $P \vee C$ 1, 3, MP
5. C 2, 4, DS

(7) 1. $H \supset (D \equiv A)$
2. $V \vee (R \supset V)$
3. $R \vee H$
4. $\sim V$ / $D \equiv A$
5. $R \supset V$ 2, 4, DS
6. $\sim R$ 4, 5, MT
7. H 3, 6, DS
8. $D \equiv A$ 1, 7, MP

(22) 1. $(C \supset M) \supset (N \supset P)$
2. $(C \supset N) \supset (N \supset M)$
3. $(C \supset P) \supset \sim M$
4. $C \supset N$ / $\sim C$
5. $N \supset M$ 2, 4, MP
6. $C \supset M$ 4, 5, HS
7. $N \supset P$ 1, 6, MP
8. $C \supset P$ 4, 7, HS
9. $\sim M$ 3, 8, MP
10. $\sim C$ 6, 9, MT

(25) 1. $\sim N \supset [(B \supset D) \supset (N \vee \sim E)]$
2. $(B \supset E) \supset \sim N$
3. $B \supset D$
4. $D \supset E$ / $\sim D$
5. $B \supset E$ 3, 4, HS
6. $\sim N$ 2, 5, MP
7. $(B \supset D) \supset (N \vee \sim E)$ 1, 6, MP
8. $N \vee \sim E$ 3, 7, MP
9. $\sim E$ 6, 8, DS
10. $\sim D$ 4, 9, MT

(4) 1. $(R \supset L) \supset (L \supset \sim F)$
2. $\sim F \vee (R \supset L)$
3. $\sim \sim F$ / $\sim R$
4. $R \supset L$ 2, 3, DS
5. $L \supset \sim F$ 1, 4, MP
6. $\sim L$ 3, 5, MT
7. $\sim R$ 4, 6, MT

(10) 1. $\sim C \supset [C \vee (J \supset D)]$
2. $C \supset (C \cdot U)$
3. $\sim (C \cdot U)$
4. $\sim D$ / $\sim J$
5. $\sim C$ 2, 3, MT
6. $C \vee (J \supset D)$ 1, 5, MP
7. $J \supset D$ 5, 6, DS
8. $\sim J$ 4, 7, MT

7

Exercise 7.2

I.

1. B 2
4. $H \vee F$ 1

7. $Q \vee K$ 1
10. $\sim L \vee M$ 1, 2

II.

1. G 2, Simp
              3, Add
4. $T \vee U$ 1, Add
              3, 4, MP

7. $\sim F$ 2, 3, MT
         1, 4, Conj
10. $M \cdot E$ 1, 3, Conj
          2, 4, MP

III.

(1)
1. $\sim M \supset Q$
2. $R \supset \sim T$
3. $\sim M \vee R$ / $Q \vee \sim T$
4. $(\sim M \supset Q) \cdot (R \supset \sim T)$ 1, 2, Conj
5. $Q \vee \sim T$ 3, 4, CD

(4)
1. $(H \vee \sim B) \supset R$
2. $(H \vee \sim M) \supset P$
3. H / $R \cdot P$
4. $H \vee \sim B$ 3, Add
5. R 1, 4, MP
6. $H \vee \sim M$ 3, Add
7. P 2, 6, MP
8. $R \cdot P$ 5, 7, Conj

(7)
1. $(\sim F \vee X) \supset (P \vee T)$
2. $F \supset P$
3. $\sim P$ / T
4. $\sim F$ 2, 3, MT
5. $\sim F \vee X$ 4, Add
6. $P \vee T$ 1, 5, MP
7. T 3, 6, DS

(10)
1. $(D \vee E) \supset (G \cdot H)$
2. $G \supset \sim D$
3. $D \cdot F$ / M
4. D 3, Simp
5. $D \vee E$ 4, Add
6. $G \cdot H$ 1, 5, MP
7. G 6, Simp
8. $\sim D$ 2, 7, MP
9. $D \vee M$ 4, Add
10. M 8, 9, DS

(13)
1. $(C \supset N) \cdot E$
2. $D \vee (N \supset D)$
3. $\sim D$ / $\sim C \vee P$
4. $N \supset D$ 2, 3, DS
5. $\sim N$ 3, 4, MT
6. $C \supset N$ 1, Simp

7. $\sim C$ 5, 6, MT
8. $\sim C \vee P$ 7, Add

(16)
1. $(C \vee \sim G) \supset (\sim P \cdot L)$
2. $(\sim P \cdot C) \supset (C \supset D)$
3. $C \cdot \sim R$ / $D \vee R$
4. C 3, Simp
5. $C \vee \sim G$ 4, Add
6. $\sim P \cdot L$ 1, 5, MP
7. $\sim P$ 6, Simp
8. $\sim P \cdot C$ 4, 7, Conj
9. $C \supset D$ 2, 8 MP
10. D 4, 9, MP
11. $D \vee R$ 10, Add

(19)
1. $(U \cdot \sim P) \supset Q$
2. $\sim O \supset U$
3. $\sim P \supset O$
4. $\sim O \cdot T$ / Q
5. $\sim O$ 4, Simp
6. U 2, 5, MP
7. $\sim \sim P$ 3, 5, MT
8. $U \cdot \sim \sim P$ 6, 7, Conj
9. Q 1, 8, MP

(22)
1. $(\sim K \cdot \sim N) \supset [(\sim P \supset K) \cdot (\sim R \supset G)]$
2. $K \supset N$
3. $\sim N \cdot B$
4. $\sim P \vee \sim R$ / G
5. $\sim N$ 3, Simp
6. $\sim K$ 2, 5, MT
7. $\sim K \cdot \sim N$ 5, 6, Conj
8. $(\sim P \supset K) \cdot (\sim R \supset G)$ 1, 7, MP
9. $K \vee G$ 4, 8, CD
10. G 6, 9, DS

(25)
1. $(\sim M \cdot N) \supset [(\sim M \vee H) \supset (K \cdot L)]$
2. $\sim M \cdot (C \supset D)$
3. $\sim N \cdot (F \equiv G)$ / $K \cdot \sim N$
4. $\sim M$ 2, Simp

5.	~N	3, Simp
6.	~M • ~N	4, 5, Conj
7.	(~M ∨ H) ⊃ (K • L)	1, 6, MP
8.	~M ∨ H	4, Add
9.	K • L	7, 8, MP
10.	K	9, Simp
11.	K • ~N	5, 10, Conj

IV.

(1)
1.	T ⊃ (Q • F)	
2.	T • C	/ Q ∨ O
3.	T	2, Simp
4.	Q • F	1, 3, MP
5.	Q	4, Simp
6.	Q ∨ O	5, Add

(7)
1.	(~C ∨ ~M) ⊃ (~C ⊃ T)	
2.	C ∨ ~T	
3.	~C	/ 1, B
4.	~C ∨ ~M	3, Add
5.	~C ⊃ T	1, 4, MP
6.	T	3, 5, MP
7.	T ∨ B	6, Add
8.	~T	2, 3, DS
9.	B	7, 8, DS

(28)
1.	(D ⊃ B) • (C ⊃ D)	
2.	(B ⊃ D) • (E ⊃ C)	
3.	B ∨ E	/ D ∨ B
4.	D ∨ C	2, 3, CD
5.	B ∨ D	1, 4, CD
6.	B ⊃ D	2, Simp
7.	D ⊃ B	1, Simp
8.	(B ⊃ D) • (D ⊃ B)	6, 7, Conj
9.	D ∨ B	5, 8, CD

(4)
1.	M ∨ P	
2.	(P ∨ S) ⊃ (R • D)	
3.	~M	/ R
4.	P	1, 3, DS
5.	P ∨ S	4, Add
6.	R • D	2, 5, MP
7.	R	6, Simp

(10)
1.	(V • ~E) ⊃ (P ⊃ E)	
2.	V ⊃ ~E	
3.	V • I	
4.	~E ⊃ (P ∨ J)	/ J • ~E
5.	V	3, Simp
6.	~E	2, 5, MP
7.	V • ~E	5, 6, Conj
8.	P ⊃ E	1, 7, MP
9.	~P	6, 8, MT
10.	P ∨ J	4, 6, MP
11.	J	9, 10, DS
12.	J • ~E	6, 11, Conj

Exercise 7.3

I.

1.	~N • ~G	2
4.	A • S	3
7.	~G ∨ ~~Q	1
10.	~(R • P)	1
13.	H ⊃ ~(L ∨ D)	2

II.

1.	C ∨ K	1, Com
		2, 3, DS
4.	L • (S • F)	1, Assoc
		2, Simp
7.	D • (M ∨ N)	1, Dist
		2, Simp
10.	(D ∨ N) • (D ∨ H)	1, Dist
		2, Simp
13.	M ∨ (G ∨ T)	1, Assoc
		2, 3, DS

III.

(1)
1. $(\sim M \supset P) \cdot (\sim N \supset Q)$
2. $\sim(M \cdot N)$ / $P \vee Q$
3. $\sim M \vee \sim N$ 2, DM
4. $P \vee Q$ 1, 3, CD

(4)
1. $\sim(N \cdot T)$
2. T / $\sim N$
3. $\sim N \vee \sim T$ 1, DM
4. $\sim T \vee \sim N$ 3, Com
5. $\sim\sim T$ 2, DN
6. $\sim N$ 4, 5, DS

(7)
1. $T \supset (B \vee E)$
2. $\sim E \cdot T$ / B
3. $T \cdot \sim E$ 2, Com
4. T 3, Simp
5. $B \vee E$ 1, 4 MP
6. $E \vee B$ 5, Com
7. $\sim E$ 2, Simp
8. B 6, 7, DS

(10)
1. $(K \cdot H) \vee (K \cdot L)$
2. $\sim L$ / H
3. $K \cdot (H \vee L)$ 1, Dist
4. $(H \vee L) \cdot K$ 3, Com
5. $H \vee L$ 4, Simp
6. $L \vee H$ 5, Com
7. H 2, 6, DS

(13)
1. $(E \cdot I) \vee (M \cdot U)$
2. $\sim E$ / $\sim(E \vee \sim M)$
3. $\sim E \vee \sim I$ 2, Add
4. $\sim(E \cdot I)$ 3, DM
5. $M \cdot U$ 1, 4, DS
6. M 5, Simp
7. $\sim\sim M$ 6, DN
8. $\sim E \cdot \sim\sim M$ 2, 7, Conj
9. $\sim(E \vee \sim M)$ 8, DM

(16)
1. $(Q \cdot N) \vee (N \cdot T)$
2. $(Q \vee C) \supset \sim N$ / T
3. $(N \cdot Q) \vee (N \cdot T)$ 1, Com
4. $N \cdot (Q \vee T)$ 3, Dist
5. N 4, Simp
6. $\sim\sim N$ 5, DN
7. $\sim(Q \vee C)$ 2, 6, MT
8. $\sim Q \cdot \sim C$ 7, DM
9. $\sim Q$ 8, Simp
10. $(Q \vee T) \cdot N$ 4, Com
11. $Q \vee T$ 10, Simp
12. T 9, 11, DS

(19)
1. $[(I \vee M) \vee G] \supset \sim G$
2. $M \vee G$ / M
3. $(M \vee G) \vee I$ 2, Add
4. $I \vee (M \vee G)$ 3, Com
5. $(I \vee M) \vee G$ 4, Assoc
6. $\sim G$ 1, 5, MP
7. $G \vee M$ 2, Com
8. M 6, 7, DS

(22)
1. $S \vee (I \cdot \sim J)$
2. $S \supset \sim R$
3. $\sim J \supset \sim Q$ / $\sim(R \cdot Q)$
4. $(S \vee I) \cdot (S \vee \sim J)$ 1, Dist
5. $(S \vee \sim J) \cdot (S \vee I)$ 4, Com
6. $S \vee \sim J$ 5, Simp
7. $(S \supset \sim R) \cdot (\sim J \supset \sim Q)$ 2, 3, Conj
8. $\sim R \vee \sim Q$ 6, 7, CD
9. $\sim(R \cdot Q)$ 8, DM

(25)
1. $E \vee \sim(D \vee C)$
2. $(E \vee \sim D) \supset C$ / E
3. $E \vee (\sim D \cdot \sim C)$ 1, DM
4. $(E \vee \sim D) \cdot (E \vee \sim C)$ 3, Dist
5. $E \vee \sim D$ 4, Simp
6. C 2, 5, MP
7. $(E \vee \sim C) \cdot (E \vee \sim D)$ 4, Com
8. $E \vee \sim C$ 7, Simp
9. $\sim C \vee E$ 8, Com
10. $\sim\sim C$ 6, DN
11. E 9, 10, DS

(28)
1. $P \vee (I \cdot L)$
2. $(P \vee I) \supset \sim(L \vee C)$
3. $(P \cdot \sim C) \supset (E \cdot F)$ / $F \vee D$
4. $(P \vee I) \cdot (P \vee L)$ 1, Dist
5. $P \vee I$ 4, Simp
6. $\sim(L \vee C)$ 2, 5, MP
7. $\sim L \cdot \sim C$ 6, DM
8. $\sim L$ 7, Simp
9. $(P \vee L) \cdot (P \vee I)$ 4, Com
10. $P \vee L$ 9, Simp
11. $L \vee P$ 10, Com
12. P 8, 11, DS
13. $\sim C \cdot \sim L$ 7, Com
14. $\sim C$ 13, Simp
15. $P \cdot \sim C$ 12, 14, Conj
16. $E \cdot F$ 3, 15 MP
17. $F \cdot E$ 16, Com
18. F 17, Simp
19. $F \vee D$ 18, Add

7

(31) 1. $(\sim R \vee D) \supset \sim(F \cdot G)$
2. $(F \cdot R) \supset S$
3. $F \cdot \sim S$ / $\sim(S \vee G)$
4. $\sim S \cdot F$ 3, Com
5. $\sim S$ 4, Simp
6. $\sim(F \cdot R)$ 2, 5, MT
7. $\sim F \vee \sim R$ 6, DM
8. F 3, Simp
9. $\sim\sim F$ 8, DN
10. $\sim R$ 7, 9, DS
11. $\sim R \vee D$ 10, Add
12. $\sim(F \cdot G)$ 1, 11, MP
13. $\sim F \vee \sim G$ 12, DM
14. $\sim G$ 9, 13, DS
15. $\sim S \cdot \sim G$ 5, 14, Conj
16. $\sim(S \vee G)$ 15, DM

(34) 1. $(M \cdot N) \vee (O \cdot P)$
2. $(N \vee O) \supset \sim P$ / N
3. $[(M \cdot N) \vee O] \cdot [(M \cdot N) \vee P]$ 1, Dist
4. $(M \cdot N) \vee O$ 3, Simp
5. $O \vee (M \cdot N)$ 4, Com
6. $(O \vee M) \cdot (O \vee N)$ 5, Dist
7. $(O \vee N) \cdot (O \vee M)$ 6, Com
8. $O \vee N$ 7, Simp
9. $N \vee O$ 8, Com
10. $\sim P$ 2, 9, MP
11. $[(M \cdot N) \vee P] \cdot [(M \cdot N) \vee O]$ 3, Com
12. $(M \cdot N) \vee P$ 11, Simp
13. $P \vee (M \cdot N)$ 12, Com
14. $M \cdot N$ 10, 13, DS
15. $N \cdot M$ 14, Com
16. N 15, Simp

IV.

(1) 1. $(S \cdot D) \vee (S \cdot H)$
2. $S \supset (I \cdot R)$ / $S \cdot R$
3. $S \cdot (D \vee H)$ 1, Dist
4. S 3, Simp
5. $I \cdot R$ 2, 4, MP
6. $R \cdot I$ 5, Com
7. R 6, Simp
8. $S \cdot R$ 4, 7, Conj

(4) 1. $G \vee (R \cdot E)$
2. $(G \vee E) \supset \sim R$ / $G \vee M$
3. $(G \vee R) \cdot (G \vee E)$ 1, Dist
4. $(G \vee E) \cdot (G \vee R)$ 3, Com
5. $G \vee E$ 4, Simp
6. $\sim R$ 2, 5, MP
7. $G \vee R$ 3, Simp
8. $R \vee G$ 7, Com
9. G 6, 8, DS
10. $G \vee M$ 9, Add

(7) 1. $R \supset (C \vee M)$
2. $\sim(I \vee C)$
3. $\sim(A \vee M)$ / $\sim R$
4. $\sim I \cdot \sim C$ 2, DM
5. $\sim A \cdot \sim M$ 3, DM
6. $\sim C \cdot \sim I$ 4, Com
7. $\sim C$ 6, Simp
8. $\sim M \cdot \sim A$ 5, Com
9. $\sim M$ 8, Simp
10. $\sim C \cdot \sim M$ 7, 9, Conj
11. $\sim(C \vee M)$ 10, DM
12. $\sim R$ 1, 11, MT

(10) 1. $\sim E \vee (B \cdot P)$
2. $\sim E \vee (G \cdot W)$
3. $\sim P \vee \sim W$ / $\sim E$
4. $(\sim E \vee B) \cdot (\sim E \vee P)$ 1, Dist
5. $(\sim E \vee P) \cdot (\sim E \vee B)$ 4, Com
6. $\sim E \vee P$ 5, Simp
7. $(\sim E \vee G) \cdot (\sim E \vee W)$ 2, Dist
8. $(\sim E \vee W) \cdot (\sim E \vee G)$ 7, Com
9. $\sim E \vee W$ 8, Simp
10. $(\sim E \vee P) \cdot (\sim E \vee W)$ 6, 9, Conj
11. $\sim E \vee (P \cdot W)$ 10, Dist
12. $(P \cdot W) \vee \sim E$ 11, Com
13. $\sim(P \cdot W)$ 3, DM
14. $\sim E$ 12, 13, DS

7

Exercise 7.4

I.

1. $G \supset Q$ 3
4. $B \equiv N$ 1
7. $\sim\sim C \vee \sim F$ 1

10. $S \supset G$ 3
13. $W \equiv \sim T$ 2

II.

1. $J \supset M$ 1, Impl
     2, 3, HS
4. $K \vee K$ 1, 2, CD
     3, Taut
7. $H \supset (C \supset R)$ 1, Impl
     2, Exp

10. $\sim H \vee \sim H$ 1, Impl
     2, Taut
13. $(N \supset A) \cdot (A \supset N)$ 1, Trans
     2, Equiv

III.

(1)
1. $(S \cdot K) \supset R$
2. K / $S \supset R$
3. $(K \cdot S) \supset R$ 1, Com
4. $K \supset (S \supset R)$ 3, Exp
5. $S \supset R$ 2, 4, MP

(4)
1. $S \equiv Q$
2. $\sim S$ /$\sim Q$
3. $(S \supset Q) \cdot (Q \supset S)$ 1, Equiv
4. $(Q \supset S) \cdot (S \supset Q)$ 3, Com
5. $Q \supset S$ 4, Simp
6. $\sim Q$ 2, 5, MT

(7)
1. $(B \supset M) \cdot (D \supset M)$
2. $B \vee D$ / M
3. $M \vee M$ 1, 2, CD
4. M 3, Taut

(10)
1. $(B \supset G) \cdot (F \supset N)$
2. $\sim(G \cdot N)$ /$\sim(B \cdot F)$
3. $\sim G \vee \sim N$ 2, DM
4. $(\sim G \supset \sim B) \cdot (F \supset N)$ 1, Trans
5. $(\sim G \supset \sim B) \cdot (\sim N \supset \sim F)$ 4, Trans
6. $\sim B \vee \sim F$ 3, 5, CD
7. $\sim(B \cdot F)$ 6, DM

(13)
1. $K \supset (B \supset \sim M)$
2. $D \supset (K \cdot M)$ / $D \supset \sim B$
3. $K \supset (\sim\sim M \supset \sim B)$ 1, Trans
4. $K \supset (M \supset \sim B)$ 3, DN
5. $(K \cdot M) \supset \sim B$ 4, Exp
6. $D \supset \sim B$ 2, 5, HS

(16)
1. $T \supset R$
2. $T \supset \sim R$ / $\sim T$
3. $\sim\sim R \supset \sim T$ 2, Trans
4. $R \supset \sim T$ 3, DN
5. $T \supset \sim T$ 1, 4, HS
6. $\sim T \vee \sim T$ 5, Impl
7. $\sim T$ 6, Taut

(19)
1. $\sim R \vee P$
2. $R \vee \sim P$ / $R \equiv P$
3. $R \supset P$ 1, Impl
4. $\sim P \vee R$ 2, Com
5. $P \supset R$ 4, Impl
6. $(R \supset P) \cdot (P \supset R)$ 3, 5, Conj
7. $R \equiv P$ 6, Equiv

(22)
1. $S \supset (L \cdot M)$
2. $M \supset (L \supset R)$ / $S \supset R$
3. $(M \cdot L) \supset R$ 2, Exp
4. $(L \cdot M) \supset R$ 3, Com
5. $S \supset R$ 1, 4, HS

(25)
1. $T \supset G$
2. $S \supset G$ / $(T \vee S) \supset G$
3. $\sim T \vee G$ 1, Impl
4. $\sim S \vee G$ 2, Impl
5. $G \vee \sim T$ 3, Com
6. $G \vee \sim S$ 4, Com
7. $(G \vee \sim T) \cdot (G \vee \sim S)$ 5, 6, Conj
8. $G \vee (\sim T \cdot \sim S)$ 7, Dist
9. $(\sim T \cdot \sim S) \vee G$ 8, Com
10. $\sim(T \vee S) \vee G$ 9, DM
11. $(T \vee S) \supset G$ 10, Impl

(28)
1. $P \supset (\sim E \supset B)$
2. $\sim(B \vee E)$ / $\sim P$
3. $\sim(E \vee B)$ 2, Com
4. $\sim(\sim\sim E \vee B)$ 3, DN
5. $\sim(\sim E \supset B)$ 4, Impl
6. $\sim P$ 1, 5, MT

(31)
1. $K \equiv R$
2. $K \supset (R \supset P)$
3. $\sim P$ / $\sim R$
4. $(K \cdot R) \vee (\sim K \cdot \sim R)$ 1, Equiv
5. $(K \cdot R) \supset P$ 2, Exp
6. $\sim(K \cdot R)$ 3, 5, MT

7. $\sim K \cdot \sim R$ 4, 6, DS

8. $\sim R \cdot \sim K$ 7, Com

9. $\sim R$ 8, Simp

(34) 1. $(F \cdot H) \supset N$

     2. $F \lor S$

     3. H / $N \lor S$

     4. $(H \cdot F) \supset N$ 1, Com

     5. $H \supset (F \supset N)$ 4, Exp

     6. $F \supset N$ 3, 5, MP

     7. $\sim N \supset \sim F$ 6, Trans

     8. $\sim\sim F \lor S$ 2, DN

     9. $\sim F \supset S$ 8, Impl

     10. $\sim N \supset S$ 7, 9, HS

     11. $\sim\sim N \lor S$ 10, Impl

     12. $N \lor S$ 11, DN

(37) 1. $(D \supset E) \supset (E \supset D)$

     2. $(D \equiv E) \supset \sim(G \cdot \sim H)$

     3. $E \cdot G$ / $G \cdot H$

     4. E 3, Simp

     5. $E \lor \sim D$ 4, Add

     6. $\sim D \lor E$ 5, Com

     7. $D \supset E$ 6, Impl

     8. $E \supset D$ 1, 7, MP

     9. $(D \supset E) \cdot (E \supset D)$ 7, 8, Conj

     10. $D \equiv E$ 9, Equiv

     11. $\sim(G \cdot \sim H)$ 2, 10, MP

     12. $\sim G \lor \sim\sim H$ 11, DM

     13. $\sim G \lor H$ 12, DN

     14. $G \cdot E$ 3, Com

     15. G 14, Simp

     16. $\sim\sim G$ 15, DN

     17. H 13, 16, DS

     18. $G \cdot H$ 15, 17, Conj

(40) 1. $A \equiv W$

     2. $\sim A \lor \sim W$

     3. $R \supset A$ / $\sim(W \lor R)$

     4. $(A \cdot W) \lor (\sim A \cdot \sim W)$ 1, Equiv

     5. $\sim(A \cdot W)$ 2, DM

     6. $\sim A \cdot \sim W$ 4, 5, DS

IV.

(1) 1. $D \supset C$

     2. $\sim(C \cdot \sim S)$ / $D \supset S$

     3. $\sim C \lor \sim\sim S$ 2, DM

     4. $C \supset \sim\sim S$ 3, Impl

     5. $C \supset S$ 4, DN

     6. $D \supset S$ 1, 5, HS

7. $\sim A$ 6, Simp

8. $\sim R$ 3, 7, MT

9. $\sim W \cdot \sim A$ 6, Com

10. $\sim W$ 9, Simp

11. $\sim W \cdot \sim R$ 8, 10, Conj

12. $\sim(W \lor R)$ 11, DM

(43) 1. $O \supset (Q \cdot N)$

     2. $(N \lor E) \supset S$ / $O \supset S$

     3. $\sim O \lor (Q \cdot N)$ 1, Impl

     4. $(\sim O \lor Q) \cdot (\sim O \lor N)$ 3, Dist

     5. $(\sim O \lor N) \cdot (\sim O \lor Q)$ 4, Com

     6. $\sim O \lor N$ 5, Simp

     7. $O \supset N$ 6, Impl

     8. $\sim(N \lor E) \lor S$ 2, Impl

     9. $(\sim N \cdot \sim E) \lor S$ 8, DM

     10. $S \lor (\sim N \cdot \sim E)$ 9, Com

     11. $(S \lor \sim N) \cdot (S \lor \sim E)$ 10, Dist

     12. $S \lor \sim N$ 11, Simp

     13. $\sim N \lor S$ 12, Com

     14. $N \supset S$ 13, Impl

     15. $O \supset S$ 7, 14, HS

(45) 1. $P \supset A$

     2. $Q \supset B$ / $(P \lor Q) \supset (A \lor B)$

     3. $\sim P \lor A$ 1, Impl

     4. $\sim Q \lor B$ 2, Impl

     5. $(\sim P \lor A) \lor B$ 3, Add

     6. $(\sim Q \lor B) \lor A$ 4, Add

     7. $\sim P \lor (A \lor B)$ 5, Assoc

     8. $(A \lor B) \lor \sim P$ 7, Com

     9. $\sim Q \lor (B \lor A)$ 6, Assoc

     10. $\sim Q \lor (A \lor B)$ 9, Com

     11. $(A \lor B) \lor \sim Q$ 10, Com

     12. $[(A \lor B) \lor \sim P] \cdot [(A \lor B) \lor \sim Q]$

         8, 11, Conj

     13. $(A \lor B) \lor (\sim P \cdot \sim Q)$ 12, Dist

     14. $(\sim P \cdot \sim Q) \lor (A \lor B)$ 13, Com

     15. $\sim(P \lor Q) \lor (A \lor B)$ 14, DM

     16. $(P \lor Q) \supset (A \lor B)$ 15, Impl

(4) 1. $D \supset P$ / $(I \cdot D) \supset P$

     2. $\sim D \lor P$ 1, Impl

     3. $(\sim D \lor P) \lor \sim I$ 2, Add

     4. $\sim I \lor (\sim D \lor P)$ 3, Com

     5. $(\sim I \lor \sim D) \lor P$ 4, Assoc

     6. $\sim(I \cdot D) \lor P$ 5, DM

     7. $(I \cdot D) \supset P$ 6, Impl

7

(7) 1. $G \supset A$
   2. $G \supset L$ / $G \supset (A \cdot L)$
   3. $\sim G \vee A$ 1, Impl
   4. $\sim G \vee L$ 2, Impl
   5. $(\sim G \vee A) \cdot (\sim G \vee L)$ 3, 4, Conj
   6. $\sim G \vee (A \cdot L)$ 5, Dist
   7. $G \supset (A \cdot L)$ 6, Impl

(10) 1. $(A \cdot U) \equiv \sim R$
   2. $\sim(\sim R \vee \sim A)$ / $\sim U$
   3. $[(A \cdot U) \supset \sim R] \cdot [\sim R \supset (A \cdot U)]$ 1, Equiv
   4. $(A \cdot U) \supset \sim R$ 3, Simp
   5. $\sim\sim R \cdot \sim\sim A$ 2, DM
   6. $\sim\sim R$ 5, Simp
   7. $\sim(A \cdot U)$ 4, 6, MT
   8. $\sim A \vee \sim U$ 7, DM
   9. $\sim\sim A \cdot \sim\sim R$ 5, Com
  10. $\sim\sim A$ 9, Simp
  11. $\sim U$ 8, 10, DS

Exercise 7.5

I.

(1) 1. $N \supset O$
   2. $N \supset P$ / $N \supset (O \cdot P)$
      3. N ACP
      4. O 1, 3, MP
      5. P 2, 3, MP
      6. $O \cdot P$ 4, 5, Conj
   7. $N \supset (O \cdot P)$ 3–6, CP

(4) 1. $(G \vee H) \supset (S \cdot T)$
   2. $(T \vee U) \supset (C \cdot D)$ / $G \supset C$
      3. G ACP
      4. $G \vee H$ 3, Add
      5. $S \cdot T$ 1, 4, MP
      6. $T \cdot S$ 5, Com
      7. T 6, Simp
      8. $T \vee U$ 7, Add
      9. $C \cdot D$ 2, 8, MP
    10. C 9, Simp
  11. $G \supset C$ 3–10, CP

(7) 1. $M \vee (N \cdot O)$ / $\sim N \supset M$
      2. $\sim M$ ACP
      3. $N \cdot O$ 1, 2, DS
      4. N 3, Simp
   5. $\sim M \supset N$ 2–4, CP
   6. $\sim N \supset \sim\sim M$ 5, Trans
   7. $\sim N \supset M$ 6, DN

(10) 1. $C \supset (A \cdot D)$
    2. $B \supset (A \cdot E)$ / $(C \lor B) \supset A$
        3. $C \lor B$ ACP
        4. $[C \supset (A \cdot D)] \cdot [B \supset (A \cdot E)]$ 1, 2, Conj
        5. $(A \cdot D) \lor (A \cdot E)$ 3, 4, CD
        6. $A \cdot (D \lor E)$ 5, Dist
        7. A 6, Simp
    8. $(C \lor B) \supset A$ 3–7, CP

(13) 1. $R \supset B$
    2. $R \supset (B \supset F)$
    3. $B \supset (F \supset H)$ / $R \supset H$
        4. R ACP
        5. B 1, 4, MP
        6. $B \supset F$ 2, 4, MP
        7. F 5, 6, MP
        8. $F \supset H$ 3, 5, MP
        9. H 7, 8, MP
    10. $R \supset H$ 4–9, CP

(16) 1. $Q \supset (R \supset S)$
    2. $Q \supset (T \supset \sim U)$
    3. $U \supset (R \lor T)$ / $Q \supset (U \supset S)$
        4. Q ACP
            5. U ACP
            6. $R \supset S$ 1, 4, MP
            7. $T \supset \sim U$ 2, 4, MP
            8. $\sim\sim U$ 5, DN
            9. $\sim T$ 7, 8, MT
            10. $R \lor T$ 3, 5, MP
            11. $T \lor R$ 10, Com
            12. R 9, 11, DS
            13. S 6, 12, MP
        14. $U \supset S$ 5–13, CP
    15. $Q \supset (U \supset S)$ 4–14, CP

(19) 1. $P \supset [(L \lor M) \supset (N \cdot O)]$
    2. $(O \lor T) \supset W$ / $P \supset (M \supset W)$
        3. P ACP
            4. M ACP
            5. $(L \lor M) \supset (N \cdot O)$ 1, 3, MP
            6. $M \lor L$ 4, Add
            7. $L \lor M$ 6, Com
            8. $N \cdot O$ 5, 7, MP
            9. $O \cdot N$ 8, Com
            10. O 9, Simp
            11. $O \lor T$ 10, Add
            12. W 2, 11, MP
        13. $M \supset W$ 4–12, CP
    14. $P \supset (M \supset W)$ 3–13, CP

7

II.

(1) 1. $H \supset D$
    2. $U \supset S$ / $(H \cdot U) \supset (S \cdot D)$
        | 3. $H \cdot U$ ACP
        | 4. H 3, Simp
        | 5. D 1, 4, MP
        | 6. $U \cdot H$ 3, Com
        | 7. U 6, Simp
        | 8. S 2, 7, MP
        | 9. $S \cdot D$ 5, 8, Conj
    10. $(H \cdot U) \supset (S \cdot D)$ 3–9, CP

(4) 1. $J \supset D$
    2. $(J \cdot D) \supset C$
    3. $(N \cdot C) \supset I$ / $J \supset (N \supset I)$
        | 4. J ACP
        | | 5. N ACP
        | | 6. D 1, 4, MP
        | | 7. $J \cdot D$ 4, 6, Conj
        | | 8. C 2, 7, MP
        | | 9. $N \cdot C$ 5, 8, Conj
        | |10. I 3, 9, MP
        |11. $N \supset I$ 5–10, CP
    12. $J \supset (N \supset I)$ 4–11, CP

Exercise 7.6

I.

(1) 1. $(S \lor T) \supset {\sim}S$ / ${\sim}S$
        | 2. S AIP
        | 3. $S \lor T$ 2, Add
        | 4. ${\sim}S$ 1, 3, MP
        | 5. $S \cdot {\sim}S$ 2, 4, Conj
    6. ${\sim}S$ 2–5, IP

(4) 1. $H \supset (L \supset K)$
    2. $L \supset (K \supset {\sim}L)$ / ${\sim}H \lor {\sim}L$
        | 3. $H \cdot L$ AIP
        | 4. H 3, Simp
        | 5. $L \supset K$ 1, 4, MP
        | 6. $L \cdot H$ 3, Com
        | 7. L 6, Simp
        | 8. $K \supset {\sim}L$ 2, 7, MP
        | 9. K 5, 7, MP
        |10. ${\sim}L$ 8, 9, MP
        |11. $L \cdot {\sim}L$ 7, 10, Conj
    12. ${\sim}(H \cdot L)$ 3–11, IP
    13. ${\sim}H \lor {\sim}L$ 12, DM

(7) 1. $(E \lor F) \supset (C \cdot D)$
    2. $(D \lor G) \supset H$
    3. $E \lor G$ / H
        | 4. ${\sim}H$ AIP
        | 5. ${\sim}(D \lor G)$ 2, 4, MT
        | 6. ${\sim}D \cdot {\sim}G$ 5, DM
        | 7. ${\sim}D$ 6, Simp
        | 8. ${\sim}D \lor {\sim}C$ 7, Add
        | 9. ${\sim}C \lor {\sim}D$ 8, Com
        |10. ${\sim}(C \cdot D)$ 9, DM
        |11. ${\sim}(E \lor F)$ 1, 10, MT
        |12. ${\sim}E \cdot {\sim}F$ 11, DM
        |13. ${\sim}E$ 12, Simp
        |14. G 3, 13, DS
        |15. ${\sim}G \cdot {\sim}D$ 6, Com
        |16. ${\sim}G$ 15, Simp
        |17. $G \cdot {\sim}G$ 14, 16, Conj
    18. ${\sim}{\sim}H$ 4–17, IP
    19. H 18, DN

(10) 1. K $/ S \supset (T \supset S)$

    2. S ACP
    3. $S \lor \sim T$ 2, Add
    4. $\sim T \lor S$ 3, Com
    5. $T \supset S$ 4, Impl
  6. $S \supset (T \supset S)$ 2–5, CP

(13) 1. $[C \supset (D \supset C)] \supset E$ $/ E$

    2. C ACP
    3. $C \lor \sim D$ 2, Add
    4. $\sim D \lor C$ 3, Com
    5. $D \supset C$ 4, Impl
  6. $C \supset (D \supset C)$ 2–5, CP
  7. E 1, 6, MP

(16) 1. $(N \lor O) \supset (C \cdot D)$
    2. $(D \lor K) \supset (P \lor \sim C)$
    3. $(P \lor G) \supset \sim(N \cdot D)$ $/ \sim N$

    4. N AIP
    5. $N \lor O$ 4, Add
    6. $C \cdot D$ 1, 5, MP
    7. $D \cdot C$ 6, Com
    8. D 7, Simp
    9. $D \lor K$ 8, Add
   10. $P \lor \sim C$ 2, 9, MP
   11. C 6, Simp
   12. $\sim C \lor P$ 10, Com
   13. $\sim\sim C$ 11, DN
   14. P 12, 13, DS
   15. $P \lor G$ 14, Add
   16. $\sim(N \cdot D)$ 3, 15, MP
   17. $\sim N \lor \sim D$ 16, DM
   18. $\sim\sim N$ 4, DN
   19. $\sim D$ 17, 18, DS
   20. $D \cdot \sim D$ 8, 19, Conj
  21. $\sim N$ 4–20, IP

(19) 1. $A \supset [(N \lor \sim N) \supset (S \lor T)]$
    2. $T \supset \sim(F \lor \sim F)$ $/ A \supset S$

    3. $A \cdot \sim S$ AIP
    4. A 3, Simp
    5. $(N \lor \sim N) \supset (S \lor T)$ 1, 4, MP
    6. N ACP
    7. $N \lor N$ 6, Add
    8. N 7, Taut
    9. $N \supset N$ 6–8, CP
   10. $\sim N \lor N$ 9, Impl
   11. $N \lor \sim N$ 10, Com
   12. $S \lor T$ 5, 11, MP
   13. $\sim S \cdot A$ 3, Com
   14. $\sim S$ 13, Simp
   15. T 12, 14, DS
   16. $\sim(F \lor \sim F)$ 2, 15, MP
   17. $\sim F \cdot \sim\sim F$ 16, DM
  18. $\sim(A \cdot \sim S)$ 3–17, IP
  19. $\sim A \lor \sim\sim S$ 18, DM
  20. $\sim A \lor S$ 19, DN
  21. $A \supset S$ 20, Impl

II.

(1) 1. $(C \cdot R) \supset (I \cdot D)$
    2. $R \supset \sim D$ $/ \sim C \lor \sim R$

    3. $C \cdot R$ AIP
    4. $I \cdot D$ 1, 3, MP
    5. $D \cdot I$ 4, Com
    6. D 5, Simp
    7. $R \cdot C$ 3, Com
    8. R 7, Simp
    9. $\sim D$ 2, 8, MP
   10. $D \cdot \sim D$ 6, 9, Conj
  11. $\sim(C \cdot R)$ 3–10, IP
  12. $\sim C \lor \sim R$ 11, DM

(4) 1. $(Z \supset C) \supset B$
    2. $(V \supset Z) \supset B$ $/ B$

    3. $\sim B$ AIP
    4. $\sim(Z \supset C)$ 1, 3, MT
    5. $\sim(\sim Z \lor C)$ 4, Impl
    6. $\sim\sim Z \cdot \sim C$ 5, DM
    7. $\sim\sim Z$ 6, Simp
    8. $\sim(V \supset Z)$ 2, 3, MT
    9. $\sim(\sim V \lor Z)$ 8, Impl
   10. $\sim\sim V \cdot \sim Z$ 9, DM
   11. $\sim Z \cdot \sim\sim V$ 10, Com
   12. $\sim Z$ 11, Simp
   13. $\sim Z \cdot \sim\sim Z$ 7, 12, Conj
  14. $\sim\sim B$ 3–13, IP
  15. B 14, DN

7

Exercise 7.7

(1)   / $P \supset [(P \supset Q) \supset Q]$

    1. P ACP
        2. $P \supset Q$ ACP
        3. Q 1, 2, MP
    4. $(P \supset Q) \supset Q$ 2–3, CP
  5. $P \supset [(P \supset Q) \supset Q]$ 1–4, CP

(4)   / $(P \supset Q) \supset [(P \cdot R) \supset (Q \cdot R)]$

    1. $P \supset Q$ ACP
        2. $P \cdot R$ ACP
        3. P 2, Simp
        4. Q 1, 3, MP
        5. $R \cdot P$ 2, Com
        6. R 5, Simp
        7. $Q \cdot R$ 4, 6, Conj
    8. $(P \cdot R) \supset (Q \cdot R)$ 2–7, CP
  9. $(P \supset Q) \supset [(P \cdot R) \supset (Q \cdot R)]$ 1–8, CP

(7)   / $[(P \supset Q) \vee (\sim Q \supset P)]$

    1. $\sim[(P \supset Q) \vee (\sim Q \supset P)]$ AIP
    2. $\sim(P \supset Q) \cdot \sim(\sim Q \supset P)$ 1, DM
    3. $\sim(P \supset Q)$ 2, Simp
    4. $\sim(\sim P \vee Q)$ 3, Impl
    5. $\sim\sim P \cdot \sim Q$ 4, DM
    6. $P \cdot \sim Q$ 5, DN
    7. P 6, Simp
    8. $\sim(\sim Q \supset P) \cdot \sim(P \supset Q)$ 2, Com
    9. $\sim(\sim Q \supset P)$ 8, Simp
    10. $\sim(\sim\sim Q \vee P)$ 9, Impl
    11. $\sim(Q \vee P)$ 10, DN
    12. $\sim Q \cdot \sim P$ 11, DM
    13. $\sim P \cdot \sim Q$ 12, Com
    14. $\sim P$ 13, Simp
    15. $P \cdot \sim P$ 7, 14, Conj
  16. $\sim\sim[(P \supset Q) \vee (\sim Q \supset P)]$ 1–15, IP
  17. $(P \supset Q) \vee (\sim Q \supset P)$ 16, DN

(10)   / $[\sim(P \cdot \sim Q) \cdot \sim Q] \supset \sim P$

    1. $\sim(P \cdot \sim Q) \cdot \sim Q$ ACP
    2. $\sim(P \cdot \sim Q)$ 1, Simp
    3. $\sim P \vee \sim\sim Q$ 2, DM
    4. $\sim P \vee Q$ 3, DN
    5. $\sim Q \cdot \sim(P \cdot \sim Q)$ 1, Com
    6. $\sim Q$ 5, Simp
    7. $Q \vee \sim P$ 4, Com
    8. $\sim P$ 6, 7, DS
  9. $[\sim(P \cdot \sim Q) \cdot \sim Q] \supset \sim P$ 1–8, CP

(13)   / $(P \supset Q) \supset [(P \supset \sim Q) \supset \sim P]$

     1. $P \supset Q$ ACP
         2. $P \supset \sim Q$ ACP
         3. $\sim\sim Q \supset \sim P$ 2, Trans
         4. $Q \supset \sim P$ 3, DN
         5. $P \supset \sim P$ 1, 4, HS
         6. $\sim P \vee \sim P$ 5, Impl
         7. $\sim P$ 6, Taut
     8. $(P \supset \sim Q) \supset \sim P$ 2–7, CP
   9. $(P \supset Q) \supset [(P \supset \sim Q) \supset \sim P]$ 1–8, CP

(16)   / $\sim[(P \supset \sim P) \cdot (\sim P \supset P)]$

     1. $(P \supset \sim P) \cdot (\sim P \supset P)$ AIP
     2. $(\sim P \vee \sim P) \cdot (\sim P \supset P)$ 1, Impl
     3. $\sim P \cdot (\sim P \supset P)$ 2, Taut
     4. $\sim P \cdot (\sim\sim P \vee P)$ 3, Impl
     5. $\sim P \cdot (P \vee P)$ 4, DN
     6. $\sim P \cdot P$ 5, Taut
     7. $P \cdot \sim P$ 6, Com
   8. $\sim[(P \supset \sim P) \cdot (\sim P \supset P)]$ 1–7, IP

(19)   / $P \equiv [P \vee (Q \cdot \sim Q)]$

     1. P ACP
     2. $P \vee (Q \cdot \sim Q)$ 1, Add
   3. $P \supset [P \vee (Q \cdot \sim Q)]$ 1–2, CP
     4. $P \vee (Q \cdot \sim Q)$ ACP
         5. $\sim P$ AIP
         6. $Q \cdot \sim Q$ 4, 5, DS
     7. $\sim\sim P$ 5–6, IP
     8. P 7, DN
   9. $[P \vee (Q \cdot \sim Q)] \supset P$ 4–8, CP
   10. {line 3} $\cdot$ {line 9}   3, 9, Conj
   11. $P \equiv [P \vee (Q \cdot \sim Q)]$ 10, Equiv

Exercise 8.1

1. Ce

4. $Jr \vee Nr$

7. $(x)(Mx \supset Tx)$

10. $(\exists x)(Hx \cdot \sim Rx)$

13. $(\exists x)Tx$

16. $(\exists x)(Sx \cdot \sim Gx)$

19. $(x)(Sx \supset Vx)$

22. $(x)(Cx \supset \sim Hx)$

25. $(x)(Tx \supset Hx)$

28. $(x)(Hx \supset \sim Ex)$

31. $(\exists x)[Cx \cdot \sim(Sx \vee Bx)]$

34. $(\exists x)[(Dx \cdot Bx) \equiv Tx]$

37. $(\exists x)[Cx \cdot (Ax \supset Tx)]$

40. $(x)[(Wx \cdot Cx) \supset Rx]$

43. $(x)[(Vx \vee Cx) \supset (Sx \cdot Ix)]$

46. $(\exists x)[(Fx \cdot Rx) \cdot Ex]$

I.

(1) 1. $(x)(Ax \supset Bx)$
  2. $(x)(Bx \supset Cx)$ / $(x)(Ax \supset Cx)$
  3. $Ax \supset Bx$ 1, UI
  4. $Bx \supset Cx$ 2, UI
  5. $Ax \supset Cx$ 3, 4, HS
  6. $(x)(Ax \supset Cx)$ 5, UG

(4) 1. $(x)[Ax \supset (Bx \lor Cx)]$
  2. $Ag \cdot {\sim}Bg$ / Cg
  3. $Ag \supset (Bg \lor Cg)$ 1, UI
  4. Ag 2, Simp
  5. $Bg \lor Cg$ 3, 4, MP
  6. ${\sim}Bg \cdot Ag$ 2, Com
  7. ${\sim}Bg$ 6, Simp
  8. Cg 5, 7, DS

(7) 1. $(x)[Ax \supset (Bx \lor Cx)]$
  2. $(\exists x)(Ax \cdot {\sim}Cx)$ / $(\exists x)Bx$
  3. $Am \cdot {\sim}Cm$ 2, EI
  4. $Am \supset (Bm \lor Cm)$ 1, UI
  5. Am 3, Simp
  6. $Bm \lor Cm$ 4, 5, MP
  7. ${\sim}Cm \cdot Am$ 3, Com
  8. ${\sim}Cm$ 7, Simp
  9. $Cm \lor Bm$ 6, Com
  10. Bm 8, 9 DS
  11. $(\exists x)Bx$ 10, EG

(10) 1. $(x)(Bx \lor Ax)$
  2. $(x)(Bx \supset Ax)$ / $(x)Ax$
  3. $Bx \lor Ax$ 1, UI
  4. $Bx \supset Ax$ 2, UI
  5. $Ax \lor Bx$ 3, Com
  6. ${\sim}{\sim}Ax \lor Bx$ 5, DN
  7. ${\sim}Ax \supset Bx$ 6, Impl
  8. ${\sim}Ax \supset Ax$ 4, 7, HS
  9. ${\sim}{\sim}Ax \lor Ax$ 8, Impl
  10. $Ax \lor Ax$ 9, DN
  11. Ax 10, Taut
  12. $(x)Ax$ 11, UG

(13) 1. $(\exists x)Ax \supset (x)Bx$
  2. $(\exists x)Cx \supset (\exists x)Dx$
  3. $An \cdot Cn$ / $(\exists x)(Bx \cdot Dx)$
  4. An 2, Simp
  5. $(\exists x)Ax$ 4, EG
  6. $(x)Bx$ 1, 5, MP
  7. $Cn \cdot An$ 3, Com
  8. Cn 7, Simp
  9. $(\exists x)Cx$ 8, EG
  10. $(\exists x)Dx$ 2, 9, MP
  11. Dm 10, EI
  12. Bm 6, UI
  13. $Bm \cdot Dm$ 11, 12, Conj
  14. $(\exists x)(Bx \cdot Dx)$ 13, EG

II.

(1) 1. $(x)(Ox \supset Sx)$
  2. $(x)(Ox \supset Fx)$ / $(x)[Ox \supset (Sx \cdot Fx)]$
  3. $Ox \supset Sx$ 1, UI
  4. $Ox \supset Fx$ 2, UI
  5. ${\sim}Ox \lor Sx$ 3, Impl
  6. ${\sim}Ox \lor Fx$ 4, Impl
  7. $({\sim}Ox \lor Sx) \cdot ({\sim}Ox \lor Fx)$ 5, 6, Conj
  8. ${\sim}Ox \lor (Sx \cdot Fx)$ 7, Dist
  9. $Ox \supset (Sx \cdot Fx)$ 8, Impl
  10. $(x)[Ox \supset (Sx \cdot Fx)]$ 9, UG

(4) 1. $(x)(Cx \supset Vx) \cdot (x)(Px \supset Fx)$
  2. $(\exists x)(Cx \cdot Gx) \cdot (\exists x)(Px \cdot Gx)$ / $(\exists x)(Vx \cdot Gx) \cdot (\exists x)(Fx \cdot Gx)$
  3. $(\exists x)(Cx \cdot Gx)$ 2, Simp
  4. $Cm \cdot Gm$ 3, EI
  5. $(\exists x)(Px \cdot Gx) \cdot (\exists x)(Cx \cdot Gx)$ 2, Com
  6. $(\exists x)(Px \cdot Gx)$ 5, Simp
  7. $Pn \cdot Gn$ 6, EI
  8. $(x)(Cx \supset Vx)$ 1, Simp

8

9. $Cm \supset Vm$		8, UI
10. Cm		4, Simp
11. Vm		9, 10, MP
12. $Gm \cdot Cm$		4, Com
13. Gm		12, Simp
14. $Vm \cdot Gm$		11, 13, Conj
15. $(\exists x)(Vx \cdot Gx)$		14, EG
16. $(x)(Px \supset Fx) \cdot (x)(Cx \supset Vx)$		1, Com
17. $(x)(Px \supset Fx)$		16, Simp
18. $Pn \supset Fn$		17, UI
19. Pn		7, Simp
20. Fn		18, 19, MP
21. $Gn \cdot Pn$		7, Com
22. Gn		21, Simp
23. $Fn \cdot Gn$		20, 22, Conj
24. $(\exists x)(Fx \cdot Gx)$		23, EG
25. $(\exists x)(Vx \cdot Gx) \cdot (\exists x)(Fx \cdot Gx)$		15, 24, Conj

(7)	1. $(x)[Gx \supset (Ix \cdot Px)]$		
	2. $(x)[(Ix \cdot Px) \supset Rx]$		
	3. $Ga \cdot Gc$		/ $Ra \cdot Rc$
	4. $Gx \supset (Ix \cdot Px)$		1, UI
	5. $(Ix \cdot Px) \supset Rx$		2, UI
	6. $Gx \supset Rx$		4, 5, HS
	7. $(x)(Gx \supset Rx)$		6, UG
	8. $Ga \supset Ra$		7, UI
	9. Ga		3, Simp
	10. Ra		8, 9, MP
	11. $Gc \supset Rc$		7, UI
	12. $Gc \cdot Ga$		3, Com
	13. Gc		12, Simp
	14. Rc		11, 13, MP
	15. $Ra \cdot Rc$		10, 14, Conj

(10)	1. $(x)[(Ax \cdot Kx) \supset Rx] \supset (x)(Gx \supset Sx)$		
	2. $(x)[(Ax \cdot Kx) \supset Fx] \supset (x)(Gx \supset Px)$		
	3. $(x)[(Ax \cdot Kx) \supset (Rx \cdot Fx)]$		/ $(x)[Gx \supset (Sx \cdot Px)]$
	4. $(Ax \cdot Kx) \supset (Rx \cdot Fx)$		3, UI
	5. $\sim(Ax \cdot Kx) \lor (Rx \cdot Fx)$		4, Impl
	6. $[\sim(Ax \cdot Kx) \lor Rx] \cdot [\sim(Ax \cdot Kx) \lor Fx]$		5, Dist
	7. $\sim(Ax \cdot Kx) \lor Rx$		6, Simp
	8. $[\sim(Ax \cdot Kx) \lor Fx] \cdot [\sim(Ax \cdot Kx) \lor Rx]$		6, Com
	9. $\sim(Ax \cdot Kx) \lor Fx$		8, Simp
	10. $(Ax \cdot Kx) \supset Rx$		7, Impl
	11. $(Ax \cdot Kx) \supset Fx$		9, Impl
	12. $(x)[(Ax \cdot Kx) \supset Rx]$		10, UG
	13. $(x)[(Ax \cdot Kx) \supset Fx]$		11, UG
	14. $(x)(Gx \supset Sx)$		1, 12, MP
	15. $(x)(Gx \supset Px)$		2, 13, MP

8

16. $Gx \supset Sx$	14, UI
17. $Gx \supset Px$	15, UI
18. $\sim Gx \lor Sx$	16, Impl
19. $\sim Gx \lor Px$	17, Impl
20. $(\sim Gx \lor Sx) \cdot (\sim Gx \lor Px)$	18, 19, Conj
21. $\sim Gx \lor (Sx \cdot Px)$	20, Dist
22. $Gx \supset (Sx \cdot Px)$	21, Impl
23. $(x)[Gx \supset (Sx \cdot Px)]$	22, UG

Exercise 8.3

I.

(1)
1. $(x)Ax \supset (\exists x)Bx$	
2. $(x)\sim Bx$	/ $(\exists x)\sim Ax$
3. $\sim(\exists x)Bx$	2, CQ
4. $\sim(x)Ax$	1, 3, MT
5. $(\exists x)\sim Ax$	4, CQ

(4)
1. $(\exists x)Ax \lor (\exists x)(Bx \cdot Cx)$	
2. $\sim(\exists x)Bx$	/ $(\exists x)Ax$
3. $(x)\sim Bx$	2, CQ
4. $\sim Bx$	3, UI
5. $\sim Bx \lor \sim Cx$	4, Add
6. $\sim(Bx \cdot Cx)$	5, DM
7. $(x)\sim(Bx \cdot Cx)$	6, UG
8. $\sim(\exists x)(Bx \cdot Cx)$	7, CQ
9. $(\exists x)(Bx \cdot Cx) \lor (\exists x)Ax$	1, Com
10. $(\exists x)Ax$	8, 9, DS

(7)
1. $(x)(Ax \supset Bx)$	
2. $\sim(x)Cx \lor (x)Ax$	
3. $\sim(x)Bx$	/ $(\exists x)\sim Cx$
4. $(\exists x)\sim Bx$	3, CQ
5. $\sim Bm$	4, EI
6. $Am \supset Bm$	1, UI
7. $\sim Am$	5, 6, MT
8. $(\exists x)\sim Ax$	7, EG
9. $\sim(x)Ax$	8, CQ
10. $(x)Ax \lor \sim(x)Cx$	2, Com
11. $\sim(x)Cx$	9, 10, DS
12. $(\exists x)\sim Cx$	11, CQ

(10)
1. $\sim(\exists x)(Ax \cdot \sim Bx)$	
2. $\sim(\exists x)(Bx \cdot \sim Cx)$	/ $(x)(Ax \supset Cx)$
3. $(x)\sim(Ax \cdot \sim Bx)$	1, CQ
4. $(x)\sim(Bx \cdot \sim Cx)$	2, CQ
5. $\sim(Ax \cdot \sim Bx)$	3, UI
6. $\sim(Bx \cdot \sim Cx)$	4, UI
7. $\sim Ax \lor \sim\sim Bx$	5, DM
8. $\sim Ax \lor Bx$	7, DN
9. $\sim Bx \lor \sim\sim Cx$	6, DM

8

	10. $\sim Bx \lor Cx$	9, DN
	11. $Ax \supset Bx$	8, Impl
	12. $Bx \supset Cx$	10, Impl
	13. $Ax \supset Cx$	11, 12, HS
	14. $(x)(Ax \supset Cx)$	13, UG
(13)	1. $(x)(Ax \cdot \sim Bx) \supset (\exists x)Cx$	
	2. $\sim(\exists x)(Cx \lor Bx)$	$/ \sim(x)Ax$
	3. $(x)\sim(Cx \lor Bx)$	2, CQ
	4. $\sim(Cx \lor Bx)$	3, UI
	5. $\sim Cx \cdot \sim Bx$	4, DM
	6. $\sim Cx$	5, Simp
	7. $(x)\sim Cx$	6, UG
	8. $\sim(\exists x)Cx$	7, CQ
	9. $\sim(x)(Ax \cdot \sim Bx)$	1, 8, MT
	10. $(\exists x)\sim(Ax \cdot \sim Bx)$	9, CQ
	11. $\sim(Am \cdot \sim Bm)$	10, EI
	12. $\sim Am \lor \sim\sim Bm$	11, DM
	13. $\sim Am \lor Bm$	12, DN
	14. $\sim Bx \cdot \sim Cx$	5, Com
	15. $\sim Bx$	14, Simp
	16. $(x)\sim Bx$	15, UG
	17. $\sim Bm$	16, UI
	18. $Bm \lor \sim Am$	13, Com
	19. $\sim Am$	17, 18, DS
	20. $(\exists x)\sim Ax$	19, EG
	21. $\sim(x)Ax$	20, CQ

II.

(1)	1. $(x)[Px \supset (Hx \lor Nx)] \supset \sim(\exists x)Cx$	
	2. Cf	$/ (\exists x)(Px \cdot \sim Nx)$
	3. $(\exists x)Cx$	2, EG
	4. $\sim\sim(\exists x)Cx$	3, DN
	5. $\sim(x)[Px \supset (Hx \lor Nx)]$	1, 4, MT
	6. $(\exists x)\sim[Px \supset (Hx \lor Nx)]$	5, CQ
	7. $\sim[Pm \supset (Hm \lor Nm)]$	6, EI
	8. $\sim[\sim Pm \lor (Hm \lor Nm)]$	7, Impl
	9. $\sim\sim Pm \cdot \sim(Hm \lor Nm)$	8, DM
	10. $Pm \cdot \sim(Hm \lor Nm)$	9, DN
	11. $Pm \cdot (\sim Hm \cdot \sim Nm)$	10, DM
	12. Pm	11, Simp
	13. $(Pm \cdot \sim Hm) \cdot \sim Nm$	11, Assoc
	14. $\sim Nm \cdot (Pm \cdot \sim Hm)$	13, Com
	15. $\sim Nm$	14, Simp
	16. $Pm \cdot \sim Nm$	12, 15, Conj
	17. $(\exists x)(Px \cdot \sim Nx)$	16, EG

(4) 1. $(\exists x)(Gx \cdot Px) \lor (\exists x)(Sx \cdot Ex)$
  2. $\sim(\exists x)Ex$ / $(\exists x)Px$
  3. $(x)\sim Ex$ 2, CQ
  4. $\sim Ex$ 3, UI
  5. $\sim Ex \lor \sim Sx$ 4, Add
  6. $\sim Sx \lor \sim Ex$ 5, Com
  7. $\sim(Sx \cdot Ex)$ 6, DM
  8. $(x)\sim(Sx \cdot Ex)$ 7, UG
  9. $\sim(\exists x)(Sx \cdot Ex)$ 8, CQ
  10. $(\exists x)(Sx \cdot Ex) \lor (\exists x)(Gx \cdot Px)$ 1, Com
  11. $(\exists x)(Gx \cdot Px)$ 9, 10, DS
  12. $Gm \cdot Pm$ 11, EI
  13. $Pm \cdot Gm$ 12, Com
  14. Pm 13, Simp
  15. $(\exists x)Px$ 14, EG

(7) 1. $(x)(Px \supset Sx) \cdot (x)(Ix \supset Gx)$
  2. $\sim(\exists x)(Sx \cdot Gx)$ / $\sim(\exists x)(Px \cdot Ix)$
  3. $(x)\sim(Sx \cdot Gx)$ 2, CQ
  4. $\sim(Sx \cdot Gx)$ 3, UI
  5. $\sim Sx \lor \sim Gx$ 4, DM
  6. $(x)(Px \supset Sx)$ 1, Simp
  7. $(x)(Ix \supset Gx) \cdot (x)(Px \supset Sx)$ 1, Com
  8. $(x)(Ix \supset Gx)$ 7, Simp
  9. $Px \supset Sx$ 6, UI
  10. $Ix \supset Gx$ 8, UI
  11. $\sim Sx \supset \sim Px$ 9, Trans
  12. $\sim Gx \supset \sim Ix$ 10, Trans
  13. $(\sim Sx \supset \sim Px) \cdot (\sim Gx \supset \sim Ix)$ 11, 12, Conj
  14. $\sim Px \lor \sim Ix$ 5, 13, CD
  15. $\sim(Px \cdot Ix)$ 14, DM
  16. $(x)\sim(Px \cdot Ix)$ 15, UG
  17. $\sim(\exists x)(Px \cdot Ix)$ 16, CQ

(10) 1. $\sim(\exists x)[Px \cdot (Gx \lor Hx)]$
  2. $(x)[Nx \supset (Px \cdot Hx)]$
  3. $(\exists x)(Px \cdot Cx) \lor (\exists x)(Px \cdot Nx)$ / $(\exists x)(Cx \cdot \sim Gx)$
  4. $(x)\sim[Px \cdot (Gx \lor Hx)]$ 1, CQ
  5. $\sim[Px \cdot (Gx \lor Hx)]$ 4, UI
  6. $\sim Px \lor \sim(Gx \lor Hx)$ 5, DM
  7. $\sim Px \lor (\sim Gx \cdot \sim Hx)$ 6, DM
  8. $(\sim Px \lor \sim Gx) \cdot (\sim Px \lor \sim Hx)$ 7, Dist
  9. $\sim Px \lor \sim Gx$ 8, Simp
  10. $(\sim Px \lor \sim Hx) \cdot (\sim Px \lor \sim Gx)$ 8, Com
  11. $\sim Px \lor \sim Hx$ 10, Simp
  12. $\sim(Px \cdot Hx)$ 11, DM
  13. $Nx \supset (Px \cdot Hx)$ 2, UI
  14. $\sim Nx$ 12, 13, MT

8

15.	~Nx ∨ ~Px	14, Add
16.	~Px ∨ ~Nx	15, Com
17.	~(Px • Nx)	16, DM
18.	(x)~(Px • Nx)	17, UG
19.	~(∃x)(Px • Nx)	18, CQ
20.	(∃x)(Px • Nx) ∨ (∃x)(Px • Cx)	3, Com
21.	(∃x)(Px • Cx)	19, 20, DS
22.	Pm • Cm	21, EI
23.	(x)(~Px ∨ ~Gx)	9, UG
24.	~Pm ∨ ~Gm	23, UI
25.	Pm	22, Simp
26.	~~Pm	25, DN
27.	~Gm	24, 26, DS
28.	Cm • Pm	22, Com
29.	Cm	28, Simp
30.	Cm • ~Gm	27, 29, Conj
31.	(∃x)(Cx • ~Gx)	30, EG

Exercise 8.4

I.

(1)
1.	(x)(Ax ⊃ Bx)	
2.	(x)(Ax ⊃ Cx)	/ (x)[Ax ⊃ (Bx • Cx)]
	3. Ax	ACP
	4. Ax ⊃ Bx	1, UI
	5. Ax ⊃ Cx	2, UI
	6. Bx	3, 4, MP
	7. Cx	3, 5, MP
	8. Bx • Cx	6, 7, Conj
9.	Ax ⊃ (Bx • Cx)	3–8, CP
10.	(x)[Ax ⊃ (Bx • Cx)]	9, UG

(4)
1.	(x)(Ax ⊃ Cx)	
2.	(∃x)Cx ⊃ (∃x)(Bx • Dx)	/ (∃x)Ax ⊃ (∃x)Bx
	3. (∃x)Ax	ACP
	4. Am	3, EI
	5. Am ⊃ Cm	1, UI
	6. Cm	4, 5, MP
	7. (∃x)Cx	6, EG
	8. (∃x)(Bx • Dx)	2, 7, MP
	9. Bn • Dn	8, EI
	10. Bn	9, Simp
	11. (∃x)Bx	10, EG
12.	(∃x)Ax ⊃ (∃x)Bx	3–11, CP

(7) 1. $(x)[(Ax \lor Bx) \supset Cx]$

  2. $(x)[(Cx \lor Dx) \supset Ex]$ $/ (x)(Ax \supset Ex)$

       3. Ax ACP

       4. $(Ax \lor Bx) \supset Cx$ 1, UI

       5. $(Cx \lor Dx) \supset Ex$ 2, UI

       6. $Ax \lor Bx$ 3, Add

       7. Cx 4, 6, MP

       8. $Cx \lor Dx$ 7, Add

       9. Ex 5, 8, MP

  10. $Ax \supset Ex$ 3–9, CP

  11. $(x)(Ax \supset Ex)$ 10, UG

(10) 1. $(x)(Ax \supset Bx)$

  2. $Am \lor An$ $/ (\exists x)Bx$

       3. $\sim(\exists x)Bx$ AIP

       4. $(x)\sim Bx$ 3, CQ

       5. $Am \supset Bm$ 1, UI

       6. $An \supset Bn$ 1, UI

       7. $(Am \supset Bm) \cdot (An \supset Bn)$ 5, 6, Conj

       8. $Bm \lor Bn$ 2, 7, CD

       9. $\sim Bm$ 4, UI

       10. Bn 8, 9, DS

       11. $\sim Bn$ 4, UI

       12. $Bn \cdot \sim Bn$ 10, 11, Conj

  13. $\sim\sim(\exists x)Bx$ 3–12, IP

  14. $(\exists x)Bx$ 13, DN

(13) 1. $(\exists x)Ax \supset (x)(Bx \supset Cx)$

  2. $(\exists x)Dx \supset (\exists x)Bx$ $/ (\exists x)(Ax \cdot Dx) \supset (\exists x)Cx$

       3. $(\exists x)(Ax \cdot Dx)$ ACP

       4. $Am \cdot Dm$ 3, EI

       5. Am 4, Simp

       6. $(\exists x)Ax$ 5, EG

       7. $(x)(Bx \supset Cx)$ 1, 6, MP

       8. $Dm \cdot Am$ 4, Com

       9. Dm 8, Simp

       10. $(\exists x)Dx$ 9, EG

       11. $(\exists x)Bx$ 2, 10, MP

       12. Bn 11, EI

       13. $Bn \supset Cn$ 7, UI

       14. Cn 12, 13, MP

       15. $(\exists x)Cx$ 14, EG

  16. $(\exists x)(Ax \cdot Dx) \supset (\exists x)Cx$ 3–15, CP

8

(16) 1. $(x)[(Ax \lor Bx) \supset Cx]$
    2. $(\exists x)(\sim Ax \lor Dx) \supset (x)Ex$ / $(x)Cx \lor (x)Ex$
        3. $\sim[(x)Cx \lor (x)Ex]$ AIP
        4. $\sim(x)Cx \cdot \sim(x)Ex$ 3, DM
        5. $\sim(x)Cx$ 4, Simp
        6. $(\exists x)\sim Cx$ 5, CQ
        7. $\sim Cm$ 6, EI
        8. $(Am \lor Bm) \supset Cm$ 1, UI
        9. $\sim(Am \lor Bm)$ 7, 8, MT
      10. $\sim Am \cdot \sim Bm$ 9, DM
      11. $\sim Am$ 10, Simp
      12. $\sim Am \lor Dm$ 11, Add
      13. $(\exists x)(\sim Ax \lor Dx)$ 12, EG
      14. $(x)Ex$ 2, 13, MP
      15. $\sim(x)Ex \cdot \sim(x)Cx$ 4, Com
      16. $\sim(x)Ex$ 15, Simp
      17. $(x)Ex \cdot \sim(x)Ex$ 14, 16, Conj
     18. $\sim\sim[(x)Cx \lor (x)Ex]$ 3–17, IP
     19. $(x)Cx \lor (x)Ex$ 18, DN

(19) 1. $(x)[Bx \supset (Cx \cdot Dx)]$ / $(x)(Ax \supset Bx) \supset (x)(Ax \supset Dx)$
        2. $(x)(Ax \supset Bx)$ ACP
           3. Ax ACP
           4. $Ax \supset Bx$ 2, UI
           5. Bx 3, 4, MP
           6. $Bx \supset (Cx \cdot Dx)$ 1, UI
           7. $Cx \cdot Dx$ 5, 6, MP
           8. $Dx \cdot Cx$ 7, Com
           9. Dx 8, Simp
        10. $Ax \supset Dx$ 3–9, CP
        11. $(x)(Ax \supset Dx)$ 10, UG
     12. $(x)(Ax \supset Bx) \supset (x)(Ax \supset Dx)$ 2–11, CP

II.

(1) 1. $(x)(Ax \supset Wx)$
    2. $(x)(Rx \supset Cx)$ / $(x)[(Rx \cdot Ax) \supset (Cx \cdot Wx)]$
        3. $Rx \cdot Ax$ ACP
        4. Rx 3, Simp
        5. $Ax \cdot Rx$ 3, Com
        6. Ax 5, Simp
        7. $Ax \supset Wx$ 1, UI
        8. $Rx \supset Cx$ 2, UI
        9. Cx 4, 8, MP
      10. Wx 6, 7, MP
      11. $Cx \cdot Wx$ 9, 10, Conj
     12. $(Rx \cdot Ax) \supset (Cx \cdot Wx)$ 3–11, CP
     13. $(x)[(Rx \cdot Ax) \supset (Cx \cdot Wx)]$ 12, UG

(4) 1. $(x)[(Sx \lor Ux) \supset (Ix \cdot Cx)]$
 2. $(x)[(Cx \lor Vx) \supset (Rx \cdot Ax)]$ $/ (x)(Sx \supset Ax)$
 3. Sx ACP
 4. $Sx \lor Ux$ 3, Add
 5. $(Sx \lor Ux) \supset (Ix \cdot Cx)$ 1, UI
 6. $Ix \cdot Cx$ 4, 5, MP
 7. $Cx \cdot Ix$ 6, Com
 8. Cx 7, Simp
 9. $Cx \lor Vx$ 8, Add
 10. $(Cx \lor Vx) \supset (Rx \cdot Ax)$ 2, UI
 11. $Rx \cdot Ax$ 9, 10, MP
 12. $Ax \cdot Rx$ 11, Com
 13. Ax 12, Simp
 14. $Sx \supset Ax$ 3–13, CP
 15. $(x)(Sx \supset Ax)$ 14, UG

(7) 1. $(\exists x)Cx \supset (x)[Ax \supset (Sx \cdot Dx)]$
 2. $(x)(Cx \supset {\sim}Ax) \supset (\exists x)(Dx \cdot Sx)$ $/ (\exists x)(Dx \cdot Sx)$
 3. ${\sim}(\exists x)(Dx \cdot Sx)$ AIP
 4. ${\sim}(x)(Cx \supset {\sim}Ax)$ 2, 3, MT
 5. $(\exists x){\sim}(Cx \supset {\sim}Ax)$ 4, CQ
 6. ${\sim}(Cm \supset {\sim}Am)$ 5, EI
 7. ${\sim}({\sim}Cm \lor {\sim}Am)$ 6, Impl
 8. ${\sim}{\sim}Cm \cdot {\sim}{\sim}Am$ 7, DM
 9. $Cm \cdot {\sim}{\sim}Am$ 8, DN
 10. $Cm \cdot Am$ 9, DN
 11. Cm 10, Simp
 12. $(\exists x)Cx$ 11, EG
 13. $(x)[Ax \supset (Sx \cdot Dx)]$ 1, 12, MP
 14. $Am \supset (Sm \cdot Dm)$ 13, UI
 15. $Am \cdot Cm$ 10, Com
 16. Am 15, Simp
 17. $Sm \cdot Dm$ 14, 16, MP
 18. $Dm \cdot Sm$ 17, Com
 19. $(\exists x)(Dx \cdot Sx)$ 18, EG
 20. $(\exists x)(Dx \cdot Sx) \cdot {\sim}(\exists x)(Dx \cdot Sx)$ 3, 19, Conj
 21. ${\sim}{\sim}(\exists x)(Dx \cdot Sx)$ 3–20, IP
 22. $(\exists x)(Dx \cdot Sx)$ 21, DN

(10) 1. $(\exists x)(Gx \cdot Px) \lor (\exists x)(Ax \cdot Px)$

2. $(\exists x)Px \supset (\exists x)[Ax \cdot (Cx \cdot Dx)]$ / $(\exists x)(Dx \cdot Cx)$

3. $\sim(\exists x)Px$	AIP
4. $(x)\sim Px$	3, CQ
5. $\sim Px$	4, UI
6. $\sim Px \lor \sim Gx$	5, Add
7. $\sim Gx \lor \sim Px$	6, Com
8. $\sim(Gx \cdot Px)$	7, DM
9. $(x)\sim(Gx \cdot Px)$	8, UG
10. $\sim(\exists x)(Gx \cdot Px)$	9, CQ
11. $(\exists x)(Ax \cdot Px)$	1, 10, DS
12. $Am \cdot Pm$	11, EI
13. $Pm \cdot Am$	12, Com
14. Pm	13, Simp
15. $\sim Pm$	4, UI
16. $Pm \cdot \sim Pm$	14, 15, Conj
17. $\sim\sim(\exists x)Px$	3–16, IP
18. $(\exists x)Px$	17, DN
19. $(\exists x)[Ax \cdot (Cx \cdot Dx)]$	2, 18, MP
20. $An \cdot (Cn \cdot Dn)$	19, EI
21. $(Cn \cdot Dn) \cdot An$	20, Com
22. $Cn \cdot Dn$	21, Simp
23. $Dn \cdot Cn$	22, Com
24. $(\exists x)(Dx \cdot Cx)$	23, EG

Exercise 8.5

I.

1. All cats are animals.
   No cats are dogs.
   No dogs are animals.

4. Some mammals are dogs.
   Some mammals write books.
   Some mammals are dogs that write books.

7. There are flowers.
   There are dogs.
   No flowers are animals.
   Some dogs are not animals.

10. Some mammals are felines.
    Some animals are not felines.
    All mammals are animals.
    Some feline animals are not mammals.

II.

(1) 1. $(x)(Ax \supset Bx)$

2. $(x)(Ax \supset Cx)$ / $(x)(Bx \supset Cx)$

For a universe consisting of one member, we have

$Aa \supset Ba$	/	$Aa \supset Ca$	//	$Ba \supset Ca$
F T T		F T F		T F F

(4) 1. $(x)(Ax \supset Bx)$
   2. $(\exists x)Ax$ $/ (x)Bx$

For a universe consisting of two members, we have

$(Aa \supset Ba) \cdot (Ab \supset Bb) \quad / \quad Aa \lor Ab \quad // \quad Ba \cdot Bb$
  T T T   T F T   F   T T F   T F F

(7) 1. $(x)(Ax \supset Bx)$
   2. $(\exists x)Bx \supset (\exists x)Cx$ $/ (x)(Ax \supset Cx)$

For a universe consisting of two members, we have

$(Aa \supset Ba) \cdot (Ab \supset Bb) \, / \, (Ba \lor Bb) \supset (Ca \lor Cb) \, // \, (Aa \supset Ca) \cdot (Ab \supset Cb)$
  T T T T T T T   T T T T T T F   T T T F T F F

(10) 1. $(\exists x)(Ax \cdot Bx)$
   2. $(\exists x)(\sim Ax \cdot \sim Bx)$ $/ (x)(Ax \equiv Bx)$

For a universe consisting of one member, we have

$Aa \cdot Ba \, / \, \sim Aa \cdot \sim Ba \, // \, Aa \equiv Ba$
  T T   (F T T)   F

For a universe consisting of two members, we have

$(Aa \cdot Ba) \lor (Ab \cdot Bb) \, / \, (\sim Aa \cdot \sim Ba) \lor (\sim Ab \cdot \sim Bb)$
  T T T T T F F   F T(F F T T F T F)T F

$// \, (Aa \equiv Ba) \cdot (Ab \equiv Bb)$
       T T T F T F F

For a universe consisting of three members, we have

$(Aa \cdot Ba) \lor [(Ab \cdot Bb) \lor (Ac \cdot Bc)] \, /$
  T T T T   T F F T   F F F

$(\sim Aa \cdot \sim Ba) \lor [(\sim Ab \cdot \sim Bb) \lor (\sim Ac \cdot \sim Bc)]$
  F T F F T T   F T F F T T T F T T F

$// \, (Aa \equiv Ba) \cdot [(Ab \equiv Bb) \cdot (Ac \equiv Bc)]$
     T T T F   T F F F   F T F

III.

(1) 1. $(x)[(Vx \cdot Px) \supset (Ax \cdot Mx)]$
   2. $(\exists x)(Vx \cdot Ox)$ $/ (\exists x)(Mx \cdot Ax)$

For a universe consisting of one member, we have

$(Va \cdot Pa) \supset (Aa \cdot Ma) \, / \, Va \cdot Oa \, // \, Ma \cdot Aa$
  T F F   T   F F T   T T T   F F F

(4) 1. $(x)(Tx \supset Hx)$
   2. $(\exists x)(Tx \cdot Hx) \supset (\exists x)(Px \cdot Ox)$ $/ (x)(Tx \supset Ox)$

For a universe consisting of two members, we have

$(Ta \supset Ha) \cdot (Tb \supset Hb) \, / \, [(Ta \cdot Ha) \lor (Tb \cdot Hb)] \supset [(Pa \cdot Oa) \lor (Pb \cdot Ob)]$
  T T T T T T   T T T T T T T   T   F F F T T T T

$// \, (Ta \supset Oa) \cdot (Tb \supset Ob)$
    T F F F T T T

Exercise 8.6

I.

1. Rcp

4. $(\exists x)Fxj \supset Fmj$

7. $(x)[Px \supset (\exists y)Sxy]$

10. $(\exists x)[Px \cdot (y)Sxy]$

13. $(\exists x)[(Cx \cdot Lx) \cdot Dpx]$

16. $(\exists x)(Fxc \cdot Icx)$

19. $(x)\{Px \supset (\exists y)[Py \cdot (Mxy \supset Axy)]\}$

22. $(\exists x)\{Px \cdot (y)[(Ty \cdot Sxy) \supset Axy]\}$

25. $(x)\{Lx \supset (y)[(Wy \cdot Cy) \supset Rxy]\}$

28. $(x)\{(Cx \cdot Fx) \supset (y)[(By \cdot Ly) \supset Rxy]\}$

II.

(1) 1. $(x)[Ax \supset (y)Bxy]$
2. Am / $(y)Bmy$
3. $Am \supset (y)Bmy$ 1, UI
4. $(y)Bmy$ 2, 3, MP

(4) 1. $(x)(\exists y)(Ax \supset By)$ / $(x)Ax \supset (\exists y)By$
2. $(x)Ax$ ACP
3. Ax 2, UI
4. $(\exists y)(Ax \supset By)$ 1, UI
5. $Ax \supset Bm$ 4, EI
6. Bm 3, 5, MP
7. $(\exists y)By$ 6, EG
8. $(x)Ax \supset (\exists y)By$ 2–7, CP

(7) 1. $(\exists x)[Ax \cdot (y)(Ay \supset Bxy)]$ / $(\exists x)Bxx$
2. $Am \cdot (y)(Ay \supset Bmy)$ 1, EI
3. Am 2, Simp
4. $(y)(Ay \supset Bmy) \cdot Am$ 2, Com
5. $(y)(Ay \supset Bmy)$ 4, Simp
6. $Am \supset Bmm$ 5, UI
7. Bmm 3, 6, MP
8. $(\exists x)Bxx$ 7, EG

(10) 1. $(x)(\exists y)Axy \supset (x)(\exists y)Bxy$
2. $(\exists x)(y)\sim Bxy$ / $(\exists x)(y)\sim Axy$
3. $(\exists x)\sim(\exists y)Bxy$ 2, CQ
4. $\sim(x)(\exists y)Bxy$ 3, CQ
5. $\sim(x)(\exists y)Axy$ 1, 4, MT
6. $(\exists x)\sim(\exists y)Axy$ 5, CQ
7. $(\exists x)(y)\sim Axy$ 6, CQ

(13) 1. $(\exists x)\{Ax \cdot (y)[(By \vee Cy) \supset Dxy]\}$
2. $(\exists x)Ax \supset (\exists y)By$ / $(\exists x)(\exists y)Dxy$
3. $Am \cdot (y)[(By \vee Cy) \supset Dmy]$ 1, EI
4. Am 3, Simp
5. $(\exists x)Ax$ 4, EG
6. $(\exists y)By$ 2, 5, MP
7. Bn 6, EI
8. $(y)[(By \vee Cy) \supset Dmy] \cdot Am$ 3, Com
9. $(y)[(By \vee Cy) \supset Dmy]$ 8, Simp
10. $(Bn \vee Cn) \supset Dmn$ 9, UI
11. $Bn \vee Cn$ 7, Add

	12. Dmn	10, 11, MP
	13. $(\exists y)Dmy$	12, EG
	14. $(\exists x)(\exists y)Dxy$	13, EG
(16)	1. $(x)(\exists y)(Ax \cdot By)$	/ $(\exists y)(x)(Ax \cdot By)$
	2. $(\exists y)(Ax \cdot By)$	1, UI
	3. $Ax \cdot Ba$	2, EI
	4. Ax	3, Simp
	5. $(x)Ax$	4, UG
	6. Az	5, UI
	7. $Ba \cdot Ax$	3, Com
	8. Ba	7, Simp
	9. $Az \cdot Ba$	6, 8, Conj
	10. $(x)(Ax \cdot Ba)$	9, UG
	11. $(\exists y)(x)(Ax \cdot By)$	10, EG
(19)	1. $(x)(\exists y)Axy \lor (x)(y)Bxy$	
	2. $(x)(\exists y)(Cx \supset {\sim}Bxy)$	/ $(x)(\exists y)(Cx \supset Axy)$
	3. Cx	ACP
	4. $(\exists y)(Cx \supset {\sim}Bxy)$	2, UI
	5. $Cx \supset {\sim}Bxm$	4, EI
	6. ${\sim}Bxm$	3, 5, MP
	7. $(\exists y){\sim}Bxy$	6, EG
	8. $(\exists x)(\exists y){\sim}Bxy$	7, EG
	9. $(\exists x){\sim}(y)Bxy$	8, CQ
	10. ${\sim}(x)(y)Bxy$	9, CQ
	11. $(x)(y)Bxy \lor (x)(\exists y)Axy$	1, Com
	12. $(x)(\exists y)Axy$	10, 11, DS
	13. $(\exists y)Axy$	12, UI
	14. Axn	13, EI
	15. $Cx \supset Axn$	3–14, CP
	16. $(\exists y)(Cx \supset Axy)$	15, EG
	17. $(x)(\exists y)(Cx \supset Axy)$	16, UG

III.

(1)	1. $(x)[Px \supset (y)(Ay \supset Oxy)]$	
	2. $Pj \cdot {\sim}Ojm$	/ ${\sim}Am$
	3. $Pj \supset (y)(Ay \supset Ojy)$	1, UI
	4. Pj	2, Simp
	5. $(y)(Ay \supset Ojy)$	3, 4, MP
	6. $Am \supset Ojm$	5, UI
	7. ${\sim}Ojm \cdot Pj$	2, Com
	8. ${\sim}Ojm$	7, Simp
	9. ${\sim}Am$	6, 8, MT

(4) 1. Po
2. $(x)[(Px \cdot Cx) \supset Sox]$
3. $(x)(Px \supset \sim Sxx)$ / $\sim Co$
   4. Co AIP
   5. $(Po \cdot Co) \supset Soo$ 2, UI
   6. $Po \cdot Co$ 1, 4, Conj
   7. Soo 5, 6, MP
   8. $Po \supset \sim Soo$ 3, UI
   9. $\sim Soo$ 1, 8, MP
   10. $Soo \cdot \sim Soo$ 7, 9, Conj
11. $\sim Co$ 4–10, IP

(7) 1. $(\exists x)\{Px \cdot (y)[(Py \cdot Kxy) \supset Fxy]\}$
2. $(x)[Px \supset (\exists y)(Py \cdot Kxy)]$ / $(\exists x)(\exists y)[(Px \cdot Py) \cdot Fxy]$
3. $Pm \cdot (y)[(Py \cdot Kmy) \supset Fmy]$ 1, EI
4. $Pm \supset (\exists y)(Py \cdot Kmy)$ 2, UI
5. Pm 3, Simp
6. $(\exists y)(Py \cdot Kmy)$ 4, 5, MP
7. $Pn \cdot Kmn$ 6, EI
8. $(y)[(Py \cdot Kmy) \supset Fmy] \cdot Pm$ 3, Com
9. $(y)[(Py \cdot Kmy) \supset Fmy]$ 8, Simp
10. $(Pn \cdot Kmn) \supset Fmn$ 9, UI
11. Fmn 7, 10, MP
12. Pn 7, Simp
13. $Pm \cdot Pn$ 5, 12, Conj
14. $(Pm \cdot Pn) \cdot Fmn$ 11, 13, Conj
15. $(\exists y)[(Pm \cdot Py) \cdot Fmy]$ 14, EG
16. $(\exists x)(\exists y)[(Px \cdot Py) \cdot Fxy]$ 15, EG

(10) 1. $(x)\{Ix \supset [(\exists y)(Cy \cdot Ay) \supset Ex]\}$
2. $[(\exists x)Tx \lor (\exists x)Wx] \supset [(\exists x)Ix \cdot (\exists x)Cx]$
3. $(x)(Cx \supset Ax)$ / $(\exists x)Tx \supset (\exists x)(Ix \cdot Ex)$
   4. $(\exists x)Tx$ ACP
   5. $(\exists x)Tx \lor (\exists x)Wx$ 4, Add
   6. $(\exists x)Ix \cdot (\exists x)Cx$ 2, 5, MP
   7. $(\exists x)Ix$ 6, Simp
   8. Im 7, EI
   9. $Im \supset [(\exists y)(Cy \cdot Ay) \supset Em]$ 1, UI
   10. $(\exists y)(Cy \cdot Ay) \supset Em$ 8, 9, MP
   11. $(\exists x)Cx \cdot (\exists x)Ix$ 6, Com
   12. $(\exists x)Cx$ 11, Simp
   13. Cn 12, EI
   14. $Cn \supset An$ 3, UI
   15. An 13, 14, MP
   16. $Cn \cdot An$ 13, 15, Conj
   17. $(\exists y)(Cy \cdot Ay)$ 16, EG
   18. Em 10, 17, MP
   19. $Im \cdot Em$ 8, 18, Conj
   20. $(\exists x)(Ix \cdot Ex)$ 19, EG
21. $(\exists x)Tx \supset (\exists x)(Ix \cdot Ex)$ 4–20, CP

8

Exercise 8.7

I.

1. $s = g$
4. $h \neq g$
5. $Wp \cdot (x)(Wx \supset x = p)$
8. $Nc \cdot Mc \cdot (x)[(Nx \cdot Mx) \supset x = c]$
11. $Sh \cdot Ph \cdot (x)[(Sx \cdot Px) \supset x = h]$
12. $Eh \cdot (x)[(Ex \cdot x \neq h) \supset Lhx]$
15. $Rd \cdot Nd \cdot (x)[(Rx \cdot Nx \cdot x \neq d) \supset Ldx]$
16. $Al \cdot {\sim}Sl \cdot (x)[(Ax \cdot x \neq l) \supset Sx]$
19. $Pc \cdot {\sim}Wc \cdot (x)[(Px \cdot x \neq c) \supset Wx]$
20. $(x)(y)[(Cx \cdot Bx \cdot Cy \cdot By) \supset x = y]$
23. $(x)(y)(z)[(Cx \cdot Mx \cdot Cy \cdot My \cdot Cz \cdot Mz) \supset (x = y \lor x = z \lor y = z)]$
26. $(\exists x)(\exists y)(\exists z)(Cx \cdot Cy \cdot Cz \cdot x \neq y \cdot x \neq z \cdot y \neq z)$
29. $(\exists x)(\exists y)\{Sx \cdot Bx \cdot Gx \cdot Sy \cdot By \cdot Gy \cdot x \neq y \cdot (z)[(Sz \cdot Bz \cdot Gz) \supset (z = x \lor z = y)]\}$
30. $(\exists x)[Wxv \cdot (y)(Wyv \supset y = x) \cdot Bx]$
33. $(\exists x)\{Ax \cdot Pxa \cdot (y)[(Ay \cdot Pya) \supset y = x] \cdot x = b\}$
35. $Sr \cdot (x)[(Sx \cdot x \neq r) \supset Srx]$
38. $Ar \cdot Er \cdot (x)[(Ax \cdot Ex) \supset x = r]$
41. $(x)(y)[(Sxh \cdot Syh) \supset x = y]$
44. $m \neq b$
47. $(\exists x)(\exists y)\{Tx \cdot Cx \cdot Ty \cdot Cy \cdot x \neq y \cdot (z)[(Tz \cdot Cz) \supset (z = x \lor z = y)]\}$
50. $(\exists x)(\exists y)(\exists z)(Sx \cdot Ox \cdot Sy \cdot Oy \cdot Sz \cdot Oz \cdot x \neq y \cdot x \neq z \cdot y \neq z)$

II.

(1)
1. $(x)(x = a)$
2. $(\exists x)Rx$ / Ra
3. Ri 2, EI
4. $i = a$ 1, UI
5. Ra 3, 4, Id

(4)
1. $(\exists x)(x = g)$
2. $(x)(x = i)$ / $g = i$
3. $n = g$ 1, EI
4. $n = i$ 2, UI
5. $g = n$ 3, Id
6. $g = i$ 4, 5, Id

(7)
1. $(x)(x = a)$
2. Fa / $Fm \cdot Fn$
3. $m = a$ 1, UI
4. $a = m$ 3, Id
5. Fm 2, 4, Id
6. $n = a$ 1, UI
7. $a = n$ 6, Id
8. Fn 2, 7, Id
9. $Fm \cdot Fn$ 5, 8, Conj

(10)
1. $(x)(Px \supset x = a)$
2. $(x)(x = c \supset Qx)$
3. $a = c$ / $(x)(Px \supset Qx)$
4. Px ACP
5. $Px \supset x = a$ 1, UI
6. $x = a$ 4, 5, MP
7. $x = c$ 3, 6, Id
8. $x = c \supset Qx$ 2, UI
9. Qx 7, 8, MP
10. $Px \supset Qx$ 4–9, CP
11. $(x)(Px \supset Qx)$ 10, UG

(13)
1. $(x)(Ba \supset x \neq a)$
2. Bc / $a \neq c$
3. $a = c$ AIP
4. $c = a$ 3, Id
5. Ba 2, 4, Id
6. $Ba \supset c \neq a$ 1, UI
7. $c \neq a$ 5, 6, MP
8. $c = a \cdot c \neq a$ 4, 7, Conj
9. $a \neq c$ 3–8, IP

8

(16) 1. $(x)[Nx \supset (Px \cdot x = m)]$

    2. $\sim\!Pm$ / $\sim\!Ne$

        3. Ne AIP

        4. $Ne \supset (Pe \cdot e = m)$ 1, UI

        5. $Pe \cdot e = m$ 3, 4, MP

        6. Pe 5, Simp

        7. $e = m \cdot Pe$ 5, Com

        8. $e = m$ 7, Simp

        9. Pm 6, 8, Id

       10. $Pm \cdot \sim\!Pm$ 2, 9, Conj

    11. $\sim\!Ne$ 3–10, IP

(19) 1. $(x)(\exists y)(Cxy \supset x = y)$

    2. $(\exists x)(y)(Cxy \cdot x = a)$ / Caa

    3. $(y)(Cny \cdot n = a)$ 2, EI

    4. $(\exists y)(Cay \supset a = y)$ 1, UI

    5. $Cam \supset a = m$ 4, EI

    6. $Cnm \cdot n = a$ 3, UI

    7. Cnm 6, Simp

    8. $n = a \cdot Cnm$ 6, Com

    9. $n = a$ 8, Simp

   10. Cam 7, 9, Id

   11. $a = m$ 5, 10, MP

   12. $m = a$ 11, Id

   13. Caa 10, 12, Id

III.

(1) 1. $(\exists x)(Nx \cdot Wjx \cdot Ix)$

    2. $Nc \cdot Wjc \cdot (x)[(Nx \cdot Wjx) \supset x = c]$ / Ic

    3. $Na \cdot Wja \cdot Ia$ 1, EI

    4. $(x)[(Nx \cdot Wjx) \supset x = c] \cdot Nc \cdot Wjc$ 2, Com

    5. $(x)[(Nx \cdot Wjx) \supset x = c]$ 4, Simp

    6. $(Na \cdot Wja) \supset a = c$ 5, UI

    7. $Na \cdot Wja$ 3, Simp

    8. $a = c$ 6, 7, MP

    9. $Ia \cdot Na \cdot Wja$ 3, Com

   10. Ia 9, Simp

   11. Ic 8, 10, Id

(4) 1. $(\exists x)\{Nx \cdot Tx \cdot (y)[(Ny \cdot Ty) \supset y = x] \cdot Wmx\}$

    2. $Ng \cdot Wmg \cdot (x)[(Nx \cdot Wmx) \supset x = g]$

         / $(\exists x)\{Nx \cdot Tx \cdot (y)[(Ny \cdot Ty) \supset y = x] \cdot x = g\}$

    3. $Na \cdot Ta \cdot (y)[(Ny \cdot Ty) \supset y = a] \cdot Wma$ 1, EI

    4. $(x)[(Nx \cdot Wmx) \supset x = g] \cdot Ng \cdot Wmg$ 2, Com

    5. $(x)[(Nx \cdot Wmx) \supset x = g]$ 4, Simp

    6. $(Na \cdot Wma) \supset a = g$ 5, UI

    7. Na 3, Simp

    8. $Wma \cdot Na \cdot Ta \cdot (y)[(Ny \cdot Ty) \supset y = a)]$ 3, Com

    9. Wma 8, Simp

   10. $Na \cdot Wma$ 7, 9, Conj

   11. $a = g$ 6, 10, MP

   12. $Na \cdot Ta \cdot (y)[(Ny \cdot Ty) \supset y = a]$ 3, Simp

   13. $Na \cdot Ta \cdot (y)[(Ny \cdot Ty) \supset y = a] \cdot a = g$ 11, 12, Conj

   14. $(\exists x)\{Nx \cdot Tx \cdot (y)[(Ny \cdot Ty) \supset y = x] \cdot x = g\}$ 13, EG

(7) 1. $Me \cdot \sim\!Se \cdot (x)[(Mx \cdot x \neq e) \supset Sx]$

    2. $Mn \cdot \sim\!Gn \cdot (x)[(Mx \cdot x \neq n) \supset Gx]$

    3. $e \neq n$ / $Ge \cdot Sn$

    4. $(x)[(Mx \cdot x \neq e) \supset Sx] \cdot Me \cdot \sim\!Se$ 1, Com

5. $(x)[(Mx \cdot x \neq e) \supset Sx]$		4, Simp
6. $(Mn \cdot n \neq e) \supset Sn$		5, UI
7. Mn		2, Simp
8. $n \neq e$		3, Id
9. $Mn \cdot n \neq e$		7, 8, Conj
10. Sn		6, 9, MP
11. $(x)[(Mx \cdot x \neq n) \supset Gx] \cdot Mn \cdot \sim Gn$		2, Com
12. $(x)[(Mx \cdot x \neq n) \supset Gx]$		11, Simp
13. $(Me \cdot e \neq n) \supset Ge$		12, UI
14. Me		1, Simp
15. $Me \cdot e \neq n$		3, 14, Conj
16. Ge		13, 15, MP
17. $Ge \cdot Sn$		10, 16, Conj

(10) 1. $Bs \cdot (x)[(Bx \cdot x \neq s) \supset Tsx]$		
2. $(\exists x)\{Bx \cdot (y)[(By \cdot y \neq x) \supset Txy] \cdot Cx\}$		
3. $(x)(y)(Txy \supset \sim Tyx)$		/ Cs
4. $Ba \cdot (y)[(By \cdot y \neq a) \supset Tay] \cdot Ca$		2, EI
5. $(x)[(Bx \cdot x \neq s) \supset Tsx] \cdot Bs$		1, Com
6. $(x)[(Bx \cdot x \neq s) \supset Tsx]$		5, Simp
7. $(Ba \cdot a \neq s) \supset Tsa$		6, UI
8. $a \neq s$		AIP
9. Ba		4, Simp
10. $Ba \cdot a \neq s$		8, 9, Conj
11. Tsa		7, 10, MP
12. $(y)[(By \cdot y \neq a) \supset Tay] \cdot Ca \cdot Ba$		4, Com
13. $(y)[(By \cdot y \neq a) \supset Tay]$		12, Simp
14. $(Bs \cdot s \neq a) \supset Tas$		13, UI
15. Bs		1, Simp
16. $s \neq a$		8, Id
17. $Bs \cdot s \neq a$		15, 16, Conj
18. Tas		14, 17, MP
19. $(y)(Tay \supset \sim Tya)$		3, UI
20. $Tas \supset \sim Tsa$		19, UI
21. $\sim Tsa$		18, 20, MP
22. $Tsa \cdot \sim Tsa$		11, 21, Conj
23. $\sim(a \neq s)$		8–22, IP
24. $a = s$		23, DN
25. $Ca \cdot Ba \cdot (y)[(By \cdot y \neq a) \supset Tay]$		4, Com
26. Ca		25, Simp
27. Cs		24, 26, Id

(13) 1. $(\exists x)(\exists y)(Ax \cdot Ox \cdot Ay \cdot Oy \cdot x \neq y)$
    2. $(x)(Ax \supset Px)$
    3. $(x)(y)(z)[(Px \cdot Ox \cdot Py \cdot Oy \cdot Pz \cdot Oz) \supset (x = y \lor x = z \lor y = z)]$
        $/ (\exists x)(\exists y)\{Px \cdot Ox \cdot Py \cdot Oy \cdot x \neq y \cdot (z)[(Pz \cdot Oz) \supset (z = x \lor z = y)]\}$

4.	$(\exists y)(Aa \cdot Oa \cdot Ay \cdot Oy \cdot a \neq y)$	1, EI
5.	$Aa \cdot Oa \cdot Ab \cdot Ob \cdot a \neq b$	4, EI
6.	$Aa \supset Pa$	2, UI
7.	Aa	5, Simp
8.	Pa	6, 7, MP
9.	$Ab \supset Pb$	2, UI
10.	$Ab \cdot Ob \cdot a \neq b \cdot Aa \cdot Oa$	5, Com
11.	Ab	10, Simp
12.	Pb	9, 11, MP
13.	$Oa \cdot Ab \cdot Ob \cdot a \neq b \cdot Aa$	10, Com
14.	Oa	13, Simp
15.	$Ob \cdot a \neq b \cdot Aa \cdot Oa \cdot Ab$	5, Com
16.	Ob	15, Simp
17.	$a \neq b \cdot Aa \cdot Oa \cdot Ab \cdot Ob$	5, Com
18.	$a \neq b$	17, Simp
19.	$Pa \cdot Oa \cdot Pb \cdot Ob \cdot a \neq b$	8, 14, 12, 16, 18, Conj
20.	$\sim(z)[(Pz \cdot Oz) \supset (z = a \lor z = b)]$	AIP
21.	$(\exists z)\sim[(Pz \cdot Oz) \supset (z = a \lor z = b)]$	20, CQ
22.	$\sim[(Pc \cdot Oc) \supset (c = a \lor c = b)]$	21, EI
23.	$\sim[\sim(Pc \cdot Oc) \lor (c = a \lor c = b)]$	22, Impl
24.	$\sim\sim(Pc \cdot Oc) \cdot \sim(c = a \lor c = b)$	23, DM
25.	$Pc \cdot Oc \cdot \sim(c = a \lor c = b)$	24, DN
26.	$(y)(z)[(Pa \cdot Oa \cdot Py \cdot Oy \cdot Pz \cdot Oz) \supset (a = y \lor a = z \lor y = z)]$	3, UI
27.	$(z)[(Pa \cdot Oa \cdot Pb \cdot Ob \cdot Pz \cdot Oz) \supset (a = b \lor a = z \lor b = z)]$	26, UI
28.	$(Pa \cdot Oa \cdot Pb \cdot Ob \cdot Pc \cdot Oc) \supset (a = b \lor a = c \lor b = c)$	27, UI
29.	$Pc \cdot Oc$	25, Simp
30.	$Pa \cdot Oa \cdot Pb \cdot Ob$	19, Simp
31.	$Pa \cdot Oa \cdot Pb \cdot Ob \cdot Pc \cdot Oc$	29, 30, Conj
32.	$a = b \lor a = c \lor b = c$	28, 31, MP
33.	$a = c \lor b = c$	18, 32, DS
34.	$\sim(c = a \lor c = b) \cdot Pc \cdot Oc$	25, Com
35.	$\sim(c = a \lor c = b)$	34, Simp
36.	$\sim(a = c \lor c = b)$	35, Id
37.	$\sim(a = c \lor b = c)$	36, Id
38.	$(a = c \lor b = c) \cdot \sim(a = c \lor b = c)$	33, 37, Conj
39.	$\sim\sim(z)[(Pz \cdot Oz) \supset z = a \lor z = b)]$	20–38, IP
40.	$(z)[(Pz \cdot Oz) \supset (z = a \lor z = b)]$	39, DN
41.	$Pa \cdot Oa \cdot Pb \cdot Ob \cdot a \neq b \cdot (z)[(Pz \cdot Oz) \supset (z = a \lor z = b)]$	19, 40, Conj
42.	$(\exists y)\{Pa \cdot Oa \cdot Py \cdot Oy \cdot a \neq y \cdot (z)[(Pz \cdot Oz) \supset (z = a \lor z = y)]\}$	41, EG
43.	$(\exists x)(\exists y)\{Px \cdot Ox \cdot Py \cdot Oy \cdot x \neq y \cdot (z)[(Pz \cdot Oz) \supset (z = x \lor z = y)]\}$	42, EG

(16) 1. $Sc \cdot \sim Pc \cdot Sn \cdot \sim Pn \cdot (x)[(Sx \cdot x \neq c \cdot x \neq n) \supset Px]$
   2. $Sn \cdot Dn \cdot (x)[(Sx \cdot Dx) \supset x = n]$
   3. $(x)\{Sx \supset [Rx \equiv (\sim Dx \cdot \sim Px)]\}$
   4. $c \neq n \qquad /(\exists x)\{Sx \cdot Rx \cdot (y)[(Sy \cdot Ry) \supset y = x]\}$
   5. Sc 1, Simp
   6. $Sc \supset [Rc \equiv (\sim Dc \cdot \sim Pc)]$ 3, UI
   7. $Rc \equiv (\sim Dc \cdot \sim Pc)$ 5, 6, MP
   8. $[Rc \supset (\sim Dc \cdot \sim Pc)] \cdot [(\sim Dc \cdot \sim Pc) \supset Rc]$ 7, Equiv
   9. $[(\sim Dc \cdot \sim Pc) \supset Rc] \cdot [Rc \supset (\sim Dc \cdot \sim Pc)]$ 8, Com
   10. $(\sim Dc \cdot \sim Pc) \supset Rc$ 9, Simp
   11. $(x)[(Sx \cdot Dx) \supset x = n] \cdot Sn \cdot Dn$ 2, Com
   12. $(x)[(Sx \cdot Dx) \supset x = n]$ 11, Simp
   13. $(Sc \cdot Dc) \supset c = n$ 12, UI
   14. $\sim(Sc \cdot Dc)$ 4, 13, MT
   15. $\sim Sc \lor \sim Dc$ 14, DM
   16. $\sim\sim Sc$ 5, DN
   17. $\sim Dc$ 15, 16, DS
   18. $\sim Pc \cdot Sn \cdot \sim Pn \cdot (x)[(Sx \cdot x \neq c \cdot x \neq n) \supset Px] \cdot Sc$ 1, Com
   19. $\sim Pc$ 18, Simp
   20. $\sim Dc \cdot \sim Pc$ 17, 19, Conj
   21. Rc 10, 20, MP
   22. $Sc \cdot Rc$ 5, 21, Conj
      23. $\sim(y)[(Sy \cdot Ry) \supset y = c]$ AIP
      24. $(\exists y)\sim[(Sy \cdot Ry) \supset y = c]$ 23, CQ
      25. $\sim[(Sa \cdot Ra) \supset a = c]$ 24, EI
      26. $\sim[\sim(Sa \cdot Ra) \lor a = c]$ 25, Impl
      27. $\sim\sim(Sa \cdot Ra) \cdot a \neq c$ 26, DM
      28. $Sa \cdot Ra \cdot a \neq c$ 27, DN
      29. $Sa \supset [Ra \equiv (\sim Da \cdot \sim Pa)]$ 3, UI
      30. Sa 28, Simp
      31. $Ra \equiv (\sim Da \cdot \sim Pa)$ 29, 30, MP
      32. $[Ra \supset (\sim Da \cdot \sim Pa)] \cdot [(\sim Da \cdot \sim Pa) \supset Ra]$ 31, Equiv
      33. $Ra \supset (\sim Da \cdot \sim Pa)$ 32, Simp
      34. $Ra \cdot a \neq c \cdot Sa$ 28, Com
      35. Ra 34, Simp
      36. $\sim Da \cdot \sim Pa$ 33, 35, MP
      37. $(x)[(Sx \cdot x \neq c \cdot x \neq n) \supset Px] \cdot Sc \cdot \sim Pc \cdot Sn \cdot \sim Pn$ 1, Com
      38. $(x)[(Sx \cdot x \neq c \cdot x \neq n) \supset Px]$ 37, Simp
      39. $(Sa \cdot a \neq c \cdot a \neq n) \supset Pa$ 38, UI
      40. $(Sa \cdot a \neq c) \supset (a \neq n \supset Pa)$ 39, Exp
      41. $a \neq c \cdot Sa \cdot Ra$ 28, Com
      42. $a \neq c$ 41, Simp
      43. $Sa \cdot a \neq c$ 30, 42, Conj
      44. $a \neq n \supset Pa$ 40, 43, MP
      45. $\sim Pa \cdot \sim Da$ 36, Com
      46. $\sim Pa$ 45, Simp
      47. $\sim(a \neq n)$ 44, 46, MT

48. $a = n$	47, DN
49. $n = a$	48, Id
50. $Dn \cdot (x)[(Sx \cdot Dx) \supset x = n] \cdot Sn$	2, Com
51. Dn	50, Simp
52. Da	49, 51, Id
53. $\sim Da$	36, Simp
54. $Da \cdot \sim Da$	52, 53, Conj
55. $\sim\sim(y)[(Sy \cdot Ry) \supset y = c]$	23–54, IP
56. $(y)[(Sy \cdot Ry) \supset y = c]$	55, DN
57. $Sc \cdot Rc \cdot (y)[(Sy \cdot Ry) \supset y = c]$	22, 56, Conj
58. $(\exists x)\{Sx \cdot Rx \cdot (y)[(Sy \cdot Ry) \supset y = x]\}$	57, EG

Exercise 9.1

II.

1. a. Has no effect.
   b. Strengthens.
   c. Weakens.
   d. Weakens.
   e. Strengthens.
   f. Strengthens
   g. Weakens
   h. Strengthens
   i. Strengthens
   j. Weakens

4. a. Has no effect.
   b. Weakens.
   c. Strengthens.
   d. Weakens.
   e. Strengthens.
   f. Has no effect.
   g. Strengthens.
   h. Weakens.
   i. Weakens.
   j. Strengthens.

7. a. Weakens.
   b. Strengthens.
   c. Has no effect.
   d. Strengthens.
   e. Strengthens.
   f. Weakens.
   g. Weakens.
   h. Strengthens.
   i. Strengthens.
   j. Weakens.

10. Hint: For Maxie's argument, concentrate on the similarities between a home and a car (a car is an extended living space with heating, air conditioning, stereo, telephone, and so on), the dissimilarities between a plane and a car (greater difficulty in controlling, ease of crossing international borders, greater danger in operating, and so on). Also, people outside U.S. borders are not accorded the same constitutional protections as people inside, and a phone message normally suggests greater privacy than a radio message. In addition, the teenagers parked in the lot were acting in plain view, and a telescope only enhances ordinary sense perception (so there was no search). Maxie, on the other hand, was talking while speeding down the freeway and was thus not acting in plain view (in the same sense), and a radio receiver (used by the agents) does not enhance ordinary sense perception.

   For the agents' argument, concentrate on the similarities between a car and a plane (both are means of transportation, both can cross state lines, both are relatively hard to keep track of, and so on) and the dissimilarities between a car or plane and a house (houses do not move, so it will stay in place while a search warrant is obtained). Also, cell phones use radio transmitters just like planes, both the cell phone message and the radio message from the plane were received inside U.S. borders, and the cell phone message was received inadvertently, just as the radio message from the plane and the image through the telescope were (thus making it impossible to plan ahead for a search warrant). Also, in a sense, Maxie *was* acting in plain view: A lip reader traveling in an adjacent car might interpret his message. Lastly, controlling illicit drugs is a high priority for the government.

13. Hint: Couch your arguments in terms of foreseeability.

For Liz's argument note that there were several events that intervened between the car accident and the amputation: Mary's being taken to the hospital, Mary's being treated by doctors for bumps and bruises, Mary's apparent mix-up with some other patient scheduled for leg amputation, the doctors' failure to check Mary's proper identity before operating, etc. Liz did not directly control any of these events, and therefore she could not have foreseen them. Liz could not have foreseen what hospital Mary would be taken to, the fact that Mary would be mixed up with another patient, etc. Because Liz should not be held liable for an event utterly unforeseen to her, she should not be liable for Mary's amputated leg. The facts are similar to those in *Gomez v. Hunt,* where Gomez could not foresee the exact route that Hunt would take when walking home, the fact that a worker would drop a brick, the fact that the brick would strike Hunt, etc. The facts are dissimilar to those in *Sacco v. Lane,* where Lane was in direct control over the flames in the barbecue, and it was those very same flames that spread to the houses.

For Mary's argument note that Liz initiated a chain of events that flowed naturally from the car accident to the amputation. Once the car accident occurred, it was foreseeable that Mary would be taken to the hospital; once Mary was in the hospital it was foreseeable that mix-ups would occur (after all, mix-ups occur in hospitals every day); given the nature of these mix-ups, it was foreseeable that Mary's leg would be amputated. Granted, Liz might not have been able to foresee each event in the chain, but once an event occurred, someone familiar with it could have foreseen the next event. Therefore, given that each event was foreseeable by *someone*—at least some hypothetical person—Liz should be held liable. The events are similar to those in *Sacco v. Lane.* When the flames were leaping from the barbecue, it was foreseeable that they would ignite the trees; once the trees were aflame, it was foreseeable that a house would be ignited, then another house, etc. Lane would not have been able to foresee the whole chain of events at the time he was tending the barbecue, but once one event occurred, the next was foreseeable. Also, even though the wind constituted an intervening event, Lane was still held liable. Finally, the facts are dissimilar to those in *Gomez v. Hunt.* When Hunt was walking home, he was in complete control over his own actions. He freely chose to walk past the building under construction, and he should have been on the lookout for falling objects. The fact that he was struck by a falling brick was partly the result of his own failure to observe. On the contrary, from the time of the accident until the amputation, Mary was in the hands of others: the person who took her to the hospital, nurses in the hospital, etc. In no sense was the amputation the result of Mary's free choices.

Exercise 9.2

I.

1. Sufficient condition. The window can also be broken by throwing a stone or baseball through it.
4. Necessary condition. For an image to appear on the film the camera must also be loaded and focused and there must be sufficient light.
7. Sufficient condition. The fire will also be extinguished if it is smothered.
10. Necessary condition. Electricity must also be supplied from the main lines.

II.

1. A = a certain make, B = a certain year, C = a certain model, D = driven 30,000 miles, E = a certain gasoline, F = a certain oil, G = a certain driver, H = certain road conditions, I = the additive.

	Possible conditions									Phenomenon (Less wear)
Occurrence	A	B	C	D	E	F	G	H	I	
1	*	*	*	*	*	*	*	*	*	*
2	*	*	*	*	*	*	*	*	−	−

Method of difference
Sufficient condition

4. A = type X circuitry, B = shipped to a coastal region, C = sold to a business customer, D = manufactured in the Kansas City plant, E = used to play computer games, F = shipped to a large city.

Occurrence	Possible conditions						Phenomenon (returned)
	A	B	C	D	E	F	
1	*	*	-	*	*	-	*
2	-	*	*	*	-	*	*
3	*	*	*	-	*	*	*
4	-	*	-	*	*	*	*
5	*	*	-	*	*	-	*
6	*	*	*	-	-	*	*
7	*	*	*	*	-	*	*

Coastal region (salty air) is the cause in the sense of a necessary condition.
Method of agreement.

7. A = camomile tea, B = late dinner, C = hot bath, D = read book, E = walk, F = wine, G = massage.

Occurrence	Possible conditions							Phenomenon (slept well)
	A	B	C	D	E	F	G	
Mon	*	*	*	*	*	-	-	*
Tu	-	*	-	*	-	-	-	-
Wed	-	-	-	-	*	*	*	-
Th	-	*	*	*	-	*	*	*
Fri	*	*	-	*	*	-	*	*
Sat	*	-	*	-	*	*	*	*
Sun	*	-	*	*	-	-	-	-

None of the possible conditions is a cause of the phenomenon.
Joint method of agreement and difference.

10. A = corporal punishment, B = siblings, C = adopted, D = male parent figure, E = sexual abuse, F = domineering mother, G = uprooted often, H = day-care center.

Occurrence	Possible conditions								Phenomenon (blurred bound.)
	A	B	C	D	E	F	G	H	
Meg	*	*	*	-	*	*	-	-	*
Sue	*	*	-	*	*	-	-	*	*
Dot	*	-	*	*	*	*	*	*	*
Jane	*	*	*	*	*	*	*	-	*
Lynn	-	*	*	*	*	-	-	*	*
Flo	*	*	-	*	*	*	*	-	*

Sexual abuse is the cause of the phenomenon in the sense of a necessary condition.
Method of agreement.

13. A = malathion, B = American Beauty, C = five years old, D = a certain location, E = a certain amount of water, F = a certain amount of sun, G = a certain kind of soil, H = a certain amount of cultivation, I = a certain amount of Bandini rose food.

	Possible conditions									Phenomenon (no aphids)
Occurrence	*A*	*B*	*C*	*D*	*E*	*F*	*G*	*H*	*I*	
1	*	*	*	*	*	*	*	*	*	*
2	–	*	*	*	*	*	*	*	*	–

Method of difference, sufficient condition.

III.

1. By the method of agreement, D is the cause in the sense of a necessary condition.
4. By the joint method of agreement and difference, D is the cause in the sense of a sufficient condition.

Exercise 9.3

I.

1. 1/6   4. .853   7. 1/4 or .25   10. Approximately $17

II.

1. $P(6 \text{ or } 1) = P(6) + P(1) = 1/6 + 1/6 = 2/6 = 1/3$

4a. $P(A_1 \text{ and } A_2) = P(A_1) \times P(A_2)$
$$= 4/52 \times 4/52$$
$$= 1/169 = .0059$$

4b. $P(A_1 \text{ and } A_2) = P(A_1) \times P(A_2 \text{ given } A_1)$
$$= 4/52 \times 3/51$$
$$= 1/221 = .0045$$

7. First compute the probability of getting no sixes:
$$P(\text{no sixes}) = 5/6 \times 5/6 \times 5/6$$
$$= 125/216$$

Then use the negation rule:
$$P(\text{at least one six}) = 1 - P(\text{no sixes})$$
$$= 1 - 125/216$$
$$= 91/216 = .4213$$

10. a. $P(R_1 \text{ and } R_2) = P(R_1) \times P(R_2 \text{ given } R_1)$
$$= 3/12 \times 2/11$$
$$= 6/132 = .045$$

b. $P(Y \text{ and } G) = P(Y_1 \text{ and } G_2) + P(G_1 \text{ and } Y_2)$
$$= (5/12 \times 4/11) + (4/12 \times 5/11)$$
$$= 20/132 + 20/132$$
$$= 10/33 = .303$$

c. $P(R \text{ or } G) = 1 - P(Y_1 \text{ and } Y_2)$
$$= 1 - (5/12 \times 4/11)$$
$$= 1 - 20/132$$
$$= 28/33 = .848$$

d. $P(G_1 \text{ or } G_2) = 1 - P(\text{not } G)$
$$= 1 - [P(R_1 \text{ and } R_2) + P(R_1 \text{ and } Y_2) + P(Y_1 \text{ and } R_2)$$
$$+ P(Y_1 \text{ and } Y_2)]$$
$$= 1 - [(3/12 \times 2/11) + (3/12 \times 5/11)$$
$$+ (5/12 \times 3/11) + (5/12 \times 4/11)]$$
$$= 1 - [6/132 + 15/132 + 15/132 + 20/132]$$
$$= 1 - 56/132$$
$$= 19/33 = .57$$

e. $P(\text{same color}) = P(R_1 \text{ and } R_2) + P(G_1 \text{ and } G_2) + P(Y_1 \text{ and } Y_2)$
$$= (3/12 \times 2/11) + (4/12 \times 3/11) + (5/12 \times 4/11)$$
$$= 6/132 + 12/132 + 20/132$$
$$= 19/66 = .288$$

13a. $P(M \text{ or } W) = P(M) + P(W) - P(M \text{ and } W)$
$$= .74 + .82 - (.74 \times .82)$$
$$= .95$$

13b. $P(M \text{ and } W \text{ and } S) = P(M) \times P(W) \times P(S)$
$$= .74 \times .82 \times 8/9$$
$$= .54$$

16. $P(N \text{ given } R) = \dfrac{P(N) \times P(R \text{ given } N)}{[P(N) \times P(R \text{ given } N)] + [P(O) \times P(R \text{ given } O)]}$

$$= \dfrac{3/5 \times 7/15}{[3/5 \times 7/15] + [2/5 \times 5/15]} = \dfrac{21/75}{21/75 + 10/75}$$

$$= \dfrac{21/75}{31/75} = 21/31 = .68$$

Answer: new urn.

19. $P(R \text{ given } N) = \dfrac{P(R) \times P(N \text{ given } R)}{[P(R) \times P(N \text{ given } R)] + [P(T) \times P(N \text{ given } T)]}$

$$= \dfrac{.2 \times .7}{(.2 \times .7) + (.8 \times .2)} = \dfrac{.14}{.14 + .16} = .14/.30 = .47$$

Exercise 9.4

I.

1. Since the water in the lake might not be circulating, the algae content of the water at one end might not be representative of the whole lake. Thus, the sample might be biased.

4. According to Table 9.7, the margin of error for a random sample of 600 is ± 5 percent. Since the sample taken indicates a difference of only 2 percent, the results of the sample are inconclusive.

7. Since no mention is made of the size of the sample or of the expected sampling error, the sample might be biased. The manufacturer might have taken 25 separate samples consisting of ten dentists per sample and reported the results of only the most favorable one.

10. The problem concerns the meaning of "average." If the average is a mean, most of the toys could be over $15, and a few very cheap toys could bring the average down to $15. If the average is a mode, there might be a few toys priced at $15, and all the other toys might have varying prices exceeding $15. Only if the average is a median can one be assured that half the toys are $15 or less.

13. Since no mention is made of the dispersion, the argument is weak. The rock pile might consist of several pieces weighing 500 pounds and enough weighing only 4 or 5 pounds to bring the average down to 50 pounds. If the range were only 10 pounds or so, the conclusion would follow.

16. If the scale on the vertical axis does not begin at zero, the conclusion does not follow.

19. Since there were many more cars on the road in 2005 than there were in 1980, the comparison is faulty.

II.

1. mean = 180, median = 170, mode = 160

4.

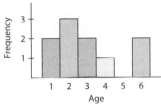

Mean age = 3, variance = 3, standard deviation = 1.73.

III.

1. False.	7. True.	13. True.	19. False.
4. False.	10. False.	16. False.	

Exercise 9.5

VI.

1. True.	7. True.	13. True.	19. False.
4. False.	10. True.	16. False.	

Glossary / Index

A proposition: A categorical proposition having the form "All *S* are *P*," 187

Abelard, Peter, 5

Absorption, 349n

Accident: An informal fallacy that occurs when a general rule is wrongly applied to an atypical specific case, 119–120, 157–158

Ackermann, Wilhelm, 424n

Ad hoc modifications, 547–548

Ad hominem. See Argument against the person

***Ad hominem* abusive:** A variety of the argument-against-the-person fallacy that occurs when an arguer verbally abuses a second arguer for the purpose of discrediting that person's argument, 117, 167–169

***Ad hominem* circumstantial:** A variety of the argument-against-the-person fallacy that occurs when an arguer cites circumstances that affect a second arguer for the purpose of discrediting that person's argument, 117–118

Adams, John Couch, 528–529, 534, 536

Addition: A valid rule of inference: "*p //
p* or *q*," 349–353, 363, 372; with relational predicates, 433

Adequacy: The extent to which a hypothesis fits the facts it is intended to explain, 535, 537, 544–545

Adverbs, translation of, 229

Advice. *See* Piece of advice

Affective terminology and definitions, 106

Affirmative statement: A statement that asserts class membership, 186–187, 190

Affirming the consequent: An invalid argument form: "If *p* then *q* / *q* // *p*," 323, 326–327, 330

"All except," "all but," 232–233, 438

Ambiguity, fallacies of, 144, 152–154

Ambiguous expression: An expression that can be interpreted as having more than one distinct meaning in a given context, 75–76, 89, 144

Ambiguous definitions, 106

Amphiboly: An informal fallacy that occurs when the conclusion of an argument depends on the misinterpretation of a statement that is ambiguous owing to some structural defect, 144, 153–154

Analogue, 452–453

Analogy, 451–461; argument from, 34, 452–454

Anecdotal evidence, 546

Antecedent: The component of a conditional statement immediately following the word "if," 20–21; the component of a conditional statement to the left of the horseshoe, 282

Appeal to force: An informal fallacy that occurs when an arguer threatens a reader or listener for the purpose of getting him or her to accept a conclusion, 113–114, 168

Appeal to ignorance: An informal fallacy that occurs when an arguer uses the fact that nothing has been proved about something as evidence in support of some conclusion about that thing, 130–131

Appeal to pity: An informal fallacy that occurs when an arguer attempts to evoke pity from a reader or listener for the purpose of getting him or her to accept a conclusion, 114–115, 168, 170

Appeal to snobbery: A variety of the appeal-to-the-people fallacy that occurs when the arguer plays on the reader's or listener's need to feel superior, 116

Appeal to the people: An informal fallacy that occurs when an arguer plays on certain psychological needs for the purpose of getting the reader or listener to accept a conclusion, 115–116, 168, 550

Appeal to unqualified authority: An informal fallacy that occurs when an arguer cites the testimony of an unqualified authority in support of a conclusion, 128–129, 170

Appeal to vanity: A variety of the appeal-to-the-people fallacy that occurs when an arguer plays on the vanity of the reader or listener, 116

Argument: A group of statements, one or more of which (the premises) are claimed to provide support for, or reasons to believe, one of the others (the conclusion), 1; cogent, 47–48; conditional statements and, 21–22; definitions and, 75–76; explanation and, 19–20; extended, 59–64; form of, 52–57, 320–324, 326–330; in science, 35; recognition of, 14–23; sound, 44, 48; strong, 44–48; valid, 41–44, 48. *See also* Deductive argument; Inductive argument

Argument against the person: An informal fallacy that occurs when an arguer verbally attacks the person of a second arguer for the purpose of discrediting his or her argument, 116–119, 167–168

Argument based on mathematics: A deductive argument in which the conclusion depends on some purely arithmetic or geometric computation or measurement, 32–33

Argument based on signs: An inductive argument that proceeds from the knowledge of a sign to a claim about the thing or situation that the sign symbolizes, 34

Argument form: An arrangement of words and letters such that the uniform substitution of terms or statements in place of the letters results in an argument, 52–57; an arrangement of statement variables and operators such that the uniform substitution of statements in place of the variables results in an argument, 321–324, 327–330; invalid, 52–55, 323, 326–327; valid, 53, 321–324, 327

Argument from analogy: An inductive argument that depends on the existence of a similarity between two things or states of affairs, 34–35, 452–454

Argument from authority: An inductive argument in which the conclusion rests on a statement made by some presumed authority or witness, 34

Argument from compassion, 114–115

Argument from definition: A deductive argument in which the conclusion is claimed to depend merely on the definition of some word or phrase used in the premise or conclusion, 33

Argument from example: An argument that purports to prove something by giving one or more examples of it, 18–19

Argumentum ad baculum. See Appeal to force

Argumentum ad hominem. See Argument against the person

Argumentum ad ignorantiam. See Appeal to ignorance

Argumentum ad misericordiam. See Appeal to pity

Argumentum ad populum. See Appeal to the people

Argumentum ad verecundiam. See Appeal to unqualified authority

Aristotelian sorites, 274n

Aristotelian standpoint/interpretation (traditional standpoint), 191–192, 209–210, 212–214, 220, 222–225, 240, 251–253, 259–260, 262; in predicate logic, 396; Venn diagrams for, 219–220

Aristotle, 5–6, 112, 191, 256, 526, 530–532

Associativity: A valid rule of inference that allows for the relocation of parentheses in conjunctions and disjunctions, 358–359, 361

Atmospheric pressure, discovery of, 530–531

Autokinetic effect, 553

Average, meaning of, 510–512

Avoiding fallacies, 168–172

Axiom of replacement: An axiom that states that logically equivalent expressions may replace one another in a proof sequence, 358

Baliani, Giovanni, 530

Bandwagon argument: A variety of the appeal-to-the-people fallacy that occurs when the arguer plays on the reader's or listener's need to feel part of a group, 116

"Barbara" syllogism, 241, 267

Barometer, invention of, 531

Bayes, Thomas, 499

Bayes's theorem: In probability theory, a rule for evaluating the conditional probability of two or more mutually exclusive and jointly exhaustive events, 499–501

"Because," 3, 19

Becquerel, Henri, 528

Begging the question: An informal fallacy that occurs when the arguer creates the illusion that inadequate premises provide adequate support for the conclusion by leaving out a key premise, by restating the conclusion as a premise, or by reasoning in a circle, 144–147, 167–168, 170–172

Begriffsschrift, 6

Benassi, Victor A., 550

Berti, Gasparo, 530

Biased sample: A sample that is not representative of the population from which it was selected, 506

Biconditional statement: A statement having a triple bar as its main operator, 282, 285; truth-functional definition of, 294; comparison of with ordinary language, 299–300; relating logically equivalent statements, 306; subjunctive, 299–300

Boethius, 5

Bolzano, Bernard, 6

Boole, George, 6, 191

Boolean standpoint/interpretation (modern standpoint), 191–192, 206, 209, 213–214, 219, 239, 246–251, 256, 260, 262; in predicate logic, 394, 396

"Both . . . not," 286–287

Bound variable: A variable that is bound by a quantifier, 395

Bouvard, Alexis, 529

Boyle, Robert, 484

Braces, 285

Brackets, 285–286

Broad definitions, 104

Broad hypotheses, 547

Bruner, Jerome S., 552

Campbell, Stephen K., 520n

Cantril, Albert H., 508n

Carroll, Lewis, 277

Categorical proposition: A proposition that relates two classes (or categories), 184–236; letter names of, 187, 190; standard form of, 184–185

Categorical syllogism: A syllogism in which all three statements are categorical propositions, 33, 237–279; exceptive propositions in, 268; figure of, 239–240; form of, 239–240; mood of, 238–239; in ordinary language, 266–268; reconstruction of, from mood and figure, 241; reducing the number of terms in, 264–265; rules for, 256–262; standard form of, 237–238; Venn diagrams for, 244–253

Causal inference: An inductive inference that proceeds from knowledge of a cause to a claim about an effect, or from knowledge of an effect to a claim about a cause, 35

Causality, 469–470

Change of quantifier rule: A rule of inference that allows one kind of quantifier to be replaced by another, provided that certain negation signs are deleted or introduced, 411–413; with overlapping quantifiers, 430, 432

Charles, Jacques Alexandre, 484

Chrysippus, 5

Circular definitions, 104–105

Circular reasoning. *See* Begging the question

Class complement, 202

Class statement, 156

Classical theory of probability: The theory according to which probabilities are computed *a priori* by dividing the number of favorable outcomes by the number of possible outcomes, 491–492, 494, 501

Cogent argument: An inductive argument that is strong and has all true premises, 47–48

Cognitive meaning: the meaning by which terminology conveys information, 72–74

Coherence. *See* Internal coherence

Cold reading, 555–556

Collective hallucination, 553

Collective predication: An attribute is predicated collectively when it is assigned to a class as a whole, 156

89, 95, 99–100; negative, 106; operational, 97–100, 104–105, persuasive, 91, 96, 99–100; precising, 89–90, 96, 99–100; purposes of, 86–91; stipulative, 87–89, 91, 95–96, 99–100; synonymous, 96–97, 99–100, 104–105; theoretical, 90–91, 96, 99–100

Definition by genus and difference: A definition that assigns a meaning to a term by identifying a genus term and one or more difference words that, when combined, convey the same meaning as the term being defined, 98–100, 104–105

Definition by subclass: A definition that assigns a meaning to a term by naming subclasses of the class that the term denotes, 95, 100

Definitional techniques, 94–100

Definitions of the logical operators, 291–295

Demonstrative definition: A definition that assigns a meaning to a word by pointing to members of the class that the word denotes, 94–96, 100

DeMorgan, Augustus, 6

DeMorgan's rule: A valid rule of inference that allows tildes to be moved inside and outside of parentheses, 286, 358–363

Denotation: Extensional meaning or extension, 83

Denotative definition. *See* Extensional definition

Denying the antecedent: An invalid argument form: "If p then q / not p // not q," 323, 327, 329

Dependent events, 495–496

Descartes, René, 532, 536

Descriptive phrases, 82

Destructive dilemma: A valid argument form/rule of inference: "If p then q, and if r then s / not q or not s // not p or not r," 324, 327, 330; refuting, 324–326

Detecting fallacies, 167–168

Difference, 98–99

Dilemma. *See* Constructive dilemma; Destructive dilemma

Disanalogy, 453

Disconfirmability criterion, 547

Disjunct: The component in a disjunctive statement on either side of the main operator, 281

Disjunction: A statement having a wedge as its main operator, 281; comparison of with ordinary language, 297; exclusive, 293, 297, inclusive, 292–293, 297,

321; truth-functional definition of, 292–293

Disjunctive statement: A statement having a wedge as its main operator, 281, 283

Disjunctive syllogism: A syllogism having a disjunctive statement for one or both of its premises, 33; a valid argument form/rule of inference: "p or q / not p // q," 321, 327–330, 338, 340–344

Dispersion: In statistics, an indicator of how spread out the data are in regard to numerical value, 512–517

Disputes, 76

Distribution: (1) An attribute possessed by a term in a categorical proposition if and only if the proposition makes a claim about all the members of the class denoted by the term, 187–190, 256; (2) a valid rule of inference that allows a conjunct/disjunct to be distributed through a disjunction/conjunction, 358–359, 361–363, 373

Distributive predication: An attribute is predicated distributively when it is assigned to each and every member of a class, 156

Division: An informal fallacy that occurs when the conclusion of an argument depends on the erroneous transference of an attribute from a whole (or class) onto its parts (or members), 145, 156–158

Dot, 281–283; truth-functional definition of, 292; comparison of with ordinary language, 296–297; use in predicate logic, 396

Double blind studies, 481, 509

Double colon: The metalogical symbol that designates logical equivalence, 358

Double colon with superscribed "c," 422

Double negation: A valid rule of inference that allows the introduction or deletion of pairs of negation signs, 329, 358–361

Drawing an affirmative/negative conclusion from negative/affirmative premises: A formal fallacy that occurs in a categorical syllogism when an affirmative conclusion is drawn from a negative premise or a negative conclusion is drawn from affirmative premises, 258–259

E proposition: A categorical proposition having the form "No S are P," 187

Einstein, Albert, 526, 535, 537, 549

Emotional disposition and avoiding fallacies, 169, 171–172

Emotive meaning: the meaning by which terminology expresses or evokes feelings, 72–74

Empirical hypotheses: Hypotheses that concern the production of some thing or the occurrence of some event that can be observed, 534–535

Empty extension: The extension of a term that denotes something that does not exist; the null class, 84

Empty intension, 84

Enthymeme: A categorical syllogism that is missing a premise or conclusion, 269–271; an argument that is missing a premise or conclusion, 21n, 269–271

Enumerative definition: A definition that assigns a meaning to a word by naming the members of the class that the word denotes, 95–96, 100

Equivalence. *See* Biconditional statement; Conditional logical equivalence; Logical equivalence; Material equivalence

Equivocation: An informal fallacy that occurs because some word or group of words is used either implicitly or explicitly in two different senses, 144, 152–153, 171, 520; division and, 158

Escaping between the horns of a dilemma, 324–325

Essential meaning, definitions and, 104

Etymological definition: A definition that assigns a meaning to a word by disclosing the word's ancestry in both its own language and other languages, 97, 100

Evidentiary support, 545–549

Exceptive propositions, 232–233; syllogisms containing, 268; in predicate logic, 438

Exclusive disjunction, 293, 297

Exclusive premises: A formal fallacy that occurs when both premises of a categorical syllogism are negative, 258

Exclusive propositions, 231–232; in predicate logic, 397–398, 438

Existential fallacy: A fallacy that occurs after the Aristotelian standpoint is adopted, when a particular conclusion is drawn from a universal premise (or premises) about things that do not exist, 212–213, 259; a formal fallacy that occurs after the Boolean standpoint is adopted when a particular conclusion is drawn from a universal premise (or premises), 198, 213, 260

Existential generalization: A rule of inference that introduces existential quantifiers, 401, 403–404, 407, 409,

430–431, 433; improper or invalid applications of, 409, 433–434; restrictions on, 406

Existential import, 191–192

Existential instantiation: A rule of inference that removes existential quantifiers, 401, 405–409; invalid applications of, 406, 409; restrictions on, 405–407

Existential names, 405–407

Existential quantifier: The quantifier used to translate particular statements in predicate logic, 395–396

Explanandum: The component of an explanation that describes the event or phenomenon to be explained, 19–20

Explanans: The component of an explanation that explains the event or phenomenon indicated by the explanandum, 19

Explanation: A group of statements intended to shed light on some event or phenomenon, 19–20

Exportation: A valid rule of inference that allows conditional statements having conjunctive antecedents to be replaced with conditional statements having conditional consequents, and vice versa, 368–372

Expository passage: A kind of nonargument consisting of a topic sentence and one or more other sentences that expand or elaborate on the topic sentence, 17–18

Extended arguments, 59–64

Extensional definition: A definition that assigns a meaning to a term by indicating the members of the class that the term denotes, 94–96, 104

Extensional meaning (extension): The members of the class that a term denotes, 83–85, 96; empty, 84

External consistency: The extent to which a hypothesis agrees with other, well-confirmed hypotheses, 536–537, 544–545

Factual claim: A claim that something is true; a claim that evidence or reasons are being presented, 14

Factual disputes, 76

Fallacies of ambiguity: A group of informal fallacies that occur because of an ambiguity in the premises or conclusion, 144–145, 152–154

Fallacies of categorical syllogisms, 256–260

Fallacies of grammatical analogy: A group of informal fallacies that occur because of a grammatical similarity to other arguments that are nonfallacious, 145, 154–158

Fallacies of presumption: A group of informal fallacies that occur when the premises of an argument presume what they purport to prove, 144–151

Fallacies of relevance: A group of informal fallacies that occur because the premises of an argument are irrelevant to the conclusion, 113–123

Fallacies of weak induction: A group of informal fallacies that occur because the connection between the premises and conclusion is not strong enough to support the conclusion, 128–138

Fallacy: A defect in an argument arising from some source other than merely false premises, 110. *See also* Fallacies; Formal fallacy; Informal fallacy

False cause: An informal fallacy that occurs when the conclusion of an argument depends on some imagined causal connection that probably does not exist, 133–135, 170, 172, 546, 550; and appeal to the people, 116

False dichotomy: An informal fallacy that is committed when an arguer presents two nonjointly exhaustive alternatives as if they were jointly exhaustive and then eliminates one, leaving the other as the conclusion, 144, 149–150, 168–170

Falsifiability criterion, 547

Feng shui, 547

Fermat, Pierre de, 491

"Few," "a few," 230

Figurative definitions, 105

Figure: An attribute of a categorical syllogism that specifies the location of the middle term, 239–240

Finite universe method: A method for proving invalidity in predicate logic that consists in reducing the universe to a single object and then sequentially increasing it until one is found in which the premises of an argument turn out true and the conclusion false, 421–424

"For the reason that," 3

"For this reason," 3

Form of a categorical syllogism, 239–240

Form of an argument, 52–57, 320–324, 326–330; invalid, 326–327

Formal fallacy: A fallacy that can be identified by merely examining the form or structure of an argument, 110–111. *See also* specifically named fallacies

Free variable: A variable that is not bound by a quantifier, 395

Frege, Gottlob, 6

Fruitfulness: The extent to which a hypothesis suggests new ideas for future analysis and confirmation, 537, 545

Galen, 5

Galilei, Galileo, 484, 530, 534

Galle, Johann, 528, 530, 534

Gallup poll, 508

Gambler's fallacy, 134–135

Gay-Lussac, Joseph Luis, 547

Geller, Uri, 554–555

General conjunction rule: In probability theory, a rule for computing the probability of two events occurring together whether or not the events are independent, 495–496, 498

General disjunction rule: In probability theory, a rule for computing the probability of either of two events whether or not they are mutually exclusive, 497–498, 501–502

General statement: A statement that makes a claim about all the members of a class, 36, 156–157

Generalization: An inductive argument that proceeds from the knowledge of a selected sample to some claim about the whole group, 34–35; in predicate logic, 404. *See also* Existential generalization; Universal generalization

Genus, 98–99

Gestalt, 552

Goclenian sorites, 274n

Goedel, Kurt, 6–7

Grammar, definitions and, 103–104

Grammatical analogy, fallacies of, 145, 154–158

Graphs, 517–518

Grasping a dilemma by the horns, 324–325

Hallucination, 553

Hasty generalization: An informal fallacy that occurs when a general conclusion is drawn from atypical specific cases, 131–133, 155–157, 170, 550

Helmont, Jan Baptista Van, 532

Herschel, William, 529

History of logic, 5–7

Horizontal pattern, 60–61

Horns of a dilemma, 324

Horseshoe, 281, 283–284; truth-functional definition of, 293–294; comparison of with ordinary language, 298–299; use in predicate logic, 394

Huff, Darrell, 513n

statement is not necessarily either true or false, given the truth value of some related statement, 195, 201, 205, 207, 210–212, 221–222

Loosely associated statements: Statements about the same general subject that lack an inferential relationship, 16

Lyons, Eugene, 520n

Maharishi Mahesh Yogi, 558

Main operator: The operator (connective) in a compound statement that governs the largest component(s) in the statement, 282, 295–296

Major premise: In a categorical syllogism, the premise that contains the major term, 237–238

Major term: In a standard-form categorical syllogism, the predicate of the conclusion, 237–238

Material equivalence: (1) The relation expressed by a truth-functional biconditional, 281, 285; comparison with ordinary language, 299–300; truth-functional definition of, 294; (2) a valid rule of inference that allows an equivalence statement to be replaced by a conjunctive statement or a disjunctive statement, 368–370

Material implication: (1) The relation expressed by a truth-functional conditional, 281–282, 284–285; comparison with ordinary language, 298–299; truth-functional definition of, 293–294; (2) a valid rule of inference that allows an implication sign to be replaced by a disjunction sign if and only if the antecedent is negated, 368–373

Maxwell, James Clerk, 536–537

Mean: The arithmetical average, 510–517

Meaning, 72–76, 83; cognitive, 72–74; emotive, 72–74; extensional, 83–85, 96; intensional, 83–85, 96; varieties of, 72–76

Median: The middle point when data are arranged in ascending order, 510–511, 513, 516

Mendeleev, Dmitri, 536

Mental carelessness, 169

Mention of a word, 82–83

Method of agreement: A method for identifying a causal connection between an effect and a single factor that is present in a number of occurrences in which the effect is present, 471–472

Method of concomitant variation: A method for identifying a causal connection between two conditions by

matching variations in one condition with variations in another, 477–479, 481–482, 484

Method of difference: A method for identifying a causal connection between an effect and a single factor that is present in an occurrence in which the effect is present and absent from an occurrence in which the effect is absent, 472–474, 480–481

Method of residues: A method of identifying a causal connection by subtracting strands of causal connection that are already known from a compound causal connection, 476–477

Middle term: In a standard-form categorical syllogism, the term that occurs only in the premises, 237

Mill, John Stuart, 6, 451, 470–471

Mill's methods and science, 479–484

Mill's methods of induction, 470–484

Minor premise: In a categorical syllogism, the premise that contains the minor term, 237–238

Minor term: In a standard-form categorical syllogism, the subject of the conclusion, 237–238

Missing the point: An informal fallacy that occurs when the premise of an argument entails one particular conclusion but a completely different conclusion is actually drawn, 121–122, 168, 170, 172, 521

Mnemonic device, for distribution, 189–190; for sufficient conditions, necessary conditions, 284–285

Mob mentality, 115

Modal logic: A kind of logic that deals with concepts such as possibility, necessity, belief, and doubt, 5–7

Mode: The value that occurs with the greatest frequency in a set of data, 510–511, 516

Modern square of opposition: A diagram that illustrates the necessary relations that prevail between the four kinds of standard-form categorical propositions as interpreted from the Boolean standpoint, 195

Modus ponens: A valid argument form/rule of inference: "If *p* then *q* / *p* // *q*," 322, 326–328, 330, 338–343, 372; in predicate logic, 402

Modus tollens: A valid argument form/rule of inference: "If *p* then *q* / not *q* // not *p*," 322–323, 327–330, 338–340, 342–343, 372

Monadic predicate: A predicate used to assign an attribute to individual things, 426

Mood: An attribute of a categorical syllogism that specifies the kind of statements (**A, E, I, O**) that make it up, 238–239

Moral reasoning, 458–461

Multiple conclusion, 61

Mutually exclusive events, 496

Names, 82, 84; existential, 405–407

Narrow definitions, 104

Natural deduction: A proof procedure by which the conclusion of an argument is derived from the premises through use of rules of inference, 338; in predicate logic, 401–450; in propositional logic, 338–391

Necessary and sufficient condition, 285; causality and, 470, 475–476

Necessary condition: The condition represented by the consequent in a conditional statement, 22, 284–285; causality and, 469–472

Needham, John, 532–533

Negation: A statement having a tilde as its main operator, 281; truth-functional definition of, 292

Negation rule: A rule for computing the probability of an event from the probability of the event *not* happening, 498–499

Negative definitions, 106

Negative statement: A statement that denies class membership, 186–187, 190

"Neither . . . nor," 286–287

Neptune, discovery of, 529–530, 535

Neurolinguistic programming, 555

Newton, Isaac, 532, 535, 537, 547

"No . . . except," 231, 438

Non causa pro causa, 134

Non sequitur, 110

Nonarguments, typical kinds of, 15–23

"None but," 231–232; in predicate logic, 397

"None except," 231–232

Nonstandard quantifiers, 230

Nonstandard verbs, translation of, 227

Normal probability distribution: A distribution of random phenomena having the shape of a bell, 481, 515–516

"Not both," 286–287

"Not either," 286–287

Numerical statements, 439–440

O proposition: A categorical proposition having the form "Some *S* are not *P*," 187

Reference, 83

Regression line, 483

Relational predicate: A predicate that expresses a connection between or among two or more individuals, 426–434

Relations, 426–427

Relative frequency theory of probability: The theory according to which probabilities are computed by dividing the number of observed favorable events by the number of observed events, 492–493, 501

Relevance, fallacies of. *See* Fallacies of relevance

Replacement, axiom of, 358; rules of, 358–363, 368–373

Replicability, 546

Report: A kind of nonargument consisting of one or more statements that convey information about some topic or event, 16–17

Restricted conjunction rule: In probability theory, a rule for computing the probability of two independent events occurring together, 494–496, 501–502

Restricted disjunction rule: In probability theory, a rule for computing the probability of either of two mutually exclusive events, 496–498

Retrospective study, 482

Robbins, Tony, 555

Roll, Charles W., 508n

Rule of inference: A rule by means of which the conclusion of an argument is derived from the premises, 338–344, 349–353, 358–363, 368–373; for identity, 441–444; for relational predicates and overlapping quantifiers, 430–434; in predicate logic, 401–409; misapplications of, 352–353

Rules for categorical syllogisms, 256–262

Rules of implication, 338–344, 349–353

Rules of replacement, 358–363, 368–373

Russell, Bertrand, 6

Samples, 506–510

Sampling error: The difference between the relative frequency with which some characteristic occurs in a sample and the relative frequency with which the same characteristic occurs in the population, 508–509

Science and superstition, 544–560

Scientific arguments, 35

Scientific reasoning, 525–537

Secondary analogue, 452

Self-contradictory statement: A statement that is necessarily false, 305; and inconsistency, 307

Sense, 83

Sherwood, William of, 6

Shirt-collar model, 239

Simple identity statements, 437

Simple noninferential passages, 15–17

Simple statement: A statement that does not contain any other statement as a component, 280

Simplification: A valid rule of inference, "*p* and *q* // *p*," 349–353, 363

"Since," 3, 15

Singer, Barry F., 550

Singleton, Donald, 554–555

Singular proposition (statement): A proposition (statement) that makes an assertion about a specifically named person, place, thing, or time, 228–229; in predicate logic, 393

Size of sample, 508

Slippery slope: An informal fallacy that occurs when the conclusion of an argument rests on an alleged chain reaction, and there is not sufficient reason to think that the chain reaction will actually take place, 135–136, 170

"Some," 56, 185, 192n

Sorites: A chain of categorical syllogisms in which the intermediate conclusions have been left out, 274–275; Aristotelian, 274n; Goclenian, 274n; standard form of, 274

Sound argument: A deductive argument that is valid and has all true premises, 44, 48

Spallanzani, Lazzaro, 532

Species, 98–99

Specific difference, 98–99

Spinoza, Benedict, 536

Spontaneous generation, 531–533

Square of opposition. *See* Modern square of opposition; Traditional square of opposition

Standard deviation: In statistics, a measure of how far the data vary or deviate from the mean value; the square root of the variance, 512–517

Standard-form categorical proposition: A proposition that has one of the following forms: "All *S* are *P*," "No *S* are *P*," "Some *S* are *P*," "Some *S* are not *P*," 184–185

Standard form of a categorical syllogism, 237–238

Standard form of a sorites, 274

Statement: (1) A sentence that is either true or false, 1–2, 48; (2) in predicate logic, an expression involving bound variables or constants throughout, 393–399, 407. *See also* Compound statement; General statement; Numerical statement; Particular statement; Simple statement; Singular statement; Superlative statement; Universal statement

Statement form: An arrangement of statement variables and operators such that the uniform substitution of statements in place of the variables results in a statement, 291

Statement function: In predicate logic, the expression that remains when a quantifier is removed from a statement, 395, 406–407

Statement of belief, statement of opinion: A kind of nonargument composed of statements that express the personal conviction of a speaker or writer without giving any evidence in support of that conviction, 16

Statement variable: A lowercase letter, such as *p* or *q*, that can represent any statement, 291

Statistical reasoning, 506–521

Stellar parallax, 557

Stipulative definition: A definition that assigns a meaning to a word for the first time, 87–89, 91, 95–96, 99–100

Stipulative use of a word, 88–89

Straw man: A fallacy that occurs when the arguer misinterprets an opponent's position for the purpose of more easily attacking it, demolishes the misinterpreted argument, and then proceeds to conclude that the original argument has been demolished, 120–121, 123, 167–168, 170

Strong inductive argument: An inductive argument in which it is improbable that the conclusion be false given that the premises are true, 44–48

Study, 482

Subalternation: The relation by which a true **A** or **E** statement necessarily implies a true **I** or **O** statement, respectively, and by which a false **I** or **O** statement necessarily implies a false **A** or **E** statement, respectively, 211–214, 222

Subcontrary: The relation that exists between two statements that are necessarily not both false, 210–214, 222

Subject, 185

Subject term: In a standard-form categorical proposition, the term that comes immediately after the quantifier, 184–185

Subjectivist theory of probability: The theory according to which probabilities are computed from the odds that people would accept on a bet, 493, 502

Subjunctive biconditionals, 299–300

Subjunctive conditionals, 299

Substitution instance: An argument or statement that has the same form as a given argument form or statement form; of an argument form, 53–57, 321–324, of a statement form, 291

Sufficient and necessary condition, 285; causality and, 470, 475–476

Sufficient condition: The condition represented by the antecedent in a conditional statement, 22, 284–285; causality and, 469–470, 473–474

Summulae Logicales, 6

Superfluous distribution rule, 260

Superlative statements, 439

Superstition, 544–560

Suppressed evidence: A fallacy that occurs when the arguer ignores relevant evidence that outweighs the presented evidence and entails a very different conclusion, 144, 150–151, 168, 170

Syllogism: A deductive argument consisting of two premises and one conclusion, 237. *See also* Categorical syllogism; Disjunctive syllogism; Hypothetical syllogism; Pure hypothetical syllogism

Syllogistic logic: The logic that deals with categorical propositions and categorical syllogisms, 5; predicate logic and, 392

Synonymous definition: A definition in which the definiens is a single word that connotes the same attributes as the definiendum, 96–97, 99–100, 104–105

System of Logic, 470

Tautologous conclusion, 311–312

Tautologous (logically true) statement: A statement that is necessarily true, 305

Tautology: (1) A tautologous statement, 305; (2) a rule of inference that eliminates redundancy in conjunctions and disjunctions, 368–369, 372; with relational predicates, 432

Term: A word or group of words that can serve as the subject of a statement, 82. *See also* Subject term; Predicate term

Term complement: The word or group of words that denotes the class complement, 202

Terms without nouns, translation of, 227

"The only," 232, 438

Theoretical definition: A definition that assigns a meaning to a word by suggesting a theory that gives a certain characterization to the entities that the term denotes, 90–91, 96, 99–100

Theoretical hypotheses: Hypotheses that concern how something should be conceptualized, 534–535

"Thus," 2, 14, 18

Tilde, 281–282, 286; truth-functional definition of, 292

Torricelli, Evangelista, 528, 530–531, 534–537

Total evidence rule, 47–48

Traditional square of opposition: A diagram that illustrates the necessary relations that prevail between the four kinds of standard-form categorical propositions as interpreted from the Aristotelian standpoint, 209–214; proof of, 220–222

Traditional standpoint. *See* Aristotelian standpoint

Translating ordinary language arguments into standard-form categorical syllogisms, 266–268

Translating relational statements, 427–430

Translating statements in predicate logic, 392–399, 426–430

Translating statements in propositional logic, 280–287

Translating statements into categorical form, 226–233

Transposition: A valid rule of inference that allows the antecedent and consequent of a conditional statement to switch places if and only if both are negated, 368–372

Triple bar, 281, 285; truth-functional definition of, 294; comparison of with ordinary language, 299–300

Truth, and strength, 44–46; and validity, 41–44. *See also* Logically true statement

Truth function: A compound statement is a truth function of its components if its truth value is determined by the truth value of the components, 291–300

Truth table: An arrangement of truth values that shows in every possible case how the truth value of a compound proposition is determined by the truth values of its simple components, 292; for arguments, 310–312; for propositions, 302–307. *See also* Indirect truth tables

Truth value: The attribute by which a statement is either true or false, 2; of

compound statements, 291–296; logically undetermined, 195, 201, 205, 207, 210–212, 221–222

Tu quoque: A variety of the argument-against-the-person fallacy that occurs when an arguer shifts the burden of guilt onto a second arguer for the purpose of discrediting his or her argument, 118

Unconditionally valid: valid from the Boolean standpoint, 196; for immediate inferences, 196, 214; for syllogisms, 239–240

Undetermined truth value. *See* Logically undetermined truth value

Undistributed middle: A formal fallacy that occurs when the middle term in a categorical syllogism is undistributed in both premises, 257

Unexpressed quantifiers, 229–230

Universal generalization: A rule of inference that introduces universal quantifiers, 401–403, 407–409; invalid applications of, 403, 407, 409, 417–418, 430–431, 433; restrictions on, 403–404, 406–407, 409, 415–417, 430–431

Universal instantiation: A valid rule of inference that removes universal quantifiers, 401–402, 406–409, 433; invalid applications of, 406, 409, 433

Universal quantifier: In predicate logic, the quantifier used to translate universal statements, 394

Universal statement: A statement that makes an assertion about every member of its subject class, 186–187, 189–190; in predicate logic, 393–395, 397–398; in a restricted universe, 422

"Unless," 231, 283, 297

Use of a word, 82–83

Vague definitions, 106

Vague expression: An expression that allows for borderline cases in which it is impossible to tell if the expression applies or does not apply, 74–76, 89, 96

Vague hypotheses, 547

Valid argument forms, 53, 321–324, 327. *See also* Rules of inference; Valid syllogistic forms

Valid deductive argument: An argument in which it is impossible for the conclusion to be false given that the premises are true, 41–44, 48

Valid syllogistic forms, 239–241

Validity, 41–44; form of an argument and, 52–53, 320–324

Value claim: A claim that something is good, bad, right, or wrong, 73

Variable, bound, 395; free, 395; individual, 394; statement, 291

Variance: In statistics, a measure of how far the data vary from the mean value, 512–515

Venn, John, 6, 192

Venn diagram: A diagram consisting of two or more circles used to represent the information content of categorical propositions, 192–195; and the Aristotelian standpoint, 219–220; for categorical syllogisms, 244–253; for particular statements in predicate logic, 396; for testing immediate inferences, 196–198, 222–225; for proving the traditional square of opposition, 220–222; for sorites, 274–275; for universal statements in predicate logic, 394

Verbal disputes, 76

Vertical pattern, 60

Viviani, Vincenzo, 531

Warning: A form of expression intended to put someone on guard against a dangerous or detrimental situation, 15

Weak analogy: An informal fallacy that occurs when the conclusion of an argument depends on an analogy (or similarity) that is not strong enough to support the conclusion, 137–138, 170, 172

Weak induction, fallacies of. *See* Fallacies of weak induction

Weak inductive argument: An inductive argument in which the conclusion does not follow probably from the premises even though it is claimed to, 44–48

Wedge, 281, 283; truth-functional definition of, 292–293; comparison with ordinary language, 297

Well-formed formula (WFF): A syntactically correct arrangement of symbols, 287

Whitehead, Alfred North, 6

Wittgenstein, Ludwig, 6, 72

Worldview, 169–172

Conditional Proof		**Indirect Proof**	

―		―	
―		―	
―	/ ―	―	/ ―
p ACP		p AIP	
―		―	
―		―	
―		―	
q		$q \cdot \sim q$	
$p \supset q$ CP		$\sim p$ IP	

Rules for Removing and Introducing Quantifiers

($a, b, c, \ldots u, v, w$ are individual constants; x, y, z are individual variables)

1. Universal instantiation (UI)

$$\frac{(x)\,\mathscr{F}x}{\mathscr{F}y} \qquad\qquad \frac{(x)\,\mathscr{F}x}{\mathscr{F}a}$$

2. Universal generalization (UG)

$$\frac{\mathscr{F}y}{(x)\,\mathscr{F}x} \qquad \text{not} \atop \text{allowed:} \qquad \frac{\mathscr{F}a}{(x)\,\mathscr{F}x}$$

Restrictions:
(conditional and indirect proof)

   (1) UG must not be used within the scope of an indented sequence if the instantial variable occurs free in the first line of that sequence.

(overlapping quantifiers)

   (2) UG must not be used if $\mathscr{F}y$ contains an existential name and y is free in the line where that name is introduced.

3. Existential instantiation (EI)

$$\frac{(\exists x)\,\mathscr{F}x}{\mathscr{F}a} \qquad \text{not} \atop \text{allowed:} \qquad \frac{(\exists x)\,\mathscr{F}x}{\mathscr{F}y}$$

Restriction: The existential name a must be a new name that has not occurred in any previous line.

4. Existential generalization (EG)

$$\frac{\mathscr{F}a}{(\exists x)\,\mathscr{F}x} \qquad\qquad \frac{\mathscr{F}y}{(\exists x)\,\mathscr{F}x}$$

Change of Quantifier Rules

$$(x)\,\mathscr{F}x :: \sim(\exists x)\sim\mathscr{F}x \qquad\qquad (\exists x)\,\mathscr{F}x :: \sim(x)\sim\mathscr{F}x$$
$$\sim(x)\,\mathscr{F}x :: (\exists x)\sim\mathscr{F}x \qquad\qquad \sim(\exists x)\,\mathscr{F}x :: (x)\sim\mathscr{F}x$$

Identity Rules

1. Prem.
$$\frac{}{a = a}$$

2. $a = b :: b = a$

3. $\dfrac{\begin{array}{c}\mathscr{F}a \\ a = b\end{array}}{\mathscr{F}b}$